University of Nebraska Press • Lincoln and London

21

The Yankees, the Giants,
and the Battle for Baseball
Supremacy in New York

LYLE SPATZ

AND STEVE STEINBERG

FOREWORD BY

CHARLES C. ALEXANDER

Library of Congress Cataloging-in-Publication Data
        Spatz, Lyle, 1937–
1921: the Yankees, the Giants, and the battle for baseball
supremacy in New York / Lyle Spatz and Steve Steinberg;
foreword by Charles C. Alexander.
        p. cm.
Includes bibliographical references and index.
        ISBN 978-0-8032-2060-7 (cloth : alk. paper)
1. New York Yankees (Baseball team)—History—20th
century. 2. New York Giants (Baseball team)—History—
20th century. 3. Baseball—United States—History—20th
century. 4. Sports rivalries—United States. I. Steinberg,
Steve. II. Title. III. Title: Nineteen twenty one.
        GV875.N4S62 2010   796.357'64097471—dc22
        2009039477

Set in Minion Pro by Bob Reitz. Designed by A. Shahan.

To
my grandson,
Timothy William Spatz,
whose smile lights up my life • LS

To the memory of Bill Kirwin:
teacher, mentor,
and friend
• SS

Contents

Illustrations

Foreword

Charles C. Alexander

One can argue that in the course of American professional baseball's long and rich history, various baseball seasons—for a variety of reasons—have been particularly significant. The 1893 season, for example, saw the distance between the pitcher and home plate set at its present sixty and a half feet, a change that established the basic features of the game as we know it today. In popular understanding, the "modern" World Series dates from 1903 (a distinction that ignores the 1883–89 postseason competitions between champions of the National League and the American Association, the second Major League of that era). How about 1941, the last peacetime season, in which Joe DiMaggio hit safely in fifty-six consecutive games and Ted Williams batted .406—achievements unequaled over the many succeeding decades? In 1946 players who had served in the armed forces during the Second World War resumed their careers at the start of the greatest attendance boom that baseball had known up to then. Certainly the next year was meaningful, since Jackie Robinson became the Major Leagues' first black player in more than sixty years.

In terms of what might be called baseball's institutional history, an argument can be made for the importance of 1958, when the Dodgers and Giants deserted New York City and, relocating in Los Angeles and San Francisco, made the Major Leagues transcontinental. In 1976 baseball's century-old reserve system was radically altered, and the advent of free agency was formalized in a new Basic Agreement negotiated between the club owners and an increasingly powerful Major League Players Association. In 1981 a players' strike tore a fifty-game hole in the season, and in 1994 another strike closed down the season and cancelled the World Series.

But for all that, Lyle Spatz and Steve Steinberg make a convincing case that the season of 1921 was a truly pivotal one. For the first time, both New York teams won pennants. The Yankees had finally come out on top of the American League, powered by Babe Ruth after eighteen mostly lackluster seasons. Both teams had to struggle through tight races; the outcome in the American League wasn't decided until the season's final days. Along the way, Babe Ruth slammed fifty-nine home runs, breaking his own record of fifty-four, which he had set the previous season, and solidifying his hold on the popular imagination of many millions of Americans, including people who had previously followed baseball only casually if at all. As Spatz and Steinberg show, Ruth's spectacular prowess with the bat worked a revolutionary effect on the way the game was played. The pitching-dominated inside baseball of the previous two decades gave way to a new big-inning, power-oriented game, in which a growing number of other sluggers would follow Ruth's example (or try to).

Besides Ruth, the 1921 World Series featured a number of memorable personalities. John McGraw, long hailed as baseball's "Little Napoleon," led his Giants into their sixth Series (the Giants had refused to play the American League champions in 1904) but their first since 1917. McGraw had won only with his 1905 team; for the imperious McGraw, 1921 would be another opportunity to answer critics who said that for all his regular-season managing skills, he faltered in postseason play. All the games in the 1921 Series would be played in the Giants-owned Polo Grounds, which the Yankees had been renting a share of since 1913. McGraw bitterly resented the ascendancy of the Yankees. Like Ty Cobb, who was king of the players in the pre-1920s Deadball Era, McGraw abhorred the way Ruth's slugging style was changing the game. Moreover, starting in 1920, when the Yankees became the first team to top 1 million in home attendance, the Giants found themselves being outdrawn—and outglamorized—in their own ballpark. Back in 1914 McGraw had been instrumental in bringing about the purchase of the Yankees franchise by Jacob Ruppert and Tillinghast L'Hommedieu Huston, but since then the relationship between the Giants and their wealthy tenants had grown increasingly unpleasant.

Much of the drama of the 1921 season and World Series had to do with the predicament of little Miller Huggins, the Yankees' long-suffering manager. Although Huggins would lead the Yankees to six pennants and three Series championships in the 1920s, he never had the confidence of T. L. Huston (who sold out his interests to Ruppert in 1923) or of a number of the baseball reporters and columnists writing for the dozen or so morning and evening newspapers published in New York City. Nor did he have the confidence or the obedience of the roisterous Ruth or of some of Ruth's almost equally roisterous teammates. For Huggins, who was frail and often ill, the 1921 season became a considerable ordeal.

One of Huggins's most difficult players was Carl Mays, an outstanding pitcher but a complex man who had no real friends and seemed not to want any. During the 1919 season, Mays simply walked out on the Boston Red Sox. Over the determined but ultimately futile opposition of American League president Ban Johnson, Boston owner Harry Frazee quickly sold Mays to the Yankees for $40,000. Mays had a reputation for trying to intimidate batters with high and tight pitches—a reputation that became infamous after August 16, 1920, when one of his pitches inflicted a fatal skull fracture on Cleveland shortstop Ray Chapman. Yet a twenty-six-game winner in 1920 and a twenty-seven-game winner in 1921, Mays remained the ace of the Yankees' staff. Although Mays's career record is superior to several other pitchers in the National Baseball Hall of Fame, there has never been much sentiment in favor of his election.

The 1921 World Series did have on the scene a total of ten future Hall of Famers. Both managers are in the Hall of Fame, both elected posthumously. The Yankees' roster listed three future Hall of Famers: Waite Hoyt, Frank Baker, and of course Ruth. The Giants fielded four of their own electees: Ross Youngs in right field, George Kelly at first base, Dave Bancroft at shortstop, and Frank Frisch at third base. (Coaches Hughie Jennings and Jesse Burkett and reserve Casey Stengel, who is in the Hall of Fame on his managing record, spent the Series on the Giants' bench)

The all–New York Series occasioned unprecedented coverage, not only from the host of local writers, but from representatives of numerous out-of-town newspapers who jammed the press section at the Polo Grounds. An especially appealing feature of Spatz and Steinberg's book is the extensive treatment they give to the way the print media—virtually the only source of daily information in that period—reported on doings in baseball, beginning with dispatches from the spring training sites in the southern climes and climaxing with detailed inning-by-inning narratives and postmortems during the "Fall Classic." Long before television and with radio still in its infancy, the vast majority of Americans who couldn't attend Major League games depended on the accounts they could read in their newspapers. This book regales us with excerpts from the work of some of the legendary figures in American sportswriting—men such as Grantland Rice, Heywood Broun, H. G. Salsinger, Damon Runyon, and a galaxy of others. Anybody reading such reportage from that long-ago time may regret what has happened to sports journalism in the age of television.

Spatz and Steinberg's *1921* also appeals to the eye. The authors include more than fifty photos, many of which have been seen only rarely if ever. Babe Ruth was the most photographed person of his day; but how many people have ever viewed sharp images of such men as Mike McNally, Johnny Rawlings, Aaron Ward, or a very young Waite Hoyt (pictured with his sister and parents)?

Spatz and Steinberg's *1921* is a finely detailed, meticulously researched and documented, and well-illustrated book that conveys a vivid feel for the times in baseball and in American society in general. It is a major addition to an exponentially growing literature in baseball history. Although the Giants defeated the Yankees in eight games (in what was scheduled as a best-of-nine World Series), never again—under McGraw or his successors—would they be masters of the city's sports scene, as they had been before Babe Ruth arrived. For the history of baseball in New York City and, to a great extent, baseball as a whole, what happened in the year 1921 was transformative. I wasn't there, but Spatz and Steinberg often made me feel that I was.

Nineteen twenty-one was a remarkable baseball season, one that signaled that a seismic shift in how the game was played was underway. Baseball was moving from low-scoring contests dominated by pitching to a power game with more hits, runs, and home runs. It was the year that New York City rose to the top of the baseball world, where it would remain for most of the twentieth century. At hand was a long-anticipated confrontation between the two New York clubs: the Yankees, led by Babe Ruth, and the Giants, led by John McGraw. They represented two very different philosophies. Sharing one ballpark, the two teams fought for the fan base of the nation's largest city, for the top of the baseball world, and for the future direction of the game.

Books have been devoted to nearly two dozen seasons between 1901 and 1966 and to virtually every season of the last four decades. Yet the story of this historically significant 1921 season has not been told until now. Highlights include two dramatic pennant races, the New York Yankees' first American League pennant, and the first all–New York City World Series. With as much drama and as many turnarounds as any postseason ever, that Series, a match between the American League's Yankees and the National League's Giants, provided a worthy climax to an eventful season.

With the end of World War I, the nation was ready to focus on less-momentous clashes, ones that were not about life and death. The election of President Warren Harding, who in his March 4, 1921, inauguration promised the nation a "return to normalcy," signified that Americans had tired of world affairs. They were ready to consider less cosmic issues and to enjoy themselves. Newspapers across the country responded with expanded sports sections. Baseball occupied an increasingly large part of the nation's newspapers, as well as its psyche. In 1921 the game provided a season for the ages.

In 1921 baseball had center stage of the sports world almost to itself. Professional football and basketball had not yet developed as popular alternatives for fan support. College football emerged each fall, but it was a plodding game with little offense. The forward pass, which would revolutionize football in much the same way the home run did baseball, was still in its infancy. Boxing was popular in the lower weight divisions in New York City; yet except for infrequent heavyweight title fights, the sport did not appeal to the nation at large. Moreover, the sport meant little to the youth of America in the way baseball did. The same was true of horseracing, which was recovering from corruption—fixed races—far worse than that of baseball's 1919 Black Sox scandal.

In New York City, it was on this stage that the larger-than-life figures of Ruth and McGraw, two of the dominant personalities of their day, took over in 1921. The Giants and McGraw, their autocratic manager since 1902, had dominated National League baseball and the New York City sports scene. McGraw's disdain for the American League dated from 1902, when he quit as an AL manager after repeated suspensions by and clashes with the league's president, Ban Johnson. McGraw's contempt for Ruth's new slugging game, which was repudiating the very style of play McGraw had helped make famous, only added to his disdain. Now the Giants were back in the World Series for the sixth time under his leadership.

The Brooklyn club had won the National League pennant in 1916 and 1920, but it was not a serious contender for the devotion of New Yorkers outside of that borough. Brooklyn remained a separate entity—not accepted as New York, by New York—even after it had joined the city in 1898. The feeling of Brooklynites was mutual.

At the start of 1921, the Yankees—who have since won forty pennants—had won none. They were a franchise with a long history of losing. By 1921, however, the allegiance of New York City's baseball fans was in play. Ruth was the force behind the Yankees' rise in the standings and at the box office. In 1920, Ruth's first year in New York, the Yankees outdrew the Giants, the team that owned and shared their ballpark, the Polo Grounds, by 360,000 fans. That year, the Yankees had become the first team to top 1 million fans in home attendance. Ruth was also the catalyst behind a shift away from the game McGraw's teams had excelled at for years. When they met in the 1921 Series—the Giants and Yankees,

McGraw and Ruth—they represented two very different styles: what the game had been and what it would soon become.

Often thought of as the season in which baseball emerged from the Great War, 1920 was dominated by the spectacular slugging of Babe Ruth. Yet 1919 was when attendance rose dramatically and Ruth first astounded the baseball world playing in Boston, where he hit an unheard of twenty-nine home runs. The year 1920 is also remembered as the season that baseball rebounded from the 1919 Chicago Black Sox scandal. However, the scandal was not exposed until the final days of the 1920 season. In fact, the year that tested the loyalty of baseball fans was 1921 not 1920.

With the arrival of the game's first commissioner, Judge Kenesaw Mountain Landis, 1921 also marked a revolution in baseball governance. Baseball's owners had selected an outsider—the maverick federal judge who himself was a big fan of the game—and had given him enormous power. Confronted with a crisis of confidence in the integrity of the game, Landis began his rule with an iron, if somewhat erratic, fist and an eye on how baseball could best recover. It was also the year that Landis, Ruth, and the sheer drama of the baseball season brought the game back from its darkest days.

In *1921: The Yankees, the Giants, and the Battle for Baseball Supremacy in New York* lies a gem of a baseball season, one that has not gotten the attention it deserves. The drama unfolds and builds to a climax, as seesaw and cliffhanger pennant races give way to another tense battle, the World Series in October. In this story, heroes are larger than life, and baseball is the undisputed king of American sport. The game was undergoing fundamental change. John McGraw personified the Deadball Era, which was not going quietly; and Babe Ruth was fueling the new power game almost single-handedly. This season was one of the great tipping points in the history of our national pastime.

Acknowledgments

Rob Taylor, our editor at the University of Nebraska Press, provided astute input that made our book stronger as we proceeded through various drafts. We want to thank the entire team at the University of Nebraska Press for their help in transforming our manuscript into a book and for bringing it to the attention of our reading audience.

Professor Charles Alexander, who wrote our Foreword, also provided a thorough read of the manuscript.

A special thank you to Jennifer McCord, who provided editorial advice and support from the start, assuring us that two writers living on opposite coasts could indeed speak with one voice.

Skip McAfee did a superb job indexing this book.

We would like to thank our readers: Mark Armour, Tom Bourke, the late Gene Carney, Rick Huhn, Dan Levitt, Skip McAfee, and Eric Sallee.

Our fact checker par excellence was Bill Deane.

The following people were most generous with their advice and answers to our inquiries: Marty Appel, Bill Ayrovainen, Cliff Blau, Robert Creamer, Richard Crepeau, Henry Fetter, Jan Finkel, Matt Fulling, Glenn Guzzo, Ed Hartig, Bill James, Mike Lynch, Norman Macht, Peter Mancuso, Roberta Newman, Dan O'Brien, Pete Palmer, David Pietrusza, Steven Riess, Ray Robinson, Chuck Rosciam, Gregory Ryhal, Gabriel Schechter, Fred Schuld, Ron Selter, Dave Smith, Fred Stein, Stew Thornley, David Vincent, Russell Wolinsky, and Marshall Wright.

Members of SABR, the Society for American Baseball Research, not only those listed above.

National Baseball Hall of Fame Library and Archives; New York Public

Library's microforms reading room; Stephan Saks of the New York Public Library; and Seattle Public Library's Interlibrary Loan Department and Magazines and Newspapers Department.

Our statistical sources were Gillette and Palmer, *The ESPN Baseball Encyclopedia*, 5th ed.; and Retrosheet.

Our photo sources included the private collections of Dennis Goldstein, Michael Mumby, Dan Levitt, Mark Stang, and Steve Steinberg; © Bettmann/CORBIS; Aaron Schmidt and the Boston Public Library; Chicago History Museum; Eva Tucholka, Harriet Culver, and Culver Pictures; Ernie Harwell Sports Collection, Detroit Public Library; Pat Kelly and the National Baseball Hall of Fame Library and Archives, Cooperstown, New York; Library of Congress, Prints and Photographs Division; Mark Rucker and Transcendental Graphics/theruckerarchive.com; and Paula Homan and the St. Louis Cardinals Hall of Fame Museum.

PART 1   The Preseason

1   Prelude to the World Series

By 1921 the World Series had become America's greatest sporting event. Even those who paid little attention to baseball during the regular season were cognizant of the multigame struggle between the champions of the American and National leagues. And while no one individual game could create the furor and excitement of the previous July's heavyweight title fight between champion Jack Dempsey and his French challenger, Georges Carpentier, no other event could hold the sporting public's protracted interest that the battle for baseball's championship could.[1]

Dempsey was one of the two 1920s athletes whom American sports fans would come to idolize and who would symbolize the era of the Roaring Twenties. The other was New York Yankee slugger Babe Ruth. No player before (or since) has so captured the imagination of the American sporting public, many of whom had begun following the Babe's at bats on a daily basis. His fame spread nationwide and even beyond, with more words written about him than about President Warren Harding. Ruth's presence in the Yankee lineup assured that the 1921 Series between the Yanks and John McGraw's New York Giants would be the most closely followed championship series ever. Even before the first pitch was thrown, fans were discussing whether McGraw's pitchers would be able to handle the Yankee sluggers as a group and in particular, Ruth.

With the Polo Grounds, the home park for both teams, hosting all the games, Ruth appeared to be even more of a looming threat to the Giants' pitchers. The seats down the right-field line at the Polo Grounds were a mere 256 feet away, not that the Babe needed the help. Fifty-two of his 113 home runs in two seasons with the Yankees had come on the road.

The glamour and prestige surrounding the World Series had come a long way since that day seventeen years earlier, when, after the Giants had won the 1904 National League pennant, manager McGraw famously announced, "The Giants will not play a postseason series with the American League champions."[2] Now the Giants were preparing to do just that. They had done so before, of course, although with limited success, much to the chagrin of McGraw, who passionately hated the American League and its president, Ban Johnson.[3] After having defeated the Philadelphia Athletics in the 1905 World Series, McGraw's Giants had lost four consecutive Series to the American League pennant winners: to the Athletics in 1911 and 1913, to the Boston Red Sox in 1912, and to the Chicago White Sox in 1917.

Back in July 1904, when McGraw, backed by owner John T. Brush, issued his refusal to play a World Series against the champion of the upstart new league, there was a strong possibility that the Highlanders, as the Yankees were then called, might be that champion. But the Highlanders lost the pennant to Boston on the last day of the season, whereupon Highlanders co-owner Frank Farrell proposed to Brush and McGraw that the Giants meet his second-place team in a postseason series. Brush's refusal was brutally and mockingly short. "Who are these people?" he asked dismissively. "We do not know them at all. The Giants do not care to play minor leaguers, so this absurd challenge from a lot of nobodies will be ignored."[4] Recognizing the new team in New York as being on a par with the lordly Giants was something neither their manager nor their owner wanted to do.

Two years later, in 1906, Farrell had his revenge. The Yankees had again been involved in an exciting pennant race, finishing in second place, three games behind the Chicago White Sox. Moreover, they had surpassed the Giants in attendance for the first time. Hoping to convert the Yankees' popularity into dollars for the Giants, Brush and McGraw suggested a postseason series between the two teams. Farrell, who had hoped the Yanks' postseason play would be against the Chicago Cubs in the World Series, turned the Giants down flat.[5] The "nobodies" had gotten their revenge.

Now that the Yankees, a team McGraw despised above all others, had won their first pennant, these two New York teams would meet, with the world championship at stake. That the Yankees' potent offense was led by Babe Ruth, the game's greatest attraction and the antithesis of the "inside baseball" McGraw had helped foster, only heightened the drama of this match.[6] There were many reasons for McGraw's current antipathy to the Yankees. Perhaps foremost was that the American Leaguers had now shed their image as New York's "other team" and taken their place as the Giants' equals in the estimation of New York's fans.

Furthermore, by 1921 the hordes of early twentieth-century immigrants who had descended on New York City, mostly Jewish and Italian, had changed not only the ethnic composition of the city but also the fan base of its baseball teams. Author Harry Golden's tales of his childhood attachment to the Giants were symbolic of a generation of newcomers to America who had taken to America's game without assistance from, and often as an act of revolt against, their old-world fathers. Eric Rolfe Greenberg touched on a similar theme in his novel *The Celebrant*, a story centering on a young Jewish immigrant's devotion to pitcher Christy Mathewson.

Neither the National League team that had been in neighboring Brooklyn since the 1890s nor the American League entry relocated to Manhattan from Baltimore in 1903 had done much to change the Giants' entrenched position as the team of choice for the vast majority of New Yorkers. Brooklyn, despite becoming a part of the city in 1898, was just too far away; and its inhabitants did not fully embrace New York either. Just four years earlier, Brooklyn had voted for the merger by only 277 votes out of more than 129,000 cast; and on the eve of 1898, the editor of the *Brooklyn Daily Eagle* had declared, "Though borough it may be, Brooklyn it is, Brooklyn it remains, and Brooklyn we are."[7]

Because the Yankees rarely generated much excitement, a good portion of the American Leaguers' attendance came from fans anxious to see the great stars of the American League rather than to watch the home team. Only by going to watch the Yankees play at Hilltop Park, located at Broadway and 168th Street, not too far from the Polo Grounds, could older fans and those youngsters new to the game have the opportunity to see players like Nap Lajoie, Ty Cobb, Eddie Collins, Tris Speaker, Rube Waddell, Cy Young, Addie Joss, and Walter Johnson.

John McGraw's constant bullying of umpires and complaints that everyone was out to get the Giants had alienated fans in the league's seven other cities. Over time, his behavior came to alienate and drive away a significant number of New Yorkers. Yet despite the defections, New York had remained a strong National League town through the end of the First World War. That began to change when the Yankees became serious pennant contenders in 1919, and accelerated with the coming of Babe Ruth to New York in 1920. Ruth's arrival had won new converts for the Yanks and the American League. On the eve of the 1921 Series, New York was evenly divided in its sentiment. "A few years ago, the Giants had the big following in New York, and the Yankees were given little consideration. McGraw and his men have still as great a grip on one part of fandom as any Giant team of the past had, but in the meantime a new army of fans has rallied to the Yankee standard where there once was a scattering few."[8]

Sid Mercer, of the *New York Evening Journal*, also recognized the inroads made by Yankee rooters and credited Ruth for bringing it about. "This is a National League town. John J. McGraw put his label on it years ago, and the Giants are firmly established. Up to a couple of years ago, the Yanks were just the 'other New York team.' But the immense personal popularity of Babe Ruth and the dynamite in the rest of that Yankee batting order have made the Yanks popular with the element that loves the spectacular."[9]

Unlike in future years, when rooting for one New York team meant rooting against the others, many New Yorkers had been happy to see both teams win. New York fans wanted and demanded winning teams, and they had not had a pennant winner since the Giants in 1917. The Brooklyn Dodgers had won the National League pennant in 1920, but that World Series had not generated much interest or excitement in New York.[10] People in Manhattan just could not get very enthused about a team from Brooklyn.

When the Dodgers reached that Series to play the Cleveland Indians, one New York newspaper noted in an editorial that "the honor will go to a new city."[11] Another paper sarcastically editorialized that there would be a World Series "in town," if Brooklyn would concede that "Manhattan is part of New York and admit the inhabitants of this inconsiderable suburb to a humble share in their triumph."[12] Should Brooklyn repeat as National League champions in 1921, "there'd be nothing but thick gloom from the Statue of Liberty to Westchester County," unless the Yankees thrashed them in the World Series, wrote sportswriter Joe Vila.[13]

This year was different. New York fans were certain of one thing: for the first time since Christy Mathewson and 1905, a New York team would be baseball's world champions.

The cleaner brand of play in the American League, along with its star-studded rosters, contributed to the Yankees gaining a foothold in New York.[14] Nevertheless, the overwhelming factor was the addition of Ruth. The bigger-than-life Babe, now playing on the nation's biggest stage, won the hearts of New Yorkers immediately. After having hit twenty-nine home runs—a record at that time—with the Boston Red Sox in 1919, Ruth shattered that mark with an unprecedented fifty-four in 1920, more than any other *team* in the American League and thirty-five more than runner-up George Sisler. He also led by similarly large margins in runs scored, runs batted in, on-base percentage, slugging percentage, and walks.

Yet despite the Babe's accomplishments, McGraw remained defiant, convinced his pitchers could handle the Yankee slugger. When asked before the Series if the Giants would pitch to Ruth, he responded, "Why shouldn't we pitch to Ruth? I've said it before, and I'll say it again, we pitch to better hitters than Ruth in the National League."[15]

Despite McGraw's disdain for Ruth, the Babe had impressed him since he first saw the young slugger back in 1914, when the Giants were playing a spring-training game against the International League Baltimore Orioles. Ruth was, of course, a pitcher then; and McGraw envisioned him some day pitching for the Giants. When Orioles owner Jack Dunn sold Ruth to the Red Sox without even contacting him, McGraw was so upset he never forgave his old Baltimore teammate.[16] Nor, seemingly, did McGraw ever again have a kind word to say about Ruth. In the spring of 1919, Ruth was pestering Red Sox manager Ed Barrow to allow him to play every day. "If he plays every day," said McGraw, "the bum will hit into a hundred double plays before the season is over."[17] The Red Sox and Giants played a series of exhibition games that spring, and whenever Ruth had a hit he would direct a "How's that for a double-play ball, Mac?" at the Giants' bench.[18]

Now a full-time outfielder, Ruth had almost single-handedly begun changing the game from the old-style inside baseball practiced by McGraw to one that featured power hitting and home runs.[19] McGraw had been the embodiment of that old style of play—a low-scoring, scientific game that had prevailed in baseball since the turn of the century, a game dominated by pitchers, many of whom threw "trick" pitches, a game where a walk, a stolen base, and a couple of sacrifices would

1. The Giants had shared their home ballpark, the oddly shaped Polo Grounds, with the Yankees since 1913. For the first time, all games of the World Series were played in one park. Since the arrival of Babe Ruth in New York in 1920, the tenant was outdrawing its landlord. *Private collection of Dennis Goldstein.*

scratch out a precious run.[20] Even the introduction of the cork-centered baseball in 1910 had not changed the style of play.

Ruth did. The Babe represented the new power-hitting game, where one swing of the bat generated runs. Twenty-five Major Leaguers had slugged ten or more home runs in 1921, a steep increase from the usual three or four who had done so during a typical year of the Deadball Era. As recently as 1917, Yankees first baseman Wally Pipp had led the American League with nine home runs.

McGraw hated this new style of play. "I do not like the lively ball," he said. "I think the game far more interesting when the art of making scores lies in scientific work on the bases." He believed that while fans liked to see home runs hit, there were times when they got weary of the long ball.[21]

But evidently the fans were not getting weary of it. More than 1 million of them had paid their way into the Polo Grounds in 1920 to watch the Ruth-led Yankees stay in contention all season before finishing third, behind the Chicago White Sox and the pennant-winning Cleveland Indians. The Yankees' failure to win that year emboldened those in the New York press who had never cared for manager Miller Huggins to call for his removal, just as they had after the 1919 season.

Huggins also had to deal with unrest among his own players, who often second-guessed his moves. Yankees co-owner Tillinghast "Til" Huston was in favor of firing Huggins, but his partner, Jacob Ruppert, had faith in Huggins and wanted him to remain. Ruppert had prevailed, and now Huggins had rewarded him and Huston with the Yankees' first American League pennant.

While the *Sporting News* complained in an October 13 editorial that "baseball is a national game, not just a diversion for Manhattanites," the *Detroit News* more accurately reflected the opinions of baseball fans everywhere: "Never before have two teams as colorful as the contending clubs in this Series met for the title. Never has personality and individuality entered so strongly into a clash for baseball supremacy."[22]

The Giants had finished in second place in each of the three preceding seasons. Over that same period, the Yankees, under Huggins and with the addition of Ruth in 1920, had become legitimate pennant contenders. As a result, supporters of both teams had spent countless hours arguing which was the better team. Now, finally, the first all–New York Series was here, and the answer would be determined on the field.[23] In one corner stood John McGraw and the old, established Giants, a fixture in the city since the Rosie O'Grady days of the Gay Nineties. In the other, stood Babe Ruth and the brash Yankees, the perfect sports symbol for what would come to be called America's Jazz Age.

Also at stake was the battle for who would be New York's team of choice. From a vantage point ninety miles away, the *Philadelphia Inquirer* wrote, "It is more than possible that the victor in this combat will plunge ahead as the chosen team of the city, and if the American Leaguers bring home the bacon it will mean much, very much to them. . . . McGraw has never lost his hold on the popular imagination of New York, and the legend that he is the greatest still exists and is still potent."[24]

2 Baseball Confronts the Black Sox Scandal

The American public first heard the shocking news of the 1919 World Series scandal in late September 1920, with but a few games left in the baseball season. Almost a year earlier, several members of the favored Chicago White Sox had conspired with gamblers to deliberately lose the 1919 World Series. The result was an upset victory by the Cincinnati Reds.

Now two of the game's best players, pitcher Eddie Cicotte and outfielder Joe Jackson, went before a grand jury, admitted their involvement, and implicated some of their White Sox teammates. In the eleven months following the end of that Series—and just before and during the Series itself, for those closer to the event—there had been hints of a fix. Chicago sportswriter Hugh Fullerton was one of the few newsmen who had raised concerns from the start. In early 1920 both Grantland Rice, one of the nation's leading sportswriters, and William Macbeth of the *New York Tribune* had called for a full inquiry.

Yet baseball's establishment, and most journalists, quickly dismissed such talk as irresponsible and absurd. The view of the *Sporting News* was typical. Just after the 1919 World Series, it wrote, "There is no such evidence of wrongdoing except in the mucky minds of the stinkers who—because they are crooked—think all the rest of the world can't play straight."[1]

Sportswriters and fans often said that baseball games could not be fixed, in part because players were above such corruption and in part because it was a team game. "I said to myself they might fix a player, but they could not fix a whole team," was the way sportswriter Fred Lieb put it.[2] A baseball fix required a greater number of participants than a boxing match or a horse race. Yet baseball always has been a reflection of society, susceptible to temptation and corruption. The game had been compromised a number of times in the past. Gamblers operated openly in ballparks, despite occasional efforts to crack down on them.

Whenever Organized Baseball had the opportunity to confront the problem, most notably in the early 1919 investigation of corrupt Giants first baseman Hal Chase, it had looked the other way. The owners had feared such scrutiny would shake the fans' faith in the game and thus the owners' pocketbooks. The exoneration of Chase had sent a dangerous message to ballplayers, that they could throw games with impunity. Like a festering wound, the problem of fixed games grew until it could be contained no longer. It broke into the open with the 1919 World Series, albeit not publicly until September 1920.

After World War I the three-man National Commission, baseball's ruling body, had become increasingly dysfunctional. Even before the Black Sox scandal had become public knowledge, there were serious discussions of changing that governing entity to a single person, probably someone outside of baseball. American League president Ban Johnson, who had been the most powerful man in the game since 1903, did his best to derail such developments. The Black Sox scandal now added a sense of urgency to those deliberations.

When the story emerged that the greatest event in sports had been compromised, the owners had a public relations nightmare—and even worse, potential financial ruin—on their hands. Respected columnist William McGeehan of the *New York Tribune* did not mince words: "Even 'Babe' Ruth cannot revive the interest that died such a violent death when it was shown that a world's series had been hawked and sold by gamblers."[3] Fan support and ticket buying were the lifeblood of baseball. The scandal had to be contained.

Most, if not all, owners knew that thrown contests had roots deep in the sport itself. Richard Crepeau explained, "For years the owners had piously proclaimed the purity of the National Pastime from the housetops, while they casually concealed misconduct. To admit otherwise now might have brought down the entire house of cards on their heads."[4] Bill Veeck Jr., whose father William Veeck Sr. was president of the Chicago Cubs at the time of the Black Sox scandal, provided insight to an age-old problem. "It is the nature of any organization in trouble to cover up its sins, to whitewash itself when exposed and, in the final extremity, to try to claim virtue for cleaning its own house when the Sanitation Department is knocking at the door."[5]

On November 12, 1920, less than two months after the scandal had come into the open, the owners asked Federal Judge Kenesaw Mountain Landis of Ohio to become baseball's commissioner, replacing the National Commission. Landis was an attractive choice. The owners considered him a friend because of his handling of the Federal League's 1915 antitrust lawsuit against Organized Baseball.[6]

Landis was a big baseball fan and hesitated tearing down the reserve clause the Federal League was attacking, which bound a player to his team year after year.[7] So he delayed ruling on the lawsuit; and by the end of the year (1915), the Federal League settled with Major League Baseball, making the case moot.[8]

The owners were also attracted to Landis because he conveyed a sense of rugged independence and integrity. While he projected the savior image they desperately needed to restore faith in the game, the owners were making an enormous bet: that whatever dirty linen Landis might find would be more than offset by the public's support of his moves to clean up the game.

The "easy" part of the commissioner's job was to stop the infighting among the owners. Toward that end, they not only granted him absolute power but also agreed not to criticize him or each other in public. Moreover, they agreed to waive recourse to the courts, should they dispute his decisions. As Leonard Koppett so aptly wrote, Landis "had all the characteristics of an effective dictator—and civil wars, sooner or later produce a dictator to restore order."[9]

The harder part of his job was to deal with the stench of scandal that was engulfing the game. Landis quickly went on the offensive to rehabilitate baseball with words, if not action. In late November, even before he formally took office, Landis made a sweeping statement directed at the accused Black Sox: "There is absolutely no chance for any of them to creep back into organized baseball. They will be and will remain outlaws."[10]

Landis's entire thrust was to paint the Black Sox scandal as an aberration.[11] Early in 1921 he spoke dramatically to federal judges at a Fort Worth dinner: "Notwithstanding what recently has happened, I believe there is a higher degree of honesty in the profession of playing ball than there is in any other that I know. And I do not except the clergy or the judiciary."[12]

And when the trial of the Black Sox seemed headed for a delay in mid-March, with the 1921 season less than a month away, the judge put the indicted players on an "ineligible list," reminding the public that "baseball is not powerless to protect itself."[13] A few days later, Landis banned for life Phillies first baseman Gene Paulette, who had dealings with St. Louis gamblers, though there was no proof that he had taken part in fixing games.

Perhaps the owners were not taking quite as much of a gamble as it seemed when they hired Judge Landis. This is not to suggest there was any conspiracy or quid pro quo between them and the new commissioner. Yet Landis surely did not want to tear down the very game he loved and now oversaw. His biographer David Pietrusza wrote that Landis understood, as White Sox owner Charles Comiskey had realized, that too many revelations could damage the game beyond repair. "He was not about to voluntarily put himself out of business any more than Comiskey was."[14]

Landis continually focused on the Black Sox players (along with a few other choice targets, players whose actions and associations were offensive and easy to attack) and thus diverted attention from a broader story and wider investigation. In retrospect, we can call them scapegoats or victims, yet Landis knew what he was doing. He instinctively understood, in the words of Koppett, that "moralistic posturing, particularly about gambling, brings greater rewards than actually trying to do something about the vice in question."[15] By focusing on the players, Landis deflected attention from the owners and their repeated failures to confront gambling in baseball.

Judge Landis often has been criticized for lumping White Sox third baseman Buck Weaver—who seemed to play his best in the Series and did not take money from gamblers, even though he knew of the fix—with the other Black Sox. The commissioner repeatedly refused to reopen Weaver's case and reconsider his verdict. Even today, more than sixty years after Landis's death, there is an active, ongoing movement for pardoning Weaver.[16] Yet Pietrusza suggests that Landis's most controversial act was also his most important, because he defined "dishonest play" so broadly. "What Landis did in banning Weaver was to *ex post facto* place guilty knowledge of crooked play on the same level as the deed itself."[17]

Landis's action with Weaver, and with Joe Jackson, whose degree of involvement in the fix is unclear and who has a groundswell of support today for the rehabilitation of his reputation, went even further. The reality is that the commissioner's solution to the problem he was hired to solve left him with no choice. Landis really could not pardon any of the Black Sox, even years later. Should the commissioner ever exonerate Jackson and admit that he was merely a scapegoat, Organized Baseball's superficial handling of a much more serious problem would be exposed.[18]

The national pastime successfully averted the looming crisis. Landis had two crucial "allies" in the process. The first was Babe Ruth, whose power game had been thrilling the nation even before the scandal broke. In the words of syndicated columnist Grantland Rice, baseball needed "a Superman, a man who could capture the imagination of the public"; and Ruth was that man.[19] The second was the nation's newspapers. They too had a vested interest in baseball's survival and prosperity. Reporting on the game was a huge source of circulation and revenue. It was also a source of employment for baseball's beat writers and columnists. So there was a rush to judgment in the press proclaiming Landis successful in cleaning up the game, even before he had done much investigating.

In a revealing editorial just before Christmas 1920 entitled "Penalties and Psychology," the *Sporting News* wrote, "Judge Landis himself has said that keeping baseball honest is largely a matter of psychology. . . . The public can be depended on if there is the right sort of propaganda used to awaken it."[20] Two weeks later, before Landis took over on January 12, the *Tribune*'s Macbeth, who had been a critic of the scandal's cover-up, wrote that fans "may rest assured" that the problem would be resolved simply because Landis promised to address it.[21]

The commissioner declared that his justice would be more demanding than the courts. Even if an indicted player were found innocent in a trial, Landis declared, "He has got to make good with the Commissioner. Juries sometimes make mistakes."[22] The following day, the judge (who still had his seat on the federal bench) made headlines that confirmed his flair for drama and his own sense of justice. Leaning on the nuisance clause of the Volstead Act that regulated Prohibition, Landis sealed twenty-one Chicago buildings worth almost $2 million for an entire year, because they had saloons operating within their walls.[23]

A month later, before Landis took office, one of the nation's leading sportswriters was already singing his praise. Sam Crane was a nine-teenth-century ballplayer who had been covering baseball for the *New York Evening Journal* for more than twenty years. He wrote that it was fortunate that a man of Landis's "firmness, strength of character, deter-mination and fearlessness" had the power "to eradicate the evil that the national game was up against. It means the salvation of the game—our game."[24] Crane's commentary was typical of the coverage Landis got early on.

Grantland Rice seemed to be an exception. When the scandal first emerged, he had been both outraged and worried. "Possibly nothing at all will be done except to throw out the crooks and call it a day's work. If this happens, we wouldn't give twenty cents for any franchise in America."[25] Yet Rice had not spoken out much during the 1920 season until the scandal became public knowledge. When Hugh Fullerton be-gan questioning the legitimacy of the 1919 Series, immediately following its conclusion, he was roundly attacked and ridiculed by the baseball establishment, including the *Sporting News* and *Baseball Magazine*. Like most of the nation's sports columnists, Rice did not come to Fullerton's defense or pursue the story.

After Landis started his job as commissioner, when other sportswrit-ers were ready to move on, Rice initially clamored for a full accounting. "The case isn't closed, by any means. Every fan in America is entitled to know the name of every crooked player and to be shown that every effort has been made to hang the branding iron upon every gambler involved, with especial attention paid to the main crooks."[26]

Yet when it became apparent that most journalists and fans were ready to put the scandal behind them, Rice fell into line. He may not have proclaimed that the game had been cleaned up, but he pulled back from criticism and rarely wrote about the Black Sox. In his autobiog-raphy, Rice wrote briefly (and inaccurately) of the scandal, that "the investigation lasted through the '20 season." Like most sports reporters and columnists, Rice did not push for an investigation in 1920, or a full accounting in 1921.

The stage was set for National League president John Heydler to declare, just before the start of the 1921 season, that the threat to the game's survival had been "throttled by heroic measures. . . . Baseball has emerged out of its ordeal in a healthier state than ever before. The whole baseball structure has been reorganized, and its government is now of a semi-public character."[27]

Yet neither the commissioner nor the courts had dug very deeply; there had been no investigation or trial. Landis was rehabilitating the game by narrowing his focus, simplifying events, and making examples of a few attractive suspects. Even Fullerton got on board, doing so with a surprising statement: "Judge Landis has no thought of waiting until a court has found a player guilty before acting. . . . In such cases the burden of proof is upon the defendant. He must prove his innocence when charged with crooked work in baseball."[28]

Black Sox researcher Gene Carney has written that the Black Sox scandal was merely "the tip of an iceberg." He notes that the scandal "was not about 'eight men out' for throwing the World Series. That is how it went down in history. The scandal was that baseball was being preyed upon by gamblers."[29] Sportswriters wanted to write about baseball, not fixed games; and fans wanted to believe in the integrity of the game.

Both groups let the owners—and even Judge Landis—off the hook. If their actions were not defensible, they were understandable. It is not surprising that almost a year had gone by before the real story of the 1919 World Series began to emerge. Nor is it surprising that Organized Baseball moved quickly to put the event behind it. As the scandal emerged, the public wanted to know its details; yet at the same time, they wished to deny that it really could have occurred. "The mythology of the episode as being aberrational, even inexplicable, began."[30]

Lest we judge the commissioner too harshly for not getting to the "bottom of the problem," his actions—and inaction—may have been the best thing for the game at the time. Bill Veeck Jr. explained, "Instead of setting out to make himself out to be a knight on white horseback, which is exactly what his critics have always accused him of doing, he did no more than the bare minimum that was necessary. Landis' great wisdom was in understanding that any attempt to investigate all of the gambling and fixing of the past would not only be impossible from a purely administrative standpoint, but would open up a can of worms that would be eating away at baseball for the next decade."[31] Had Landis gone after every dirty player and every thrown game, the very fabric of baseball might have unraveled.

3 The Shady Side of Baseball's Flagship Franchise

Since arriving in the city in 1883 and continuing through the years of the First World War, the Giants had "owned" New York.[1] Following some lean years, John McGraw took over as manager in 1902, and the Giants had been on or near the top of the National League ever since. Their winning ways had helped make them the team of choice for the city's commercial, theatrical, and political power elite, many of whom had established friendships, and in some cases business relationships, with McGraw.

Additionally, the Giants had always been the darlings of Tammany Hall, dating back to former owner Andrew Freedman's involvement with the corrupt Democratic political machine that ran New York City. Several generations of boys had grown up following the exploits of a never-ending parade of Giants heroes. It began with those late nineteenth-century teams that featured star players such as Buck Ewing, Roger Connor, Mickey Welch, Tim Keefe, and John Montgomery Ward. The progression continued through Amos Rusie, George Davis, and Mike Tiernan, and more recently to Larry Doyle, Fred Snodgrass, and the most beloved of all, Christy Mathewson. Now the heroes were named George Kelly, Ross Youngs, Frankie Frisch, George Burns, and Art Nehf.[2] Boys whose fathers took them to see the Giants play at the Polo Grounds in its various incarnations grew up to take their own sons to see the Giants play, and so it had always been.[3]

In his 1976 memoir, *For 2 Cents Plain*, author and social critic Harry Golden, a longtime Giants fan, recalled growing up in New York in the first decades of the twentieth century. "The Giants represented the New York of the brass cuspidor," he wrote, "that old New York that was still a man's world before the advent of the League of Women Voters; the days of swinging doors, of sawdust on the barroom floor, and of rushing to the growler."[4]

Not only did McGraw represent an old-fashioned style of baseball that was being replaced by one represented by Babe Ruth, he was also a part of the pre–World War I New York that was rapidly changing. Jerome Charyn writes about the changes taking place in New York at the beginning of the 1920s. Among them were the closing down of traditional New York gathering places of the sporting and theater crowds such as Rector's and Delmonico's, as the introduction of Prohibition spawned speakeasies and nightclubs. A new midtown-Manhattan landmark eatery, Lindy's, opened in 1921 and quickly became the major hangout for the Broadway crowd, especially the notorious Arnold Rothstein.[5] David Pietrusza, in the subtitle of his biography of Rothstein, called him "the criminal genius who fixed the 1919 World Series."[6]

The year 1919 was also marked by a change in ownership for the Giants. The relatively unknown Charles A. Stoneham was a forty-two-year-old newcomer to baseball when he bought controlling interest in the club that year. After John T. Brush, who had owned the team since 1902, died in 1912, his son-in-law, Harry Hempstead, had assumed control. Hempstead ran its operations until late in 1918, when he announced that the team was for sale. Several well-known people professed interest in buying the ballclub, including a group headed by two Broadway mainstays: singer, dancer, actor, and producer George M. Cohan and his partner, producer Sam Harris.

Also among the list of potential buyers were two prominent American industrialists: George W. Loft, of the Loft Candy Corporation, and Harry F. Sinclair, founder of the Sinclair Oil Company.[7] Loft appeared to be the front-runner, but his negotiations with Hempstead broke down. Cohan, a friend of McGraw's and a longtime Giants fan, claimed he was still negotiating with Hempstead when on January 14, 1919, the announcement came that Stoneham had purchased the team for $1,030,000.[8] "There were no less than ten different people after the club," manager John McGraw said following the announcement.[9]

McGraw had helped facilitate the sale, just as he had helped facilitate the sale of the Yankees to Jacob Ruppert and T. L. Huston four years earlier. He was also a friend of Stoneham; and as part of the deal, Stoneham named him the team's vice president. McGraw paid $50,000 to acquire seventy shares of the club, thus fulfilling his longtime desire to be part of the Giants' ownership. New York City magistrate Francis X. McQuade,

2. Charles A. Stoneham used profits from dubious stock dealings, his ties to Tammany politicians, and his relationship with "criminal genius" Arnold Rothstein to become the Giants' majority owner in 1919. *Private collection of Dennis Goldstein.*

a Tammany Hall–connected judge in magistrate's court and a McGraw crony and diehard Giants fan, also bought a small share of the team.

Stoneham and his group now owned 58 percent of the National Exhibition Company, which operated the Giants. Hempstead retained one-third, while the heirs of Arthur Soden continued to hold most of the remaining stock. Soden, owner of the Boston Beaneaters of the National

League, had helped bail out the Giants when they were in financial trouble during the Player League war of 1890.[10]

At the Giants' annual meeting in November 1920, the National Exhibition Company reelected Stoneham as president and McGraw as vice-president. They also reelected McQuade as treasurer and Leo G. Bondy, one of Stoneham's attorneys, and Horace Stoneham, his son, as directors.

Who exactly was Charles A. Stoneham? For one, he was an ally of New York governor Al Smith, both of whom had ties to Tammany Hall. "No one had ever owned a major ball club in New York City without the blessing of the Tammany Tiger," wrote author Noel Hynd.[11] Stoneham, the owner of a brokerage house, had gotten rich in a series of dubious stock maneuvers. Newspaper reports identified him as a Wall Street broker, but he was actually the proprietor of a bucket shop. Although bucket shops were legal at the time, what Stoneham and others who ran these operations did was certainly sleazy. They would accept buy-and-sell orders for stocks but not execute them. Instead, they would hold onto the money and cash in when the customers' selections proved unwise. "Bookmaker," rather than Wall Street broker, would have been a better description of Stoneham's profession. The only difference was that he took bets on stocks instead of sporting events.

Several of Stoneham's clients had filed suits against him, and in 1923 he would be indicted on charges of mail fraud and perjury related to his dubious stock transactions. The most flamboyant lawyer of the time, William J. Fallon, would defend Stoneham and win his acquittal. Fallon, known as the Great Mouthpiece, was the Giants' counsel. In his 1931 biography of Fallon, *The Great Mouthpiece*, author Gene Fowler wrote, "He became the Great Mouthpiece for the grand dukes of Racketland."[12]

Fallon was also McGraw's defense attorney in the notorious Lambs Club brawl of 1920 and the lawyer who helped Arnold Rothstein avoid indictment by the grand jury investigating the 1919 World Series.[13] Rothstein's claim of innocence convinced not only the grand jury but also Ban Johnson. "I found the man Arnold Rothstein and after a long talk with him, I felt convinced he wasn't in any plot to fix the Series," said the credulous Johnson. "He did admit to me that he'd heard of the fixing, but in spite of that, declared he had wagered on the White Sox."[14]

Running a bucket shop, as Stoneham did, allowed many disreputable characters to make a lot of money and inevitably to encounter other shady characters. Moreover, Rothstein was involved with much questionable enterprise that went on in America, and especially in New York City. He was Stoneham's partner in the bucket shop enterprises and had served as a go-between in Stoneham's purchase of the Giants. Once Stoneham took control of the club, Rothstein often was a guest in the owners' box at the Polo Grounds.

In fact, Rothstein had a relationship with all three of the Giants' new owners. In addition to his partnership with Stoneham, at one time he had been partners with McGraw and discredited-jockey Tod Sloan in a billiards parlor at Herald Square in Manhattan.[15] The dealings between Rothstein and the Tammany-controlled McQuade had been mostly indirect until June 1919. It was Magistrate McQuade who allowed Rothstein to walk away from charges that he had shot and wounded three policemen at the Partridge Club, one of Rothstein's illegal casinos. Perhaps McQuade was bribed into doing so, or maybe he was just acting on orders from his superiors at Tammany. Whatever the case, a group of men who were indebted in one way or another to America's most notorious gambler were now running baseball's flagship franchise.

4 Ruppert and Huston Arrive, Ready to "Go to the Limit"

For the Yankees 1921 was the culmination of a journey that began when the franchise relocated from Baltimore to New York City in 1903.[1] While the club had come close to the American League pennant in 1904 and 1906, it then floundered for many years, becoming almost an afterthought to New York baseball fans. Owners Frank Farrell and Bill Devery were hampered by financial constraints, their own deteriorating relationship, and their meddling in the clubhouse. The franchise also suffered from poor personnel decisions, buying and trading for players of limited ability, and from a revolving door of managers, seven between 1908 and 1914 alone.[2]

Colonel Jacob Ruppert and Captain Til Huston arrived on the scene in 1915 with deep pockets, business sense, and a commitment to winning. The Giants' John McGraw played a key role in bringing the old and new Yankees' owners together. Ruppert was a Giants' fan who often attended their games at the Polo Grounds, sometimes as McGraw's guest. Several years earlier, when he had an opportunity to buy the Chicago Cubs, Ruppert declined, saying he was not interested "in anything so far from Broadway."[3] McGraw introduced Ruppert to Huston, and the two men later made him a proposal to buy the Giants. McGraw quickly let them know the Giants were not for sale.

"But if you really want to buy a ball club," McGraw said, "I think I can get one for you. How about the Yankees?"[4] Neither Ruppert nor Huston was interested in the sorry franchise. Ruppert had seen the Yankees play only twice; like many New Yorkers, he went to their games to see visiting teams' star players.[5] In his history of the Yankees, Frank Graham described McGraw's efforts to persuade these reputable businessmen to buy the Yankees: "McGraw's vision was broader than theirs. He set about convincing them that, under proper direction and with fresh

3. John McGraw (*center*) played a key role in facilitating the sale of the Yankees to Jacob Ruppert (*left*) and Til Huston in early 1915. New York's American League club had had little success since George Stallings (*right*) managed them in 1910, when they finished second. *Library of Congress, Prints and Photographs Division, George Grantham Bain Collection,* LC-B2-5171-9.

money—in the amount they had, for instance—much might be done with the Yankees. At last they weakened."[6]

Ruppert was a former New York City congressman with strong Tammany connections and a controlling interest in his family's large brewery.[7] He was an impeccably dressed bachelor with extensive real estate holdings and eclectic collections of rare jade, porcelain, monkeys, and Saint Bernards. Huston was an engineer and self-made millionaire, who made his fortune dredging Havana harbor after the Spanish-American War. Huston was as unkempt and indifferent about his appearance as Ruppert was fastidious about his. Huston was usually the face of the franchise to the press and the public in the early years.

For $450,000 the two men had acquired a seventh-place team that played in the New York Giants' ballpark, the Polo Grounds.[8] The Yankees had a reputation of losing and of being an ill-fated team during the second decade of the twentieth century. References to "the immortal Yankee jinx" were not uncommon.[9] Even Frank Chance, "the Peerless Leader," of the world champion Chicago Cubs of 1907 and 1908, who took over as manager of the Yankees in 1913, could not get them to play winning ball. He soon lamented, "I know there are boneheads in baseball, but I didn't believe so many could get on one club. Mine."[10]

As Ruppert later said, he and Huston had bought "an orphan ball club, without a home of its own, without players of outstanding ability, without prestige."[11] In their first two years, they spent more than $75,000 for stars of the defunct Federal League and for minor league prospects.

Ruppert and Huston also hired the genial, former Detroit Tigers pitching star of the early twentieth century, Bill Donovan, to manage the club. Except for a tantalizing few weeks in June and July 1916, when the Yankees were in first place, the new owners had little to show for their expenditures. Donovan's easygoing ways didn't produce a winner, and he was let go after a sixth-place finish in 1917.[12] Ruppert and Huston had inherited a 70-84 team and three years later had only a 71-82 team, despite all their spending and efforts.[13]

The year 1921 was also the culmination of a long upward struggle for Miller Huggins, who was in his fourth year as the Yankees manager. The diminutive Huggins had been a successful leadoff hitter and second baseman in the National League from 1904 to 1916.[14] He had moderate success managing the St. Louis Cardinals from 1913 to 1917, overcoming, among other things, his size. "Hug is a tiny fellow, and there's the rub. There are giants on the field who resent an order from a little guy," wrote St. Louis Times sports editor Sid Keener.[15] Despite the team's severe financial problems, he guided them to third-place finishes in both 1914 and 1917. Huggins gained a reputation as a developer of talent, a necessity in a club that had limited resources to buy and keep established stars.

Huggins was not a popular figure in New York with either the fans or the press, or even with his own players. In contrast to his predecessor, the immensely popular and gregarious Donovan, Huggins was an aloof and introspective man. He was a bachelor and lived with his spinster-sister Myrtle. He seldom mingled with others, except for a small circle of friends, which included longtime scout Bob Connery.

Damon Runyon captured the Huggins personality at the start of his first season at the Yankees helm: "Off the field he is quite self-effacing, and rather given to solitude. He is no mixer with the world at large. His exterior manner suggests the crustacean known as the crab."[16] Runyon did add that Huggins conveyed a sense that he knew his baseball. Other writers, while agreeing, were less generous. Hugh Fullerton would write in the heat of the 1921 season, "He is a crabby little man, who knows about as much baseball as there is to be known, a superior sort of fellow who does not mix well, either with fans or players."[17]

After joining the Yankees, Huggins began to mold a winning team, a long and slow process of evaluating, trading, releasing, and acquiring players. Colonel Ruppert had authorized him to "go to the limit" to build a championship team.[18] In this era, the modern-day position of general manager did not exist. Business managers handled everything from ticket sales to equipment to travel arrangements, and field managers usually made the personnel decisions and trades on their own, subject to agreement by the teams' owners. Huggins took over, "nursing no delusions concerning . . . exploded phenoms" or "false hopes regarding pastimers who should be, but are not, great stars."[19] He quickly began cleaning house. By 1919, the start of his second season, seventeen of the Yankees Huggins had inherited were gone; and new faces—players of his choosing—had been brought in to take their place.

Huggins's club also began to establish a close working relationship with Harry Frazee, the owner of the Boston Red Sox, an association that would prove to be extremely beneficial for the Yankees. In their first trade, in December 1918, the Red Sox sent former stars Duffy Lewis and Ernie Shore to New York in a seven-player deal. The key Yankee player in the transaction was their former ace Ray Caldwell, who had worn out his welcome in New York because of his repeated bouts of drinking.[20]

In late July 1919 the Yankees acquired Red Sox pitcher Carl Mays, who had won sixty-one games for Boston over the previous three seasons.[21] He also had two victories in the 1918 World Series, including the clincher in what would be the Red Sox's last world championship of the twentieth century.

An agitated Mays had walked out on manager Ed Barrow and his teammates on July 13, 1919, during a difficult summer in Boston. Mays was facing various personal problems at the time, and he later explained,

"At that particular moment my whole world was falling down."[22] The defending world champions were hampered by injuries and mired in sixth place at the time. Mays was frustrated by poor run support; he had a 5-11 record, despite a very respectable 2.47 earned run average.

The Yankees owners, intent on building a winning team, knew how much a pitcher like Mays could move them in that direction. They were willing to risk legal battles and spend whatever it took to achieve their goal. Their acquisition of Mays on July 29 set off a bitter dispute between the Yankees, on one side, and American League president Ban Johnson, on the other. Johnson ordered Mays suspended, in part to teach rebellious players that they could not change teams on their own and in part to punish Boston owner Frazee, who was too independent for Johnson's liking. Both the Yankees and the Red Sox felt they had the right to consummate the Mays deal and went to court to prevent Johnson from interfering.

For one of the few times since he founded the American League in 1900, Johnson's authority had been seriously challenged. Historically, the owners had accepted their president's direction almost without question, but not Frazee. The previous winter, Frazee had led an unsuccessful effort to replace the autocratic Johnson and the National Commission with one commissioner. The man he proposed for the job was former United States president William Howard Taft. Frazee had the novel theory that the league president should follow the wishes of the owners, rather than vice versa. "I am one of the eight employers of Ban Johnson," he declared.[23]

The case ultimately went to the New York State Supreme Court for the Manhattan District, where future United States senator Robert Wagner granted the Yankees a permanent injunction preventing Johnson from stopping the trade.[24] It has often been said that Yankee owners Ruppert and Huston agreed on virtually nothing. Yet they were totally in alignment on two issues, matters in which Huston took the lead role: the 1919 court battle over Carl Mays and the 1922 construction of Yankee Stadium.

Mays gave New York another frontline pitcher to go along with Bob Shawkey and Jack Quinn. Shawkey was the best early acquisition of the new Yankees' owners, a young pitcher they had purchased from the Philadelphia Athletics in the summer of 1915. Quinn was an aging spitball pitcher who had been a Yankee a decade earlier and had rejoined the team in 1919. In 1919 the three hurlers combined for forty-four victories for New York, though Mays had been a Yankee for only two months that season. These would be the top three hurlers the team would count on for 1920.[25]

The Yankees had some powerful bats in their lineup late in the second decade of the twentieth century. "Murderers' Row" was a phrase New York sportswriters began calling the Yankees as early as 1918, long before Babe Ruth joined the team. "The renowned 'Murderers' Row'—this mob of baseball criminals and pitcher beaters," wrote columnist and cartoonist Robert Ripley that year, "are apt to break out at any moment."[26] Less than two weeks later Fred Lieb also used the phrase. On June 23 he wrote of "Murderers' Row, the greatest collection of pitcher thumpers in baseball to-day."[27]

This group consisted of outfielder Ping Bodie and the entire Yankees infield: first baseman Wally Pipp, second baseman Del Pratt, shortstop Roger Peckinpaugh, and third baseman Frank Baker.

First baseman Pipp joined the Yankees from the Detroit Tigers, when the Yankees' new owners took over in 1915. The American League promised Ruppert and Huston talented personnel from the league's other clubs to strengthen the downtrodden franchise and help establish a team that could compete for fans with John McGraw's Giants in the nation's biggest city. Yet only the Tigers came through with players for the Yankees, providing Pipp and outfielder Hugh High.[28]

Pratt had come to New York in a seven-player deal with the St. Louis Browns in the winter of 1917–18, in Miller Huggins's first trade as New York's manager.[29] While the Yankees gave up a lot of talent to get him—especially promising young spitball pitcher Urban Shocker—Pratt solidified the team's middle defense. Huggins said that Pratt was "the man who put the ball club on its feet."[30]

Peckinpaugh was the only Yankee starter in 1919 who had been a regular on the team before Ruppert and Huston bought the club. Frank "Home Run" Baker was the one legitimate star on the Yanks from 1915 to 1919. He had earned his nickname by hitting two dramatic home runs for the Athletics in the 1911 World Series. Like Shawkey, he had come from Philadelphia in a straight cash deal, before the 1916 season.

Miller Huggins had overseen a steady rise in the standings for the

Yankees, to fourth place in 1918 and to third in 1919. Yet the New York press blamed him for the team's midseason swoons both seasons, which followed a similar pattern. In both seasons, the Yanks were in first place as late as early July and then soon fell out of contention. As the decade came to a close, the Yankees were improving; but their outfield was weak and their pitching lacked depth. They were still not a championship-caliber team.

5

"You can't compare him with anybody else. He's Babe Ruth."

Babe Ruth joined the New York Yankees in January 1920, as Prohibition became the law of the land. Yet New York City was anything but dry. Estimates of the number of speakeasies in the city were around 32,000 in the 1920s, far more than the number of pre-Prohibition bars in town. "Prohibition, passed into law in 1919 and not repealed until 1933, was a joke in most of urban America, but in New York it was an all-out full-scale farce."[1]

Ruth was a great fit for and reflection of the nation's biggest city with his uninhibited personality and enormous zest for life. Whether he was hitting baseballs on the field or relishing life off it, no ballpark or city seemed able to contain or restrain him. As appealing off the field as he was dominant on it, Ruth naturally attracted fans, especially women and youngsters. He may have been the Colossus of Clout and the Sultan of Swat—just two of the many nicknames sportswriters bestowed on him when he arrived in New York City. Yet he was also simply the Babe.[2]

Ruth began his big league career as a pitcher for the Boston Red Sox and soon became one of the game's best left-handers. From 1915 to 1918 he won 78 games with only 40 losses as well as 3 victories without a loss in the World Series.[3] Yet from the start, his batting prowess was evident to all, and he seemed to deliver some of his most dramatic drives against the Yankees. In 1915 he hit his first big league home run off New York's Jack Warhop at the Polo Grounds. That year, he had four home runs (three against the Yanks) in only 92 at bats, while the league leader, Braggo Roth, had seven in 384 at bats (playing for Chicago and Cleveland). "With Babe Ruth's ability to murder the ball," the *New York World* wrote that summer, "it seems a pity that his family did not raise him to be an outfielder instead of a pitcher."[4]

In 1918 Ruth, now primarily an outfielder, led the league with eleven homers, while he still pitched in twenty games, winning thirteen of them.[5] The following year, his Boston manager, Ed Barrow, moved him out of the pitching rotation and into the everyday lineup as an outfielder. He hit an amazing twenty-nine home runs that year, and many were long-distance blasts that traveled well beyond the playing field.

On September 24, 1919, the Yankees played the Red Sox in a double-header at the Polo Grounds. The games, which had no bearing on the pennant race, drew only about 6,000 fans. The defending world champion Red Sox, devastated by injuries, were in fifth place, twenty and a half games behind the Chicago White Sox. The Yankees had faded badly after their fast start and were eleven and a half games out of first, fighting the Detroit Tigers for third place. Yet the second game, a 2–1 Yankee win in thirteen innings, was marked by a couple of spectacular individual performances.

A relatively unknown Red Sox pitcher named Waite Hoyt threw a complete game. While he eventually lost, 2–1, in thirteen innings, Hoyt, at one point, retired twenty-seven men in a row, in essence pitching a nine-inning perfect game within a game.[6]

That game must have made quite an impression on Yankees manager Miller Huggins, not simply for Hoyt's performance, but also for a mammoth home run Ruth hit off Bob Shawkey in the ninth inning to send the game into extra innings. It was the longest drive ever hit in the New York ballpark, or—more accurately—out of it. The ball sailed over the right-field roof and landed in adjacent Manhattan Field, site of an earlier Polo Grounds. Newspapers reported that the home run broke Ed Williamson's Major League record of twenty-seven, set in 1884 in a small Chicago ballpark, just as they had noted a couple of weeks earlier that Ruth's twenty-sixth home run (also hit off the Yankees) had smashed Buck Freeman's record of twenty-five, set in 1899.[7] Long home runs like this were fueling Ruth's growing popularity and bringing out souvenir hunters. The slugger said he was being "pestered to death" by them; one enterprising Baltimore fan offered $2,500 for the bat that Ruth had used to set the record.[8]

It was no secret that Ruth was having a number of disputes with Red Sox management.[9] Huggins told the Yankees' owners that if Ruth were to become available, they should try to acquire him, whatever the cost. Huggins later told Ruppert that Red Sox owner Harry Frazee would consider $100,000 as a fair price for Ruth. "Huggins, you are crazy," ex-

4. "Feels like a Lot of Homers" read the caption of this February 1921 photo. As the season progressed, Babe Ruth's walloping continued; but Miller Huggins rarely smiled. Some in the press accused several Yankees, including the Babe, of undermining Huggins's authority. *Private collection of Steve Steinberg.*

claimed Ruppert, "and this man Frazee is even crazier. Who ever heard of a ball player being worth $100,000 in cash?" Huggins was quick with his reply: "Colonel, take my advice. Buy Ruth. Frazee is crazy, yes. He's crazy to let you have the Babe for so little."[10]

Miller Huggins was a Deadball Era player, who had mastered the low-scoring, hit-and-run style of play. He had led the National League in walks four times, stolen twenty or more bases nine seasons, and hit a grand total of nine home runs in his career. When he came to New York in 1918, many people expected that he would bring that same game of inside baseball to the Yankees. Yet before he had managed a single game with the Yankees, he explained that his team's style of play would be determined by the strengths and weaknesses of his players.[11] In the next couple of years, Huggins had the flexibility and foresight to see just what kind of an impact Babe Ruth could make. In 1920, with Ruth now a Yankee, Huggins had the opportunity to benefit from that impact.

"Take all the adjectives there are in the language which could be used to describe a slugger," Huggins said in the summer of 1920, "plaster them all on and then wish there were a few more for good measure. You can't describe him, you can't compare him with anybody else. He's Babe Ruth."[12] Years later, Jacob Ruppert would pay tribute to his deceased Yankees manager: "Huggins had vision. . . . Far-seeing judgment. He planned on a big scale. . . . I doubt if anybody except Huggins had any foreknowledge of just how predominant Ruth could become in the baseball world."[13]

Ruth did become available in late 1919, when his contract demands and generally combative behavior proved too much for Frazee, especially with Boston's fifth-place finish that season.[14] The Yankees acquired Ruth for $100,000 plus a $300,000 loan, secured by a mortgage on the Red Sox's Fenway Park.[15]

Ruth did not hit his first home run as a Yankee until May 1, 1920; but he then caught fire and showed that 1919 was a mere warm-up now that he was on the main stage, New York City. He hit his thirtieth home run on July 19, 1920. Fans everywhere were turning out in large numbers, nowhere more than at home in the Polo Grounds. "His name glowing on the score card," wrote the *New York Evening Telegram*, "carries all the magnetism of [Douglas] Fairbanks or [Mary] Pickford or [Charlie] Chaplin glittering from a theatre."[16]

Fans were also attracted to Ruth's boisterous and almost childlike personality. He did everything—from eating, drinking (illegal alcohol), and womanizing to hitting home runs and pop flies and even striking out—with exuberance. Heywood Broun captured Ruth this way in *Vanity Fair* in 1921: "There is no compromise in his method. His intent is constantly All or Nothing. . . . A hair-line divides the great and the ridiculous. Magnificence will never be achieved except by those who are willing to run the risk of spectacular failure."[17]

In the past, most players had choked up on the bat, trying to punch the ball through the infield. Along came Ruth, who combined enormous upper body strength and the full extension of his arms, to send baseballs to places they had not gone before.[18]

Ruth was attracting to the ballparks, both home and away, a new and less-knowledgeable fan. It was far easier to understand the power game of the home run than the more-subtle game of the walk, the steal, the sacrifice, and the hit and run. "To someone new to the game—children, perhaps a recently arrived immigrant, or a casual fan unfamiliar with the intricacies of baseball . . . Babe Ruth made it easier to be a baseball fan than it ever had been before."[19]

One man who did not care for this new game was the manager of the New York Giants, John McGraw. As Robert Creamer wrote in his Ruth biography, "The term 'inside' baseball was almost sacred, and John McGraw was its high priest. It meant playing for a run, a single run."[20] While the Giants' skipper often belittled Ruth's baseball skills, he was able to recognize Ruth's appeal. When McGraw took members of his team on an exhibition tour of Cuba after the 1920 season, he added Ruth to his squad and gave the slugger top billing.[21]

While McGraw was frustrated that, with the addition of Ruth, the Yankees were outdrawing the Giants by a large margin at the Polo Grounds, that trend did not crystallize until later in the 1920 season. What had become obvious to the Giants during the 1919 season was that they were losing significant revenue by sharing their lucrative Sunday playing dates with the Yankees. Sunday baseball in New York City had been legalized before the start of the 1919 season, and New York teams were soon drawing large crowds on Sundays.[22]

Equally important was the new class of fans that attended Sunday games. The working class, whose workweek was usually six days, now had the time and opportunity to see a ball game on their day off. On May 4, 1919, the *New York Tribune* described the scene at the Polo Grounds' first Sunday game: "Up to yesterday, baseball in greater New York was for the semi-idle. . . . Yesterday those bleachers teemed with life. The men from the docks and the factories came and they brought their wives and children. Those dark green benches held thousands of fans who never in their lives had seen a big league game."[23]

On May 14, 1920, the Giants informed the Yankees that they would not renew their lease after this season. With such short notice, there was no way the Yankees could find a location and build in time for the 1921 season. The Giants then relented, albeit with a large rent increase.[24] The Yankee owners resolved to not be put into such a position again. And with the arrival of Ruth and the rise of their team to contender status, it was time for them to have a home of their own, and a large one. Nine months later the New York Yankees closed a deal on the Bronx site of Yankee Stadium, which they purchased from the estate of William Waldorf Astor.[25]

The Yankees' infield of 1920 was a solid one. Wally Pipp, Del Pratt, and Roger Peckinpaugh again had strong seasons. At third base, two youngsters were vying to replace Frank Baker, who had left baseball for the season, which he also had done in 1915.[26] "Phenoms of 1920: Yankee Hopes Rest on Two Youthful Recruits," headlined an early season article about Bob Meusel and Aaron Ward.[27]

The Yankees of 1920 had sufficient pitching to stay in the race until the final weeks of the season. Bob Shawkey won twenty games for the second year in a row, despite missing almost a month to injury from a strained side muscle. At one point, he reeled off eleven consecutive victories. "Old" Jack Quinn won eighteen games, the same number that he had won for New York exactly ten years earlier. Carl Mays was the ace of the staff, with twenty-six victories and a league-leading six shutouts. In just one season, he paid back the Yankees for all they had gone through to secure him.

On August 16, 1920, Mays was on the mound in the Polo Grounds, in a key game against the Cleveland Indians, who were tied for first with the Chicago White Sox. The Yankees were only a half game back. The three teams had been battling for first place all season. Ten-game and nine-game winning streaks earlier in the year had kept the Yankees close, with brief stays in first place.

Popular Cleveland shortstop Ray Chapman, known to crowd the plate, stepped up to bat in the fifth inning, with the Indians leading, 3–0. He never saw Mays's first pitch; he seemed to freeze, according to witnesses. When the ball hit his temple, it made such a crisp sound that Mays thought it had come off Chapman's bat. Mays fielded it and threw to first base, but he quickly realized what had happened when he saw Chapman collapse at home plate. By the next morning, Ray Chapman was dead from a massive skull fracture, the only on-field Major League fatality in baseball history.[28]

Mays immediately came under attack from many quarters. The Detroit Tigers and the St. Louis Browns talked of boycotting the games he would pitch in. Though Mays was known for throwing the beanball, most observers felt that was not the case with this tragedy.[29] With Chapman's batting stance, the pitch may very well have been a strike, or very close to one. League president Ban Johnson, who had fought Mays a little more than a year earlier over his quitting the Red Sox, now came to his defense against the proposed boycotts. Mays was exonerated by both baseball and government authorities. While Chapman's death shook the pitcher, remarkably he was able to continue pitching at his high level of effectiveness.

After sweeping the Tigers in Detroit, the Yankees were in first place on September 14. The White Sox then swept them in Comiskey Park, dropping the Yankees to third place, where they finished the season, a game behind Chicago and three behind the Cleveland Indians.

Ruth hit fifty-four home runs in 1920, shattering his own record and accounting for an almost-unbelievable 15 percent of all homers hit in the American League that year.[30] He batted .376, drove in 137 runs, and scored 158. He also excelled in some of the measures that baseball researchers have popularized in recent years, with an on-base percentage of .532 and a slugging percentage of .847.[31] The list of hurlers he hit home runs against included the league's best; Walter Johnson, Stan Coveleski, Red Faber, Herb Pennock, Urban Shocker, and Lefty Williams were just a few of the illustrious group.[32]

Pitchers feared Ruth; opposing managers respected him. "I have seen hundreds of ball-players at the plate," *New York Daily News* sports editor Paul Gallico wrote in his retrospective, "and none of them managed to convey the message of impending doom to a pitcher that Babe Ruth did with the cock of his head, the position of his legs and the little, gentle waving of the bat, feathered in his two big paws."[33] The fear he inspired in pitchers led them to begin walking him, many times intentionally or semi-intentionally.[34]

The opposition preferred giving him one base, rather than having him swinging for the fences and taking four bases. When the Yankees were on the road and opposing pitchers walked Ruth, fans of those teams booed their own. Even though a pass to the Babe may have made sense for those teams, their fans wanted to see Ruth hit . . . or miss, but at least have a chance to swing for the fences.

With his record-breaking season and with the Yankees in the 1920 pennant race until the final week of the season, they drew a record 1,289,422 fans. That was more than double what they had drawn in 1919, and almost 360,000 more than New York's more established team, the Giants, had attracted.[35] The Yankees generated home gate receipts of $864,830 and an operating profit of $374,079 in 1920.[36] They had rewarded Ruth with a $20,000 salary in 1920 and 1921, double what he had made with the Red Sox a year earlier; and they also had paid him a $5,000 bonus each of his first two seasons.[37]

Ultimately the Yankees fell short of the 1920 pennant because of the inspired play of the Cleveland Indians. Tris Speaker, their player-manager, guided them through the Chapman tragedy with spirited and skilled leadership, as well as his contribution with the bat (he hit .388) and center-field play. In September a rookie from the University of Alabama named Joe Sewell took over at shortstop for Chapman and started a Hall of Fame career. Cleveland, led by Stan Coveleski's three complete-game victories, went on to beat Brooklyn in the World Series, five games to two.

The Yankees also fell short because of their own weaknesses. Damon Runyon succinctly observed that the 1920 Yankees were somewhat over-rated, a team with weaknesses in several areas.[38] Beyond their top three pitchers, who won sixty-four games, they got few contributions from the rest of the staff.

The Yankees' outfield, with Ping Bodie and Duffy Lewis or Bob Meusel playing alongside Babe Ruth, was not the fleetest afoot or the surest in judging fly balls. The team was weak behind the plate, with the small (five feet nine and 150 pounds) Muddy Ruel sharing duties with the weak-hitting Truck Hannah. They were also one of the slowest teams in baseball; only one big league team, the Philadelphia Athletics with fifty, had fewer stolen bases than the sixty-four they had.

Babe Ruth's timing was impeccable. He began making the transition from pitcher to everyday player in 1918 and 1919, at the end of the Deadball Era, and arrived in New York in 1920, the start of the Lively Ball Era. A close look at the numbers suggests that this transition occurred over three seasons. In 1919 batting averages and earned run averages began to rise. The jump was more significant in 1920, and 1921 continued and confirmed the trend. The pivot point of the game of baseball, the central matchup, is that between pitcher and batter. Irving Sanborn, the veteran sports editor of the *Chicago Daily Tribune* and 1920 president of the Baseball Writers' Association of America, wrote in *Baseball Magazine*, "The fight against the predominance of the pitcher is almost as ancient as baseball itself."[39] It is cyclical in nature, and the cycle was swinging away from the pitcher.

Hitting was gaining the upper hand for a combination of reasons. Starting with the 1920 season, a ban was placed on trick pitches, from the shine ball to the spitball, all pitches that gave the ball added and unusual movement as it approached the plate.[40] Hitters quickly gained confidence because they could dig in; they would no longer be intimidated by hard-to-control trick pitches.

Moreover, fresh, white balls were to be kept in play at all times.[41] Pitchers could no longer doctor the ball to make its path unpredictable, and they could no longer depend on moistened and darkened balls that were hard for the hitters to see. The Lively Ball Era is somewhat of a misnomer since these two factors were probably driving the change.[42] At the end of the decade, *Baseball Magazine* editor F. C. Lane looked back on the 1920s and noted, "Pitchers will tell you that the lively ball troubles them much less than the everlasting 'new' ball."[43]

The ball did change somewhat. The use of better raw materials after the war (such as Australian wool, which could be wound tighter) added more spring to the ball.[44] Ruth himself contributed to the new era by trying to hit the ball over the fence, rather than aiming for the open spaces between the fielders. He was soon widely emulated at the plate. In essence, he showed hitters how to take advantage of the changes to the rules and the ball. His success was bringing him fame and money. Why not "Be like Babe"? Managers began designing their offense around the home run and the big inning, rather than around the inside game of playing for one run. The game of bunt, steal, and hit-and-run was quickly disappearing.[45]

In the end, the rule changes, to ban trick pitches and to keep bright balls in play, were driven by the owners' desire to redress the balance between pitching and hitting. The new rules would bring more fans into the ballparks at the very time that rumors of the 1919 World Series fix were swirling. There is no hard evidence that the rules were adopted to combat a possible scandal with increased scoring, which would bring new fans to the ballparks. The corruption of the 1919 Series would not break into the open until the very end of the 1920 season. Yet the owners surely were aware of the whispers and rumors, if not more, when they enacted the new regulations before the start of the 1920 season.

Irving Sanborn did make an intriguing connection. He wrote in the September 1920 *Baseball Magazine*, which went to press a few weeks before the scandal became public, that the rules to increase offense were the result of increased concerns about fixed games. He stated, "Some handicap on the pitchers was necessary last winter because baseball was becoming too attractive to the gamblers."[46] He explained that the low-scoring games of the Deadball Era were vulnerable to fixes. A gambler merely had to know who the starting pitchers would be and then place his bet. Moreover, a game dominated by one player (i.e., the pitcher, in this era of low scoring) could be more easily fixed (by "reaching" that one player) than one in a higher-scoring era in which no one player dominated.

Babe Ruth and the crowds he drew in 1919 had whetted the appetites of the owners. Even the great pitcher Walter Johnson admitted, "The baseball public likes to see the ball walloped hard. The home runs are meat for the fans. . . . 'Babe' Ruth draws more people than a great pitcher does."[47] W. R. Hoefer in *Baseball Magazine* wrote, "There is very positive evidence in the jammed ballyards that the multitude finds the cruder, more robust, freer walloping game of the present more attractive. And in baseball, more perhaps than in any other sphere, the majority rules."[48]

Colonels Ruppert and Huston were determined to bring an American League pennant to New York.[49] They had turned over the controls to the cerebral and colorless manager Miller Huggins, who was making steady progress. He, in turn, was building his offense around Ruth, a man who was proving hard to control, by both opposing pitchers and his own team's management. As 1920 came to a close, anticipation for 1921 was already building. Would Ruth be able to replicate his 1920 season? Would his Yankees win their first pennant?

Babe Ruth was changing the game just as the pitcher was losing some of his most effective weapons, the trick pitch and the dirty ball. While many hitters began to copy his big-swing style, for the long ball, there still was only one Ruth. Paul Gallico saluted Ruth in this way: "You might think, perhaps, that this plethora of home runs would cheapen them and satiate our appetites. Far from it; every time Ruth came to bat he was on his way to some kind of record. Every ball he expelled from the stadia was one more link in the chain of continuing and progressing miracles. The impossible was becoming the probable, and for the price of admission would take place before one's very eyes. And the Babe's utter demolishing of every prior home run record was just another verification of the opulence of our times."[50]

6

The Giants Fail to Get Rogers Hornsby

The personnel that make up baseball teams are always in flux. Rosters change not only from season to season but also within seasons. Field managers and business managers are continually attempting to improve their teams through trades and additions from the minor leagues. One of the key decisions managers must make is when to replace an aging veteran with a promising newcomer. In business manager Ed Barrow and field manager Miller Huggins, for the Yankees, and John McGraw, who, in effect, occupied both roles for the Giants, the two New York teams had excellent judges of baseball talent making those decisions. Their shrewdness and good judgment played a big part in the early 1920s success of their teams. McGraw in particular was "perfectly ruthless in his methods of destroying a ballclub and building a new one," wrote F. C. Lane in *Baseball Magazine*.[1] But in 1920 his replacing two veteran infielders with a pair of rookies was mainly the result of forces beyond his control.

On the morning of August 31, 1920, Major League Baseball's two defending league champions found themselves holding narrow leads over two strong challengers. In the American League, the Chicago White Sox led the Yankees by one game and Cleveland by one and a half games. In the National League, the world champion Cincinnati Reds had a half-game lead over Brooklyn and a one-and-a-half-game edge on the Giants. That afternoon, the last-place Philadelphia Phillies and the fifth-place Chicago Cubs played at Cubs Park in a game that appeared to have little effect on the National League pennant race.[2] However, events surrounding that Phillies-Cubs game turned out to have a very significant impact on the American League pennant race and eventually led to the exposure of baseball's worst-ever scandal.

Before the game, gamblers in Detroit and Cleveland reported that the odds had shifted from 2–1 in favor of Chicago to 6–5 in favor of Philadelphia. A few days later, on September 5, the *Chicago Daily Tribune* reported that gamblers had bet large amounts of money on the Phillies to win. To insure winning those bets, reported the *Tribune*, they had attempted to bribe several Chicago players into deliberately losing the game. Cubs president William Veeck had received several telegrams warning him of the planned fix. Anxious to thwart it, Veeck ordered his manager, Fred Mitchell, to replace scheduled starting pitcher Claude Hendrix with his ace, Grover Alexander, and promised Alexander a $500 bonus if the Cubs won.[3] Despite the switch from Hendrix to Alexander, the Phillies won, 3–0.

The incident revived suspicions that gamblers had successfully rigged the outcomes of several games over the years and led Chicago's Cook County to convene a grand jury to investigate. The grand jury announced that, along with exploring baseball gambling in general, it would specifically look into rumors that the hometown White Sox had intentionally lost to the Reds in the 1919 World Series. The investigation resulted in indictments for eight members of the White Sox. Team owner Charles Comiskey, who, evidence suggests, was aware of the Series fix all along, suspended the eight men for the last week of the season.

Among those suspended were four members of the starting lineup—left fielder Joe Jackson, who was batting .382 at the time; center fielder Happy Felsch; shortstop Swede Risberg; and third baseman Buck Weaver—along with a pair of twenty-game winners, Lefty Williams and Eddie Cicotte. Comiskey's decision made it necessary for manager Kid Gleason to use bench players to replace the suspended men. The White Sox, a half game out of first place at the time of the suspensions, finished second, two games behind the pennant-winning Indians. The Yankees finished third, three games back.

As part of the September hearings on the alleged fix, the panel called Giants manager John McGraw to testify. McGraw's statements about gambling in baseball confirmed what many newspapermen covering the 1919 Giants had long suspected. Two key members of that team, first baseman Hal Chase and third baseman Heinie Zimmerman, had been conspiring with gamblers to lose specific games. Those gamblers had bet heavily that Cincinnati would win the pennant; and any losses by the Giants, the Reds' closest competitors, would help them win those bets.

The Giants were in second place in September 1919; nevertheless, McGraw dismissed Zimmerman from the team. He did so after pitcher Fred Toney told him that Zimmerman had tried to get Toney and two other Giants, pitcher Rube Benton and outfielder Benny Kauff, involved in the scheme.[4] Zimmerman later admitted to all the charges against him to the grand jury investigating the Black Sox. Yet despite Chase's reputation for associating with gamblers and not always playing to win, McGraw kept him around for the rest of the season, though he limited him to one pinch-hitting appearance over the final two weeks. McGraw and his wife, Blanche, had known Chase for thirteen years, so he seemed surprised that Chase would betray him by intentionally losing games. "In my opinion Chase deliberately threw us down," he later said. "I was never more deceived by a player than by Chase."[5]

Neither Chase nor Zimmerman returned to the Giants in 1920, nor did they ever play another Major League game.[6] "As far as the Giants are concerned, Chase and Zimmerman are through," said McGraw.[7] The Giants assured their nonreturn to New York by offering them contracts for significantly less money than they had received in 1919.[8] After ridding the team of the two tainted and aging one-time stars, McGraw replaced them with a pair of promising youngsters. Twenty-four-year-old George Kelly took over at first base for the thirty-seven-year-old Chase; and twenty-one-year-old Frankie Frisch replaced Zimmerman, who was thirty-three, at third. The change did not bring a pennant in 1920, as the Giants finished in second place for the third straight year.

Frisch had been a shortstop and second baseman in college and was not particularly happy about playing third, but he was willing to play anywhere McGraw wanted him. "I can stand it if you can," he told McGraw. "I'll do my best to stop the ball any time it's hit near me, even if I have to fall on it."[9] While Frisch was not an especially smooth or graceful infielder, very few balls got by the hustling youngster. "My motto is the hell with technique," he said. "Get the ball!"[10] Fans loved his approach to the game and the all-out effort he gave on any ball hit anywhere near him. "There's more to this game than hitting," he would later say.[11]

Unfortunately, during the second week of the 1920 season, Frisch suffered an attack of appendicitis while on a train returning the Giants from Boston. Doctors operated on him (at his home in the Bronx) on

April 26, and he did not return to the lineup until mid-June. While Frisch recovered, two undistinguished utility players, Fred Lear and Ed Sicking, played third base.

When Frisch came up as a pinch hitter on June 14, as the Giants were losing at home to the Cardinals, the New York fans welcomed him back with a long, loud ovation. Barely into his first full season, the college boy from Fordham University had become a very valuable player for the Giants both on the field and at the box office. The Giants' loss that afternoon dropped their season's record to 21-29, a testament to how much they had missed their budding young star.

Zimmerman had been available as a replacement for Frisch, yet McGraw never considered bringing him back to the team. The fans supported McGraw's decision, as did most of the New York sportswriters. Joe Vila commended McGraw and the Giants for what he saw as their determination to rid the club of disloyal players.

Frisch's absence inspired McGraw to go after St. Louis Cardinals second baseman Rogers Hornsby, the league's best young hitter, who was on his way to his first batting championship. McGraw had long filled the role of a modern-day general manager, who has the responsibility for all player signings and trades. The transition from Brush and Hempstead to Stoneham had given him even more latitude in running the team as he saw fit.

The Giants reportedly offered St. Louis more money for Hornsby than the $100,000 the Yankees were reported to have paid the Red Sox for Babe Ruth a few months earlier. Unwilling to part with Hornsby, the Cardinals refused the offer. Thwarted in his attempt to land Hornsby, McGraw traded Art Fletcher, his longtime shortstop and team captain, on June 7 to the Phillies for their shortstop, Dave Bancroft. A later report in the *Washington Post* said McGraw also had sent $75,000 to the Phillies.[12]

Fletcher was a feisty and aggressive player who had been with the Giants since 1909 and had been their regular shortstop for the last ten seasons. But he was now thirty-five years old; and McGraw, always looking to improve his team, made a good deal in swapping him for the twenty-nine-year-old Bancroft. There had been no previous hint of the trade in the newspapers; in fact, Phillies president William Baker, a former New York City police commissioner, had said repeatedly that

Bancroft was unavailable for any price. Bancroft's clash with manager Gavy Cravath, when the Phillies were in Chicago in late May, changed Baker's mind. Cravath accused Bancroft of loafing; Bancroft denied it; the two men argued; and Cravath removed him from the lineup. Bancroft bitterly resented Cravath's charges.

"Cravath says I laid down on the job—stood around in the shortstop's position with my arms folded," Bancroft said after reporting to the Giants. "I'll tell you it hurts to be called a quitter by the manager of the ball club to which you have given your best efforts for almost six years. I never 'jaked' on a baseball job in my life, and Cravath knows it. As for playing ball with my arms folded, why Cravath is the man who invented that style of playing."[13]

Bancroft was a reliable switch hitter whose .299 average at the time of the trade and solid fielding made him a valuable addition to the Giants. Splitting the 1920 season between Philadelphia and New York, he had set the Major League record for the most assists by a shortstop, with 598.[14] Possessing quick hands, quick feet, and quick reflexes, he had an awareness of everything that was happening on the field. By the end of the season, Grantland Rice wrote that the combination of Bancroft's batting and fielding skills, aggressiveness, and mental alertness made him the best shortstop in baseball.[15]

After Frisch's return and with the addition of Bancroft, the Giants came on strong, overtaking Cincinnati, the team that had been the Dodgers' early challengers. Still, for the third consecutive season the New Yorkers finished second; this time seven games behind a Brooklyn team that won twenty-four of their final thirty. McGraw had retooled three-fourths of his infield in 1920. Now he would go after the final piece: a replacement for Larry Doyle, his popular veteran second baseman.

The National League's premier second baseman of the past decade, Doyle had manned that position for the Giants since 1907, except for a brief stint with the Cubs in 1916–17. A five-time .300 hitter and winner of the 1912 Chalmers Award, he was coming off another solid season, batting .285 in 137 games.[16] Nevertheless, Doyle—who famously once told Damon Runyon, "it's great to be young and a New York Giant"—was no longer young and soon would no longer be a Giant.[17] At thirty-four, he had chosen to retire as an active player to try his hand at managing.

5. Despite repeated attempts, John McGraw was unable to pry Rogers Hornsby away from Branch Rickey and the Cardinals. Hornsby was the best player in the National League, but he was no match for Ruth's power or popularity. *Culver Pictures*.

Not wishing to stand in the way of the man who had captained his pennant-winning teams of 1911–13, McGraw gave Doyle his unconditional release. Doyle then signed to manage the International League Toronto Maple Leafs for the 1921 season. At his retirement, Doyle was the Giants' all-time leader in games played, at bats, and doubles. He was also the career leader among National League second basemen in slugging percentage, hits, doubles, triples, total bases, and extra-base hits.

During the 1920 Brooklyn-Cleveland World Series, McGraw, with the full backing of Giants majority owner Charles Stoneham, again set his sights on bringing Rogers Hornsby to New York. Both men knew that adding Hornsby would not only help the Giants win a pennant but that it would also give them the big-name star they needed to help offset the rise in popularity of the Yankees created by Babe Ruth.

If Ruth was the best and most exciting young hitter in baseball, Hornsby, Doyle's successor as the National League's premier second baseman, was not very far behind. While not in the Babe's league as a home run hitter (who was?), Hornsby had dominated the National League's offensive categories in 1920 in much the same way Ruth had dominated them in the American League. He too had led in slugging percentage and on-base percentage, along with runs batted in, hits, and doubles; and his .370 batting average earned him the first of what would be six consecutive batting titles.

Yet if the Giants were depending on Hornsby for increased attendance, it would have to come from the firepower he would bring to the offense. Unlike the popular and outgoing Ruth, Hornsby was a dour loner who shunned the press. "Even his longest hits seem somehow of no consequence," wrote sportswriter Heywood Broun in comparing Hornsby's fan appeal to Ruth's. "A Hornsby homer contains less of human fervor than a strikeout by Babe Ruth."[18]

St. Louis had twice refused McGraw's offer to acquire Hornsby early in the 1920 season; but McGraw, not a man easily discouraged, traveled from Cuba to try again at baseball's winter meetings in New York. According to one report, he offered $200,000 and four players for Hornsby; but he backed off when Cardinals owner and president Sam Breadon said one of those players had to be Frisch. "If you will include Frank Frisch in the deal you are at liberty to take up the matter with Mr. [Branch] Rickey, our manager," said Breadon.[19] Rickey, who was also the team's vice president, confirmed the offer but insisted that "Hornsby is absolutely not on the market."[20] Treasurer McQuade's response to Breadon's request for Frisch was to the point: "McGraw wouldn't trade Frisch for Hornsby even up. That's what we think of their return proposition."[21]

Giant business manager Joseph D. O'Brien confirmed McQuade's statement that McGraw would not trade Frisch even up for Hornsby. He said McGraw considered Frisch "one of the best looking players picked up in years" and predicted future stardom for him.[22]

Nevertheless, the Cardinals accused McGraw of working on Hornsby during the 1920 season to try to drive a wedge between the second baseman and St. Louis management. Over the years, other National League clubs had accused McGraw of this kind of "tampering"; but McGraw, of course, denied it. "It isn't our policy to keep driving after a man in a way to break up another owner's ball club," he said, ignoring much evidence to the contrary.[23] In the situation between Hornsby and the Cardinals, the "wedge" was already there. Hornsby was a difficult man to get along with, and in the past he had clashed several times with both Breadon and Rickey.

The Giants' very generous offer for Hornsby made sense, not only from a baseball standpoint, but also from an economic one. The Giants had had a very profitable season in 1920, requiring them to turn over at least $200,000 to the federal government in excess profits taxes. As sportswriter Dan Daniel saw it, by investing in improvements (an accepted practice in business circles), they would in a sense get Hornsby for nothing.[24] In his January 8, 1921, column in the *New York Herald*, Daniel wrote that Stoneham and McGraw had raised their offer to an astounding $300,000 and four players for Hornsby; but Breadon and Rickey had again turned them down. Breadon's assertion that he would not sell Hornsby to New York even for a million dollars dumbfounded Daniel, who noted that the new Cardinals' ownership was still heavily in debt to former owner Mrs. Helene Britton.

The Giants' failure to lure Hornsby from St. Louis had forced them to look elsewhere for someone to round out their infield. In November they purchased third baseman Goldie Rapp for a reported $15,000 from St. Paul of the American Association. Rapp had shown well with Cincinnati in spring training in 1919 as a fill-in for the injured Heinie

Groh. However, Reds manager Pat Moran felt he was not ready for the big leagues and sent him back to St. Paul. Rapp batted a league-leading .335 for the Saints, stole forty-nine bases, and played an excellent third base. Giants scouts considered him the best infield prospect available in all the Minor Leagues. Dick Kinsella, McGraw's most trusted scout, had tracked Rapp at St. Paul and highly recommended him. Kinsella had discovered Ross Youngs as a sixteen-year-old, and his recommendation was good enough for McGraw.

Although Rapp had been a third baseman at St. Paul, McGraw's initial reaction was to move him to second and keep Frisch at third. "I understand he can play any infield place," said McGraw. "If I placed him at third and Frisch at second I would have to school both men in places strange to them, for third base in the National League is far different than third base in the minors. By keeping Frisch at third, where he has made good, and placing Rapp at second, I will have to break in only one new man."[25]

Signing Rapp did not prevent McGraw from trying to add another top-drawer infielder to his team. His primary targets at the December 1920 National League meetings, held at New York's Waldorf-Astoria Hotel, were Reds star third baseman Heinie Groh and Braves shortstop Rabbit Maranville. Neither man was the caliber of Hornsby, but both had been longtime National League stalwarts. The Pittsburgh Pirates were also after Maranville, as were the Reds.

In one rumored deal—a three-way affair among the Giants, Braves, and Reds—Maranville would go to Cincinnati, Groh would go to New York, and a group of unnamed players from the Giants and Reds would go to Boston. As Groh was the man the Giants wanted, this seemed a likely scenario. Their only reason to acquire Maranville would have been to use him in a trade with Cincinnati in which New York would receive Groh. McGraw also talked to the Reds about separate deals that would bring either Groh or outfielder Edd Roush to New York, though clearly his preference was for Groh.[26]

Speculation about Maranville ended on January 23, 1921, when the Braves traded him to Pittsburgh for outfielders Billy Southworth and Fred Nicholson, infielder Walter Barbare, and $15,000. McGraw viewed the Pirates as his major competitor for the 1921 pennant and was not happy to see them add a player such as Maranville, a veteran shortstop with World Series experience.[27] Rumors persisted that the Braves-Pirates trade was part of a larger deal that would send Maranville from Pittsburgh to the Giants.

Pirates owner Barney Dreyfuss, whose dislike for McGraw went back many years, just laughed at the notion that he would do anything to help McGraw or the Giants. One reason for Dreyfuss's contempt was that he had never forgiven McGraw for "stealing" his star third baseman, Jimmy Williams, back in 1901, when McGraw was the manager of the new Baltimore Orioles of the American League.

Maranville's going to Pittsburgh was a double blow to the Giants: it greatly strengthened their chief rival and at the same time prevented them from strengthening themselves by adding Groh in exchange for Maranville. Groh, who had broken in with the Giants in 1912, wanted to return to New York. Although he enjoyed living in Cincinnati, he was aware the Giants were more likely to earn him World Series money in the next few years. McGraw was dismayed at not getting Groh and even more so at not getting Hornsby, but the team's official position indicated otherwise. "The club tried hard to get a good infielder, but did not succeed, as the club owners [of St. Louis and Cincinnati] would not consider even a fortune for Rogers Hornsby or Heinie Groh. However the Giants can win without them," said club secretary Joe O'Brien.[28]

Because Braves owner George W. Grant was a close friend of both McGraw and Stoneham, some National League owners and managers viewed his selling Maranville to Pittsburgh, rather than to New York, as a positive step for the league. They saw it as a sign that Boston was an independent team and not, as sometimes had been suggested, just a farm club of the Giants controlled by Stoneham and McGraw.[29] Moreover, a "let's not help McGraw" clique, whose slogan was "Squelch New York!" existed among several National League clubs.

Not all the owners agreed. Some thought it would be in the league's best interest to build up the Giants in their battle with Ruth and the Yankees for the affection (and the dollars) of the New York fans. That sentiment, in turn, fed into the suspicion in other league cities that some clubs were subsidizing the New York teams to help increase the league's riches. The Giants had not won a pennant since 1917, and the Yankees had never won one. Yet there remained a constant barrage of conspiracy theories, criticism, and whining, for want of a better word, about the Giants and Yankees in the *Sporting News* editorials and by baseball columnists in other cities.

The comments of Oscar C. Reichow, who covered the Chicago teams for the *Sporting News*, were typical. Reichow claimed that New Yorkers had heard so many stories about the wealth of Stoneham and Ruppert that they believed all the Giants or Yankees had to do was name the players they wanted and those players would come to them automatically. Reichow went on to decry the deals that brought Babe Ruth and Carl Mays to the Yanks, charging that the effect of those deals was to ruin baseball in Boston. It seemed "to be the impression in the East," he wrote, "that the leagues cannot exist unless New York teams are leaders in the scrap for the championships."[30]

7 Ed Barrow Comes to New York

Baseball has always had its "buying" teams, those wealthy enough to pay other teams for their better players, and "selling" teams, those that need cash infusions to stay afloat. The Yankees, like the Giants, were a "buying" team. Yet their most significant acquisition during the 1920 off-season was not a ballplayer. On October 28, 1920, Ed Barrow, the Red Sox's field manager who led them to the 1918 world championship, joined the Yankees as their business manager. He replaced Harry Sparrow, who had died unexpectedly earlier that year. Sparrow, a friend and associate of McGraw's, had held the position since McGraw recommended him to Jacob Ruppert and Til Huston when they bought the team.

Barrow brought more than thirty years of baseball experience to the Yankees. Besides managing in both the Major and Minor leagues, he had owned Minor League teams and had been president of the International League. Fred Lieb observed that Barrow had a stronger background and better training for his new job than did any other business manager in baseball.[1] He was a shrewd and tough negotiator who rarely backed away from a confrontation. Barrow once challenged Ruth to a fight, when the two were scrapping over discipline on the Red Sox. Ruth wisely backed down.[2]

Barrow's move from Boston to New York surprised most observers because he and Frazee were close friends.[3] Yet he had been disappointed when Frazee sold Ruth to New York in January 1920. From the Yankees' perspective, hiring Barrow made sense. After Sparrow's death, Huston ran the team's day-to-day operations during the 1920 season. And he did not want to be bogged down doing it again; Ruppert, for his part, did not want to cede too much power to his partner.[4] Even though Barrow was a friend of Huston's, his reputation for competence and impartiality made him acceptable to Ruppert.

6. When Ed Barrow joined the Yankees in October 1920, wrote sportswriter Frank Graham, "the future greatness of the club was sealed" (*New York Yankees*, p. 57). He was a skilled evaluator of personnel, especially that of the Boston Red Sox, Barrow's former team. Within sixty days, the Yankees acquired Red Sox pitcher Waite Hoyt in a trade. *Private collection of Dan Levitt.*

Whether Frazee suggested that Barrow approach the Yankees or whether they first contacted Frazee about Barrow, the Red Sox owner was not going to stand in the way of this opportunity for his manager. Nor was he going to do anything that might sour his burgeoning working relationship with the Yankees' owners.

The move to New York made sense for Barrow too. "It was not a hard decision to make," he wrote more than three decades later.[5] "The Yankee colonels were the richest owners in baseball and they were building. They had Ruth." It was also a good career move for another reason. Temperamentally, Barrow was probably better suited to managing a team's business affairs (e.g., its contract negotiations and acquisitions) than its players on the field. In his Yankees team history, sportswriter Frank Graham later wrote of the Barrow hiring, "On that day [when Barrow was hired] the future greatness of the club was sealed."[6]

As a former manager, especially one who had clashed with both his owner and his players when he had managed the Detroit Tigers back in 1903–4, Barrow brought a broad perspective to his new position. He would become a key ally of beleaguered manager Miller Huggins. Barrow provided a buffer between Huggins and Yankees co-owner Huston, who continued to be critical of the little skipper. Barrow insisted that the Yankees' owners (and Barrow himself) stay out of the clubhouse, which was the manager's domain. He also supported Huggins in his efforts to establish his authority among the team's raucous and rebellious players.

Barrow's arrival could have become a source of friction and frustration for Huggins, who had had total control over personnel decisions until now. In 1917 Branch Rickey's arrival in St. Louis and assumption of such a role for the Cardinals had led to Huggins's departure from that team.

Yet early on, Barrow told Huggins how he saw their relationship—a partnership and separation of powers that was definitely ahead of its time. "No ship can have two captains, and no baseball organization a divided authority. You're the manager, and you're going to get no interference or second-guessing from me. Your job is to win and part of my job is to see that you have the players to win with. You tell me what you need, and I'll make the deals."[7]

Barrow expanded his role far beyond the functions Harry Sparrow had dealt with. Active with the team's finances and player moves and negotiations, Barrow was very much of a modern-day general manager, one of only a handful of such executives in 1921.[8]

In Barrow and Huggins, the Yankees now had two of the sharpest evaluators of talent in the game. Less than two months later, they made their first deal. On December 15, 1920, the Yankees made a trade that some historians have described as a key part of the "Rape of the Red Sox."[9] It was a blockbuster eight-player transaction, their fourth major deal with Frazee's club.[10] The Yankees sent second baseman Del Pratt, catcher Muddy Ruel, and two other players to Boston for pitchers Harry Harper and Waite Hoyt, catcher Wally Schang, and utility infielder Mike McNally.[11]

While the trade gained this moniker because Hoyt went on to a Hall of Fame career in New York, it was viewed very differently at the time, without the benefit of hindsight. Both the Boston and the New York newspapers were evenly split on the deal. Burt Whitman of the *Boston Herald* was ecstatic and gushed that the Red Sox clearly got the better of the deal. He felt it must have been "a conscience payment" from New York for the Ruth sale.[12] On the other hand, Joe Vila declared in the *Sporting News*, "Miller Huggins got out the old chloroform bottle. . . . Huggins actually gave up nothing for something."[13] Others were more neutral and less opinionated. F. C. Lane, for example, declared in *Baseball Magazine* that no one could really predict how the deal would turn out.[14]

Del Pratt was one of the best second basemen in the game and a key to the trade for the Red Sox.[15] Yet his relationship with Huggins had become severely strained; the two men had almost come to blows a few times during the season. One Boston paper described the Yankees as "a club now famous for its cliques."[16] It was no secret that Pratt was a leader of the anti-Huggins agitators in the New York clubhouse, even jockeying for position as the next Yankees manager. A few years later, John Kieran would call Pratt "the greatest clubhouse lawyer baseball ever knew."[17]

In his three years with the Yankees, Miller Huggins had learned that New York fans and sportswriters demanded a winner and did not permit a manager the luxury of time to develop players in key positions. Even though some felt that in five years Muddy Ruel would become a better catcher than Schang, "New York is too valuable a territory to waste on architectural plans."[18] Win and win now. Wally Schang was the experienced catcher Huggins needed. He had been the backstop for two world champions, the 1913 Philadelphia Athletics and the 1918 Red Sox.

Mike McNally would provide the Yankees with infield reserve strength, and Harry Harper would be their only left-handed pitcher in 1921. For New York, the other key man in the deal (besides Schang) was twenty-one-year-old Waite Hoyt. He was also the trade's biggest question mark. A pitcher of enormous talent, Hoyt had missed a good part of the 1920 season with a stomach abscess and double hernia. He also had a reputation for being temperamental, and there was some concern that the Yanks were exchanging one difficult player (Pratt) for another (Hoyt).

Hoyt's Red Sox record was only 10-12 over the past two seasons, yet he had shown flashes of brilliance in Boston. Huggins was well aware that Hoyt had potential. "Young Hoyt is a pitcher of infinite promise," he said.[19] Even Burt Whitman acknowledged that Hoyt could give the edge in the trade to the Yankees.[20] But two questions remained. Would Hoyt take direction? And would he recover from his medical problems? The *New York World* captured the essence of this deal when it wrote, "The value of the trade from a New York point of view hinges entirely on Waite Hoyt. The possibilities of this youthful pitcher cannot be overestimated."[21]

The second off-season move for the Yankees, which came just two weeks later, was the December 31, 1920, acquisition of speedy outfielder Bobby "Braggo" Roth from Washington, in exchange for left-handed pitcher George Mogridge and outfielder Duffy Lewis. Mogridge had won only five games in 1920 and had not lived up to his potential.[22] And like pitcher Ernie Shore, Lewis had not delivered on his past performance on championship Red Sox teams.[23]

Roth was a talented and temperamental player whose nickname reflected his high opinion of himself. He had moved from team to team because of his frequent run-ins with managers; the Yankees would be his sixth team in eight seasons. In 1915 he led the American League in home runs, yet the White Sox traded him to Cleveland in the middle of that season.[24] A "clever fielder and dangerous hitter," he was perhaps "too colorful for his own good."[25] Roth, whose brother Frank was a Yankees coach, would bring the speed that the Yankees sorely lacked both in the outfield and on the base paths. He had stolen 20 or more bases in each of the past six seasons, including 51 in 1917. Huggins planned to start him in the outfield alongside Ruth and, probably, Ping Bodie.

On January 27, 1921, the Yankees completed their third trade of that off-season, a complicated deal to acquire shortstop Johnny Mitchell, a player that some felt was the most promising youngster to emerge from the Minors in many years.[26] While it was not clear if he would be a regular or just what position he would play, Mitchell would supply the Yankees with added depth. He had spent the last three seasons with the Vernon club in the Pacific Coast League, where he averaged more than thirty-two stolen bases and twice had more than two hundred hits.

In return, New York sent pitcher Ernie Shore and several other players to Vernon.[27] Shore had been a major disappointment in New York after starring on the world champion Red Sox of 1915 and 1916. Perhaps more than any player who went off to war, Shore was unable to regain his old form. His fastball somehow lost its speed while he was in the navy in 1918.[28]

This deal was even more intricate. The Yankees had to give up a pitching prospect named Lefty O'Doul, who also had shown some potential with the bat. The Yanks did retain the right to recall O'Doul.[29]

Because so many players were involved, Harry A. Williams of the *Los Angeles Times* called it one of the most significant trades ever made. While he felt Vernon got the better of the deal, he noted that if Mitchell were to become the missing piece that makes the Yankees, "he is dirt cheap at the price, and very poor dirt at that."[30] While the Yankees were set at shortstop with Roger Peckinpaugh, Mitchell (along with McNally) gave them infield flexibility, especially since it was unclear if Frank Baker would return to baseball. A number of other teams had coveted Mitchell as well, so he also provided New York with some trading options.

The Yankees made other additions to their team before the season began. In early February, they hired a young hunchback by the name of Eddie Bennett as the team's mascot and batboy, and they agreed to pay him $100 a month.[31] A number of teams employed midgets and hunchbacks as mascots, since they were thought to bring luck to their teams.

Bennett brought along an impressive résumé. Early in 1919 in Chicago, White Sox outfielder Happy Felsch brought Bennett into Comiskey Park. Bennett had given a positive response to Felsch's question, "Hey, kid, are you lucky?"[32] Many ballplayers believed that rubbing the hump of a hunchback brought good luck to a batter. The White Sox won the pennant that year; Bennett claimed that crooked gamblers undercut his "luck efforts" for the White Sox to win the World Series.

In 1920 Bennett joined the Brooklyn Dodgers, who then also won the pennant. After they won two of the first three World Series games, all played in Brooklyn, the Series moved to Cleveland. The Dodgers decided not to spend the money to take Eddie along. They lost the next four games and the Series, five games to two. Now Eddie was bringing his good-luck charm to the Yankees.

Babe Ruth also brought his own mascot on board in 1921. Driving along Manhattan's Riverside Drive one afternoon, he spotted a man playing catch with his three-year-old son. The Babe invited the man and his son Ray to the Polo Grounds, where they watched the game. More than seventy years later, Ray Kelly recalled, "He asked my dad that day, 'Would you mind if I had your son, Little Ray, as my personal mascot?'"[33] For the rest of the 1920s, Little Ray Kelly became a fixture at Yankee games, often posing in his own uniform for pictures with Ruth.

Early in 1921 Ruth also began a business relationship with what is now known as a player's agent. Before he headed south to Hot Springs, Arkansas, to shed some pounds before spring training, the Babe agreed to let a young, unemployed advertising man by the name of Christy Walsh represent him in marketing opportunities.[34] Walsh's sole experience at agenting and ghostwriting was with auto racer and World War I flying ace Eddie Rickenbacker. After repeated failed attempts to meet Ruth at his residence in Manhattan's Ansonia Hotel, Walsh got lucky when he was hanging out at the nearby neighborhood grocery store. Ruth called the store, whose owner exclaimed, "Baby Root vants a case of beer. Right away, right away, and mine boy is gone. Yoi, Yoi, Yoi."[35] Walsh offered to do the delivery. Once inside Ruth's apartment, Walsh promised to pay the Babe $500 for each article, rather than the mere $5 he had been receiving.

The Christy Walsh Syndicate, as he would call his company, would hire ghostwriters to pen columns under Babe Ruth's name and sell them to newspapers.[36] Walsh always defended his profession, noting that he never misrepresented the authors' identities to editors (though the public was not told about the ghosts). He also emphasized that he hired top writers who stayed in contact with and could speak for their ballplayers. Before opening day 1921 at the Polo Grounds, Walsh presented a thrilled Ruth with his first check, for $1,000. Walsh later confessed that he had to borrow the money to make that payment.[37]

The Yankees had added a veteran backstop in Schang, speed with Roth, and versatility and depth with Mitchell and McNally. They also felt their pitching staff was improved. Ed Barrow knew the Red Sox's personnel, and he knew it well. He understood the guidance Schang would provide for pitchers and was able to corroborate Huggins's evaluation of Hoyt.

As spring training approached, the Yankees and the Giants, both of whom had contended in 1920, seemed to be stronger than they had been the year before. Miller Huggins felt his team had improved not only on the field but also in the clubhouse, where harmony previously had been hard to come by. John McGraw believed his team was as good as any in the National League. For those in the press and for those fans around the country who disliked New York and New Yorkers, their fears of an all–New York World Series in 1921 seemed to be well founded.

8 "We fear only Cleveland"

After coming close to winning the pennant the past two seasons, both the Giants and the Yankees were setting their sights on nothing less than winning the World Series in 1921. For their front offices and for those of other teams, the off-season was anything but a quiet time. It was a season of making personnel moves—trades and acquisitions—and a time to evaluate their strengths and weaknesses, where their teams stood relative to the competition. Were their young players ready to step into the lineup? Were their veterans capable of another good season? Spring training, beginning in early March, would allow Miller Huggins and John McGraw to see how the new mix of players they had assembled would perform.

The owners of the Yankees had made it very clear that after finishing in third place in 1920, just three games short of the pennant, they expected to win it all in 1921. Jacob Ruppert declared just after New Year's Day, "Colonel Huston and I have but one object in mind. That is to win the world's championship. We shall not be content to finish second or third. We want that title."[1] Huston raised the level of expectations even higher. "If we don't win this year, I cannot see how we could ever win."[2]

While acknowledging his team's powerful offense, Huggins realized that their success would depend on the arms of his young pitchers. He made no claims for the American League pennant, in part because of his understated style and in part because he recognized his team's shortcomings. "The Yankees are wonderfully well equipped this year to make a hard and determined fight of it," he said. "They are not even yet an ideal ball club."[3] And in a moment of candor, Huggins admitted, "We fear only Cleveland."[4]

The Indians had gotten a big boost in the off-season when their best pitcher, Stan Coveleski (who had won 104 games for them the past five years), was assured of being allowed to retain his main weapon, the spitball. Baseball's owners decided to permanently grandfather the game's seventeen spitball pitchers, thereby excluding them from the 1920 ban on that pitch.

Coveleski, the 1920 World Series star (with three complete-game victories), depended on the pitch more than any other spitballer did. He used it almost exclusively and would not have been able to develop an effective replacement. "Why, he could make that spitball talk," marveled his teammate Joe Sewell years later.[5] The *Sporting News* declared that without Covey's spitter, the Indians' prospects to repeat as pennant winners would have been seriously damaged.[6] The absence of that pitch from Coveleski's repertoire, wrote American League umpire and syndicated columnist Billy Evans, "will mean the making of a mediocre pitcher out of a star."[7]

When trick pitches were banned before the start of the 1920 season, spitballers were given only a one-year reprieve, during which they were to develop replacement pitches. Those pitchers then organized a "Spitballers' Fraternity," which petitioned the owners, framing the issue as one of fairness and equity. If they were to lose their main pitch, they argued, Organized Baseball would be depriving them of their livelihood. The *Sporting News*, however, urged the owners to hold their ground and ban the pitch outright in 1921, as they originally had legislated. In a November 1920 editorial, the paper described "the piteous pleas of the spitballers, who have figuratively applied their slippery elm to their tear ducts and are weeping over their fate."[8]

The spitballers succeeded in turning their one-year reprieve into a permanent exemption from the ban. Veteran umpires Billy Evans and Bill Klem rallied to their defense.[9] It did not seem fair that—virtually overnight—these pitchers would lose a tool they had worked on most of their adult lives.[10] That the two leading 1920 World Series pitchers, Coveleski and Brooklyn's Burleigh Grimes, were spitball pitchers did not hurt their cause; and the owners did not want to limit or possibly eliminate two of the game's stars. Baseball's Rules Committee decided to let the spitball die a natural death. These men would be allowed to throw the pitch for the rest of their careers.[11]

Other spitball stars would also benefit from the reprieve, including Red Faber (Chicago White Sox), Urban Shocker (St. Louis Browns),

"Spittin'" Bill Doak (St. Louis Cardinals), and Ray Caldwell (Cleveland Indians), all of whom won twenty or more games in 1920. Caldwell had a stunning comeback that year, after his career seemed to be at an end when the Red Sox released him in 1919. The Yankees' Jack Quinn and the Giants' Phil Douglas were also top spitballers, with eighteen and fourteen wins, respectively, in 1920.

The coaches of the Yankees were not conspicuous or pugnacious men. They reflected the subdued nature of their skipper. Late in 1920 the Yankees hired Frank Roth (Braggo's older brother by fourteen years) to coach the team's pitchers and catchers. Roth had been a part-time catcher for six seasons and played on the 1906 world champion White Sox. He joined that team a year earlier as the proverbial "player to be named later." The White Sox had sent marginal catcher and future front-office great Branch Rickey to the Browns and later got Roth in return.

Roth joined Charley O'Leary, who was in his second year as a Yankee coach. O'Leary had been an infielder with the Detroit Tigers for nine seasons (six of them under manager Hughie Jennings) and ended his playing career with the Cardinals under Huggins in 1913. While Roth would spend most of his time in the bullpen, O'Leary would continue to work in the third base coaching box. Huggins considered O'Leary his confidant and sounding board. "Canny, quiet, and immobile, O'Leary is ideal in transmitting signals from Huggins on the bench."[12] Shortly after Ed Barrow joined the Yankees, the club added another member to their nonplaying team; he brought over his Boston coach, Paul Krichell, to scout the colleges for prospects.[13]

As Prohibition rolled into its second year, New Yorkers were rallying to circumvent the law with a vengeance. The Dry Movement's rural and nativist origins had a challenging foe in the nation's biggest city. Jimmy Walker, New York state senator and future New York City mayor, had fought Prohibition well before it became law, calling it a "measure born in hypocrisy, and there it will die."[14] Newspapers, led by the *New York Times*, regularly had articles on the easy availability of liquor in the city, obtained everywhere from taxicabs to candy stores.

Of the city's 6 million residents, 2 million were foreign born, and another 2 million were children of immigrants. Perhaps it was no surprise that one Prohibition publication called the nation's biggest city "the least American part of the United States."[15]

New York governor Nathan Miller, a Republican, announced in January 1921 that if Commissioner Richard Enright, of the New York City police—appointed by Democratic mayor John Hylan—would not enforce the Volstead Act in the city, he would appoint a new police commissioner. A few weeks later, perhaps as a response to that threat, Enright announced that the city would soon be dry. New York City police and court records confirm that arrests and hearings for Prohibition-related violations were steadily rising in the early 1920s.

Sportswriter Irving Sanborn was one of the deans of American sportswriting, having written for the *Chicago Daily Tribune* since the 1890s. He declared that Prohibition was having a negative impact on the national pastime. Ballplayers who had previously been "temperate consumers of low voltage beer" were now "inhalers of high tension liquor."[16] And such was the case especially in Major League Baseball's big cities, where whiskey was readily available. The main change during Prohibition was the price and quality of the booze, not its availability.

Prohibition was also having an effect on one of the Yankees' owners, Jacob Ruppert, whose Ruppert Brewery had been one of the nation's largest and was now severely affected, limited to making only near beer. The colonel sold his rare-book collection of 1,500 bindings, to cover $1 million of saloon mortgages that were now rendered useless.[17]

Yet Ruppert had enormous real estate holdings, and the two colonels had made large profits from the Yankees' 1920 season with its record-breaking attendance. On February 6 they announced that they had acquired more than ten acres in the Bronx, just across the Harlem River from the Polo Grounds, for the future home of the Yankees. They planned for the Yankees to begin playing in their new park in 1923. Joe Vila had been covering sports in New York City since 1890. He noted that this Astor Estate location had been considered as a possible home for the Brotherhood (Players' League) team back in 1890 and for Frank Farrell's New York Americans in 1903. There was no rapid transit across the Harlem River from Manhattan back then, but by 1920 the subway service made the Bronx site easily accessible.

"We aim to make our new park the finest baseball plant in the world," said Ruppert. "The remarkable rise of the Yankees in popu-

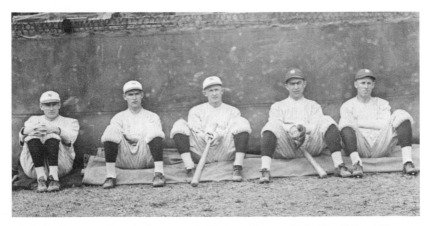

7. Babe Ruth was not the only slugger on the Yankees. Veterans Wally Pipp (*left*) and Home Run Baker (*second from right*) had six American League home run titles between them. Aaron Ward (*second from left*) was emerging as a classy infielder, and Johnny Mitchell (*middle*) was a highly touted prospect. Al DeVormer (right) was a backup catcher to Wally Schang. *Library of Congress, Prints and Photographs Division, George Grantham Bain Collection,* LC-B2-5687-2.

larity last year convinced us that the old must give way to the new."[18] Newspapers reported that the new facility would accommodate 75,000 fans and that only the Yale Bowl in New Haven, Connecticut, had a greater capacity. The Yankee owners sensed that the city and nation were entering a postwar era of economic prosperity and sports popularity. As the *New York World* noted, "Sports are running wild. A battle of ping-pong would draw a crowd these days. . . . THESE are the golden days."[19]

Because the Yankees and the Giants did not have separate ballparks, the emergence of clear and contrasting fan bases had been hindered. "Since both clubs have been using the same field the same people have gone to see them both play. This condition has killed the fierce partisan rivalry," wrote James P. Sinnott in the *New York Evening Mail*.[20] In Chicago, by contrast, the North Side Cubs and the South Side White Sox had separate geographic strongholds. Now that the Yankees were getting their own home, their rivalry with the Giants would intensify. Yet the future Yankee Stadium's proximity to the Polo Grounds would curb the rise of distinct groups of team partisans, suggested Ed Van Every in the *Evening Mail*. The home parks were not far enough away from each other to create "the proper factional spirit," he wrote.[21] Had the Yankees located their new ballpark closer to the East River, they would have created an east side versus west side rivalry.

While the Yankees knew where they would be playing in 1923, Miller Huggins's challenge was to decide who would be playing—and how he would construct his lineup—in 1921. Who would start, and at what position? He was set at first base with Wally Pipp, at shortstop with Roger Peckinpaugh, and at catcher with Wally Schang. But where would he play Bob Meusel, after Meusel's poor showing in the outfield in 1920? Would third baseman Frank Baker emerge from retirement? If he did, should he start? If Huggins were to play Aaron Ward at third base, which of the three youngsters—Chick Fewster, Mike McNally, or Johnny Mitchell—should start at second base?

When Braggo Roth went down with a knee injury on a bad field in a spring-training game at Lake Charles, Louisiana, Meusel and Fewster, who had played in the outfield in the past, moved up on the outfield depth charts. Roth's condition developed into a nagging case of water on the knee and showed signs of lingering and permanently impairing what had been his strongest asset, his speed. The Yanks' quest for more speed—on the base paths and in the field—was falling by the wayside before the season had begun. Roth had stolen 189 bases in his career, including eleven steals of home. He would steal only one more base as a Major Leaguer.

Frank Baker, the Yankees' aging third baseman, had missed the entire 1920 season to tend to his two young daughters, after his wife, Ottalee, died of scarlet fever in February. When his older daughter developed double pneumonia early in 1921, he hesitated straying far from his farm in Trappe, Maryland. When she recovered, he joined the Yankees at their spring-training headquarters in Shreveport and applied for reinstatement—merely a formality, he thought, since he had gone on the Voluntary Retired list when his wife died.

Commissioner Landis then announced he was investigating Baker's status, because he had played for an independent team in Upland, Pennsylvania, in 1920. Colonel Huston came to Baker's defense, declaring, "No baseball player has a more honorable record in baseball" than Baker.[22] Baker himself, miffed that he was being investigated, considered quitting.

Ultimately, he was cleared and reinstated on April 21, a week into the season. His biographer, Barry Sparks, wrote, "While Baker wouldn't enhance the team's speed or youth, he would add power and character."[23] However, by the time Baker rejoined the team, Aaron Ward was firmly ensconced at third base; and Baker would not start in a game until early May.

Another question mark for the Yankees revolved around their lack of a frontline left-handed pitcher. While Harry Harper had more than seven years of big league experience, only once had he won more than eleven games. While the press harped on the importance of having a top left-hander on the staff, Huggins was not particularly concerned. He was satisfied with his pitchers and noted there were not any good lefties available anyway. His top-of-the-rotation starting pitchers, he felt, were solid: Carl Mays, Bob Shawkey, and Waite Hoyt.

The Yankees had just moved their spring-training camp to Shreveport. In 1919 and 1920 they had trained in Jacksonville, Florida, where many of the players' rowdy nighttime behavior prompted Huggins to move to a smaller (and supposedly drier) town. Yet the new setting did little to reduce the players' boisterous partying and once again fueled discussions that the little Yankees manager was unable to control his men.

In Shreveport—an oil boomtown of 50,000, where the Minor League team was called the Gassers—there were three topics of conversation: oil, horseracing, and baseball. Louisiana railway commissioner (and future governor and senator) Huey Long had just won a lawsuit against the Shreve Railway Company, to keep streetcar fares at five cents rather than six. While the case was being decided, Long urged his constituents, "Get on the street car, drop a nickel in the slot and ride. Don't get off."[24] Sid Mercer described the southern city as one where alcohol could be found, "but the quality and price would make a piker out of even a New York bootlegger." "Shreveport," he wrote, "has the hustle and bustle of a western town, and not many of the old prejudices that linger in many parts of the old south."[25]

The Yankees played a series of exhibition games against the Brooklyn Dodgers throughout the South that spring. They drew huge crowds in the region's biggest cities, including Atlanta, Birmingham, and New Orleans. More than 100,000 fans saw the teams play. Some fans turned out for the National League champions, yet Babe Ruth was the player they most wanted to see. They came to see him swing for the fences; they came to see his power. In New Orleans his long foul cleared the right-field fence, and the fans cheered as he walked back to the plate. "If you have never seen Ruth hit the ball it is difficult to explain to you the surge of satisfaction that expands the heart," wrote Damon Runyon that spring. "Even when Ruth fails to knock a home run your disappointment is smothered by the mighty effort he puts behind each attempt."[26]

Some reporters had raised the issue of the Babe's physical condition when he reported to camp. While modern-day fans think that Ruth did not pack a lot of weight until late in his career, such was not the case. Ruth's playing weight (185 pounds in Baltimore and 198–212 in Boston) rarely dipped below 220 pounds once he joined the Yankees and was often around 230 pounds or more. Robert Creamer notes that the Babe had such a good time in Cuba in late 1920 that he returned to New York weighing "a jarring 240 pounds."[27]

Yet it took Ruth just a few days to hit his stride. In a March 13 game against the Gassers, Ruth rocked Shreveport pitching for three home runs and three singles in a 21–3 romp. Heywood Broun would write later in the year, "For all those who pine and worry about waistlines there is solace in the performance of Ruth. He is a large fat man, and growing fatter, but in many respects he is the greatest baseball player of all time."[28]

Fans everywhere were talking about the Babe, wondering if he would match his 1920 numbers. *Baseball Magazine*'s article "Can Babe Ruth Repeat?" hit the newsstands as opening day was approaching. The monthly noted that Ruth was a greater player than any man who ever played the game. "Babe is a true superman, a prodigy, a player who has never been remotely paralleled. . . . Ruth will not race a visible competitor. He will race against time. He will race against Ruth, the Ruth of 1921 against the Ruth of 1920."[29]

When the Yankees came to town, the day became a festive holiday. In Winston-Salem, where the ballpark was on the fairgrounds inside the racetrack, the tobacco factories declared a half-day holiday, "and the whole town was out."[30] As the Yankees worked their way back to New York, they stopped in Baltimore, where Ruth was born and reared, for a game against Jack Dunn's Orioles. Fewster—the other local boy—homered, as the Yankees won, 8–1. Baltimore pitcher Lefty Grove, yet another native Marylander, struck out the Babe three times.

The Yankees and Dodgers ended their series with two games at Brooklyn's Ebbets Field before large crowds of 15,000 and 21,000 fans. The final game was marked by Ruth's home run on the first pitch he saw in the first inning. The teams split the two games, and the series that had continued across a thousand miles ended with the Yanks winning nine of fourteen games.

Many onlookers examined the powerful Yankee lineup and saw what they believed was the best team in baseball. Hugh Fullerton wrote that the team's explosive offense would hide its weaknesses.[31] With the addition of Braggo Roth, the development of Bob Meusel, and the likely return of Frank Baker to surround Babe Ruth, Fred Lieb felt that by the end of the season, New York fans would see "the greatest combination of clouters in history."[32] The thirty-three-year-old Lieb was a young original member of the Baseball Writers' Association of America (the BBWAA, founded in 1908) and had covered the Yankees since 1915.

Not everyone saw the Yankees as sure winners. A number of baseball observers picked the world champion Cleveland Indians to repeat as American League pennant winners. Their player-manager, Tris Speaker, was as talented a skipper as he was a ballplayer; he was able to get tremendous performance out of his men.[33] A Pittsburgh sports editor reflected the thinking of many newspapers, including some in New York, when he wrote, "Cleveland wins largely because of Speaker. . . . If the Yankees win, it will not be because of Miller Huggins, but in spite of him."[34]

After the 1920 season, rumors had swirled for the third consecutive year that the Yankee skipper would be replaced. Many respected New York reporters openly questioned Huggins's leadership. Sid Mercer, a New York sportswriter since 1906 and a charter member of the BBWAA, wondered if the Yankees manager, who had never been "a commanding figure among men," could control the strong personalities. "Do the Yankees need a professor of baseball or a disciplinarian?" he asked.[35]

Like many writers, Grantland Rice rated the American League pennant race a toss-up. He gave the slight edge to the Indians because they would be as good as they were in 1920, "plus Mails."[36] Walter "Duster"

Mails—the colorful, self-proclaimed Walter the Great—had joined Cleveland late in the 1920 season. His nickname was well earned; he lacked control early in his career.[37] His Brooklyn manager, Wilbert Robinson, said, "I loved Walter as a person and a pitcher, but when he didn't have his stuff, he was so wild I started ducking in the dugout."[38]

In the home stretch of the 1920 pennant race, the lefty started eight games for Cleveland and had a perfect 7-0 record, with two shutouts and a 1.85 earned run average.[39] In the World Series against his old team, Mails pitched fifteen and two-thirds innings of shutout ball, including a 1–0 three-hit win in Game 6. Billy Evans wrote that Mails had so much talent that he had a chance to be another Rube Waddell.[40] In 1921 the Indians would have Mails from the start of the season.

Tris Speaker was confident his Cleveland Indians would repeat. He realized the powerful and hungry Yankees, led by Babe Ruth, would give his club a battle, though he doubted that Ruth could top his individual season totals of the year before. Speaker was "standing pat" with his team and took only thirty-two men south to Dallas. Mails was not the only youngster the team would have for the entire season. Shortstop Joe Sewell was only twenty-one when he had taken over Ray Chapman's position on September 10, 1920, and hit .329 in twenty-two games.[41]

Baseball Magazine noted the strengths of the Indians, who looked like "real repeaters" because of their balanced strength, class, and confidence. "The Cleveland clan, we trust, are made of sterner steel and won't go wild with success or get their craniums unduly inflated."[42]

When second baseman Bill Wambsganss ("Wamby") broke a bone in his arm in early April, before the season even began (he had missed only one game in the previous two years), Speaker turned to the president of the University of Alabama, Sewell's alma mater. The Indians received permission to sign Sewell's former Alabama teammate, Riggs Stephenson, who joined the Tribe as Sewell's double play partner and played regularly until Wambsganss recovered. And early in the summer of 1921, a third University of Alabama man would join the Indians—Joe's twenty-year-old brother, Luke.[43] Each of the three men would play in the Major Leagues for at least fourteen seasons.

Hugh Fullerton noticed a peculiar condition in the American League that year. American League teams wanted to beat Cleveland, but they wanted to beat the free-spending Yankees even more.[44] Other teams and their supporters had an ongoing love-hate relationship with New York. Visiting teams often earned more money from gate receipts in New York than they did from their own home games. Visiting teams needed strong and competitive New York clubs to draw large crowds in the big city.[45]

Yet there was a natural jealousy of the wealthy, winning New York clubs. Anti–New York sentiment gained an unlikely spokesman in Connie Mack, the soft-spoken manager of the Philadelphia Athletics. Early in 1921 he was dealing with his moody third baseman, Joe Dugan, who wanted to be traded to a contending team and whom the Yankees were trying to acquire.[46] Mack railed against wealthy teams that created unrest by tempting talented players from other clubs with promises of higher salaries: "First division teams think that whenever a star is developed, all they have to do is advertise that they will pay thousands of dollars for him and then double the salary he's getting from his present club. To my mind that is the biggest menace baseball faces right now."[47]

The next day, George Daley noted in the *World* that in the past, Mr. Mack did not hesitate to sell his stars, including Eddie Collins, Frank Baker, and Jack Barry, for tidy sums. When Dugan quit the Athletics (temporarily) during the 1921 season, Hugh Fullerton agreed with Mack. Charges that certain managers were "tampering" with players from other teams were ongoing. "What will become of organized baseball if players begin to dictate to owners as to which club they prefer? It means perpetual championships for New York and Chicago."[48]

As the Yankees prepared for the 1921 season, only four men remained from the squad Miller Huggins had inherited after the 1917 season: pitcher Bob Shawkey and infielders Roger Peckinpaugh, Wally Pipp, and Frank Baker. The Yankee skipper had sold, traded, or released forty men since he took over. Remarkably, ten men from the 1920 Yankees' team that fell just short of the pennant were gone from the 1921 team. Huggins was continuing his ongoing process of evaluating and adjusting, assembling the best team on the field and in the clubhouse.

Clearly, the ballclub had the talent to compete for the pennant; but questions remained: Would the players jell as a team? Did they have the drive and determination to wage a season-long fight for the pennant?

Would Huggins be able to meld an unruly group of stars and prima donnas, as well as ordinary and everyday players, into a championship team? As William B. Hanna of the *New York Herald* wrote of the Yankees, "Their pennant chances depend chiefly on how they fight and hustle and their steadfastness in keeping it up."[49]

9 "I do not fear any club in the National League"

For many players, the off-season did not signal the end of baseball for the year. To supplement their income, they continued to play various types of exhibition games, weather permitting. The year 1920 was no different. When the Yankees and the Giants finally were eliminated from their respective pennant races, players on both teams had the idea to meet in a postseason city series. Though unwilling to issue the challenge themselves, the Giants' players eagerly accepted it from the Yankees. The teams agreed that they would not play on the days that Brooklyn was playing their home World Series games against Cleveland.

The idea for a postseason series had the full support of Yankee owners Jacob Ruppert and Til Huston, who saw it as a way for the players to supplement their incomes, while adding to the club's revenue. But National League president John Heydler, a member of the three-man National Commission that ruled baseball, opposed the series. He decried it as an unnecessary money-making scheme, especially in light of the World Series shares the second-place Giants and third-place Yankees would be receiving. He also cited the recent revelations concerning the 1919 World Series and a possible distraction from this year's World Series as reasons for his opposition.

The teams could have played despite Heydler's resistance, but that likelihood faded considerably when Giants owner Charles Stoneham said he too opposed the idea. The final blow came on October 1 by way of a statement from the Yankees: "Inasmuch as President Heydler of the National League and President Stoneham of the Giants think it inadvisable to play the series, Colonel Jacob Ruppert and Colonel T. L. Huston have notified their players that the series is off."[1]

Two weeks later, a dozen Giants headed to Cuba for a barnstorming tour of the island. Leading the contingent was Johnny Evers, who had served as John McGraw's assistant manager during the 1920 season.

This would be Evers's last duty as a member of the club. McGraw had agreed to his leaving to manage the Chicago Cubs in 1921, the team he had played for as a member of the famous (Joe) Tinker to Evers to (Frank) Chance double play combination. The Giants played to mostly small crowds on the island until the end of October when Babe Ruth joined them. (Ruth had participated in his own lucrative barnstorming tour in the states earlier that month.) Ruth's arrival caused attendance to rise significantly, as Cuban baseball fans jammed the parks where the Giants were playing to see the great American star.

McGraw skipped this trip but in mid-November traveled with Stoneham to Cuba, where the two, both lifelong horseracing aficionados, owned a controlling interest in Havana's Oriental Park Race Track and Casino.[2] They would arrive in time for the racing season, which opened on Thanksgiving Day; come back to New York for baseball's December winter meetings; and then return to Cuba.

Coaches were relatively recent additions to baseball teams, but they quickly became key lieutenants for their managers. With Evers leaving to manage the Cubs, McGraw signed Hughie Jennings to take his place. Jennings, who had a law degree from Cornell, had resigned as manager of the Detroit Tigers, a position he had held for fourteen years.[3] The two men's friendship had begun when shortstop Jennings and third baseman McGraw made up the left side of the infield for the great Baltimore Orioles teams of 1894–98.[4]

McGraw also added another old acquaintance to his staff. He signed Jesse Burkett, a lifetime .338 hitter over sixteen seasons (1890–1905), to serve as a batting coach. Nicknamed "the Crab" for his surly disposition, Burkett had been a very successful head baseball coach at Holy Cross College in Worcester, Massachusetts, and had tutored Giants recruits in 1920.[5] McGraw and his two new coaches had been among baseball's biggest stars of the late nineteenth and early twentieth centuries, with twenty-five seasons of batting better than .300 among them.[6]

Most players of this era were the sons of farmers, miners, factory workers, and other members of the working class. Few were well educated and even fewer had grown up in privileged circumstances. Baseball had given them a chance to get off the farm or out of the mines and make a better life for themselves. The tendency to coddle players or attempt to improve their performance by boosting their morale was still a long way off. Nevertheless, McGraw, Jennings, and Burkett had to be, for members of the 1921 Giants, three of the most difficult men ever to play under. Very few days went by when some player was not on the receiving end of one of McGraw's legendary tongue-lashings or the object of a sarcastic put-down from Burkett or Jennings. "Burkett was so hated for his venomous tongue that the players refused to vote him a share of their World Series money."[7]

After eleven years in Marlin, Texas, and a year in Gainesville, Florida, McGraw had moved the Giants' spring-training site to San Antonio in 1920. He had been satisfied with the weather and hotel arrangements in San Antonio, and with the condition of his players when they broke camp to head north, though he was still not satisfied with the cramped space in the players' clubhouse. Eager to have the Giants return to their city, the local chamber of commerce agreed to improve both the clubhouse and an inadequate heating system that McGraw had complained about. Pleased with the upgrades, McGraw brought the Giants back to San Antonio in 1921.

On February 27 coaches Jennings and Burkett led a core group that departed New York for Texas. Aboard the train were those Giants who lived in the New York and New England areas. Several players boarded along the way, with the bulk of the others joining the entourage in St. Louis, where all boarded the *Sunshine Special* and arrived in San Antonio on March 1. Workouts began the next day.

McGraw was in Havana looking after his racing interests; he and wife Blanche arrived on March 5. McGraw's plan was to have the Giants spend two and a half weeks working out at their base camp, before playing a series of exhibition games against Major and Minor League teams in cities across Texas, Louisiana, and Alabama.

On first impression, McGraw was pleased with the team he would lead in 1921. "I have a better ball club by a lot than I had at this time last spring," he said several days after arriving from Cuba.[8] Stoneham was equally confident. "The Giants have only the Reds and the Pirates to fear in the 1921 race. We are the only club that has improved all around over last year," Stoneham said from his New York office. "The Giants are better in pitching, in catching, stronger on defense and offense, and we have a fighting club," he added.[9]

8. The Giants look relaxed at this exhibition game. But as Frankie Frisch (in the *center* of those players seated on the bench) remembered, the paunchy, white-haired McGraw drove them hard during spring training. *National Baseball Hall of Fame Library, Cooperstown, New York.*

McGraw was a firm believer in the value of spring training. As a member of the 1894 champion Baltimore Orioles, he had seen manager Ned Hanlon put that team through an extensive eight-week stint in Macon, Georgia. McGraw attributed much of the rise of that Orioles team—from an eighth-place finish in 1893 to champions in 1894—to their fast start that spring.[10] He credited Hanlon's strict regimen in Macon as the main reason for that start.

Frankie Frisch attested to how hard McGraw drove his players, while reminiscing about his first spring training in San Antonio in 1920: "I woke at seven and walked four miles to the field. At nine, I jogged five laps. I hit, fielded, threw, and slid until noon. Then I walked four miles back to the hotel."[11] Despite all that, Frisch remembered McGraw berating him at lunch one day after he had hitchhiked from the field to the hotel. "You rockhead. Next time I catch you riding anywhere, I'll fine you five bucks a mile. You know what legs are for . . . baseball," he recalled McGraw screaming.

Though long past his playing days, McGraw would take batting practice with the players and spend time at third base, the position he had manned so well for the Orioles of the 1890s. A strict disciplinarian both on the field and off, McGraw demanded that his players be in their rooms by eleven o'clock at night. To make certain they were following his rules, he was not above sitting near the hotel entrance each night to monitor the night owls.

Jennings's former team, the Tigers, were also training in San Antonio and staying at a hotel a block away from the Giants. Normally, two teams training in the same city would play exhibition games against each other. However, because Ty Cobb had replaced Jennings as Detroit's manager, that would not be the case in San Antonio in 1921. "Mr. Cobb said nothing to me about any such games," McGraw said on arriving in camp. "When he does, I will give him my answer."[12] Had Cobb asked, which is highly unlikely, McGraw no doubt would have refused.

A feud between McGraw and Cobb, two of baseball's most volatile and aggressive men ever, dated back to a fiery confrontation at a spring-training game in Dallas in 1917. The resulting rift between them had never healed. Cobb and Giants infielder Buck Herzog had gotten into a fight on the field, which the two men continued that night at the Oriental Hotel, where both teams were staying. All reports had Cobb, who was at least twenty-five pounds heavier than Herzog, clearly getting the better of it. Cobb's biographer, Charles C. Alexander, wrote, "The next morning John McGraw confronted Cobb in the hotel lobby and was so abusive that Cobb told the Giants manager that if McGraw were younger, he'd kill him."[13]

Fans had filled the park the next day to see Cobb and Herzog renew their battle. But Herzog was too bruised and battered to play, and Cobb took a seat in the stands, refusing to play against the Giants. "McGraw is a mucker and always has been and I don't intend to stand for his dirty work," said the suddenly peace-loving Cobb.[14] Not only would the two teams not meet on the field, the feelings of McGraw and Cobb toward each other were so bitter, they even forbade any intermingling of their players with members of the other team.

There was good reason for the optimism in the Giants' camp. They were a team of excellent players at almost all positions. George Kelly had become the full-time first baseman in 1920, leading the league in runs batted in and games played and figured only to get better. Kelly was no longer the awkward young man he had been, having reaped the benefits of all the hours McGraw had devoted to his improvement. With Larry Doyle now managing in Toronto, Frisch would be back at second base. Frisch preferred playing second, despite having established himself as one of the league's better third basemen.

At McGraw's invitation, Albert "Cozy" Dolan, a thirty-one-year-old former big league outfielder–third baseman, joined the Giants in San Antonio. Dolan, who had been a coach for the Chicago Cubs in 1920, was there to work with the infielders, primarily with Goldie Rapp, the rookie third baseman.[15] Rapp, the only question mark in the infield, would have to prove he could hit Major League pitching. "If Rapp shows more skill at third, Frisch will be moved over to second," McGraw said on his first day in camp.[16] Rapp's fine play during the early workouts did allow McGraw to move Frisch back to second and to feel secure in opening the season with Rapp at third.

Frisch had been the second Giant to sign for 1921, doing so coincidentally on the same day of the Maranville trade to Pittsburgh. Unhappy with the Giants' first offer, he returned the contract unsigned. A chat with McGraw and some more money convinced him to sign. This was in sharp contrast to 1920, when the club had been unable to sign him until the second week of spring training. Frisch had threatened to leave baseball unless the Giants met his terms. Unwilling to risk losing him, they did so. Though he had been with the team for just one and a half seasons, the twenty-two-year-old Frisch's spectacular play, and his status as a rare native New Yorker on the club, had made him especially popular among Giants fans.

The only Giant to sign before Frisch had been veteran shortstop Dave Bancroft, who had also assumed the duties of team captain, a role formerly held by Doyle, along with the $500 stipend that the Giants awarded the occupier of that position. However, Bancroft had been late in reporting to camp due to an undiagnosed stomach problem. Several doctors believed the trouble stemmed from his infected tonsils, so in late March Bancroft underwent a tonsillectomy. The procedure left him sidelined for a few days but ready for the regular-season opener.

Otherwise, aside from the usual bumps, bruises, twisted ankles, and pulled muscles, the Giants left spring training free of any serious injuries. Rookie second baseman John Monroe took advantage of a minor Frisch injury to earn a spot on the opening-day roster. Manager McGraw was especially pleased that three of his four infielders—Bancroft, Frisch, and Rapp—were switch hitters.

Right field belonged to left-handed-hitting Ross Youngs, the sensational twenty-four-year-old Texan who had batted better than .300 in each of his first three full seasons. George Burns would be the left fielder, just as he had been for the past eight seasons. A reliable lead-off man who stood only five feet seven, he had led the National League in runs scored in five of the past seven seasons, and in bases on balls in three of the past four.

McGraw had used several players in center field in 1920, primarily Lee King and Benny Kauff, and figured to do so again in 1921. The right-handed-hitting King, a .276 batter in 1920, would indeed be back; but Kauff would not. Although he was working out with the team in San Antonio, Kauff was under a temporary suspension by Commissioner Landis because of his alleged involvement in an automobile theft scheme. The charges had surfaced in February 1920; and despite the ongoing criminal investigation, Kauff had played the first half of the 1920 season with the Giants. On July 2, 1920, McGraw sent him to Toronto of the International League, where he batted .343 and stole twenty-eight bases for the Maple Leafs.[17]

Kauff had a most interesting history. He had appeared in five games for the 1912 Yankees and then returned to the big leagues in 1914 with the Federal League's Indianapolis Hoosiers. He led the league in batting (.370) and stolen bases (seventy-five), as the Hoosiers captured the Federal League pennant. *Sporting Life* wrote of him, "Kauff is the premier slugger, premier fielder, premier base-stealer and best all-round player in the league. He is being called a second Ty Cobb, yet there are many followers of the Federal clubs who say that within next season Kauff will play rings around the Georgia Peach."[18] Transferred to the Brooklyn Tip-Tops for the 1915 season, Kauff again led in batting (.342) and stolen bases (fifty-five), though the Tip-tops finished seventh. When the league folded following the 1915 season, the Giants purchased his contract from Brooklyn.

The Giants had reacquired Kauff from Toronto after the 1920 season, and McGraw said he would use him as New York's regular center fielder in 1921. Kauff's name had been mentioned in several gambling schemes, including the Black Sox scandal; yet McGraw, no stranger to the ethically challenged, was quick to proclaim Kauff's innocence. "Kauff is innocent of the charge of buying stolen automobiles," McGraw contended. "He simply got in with evil companions who mixed him into the case before he knew it."[19] A jury acquitted Kauff on May 13; nevertheless, Judge Landis, who had ruled him ineligible to play in 1921 pending the jury's decision, banned Kauff from baseball permanently. Citing Kauff's undesirable character and reputation, Landis said the jury's verdict "smelled to high heaven," while calling it "one of the worst miscarriages of justice" he had ever seen.[20]

"Judge Landis has recognized the essential fact that a ball player who is a mucker and worse in private life is liable to carry the same system of ethics into baseball," wrote Hugh Fullerton.[21] Fullerton also took McGraw to task for the many questionable players he had employed over the years: "McGraw has nourished a half-dozen men whose private lives were disgraceful merely because they could play ball. The question is whether a man who is disreputable in one line of endeavor can be pure in another."[22]

Rookies Ed Brown and Curt Walker, both of whom had made brief appearances the previous September, would contend with King for the center-field position. Brown was a rangy six-feet-three right-handed hitter, with a weak throwing arm that had earned him the nickname "Glass Arm Eddie." He was already twenty-nine, as opposed to the speedy left-handed-hitting Walker, who was just twenty-four. The Giants had thought enough of Walker to pay the Augusta Georgians of the Class C South Atlantic League $7,000 for him, a hefty price for someone in that league. The Detroit Tigers had paid that same Augusta club only $700 for Ty Cobb back in 1905. And that came with a contingency: the Tigers would pay the money only if Cobb demonstrated he had the ability to play at the big league level. While prices for everything had risen in fifteen years, people who followed the South Atlantic League believed that Walker was a better prospect than Cobb had been at that stage of his career.

McGraw, who placed such a high premium on pitching, was satisfied with the staff he had. Fred Toney, Jesse Barnes, Art Nehf, Rube Benton, and Phil Douglas had started 151 of the Giants 155 games in 1920 and

9. Manager John McGraw used pitchers Art Nehf, Jesse Barnes, Rube Benton, Fred Toney, and Phil Douglas (*left to right*) to start all but five games in 1920. Nehf, Barnes, Toney, and Douglas would anchor the Giants' starting pitching staff in 1921. *Private collection of Dennis Goldstein.*

accounted for eighty-five of their eighty-six wins. All would be back, and all reported to San Antonio healthy. Working out of the bullpen and ready to step in if needed were veteran left-hander Slim Sallee, a former Giant picked up on waivers from Cincinnati in September, and a pair of promising right-handed rookies, Bill "Rosy" Ryan and Pat "Red" Shea.

Ryan had been especially impressive during the exhibition season. After one game, Bill Klem remarked that no young pitcher had "ever showed me anything like the stuff 'Rosy' Bill Ryan served to the Red Sox in the game at Mobile."[23] Right-handed hitter Frank Snyder and left-handed hitter Earl Smith, both seasoned veterans, would share the bulk of the catching duties, just as they had the year before.

Along with Ryan, Shea, Rapp, Brown, and Walker, several other rookies were in camp with varying chances of making the jump to the Major Leagues. During the winter, Hugh Fullerton had paid homage to McGraw's willingness to try new players: "John McGraw, manager of the Giants, has his enemies and his friends. He is, perhaps, the most hated and the most ardently admired of all managers—and with cause. But there is one thing he does in the handling of ball teams which puts him head and shoulders above all other managers. That is the fact that he gives the kids a chance."[24]

Beginning on April 4, the Giants and Washington Senators headed north together, playing in Tennessee and Virginia, before concluding the exhibition season with a three-game home-and-home weekend series. After the final game of the trip, in Norfolk, Virginia, the teams traveled to Washington—the Giants by boat and the Senators by rail. The Giants' win on that Friday in Washington marked the home debut for new manager (and former longtime Senators shortstop) George McBride, who had replaced Clark Griffith. Frankie Frisch's ninth-inning home run gave the Giants a victory on Saturday in New York, and a surprisingly large crowd of 22,000 was at the Polo Grounds on Sunday to see the home team win again. Bad weather cancelled the next day's scheduled game with Princeton, before the Giants concluded their exhibition season with an easy win against the Art Devlin–coached Fordham Rams.

Most prognosticators were picking the Giants to win the National League pennant, an opinion shared by Indians manager Tris Speaker. "Everybody with whom I have discussed the National League situation has picked the Giants," he said following a spring game against them at Dallas. "Nobody seems to give [defending-champion] Brooklyn a look in; nor are the Reds considered formidable contenders. It's nothing but the Giants," said Speaker, while making no mention of the Pirates or Cardinals.[25]

While his contention that most sportswriters were picking the Giants to win the pennant was accurate, Speaker's assertion that nobody was paying much attention to Brooklyn was not. Many saw it as a three-team race, with the Giants winning by a close margin over Brooklyn and Pittsburgh. Grantland Rice's prediction of the Giants finishing on top, with the Dodgers second and Pittsburgh third, was representative of many early assessments.

Rice noted that the Giants had led the league in runs scored in 1920 but were hurt by their defense. He believed that having Frisch and Bancroft from the beginning of the season, plus the addition of Rapp and a pitching staff that appeared to be in excellent physical condition, would be enough to propel the New Yorkers to the top. "The New York Giants look strong enough once more to win their first pennant in four years," Rice said during the first week of the season.[26]

Slugging outfielder Zack Wheat led a veteran Brooklyn team that was largely the same club that had romped home seven games ahead of the Giants in 1920. The club's one major off-season deal had been a swap of left-handers with Cincinnati. The Dodgers sent thirty-four-year-old Rube Marquard, a ten-game winner in 1920, to the Reds in exchange for twenty-seven-year-old Dutch Ruether, who was 16-12 in 1920. Marquard had become persona non grata in Brooklyn after he was arrested in a Cleveland hotel lobby for scalping World Series tickets. A judge gave him what amounted to a slap on the wrist, but Dodgers owner Charles Ebbets vowed that Marquard would never pitch another game for Brooklyn.

Staff ace Burleigh Grimes, a twenty-three-game winner, was back after a protracted salary holdout, as were Leon Cadore, Al Mamaux, Sherry Smith, and Jeff Pfeffer, all of whom had won at least eleven games for the defending champions. "It is too early too claim a pennant, but we hope to repeat," said manager Wilbert Robinson just before the opener. "We expect a hard battle from the Giants," he said, "but our team has the pitching strength, and that always is a big factor in a pennant fight."[27]

Pitching strength was also the key to manager George Gibson's Pirates. Returning was twenty-four-game winner Wilbur Cooper, who was quietly emerging as one of the game's best hurlers, along with double-digit winners Babe Adams, Hal Carlson, Earl Hamilton, and Elmer Ponder. Adams was continuing his career as one of the great control pitchers of all time, giving up far fewer walks per game than any other pitcher.[28] Gibson also had a group of impressive rookie pitchers in camp, several of whom—Whitey Glazner, Moses Yellow Horse, and Jimmy Zinn—would make the squad.

Shortstop Rabbit Maranville had been the key off-season acquisition, joining fellow prankster and nighttime-carouser first baseman Charlie Grimm, with Clyde Barnhart at third and either George Cutshaw or Cotton Tierney at second. Carson Bigbee and Possum Whitted would flank captain Max Carey (who had just won his sixth stolen-base title in 1920) in the outfield. Walter Schmidt would again be expected to do most of the catching. The weather in Hot Springs, Arkansas, where the Pirates trained, had been good; and they had come through it and the trip north injury free. "There is no question as to the Pirates being stronger than they were a year ago," wrote the *Sporting News*.[29]

Not since his pennant-winning clubs of 1911–13 had John McGraw assembled a team that blended so much youth and speed with a veteran pitching staff. Frisch (twenty-two years old), Youngs (twenty-four), and Kelly (twenty-five) supplied the youth, while Bancroft and Burns (the lone remaining member of the 1913 team), along with the pitching staff, furnished the veteran experience necessary to win a pennant. "I never make predictions," said McGraw. "My job is to give New York the best ball club I can."[30]

He had done his job. With Frisch, Bancroft, Youngs, Burns, and Rapp, the Giants were the speediest team in the league. They also had the league's strongest infield and potentially the best outfield. McGraw knew their success, as it usually does in baseball, would depend on their pitching. "Unless we have bad luck, I do not fear any club in the National League," he said a few days before the season opener.[31]

PART 2 The Season

10 "My job is to knock 'em a mile"

Miller Huggins had just observed his forty-third birthday in March, yet he looked years older. His wrinkled forehead and the creases around his eyes suggested a life of struggles or health problems, or both. He was not a natural leader, and managing a big league ballclub had not come easy for him. Doing so these past three years in New York, a city with an unforgiving press and demanding fans, only added to the stress. "Huggins largely is to blame for the fact that he has not won more popularity in New York," wrote the *New York Sun* in 1919. "He discounts both popularity and publicity. Despite the fact that he is one of the smartest men that ever trod on a ball field, and is a lawyer in the bargain, he does not seem to realize what assets popularity and publicity can be to a successful manager."[1]

Late in spring training, as the Yankees were preparing to leave Shreveport, Huggins was bedridden with what one paper termed a "catarrhal attack of the appendix."[2] Yet he was dealing with far more serious health issues. A nervous man, he had found the strain of the 1920 pennant race too much to handle, though his "nervous collapse" was reported only after the 1921 season and only by one paper.[3] And veteran reporter Bill Slocum divulged after Huggins's death that the little manager had almost ended his relationship with the Yankees that winter of 1920–21, when his health was so bad.[4] At the same time, Yankees co-owner Til Huston still wanted the team to sign Brooklyn manager Wilbert Robinson, whom Huston had wanted to hire, rather than Huggins, after the 1917 season. But Brooklyn owner Charlie Ebbets was not going to let Uncle Robbie get away after his pennant-winning season of 1920. When the Dodgers re-signed him, reported Sid Mercer, the deadlock between the pro-Huggins Jacob Ruppert and the anti-Huggins Huston ended, at least for the time.[5]

As opening day approached, Huggins surely had hopes that the 1921 season would be less of a strain than 1920 had been. The *Sporting News* front-page headline on January 13 announced, "Mite Manager Has Strengthened Himself on Field and at Same Time Has Rid Himself of Some Unruly Spirits." Yet the reality was that Huggins still had a group of headstrong prima donnas on his roster, led by Babe Ruth and by an owner who would continue to undercut his authority.

The Yankees and Giants had been rotating opening at home since the Yanks moved to the Polo Grounds in 1913. And because the Giants had opened at home in 1920, it was the Yankees' turn this year. But the Giants, anxious for a lucrative payday, asked the commissioner's office to allow them to open at home again in 1921. As a precedent, they cited the Yankees' having done it two years in a row in 1916 and 1917. Their appeal was denied, and on April 13 the Yanks opened the season at the Polo Grounds against Connie Mack's Philadelphia Athletics.

The game provided immediate evidence of the ever-increasing popularity of baseball in general and of the Yankees in particular. The crowd of almost 40,000 was the largest ever to see an opener in New York. After several window panes at the 155th Street el station were broken, the police prevented anyone without a ticket from approaching the ballpark and thus turned away 15,000 people.[6]

The crowd, in the holiday mood that always accompanied opening day, cheered each Yankee player as he came on the field. Contrary to the myth that the Yankees had adopted pinstripes to make Babe Ruth look slimmer, they had been wearing them continually since 1915, five years before Ruth joined the team. Their home whites with the blue pinstripes had no lettering of any kind on them. Only the blue interlocked "NY" on their white pinstriped caps (the bills were solid blue) suggested that they represented New York.[7]

Frank Baker—who was hoping to return from his self-imposed, one-year exile—drew an especially warm greeting, although, as usual, the loudest cheers were for Ruth. The hordes of photographers covering the game also focused on the Babe, recording his every move on film. Playing to the crowds, the gregarious Ruth interrupted his pregame routine to chat with spectators, including Jackie Coogan, child star of Charlie Chaplin's new hit movie, *The Kid*. Damon Runyon noted all the Broadway celebrities in the box seats, a reminder that John McGraw's Giants no longer had a monopoly on the city's rich and famous fans.[8]

10. Here was the scene on opening day 1921 at the Polo Grounds. New York City mayor John Hylan (*front left*) and Jacob Ruppert pose with two of the nation's biggest celebrities, child actor Jackie Coogan and slugger Babe Ruth. "Ruth, the man-boy," wrote Grantland Rice, "was the complete embodiment of everything uninhibited" (*Tumult and Shouting*, p. 114). © *Bettman/CORBIS*.

New York's mayor, John F. Hylan, was present, seated in the owners' box along the first base line with Colonels Ruppert and Huston. At three thirty, Hylan arose and launched the season with a shaky toss to Yankees catcher Wally Schang. Huggins gave the honor of pitching the opener to one of his unruly spirits, Carl Mays, based on Mays's twenty-six-win season in 1920. Two years earlier on opening day in 1919, Mays, then a member of the Boston Red Sox, had shut out the Yanks, 10–0, in this same park. Mays's catcher that day was Schang, who had four hits, including three doubles. Ruth, who had a home run, was Boston's left fielder. All three were in those same positions that opening day in 1921, only now they were Yankees.

Mays was almost as good on opening day 1921 as he was on opening day 1919, tossing a three-hit, 11–1 gem, while matching the Athletics' hit total with three of his own. A very good-hitting pitcher, Mays would have the best year of his career at the plate in 1921, hitting .343.

Carl Mays had a unique underhanded delivery, releasing the ball near the ground, from where it rose up to the batter at difficult angles. Mays threw "with a submarine sweep of his arm that made a hitter think the ball was coming up out of the dirt at him. He was a rough, tough competitor who played for keeps."[9]

Mays was among the most disliked players in the game. He had a reputation as a "headhunter," a pitcher who threw at batters' heads to intimidate them and keep them off balance. He led the American League in hit batsmen in 1917 and was second in both 1918 and 1919.[10] In his rookie season of 1915, in a crucial September home game against the Detroit Tigers, Mays repeatedly threw at Ty Cobb, the league's leading hitter, finally smacking him on the wrist. When the volatile Cobb had retaliated by throwing his bat at Mays, a near riot ensued.[11]

A year later, in 1916, after Mays had hit Senators shortstop George McBride, triggering a brawl, Washington manager Clark Griffith criticized Mays publicly. "The instant one of my players is hit by a pitched ball, I will take a bat and hammer some sense into the head of the Boston pitcher," he said. "There is nothing sportsmanlike in seeing how close one can come to hitting a batter just to frighten that batter."[12]

A May 3, 1917, editorial in the *Sporting News* accused the Red Sox pitchers of using the beanball as a tactical weapon of choice. Earlier that year, Mays had hit Athletics outfielder Frank Thrasher in the head and knocked him unconscious. Thrasher's manager, the soft-spoken Connie Mack, then joined the growing list of Mays's critics.[13] The following season, Mays hit Cleveland outfielder Tris Speaker in the head. When Mays tried to apologize, claiming that it was unintentional, his former teammate was infuriated. "I worked on the same team with you long enough to know different," growled Speaker.[14]

The opposition's dislike of Mays was a feeling shared by his own teammates. Sportswriter Tom Meany recalled that Ed Barrow considered Mays "a chronic malcontent" when he had managed the pitcher in Boston.[15] Barrow, who later became the Yankees business manager, wrote in his autobiography, "Mays was a peculiar fellow, moody and irascible and not very popular with his teammates, but he could pitch."[16] After the 1920 season, Mays acknowledged that he lacked tact and did not make friends easily. He lamented the "unpopularity which had come to be as natural as my own shadow."[17]

On opening day the Yankee batters gave an early indication of their power. Aaron Ward, Baker's replacement at third base, batted in the team's first runs with a home run. Babe Ruth, as he inevitably did, captured the headlines with a perfect day. He had five hits in five at bats, including two doubles, though he had no home runs.[18] A six-run eighth inning secured the game for New York, and Ping Bodie's bases-clearing triple was the big blow.

The Yankees were expecting major contributions from Bodie after his strong 1920 season at the plate.[19] The colorful Italian American, who was born Francesco Stephano Pezzolo, had been a member of the Yanks' Murderers' Row since 1918. A stubby five feet eight and 195 pounds, he had a reputation as a long-ball hitter from slugging thirty home runs for the San Francisco Seals of the Pacific Coast League in 1910.[20]

Bodie was also known for his humorous remarks decades before another Yankee Italian American, Yogi Berra, became famous for his aphorisms.[21] Sportswriters enjoyed writing about him; the engaging Bodie made for good newspaper copy. Observing Bodie's lack of speed on the base paths, columnist and cartoonist Bugs Baer noted, "There was larceny in his heart, but his feet were honest."[22]

When he had struck out in a 1918 spring-training game, Bodie shouted some obscenities, which were overheard by Colonel Ruppert. "My word, we have a man who swears. What are the Yankees coming to?" said the colonel. What they had become with the addition of the "swash-buckling" Bodie was a colorful club, one with a real personality.[23]

Then there was Bodie's fielding, which the New York press had tried to prepare fans for, explaining he was not a Peckinpaugh, Pipp, or Baker in the outfield. "He may lose a fly ball now and then, and the chances are that he'll throw to the wrong base on more than one throbbing occasion."[24]

Overall attendance for the seven Major League openers (Chicago at Detroit was rained out) exceeded 160,000. Opening day was the first sign that the fans had not abandoned the game and that the owners'—and Commissioner Landis's—public relations campaign was working. Landis himself was part of the record-breaking crowd in Chicago that saw Grover Alexander pitch the Cubs to a 5–2 win over the St. Louis Cardinals.

Ruth hit his first 1921 home run off Philadelphia's Slim Harriss in the season's third game. Afterward, a peeved Connie Mack asked Harriss why he had thrown Ruth a fastball with an 0-2 count. Harriss answered, "I tried to slip it past him," whereupon Mack replied with understated sarcasm, "How marvelously you succeeded!"[25] Harriss gave up only four hits in the 3–1 loss, but two were home runs. Bob Meusel also homered, making it the first of eight games in 1921 in which both he and Ruth would hit home runs.[26]

Five days later, when the Yankees and Mays again beat Philadelphia in the A's home opener, Ruth and Meusel each hit two doubles; and the Babe added a home run that cleared the Shibe Park right-field fence by twenty feet. That loss dropped the Athletics to a 1-6 record; and the *New York American*, like many observers, was ready to concede last place to them: "The Athletics may be going somewhere this year, but if so they're keeping their destination a secret."[27] The A's had finished at the bottom of the American League the past six years. After winning four pennants in five seasons (1910–14), Mack was finding the rebuilding task far more difficult than he had envisioned.

The A's and their knuckle-balling pitcher Eddie Rommel did manage to beat New York and twenty-one-year-old Waite Hoyt (in his first Yankee appearances) twice in April. Rommel had developed a knuckle ball after he had badly scalded his hands in a steam-fitting accident on a ship during World War I.[28] He had good control with his knuckler, which he actually threw off his fingernails (as did most so-called knuckleballers), not his knuckles. He was not the first to throw the pitch; but he revived it in the 1920s, when it was dying out.[29] Rommel also had an effective change of pace and underhand curve.

The Yankee sluggers loved to feast on fastballs, and Rommel's slow pitches seemed to keep them off balance. Yet Ruth did manage to hit a home run against him on April 22.[30] Late in 1920 Walter Johnson had said, "I very much doubt if 'Babe' has a real batting weakness," and the pitcher noted that two of the three homers he had given up to Ruth had come off slow curves.[31]

The blast off Rommel was Ruth's fourth of the season, putting him well ahead of his 1920 pace, when his first home run did not come until May 1. When a reporter asked the Babe why he did not shoot for a "fat average" by settling for "shorter hits and more of them," the slugger replied, "I am determined to stay just what I am. . . . My job is to knock 'em a mile, and that's what the fans expect."[32] Years later Joe Sewell, who played both with and against the Babe, said, "I honestly believe that if Ruth had gone for a batting average rather than home runs, he could have hit .500."[33]

Carl Mays had started the season in spectacular fashion, with three consecutive complete-game victories, in which he allowed only two earned runs in twenty-seven innings. He was almost untouchable with his sweeping "underhand grass-clipping delivery."[34] Two of his wins came against the Athletics, as he was in the midst of an incredible run of dominating another team, even if it was a weak one. From August 30, 1918, until July 24, 1923, Mays would beat the A's twenty-four straight times.[35]

The rest of the Yankees' pitching staff, always a key predictor of a team's success, was far less reliable. Hoyt had pitched decently in his two losses; but Jack Quinn—known as a good early-season, cool-weather pitcher—was inconsistent. Bill Piercy finally won a big league game, the 3–1 victory over Harriss. It came four years after he first pitched for New York (just one game in 1917, which was the extent of his Major League experience until 1921). In the interim, he had pitched for various Minor League clubs, including Sacramento in 1919, when he won twenty-six games. The Yanks had kept a string on Piercy since drafting the highly coveted youngster from Vernon of the Coast League in November 1915. Faced with Bob Shawkey's ongoing arm problems, they were hoping that Piercy had developed the maturity to take his turn in a Major League rotation. Back in 1916 "his main occupation was raising cain—not sugar."[36] Now, after this first victory, one New York paper raved, "This boy is game. As the scouts say, he has the nerve of a burglar."[37]

Losing the first four games of a five-game series with Washington dropped the Yankees' record to 3-5 and extended their losing streak to five games. The Washington series highlighted the team's weaknesses and signaled that their fight for the pennant would not be an easy one. The second game, on Monday April 25 at the Polo Grounds, was a scintillating matchup between two of the game's best pitchers, Mays and Walter Johnson.

Johnson, now in his fifteenth season, was attempting a comeback from serious arm problems in 1920. He had appeared in only twenty-

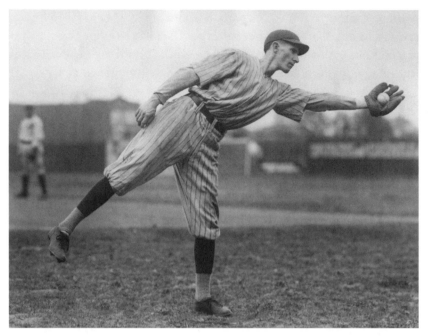

11. Chick Fewster was attempting a comeback from a near-fatal beaning he suffered in the spring of 1920. The spunky Fewster had difficulty holding up to the rigors of the season, but he was a key Yankees reserve in both the infield and the outfield. *Private collection of Dennis Goldstein.*

one games that year, with an 8-10 record and by far the highest earned run average of his career to that point, 3.13.[38] Many observers feared that Johnson's long career was coming to its end. With pitchers such as Joe Wood and Ed Walsh in mind, the *Sporting News* wrote as the 1921 season began, "Old Man History says they never come back."[39]

Through seven innings, Mays allowed no hits, as he continued his masterful early-season work. Then suddenly he weakened, and the Senators emerged with a 5–3 win. Ruth hit his fifth home run in the loss, off the first pitch he saw from Johnson. When Johnson retired Schang to end the game, the New York crowd gave him a rousing ovation. After beating the Yankees, Johnson politely disagreed with those who were predicting his demise. "I have found my arm as good as ever it was," he declared.[40]

According to the *New York Herald*, Mays's "work depreciated so much in the last two innings, it didn't seem like the same pitcher."[41] Even his fielding suffered, as he threw away an easy tap back to the mound. Yet Mays was not the only Yankee who faltered. Chick Fewster made three errors, including two in the ninth. After an impressive spring, Fewster had "suddenly flopped in a truly amazing fashion and [was] a menace" at second base.[42] Fewster would make eight errors in four games against Washington.

It was no secret that Miller Huggins had a fondness for the Baltimore kid Chick Fewster. Maybe Huggins identified with the skinny, almost gaunt, infielder. "Chick has everything," Huggins had said when he first evaluated Fewster before the 1918 season. "I have never seen a greater prospect."[43] Fewster had many fans rooting for him as he was attempting a comeback from a near-fatal beaning in spring training 1920.

In an eerie foreshadowing of Ray Chapman's death, a fastball from Brooklyn's Jeff Pfeffer had fractured Fewster's skull in a game in Jacksonville, Florida, on March 25. Like Chapman, Fewster had a reputation for crowding the plate. In both cases, the damaging pitches may have been strikes. In 1919 Fewster had been hit by pitches seven times. Like Carl Mays, Pfeffer was among those pitchers who hit many batters (he had hit fifty men from 1915 to 1917); they both had led their leagues in that category in 1917.

Originally, Fewster's injury was not deemed life threatening. Yet he could not talk, an indication that his vocal chords might have been paralyzed. The Yankee owners insisted that he return to Baltimore, his home and the home of Johns Hopkins, one of the nation's top hospitals. Doctors at Hopkins diagnosed Fewster's worsening condition, operated to relieve the swelling and bleeding in his skull, and saved his life. While many newspapers predicted that his career was over, Fewster did return to play in 1920, albeit with only twenty-one at bats. Huggins planned to play him at second base and in the outfield in 1921, as he had in 1919 when Fewster hit .283.

Fewster was offered a few "head guards" made of cork and felt in the spring of 1921, but he refused them all.[44] Observers were wondering if he would be plate shy, since many previously beaned players could not avoid the urge to pull out of their batting stance as the ball approached. Yet when he faced Pfeffer almost a year to the day after the beaning, it was the pitcher who seemed tentative, not his former victim. Fewster crushed Pfeffer's first pitch for a triple. "There are many kinds of courage in this world. . . . Chick Fewster possesses all the kinds there are," wrote James P. Sinnott in the *New York Evening Mail*.[45]

On April 27 the Senators rallied for their fourth straight come-from-behind win over New York, once again by a 5–3 score. Bob Shawkey got his first start of the season. Not surprisingly, he was not sharp and issued six walks. He faltered in the eighth with the Yanks ahead, 3–1, and gave up a two-run triple. With two men on base in the ninth, Huggins rushed Mays in. But he gave up a two-run double and lost the game. To add to Huggins's misery, former Yankees were the day's heroes. George Mogridge got the win in relief. And Duffy Lewis scored to tie the game in the eighth, and his double won it in the ninth.

The following day, Jack Quinn was ineffective against the Senators, as the Yankees lost their fifth straight game. Of immediate concern to Huggins was the state of the Yankee pitchers. "The celebrated right-handed pitching staff is as shot full of holes as a Swiss cheese," declared Sid Mercer.[46]

The Yankees' fielding was exposing its weaknesses, and not just in the infield where in addition to Fewster shortstop Roger Peckinpaugh had flubbed some grounders. It was becoming apparent that the team's outfield was below average in its fielding.[47] Bob Meusel had lost a fly ball that cost the team a game against the A's. Ruth had struggled too. On Lewis's game-winning hit in the Washington series, one New York paper lamented that Ruth was unable to bring it down, even though it "was not an impossible catch for a first grade outfielder."[48] Bodie, the slowest Yankee outfielder, had his own well-known difficulties covering ground.

The one bright spot in the field for New York was Aaron Ward's sensational play at third base. In a win over the Athletics, "He made plays that only the masters attempt and he made them with a slick assurance that drew the repeated outbursts of applause."[49] While Frank Baker had been reinstated by the commissioner that very day, Huggins said, "It would be a crime to make a switch."[50]

Ward had joined the Yankees in 1917 at the age of twenty. In his first three seasons, he appeared in a total of only fifty-five games and hit a microscopic .152. He started 1920 on the bench; but six weeks into the season, he took over at third base. "I never met a more ambitious kid than Aaron. That boy wants to play so badly that he actually suffers when he has to sit on the bench," said Miller Huggins. "I just have to get that aggressive kid, Ward, into my line-up."[51] He played in 127 games that year—114 of them at third base, where he covered a lot of ground.[52] He hit .256 with eleven home runs.

Fred Lieb felt that both Ward and Baker should be in the lineup. He had expressed admiration for Fewster's gameness, but noted that baseball was a survival of the fittest. "We do not believe that Huggins is using his full strength while Baker collects splinters on the bench and Fewster kicks around balls at second," Lieb wrote.[53]

As May began, Huggins made his moves, benching Fewster and moving Ward to second base, creating the opening at third that allowed the veteran Baker to return to the lineup. Huggins also benched Bodie, the weakest of the starting outfield bats (and gloves). He planned to use either rookie Nelson "Chicken" Hawks (who had a weak arm), youngster Tommy Connelly (a veteran of only one game, who had a weak bat), or—if his knee would cooperate—Braggo Roth. On May 3, with Ruth in left field, Roth in center, Pipp at first base, and Baker at third, the team had the distinction of having every American League annual home run leader of the past decade in the starting lineup.[54]

After three days of rainouts, New York did bounce back with two solid pitching performances in Boston on May 2 and 3. Mays pitched well but again weakened late in a 2–1 loss to Sam Jones. The next day, Piercy led the Yanks to a 2–0 win over Herb Pennock for his third victory of the season. Despite trading away many of its stars, Boston still had three fine pitchers from their 1918 championship season—Jones, Pennock, and Joe Bush.

After two more rainouts, the Yankees closed out their initial East Coast stretch of games with two thrilling weekend contests. On Saturday, May 7, they edged Washington, 6–5, in Griffith Stadium.[55] It was a seesaw battle highlighted by Ruth's eighth home run and Meusel's hitting for the cycle, including a ninth-inning triple that knocked in the tying and go-ahead runs. The press proclaimed Ruth's blast to be the longest ball ever hit in that ballpark, easily clearing the center-field wall. The Yankees battered Walter Johnson, who, despite weakening in the late innings, was left in the game by manager George McBride. Jack Quinn was again ineffective, forcing Huggins to remove him in the second inning. Hoyt pitched most of the rest of the way, with Mays retiring the side in the ninth.

Former president Woodrow Wilson attended the game, his first since his debilitating stroke in 1919. Because of Wilson's limited mobility, his auto entered the park through the center-field gate and drove his party across the playing field to his box seats. A couple of days earlier, President Warren Harding, also a big baseball fan, had visited with the Yankees at the Arlington Hotel, located a few blocks from the White House. Harding talked baseball in general and reminisced with Yankees coach Frank Roth, whom he remembered as a member of the 1906 world champion Chicago White Sox.[56] The president had recently drawn on baseball and the Babe in one of his speeches, urging Americans to "strive for production as Babe Ruth strives for home runs."[57]

On Sunday, May 8, the Yankees returned to the Polo Grounds to again face Philadelphia's Eddie Rommel. He seemed on the verge of a third win against New York, until Fewster, pinch-running for Baker in the ninth inning, stole home with two outs to force extra innings. When the dust settled, wrote Dan Daniel, "the scene resembled an asylum for roving maniacs. . . . The air became thick with score cards and newspapers torn into stage snow."[58] But Cy Perkins's triple in the fourteenth inning—a drive on which Braggo Roth did not seem to get a good jump—won the game for the A's, 5–4. Rommel went the distance, and New York fans gave him several ovations for his efforts.

Besides their disappointing play, or perhaps because of it, all was not well in the Yankee clubhouse. Once again, Miller Huggins was dealing with unrest among his players. One paper reported that on May 2 Mays had ignored Huggins's signal to walk Boston's Tim Hendryx, with two outs and first base open in the ninth inning of a 1 1 game. Hendryx, a former Yankee, then drove in the winning run.[59]

More significant were problems with the game's biggest star. Ruth had disregarded orders to sacrifice in an early-season game, reported Hugh Fullerton. Instead, he swung away and hit a home run. Though the fans cheered, Huggins berated Ruth and fined him. "No player is a good player who disobeys orders or who plays for personal glory at the expense of team work," wrote Fullerton. The New York Evening Mail sports editor had already gained the reputation for speaking out when others would not.[60]

There were also reports that Ruth was "not staying in condition" and was "violating training rules," euphemisms of the time for drinking and late-night carousing. During his career, such stories were usually kept out of the newspapers, making this glimpse behind the scenes very unusual. Even Damon Runyon, who was usually complimentary of Ruth, criticized the Yankees' star in the spring of 1921. While acknowledging his spectacular play and enormous box-office draw, Runyon wrote, "Ruth is not bigger than the game which gives him his livelihood. No man in baseball is bigger than baseball. Ruth must obey the rules of discipline. . . . The bigger the man, the better should be his example."[61]

Another paper was more concerned and more direct. In an article entitled "Babe Ruth—Liability or Asset?" the *New York Evening Telegram* wrote that some of the Yankees, including Ruth, were "kicking over the traces." The Babe "wasn't taking the prohibition movement any too seriously. . . . He is still looking upon the rye while it is ribald."[62] The paper continued, "John Barleycorn takes 'em" without considering who the violators may be.[63]

As the Yankees headed out on their first western road trip, their record stood at 9-8, with another eight games lost to rain. The rainouts would generate a burdensome schedule of doubleheaders and fewer days off later in the season, creating added pressure on an already thin and struggling pitching staff. The team was exasperating its fans and even neutral observers. "They have played about as careless ball as any team I ever watched," wrote Hugh Fullerton.[64]

AL STANDINGS AT CLOSE OF PLAY OF MAY 8, 1921

TEAM	G	W	L	T	PCT	GB
Cleveland Indians	21	15	6	0	.714	-
Washington Senators	21	11	9	1	.550	3.5
Boston Red Sox	15	8	7	0	.533	4.0
New York Yankees	17	9	8	0	.529	4.0
Detroit Tigers	21	11	10	0	.524	4.0
St. Louis Browns	19	8	11	0	.421	6.0
Philadelphia Athletics	19	7	11	1	.389	6.5
Chicago White Sox	17	5	12	0	.294	8.0

11 "This home run business is being carried too far"

For a team to prevail over a 154-game season, much has to go right, including players performing at their expected level and the avoidance of injuries to key personnel. While these concerns are true for all teams, the Giants had an additional burden to overcome—the personality of John J. McGraw.

McGraw had celebrated his forty-eighth birthday during spring training, though he, like Miller Huggins, had the appearance of a much older man. Beginning his twentieth season as the team's manager, he was now paunchy, jowly, and white haired. Long gone was the lean youngster who had been one of the most aggressive base runners in the National League during his playing career. Only Connie Mack—the man who had opposed him in the World Series of 1905, 1911, and 1913—was still managing from the group in place when McGraw succeeded Heinie Smith on July 19, 1902.[1]

In an opening day statement, McGraw appeared optimistic about his team's chances of being back in the World Series for the first time since 1917. "We were runners-up last year and I think we should finish the season with a better record this year," he said. "We have plenty of strength in every department, and plenty of speed and pitching power, and I am sure that New Yorkers will find the club worthy of its confidence and support."[2]

Still, sportswriter Harry A. Williams estimated that the Giants had to be 15 percent stronger than any other club to overcome the hostility other teams and fans had toward New York in general and McGraw in particular.[3] "Much of this is personal, due to his [McGraw's] intense aggressiveness and his long run of success, but has its chief inception in a small-town desire to beat a big-town ball team," said Williams. "The Colossus of the Hudson is wholly friendless and alone in the National League circuit."[4] He suggested that teams seemed to save their best pitchers to face the Giants and that opposing players seemed to exude extra effort in trying to beat them. In addition, the Giants had to endure fan hostility that in many cases reached "threatening proportions."[5] So while the Giants entered the 1921 season as the favorite to win the pennant, that also had been the case the previous four seasons, and they had won only in 1917.

Conversely, the Phillies, the team the Giants faced in their opener, had finished last the previous two seasons and would again in 1921. Nevertheless, more than 25,000 fans came out for the game, the largest crowd to see the Phillies play at Baker Bowl since the 1915 World Series.[6] The Giants were sporting a new look on the road this season, with blue replacing red as the dominant color. The uniforms, designed by McGraw himself, no longer had the red pinstripes and red block-lettered "GIANTS" across the front, worn the previous two seasons. They were now solid gray, and the color of the block-lettered "GIANTS" was blue. Stockings went from red on top and white on bottom to blue on top and gray on bottom. Caps—which had been gray with red pinstripes, a red interlocking "NY," and a red bill—were now gray with blue pinstripes, an interlocking blue "NY" on the crown, and a blue bill. The Phillies' home uniform also had a new look, as they too had changed their dominant color from red to blue.

Former star pitcher Bill Donovan—winner of 185 Major League games, mostly for Brooklyn and Detroit—had replaced Gavy Cravath as the Phillies' manager. Donovan had managed the Yankees in the first three years of the Ruppert-Huston ownership (1915–17), before Ruppert replaced him with Miller Huggins. His best season in New York was a fourth-place finish in 1916; however, no one in or out of Philadelphia was expecting the 1921 Phillies to reach such "lofty" heights. Just getting this team, which had little aside from slugging outfielders Cy Williams and Irish Meusel, out of the cellar would be considered a great success for the popular Donovan.[7] His best infielder should have been Art Fletcher, the veteran shortstop who had come over from the Giants in the June 1920 trade for Dave Bancroft. Unfortunately for Donovan and the Phillies, Fletcher was sitting out the season to run his family's business, following the deaths of his father and brother.

Donovan's opening-day pitcher was Jimmy Ring, a seventeen-game winner for Cincinnati in 1920, whom the Phillies had obtained in a trade for Eppa Rixey. McGraw's choice was Phil Douglas, a huge (for the time) six-feet-three, 190-pound right-hander, who had a 14-10 record in 1920.

Douglas, whose best pitch was a spitball, was a farm boy from the Georgia-Tennessee border region. A weakness for alcohol helped account for his having pitched for the White Sox, Reds, Dodgers, and Cubs since making his debut in 1912. His manager at Brooklyn during his three-month stay there in 1915 was Wilbert Robinson, a former big league catcher and an excellent judge of pitching talent. Robinson was well aware of what he was getting when he purchased Douglas from the Reds in June, both the talent and the alcoholism. "If I ever can get this fellow sober, I've got the best pitcher in the league," he said.[8]

Regrettably, Douglas could not remain sober. He was a periodic heavy drinker whose penchant for leaving his team for weeklong drinking sessions—he called them "vacations"—had kept him from realizing his potential. Douglas won only five games for Brooklyn before Robinson sold him to the Cubs in September 1915.

The Giants acquired Douglas in a July 1919 trade for outfielder Dave Robertson. A decade earlier, in 1909, McGraw had dealt for Bugs Raymond, another pitcher with a great spitball and an unquenchable thirst. Raymond had a solid first season in New York, but he was unable to curb his drinking sprees and died two years later in Chicago from a skull fracture and cerebral hemorrhage after being beaten at both a bar and a sandlot game. Warnings that dealing with Douglas would be similar to dealing with Raymond did not dissuade McGraw from making the trade. His reply—"He can win the pennant for me"—pinpointed the only logic that mattered to him.[9]

McGraw, no teetotaler himself, was familiar with hard-drinking men. He had been around them most of his life and believed he knew how to cope with alcoholic ballplayers and how to get the best out of them. "I know I am getting myself in for something when I take on Douglas," he said after the trade, "but I am sure I can handle him."[10] His methods of "handling" players like Raymond and Douglas included scolding, fines, suspensions, and having them trailed by private detectives or shadowed by team coaches. He would eventually assign Coach Jesse Burkett as Douglas's keeper.

"Such projects meant a good deal to McGraw," wrote John Lardner in a May 1956 *New Yorker* magazine article on Douglas. "Long after most managers of the modern era, he [McGraw] kept up the practice of gambling on rogue athletes, especially pitchers, for quick profits. He was a man of great ability, energy, and self-confidence. There is some evidence that it was his egotism, as well as the hope of winning pennants, that led him to sign up men other managers were afraid to hire or keep." In an excellent assessment of the McGraw persona, Lardner wrote, "Unfortunately, McGraw had a jealous violence of temperament that was as characteristic of him as his vanity or wisdom."[11]

Looking ahead to 1921, McGraw had said back in November, "George Kelly will remain on first base next year. He still is a trifle slow, but he can hit the ball and is a good fielder. He drove in many runs this year, and I'll bet he prevented more wild throws than any other first baseman in the big leagues."[12]

Kelly was indeed a fine first baseman, but it was his early-season slugging that would capture the nation's attention. It began on opening day. After he missed the club's final preseason game against Fordham because of an injured finger, his home run powered the Giants to an eleven-inning 10–8 win.

The game was tied, 7–7, when the Giants got three runs in the eleventh and the Phillies got only one against reliever Fred Toney. Kelly's long drive to center field that went for an inside-the-park home run and scored Frankie Frisch ahead of him was the big blow. An injured right knee that caused Ross Youngs to miss the last few exhibition games kept him out of the opener, and it would keep him out of the starting lineup for the first two weeks of the season as well. Rookie Curt Walker played right field in Youngs's place, with Eddie Brown, the third rookie in the starting lineup, in center. Several weak throws from that position demonstrated to all how Brown acquired his nickname, "Glass Arm Eddie."

Philadelphia's best pitcher, Lee Meadows (16-14 for the last-place Phillies in 1920) started the next two games, with widely differing results. In the first, Meadows, the first bespectacled modern-day player, gave up four hits and a walk to the first five batters before Donovan yanked him. Led by Curt Walker and Frank Snyder, each with three hits, the Giants coasted to a 10–2 victory behind Art Nehf. Walker's play in the first two games had McGraw comparing him to George Burns: "Curtis Walker is a day-in-and-day-out player. Like Burns, Walker seldom has what you might call an off day. Walker is as steady as a clock and as dependable as Burns."[13]

Following a day off, Meadows defeated the Giants, 11–5, with Kelly's second home run of the season—a three-run blast—the only bright spot for the Giants. It was a disappointing start for rookie Bill "Rosy" Ryan—the highly touted, hard-throwing right-hander whom the Giants considered a can't-miss prospect.

A former collegian at Holy Cross, where he played under Jesse Burkett, Ryan had gone to Hot Springs, Arkansas, to get ready for the upcoming season a month before the start of spring training. Prior to his late-season call-up in 1920, he had gone 19-9 for the Toronto Maple Leafs of the International League. Former big league star Hugh Duffy, his manager at Toronto, was effusive in his praise for Ryan. "He will be one of the greatest pitchers in the game," said Duffy, with no qualifications added.[14]

Following their opening series in Philadelphia, the Giants had one more stop before returning home, a scheduled four-game series at Boston that included a morning–afternoon Patriots' Day doubleheader.[15] Since their "miracle" sweep of the Philadelphia Athletics in the 1914 World Series, the Braves had been mostly a second-division team. George Stallings, manager of that 1914 team, had finally opted out after another seventh-place finish in 1920. He purchased the Rochester Colts and became the manager of that International League club. Fred Mitchell, whom the Cubs had let go after three years (including the pennant-winning season of 1918), was the new manager in Boston. The Braves had gotten off to an excellent start, winning four straight games against Brooklyn after dropping their opener. Their 4-1 record virtually tied them with the 3-0 Cubs for first place.

After snow canceled the opening game of the Boston–New York series, heavy rain washed out the morning game of the Patriots' Day doubleheader. By afternoon, the weather was cold and windy and the field was soggy; but the teams did play. Phil Douglas, looking much more impressive than he had in the opener, held the Braves to one unearned run as the Giants won, 9–1. Frisch, Walker, and Kelly had three hits apiece; and Kelly added two more runs batted in, giving him a total of ten after just four games. The Giants won again the next day behind Nehf, with late-inning help from Jesse Barnes, who earned a save.[16] In their first five games, McGraw's crew had scored forty-three runs on sixty-one hits. As they traveled to New York to open their home season with the Phillies, the Giants had a 4-1 record and were in first place by percentage points.

The weather for the Giants' Polo Grounds opener on April 21 was perfect, but the team was not. An eighth-inning error by shortstop Bancroft allowed the winning run in Philadelphia's 6–5 victory. Charles Stoneham had invited Judge Landis to throw out the first ball, but the judge was unable to rearrange his schedule. He promised, however, to be at the Polo Grounds on May 30 when the Giants would unveil a plaque dedicated to Eddie Grant, their former player and a deceased war hero.

New York's former governor, Al Smith, substituted for Landis in throwing out the first ball. As he did, the band serenaded him with the tune "How Dry I Am," a wry reminder that the effects of Prohibition were now being felt throughout the country. Also present were John Montgomery Ward—a nineteenth-century Giants' star—and General Douglas MacArthur, the superintendent of the U.S. Military Academy at West Point.[17]

As was the case with the Yankees' Polo Grounds opener, red, white, and blue decorations were displayed prominently around the park. And as it had been for the Yankees, the crowd was predominantly male, though in both openers there were far more women in attendance than there would be at most regular-season games.

Almost two years had elapsed since the passage of the Nineteenth Amendment, giving women the right to vote. Evidently, the American public assumed that women had knowledge enough to elect the country's leaders, yet the reporter from the *New York Times* did not give them credit for the ability to follow a baseball game. The *Times* condescendingly reported that the women did not quite know when to applaud, but added that they were "properly garbed, despite recent captious criticisms of women's wear."[18] There was no captious criticism of the Giants' wear. Unlike their road uniforms, their home uniforms were unchanged: blue pinstripes with an interlocking blue "NY" on the left sleeve, socks that were blue on top and white on bottom, and blue-pinstriped white caps with an interlocking blue "NY" on the crown and a blue bill.

12. After leading the National League in runs batted in for the 1920 season, a newly confident George Kelly was an early-season challenger to Babe Ruth's home run supremacy in 1921. *Private Collection of Dennis Goldstein.*

McGraw chose a relatively slimmed-down Fred Toney, 21-11 in 1920, to pitch the home opener. One of New York's three twenty-game winners in 1920 (Nehf and Barnes being the other two), Toney had won in relief on opening day at Philadelphia. Making his first start of the season, he quickly fell behind, 4–0, but settled down as the Giants battled back to even the score at 5–5 after seven innings.

Irish Meusel led off the Phillies' eighth with a triple. Then, with the bases loaded and two outs, Bancroft booted an easy grounder while Meusel raced home with what would be the winning run. Kelly had a triple and a home run, his third of the season; but perhaps the best news for the Giants was the ninth-inning, pinch-hit single by Ross Youngs, making his 1921 debut.

Both clubs got well-pitched games in the series' final two meetings, with the Giants winning both. In the first of those games, Barnes edged Red Causey, 2–1, as Kelly and Earl Smith each hit home runs for the New Yorkers. And in the final game, Douglas pitched a one-hitter (a second-inning single by backup shortstop Ralph Miller) that beat Lee Meadows, 1–0. Douglas's gem was on a Sunday before a full house at the Polo Grounds. All the Phillies looked futile in trying to hit his spitball, none more than Casey Stengel. Batting leadoff, the clownish outfielder struck out three times and hit into a double play. A former Dodger, Stengel was that rare Brooklyn player who was not hated by the Polo Grounds crowd and more often was the target of good-natured joshing by the fans. His ineffectual at bats this day allowed the fans to give full voice to razzing one of their favorite opposition players.

The recipient of most of the fans' vocal efforts, however, was Kelly; and they were all cheers. It was a welcome change for the big first baseman, whom these same fans had booed so often in previous seasons. Kelly's sixth-inning triple drove in the winning run, just as his seventh-inning home run had the day before. The newly acclaimed Giants' hero had become so feared that Meadows twice walked him intentionally. After eight games, Kelly was batting .452 and leading the league in home runs (with four) and runs batted in (with sixteen). Kelly's four home runs tied him with Babe Ruth for the Major League home run lead, putting both men well ahead of Ruth's record-setting pace of 1920. Yet unlike the Babe, who reveled in the adulation, Kelly seemed almost shy about acknowledging the crowd's applause. Whereas Ruth would often take off his cap, bow, and smile broadly after a home run, Kelly would hurry to the dugout, often forgetting even to tip his cap.

George Lange Kelly was a nephew of Bill Lange, an outstanding outfielder who, between 1893 and 1899, batted .330 for Cap Anson's Chicago Colts. Lange was a complete player, one whom some historians have called the best defensive outfielder of the nineteenth century and the Willie Mays of his day.[19] The eminent early-twentieth-century sportswriter Tim Murnane included Lange with Ty Cobb and Joe Jackson in his all-time outfield.[20]

In 1914, when Kelly was just eighteen, he elected to skip his senior year in high school to play professionally. He batted a modest .250 in 141 games for the Victoria (British Columbia) Bees of the Class B Northwestern League, but he was at .296 in August 1915 when McGraw paid the Bees $15,000 for him. Kelly did not play much over the next season and a half as he struggled with learning to hit a Major League curve ball. He produced identical .158 batting averages in a combined 114 at bats in 1915 and 1916. In 1917 McGraw sent him to bat only seven times, all of which were unsuccessful; and Kelly continued to be the target of frequent booing by the New York fans. With Walter Holke holding down first base, most games found Kelly on the bench seated next to McGraw. Recognizing that the six-feet-four San Franciscan had the raw talent necessary for baseball stardom, McGraw set about teaching him the intricacies of the game.

"Those first two years I was with the Giants, McGraw kept me on the bench alongside him, much as he was later to do with another teenager, Mel Ott," Kelly later recalled. "He talked to me about what was going on out there on the field, and I never learned so much about baseball. I was always by his side in those days, and sometimes I got a good ribbing about it, too. But I didn't care. It was worth it."[21]

Kelly's education was interrupted for a ten-day period in mid-1917, when McGraw either sold him to the Pirates or sent him there on temporary loan. More than forty years later, the memory was still fresh in Kelly's mind: "On a day in July, 1917, McGraw looked me up and down when I returned to the bench—and spat. My stature was hammered down from a 12-foot Giant to that of a dwarf. I was released to Pittsburgh. It was just a train ride. I went to the Pirates July 25, and returned to the Giants in time to be optioned on August 4 to Rochester."[22]

A 1934 *Daguerreotypes* profile of Kelly says, "In 1917, George dropped to .067 for 17 games, and McGraw almost gave up on him. Mac sent the big fellow to Pittsburgh, the Pirates to pay for him if he made good. After he played half-dozen hitless games, Barney Dreyfuss returned him, saying: 'I've heard of no-hit pitchers, but he's the first no-hit first baseman I ever saw.'"[23]

So while the administrative details of Kelly's move to Pittsburgh and back are unclear, his stay there was short-lived, unpleasant, and unsuccessful. He had only 2 hits in 23 at bats, and the local fans were extremely vocal in showing their displeasure with him.

After joining Rochester, he batted .300 in thirty-two games and began showing signs of the player he was to become. Kelly served in the army in 1918 but blossomed on his return to Rochester in 1919. He was batting .356 with fifteen home runs for the Hustlers when the Giants called him back to New York.[24] Replacing Hal Chase for the last month of the season, he batted a respectable .290.

Kelly started slowly at the plate in 1920 and often seemed unsure of himself in the field. He would eventually become an outstanding defensive first baseman; but at this point in his career, he was awkward, especially when contrasted with the now-departed, slick-fielding Chase. The fans noticed the difference between the two men, as did the reporters covering the team. Members of each group were quick to let Kelly know about it. When the youngster began to brood, McGraw stepped in. "I just wanted to remind you," he told Kelly in a meeting in his office, "I'm the only one you have to care about around here. I'm running this ball club. Not the fans behind first base, the gamblers behind third, or the writers in the press box."[25] Reassured and now fully established as the Giants first baseman, Kelly rewarded McGraw's faith in him by tying Rogers Hornsby for the National League lead in runs batted in, with ninety-four.[26]

At 6-2 with a .750 winning percentage, the Giants were in first place, although they were a half game behind the 8-3 (.727) Pirates. New York's eight games had been against Boston and Philadelphia, teams that finished seventh and eighth the year before. Now they headed to Brooklyn, where they would play four games against the Dodgers. McGraw and his lieutenants were aware that the April 25–28 series against the defending National League champions would give them a better read on how good this Giants' team was. After winning their opener, the Dodgers had dropped five straight, but had rebounded to win their last four to even their record at 5-5.

New York versus Brooklyn was baseball's most heated rivalry, one that did not need modern-day hype to express it. Long before shows of "hatred" for the other team were a way for fans to get their faces on television, the fans of each of these two clubs truly detested the fans and players of the other and were quite willing to show their feelings. While relative position in the league standings was mostly irrelevant when the two teams played, the fact that they were two of the leading contenders for the pennant, as they had been the year before, only heightened the sense of drama. On two occasions in 1920, once at Ebbets Field and once at the Polo Grounds, police had to be called to end fights that had broken out in the stands.

The antagonism between the fans of the two National League clubs dated from well before the 1898 incorporation of the then independent city of Brooklyn into Greater New York. Losing their independent status likely inflamed the sense of inferiority many Brooklynites harbored when comparing their city-turned-borough, large parts of which were still farmland, to Manhattan, the "sophisticated" colossus across the East River. Similarly, those living in Manhattan had little or no interest in what went on in Brooklyn. Joe Vila, writing after the Dodgers' loss to Cleveland in the 1920 World Series, said this: "Dyed-in-the-wool New Yorkers didn't enthuse over the World's Series because the Giants and Yankees were not the participants. They were lukewarm in their sentiment for the Brooklyns for the reason that nothing on Long Island except the race tracks ever interests residents of Manhattan and the Bronx."[27]

Bill Dahlen, the great turn-of-the-century shortstop, summed up the feelings of many, following his December 1903 trade from Brooklyn to the McGraw-led Giants. Dahlen, who had played on some of Brooklyn's greatest teams, exacerbated the borough's self-image of second-class citizenship by announcing, "It has always been my ambition to play in New York City. Brooklyn is all right, but if you're not with the Giants, you might as well be in Albany."[28]

Adding fuel to the fire was the enmity between John McGraw and

Wilbert Robinson, the two managers. Robinson had been yet another of McGraw's teammates on the great Orioles teams of the 1890s. Despite the difference in their ages—Robinson was ten years older than McGraw—the two men developed a close friendship and later became business partners in a Baltimore billiards parlor.[29] In 1911 McGraw added Robinson to his coaching staff, where he remained through 1913. Often at odds with each other during that last season, things came to a head after the last game of the World Series, which the Giants lost to the Philadelphia Athletics. At a reunion of some former Orioles at a New York saloon, a drunken McGraw criticized Robinson's coaching at third base in that afternoon's 3–1 loss. Robinson snapped back that McGraw's managing had been "pretty lousy" too. "This is my party. Get the hell out of here," snarled McGraw.[30] Not to be outdone, Robinson showered him with a glass of beer on the way out. The feud would last for seventeen years before the two aging skippers would reconcile at the National League winter meetings in 1930.

Dutch Ruether, Robinson's new pitcher, may or may not have known it—but the surest way for a Brooklyn player to win the hearts of the local fans was to do well against the Giants. Ruether did just that, tossing complete-game victories in the first and last games of the series. The left-handed Ruether topped Nehf, McGraw's ace left-hander, 4–1, in the first game and the rookie Ryan, 2–1, in the finale. Like Rube Marquard, the man for whom he was traded, Ruether had a taste for high living. "He never cared much for training rules," said sportswriter Frank Graham, "but he knew how to pitch, and he never really got out of hand. He was a big southpaw with plenty of stuff and plenty of moxie."[31]

The Brooklyn fans booed George Kelly heavily throughout the series, befitting his new status as a feared slugger. (His fifth home run of the season had again tied him with Ruth for the Major League lead.) The booing of Kelly during the four games was so vociferous it appeared that he now had surpassed McGraw as the number-one target of the Ebbets Field boobirds.

In stretching their winning streak to eight, the Dodgers had outplayed their interborough rivals in all phases of the game. The Giants committed both physical and mental mistakes, yet all four games had been close and exciting. One Giants rooter leaving the park after the final game expressed the eternal April optimism of fans. "Did you ever see such a splendid exhibition as was given in these four games?" he asked. "They couldn't possibly be beaten from a spectacular point of view. I am satisfied that the Giants have the better team, although they were beaten four in a row."[32]

The Giants limped out of Brooklyn in fourth place, three and a half games behind Pittsburgh, while the Dodgers were now second, just a game and a half behind. McGraw's club had not done well at Ebbets Field in 1920 either, losing eight of the eleven games played there. Overall, the Dodgers' fifteen wins in twenty-two games against the Giants that season was obviously a major contributor to their seven-game bulge over the second-place New Yorkers. And after losing this four-game set to the Dodgers, McGraw had to be wondering if his team could do any better this season.

Moreover, Brooklyn had accomplished the sweep without using their ace right-hander, Burleigh Grimes, relying instead on left-handers to start each game. Grimes, a twenty-three-game winner in 1920, had held out all spring before signing a contract the day before the season opened. His first game was on April 21, eight days into the season, when he went all the way to beat Boston in Brooklyn's home opener.

Despite the debacle in Brooklyn, the Giants had encouraging news when they returned home to begin a four-game series with Boston. Ross Youngs, limited by a knee injury to one pinch-hitting appearance in the Giants' first twelve games, was back in the starting lineup. Delighted at the return of one of their best players, the fans gave him a standing ovation when he trotted out to his familiar spot in right field to begin the game. Batting fourth, Youngs doubled in his first at bat and scored the Giants' first run. But once more, it was Kelly who provided the big blow for the Giants. His seventh-inning, bases-loaded home run was his sixth of the young season and put him one up on Ruth.

Much as Yankee fans did with Ruth, Giant fans were now expecting a home run from Kelly each time he came to bat. He failed to hit one the next day during a 7–2 thrashing of the Braves. Hugh McQuillan and Dana Fillingim held him hitless, ending his thirteen-game hitting streak that began on opening day. Kelly renewed his long-ball slugging in the first inning of game three of the series. The cheers were so loud that he stopped to take off his cap in acknowledgement as he followed Frisch across the plate. He now had seven home runs in fifteen games and remained one ahead of Ruth, who blasted number six at Fenway Park that afternoon. The Ruth-Kelly home run race had so captivated the fans that the *New York American* was running a graphic called the "Ruth-KellyOmeter" chronicling their progress.

That two players had so many home runs so early in the season was unprecedented. Ruth had reached the point where nothing he accomplished in that department surprised anyone, but Kelly being at that level shocked the baseball world. Unlike the Babe, who "swung from the heels," Kelly was more of a slash-type hitter; and Kelly, in fact, choked up a bit on the bat. Yet there he was, one home run up on Babe Ruth. "Who in the wildest flight of fancy could dream that another batter could challenge the Home Run King and beat him at his own particular specialty?" wrote John J. Ward in *Baseball Magazine*.[33]

Kelly attributed his home run splurge to confidence and a change in his swing. "I guess it's just more confidence this year. That and some luck and a good swing at the ball. I'm standing up straight this season too—that is I'm bending my right leg to get the spring, but I'm not crouching."[34]

Describing Kelly's power, John B. Foster wrote, "Kelly is without grace but hits with the force of a double cylinder mogul going head on into the rear of a freight in front."[35]

The Ruth-Kelly home run race was the most talked about happening of the young season, though not everyone was convinced of the legitimacy of these home runs. Some in the press believed that the owners had concocted the race as a way to bring fans shaken by the Black Sox scandal back to the ballparks. Cliff Wheatley made the case for these conspiracy theorists in the *Atlanta Constitution*.[36] Wheatley claimed that the National League owners believed a home run rival for Ruth would be a great asset in raising league attendance, particularly if that rival played in New York. He said those NL owners had been disappointed when the Cardinals had refused to trade Rogers Hornsby, the man most likely to challenge the Babe, to the Giants. Instead, he suggested, they had settled on Kelly to fill that role.

Wheatley found it fishy that someone like Kelly, who had hit only eleven home runs in all of 1920, already had seven after just fifteen games. According to his conspiratorial "analysis," many of the home runs that Ruth and Kelly had hit this season had been staged. Contrary to fact, he claimed they had come mostly when their teams were well ahead or well behind and therefore did not have a great affect on the game. He also did not bother to explain how the owners would transmit these orders to their managers, who would then have to order their pitchers exactly when to groove a pitch to Kelly or Ruth.

Several longtime baseball observers also expressed concern that the game had swung too far in the direction of high scores and frequent home runs: "This home run business is being carried too far, with all due respect to the thrills and chills the big blows bring."[37]

Questioning the legitimacy of Kelly's home runs was odious in its own right, but doing so to Ruth was an indication of how much suspicion remained in baseball. In an eerie precedent to the Barry Bonds story of eighty-plus years later, Fuzzy Woodruff, also of the *Atlanta Constitution*, called for Judge Landis to investigate Kelly's home run surge, lest the game be tarnished with another scandal.[38]

While these accusations had no factual basis, it was nevertheless true that if Kelly could indeed maintain a home run pace similar to Ruth's, it would be a financial windfall for the Giants and the National League. Though the Giants had enjoyed their greatest profit-making year ever in 1920, they still trailed the Yankees in both home and road attendance. The difference was Ruth, and having a slugger of Ruth's caliber might allow them to equal or even surpass the American Leaguers in attendance and popularity.

Strong attendance early in the 1921 season suggested that fans did indeed like the long ball. The numbers were close to the record figures of 1920, despite the mild recession the nation was experiencing. Hugh Fullerton was a sophisticated baseball analyst, a purist who might have preferred a 1–0 contest to a 9–8 game. Yet he explained the matter succinctly when he said, "Whether it is good baseball or bad baseball, the public likes it."[39]

NL STANDINGS AT CLOSE OF PLAY OF MAY 2, 1921

TEAM	G	W	L	T	PCT	GB
Pittsburgh Pirates	16	13	3	0	.813	-
Brooklyn Dodgers	17	12	5	0	.706	1.5
New York Giants	15	9	6	0	.600	3.5
Chicago Cubs	13	6	7	0	.462	5.5
Cincinnati Reds	17	7	10	0	.412	6.5
Boston Braves	17	6	11	0	.353	7.5
Philadelphia Phillies	15	5	10	0	.333	7.5
St. Louis Cardinals	12	3	9	0	.250	8.0

12   The Trials and Tribulations of John McGraw

Larger-than-life figures who are closely identified with their teams are part of baseball culture and have enriched the history of the game. Both the Giants and the Yankees of 1921 had such a figure. John Mc-Graw and Babe Ruth were immensely talented men who contributed to their teams' winning ways. They also constantly attracted fan attention and newspaper headlines. America was entering an "Era of Celebrities," with men "who kept the myth of American individualism alive and well."[1] When Sid Mercer wrote in *Baseball Magazine* about "The Supreme Value of 'Color' in Baseball," McGraw and Ruth were two of the leading exponents of this quality.[2] Call it personality or stage presence; they had it.

Yet because they pushed the boundaries of convention with their behavior, McGraw and Ruth created problems for their teams. In addition to his own drinking problem and his many associations with questionable characters, McGraw was also willing to sign talented ballplayers whose links to scandal and alcoholism detracted from the team's reputation.

"It has been my fortune—perhaps misfortune—to harbor some of the most picturesque characters in baseball," admitted McGraw in his autobiography. "Always I have had a weakness for these odd personalities."[3]

One of these "odd personalities" was Rube Benton, whose three-hitter on May 3 completed the Giants' home sweep of Boston. The slugging New Yorkers had massacred the Braves in the four games, outscoring them 31 to 9. It was the first start of the year for Benton, yet another of McGraw's parade of rehabilitation projects.

A drinker and a gambler, Benton was often involved in controversy. In late September 1920 he had testified to the Chicago grand jury investigating baseball gambling that three years earlier, in September 1917,

Giants teammate Buck Herzog and Cincinnati's Hal Chase had offered him a bribe to throw a game against the Chicago Cubs. Benton said he refused the offer and won the game. Herzog denied the charge and countered with one of his own, claiming that Benton had won $3,800 betting on Cincinnati in the 1919 World Series. Benton later admitted knowing that the 1919 World Series had been fixed, though he denied betting on the Series himself.[4]

The National League absolved Herzog of the charges made by Benton, while retaining a strong suspicion that he had been involved in other fixed games as a member of the Cubs. Herzog, another character-challenged former McGraw employee, did not return to the Cubs in 1921; and there were those in the press who believed the National League should not have allowed Benton to return to the Giants. James J. Long of the *Pittsburgh Sun* raised the old specter of New York favoritism: "Evidently the New York club is still a privileged character in the National League and can get away with anything. Anything New York needs seems to be OK in the National."[5]

At this time, McGraw was having an encounter of his own with the legal system, one that dated to his drunken brawl at the Lambs Club the previous summer. Established in New York in 1874, the Lambs Club—at 128 West 44th Street, bordering Times Square and the theater district—was America's first professional theatrical club. From its beginning, its members included the biggest names in show business, along with a smattering of nontheatrical people. A member since 1914, McGraw spent many evenings at the club when he was in New York.

John McGraw was a troubled man on the evening of August 7, 1920. Earlier in the day, the Giants had dropped a game to the Cubs and now trailed the first-place Dodgers by three games. At the same time, two events that were unfolding beyond his control were also on his mind. For one, Babe Ruth was drawing all the headlines in New York; he had just hit two home runs the day before, his fortieth and forty-first of the season. More importantly, his Yankees were drawing more people to the Polo Grounds than McGraw's Giants.

In addition, McGraw's friend and former star, Christy Mathewson, had gone to Saranac Lake in upstate New York in an attempt to improve his failing health. That evening, a Saturday, McGraw and his wife,

Blanche, dined out. Rather than go home with Blanche after dinner, McGraw chose to spend the evening at a few places where he knew he would find kindred souls, men with whom he could drink beer and whiskey and talk sports.

In all likelihood, McGraw had already had too much to drink when he entered the Lambs Club early Sunday morning; nevertheless, he continued drinking bootleg alcohol after he got there. His inebriated condition may explain, though not excuse, what ensued. McGraw got into a scuffle with actor William Boyd, a friend whom he mistook for someone else.[6] It began when Boyd took offense at the foul language McGraw was using in front of some cleaning women. Boyd got much the better of the exchange of blows, and McGraw ended up on the floor, bleeding.[7]

Comedian John C. Slavin—also a friend of McGraw's—and another man hustled McGraw into a cab and escorted him to his apartment at Broadway and 109th Street. In an argument over who would pay the fare (each man offered to do so), Slavin somehow ended up unconscious. He was rushed to nearby St. Luke's Hospital in critical condition and eventually recovered. The police questioned McGraw, while Prohibition agents accused the Lambs of having liquor on the premises. Club officials expressed "shock" that liquor had been consumed there, claiming that if it was, it would have had to have been brought in from the outside.

A bruised McGraw later confessed that he had indeed purchased and consumed alcohol, which was a federal offense. However, lawyer William J. Fallon, "the Great Mouthpiece," managed to get everything quieted down and maneuvered to have the trial postponed until the following year. The entire sordid incident ended on May 2, 1921, after Fallon had secured several additional postponements. McGraw, suffering from a badly sprained ankle and on crutches, finally appeared before Judge Learned Hand in the U.S. District Court for the Southern District of New York on charges of violating the Volstead Act.[8] The jury took all of five minutes to dismiss the charges after Fallon argued that the indictment had failed to specify where McGraw was when the alleged liquor was in his possession. McGraw—who had caused embarrassment to himself, to the Giants' organization, and to baseball—did not go completely unpunished. The Lambs Club barred him for three years.

With the advent of Prohibition, drinking clubs had sprung up in cities across America; and the Lambs Club was an example of the more upscale ones. The well-off in major metropolitan areas had easy access to good quality liquor, and they were able to violate the Volstead Act with impunity.[9] Those of lower income, many of whom were immigrants, did not and could not. Author Geoffrey Perrett wrote, "The upper classes had supported Prohibition in order to save the workers by denying them drink. They never intended it to apply to themselves."[10] Yet Perrett may have greatly oversimplified the reason for upper-class support, which involved aspects of religion, economics, and sociology.

Franklin P. Adams—who wrote "Baseball's Sad Lexicon," with its "Tinker to Evers to Chance" refrain—summed up the absurdity and futility of Prohibition, in another poem:

PROHIBITION

Prohibition is an awful flop; we like it.
It can't stop what it's meant to stop. We like it.
It's left a trail of graft and slime, it don't prohibit worth a dime,
It's filled our land with graft and crime;
Nevertheless, we're for it.[11]

After three weeks of play, the National League race was shaping up as a three-team battle among New York, Pittsburgh, and Brooklyn, just as many had predicted. The Pirates had started the season in spectacular fashion. Winners of thirteen of their first sixteen games, they led the Dodgers by one and a half games and the Giants by three. On May 4 the Dodgers invaded the Polo Grounds to take on the Giants, a team they had swept in a four-game series at Ebbets Field a week earlier.

The spring of 1921 had been one of the rainiest in memory in the Northeast and Midwest (the only areas of the country where Major League Baseball was played), leading to the rescheduling of many games. Although rain was in the forecast for New York City, the Giants and Dodgers were able to play the first game of this series. The threatening weather held the crowd to just 10,000, and those who came had to sit through a heavy downpour that interrupted play in the sixth inning.

The game was a rematch between the Dodgers' Dutch Ruether, who had tossed two complete-game victories in the Ebbets Field sweep, and

Rosy Ryan. Ruether had edged Ryan, 2–1, in the last game of that series, a game the Giants felt they should have won. This time they did, scoring three eighth-inning runs to win, 3–2. The Giants' fifth consecutive victory also ended the Dodgers' winning streak at eleven.

Rain prevented the teams from playing either of the next two days; but when the sun came out on Saturday, thousands of fans descended on the Polo Grounds. More than 38,000 wedged their way in, while thousands more were denied admission.

Fred Toney continued his strong pitching, stopping Brooklyn, 3–1. Thirty-five-year-old Ed Konetchy, one of the Deadball Era's best first basemen, now in his final season, was the only Dodger to solve Toney. Konetchy had half of the six hits Toney allowed, and his home run accounted for Brooklyn's lone run. Kelly failed to hit a home run against Brooklyn's Sherry Smith, but he did drive in his league-leading twenty-sixth run. He also continued to lead the National League in home runs (with seven) and runs scored (with eighteen). The win, their sixth straight, moved the Giants past the Dodgers into second place; but they were still three and a half games behind the Pirates.

The teams moved to Ebbets Field for Sunday's game, while the Yankees, in the middle of a twenty-five-day road trip, came home to host the Philadelphia Athletics at the Polo Grounds. Brooklyn fans turned out en masse to see their Dodgers battle their bitter rivals. The home team's 2–0 win made it as enjoyable an afternoon for them as it had been for the Giants' rooters the day before. They began razzing the New York players as soon as they appeared and never stopped, not even after the final out.

Although frequently in trouble (he allowed ten hits), spitball pitcher Clarence Mitchell raised his record to 3-0. The visitors had at least one hit in every inning but could not get the big one when they needed it. Jesse Barnes was the hard-luck loser for the Giants, who saw their six-game winning streak end as they dropped back behind Brooklyn into third place. It had been a well-attended, well-played three games, absent the usual bickering and umpire baiting that accompanied most Dodgers-Giants battles. "There was never a more sensational series played, not excepting a world's series," wrote Sam Crane.[12]

Both New York teams would now face the western clubs for the first time. The westernmost city in the Major Leagues was St. Louis, which

13. John McGraw called Ross Youngs an "ideal ballplayer" and paid him accordingly. But a knee injury kept the speedy, hard-hitting Texan out of the starting lineup for the season's first two weeks. *Library of Congress, Prints and Photographs Division, George Grantham Bain Collection, LC-B2-6169-10.*

was the home to both the American League's Browns and the National League's Cardinals. The other American League cities out west were Detroit, Cleveland, and Chicago. In the National, the other western clubs were in Cincinnati, Chicago, and Pittsburgh. The Yankees were the first New York team to travel west. The Giants would face western opposition in May, but at home. They would not leave the East Coast until June.

Branch Rickey led the St. Louis Cardinals into the Polo Grounds on May 10, for the start of what would be a fourteen-game home stand for the Giants against the National League's western clubs. St. Louis had started the season horribly, losing twelve of sixteen games. They were already ten games behind league-leading Pittsburgh, owing primarily to having lost all five games played against the Pirates. The Giants dropped them even further behind, winning three of the four games.

St. Louis's only win came in the first game, one that served to remind McGraw why he had tried so hard and so long to acquire Rogers Hornsby. The slugging second baseman went 4-4 (including a double and a triple), plus a walk, raising his league-leading batting average to .478. In a game clearly dominated by hitting, the defense of second baseman Frankie Frisch and left fielder George Burns stood out. Then again, it seemed Frisch and Burns were each making at least one great play in almost every game. In their 7–6 loss, the Giants had fourteen hits, including Ross Youngs's first home run of the season.

Youngs was coming off a spectacular 1920 season, one in which his .351 average, 204 hits, and .904 ops (on-base percentage plus slugging percentage) trailed only Rogers Hornsby in those categories.[13] He was also second in singles, walks, and on-base percentage; and he led the league in number of times reaching base safely.[14] An exceptionally speedy outfielder with an outstanding throwing arm—"He is fast, covers great stretches of ground and makes innumerable spectacular catches," was how sportswriter Sam Crane described Youngs—he also would lead the National League in assists (and errors) in 1921.[15]

McGraw, who nicknamed Youngs "Pep" because of his hustle, had been enamored of him from the beginning. As Youngs was compiling a .356 batting average for Rochester in 1917, his second full professional season, McGraw told Rochester manager Mickey Doolan, a former Major League infielder, to "not mess this kid up." McGraw called him "a great baseball player" and "a most willing athlete with a disposition that is almost flawless."[16] In 1917 McGraw signed Youngs to a three-year contract at an annual salary higher than Youngs had requested. The last Giant into the fold, Youngs had quickly become a favorite of McGraw's; and the manager was effusive in his praise after the signing: "Youngs is getting one of the best salaries paid to an outfielder in the majors and at the expiration of the new contract he will be offered an even better salary by the New York club. We appreciate his work and above all his spirit and willingness to do anything asked of him. He is the ideal ball player."[17]

The Giants won the next three games from St. Louis, including Toney's 4–1 win in the second game of the series and Ryan's 5–1 win in the fourth—a rain-shortened, six-inning affair. Rain had also threatened to cancel the previous day's game; it did not, though the threatening weather did hold down what was expected to be a larger-than-usual weekday crowd. That was unfortunate, as both the Giants and the Cardinals were donating the game's proceeds to the American Committee for Relief in Ireland. The committee was allegedly trying to alleviate economic hardship and starvation in Ireland during its rebellion against British rule. However, New York's Irish Americans may have seen this more as an opportunity "to help spread rebellion than to spread peace and goodwill."[18]

Present at the game to lend their support to the relief fund were Mayor John Hylan, General Douglas MacArthur, and Nathan L. Miller and Al Smith, New York's present and former governors. As part of the fund-raising, Father Francis Duffy, chaplain of New York's famous Fighting Sixty-ninth Regiment, auctioned off a ball signed by President Harding and General John J. Pershing. The regiment's band paraded and provided the music. The highlight of the Giants' 7–5 victory was Kelly's first-inning, bases-loaded home run. The blow, Kelly's eighth home run of the year and second with the bases loaded, set his fellow Irishmen in the crowd dancing, as the band played a traditional Irish jig. Meanwhile, in Detroit, Babe Ruth hit his tenth home run of the season. His lead over Kelly would steadily increase to the point where no longer would anyone be talking about a Ruth-Kelly home run race.

The four-game sweep of Pat Moran's Cincinnati Reds, who followed the Cardinals into New York, featured the Giants at their best. Benton won the opener, 5–0, as Frisch had three hits, including two triples, to raise his batting average to .340. The next day, May 15, was cut-down day. To bring his roster down to the required twenty-five players, McGraw optioned rookie pitcher Pat Shea, whom he had yet to use, to St. Paul of the American Association. Shea would return to New York in August and be a big help for the Giants down the stretch.

That afternoon, the Giants delighted Sunday's capacity crowd by scoring two runs against ex-Giant Rube Marquard in their last at bat to pull out a 4–3 win. Dave Bancroft's fourth hit of the afternoon was the game winner, generating more noise among the fans than at any time since the scoreboard showed that the Cardinals had scored six runs in the first inning at Brooklyn. As always, Giant rooters wanted to see not only their team winning but also the Dodgers losing. Two more wins completed the sweep of the Reds.

During the May 16 game, the authorities took into custody a fan named Reuben Berman when he refused to give an attendant a foul ball he had caught. At the time, most parks, including the Polo Grounds, did not allow fans to keep foul balls hit into the stands. Berman sued the Giants for $2,000, a case that came before the New York State Supreme Court in Manhattan on July 27, 1921.

Berman's suit alleged that the Giants had "wrongfully and unlawfully imprisoned and detained the plaintiff . . . and threatened the plaintiff while detained and imprisoned, with arrest." He added that he was "greatly humiliated before a large crowd of people in attendance . . . and thereby was caused mental and bodily distress and was thereby greatly injured in his character and reputation and in his physical health."[19] Berman won his case, but the court awarded him just $100. Before long, fans in all parks were allowed to keep balls hit into the stands, a policy that became known as "Reuben's rule."

After their sweep of the Reds, the Giants had won seven in a row and thirteen of their last fifteen since the late-April disaster at Ebbets Field. But they were still one and a half games behind the 20-6 Pirates, who were playing at a dazzling .769 pace. The Giants' winning streak reached eight with a 3–2 win over the Johnny Evers–led Chicago Cubs. Earl Smith's home run, the team's second game ender in two days, won it for the Giants.

Trailing, 1–0, the Giants scored two in the eighth to take the lead. During the inning, McGraw had Eddie Brown bat for Rube Benton, who had pitched the first eight innings. He then called on Phil Douglas to pitch the ninth, a questionable decision. Douglas had not pitched since shutting out the Phillies on April 24, and his rustiness showed.[20] After he walked two of the first three Chicago batters, McGraw replaced him with Slim Sallee, who retired the side. However, the Cubs had tied the score, setting up the Smith home run, which crashed off the roof of the right-field grandstand.

McGraw used Douglas again the next day, bringing him in for the final two innings with the Giants down, 5–2. That surely seemed a better spot to use a pitcher who had not been in action for two weeks than in the ninth inning of a 2–1 game. Douglas allowed two hits and a walk, but no runs. Nevertheless, the Giants lost, 5–3, ending their winning streak at eight games.

A split in the final two games with the Cubs, combined with Pittsburgh's four-game sweep at Brooklyn, left the Giants three and a half games behind the Pirates, while the Dodgers had dropped to eight games off the pace.

On Sunday, May 22, McGraw and his players turned their attention to the league-leading Pittsburgh Pirates, who were making their first 1921 visit to the Polo Grounds. Four games were scheduled, but they would play only two. The teams would make up the two rained-out games as part of a five-game series in late August, a series that would prove to be the most crucial of the season for both teams.

Forty-year-old George Gibson was in his second season as the Pirates' manager, having replaced Hugo Bezdek. A native of London, Ontario, Gibson was only the fourth Canadian to manage in the Major Leagues.[21] An outstanding defensive catcher with Pittsburgh between 1905 and 1916, he finished his career with a brief stint as a player-coach under McGraw in 1917–18. Gibson managed the International League's Toronto club to a second-place finish in 1919, before Pirates owner Barney Dreyfuss brought him back to Pittsburgh. After three consecutive fourth-place finishes (under Bezdek in 1918 and 1919 and under Gibson in 1920), the Pirates had jumped off to a spectacular 24-6 start in 1921. The acquisition of shortstop Rabbit Maranville had solidified their infield; and their outfield of Max Carey, Carson Bigbee, and George "Possum" Whitted was as good as any in the National League.

Maranville, the shortstop for the 1914 Braves, believed this Pirates team was better than the Boston club that had swept the Philadelphia Athletics in that World Series: "No team could have more spirit than the Braves of that year, but this team's got just as much. Our whole success this year is that we're hustling. Gibson is a real manager. He's a wonder at handling men and he's smart in a baseball way. The boys all like him."[22]

The key ingredient to Pittsburgh's early-season success had been its pitching, a fact that Maranville readily acknowledged: "I should say our pitching staff is the best in the league and they are all in good shape. . . . It is a stronger staff, in my opinion, than Brooklyn's or New York's, and they are the two teams we have to beat."[23]

Pittsburgh's number-one pitcher was Wilbur Cooper, who at 6-0 was on pace to top the twenty-four wins he had in 1920. The left-handed Cooper had been discovered by no less a personage than a future president of the United States. Cooper broke into baseball in 1911 with the Marion Diggers of the Class D Ohio State League. Warren Harding was a part owner of the Diggers that year and took a liking to Cooper, a seventeen-game winner. Harding secured a tryout with Cleveland for Cooper; but although he failed to impress the Indians, Pittsburgh's Dreyfuss jumped in and signed him. Harding and Cooper, both of whom had come a long way since their days in Marion, remained mutual admirers. Moreover, while the president lived in Washington and was an Ohio native, he admitted that he was rooting for a Pittsburgh world championship. Harding joked that if he could pick office holders as well as he could ballplayers, his administration would be safe.[24] The country would soon learn that he could not.

Given their first opportunity to see the team that was shaping up as the Giants' biggest obstacle to the pennant, New Yorkers turned out in full force. All seats were sold well before game time, necessitating the police to set up barriers outside the Polo Grounds and inform would-be attendees without tickets that they were too late. Several newspapers reported that the number of fans denied entrance to the game appeared to be as large a group as the 38,000–40,000 who did gain admission.

For seven innings, they saw a gritty pitching duel between Cooper and Jesse Barnes, although neither pitcher was overpowering. Each allowed multiple base runners; however, only the Giants, with single runs in the first and seventh, had been able to bring any home. The game then suddenly turned from a pitchers' duel to a slugfest. The two clubs combined to hit four home runs and score twelve runs total over the final two innings, with Pittsburgh winning, 8–6. Cooper's complete-game effort on this very warm afternoon raised his record to 7-0 and gave him one win against each of the other teams in the league.

Sandwiched between two rainouts, the Giants won the second game of this weather-abbreviated series, 5–3. Unlike the first game, a crowd of only 8,000 fans showed up on a very chilly Tuesday afternoon. Among them was National League president John Heydler, who looked on as Nehf pitched a complete-game five-hitter. Babe Adams, one week past his thirty-ninth birthday, was the loser. The win brought the Giants back to within three and a half games of the Pirates, as they finished this first home stand against the western clubs with ten wins in fourteen games. The two clubs would meet again nine days later in Pittsburgh.

Before facing the Pirates, the Giants would play five games at Boston and then five back at the Polo Grounds against Philadelphia. During the Giants' first visit to Boston, bad weather had wiped out two games, which the teams would make up by playing five games in three days. New York won the opener of the May 26 doubleheader, their sixth win against the Braves this season without a loss. Rube Benton—who had a complete-game, three-hit win over the Braves earlier in the season—went eight and two-thirds innings but needed help from Phil Douglas, who got the final out.

Evidently satisfied with Douglas's one-batter relief effort in the first game, McGraw sent him out to pitch the second game. Making his first start since his one-hit, 1–0 shutout of the Phillies back on April 24, Douglas lasted just one inning. The inconsistency of McGraw's pitching staff remained on display in the final three games at Boston. The Giants won two of the three; but it was thanks to their bats, as their pitchers allowed twenty-one runs.

Desperate for pitching, McGraw started veteran right-hander Pol Perritt in the final game. For Perritt, who failed to hold an early 3–0 lead, this start would be the only one he would make before the Giants sold him to Detroit on waivers in June.

Both Pol Perritt and Slim Sallee had come to New York from the Cardinals in roundabout ways that reflected McGraw's creative recruitment practices. A sixteen-game winner for Miller Huggins's Cardinals in 1914, Perritt jumped to Pittsburgh's Federal League club in 1915. McGraw took advantage of the Federal League war and approached Perritt, convincing him to stay with Organized Baseball and come to the Giants.

Without the war, the manager's action would have been considered a clear case of tampering. But since the Cardinals had already lost Perritt to the upstart league, Huggins had little leverage. He reluctantly accepted outfielder Bob Bescher as compensation for the loss of Perritt, who then won sixty-five games for the Giants between 1915 and 1918.[25] However, Perritt had become rich after discovering oil on his farm near Shreveport, Louisiana, and had not pitched much since 1918.[26]

A year later, in 1916, the Federal League had ceased to exist; nevertheless, McGraw was able to lure Sallee to the Giants. In June of that year, Sallee, winner of eighty-one games for the Cardinals from 1911 to 1915, suddenly announced he was unhappy with the team and "retired" to his Ohio farm. Once again, Huggins's hand had been forced; and in July McGraw paid the Cardinals $10,000 for the pitcher, who then emerged from retirement. Sallee and Perritt won thirty-five games for the pennant-winning 1917 Giants. Just when McGraw first had contact and contract discussions with them is unknown.

Between games of the Giants' sweep of a morning-afternoon Memorial Day doubleheader with Philadelphia, the Giants unveiled a memorial dedicated to U.S. Army captain Eddie Grant, which they had erected on the playing field out by the center-field bleachers. Grant, a Harvard-educated lawyer, had been a player for the Giants (and for the Reds and the Phillies). He was killed in the Great War while conducting a rescue mission in France's Argonne Forest on October 5, 1918, little more than a month before the armistice. Led by a military band, a group of soldiers and the players from both teams paraded out to the flag-draped monument. Several of Grant's comrades offered testimonials, as did McGraw and Judge Landis. Grant's two sisters removed the flag from the memorial, revealing a bronze plaque that read, "Soldier, Scholar, Athlete," as the band played "America."

As they had against the Braves in the previous series in Boston, the Giants would play two doubleheaders against the Phillies with a single game in between. Curiously, the single game took almost as long to play as some doubleheaders. The chief culprit for the two-and-a-half-hour struggle was Phillies pitcher Lee Meadows, who took a great deal of time between pitches and was the center of several conferences at the mound.

"He was slower than mud yesterday and caused the game to drag along most tiresomely," said Sam Crane. "Umpires [Ernie] Quigley and [Hank] O'Day would do well to make players hustle more than they did yesterday," he added.[27] According to Crane, "National League games have been noted for being played much quicker than in the American League and favorable comment has been made on that fact. President Heydler's organization does not want to lose that prestige. It is a big asset."[28]

A day later, Crane retracted his criticism of Meadows when he learned that the pitcher was working with a sore arm. He shifted his words of censure to manager Donovan for allowing Meadows not only to start the game but also to stay out there for seven innings. Sore arm and all, Meadows limited the Giants to three runs in those seven innings. Meanwhile, the Phillies pounded Barnes, Sallee, and Perritt and came away with a 10–5 victory.

The Giants bounced back the next day, on June 1, to sweep the doubleheader. Bancroft was the offensive star of the second game, batting for the cycle, while Kelly broke his long home run drought in the first game, hitting his first homer since May 12. That gave Kelly nine for the season, tying him for the National League lead with Philadelphia's Irish Meusel, who had passed him the day before. Over in the American League, Ruth now had fifteen; and not only had home run comparisons between Kelly and the Babe faded, the irresponsible speculation about the legitimacy of either's blasts had also mercifully disappeared. With forty-eight runs batted in, Kelly still had a comfortable lead in that department over the Cardinals' Austin McHenry, who had thirty-one.

NL STANDINGS AT CLOSE OF PLAY OF JUNE 1, 1921

TEAM	G	W	L	T	PCT	GB
Pittsburgh Pirates	39	29	10	0	.744	-
New York Giants	43	29	14	0	.674	2.0
Brooklyn Dodgers	44	22	22	0	.500	9.5
Boston Braves	39	19	20	0	.487	10.0
St. Louis Cardinals	37	17	20	0	.459	11.0
Chicago Cubs	37	16	21	0	.432	12.0
Philadelphia Phillies	39	14	25	0	.359	15.0
Cincinnati Reds	42	14	28	0	.333	16.5

13 Cobb and Speaker Await as the Yankees Head West

On May 9 the Yankees arrived at Detroit's Michigan Central train station. They were entering a city that was experiencing enormous growth and a baseball renaissance. Between 1910 and 1920, driven by the booming automobile industry, Detroit had risen from the country's ninth most populous city to its fourth.[1] After fourteen years of Hughie Jennings as the Tigers' skipper, center fielder Ty Cobb had taken over as manager of the club. Jennings's early years were very successful, three pennants in his first three seasons, 1907–9. The Tigers lost all three World Series, however; and there had been no pennants for the Motor City since, though the Tigers came close in 1915 and 1916.[2] Jennings's final season (1920) was one of their most disappointing ever. The Tigers started by losing their first thirteen games and finished in seventh place, thirty-seven games behind the pennant-winning Indians. Tigers owner Frank Navin decided it was time for a change.

Cobb accepted the managerial job reluctantly. He really did not want the responsibility, which, he felt, would detract from his main focus of hitting. He told Damon Runyon, "It's anything but a present. This thing has been forced on me."[3] Not quite. Navin had offered him a large salary increase, from $20,000 to $35,000. (Babe Ruth, by comparison, was making $20,000 in 1920 and 1921.)[4]

Cobb and John McGraw may have had a strong dislike for each other, but they agreed on two things. They both personified and excelled at the Deadball Era style of play, which was becoming endangered. And they both disliked Ruth—his personality and popularity as well as his style of hitting. In his Cobb biography, Charles Alexander writes of "the special rivalry of two men who represented radically contrasting approaches to the game." Ruth posed "a fundamental threat . . . to his [Cobb's] whole set of values, both as to how baseball ought to be played and how successful ballplayers ought to behave."[5]

14. Ty Cobb is captured here in a rare light moment in 1921 with baseball's new ruler, Commissioner Kenesaw Mountain Landis. Despite Cobb's added burden in his new role as the Tigers' player-manager, he raised his batting average from .334 to .389. Yet his success as a player was far greater than that as a manager. *SDN-057051A, Chicago Daily News negatives collection, Chicago History Museum.*

Ruth was showing a way to tour the bases other than with a hit or walk and steals, focusing the excitement instead on one swing of the bat. Cobb was one of the most intense men ever to play the game, and now Ruth was overshadowing him. Cobb approached every game "the way Dempsey climbed into a ring, full of fury and blood-lust, filled with a burning desire to win at all costs."[6]

Once Cobb assumed the position of manager, there was lively debate in the off-season about his chances of success. *Baseball Magazine* framed the issue in its article entitled, "Will Ty Make Good as a Manager?" Making no prediction, the article noted it would be a fascinating experiment.[7] Many observers felt that Cobb had too fiery a personality to succeed. Yet others, such as Damon Runyon, pointed to the success of another temperamental manager—John McGraw.[8]

As the Yankees headed west, they stopped for an exhibition game in Toronto on May 9 against Larry Doyle's Maple Leafs. Toronto fans were rewarded with what they wanted to see—a Babe Ruth home run. It was a common practice for Major League teams to play such games on off days during the regular season, since they generated additional revenue for the ballclubs and exposed smaller cities to big league ball and its stars.

The early returns in Detroit were somewhat promising. When the Tigers opened their four-game series with New York, they were tied with the Senators for second place with a 12-10 record, three and a half games behind the league-leading Cleveland Indians. The Yankees were another half game back, tied with the Red Sox.

The intentional base on balls was becoming a controversial tactic among reporters and fans alike.[9] It was becoming a defensive weapon for a team to neutralize the slugger's bat. Respected sportswriter John B. Sheridan wrote that he had not known a technical baseball question that generated as much debate as the intentional walking of Ruth.[10]

A pass for Ruth often gave a team a better chance of beating the Yankees than pitching to him did. Yet fans everywhere came to the ballpark to see Ruth swing. Even when he swung and missed, he provided thrills. "When he misses the ball," wrote Runyon, "he is staggering like a horse suddenly brought up at the end of a tether."[11] At one point in the 1920 season, when the Babe was getting a number of walks in a series against the Browns, one St. Louis paper ran a headline, "Pay a Dollar at Sportsman's Park to See Babe Ruth Walk."[12]

The four games between the Tigers and Yankees provided many thrills and Ruth heroics. After the Babe's two-run home run helped Carl Mays win the first game, Cobb gained a measure of revenge the next day. His "Tygers," as they were often called in newspapers, won a pitchers' duel between Waite Hoyt and Suds Sutherland by the same 2–1 score.[13] Ruth was thrown out twice, trying to stretch a single into a double and attempting a daring steal of home. H. G. Salsinger declared, "While to many people Ruth is faster than they think he is, Ruth is not quite as fast as Ruth thinks he is."[14]

The Yankees received some bad news as they headed west. Bill Piercy was joining Bob Shawkey on the sidelines with a sore shoulder. X-rays on both men showed nothing wrong beyond strained muscles. Dr. George Stewart, the Yankees' team physician, wanted to blister

Shawkey's arm and shoulder—a process similar to the one used to treat horses with sore legs, he explained. The Yankee pitcher talked him out of that, persuading Stewart that the warm weather would help round him into form. Since the doctor felt that the pitchers had "colds that settled in their arms," he agreed.[15]

With his pitching options limited by the injuries, Miller Huggins turned to Tom Sheehan for the third game. Sheehan had won nineteen games for the Atlanta Crackers of the Southern Association a couple of years earlier. The youngster did not survive the fourth inning; but thanks to the Babe's home run and triple, the Yankees won a slugfest by the score of 11–10. The game took two hours and thirty-one minutes to play, a long time for 1921, yet a speedy contest for a twenty-one-run game by today's standards.

The Yankees won the final game, 6–4. While Tigers ace Howard Ehmke pitched cautiously to the Babe and walked him three times, Ruth hit a bases-clearing triple that proved to be the game-winning blow. The Tigers had two men on and two men out in the ninth when Huggins rushed Mays to the mound; and he secured the victory in relief for the second straight day, this time with just one pitch.

Harry Harper, the Yanks' only lefty, got the win in his first start of the season. When the Yankees had acquired him in the December trade, Huggins obtained a pitcher he could use only six days a week. Harper had a clause in his contract that excused him from playing on Sundays for religious reasons.

Though Harper had recently turned twenty-six, he had already been with the Washington Senators for seven years before moving to Boston. Hackensack Harry, as he was known, had starred on the sandlots of New Jersey before turning pro. He then gained notoriety in the Minors when he walked twenty men in eight innings.[16]

It was a costly victory for New York, however. Harper fractured the thumb on his pitching hand, trying to stop a line drive in the sixth inning. He was expected to be out for at least six weeks. However, the thumb would heal slowly, and he would be unavailable for a considerably longer time.

Ruth had been a one-man wrecking crew in the Tiger series. He had 7 hits in 15 at bats, including two home runs, two triples, and a double.

(Cobb, by comparison, went 4-15, including a triple and two doubles.) Perhaps Cobb's pride and condescending attitude toward Ruth had prevented him from walking the Yankee slugger, even if the game's circumstances warranted such a move. Damon Runyon had noted that Cobb had an "inordinate desire to be a little better than anyone else."[17] Surely these games grated on him; and he could not wait for his next shot at Ruth and the Yankees, which would come in New York in a month.

The defending world champion Cleveland Indians had served notice early in the season that they would be formidable defenders of their title. Their spirit and ability to rally from behind was remarkable, and there seemed to be a different star each day. Leading them was their player-manager, center fielder Tris Speaker, who had a special ability to instill a fighting spirit into his men, while still keeping the club on an even keel.[18]

On April 14 in St. Louis, down, 9–2, to Allan Sothoron and the Browns, the Indians fought back for a 12–9 win. Leading the way with a double, triple, and home run was second-year shortstop Joe Sewell. Ed Bang of the *Cleveland News* felt that the key to the Indians' chances this season would be the young Sewell's performance.[19] Could he sustain for an entire season what he had done so well the previous September, when the rookie had replaced Ray Chapman?

Speaker used eighteen men in the game. Less than two weeks later, he played twenty-three men—an American League record at the time—in rallying from a 6–1 deficit to beat Detroit, 9–8. Long before it became prevalent, Speaker believed in platooning.[20]

The double batting shift—or use of interchangeable players, as it was called at the time—had its detractors. John B. Sheridan said that treating a player as a "specialist" ruined his development and made him a "half man." "It is a farewell, a long farewell to all that player's chance of greatness . . . destroying their most precious quality—confidence in their ability to hit any pitcher, left or right, alive, dead, or to be born."[21]

Most likely Speaker had adopted the shift to accommodate his teammate and roommate on the Red Sox, Joe Wood. Smoky Joe had made a remarkable shift of another kind. As a pitcher, he had one of the all-time great seasons in 1912, with a 34-5 record, ten shutouts, and a 1.91 earned run average. He capped off the season with three wins over McGraw's Giants in the World Series.

15. Joe Wood was no longer the "Smoky Joe" sensation of 1912, when he had a 34-5 record. After a serious arm injury, he made a comeback as an outfielder with Cleveland, where he hit .366 in 1921. Wood was just one example of the overlooked players from whom manager Tris Speaker obtained significant contributions. *Private collection of Dennis Goldstein.*

A few years later, at the age of twenty-six, Wood was out of baseball with a serious shoulder injury. Back home in 1916, he thought to himself, "Doggone it, I was a ball player, not just a pitcher."[22] He decided that if he could not make it as a pitcher, he would come back as an everyday player. At Speaker's urging, Cleveland had purchased Wood in 1917; and he joined his good friend in the Indians' outfield the following year. Starting in 1919, after players returning from the war and wartime industries replenished rosters, the right-handed-hitting Wood faced primarily left-handed pitchers and performed well at the plate. While pitchers in college and the Minors have become stars as position players, it is exceedingly rare for a star pitcher in the Majors to excel later as an everyday player.

By early May, Bill Wambsganss was ready to return to the lineup. But rookie second baseman Riggs Stephenson was hitting close to .500, and Speaker did not want to break up the University of Alabama double play combination. The *Sporting News* noted that "Bill Wamby" would have a hard time getting his job back if Stephenson kept playing so well.[23]

The Indians won fifteen of their first twenty-one games. The Cleveland bats were potent. In nine of those games, they scored at least eight runs, with pitcher George Uhle contributing at the plate as well as on the mound. When he won two games early in the season, he had three hits in each game, including a bases-loaded home run, a triple, and a double.[24]

The Indians did have shortcomings, which centered on pitching. Stan Coveleski, coming off a twenty-four-win season, won five games in the first month of the 1921 season. But Jim Bagby was not as effective as he had been in his thirty-one-win season of 1920, and Duster Mails had not shown the same form he had the past September.

One and a half games behind the first-place Tribe, the Yankees arrived in Cleveland on May 14 with a depleted pitching staff and a slugger on fire. The Babe was hitting .418; Tris Speaker was not far behind at .400, though Harry Heilmann was far ahead of both with a .512 average. To add drama to the series, Carl Mays was going to pitch in Cleveland for the first time since his pitch had killed Ray Chapman in the Polo Grounds the previous August. "Mays is going to pitch just as sure as my name is Miller Huggins," declared the Yankee skipper. "They [Cleveland fans] are big enough to allow the incident to remain forever closed."[25] He explained that the Yanks were "morally obliged" to pitch Mays, because to do otherwise would be a tacit admission of guilt.[26]

American League president Ban Johnson, recognizing the fierce rivalry and significance of this first meeting between the league's top two teams, had scheduled three umpires for the series, rather than the usual two. Before 25,000 fans, Jack Quinn was solid, if not spectacular, in the first game. Down, 4–2, in the eighth inning, the Yanks rode to a 6–4 victory on Ruth's mammoth three-run homer off Bagby, the first home run ever hit to Dunn Field's center-field bleachers.[27] The huge Saturday crowd then gave a big ovation to the man the *Cleveland Plain Dealer* called "the world's most phenomenal batter."[28] Before the cheering subsided, Wally Pipp followed with another home run.

Speaker made a catch off a Quinn drive in the eighth to keep the game close. The *New York Tribune* called it one of the best catches ever seen in Cleveland.[29] When Speaker caught up with the ball, it actually popped out of his glove; he completed the putout by grabbing the ball on the run with his bare hand. He had gained fame as the greatest defensive player at his position in the history of the game. "He is just as far above the average centre fielder as the Woolworth Building is above the subway" was how one New York paper described his play.[30]

Speaker played a very shallow center field, almost like a fifth infielder. He occasionally executed unassisted double plays, catching a fly and then tagging out a base runner or beating him back to second base. (His six career unassisted double plays are the record for an outfielder.) When a ball was hit over his head, Speaker had a sixth sense, running toward the outfield wall with his back to the infield and bringing the ball down. "He'd turn and glance over his shoulder at the last minute," said Joe Wood, "and catch the ball so easy it looked like there was nothing to it, nothing at all."[31] Now, with hitters swinging for the fences and balls going further, Speaker did adjust his position and played deeper. He was now playing as much as 150 feet deeper—a huge concession, if accurate, to the emerging new game.[32]

On Sunday, May 15, before an even larger crowd of 28,000, New York pulled even with the Tribe, as Waite Hoyt secured his first Yankee win.[33] He had an impressive assortment of pitches: a blazing fastball, a sharply breaking curve, a deceptive change of pace, and a reliable slow ball.[34] The *New York Evening Journal* headline shouted, "Yankees with Wrecked Mound Staff Sweep into First Place."[35]

Mays started the third game. He had gotten many threatening letters with Cleveland postmarks, and Huggins held him back for the Monday game and the smaller weekday crowd. Mays strode to the mound before 12,000 silent fans. When he came to the plate for the first time, there was faint applause, started by his Yankee teammates. And when Duster Mails sent Mays to the ground with a high and tight pitch, the Cleveland fans booed their own. The only time Mays heard catcalls was when he intentionally walked Stephenson in the eighth inning. Stan Coveleski had heard the same jeers when he had walked the Babe a day earlier. The Cleveland police provided a cordon around the Yankees' clubhouse after the game. It was not needed.

Mays and the Yanks prevailed, 6–3, with the help of a Meusel home run and a Ruth triple, his third in three games. Cleveland had now lost five straight games. On this same day, May 16, the Yankees completed the purchase of the land for their new ballpark with a $500,000 payment.[36]

The Indians salvaged the final game of the series with a 4–2 win by Uhle, despite Ruth's twelfth home run of the season. Most notable in the game was a near fight between Speaker and Ruth, two of the game's biggest stars. It resulted in part from the Cleveland manager's aggressiveness and in part from a misunderstanding. In the sixth inning, Uhle almost picked Ruth off second base. (Remarkably, he had picked off both Peckinpaugh and Ruth in the first inning.) In scampering back to second, Ruth collided with Joe Sewell, causing the second baseman's nose to bleed. When Ruth tried to apologize, Speaker came running in from his outfield position and accused the Babe of "playing dirty." He challenged the Yankee slugger to a fight after the game (the way players sometimes settled matters during those days), and the benches emptied before order was restored. There was no postgame fight—that was not Ruth's style—and the New York club (15-10, .600) left Cleveland in a virtual tie with the Indians (17-12, .586).

Wherever Ruth went, his towering blasts brought cheers from the crowds. Fans were like addicts: they wanted to see the Prince of Pounders hit more and more home runs that travelled farther and farther.[37] Damon Runyon, with his incisive and humor-laden style, put it this way: Willie Keeler's "idea was to 'hit 'em where they ain't.' . . . Ruth has improved on it to this extent: He hits 'em where there's no chance of them being."[38]

The ongoing debate about the reasons for so many home runs that year, as well as whether they were good for baseball, continued. Hugh Fullerton noted that the 1921 balls were more tightly wound and seemed livelier than those of previous years, and National League president John Heydler agreed. In that same article, Cliff Wheatley noted that batters were fouling off pitches to get new balls put into play.[39] George Reach, whose company made the American League balls, was quoted in an editorial in the *Sporting News*: "We are manufacturing the best ball now we ever made." And as the baseball weekly realized, "The better the ball, the livelier it is likely to be."[40]

The Yankees then split four games in Chicago. The brilliant White Sox spitballer Red Faber had another win for his lowly team, his seventh of the season. (He had also recently shut out the Indians twice.) His league-leading earned run average was a sparkling 1.22; Bill Piercy and Carl Mays were next in line with respective earned run averages of 1.43 and 1.67. Tom Meany, whose long New York sportswriting career would begin in 1923, described Faber as "quite possibly one of the most unassuming men ever to reach stardom in the major leagues."[41] The White Sox had been decimated by the suspension of the Black Sox (including pitchers Eddie Cicotte and Lefty Williams, who each had won at least twenty games in both 1919 and 1920), but they still had Faber. Unfortunately for him, they were missing many from the supporting cast of the pennant winners of 1917 and 1919, hitters who could generate runs.

The Yankees also fell to little Dickie Kerr, all of five feet seven and 150 pounds. Like Eddie Rommel, Kerr threw a lot of off-speed pitches. He was one of the 1919 Clean Sox and a surprise winner of two World Series games. Gamblers had lost a lot of money when he won Game 3; and he emerged as a legitimate star in 1920, when he won twenty-one games. Years later he said, "Honesty isn't like a curve ball or control. You don't develop it. You are born with it, and no man ought to brag about having it, or be honored because he does."[42]

The Yankees moved on to St. Louis, where they split four games with the Browns. St. Louis had a devastating offense led by first baseman

16. Like Dickie Kerr of the White Sox and Eddie Rommel of the Athletics, the Browns' Urban Shocker used off-speed pitches to keep the fastball-feasting Yankees off balance. He had "Murderers' Row spellbound," wrote Damon Runyon, "with a sling so slow you could almost see the elastic in the ball" (*New York American*, July 28, 1921). *Courtesy of the Ernie Harwell Sports Collection, Detroit Public Library.*

George Sisler, who was coming off a terrific 1920 season, when he led the American League with a .407 batting average and 257 hits.[43] Outfielders Ken Williams, Baby Doll Jacobson, and Jack Tobin were in the midst of a remarkable run: From 1919 to 1925, they would each hit at least .300 every season, with the exception of Tobin's .299 in 1925 (one hit shy of .300). And they did not simply exceed .300; they went well above it. Williams would hit .347 in 1921, and Jacobson and Tobin would achieve .352 batting averages in that same year.

Two of the games were thrillers against Urban Shocker, the "Yankee jinx." He had gained that reputation because of the success he had against his former team and the pleasure he took in beating them. Shocker had emerged as one of baseball's best pitchers; he won twenty games in 1920, despite missing the entire month of September with a leg injury. He was also a workhorse who insisted on pitching the first and last games of every four-game series against the Yanks.

Shocker was as colorful as Faber was not. He reveled in challenging the game's best hitters. He had gained notoriety in July 1920 when he struck out Babe Ruth three times in a game. The cocky pitcher even waved in his outfielders during one of those at bats.[44] "No Bush League batter was ever more thoroughly or hopelessly discomfited than the powerful home run king on that occasion," wrote *Baseball Magazine*.[45] On May 5, 1921, Shocker had taunted Ty Cobb and dared him to hit his slow ball, or floater. This time Cobb got the better of Shocker, hitting it for a home run. These showdowns were vintage Shocker, who won some and lost some but always pitched his best to the best.

In the first game, Bob Shawkey returned to the mound for his first start in almost a month. He pitched into the seventh inning before tiring. After the game, he gave reporters a none-too-positive report, saying his arm felt like someone was gripping it.[46] Miller Huggins faced a hard truth—until Shawkey and Harry Harper recovered from their injuries, he could not accomplish much.[47] Shawkey had led the American League in both 1919 and 1920 with the longest winning streaks, with ten and eleven wins, respectively. Now there was concern whether he would regain his old form. "There never is any telling when a star will fade. Some pitchers [such as Ed Walsh and Joe Wood] lose their ability almost over night," wrote the *Evening Telegram*.[48]

A few days later, the Yankees received somewhat good news about

Shawkey. John "Bonesetter" Reese—the respected Youngstown, Ohio, muscle and ligament man—reported that he had found nothing seriously wrong with Shawkey's arm. He said he had never seen a veteran curve ball pitcher with as sound an arm as the Yankee hurler had.[49]

After the Yankees edged Shocker and the Browns in ten innings, they won their next game to make it two straight in St. Louis by beating another nemesis, Dixie Davis. It was Wally Pipp's bases-loaded single in the ninth that won the game, 6–4. Davis had almost single-handedly kept the Yankees from the 1920 pennant, going 5-0 against them that year.[50]

The Yankees had made a change in their lineup when they came to St. Louis. Frank Baker, who had not been hitting that well, had strained his leg in Chicago while chasing down a foul ball. Aaron Ward moved over to third base, and Johnny Mitchell got the start at second.

But the man whom Miller Huggins had called "the best infielder in the minors," the highly touted Mitchell, simply could not get the job done.[51] In the third game with the Browns, he mishandled three balls in the first two innings. "A comedy of errors, a travesty of fumbles" was how the *New York Times* described his performance.[52] As was the case with Chick Fewster a month earlier, a promising Yankee youngster could not handle the demands of playing second base.

The Browns seemed to have learned from the Detroit and Cleveland series; they pitched very carefully to Ruth. After the first three games, Ruth had walked seven times and was hitless with only seven at bats. Now in the final game of the series, Shocker once again started for St. Louis. He challenged Ruth and struck him out in both this game and the first one. Now Shocker had a 4–3 lead, thanks in part to two more Mitchell errors. Browns manager Lee Fohl signaled for Shocker to give the Babe a pass in the seventh. Fohl was a modest and unassuming man, a "cup-of-coffee" catcher in the Majors, and a sharp handler of pitchers.[53] He yielded to Shocker's request to pitch to Ruth; and the hurler then yielded a 550-foot blast over the center-field sign at Sportsman's Park, the longest home run ever hit in St. Louis. It was a three-run shot that gave the Yankees the 6–4 lead.

With New York's pitching woes, Alex Ferguson had gotten the start, his third game in eight days. His manager in Jersey City, where he won twenty-one games in 1920, was former Yankee skipper Wild Bill Donovan, who had labeled the youngster as "can't miss."[54] In the bottom of the ninth, after the Browns had tied the game at 6–6, reliever Jack Quinn intentionally walked the bases full. Facing the dangerous Jacobson, Quinn uncorked an errant pitch that even hit Jacobson (it was ruled a wild pitch); and Shocker had a hard-fought, complete-game 7–6 victory. It was his eighth of the season, tying him with Red Faber for the league lead.

The game included a surprising case of insubordination from a Yankee not known for such behavior. Huggins did not want Quinn to walk the bases full, but the pitcher disregarded his manager's order. "Huggins wig-wagged to Quinn in disgust and stepped down into the dugout, and what a calling down the veteran pitcher received from the mite manager after the wild pitch." Huggins did not wait to get to the clubhouse and shouted down Quinn out on the field.[55]

Braggo Roth had started the opening game in St. Louis and made two errors. The Yankees lost their lead in that first game, in large part because Roth had misplayed a Sisler drive that rolled to the wall. He was then replaced by Ping Bodie in the second game; and by the final game, Huggins had rookie Californian Chicken Hawks in center. That position was an ongoing source of exasperation for the Yanks' manager.[56] It was becoming increasingly clear that neither Roth nor Bodie was adequate in the outfield. "The Wonderful Wop," as many papers affectionately called Bodie, "never notably fast, has lost what little speed he had."[57]

Roth, from whom so much was expected, was finished. The *Evening Telegram* took a long view of his failure: "Roth started with a flourish of trumpets. . . . Then, for some reason or other, he cracked. Other players have done it, others will do it, as long as the great old game is played, but it is never pleasant to contemplate."[58] As Huggins kept on shifting different players in and out of center field (his latest candidate was Chick Fewster), he was choosing among poor options. He simply had to find another outfielder.

As the Yanks closed the month of May, the pitching staff was showing encouraging signs. Bob Shawkey edged Eddie Rommel, and Waite Hoyt gained his fourth straight complete-game win in less than two weeks. While he was not overpowering, he was improving in consistency and durability. On May 30 Rip Collins got his first start and was impressive in a 2–1, four-hit win over the Senators. Collins, who had a reputation for enjoying the nightlife, was nicknamed after Old Ripy Whiskey, which he was known to enjoy. Years later his obituary would describe Collins as a pitcher "with a million dollars worth of talent and 25 cents worth of enthusiasm."[59]

With the benching of Johnny Mitchell after all his miscues, little-used Mike McNally was playing second base in the game. His daring theft of home on the front end of a double steal in the third inning proved to be the winning run. Bob Meusel made a spectacular one-handed catch of a Sam Rice drive in the eighth, with his back to the diamond, to preserve the win. He then threw back to the infield and doubled up a runner off second. This was but one of Meusel's league-leading twenty-eight outfield assists in 1921.

Jack Quinn pitched brilliantly in the second game that day; yet he lived up to his reputation of being a hard-luck pitcher, walking away with a 1–0 loss. There was a bright side to the day. If Collins and Quinn could maintain this form during the rest of the season, the Yankees' pitching woes would be resolved.[60] Despite playing six games in four days, the Yankees had won five and had given up only thirteen runs.

The team's pitching success was short-lived. The Yankees opened June with a tough 8–7 loss to Walter Johnson. It was a shame to lose "as game a fight as they have made all year."[61] The Yankees scored five runs in the eighth. After Ruth was given an intentional pass, Wally Pipp's bases-clearing triple was the key blow off a tiring Johnson. Once again, an error by Mitchell—who was playing shortstop in place of the injured Roger Peckinpaugh—opened the floodgates, this time in the ninth inning on what should have been the final out. And once again, Carl Mays weakened badly late in the game, letting a 7–3 lead slip away. Mays then gave up four hits, including a double and a triple (after giving up a triple just before the error).

Huggins made no move to pull his struggling pitcher. After all, his primary and dependable save man was already pitching. One of the weaknesses of the Yankees seemed to be their lack of a dependable relief pitcher. "For years beyond reckoning this has been one of the cardinal failings of the Yanks," wailed the *New York Globe and Commercial Advertiser*.[62]

Yet the reality was that in 1921 no team had a designated closer, other than some clubs using their best starting pitcher in that role.[63] In his Ruth biography, Marshall Smelser wonders why managers of the early 1920s did not react to the rise of hitting with a new approach to pitching, bringing in fresh arms late:

> In practice the managers of the 1920s used only three-quarters of their pitching manpower. They kept the starter in until everybody knew he was tired. . . . A manager could do nothing about the lively ball, but he could have used fresh pitchers in sequence to keep batting averages down. . . . As it was, with hits of all kinds more frequent, pitchers threw more pitches and tired sooner. Rested and rarely used pitchers watched the season roll by as daily spectators. The batting heroes of the 1920s looked even more heroic when they hit against so many weary pitchers.[64]

The Yankees then hosted the Browns just eight days after their last game in St. Louis. They would again face Shocker twice. Shawkey beat him convincingly in the first game, as the Browns' pitcher went only five innings. In the fifth, Shocker dared Ruth to hit his pitch, and the slugger hammered it off the wall for a triple.[65] He also gave up home runs to Shawkey and Pipp. Shocker had now yielded thirteen home runs this season; no other American League hurler had given up more than six. Sam Crane felt that with the Yankees mastering the Shocker jinx, "the pennant for the home folks is about ready to be picked. That is what we think of Urban Shocker."[66]

But the very next day, the Yankees' other Brownie jinx, Dixie Davis, beat Hoyt, 9–8. The Yankees rallied from a 7–1 deficit, only to fall just short. Ruth hit another triple and a home run off Davis. The latter blast gave him 16 for the season and 119 for his career. Most newspapers noted that he had tied Gavy Cravath's career mark.[67]

Al Munro Elias, along with his brother Walter, supplied statistics for the newspapers; Elias's most popular feature was the five leading hitters in each league each day. He was known for his flawless accuracy. He had started his company in 1913, and the Elias Sports Bureau is the Official Statistician of Major League Baseball today. In 1923 *Baseball Magazine*'s F. C. Lane, ahead of his time, saw the importance of this new type of baseball analyst: "They have just unearthed the body of an ancient Egyptian King [King Tutankhamun]. Thousands of years ago that body was prepared for the imperial tomb by Egyptian embalmers so skillfully that it has withstood the lapse of thirty centuries. The statistician performs an equal miracle with the happenings on the diamond. He embalms them in imperishable records that become increasingly valuable with the lapse of time."[68]

Two days later, the Yankees faced Shocker again and defeated him again, 5–4, with Mays making his first appearance since his meltdown against the Senators. Ruth led the way with a double and a triple (his third triple in four games), and Bodie's triple won the game in the seventh. While Bodie muffed a ball in the third inning, which led to a run, Sam Crane still championed the lumbering Yankee, writing that "Ping is far from a has-been."[69]

The next day, the Yankee bats went silent, as Davis tossed a two-hitter. They had mastered one jinx twice in four days, only to fall to another jinx two times in the five-game series. This season, the unpredictable Yankees seemed to be "consistent only in their inconsistency."[70] As they prepared to host the Indians for the first time on June 7, the Yanks were two and a half games behind Cleveland and in second place, where they had been since Red Faber had beaten them on May 18. Both New York teams had been inconsistent and especially unreliable with their pitching. When the *New York Tribune* wrote on June 3, "Baseball is uncertain and the Yanks are just about the most uncertain team in baseball," it just as well could have been speaking of the Giants.

AL STANDINGS AT CLOSE OF PLAY OF JUNE 6, 1921

TEAM	G	W	L	T	PCT	GB
Cleveland Indians	47	30	17	0	.638	-
New York Yankees	46	27	19	0	.587	2.5
Washington Senators	49	26	22	1	.542	4.5
Detroit Tigers	50	27	23	0	.540	4.5
Boston Red Sox	41	20	21	0	.488	7.0
St. Louis Browns	47	21	26	0	.447	9.0
Chicago White Sox	45	18	27	0	.400	11.0
Philadelphia Athletics	47	16	30	1	.348	13.5

"The Yanks are the best worst team in either league"

By the first week of June, the two major obstacles to baseball's first all–New York World Series were becoming ever clearer. The Cleveland Indians posed the primary threat to the Yankees winning their first pennant, while the Pittsburgh Pirates were the major roadblock to John McGraw's Giants capturing their seventh flag. Both New York clubs had displayed powerful offenses, yet managers Miller Huggins and McGraw continued to fret over their teams' inconsistent pitching.

A number of injuries had hampered the Cleveland Indians this season, including one to second baseman Bill Wambsganss. Yet they continued to find a way to win. On May 23 a pitch from Boston's Hank Thormahlen hit Tris Speaker on the wrist. The bad bruise sent the Indians' manager to the bench; but his replacement, fan favorite Jack Graney, got the winning hit in the next game and hit two home runs four days later. After their leader was hurt, the Indians hammered St. Louis pitching for forty-five runs in a four-game sweep and were in the midst of compiling an eight-game winning streak.

The last of those eight wins was a costly one. Tigers pitcher Howard Ehmke hit Cleveland's catcher Steve O'Neill in the hand, breaking one of O'Neill's fingers and putting him out of action for six weeks. Ehmke would lead the league in hit batsmen six times in his career, including both the 1920 and 1921 seasons. (The often-maligned Carl Mays did so only once.) F. C. Lane once noted, "Perhaps the most conspicuous trait about Ehmke is his lack of control."[1] Perhaps second only to Speaker, O'Neill was the heart and soul of the Cleveland team. *Baseball Magazine* had chosen him as baseball's best catcher of 1920 and would do so again for 1921.[2]

O'Neill's great arm, skill at blocking the plate, and guidance of the team's pitchers made his loss a devastating blow. With Speaker's coach-

17. Second only to Cleveland player-manager Tris Speaker, Steve O'Neill (seen here with his daughter, Madeline) was the Indians' most valuable player. His broken finger was one of several key injuries the Tribe had to overcome to stay in the 1921 pennant race. After the death of Ray Chapman, the Indians wore black armbands to honor their fallen teammate. *Private collection of Dennis Goldstein.*

ing, the catcher had also become a much improved threat with the bat; and it would be sorely missed. "The effect of O'Neill's injury on the Indians," wrote Hugh Fullerton, "shows in everything. . . . The absence of O'Neill hurts the Indians worse than anything that could happen to it."[3]

The Indians staggered into New York after dropping three straight games to the Red Sox, who were below .500 on the season. On the positive side, Cleveland would have Speaker back in the lineup for the Yankee series. He had returned to action a day earlier, going 4-5 and raising his batting average to a torrid .431. Speaker was leading the league in on-base percentage with a .516 mark, just ahead of Ruth's .488.

On June 7, the Yanks won the first game with ease, 9–2, as Bob Shawkey went the distance. The Yanks stole three bases on backup catcher Les Nunamaker. More significantly, New York again knocked Indians ace Stan Coveleski out of the box early, this time in the fourth

18. Babe Ruth's performance on the field was matched by his larger-than-life behavior off it. The nation's youth adored him, and he loved fast and fancy cars. Whether the authority he challenged was his manager's or the traffic court's, the Babe often got his way.
© *Bettmann/CORBIS*.

inning. The only bright note for Cleveland was the season's first appearance of Wambsganss, who had been hurt in spring training.

Babe Ruth was not in the starting lineup when Waite Hoyt and George Uhle faced off the following day. For the second time this season, the police had stopped Ruth for speeding in his new maroon Packard ("set me back $13,000, kid," he said), this time on Manhattan's Riverside Drive.[4] In late April he had paid a $25 fine for speeding up Broadway. Ruth later announced that he liked driving fast, prompting Hugh Fullerton to suggest, "He ought to be more careful of the assets."[5] The same magistrate who had levied the earlier penalty now fined the Babe $100, sentenced him to a day in jail, and sternly said, "Just because you are prominent is no excuse for speeding, Mr. Ruth."[6]

But at around four o'clock in the afternoon, "with a severe face but a glint of humor in his sharp grey eyes," the judge ordered the Babe's release. While a group of kids yelled and waved, Ruth jumped into his car and, with the help of a police escort, sped to the Polo Grounds. A Yankee official had brought Ruth's uniform to the traffic court's prison at 300 Mulberry Street in lower Manhattan, about eight miles south of the ballpark. The Babe arrived in the sixth inning, in time to pinch-hit and stay in the game.

Ruth was not a factor in the contest, though the Yankees rallied from a 3–2 deficit to a 4–3 victory after his arrival. The game ended in controversy and a formal protest by Speaker. With one out in the bottom of the ninth, Bob Meusel on first, and Frank Baker at bat, Huggins jumped out of the dugout to argue a called strike. Umpire Frank Wilson tossed the Yankee skipper out of the game. Moments later, with a two-strike count, Baker apparently swung at a ball that broke into the dirt, and started walking back to the dugout. But Wilson ruled that Baker had checked his swing; it seemed that he was evening things out by calling the pitch a ball.[7] After an extended argument, Baker singled; and the Yankees rallied for the win. "Nothing in a game of baseball could possibly be more thrilling than such a magnificent climax," crowed the *New York Evening Journal*.[8]

With the victory, the Yankees moved to within a half game of first place. Perhaps the "Worlds Champions" emblazoned across the Indians' home and road jerseys was bringing them bad luck. After all, the only other team to flaunt their championship across their chests was John McGraw's 1905 winners in 1906. That year, they finished twenty games behind the Chicago Cubs.[9] Since then, no World Series champions had worn such jerseys, though whether this was "from motives of taste or superstition was unknown."[10]

The following day, the Indians stopped their five-game losing streak, as veteran spitball pitcher Ray Caldwell beat the Yankees, 14–4, in his best outing of the year. Caldwell had been one of Speaker's prized reclamation projects. He had been the ace of the Yankees in 1914–15, when he won thirty-seven games for weak New York teams. The Yankees had even turned down Washington pitcher Walter Johnson in a straight-up trade early in 1915.[11] But Caldwell's career was derailed by his heavy drinking. "Caldwell's flashes of brilliance were usually followed by frustrating 'outbreaks of misbehavior,' and he never realized his immense potential."[12]

Huggins had tired of his antics in 1918 and traded Caldwell to the Red

Sox in the Ernie Shore–Duffy Lewis deal that December. The following August, the Red Sox gave up on him, too, and released him. Caldwell's career seemed to be over.

However, Tris Speaker saw something in Caldwell and picked up the lanky thirty-one-year-old hurler late in the 1919 season. Speaker used a remarkable approach of reverse psychology in dealing with Caldwell, stating in his contract that the pitcher "must get drunk" after every game he pitched.[13] It worked. Caldwell won five games that year, including a no-hitter against the Yankees. In the championship season of 1920, he won twenty games.

The New York press criticized Huggins for starting Jack Quinn in that third game; he did not get out of the first inning. Fred Lieb noted that he had often joined the critics of Huggins's pitching choices, while admitting there was usually no obvious alternative.[14] On this day, the relievers—Alex Ferguson, Rip Collins, and Tom Sheehan—were not much better than the aging spitballer. The only bright spot for New York was Frank Baker's first home run of the year.

The final game of the series on June 10 was a thriller, and this time the Indians prevailed. Ruth hit his seventeenth home run in the third inning; and newspapers noted that as his 120th career home run, it had moved him ahead of Gavy Cravath as the all-time leader. Dan Daniel wrote that the Babe was now in a class of his own: "Ruth now holds every home run mark there is on the books, and henceforth his efforts will be devoted to putting his records beyond the reach of posterity."[15]

Carl Mays's eighth-inning home run gave the Yankees a 6–3 lead, and the game seemed to be theirs. But a ninth-inning error by shortstop Roger Peckinpaugh seemed to unsettle Mays. The Indians rallied, and New York could not stop the onslaught. After Mays gave up a double to Speaker, Bob Shawkey came in and proceeded to give up three singles, allowing Cleveland to knot the score at six.

Larry Gardner, now thirty-five years old, won the game with a home run in the eleventh. Gardner was another veteran whose career the Indians' leader helped nurture and extend. A teammate of Speaker's on the 1912 champion Red Sox (along with Joe Wood), Gardner had "a way of rising to the occasion, as a trout rises to a fly in one of his Vermont streams," in the words of Boston sportswriter Tim Murnane.[16]

Cleveland's starter, 1920 ace Jim Bagby, had another unproductive

19. Harry Heilmann emerged as a star in 1921 after more than five seasons of modest success at the plate. He won the batting title with a .394 average, finishing ahead of Ty Cobb, Babe Ruth, George Sisler, and Tris Speaker. Heilmann stayed among the batting leaders for the rest of the decade. *Photo by Charles M. Conlon. Private collection of Dennis Goldstein.*

outing, giving up thirteen hits in seven and two-thirds innings. Like the Yankees' Quinn, Bagby would struggle in 1921 and not come close to his 1920 numbers.[17] With the teams splitting the four games, each winning one blowout and one cliffhanger, the Indians left town with their two-and-a-half-game lead intact.

The Detroit Tigers followed Cleveland into the Polo Grounds for a series that started on Saturday, June 11. With Detroit tied for third place, four and a half games out of first, and Cobb at the helm, the series figured to be as dramatic as the one against Cleveland. The press was hailing Cobb as a miracle man for having taken a team that finished seventh in 1920 into this year's pennant race.[18] Sid Mercer wrote of Cobb's positive approach: "When a pitcher wavers, Cobb comes in from center field with cheerful words calculated to allay nervousness."[19] The rookie manager told *Baseball Magazine*, "I have worked hard to get the spirit of confidence into the boys. . . . I consider now that I have one of the best pitching staffs potentially in the League."[20]

The added responsibility was not affecting Cobb's hitting, as he had feared it would. After an "off year" (at least for him—his .334 1920 batting average was his lowest since 1908), he was once again hitting close to the .400 mark. More importantly, Cobb was able to teach batting to his team; the Tigers came to New York hitting above .330 for the year.[21]

There was a new name atop the batting average leaderboard this year, Detroit outfielder Harry Heilmann. When the Tigers arrived in New York, he was leading the league with a .440 mark, while Cobb was fourth (behind Speaker and George Sisler) with .393. While this was Heilmann's seventh year in the league, he had hit above .300 only twice (.320 in 1919 and .309 in 1920). "The three-cornered fight between Ty Cobb, Tris Speaker and George Sisler for the batting championship has taken on an extra corner," wrote F. C. Lane in *Baseball Magazine*.[22] Still, virtually no one expected Heilmann would stay in that rarified company—and so close to .400—for long. Damon Runyon spoke for many when he stated that no one expected Heilmann would keep up the pace all season. Compared to Cobb and Speaker, "He is not in that particular class."[23]

Years later, White Sox pitcher Ted Lyons, who pitched against Heilmann from 1923 through 1929, had this to say about his fellow Hall of Famer: "He was a different type of hitter than, say, Hornsby; Hornsby had a smooth stroke with a beautiful follow-through; Harry had a choppy stroke, but powerful."[24]

Heilmann would prove Runyon and his other doubters wrong. He would win the first of four batting titles in 1921 with a .394 mark. Cobb would not be far behind, at .389. Hampered by a late-season injury, Speaker would tail off and finish fifth, at .362, although he would again lead the American League in doubles with fifty-two.[25]

The Yankees rallied to win the opening game before 30,000 fans. Ruth hit a slow curve for a three-run home run to tie the game at six, and Peckinpaugh won it in the ninth with a single through a drawn-in infield.

Roger Peckinpaugh went about his job without gathering headlines, except when he won games with his bat or glove. At the age of thirty, he was in his ninth season as a Yankee. He batted second most of the season, ahead of Ruth, and therefore saw a lot of good pitches. Still, Peckinpaugh had the patience to pass on bad ones and would walk eighty-four times this year.[26]

Early in his career, Peckinpaugh's bat had left something to be desired: in his first six Yankee seasons, he hit between .220 and .268. Then he jumped to .305 in 1919 and began getting rave reviews as the best short-stop in baseball.[27] "Peckinpaugh combines one of the most remarkable pair of fielding hands in baseball, with an arm that would make many vaudeville strong men green with envy," wrote the *New York Sun* in 1919.[28] That paper waxed on about his amazing ability to handle bad-bouncing balls.

Peckinpaugh was not a colorful man. He went about his work, making terrific plays look routine.[29] When *Baseball Magazine* featured Peckinpaugh in February 1920, the article was entitled, "The Baseball Plodder Who Became a Star."

Sunday's game drew an even larger crowd, with 34,000 in attendance. It was a war of words between members of the two teams, as well as between men on the same team. Ruth refused to have his picture taken with Cobb before the game and offered the cameraman "a few added remarks that were innuendos to say the least."[30] Cobb then mocked the Yankee slugger, pantomiming like a gorilla and pushing his nose up when the Babe ran past him. Cobb explained in his biography, "Whenever I'd pass near him on the field, I'd make some little remark or gesture, such as, 'Do any of you fellows smell something? Seems to me there's a polecat around here.'"[31]

At one point during the game, the two squared off to fight, only to have umpire Bill Dinneen come between them. When Ruth struck out in the fourth, Cobb whistled and roared. He also carried on a running repartee with Carl Mays, who was in the Yankee dugout. (Their relationship had not improved since they first "met" in 1915. Mays hit Cobb with a pitch, and Cobb retaliated by throwing his bat at Mays.)

They also played a ball game, and Peckinpaugh was again the star. His bases-clearing triple in the fifth put the Yankees in the lead. After the Tigers had clawed back to tie the game at eight in the top of the eighth, Peckinpaugh homered in the bottom of the inning off Hubert "Dutch" Leonard, the Detroit reliever, to seal the win, 12–8. Leonard was now on the downward side of a meteoric career. A teammate of Ruth and Mays on the world champion Boston Red Sox of 1915, 1916, and 1918, he won World Series games in both 1915 and 1916. His 0.96 earned run average in 1914 is still the lowest single-season mark ever for a starting pitcher.[32]

After Peckinpaugh's triple, Cobb finally agreed to give the Babe a pass. Suds Sutherland threw three wide ones, but the fourth ball was not wide enough. Ruth clubbed it for his nineteenth home run and his third in three days. First, Cobb argued with the umpires that the ball was foul; he did not win that argument. Then, he berated his pitcher. Sutherland had given up four straight hits; yet Cobb left him in, possibly as punishment. Before the inning had ended, he gave up another four. So much for allaying nervousness and instilling confidence.

The Yankees had their own soap opera at work in that Sunday game with the Tigers. When Huggins pulled starter Bob Shawkey after he gave up a triple to Heilmann in the eighth, Shawkey did not go quietly. His yelling at his manager was easily heard by many fans. Quinn finished the game, pitching two scoreless innings to nail down the wild win.

Things did not get any better the next day, either for the Tigers or for Huggins. The Yankees' starting pitcher was none other than Babe Ruth. After putting up with Cobb's mocking behavior, the Babe probably wanted to show the full panoply of his skills. He tossed four shutout innings, though he was wild and walked five men. (He would walk two more before he left in the sixth.) While he tired in the fifth and gave up four runs, he struck out Cobb in that inning. It was the final time in his career that Cobb faced Ruth as a pitcher.[33]

Ruth homered in the third off Howard Ehmke, as the Yankees jumped out to a 6–0 lead. He gave way to Carl Mays on the mound in the sixth and moved to center field. Ruth was not done with his bat. In the seventh, he hit a tremendous home run to center, off an Ehmke slow curve. He briefly stopped at second base and laughed at Cobb, who once again responded with his pantomime deriding the Babe's nose and waistline.

Personalities aside, the Ruth home run was a remarkable hit, the longest ever in New York. "Never before has human power propelled a baseball from the home plate into those wooden stands," wrote Frank O'Neill of the *New York Sun*. "Hitting to centre field has become something of a fad with Ruth this season."[34]

Many people think that the Babe's home run totals were made possible by the short right-field "porch" at the Polo Grounds. Yet he now had twenty-one home runs, eleven of which had come on the road. Moreover, his record-breaking blasts—in Washington, Cleveland, St. Louis, and New York—were hit to the deeper center field, not right field; and some of his blasts cleared the left-field fences. The Babe explained that he was taking what he was being offered. "The fans seem surprised that I am hitting to center field and left center field. . . . The pitchers have about made up their minds that it is folly to pitch inside to me."[35] He now had five homers in four games, breaking his own 1918 record of four in four days (in a season in which he hit only eleven.)[36] One of those 1918 blows had come off Hooks Dauss, whom Ruth would face in the final game of this series.

The Yanks had a real scare in the third inning, when an Ehmke pitch hit Wally Schang. Besides also putting Steve O'Neill out of commission for a few weeks, Ehmke had hit the Browns player-coach Jimmy Austin this spring, breaking his arm and putting him out of the game for two months. The pitch appeared to be a rising curve that broke directly into Schang's face.[37] At the last minute, the Yankee catcher raised his arm to protect his face, and the ball hit him in the wrist. While some papers reported that the wrist had been broken, x-rays proved those reports to be both premature and incorrect.

When the Tigers staged a minirally in the eighth and Huggins pulled Mays, the Yankee ace shouted derogatorily at his skipper. New York held on for a 13–8 win; but for the second straight day, a top Yankee pitcher had publicly challenged his manager. An unnamed Yankee told the *Detroit News*'s H. G. Salsinger, "I don't envy Huggins. You have no idea what a gay little troupe we have. It is packed with temperamental characters." Added the veteran Detroit sportswriter, "Huggins is up against it. Ruth, of course, does what he pleases."[38]

Babe Ruth was as colorful as John McGraw and even more unruly. "The problem of Ruth," wrote Hugh Fullerton, "is as old as the ages. . . . He is suffering from an ailment which is quite common in baseball, which is too much admiration."[39] The Babe's unrestrained behavior was also setting the wrong example and creating behavior problems among other Yankees.[40]

The *New York American* cut through all the events of the day and boiled them down to the core: "Yesterday Cobb was called to judgment. And, forever, it was impressed upon him that for all time in comparison to Gotham's bambino he is passé."[41]

Yet the Babe was not done. On June 14 the Yanks completed the sweep of the Tigers and made it seven out of eight against them this year with a 9–6 win. Ruth homered his first two times up, giving him three home runs in three at bats and seven in five games. The first shot almost cleared the distant left-field bleachers. The second blast went to virtually the same spot in the center-field bleachers, perhaps even a little farther than the previous day's home run had reached. Home runs number twenty-two and number twenty-three for the season also gave the Babe the league lead in runs batted in over Heilmann, 59–58. The home runs were numbers nine and ten of his career against his favorite pitcher—the veteran Dauss, whose 223 wins is still the most in Tigers history.

Detroit never recovered from this sweep. The Tigers lost their next five games, running their losing streak to nine; and they fell ten games out of first. A month later, they were fifteen games back; and at the end of the season, they would finish twenty-seven games out of first place.

In his Cobb biography, Al Stump wrote that during this series, the Tigers' manager was so angry that he was smashing clubhouse chairs and windows.[42] While Cobb had a good series, going 7-18, Ruth went 8-12 with six home runs. Walter Trumbull paid homage to the Babe:

'Barry to Collins to Davis'
Is only a vanished romance.
Some like the rhyme they gave us
of Tinker to Evers to Chance.
But a new one has since been invented—
The Yankees all think it immense—
Though it drives many hurlers demented.
It's 'Pitcher to Ruth to the fence.'[43]

The biggest sports headlines as spring turned to summer were coming out of New Jersey. Heavyweight champion Jack Dempsey's title defense against Georges Carpentier of France was dominating the sports pages as the July 2 bout approached. The French champion, a World War I hero, had captured the fancy of many in this country. As Walter Trumbull wrote, "To the casual glance, it looks like a meeting between a greyhound and a wolf. . . . He [Carpentier] is a man of mystery, and more than that, he appears to be a man of destiny."[44] Yet the reality was that the "casual glance" was probably correct; the undersized Frenchman had little chance. But promoter Tex Rickard, "the master of ballyhoo," showed the rising power of marketing in the 1920s. "He made boxing promotion an art form. The Carpentier-Dempsey fight in 1921 ranks as the pièce de résistance of his creation."[45] The press jumped on his bandwagon and created a groundswell of interest in the upcoming match.

Carpentier also had many connected to the fight game, as well as ballplayers, convinced he would win. Still the majority backed the champion. Giants shortstop Dave Bancroft spoke for many when he predicted that Dempsey would retain his title by a knockout: "It seems to me that Dempsey is too strong, too heavy, too hard a hitter and too rugged for Carpentier. The fight should be over in six rounds, with Dempsey the winner by a clean knockout."[46]

Another sport had been gaining in popularity, and that was golf. Some baseball observers feared golf's popularity with fans would hurt baseball. Many baseball players enjoyed the game, too, though many managers found it detrimental to the players. Miller Huggins was one of them; and he now ordered Carl Mays to put his clubs away, at least until the end of the season. Huggins's action renewed a debate, whether the two sports mix. John McGraw and Rogers Hornsby felt the game was bad for a ballplayer's baseball swing.[47] Other concerns were that golf was bad for a player's temper and that ballplayers became too preoccupied with the game; the term "golf addict" was often used. A few years later, *Baseball Magazine* would run an article entitled, "Does the Game of Golf Hurt Batting?" It concluded, "Oil and water are both necessities of life—but they won't mix. The same goes for baseball and golf."[48]

The seventh-place Chicago White Sox became the last Major League club to make their 1921 Polo Grounds debut when they arrived on Wednesday, June 15. The Yankees faced Dickie Kerr twice and Red Faber once and lost all three. Faber's victory was his fourteenth of the season against only three losses; his White Sox had won but twenty-four. During the entire series, New York had a steady diet of curves and low and slow balls. Fastballs were either wasted or inside pitches used to drive Yankee batters from the plate. And Faber's spitters were breaking just above the knees.

Hugh Fullerton explained the keys to the success of Faber, one of the game's best pitchers in 1921. He was mixing up a high fastball with a low slow ball, and the latter had a big downward break. Most importantly, Faber did not let batters get comfortable in the box. "Faber seems to use his speed to prevent them from setting themselves to hit. He keeps them stepping around and dodging and then curls a slow one up to them, and they do not hit largely because they are not balanced."[49]

It was becoming increasingly obvious that the Yankee sluggers had problems with slow-ball pitchers.[50] "A pitcher with a change of pace is an abomination for the Yanks," said the *New York Herald*.[51] Surely, John McGraw read these New York papers and filed the information away for future reference.

The phenomenon of a top team having trouble beating a weak opponent is not that rare in baseball. In the case of the Sox, they had a preset pitching strategy against the Yanks and a couple of arms to execute it. Hugh Fullerton noted what has been a truism in the national pastime: good pitching beats good hitting. "A pitcher is a huge asset to a ball club these days," he wrote, "and a good pitcher counts for more than many sluggers."[52] While Ruth hit no home runs in the series, his bat was not completely quieted. He had 6 hits in 14 at bats, including four doubles. White Sox pitchers also walked him three times. Ruth now had fifty-nine passes, twenty more than any other player.

As the Black Sox trial was finally approaching (it would start on June 27), Fullerton wondered what might have been, had the team stayed intact. Had the Black Sox not been suspended, with Faber in top form, the club "could have thrown two games a week and then won the pennant."[53]

After the Chicago series, the Yankees headed north to Fenway Park for six games with the Red Sox, including back-to-back doubleheaders. In the first game, the Yankees led, 6–3, until another late-inning Mays meltdown. Burt Whitman noted that Mays's secret was his control and ability to keep the ball low. When he tired, wrote the Boston reporter, his ball rose too much, and he was hit.[54] With the game tied, 6–6, in the tenth, the Babe led off with what would be the game-winning home run. The blow brought cheers from the Boston fans, who still considered him one of their own.

A couple of days later, Huggins started the erratic Quinn, who would be facing eleven-game winner Sam Jones, one of the league's best pitchers. Yet in "a startling reversal of form," the aging spitballer prevailed, 8–2.[55] The Yankees gained a series split in the finale, led by Ruth's twenty-fifth home run, one of the longest home runs ever hit at Fenway. Once again, the Boston crowd roared in appreciation.

Back home for a weekend set with Washington, New York's Jekyll and Hyde personalities were in full view. On Saturday, June 25, the Yankees made an incredible six first-inning errors, including three by pitcher Bob Shawkey. The Senators had a five spot and were on their way to a 6–4 win. Ruth hit his third home run of the year off Washington starter Walter Johnson in the losing cause. When the pitcher was once asked to compare the Babe with other sluggers, he replied, "All I can say is that the balls Ruth hit out of the park got smaller quicker than anybody else's."[56]

So far this season, the Babe had hit a number of what today are called tape-measure home runs—arguably the longest blasts ever hit—in ballparks in New York, Washington, Detroit, Cleveland, St. Louis, and Boston. As *Baseball Magazine* would write in looking back on Ruth's 1921 season, "He found this [smashing home run records] too tame an occupation and introduced the super home run."[57]

He was also becoming a national treasure. Harry Schumacher was one of many sportswriters who recognized the Babe's new status. "Babe

Ruth is no longer the exclusive property of the Yankees. He is now a national institution and the common idol of all American League fans save those who support the Cleveland Indians. Cleveland fanatics regard him as a pest, a horrible thing who should be suppressed by act of congress."[58]

On Sunday, Waite Hoyt beat ex-Yankee George Mogridge, 9–1. Ruth and Meusel, "the thumping twins," both homered. The Babe, who had trouble fielding in recent days, made a great catch of a Bucky Harris drive. Both Sam Crane and Fred Lieb noted that Ruth's weakness was grounders, not fly balls. Two days, two games, two vastly different Yankee teams. Or so it seemed. As one former big leaguer said, "The Yanks are the best worst team in either league."[59]

After the game, manager Huggins headed out west in search of a player to bolster his team. He refused to disclose where he was going or whom he was looking for. He left the team in the hands of coach Charley O'Leary. Washington owner Clark Griffith had just returned from a similar scouting trip, looking specifically at pitchers in the International League. He had found the trip unproductive and the pickings slim: "I wouldn't give twenty cents worth of dog meat for all the pitchers I looked at."[60] This assessment was interesting, because one of his stops had been in Baltimore to see the red-hot Orioles, winners of twenty-seven games in a row in May and June. Apparently, Lefty Grove, on his way to a twenty-five-win season, had not impressed Griffith.

The Yanks ended June and started July with a pair of doubleheader sweeps of the Red Sox. Eight days after Herb Pennock and Joe Bush had swept them at Fenway Park, the Yanks got even, defeating both Boston hurlers at the Polo Grounds. Roger Peckinpaugh led the sweep with home runs in both games.

The second twin bill was overshadowed that afternoon and in the newspaper headlines the next day. Those belonged to Jack Dempsey. Ruth hit home runs in both games, numbers twenty-nine and thirty, while the announcement of Dempsey's fourth-round knockout of Georges Carpentier that afternoon brought cheers from the fans. While the European challenger had appealed to many, ultimately the victory of the American fighter met with widespread approval in this country. Though Dempsey was once derided as a slacker for his failure to serve in the Great War, this victory set him on the road to becoming the second-most idolized athlete of the 1920s. The first, of course, was Babe Ruth.

The Yankees then swept the Philadelphia Athletics (or the "Pathetics," as the *New York Tribune* tagged them) in New York's fifth doubleheader in two weeks, as they scrambled to make up the April rainouts. Connie Mack saw Frank Baker, his third baseman of 1908–14, become Home Run Baker once again, at least for a day.[61] Baker hit two homers in the first game and went 5-9 for the day.

Until recently, inconsistent pitching had been the bane of the Yankees this season. Miller Huggins really had no more than two reliable pitchers to call on all season long; and for stretches, he did not have even that many.[62] On June 29 the *New York Evening Journal* headline shouted, "Double-Headers Will Test Huggins Clan Pitching Strength." The Yanks passed the test with flying colors. They swept the three doubleheaders in six days and had a seven-game winning streak. Moreover, their starting pitchers had tossed ten complete games in a row. (This in a season in which the Yankees' starting pitchers would complete only 60 percent of their starts, though they would lead the league in that category.)

Throwing ten consecutive complete games was probably the high point for Yankee pitching in 1921. The next day, July 5, as the Yanks extended their winning streak to eight, Bill Piercy pitched to only two men before leaving with pain in his shoulder. It was a recurrence of the ailment that kept him out for much of the early season. His replacement, Quinn, also failed to survive Philadelphia's four-run first inning. But with the help of two Frank Baker doubles and Hoyt's sparkling eight and two-thirds innings of relief, New York rallied for the win.

Ruth was spectacular in the field as well as at the plate. He made two stunning catches and threw out a runner at the plate.[63] His fourth-inning double provides a fascinating footnote to his glorious career. The ball was heading for the Polo Grounds seats—a home run—when a fan reached out and touched the ball, which fell back onto the field. It was ruled a double. Had there been no interference, the Babe would have hit sixty home runs in 1921.[64]

Meanwhile, the Indians continued their hold on first place. They were in a stretch of eight wins in ten games, highlighted by a July 4 rally from a nine-run deficit to beat Chicago, 11–10. When the Indians completed their sweep of the White Sox the next day, their lead over New York was two games. In a month, the Yankees had shaved but a half game off the Indians' lead.

AL STANDINGS AT CLOSE OF PLAY OF JULY 5, 1921

TEAM	G	W	L	T	PCT	GB
Cleveland Indians	74	48	26	0	.649	-
New York Yankees	74	46	28	0	.622	2.0
Washington Senators	79	42	36	1	.538	8.0
Detroit Tigers	75	38	37	0	.507	10.5
Boston Red Sox	71	32	39	0	.451	14.5
St. Louis Browns	76	32	44	0	.421	17.0
Chicago White Sox	71	29	42	0	.408	17.5
Philadelphia Athletics	74	29	44	1	.397	18.5

Setbacks on the Road and in the Commissioner's Office

The Giants' first swing through the West began with three wins in Pittsburgh and finished with two wins in Chicago. However, eight losses in the ten games in between made for an overall unsuccessful road trip. The New Yorkers had opened up a game-and-a-half lead on the Pirates after winning their third straight against them on June 4; but by the time they returned home to play Boston on June 21, they would trail the Pirates by three and a half games.[1]

Because pitching appeared to be the Giants' one possible weak spot, McGraw had to be pleased with what he saw in the first three games of the trip. Art Nehf and Phil Douglas threw shutouts, while Fred Toney allowed only a single run, as the three combined to limit the Pirates to just nine hits in twenty-seven innings. Douglas's effort was a one-hitter, a scratch single by Pittsburgh's first batter of the game.

The first two games of the series followed a similar track. Each featured well-pitched efforts by both sides that the Giants broke open with a late-inning bevy of runs. In addition, a two-run triple from one of the lesser Giants' batters was the big blow in each—Goldie Rapp in the first game and Lee King in the second. For both King and Rapp, it would be their last major contributions to the Giants.

After Nehf tossed a shutout in the first game, Toney faced Earl Hamilton in a matchup of physical opposites. The right-handed Toney stood six feet one and weighed over 200 pounds, while the left-handed Hamilton was just five feet eight and weighed 160 pounds. Equipped with an excellent curve ball, Hamilton had been among the St. Louis Browns' best pitchers in the early years of the previous decade. But after he lost all nine of his decisions in 1917, the Browns sold him to Pittsburgh. Hamilton got off to a phenomenal start with his new team in 1918. He made six starts, all complete-game victories; and he had allowed less than an earned run per game before the military called him into service. Returning in 1919, he compiled an 18-24 record over the next two seasons.

Hamilton allowed a run and three hits through eight innings. With Toney equally difficult for the Pirates to solve, the game entered the ninth tied at 1–1. It was then that Hamilton weakened. The Giants pushed across three runs, highlighted by King's triple, to come away with a 4–1 victory. For King, a former Pirate, it was a most satisfying hit. The fans had been riding him hard for what they considered his interfering with George Cutshaw on a play at second base earlier in the game. His answer was to make an exaggerated bow to the crowd, while executing a few dance steps on the third base bag. With the win, Toney, as Nehf had the day before, raised his record to 7-2.

Douglas's gem, before an overflow Saturday crowd, gave the Giants undisputed possession of first place. The 12–0 romp was his second one-hitter in what had so far been an erratic season for him, despite his 4-0 record. Unlike the first two games of the series, this one lacked any drama or suspense. Once the Giants unloaded on Pirates ace Wilbur Cooper for seven runs in the second inning, any question as to the outcome was effectively over.

For Cooper, it was his first loss of the season after eight consecutive wins. Ross Youngs, who had three hits in the first game of the series, added three more today. Douglas, a career .161 hitter, had three hits and three runs batted in; still, it was his pitching that made the day memorable. The one hit he allowed was an infield single by Carson Bigbee, the Pirates' first batter.

Bigbee was a speedy left-handed hitter whose 161 singles would lead the National League in 1921. He led off the Pittsburgh first with a slow-hit ground ball to first baseman George Kelly, who fielded it cleanly and tossed it to pitcher Douglas covering the bag. It was a routine play, one that Major League pitchers execute dozens of times each season. However, this time Douglas somehow missed stepping on first base. The scorer ruled it a hit, rather than charging Douglas with an error. It was a questionable call, one that might have been decided differently had it occurred later in the game. The only other time a Pirate got on base was, again, when Bigbee reached on Kelly's error with two men out in the ninth inning.

Between those two Bigbee at bats, Douglas retired twenty-six batters in a row. Because of the huge crowd, one of the largest to date at Forbes

Field, 5,000 or so fans were allowed to stand in the outfield. This necessitated specific ground rules for balls hit into that group of standees, making Douglas's effort even more impressive. Possum Whitted's liner in the second inning, on which George Burns made a shoestring catch, was the only other Pirate blow that came close to being a hit.

With no Sunday baseball in Pittsburgh because of Pennsylvania's blue laws, the Giants used the off day to cross the Mahoning River and play an exhibition game against a semipro team in Youngstown, Ohio.[2] When they returned to Pittsburgh the next day for the final game, McGraw's club had a 4–3 lead after seven innings and appeared on their way to a series sweep. But an excellent relief effort by Babe Adams, who picked up his fifth win of the season, enabled the Pirates to retake first place.

Adams was the last remaining active player from the Pirates' World Series champions of 1909.[3] Player-manager Fred Clarke had used Adams, a rookie that year, mostly in relief and as an occasional spot starter. So it was a surprise to all when Clarke named him to start Game 1 of the World Series against the American League's Detroit Tigers, a team led by AL batting champion Ty Cobb. Adams not only won the opener, he pitched three complete-game victories against the Tigers and remains the only rookie ever to win three games in a World Series. His earned run average for the Series was a sparkling 1.33, and his 8–0 shutout of the Tigers in Game 7 gave the Pirates their first World Series title.

The futility shown by Giants batters against Babe Adams in their final game in Pittsburgh continued in Cincinnati, where they collected just nine hits in losing to left-handers Rube Marquard and Eppa Rixey.[4] Oddly enough, despite their loss in the first game, the Giants gained ground on Pittsburgh. After taking three of four games from the Pirates, New York, at 32-15, had a win-loss percentage of .681, while the 30-14 Pirates were at .682. With that first-game loss on June 7, the Giants were now 32-16; but Pittsburgh's loss to Boston that day dropped them to 30-15. Both teams now had a winning percentage of .667, tying them for first place. It would be seven and a half weeks before the Giants would again achieve a first-place tie with the Pirates.

As if scoring two runs in eighteen innings was not discouraging enough, the Giants received some more bad news while in Cincinnati. During the previous winter, McGraw had tried to trade for the Reds' Heinie Groh, a player whom he had traded to Cincinnati back in 1913 and who had developed into the National League's top third baseman in the later years of the Deadball Era. Groh, in turn, wanted to leave Cincinnati and return to New York. Involved in a seemingly insoluble salary dispute with owner Garry Herrmann, he vowed he would never again play for the Reds. He would sign with them, he said, only with the proviso that they would trade him to the Giants. When the two teams could not work out a trade, Groh held out.

Early in June, McGraw called Herrmann to propose a mutually satis-factory solution. "Groh is doing you no good sitting in his apartment," he said. "I can satisfy him, and I am willing to make a profitable deal with you."[5] According to newspapers in both cities, the two men then worked out a tentative trade. Groh would sign with Cincinnati, where-upon, the papers speculated, the Reds would trade him to the Giants for third baseman Goldie Rapp, outfielder Curt Walker, catcher Mike Gonzalez, and $100,000.

Commissioner Landis had been tracking the Groh affair from its beginning and reacted immediately. He canceled any proposed trade that would send Groh to New York, and told Groh that his reinstate-ment was dependent on his playing the remainder of the 1921 season with Cincinnati. It was, believed Landis, "an unhealthy situation if a dissatisfied player could dictate his transfer to a strong contender before he agreed to sign a contract."[6] This was not the first time he had taken a firm stand against the powerful Giants, having previously banned outfielder Bennie Kauff.

Not surprisingly, Groh was furious with Landis's ruling. "I will never play ball till that decision is reversed," he said. "Judge Landis has no right to order me to play where I don't want to play, nor make me accept a salary that does not suit me. Let him render a square decision in my case. Till he does, I am through."[7] After reconsidering his position, Groh was in uniform and on the bench the next day, and three days later he played for the Reds against Brooklyn.

However, sportswriters, even those in New York, were nearly unani-mous in their praise of Landis's decision. Despite the ruling's adverse effect on McGraw and his Giants, Sam Crane wrote, "Commissioner Landis inaugurated a new era in the national game when he decided that Groh, in having his suspension as a holdout raised, must play this season out with the Cincinnati Reds, by which club he was, by baseball law, rightfully owned." Crane praised the decision for removing politics from the game and eliminating doubt among the club owners as to each other's good intentions.[8]

Hugh Fullerton went even further. He said that the Landis ruling in the Groh case "is to baseball what the Magna Carta was to English liberty. . . . He has struck at the root of one of the greatest evils of organized ball."[9] *Baseball Magazine* also supported the ruling and noted the complexity of the case. If players were able to move from club to club, the publication stated, the reserve clause—the very foundation of Organized Ball—would be threatened.[10]

Crane, nevertheless, defended McGraw and the Giants against charges that they had "been guilty of negotiating with players of rival clubs for future employment, with the direct purpose of disrupting the team of a rival by making the 'approached' players dissatisfied."[11] The Cardinals had made similar accusations against McGraw when the Giants were pursuing Rogers Hornsby, and Crane blamed it on antagonism toward New York: "Western writers have long been jealous of our big city and take gladly to any occasion to knock it. All of the many deals for players the New York National League Club has made either by purchase or trade, or both, have been strictly above board and with honest business intentions."[12]

Crane was correct in his description of the antipathy that existed toward McGraw and the Giants in the league's other cities. He was also correct that there was dislike and distrust of the "big city" in the hinterlands. However, it seems disingenuous to claim that all of McGraw's baseball dealings were completely aboveboard. With his win-at-all-costs mentality, it is highly likely that McGraw would bend any rule and abandon any sense of fair play if it interfered with an effort to improve his team.

Landis's ruling in the Groh case sent a strong message to owners and players alike. Yet, because American League president Ban Johnson had tried, unsuccessfully, to do the same thing in 1919 with Carl Mays, it contained a certain amount of hypocrisy. While Johnson would feud with Landis for years and be on the opposite side of him on virtually every issue, they were in alignment on this topic. They agreed that play-

20. On June 11 the Giants made their first visit of the season to St. Louis. At the time, the Cardinals had the top two hitters in the league, Rogers Hornsby (*center*) with a .424 average and Austin McHenry (*right*) with a .381 average. First baseman Jack Fournier (*left*) was not far behind at .360. *St. Louis Cardinals Hall of Fame Museum.*

ers should not be able to force trades by holding out or (as in the case of Mays) sitting out.

Johnson's biographer, Eugene Murdock, notes the similarity of the Mays and Groh cases and states that by his action in the latter, Landis vindicated his rival's position.[13] Nevertheless, Johnson's veto of Mays's trade to the Yankees was the beginning of the president's downfall. The Yankees not only challenged him but also prevailed in court. That the Giants did not challenge the Groh ruling was a reflection of Landis's growing power.

Having lost the final game in Pittsburgh and two in Cincinnati and minus Heinie Groh, the Giants moved on to St. Louis. The Cardinals, winners of seven straight and fourteen of their last seventeen, had been ten wins below the .500 mark earlier in the season. Now, on June 11, they were two wins above it and had climbed to third place. They also boasted the top two hitters in the National League: Rogers Hornsby, with a .424 batting average, and outfielder Austin McHenry, with a .381 average.

Cardinals manager Branch Rickey, well aware of the Giants' recent difficulties with left-handed pitching, started little-used Ferdie Schupp in the series opener.[14] The Cardinals' 8–3 victory was followed by two more, increasing their winning streak to ten and stretching the Giants' losing streak to six.

The first of the two additional Giant losses was a heartbreaker in which the Cardinals scored the tying and winning runs in their last at bat. With Youngs nursing an injured knee, McGraw was looking for offensive help wherever he could find it. He benched Rapp, whose batting average had dropped to .224, and replaced him with rookie John Monroe. Frisch moved from second to third, while Monroe played second. It seemed a desperate move, as Monroe had not started a game all season and had only three at bats. Yet McGraw's maneuver paid immediate dividends. With the Giants trailing St. Louis, 2–1, in the ninth inning, Monroe connected against Bill Pertica for a two-run homer, giving the Giants a 3–2 lead. Reliever Slim Sallee needed just three outs to end the two streaks; but he allowed a two-out, two-run double to Milt Stock, turning a potential victory into a bitter 4–3 defeat.

The following day, Les Mann hit two home runs, leading St. Louis to its tenth straight win. It gave the Cardinals the National League's second-longest winning streak thus far this season, trailing only Brooklyn's earlier eleven-game streak. The one bright note for the Giants came in the eighth inning, when Monroe snared a line drive by Hornsby and turned it into a triple play.

When Mann hit the two home runs against the Giants on June 13, he was one of three Major Leaguers to hit two that day. The others were Babe Ruth and Pittsburgh's Possum Whitted. It was only the second time that three players at the Major League level had hit two home runs in a game on the same day.[15] This led the *New York Herald* to lament what it saw as the disappearance of pitchers battles and tight games: "Gone are all the keener points of baseball while the club owners believe the fans want the slugging, which is making a joke of the game. And never a game less than two hours long."[16] As if to emphasize the *Herald*'s point, it happened again the next day, when Jimmy Dykes of the Athletics, Walton Cruise of the Braves, and Ruth again all had two–home run games.

Two-hour games were also on the mind of John McGraw, who blamed them on the new lively ball. He said such long, drawn-out contests were tiring to fans and were causing many of them to leave in the sixth or seventh inning. McGraw also claimed that the new ball had affected infield play. Balls hit on the ground now traveled so fast that the infielder was lucky to hold onto them, he said. In the mind of the Orioles' third baseman of the 1890's, many of the ground balls that went through for base hits would have been converted into putouts with the old-style ball.

Johnny Evers, a McGraw disciple, agreed about what he called the "rabbit ball." One of the iconic figures of the Deadball Era, Evers blamed the new ball for the increase in home runs and the resulting high-scoring games. "They can never convince me that the ball we are playing with is not a rabbit. I played the infield long enough to know the difference in the way they used to come at you and the way they come now."[17]

Sam Crane had a different take on whether these slugfests were tiring fans out or keeping them in their seats. Writing about the unpredictability of ball games in this era of hitting, he wrote, "One cannot tell from one day to another what a pitcher is going to get—the victory or the gate. . . . There no longer are any cinch victories even for the biggest star pitcher in the country."[18] This very volatility, he noted, was drawing fans to the ballparks and keeping them in their seats until the final out. Still, a number of owners were expressing concern that the pendulum had swung too far away from the pitcher.[19]

Around this time, Major League Baseball took small steps to redress the imbalance between pitching and hitting. Both Spalding and Reach, makers of baseballs, insisted there had been no change in their manufacture, other than the use of better raw materials, primarily Australian yarn. That yarn could withstand more strain than inferior material and therefore could be wound more tightly. One unnamed Yankee pitcher commented wryly on this explanation, calling it "a good yarn."[20] Others insisted that the pitcher, not the ball, was the key. The liveliness of the ball, they believed, was dependent on the skill of the pitcher.[21]

A *Sporting News* editorial agreed that the score of a game was more a function of the pitcher's abilities than the ball being used. "We attended two games of ball played within a few days of each other in the same ball park last week. In one the score was 16 to 8, in the other it was 1–0. The same make of baseball was used in both games. That ought to dispose of the livelier ball question."[22]

Ban Johnson sent a bulletin to his umpires in June instructing them to limit the practice of replacing balls with minor blemishes. (He had sent a similar directive a year earlier, just before Ray Chapman was killed.) Not only would this practice save the owners money, it would also keep dirtier and rougher balls (harder for the batter to see and easier for the pitcher to grip) in the game. He acknowledged pitchers' complaints that they could not get a grip on glossy new balls.[23]

Also in June, both leagues began testing substances that umpires would use to take the gloss off the balls. Since the start of the 1920 season, when "freak" pitches were banned, so too was rosin, the powdery substance pitchers used to get a good grip on the ball. Now the American League started having umpires rub the baseballs before games, using a moist, chalk-like substance that was formulated by a Philadelphia chemist. The National League was using a mixture of molder's clay and tobacco juice; the league was also testing moistened earth.[24] The intent was to let the pitchers get a grip on the ball and thus be able to throw curve balls, with a substance that did not discolor the ball and was not too sticky.[25]

In the month since May 17, when his batting average stood at .340, twenty-two-year-old Frankie Frisch had been slumping. The 10 hits in his previous 45 at bats had dropped his average to .287 by June 14, the eve of the Giants' first visit to Chicago. Frisch had not done well against the Cubs earlier in the season, garnering just one hit in the four games; but he would have five spectacular games against Chicago pitching at Cubs Park. Despite going hitless in one of the games, he banged out 13 hits in 22 at bats and raised his average to .316. It would never drop below the .300 level again in this, Frisch's breakout season. He would finish with a .341 mark, seventh best in the National League.

The Giants captured three of the five games against Johnny Evers's club, including two of the three that went into extra innings. Their one extra-inning loss came in the second game of the series. The Giants had broken a 2–2 tie with two runs in the top of the thirteenth, only to have the Cubs come back with three and win, 5–4. Starter Phil Douglas allowed only one run in six innings, but he got into an argument with umpire Bill Klem following a walk to John Kelleher leading off the seventh. Douglas disputed Klem's ball-four call, and Klem threw him out of the game.

With a larger-than-life umpire, like Klem, and a larger-than-life manager, like McGraw, clashes between the two were inevitable. And, while McGraw, the game's most obnoxious and vociferous umpire baiter, initiated many conflicts over the years with Klem and others, there was not one this day.[26] He simply summoned Rube Benton to replace the ejected Douglas.

Thirty-four-year-old Grover Alexander went the distance for the Cubs, although he allowed fourteen hits, including five by Frisch. It was the fifth win of the season for Alexander, who was well behind his 1920 pace, when he led the National League with twenty-seven wins. Over the next three games in Chicago, June 17–19, the Giants' offense moved into high gear, scoring twenty-nine runs.

Bill Klem was baseball's most recognizable umpire of the first half of the twentieth century. In a National League career that lasted from 1905 to 1941, he established his reputation early, one based on excellent umpiring skills and an unwillingness to put up with any challenges to his authority. He was particularly proud of his ability to call balls and strikes, so complaints like those made by Douglas were often invitations for an ejection. During his lengthy career, Klem threw a total of 239 players and managers out of games, which was more than any other Major League umpire.[27]

Klem's no-nonsense approach helped speed games along, a fact noted by Hugh Fullerton. Joining the chorus of those lamenting that games were dragging on and were now taking two hours or more to play, Fullerton placed much of the blame on the umpires: "In this season the umpires, instead of insisting on speeding up play, have even aided in the delay, particularly [American League umpire Tom] Connolly. Klem is a remarkable exception to the practice. Teams play games an average of ten minutes faster with Klem umpiring than with other umpires in charge of the play."[28]

Before returning home from their final stop in Chicago, the Giants stopped off in Detroit for a June 20 exhibition game against the slumping Tigers. Ty Cobb's club had lost its last nine games and now trailed the first-place Indians by ten games.

Despite McGraw's and Cobb's deep dislike for one another, there were no incidents in Detroit's 8–6 win. Before the game, the local Knights of

Columbus presented fellow member Hughie Jennings, the long-time Tigers manager and current Giants coach, with a new set of golf clubs. While the Giants were playing this meaningless game in Detroit, the Pirates were beating the Phillies, 3–2, stretching their lead over New York to three and a half games.

Finishing with seven wins in fifteen games on the trip west had been a disappointment for the Giants, particularly after winning the first three at Pittsburgh. Overall, the offense had been the team's strong point, while the pitching remained inconsistent. By June 20 they had scored a National League–leading 318 runs, and three of the top four individual runs-scored leaders were Giants: Dave Bancroft and George Burns were tied for first with forty-eight and Frankie Frisch was fourth with forty-five.[29] Ross Youngs, with a batting average of .373, was third behind Rogers Hornsby in that category; and he was also third behind the Cardinals' star second baseman in on-base percentage. George Kelly still led the runs-batted-in race with fifty-five, but his nine home runs were now two behind Philadelphia's Irish Meusel. (Meanwhile, at Fenway Park on this day, Babe Ruth hit his American League–leading twenty-fourth home run of the season.)

Among the Giants' pitchers, Jesse Barnes led the league with a 2.47 earned run average, though he had done no better than split his eight decisions. With an 8-3 record, Fred Toney had been the team's most consistent pitcher. Only Pittsburgh's Wilbur Cooper, with ten wins, had more than Toney. Art Nehf had 7 wins (and only 4 losses), but he had been a model of inconsistency. All season, he had alternated between flashes of his former brilliance in one game and complete ineffectiveness in the next.

When the Giants returned home to play Boston on June 21, they were facing a team on the way up. Winners of eleven of seventeen out west, the Braves had just taken three of four from St. Louis to climb over the Cardinals into third place. This Boston team bore little resemblance to the struggling group that the Giants had clobbered in a four-game sweep during their first visit in early May.

In the series opener, the Braves continued their road success by thumping the Giants, 16–5, dealing the home team its worst defeat of the season. The sixteen runs they allowed would be the most any team scored against them in 1921; and the eleven-run margin, their biggest single-game deficit. Sitting through typically hot, sticky weather this first day of summer in New York City, the suffering crowd saw the Giants make six errors, including four by rookie second baseman John Monroe.

Monroe was in the lineup despite McGraw's known reluctance to play rookies, particularly in the infield. McGraw believed it was better to keep youngsters on the bench for a year or two to allow them to learn, as he had done with George Kelly. (Frisch, rapidly becoming one of the league's best players, had been an exception.)

McGraw had begun using Monroe in the St. Louis series because of Rapp's failure to hit anywhere near as well as he had done in the Minors. When he did play Monroe at second base, he moved Frisch to third. McGraw had also tried another approach during the St. Louis and Chicago series. He kept Frisch at second and used yet another rookie, Pat Patterson, at third. The switch from Rapp to Monroe was an attempt to boost an already strong offense; but after Monroe's disastrous defensive performance in the loss to Boston, McGraw would never start him in another game.

Third baseman Patterson impressed the crowd with his fielding ability during the Giants' split of the remaining two games with the Braves. Meanwhile, Frisch, sometimes called "the Fordham Flame" by sportswriter Sam Crane, continued the sensational play the fans had come to expect.[30] His four hits and four runs batted in helped Toney gain his ninth win in the finale. With Pittsburgh losing a doubleheader at St. Louis, the Giants picked up a game and a half but still trailed the Pirates by three and a half games.

The Giants' offensive onslaught continued in Philadelphia, where in the first three games—a single game on June 24 and a Saturday doubleheader the next day—they outscored the last-place Phillies, 37–10. The Giants' 12–8 loss in the final game prevented a sweep.[31] McGraw's lineup accounted for an amazing sixty-six hits in the four games, including ten by Burns, nine by Kelly, and eight each by Frisch and Bancroft. Among those sixty-six hits were eighteen doubles and ten home runs, including one home run by Patterson, who started all four games; George Kelly's tenth; and a pair of two–home run games by Frank Snyder. Earl Smith's sixth home run in the final game gave the Giants' catchers five for the series.

The twenty-four-year-old Smith—a rough-hewn, hard-drinking Arkansan—was in his third year with the Giants. One of those men who seemed to have a permanent chip on his shoulder, he feared no one, including McGraw, whom he despised and whose signals and bed checks he often would ignore. During the sixth inning of the opening game of the doubleheader, he got involved in a near fight with Philadelphia slugger Cy Williams. Williams, who was leading off the inning, claimed that the catcher, Smith, was too close to the plate and was interfering with him. Smith disagreed, and the two men began to argue. Williams then took a swing at Smith that failed to land; but before Smith could retaliate, umpire Barry McCormick kicked Williams out of the game. Williams got some measure of revenge in Philadelphia's final-game win, banging out four hits, including a home run. In total, the Phillies had nineteen hits, including five home runs, all of which were against Phil Douglas, whom McGraw kept out on the mound the entire game.

McGraw's dictatorial personality had made him almost paranoid about the need to keep track of his players, and he often hired private detectives to follow them. Douglas, given his penchant for breaking training rules, drew the most scrutiny on this current Giants club. "Well, there was detectives on everybody, more or less," said George Kelly, while reminiscing about his former manager. "That's the way he kept things. But that was at home, mostly at home that he had fellows like those ones he had on Phil. Phil he had followed on the road too."[32]

Naturally, Douglas resented being spied on, and he hated McGraw for sanctioning it. "No man owns another man," he said.[33] So when he spotted the detective assigned to trail him outside the Giants' hotel in Philadelphia the night before he was scheduled to pitch, Douglas grew livid. Grabbing the startled detective by the coat, he screamed, "Listen, if I ever catch you doggin' me around again, I'll stomp you right through the sidewalk. And you can tell McGraw what I said."[34] The detective wisely left, and Douglas was free to do as he pleased.

Douglas's biographer, Tom Clark, suggests that what pleased Douglas that night was to go drinking, resulting in his pitching the next day's game hung over. In addition, he had upset McGraw earlier in the week by failing to travel with the team when it left New York for Philadelphia. Having him absorb the thrashing he did may have been McGraw's less-than-subtle way of disciplining his pitcher. And if Douglas did not get the message, McGraw berated him loudly after the game. Douglas's reaction was to leave the team and threaten never to return.

Speculation began that Douglas's career in New York was over. But five days later, he showed up at the Hotel Brunswick in Boston, where the Giants were staying. McGraw, the first to spot him, scolded Douglas for his absence, fined him, and told him his next paycheck would be reduced to reflect the five days he was gone. By contrast, the rest of the Giants were delighted to see him. Despite his escapades, Douglas was one of the best-liked players on the team.

"Don't write no funny stuff in the papers about me, because I'm back," Douglas told the reporters gathered around him. "Since I been away there has been some awful stories written about me. Where do you fellows get that stuff, anyhow? It's killing me." He went on to say that he had a personal matter to attend to in New York and thought this was the best time to do it. "Didn't I tell McGraw on the phone the other night that I'd come back? And I did."[35]

Douglas had indeed come back; and before the year was through, he would account for several of the most significant pitching wins in Giants history.

NL STANDINGS AT CLOSE OF PLAY OF JUNE 27, 1921

TEAM	G	W	L	T	PCT	GB
Pittsburgh Pirates	64	43	20	0	.683	-
New York Giants	65	40	25	0	.615	4.0
Boston Braves	63	34	29	0	.540	9.0
St. Louis Cardinals	65	33	32	0	.508	11.0
Brooklyn Dodgers	67	33	34	0	.493	12.0
Chicago Cubs	60	27	33	0	.450	14.5
Cincinnati Reds	64	25	38	0	.397	18.0
Philadelphia Phillies	62	19	43	0	.306	23.5

16   The Giants Solidify Their Lineup

As the pennant races moved into July, both the Giants and the Yankees now had the opportunity to make up ground and even overtake the leaders—the Pirates in the National League and the Indians in the American. Each New York club was scheduled to meet their rivals eight times in the next month.

Pittsburgh's two wins over Cincinnati on the last day of June had lengthened the Pirates' lead over the rained-out Giants to five games. The first win was a continuation of the protested game played on May 28, "won" by the Reds, 4–3, in ten innings. National League president John Heydler upheld Pittsburgh's protest and ordered the game continued from the point of the protest—with the visiting Reds leading, 3–2, after seven and a half innings. The Pirates got a run in the eighth inning and a Charlie Grimm home run in the ninth to win, 4–3. Pittsburgh then won the regularly scheduled game.

Cincinnati's Dolf Luque, whose "complete-game win" Heydler's decision erased, gave up both runs and took the loss. Luque was also the starter and loser in the regularly scheduled game, with rookie right-hander Chief Yellow Horse picking up the win. It was the fifth and final win of the season for Yellow Horse, a full-blooded Pawnee Indian. Unfortunately for the Pirates, Yellow Horse injured his arm in his next start, necessitating surgery and causing him to miss most of the season. Another arm injury during the 1922 season, which may have come as the result of a drunken fall, would end his Major League career. (The twenty-three-year-old Yellow Horse had fallen under the influence of veteran Rabbit Maranville, Pittsburgh's fast-living and hard-drinking shortstop.)

Though the Giants were idle on the field on July 1, they improved themselves significantly. Aware that he could not win the pennant with his current roster, John McGraw acquired veteran second baseman

Johnny Rawlings in a trade with the Phillies. Also coming to New York in the five-player deal was outfielder Casey Stengel. Going to Philadelphia were rookie third baseman Goldie Rapp, outfielder Lee King, and Minor League infielder Lance Richbourg.

McGraw's prime motivation in making the trade was Rapp's failure to hit Major League pitching, which had prevented him from becoming the team's full-time third baseman. However, the move from the contending Giants to the last-place Phillies would prove a beneficial one for Rapp. He made an immediate impression with his new team by batting safely in his first twenty-three games. At the time, Jimmy Williams of the 1899 Pirates, with streaks of twenty-six and twenty-seven, was the only rookie with a longer consecutive-game batting streak.[1] Saddled with a .215 average when the Giants traded him, Rapp would bat a solid .277 for Philadelphia during the second half of the season.

In replacing Rapp with Rawlings, McGraw was getting an aggressive, pugnacious player who would fit right in with his preferred style of play. Rawlings had never hit for a high average, though he was batting .291 this season. He was, however, a smart, seasoned player and a fine fielder who would team with shortstop Dave Bancroft to give the Giants an excellent double play combination. Playing Rawlings at second base would also allow McGraw to move Frankie Frisch back to third, thereby solidifying the Giants' infield.

Casey Stengel was a popular veteran, now in his tenth big league season; but neither the press nor the fans expected him to be of much help to the Giants. Hampered by a leg injury since the first week of the season, he was batting .305; but he had appeared in just twenty-four games with fifty-nine at bats. Stengel likely suspected that he would see even less action with the Giants; nevertheless, he was thrilled to hear he was leaving Philadelphia for New York.

Stengel was having his leg worked on by the Phillies trainer when team secretary Jim Hagan handed him a note. His first thought was that the Phillies were sending him to the Minor Leagues. When he read that he had been traded to the Giants instead of being demoted, Stengel began jumping around the room. "I thought your leg hurt," said the trainer. "Not anymore," replied Stengel. "Not anymore. I've been traded to the Giants."[2]

The Pirates also made a trade on July 1; and like the Giants' deal for

Rawlings, it would work out very well. Pittsburgh traded Elmer Ponder, a pitcher who had appeared in only eight games, to the Cubs for thirty-one-year-old outfielder Dave Robertson. The left-handed-hitting Robertson was a onetime Giant, who had shared the National League home run crown in 1916 and 1917.[3] Despite his lowly .222 average in twenty-two games with the Cubs, he filled an immediate need for the Pirates, replacing the injured Possum Whitted. Robertson would appear in sixty games for Pittsburgh in 1921, compiling a .322 batting average and batting in forty-eight runs.

Rawlings and Stengel joined the Giants in Boston, but a couple of rainouts prevented them from making their debuts until the teams moved to the Polo Grounds for a July 3 doubleheader. The Giants won the opener, 2–1, behind Art Nehf, with Stengel and Rawlings scoring the two runs. Giants fans, who had good-humoredly ridiculed and jeered Stengel as a visiting player, loudly cheered him when he appeared in his new home-white uniform. George Burns, with four runs batted in, and Bancroft, with three, led the New Yorkers to a win in the second game and a sweep of the doubleheader. George Kelly was hitless in eight at bats and, for the first time this season, heard a smattering of boos at the Polo Grounds.

The next day, Monday, was the Fourth of July; and the Giants celebrated the holiday with another doubleheader sweep, this one at Brooklyn. Kelly followed his 0-8 day with six hits and two home runs, giving him twelve homers so far on the season, which tied him for the National League lead with Irish Meusel. His five runs batted in on the day raised his total to seventy-five, twenty more than runner-up Rogers Hornsby. New York's two victories were at the expense of Clarence Mitchell in the first game and Sherry Smith and Dutch Ruether in the second game. All three were left-handers who had handled the Giants easily earlier in the season.

Meanwhile, the Pirates were splitting their July 4 doubleheader with the Cardinals. So at the traditional (if not the actual) midpoint of the season, Pittsburgh's lead over New York was three and a half games. Scheduled to play their next eighteen games at the Polo Grounds, the Giants were poised to make their run at the Pirates. But the home stand got off to an inauspicious start with two losses against the Dodgers, including one to Burleigh Grimes, who raised his record to 11-2 with his seventh consecutive win. Fifteen games against the western clubs would follow, before the home stand would conclude with a single game against Philadelphia.

First in from the West was Chicago, whom the Giants defeated in three consecutive one-run games, before dropping the finale. Art Nehf defeated Grover Alexander, 1–0, in the series opener, a marvelous pitching duel that took just one hour and thirty-seven minutes to play. Nehf allowed just three hits and no walks. New York's lone run on this blistering hot day came in the last of the ninth and was unearned. Nehf's tenth win of the season raised his overall record as a Giant to 40-18 since McGraw "stole" him from Boston in one of the best trades he ever made.[4]

The Giants-Cubs series saw the final big league appearance of Chicago's Jim "Hippo" Vaughn—a five-time twenty-game winner, who began his career with the Yankees back in 1908. Manager Johnny Evers removed him after he gave up back-to-back home runs to Frank Snyder (with the bases loaded) and pitcher Phil Douglas. Vaughn suffered his eleventh loss of the season, against just three wins; and his earned run average was a bloated 6.01. Those numbers constituted a huge reversal of form for a pitcher who had won at least seventeen games in each of the previous seven seasons and was the team's biggest winner in six of them. Vaughn was not an easy man to get along with for any manager; the massive left-hander's relationship with Evers had been especially prickly and may have accounted for some of his deterioration on the mound.[5]

The three low-scoring games between the Cubs and Giants did not prevent Evers from lamenting the loss of two of the Deadball Era's major offensive weapons, the bunt and the steal. Grover Alexander joined his manager in criticizing the new style of play, the one Babe Ruth was making popular. Alexander's position, of course, was consistent with that of most every other Major League pitcher.

A number of veteran observers also pined for the lower-scoring games of the Deadball Era. Joe Vila wrote, "The making of home runs by other players, who would not often enjoy the sensation of circling the bases under former conditions, was an insult to the intelligence of baseball students."[6] Even Miller Huggins was quoted as stating that the pitching restrictions imposed in 1920 had to be removed.[7]

The July 1921 issue of *Baseball Magazine* concluded that it was Babe Ruth, not the ball, who was driving the change. Ruth had "taken the place-hit from its pedestal as the batter's universal model" and replaced it with the home run.[8]

During the summer, there were reports that baseball's attendance figures were lower than in 1920. Those who disliked the new style of play and the "excessive" hitting were quick to place the blame there. A number of papers asked their fans to write in with the reasons they were going to fewer games (assuming that they were). Hugh Fullerton reported that 307 of 480 letters pointed to high prices.[9] Typical respondents to the *New York American*'s inquiry suggested the same. "The problem with baseball is its degeneration, its dollar diplomacy, its patent commercialism," said one. "$2.20 for a box [seat] is outrageous," wrote another.[10] The second-most common reason given was the slowness of games, many of which were stretching beyond two hours.

There was little mention of the Black Sox scandal in these accounts, which surprised Fullerton. This was a hopeful sign, he said, that fans believed that the game was still "clean." There was almost no mention of the high-scoring games or the increase in home runs as a reason that fans were staying away. Damon Runyon suggested that the men running the game had instituted "artifices designed to make mediocrity stack up with real ability."[11] Yet even Runyon had to admit that the fans were as excited as ever over a home run.[12]

Ultimately, the discussion about falling attendance was much ado about not very much, particularly as it affected the Giants. Owner Charles Stoneham issued a statement on the club's financial health in which he cited several examples of its drawing power. According to Stoneham, the Giants' four-game series in Pittsburgh and St. Louis in early June had drawn as many people in each city as had attended the entire season series there in 1920.[13] At home the Giants' National League–leading attendance would increase from 929,601 in 1920 to 973,477 in 1921.

On the morning of July 15, after three straight wins against the Cardinals, the Giants' record stood at 50-29. They were now twenty-one wins above .500, but they still trailed Pittsburgh by three games. The upcoming four-game set with the Pirates presented them with the opportunity to take over first place—if they could sweep. Behind them, third-place Boston was gaining ground on both teams. The surprising Braves had won eight straight and ten of eleven and were just four games behind New York. However, the Giants' focus was on Pittsburgh, and they went into the series full of confidence. Their success against the Pirates (they had won twenty-eight of their last forty-eight games with Pittsburgh) had continued with four wins in six games this year. Moreover, they believed that they had a deeper and stronger pitching staff than the Pirates and that overall they were the better team.

McGraw made a couple of minor moves in an effort to bolster his club for the second half of the season. In one, he purchased outfielder Bill Cunningham from the Seattle Rainiers of the Pacific Coast League. He also acquired pitcher Red Causey from the Phillies in exchange for John Monroe, who was his little-used rookie second baseman, and pitcher Jesse Winters, who was currently in the Minor Leagues. Causey, 20-9 for the Giants in 1918–19, had been part of the package McGraw sent to Boston in 1919 to get Art Nehf. He was 3-3 in seven starts for the Phillies this season, but his role in New York would be as a reliever.

The Pittsburgh series opened on Saturday, July 16, before a Polo Grounds crowd of 33,000. Pirates skipper George Gibson, equally aware of the importance of these four games, led with his ace, Wilbur Cooper, as he almost always did. On the Pirates' first swing through the east, Cooper had opened each of the four series and won them all. On this second swing, he had already won the openers at Philadelphia and Brooklyn. With a league-leading fifteen wins (15-3), Cooper seemed a good bet to exceed the twenty-four wins he had in 1920.

McGraw opened with Phil Douglas, who allowed a first-inning run; but then the Giants took over. They jumped on Cooper for four first-inning runs and went on to win, 13–4. Frisch's eighth-inning steal of second was his twenty-fourth of the season, breaking the tie he had with the Pirates' Max Carey for the league lead. Frisch then stole third to raise his total to twenty-five. Although Frisch would lead the league in stolen bases this season, Carey remained the National League's most prolific base stealer of his era. Between 1913 (in the midst of the Deadball Era) and 1925 (when the home run was gaining supremacy), Carey led the league a record ten times.[14]

Sunday's near sellout crowd saw Pittsburgh win, 4–2, in ten innings.

Relying primarily on his slow curve, lefty Earl Hamilton took a 2–1 lead into the last of the ninth. The Giants were down to their final out when Youngs singled. Kelly followed with a pop fly that landed just beyond the reach of second baseman George Cutshaw, right fielder Dave Robertson, and center fielder Carey. Youngs, running on contact, raced around to third. Next up was center fielder Bill Cunningham, a recent addition, who had already heard the cheers of the crowd after making two outstanding running catches. Despite Cunningham's impressive .341 batting average at Seattle, many in the crowd expected to see a pinch hitter; but McGraw stayed with the youngster. A few pitches after Cunningham just missed winning the game with a long drive into the left-field seats that landed barely foul, he justified McGraw's faith in him with his second Major League hit, a clean single to center. The game-tying hit sent the fans into a frenzy, as many sailed their straw hats into the air. With Kelly at second, Rawlings had a chance to win the game; but he flied harmlessly to left fielder Carson Bigbee.

The crowd's euphoria soon turned to sadness. Causey, who had replaced Jesse Barnes an inning earlier, allowed two tenth-inning runs; but the fans came alive again in the home tenth when Frisch batted with two out and the tying runs aboard. However, Hamilton got the final out on a pop foul to first baseman Charlie Grimm. Instead of reducing Pittsburgh's lead to one game, the Giants were again three back; and any chance of finishing this series in first place was gone.

By the time the series ended, gone too was the opportunity to at least have closed the gap. For after Nehf's easy 12–1 win on Monday, the Pirates, behind Babe Adams, responded with a just-as-easy 10–1 win on Tuesday. The complete-game effort by the thirty-nine-year-old Adams was particularly impressive, given that he had tossed almost a complete game in the bullpen during Hamilton's start two days earlier. Pittsburgh left town with the same three-game lead with which they had arrived, and now there were four fewer games left on the schedule. By taking three of four from St. Louis, the Braves now trailed Pittsburgh by six games and New York by only three.

The Pirates moved on to Boston, where on July 20 they increased their lead over New York to four games. Cooper bounced back from his disastrous start against the Giants to toss a shutout, while in New York, Cincinnati's Eppa Rixey outdueled Fred Toney, 2–1. A day of rain did not revive the Giants' offense. Although they compiled ten hits against Dolf Luque, among which was Kelly's fourteenth home run, the Giants managed to score just two runs and fell to the Reds, 11–2. In their last three games, the Giants had scored one, one, and two runs.

The rainout necessitated a doubleheader on July 23, which the Giants swept to earn a split of the four games. The second game was called after five innings to allow the Reds to catch their train home to Cincinnati. (In the days when teams traveled by train, it was sometimes necessary to shorten games to allow a team to meet a train schedule. The teams would agree that no inning would start after a preset time.)[15]

On July 24 Rosy Ryan ended the Giants' long home stand with a 4–3 win over Philadelphia. George Kelly's sixteenth home run, his third in four days, extended his lead over runner-up Irish Meusel to four. (By contrast, Babe Ruth now had thirty-six.) Kelly also drove in all four New York runs, raising his league-leading total to ninety.

In addition to trailing only Kelly in home runs, Irish Meusel was having an outstanding season at the plate. Yet Meusel was noticeably absent from the Phillies' lineup in their July 24 loss to the Giants. Club owner William F. Baker had suspended his star outfielder for allegedly breaking club rules. Meusel's absence heightened already existing rumors that he and pitcher Lee Meadows would be traded to the Giants.

The story out of Philadelphia was that Meusel had been "loafing" in the field, the same charge that then manager Gavy Cravath had leveled against Dave Bancroft before trading him to New York a year earlier. Perhaps Meusel had decided to follow the same route as Bancroft, in hopes that the hapless Phillies would also ship him to the contending Giants. After all, the teams had made several deals in the past two years. Former Giants Goldie Rapp and Lee King were in the Phillies lineup, while John Monroe and pitcher Jesse Winters were on the Phillies' bench. Conversely, New York's double play combination consisted of shortstop Bancroft and second baseman Johnny Rawlings, both of whom they had obtained in trades with Philadelphia.

Having gone 11-7 on the home stand, the Giants headed to Pittsburgh trailing by three games, the same deficit they had faced a week earlier when the Pirates were at the Polo Grounds. It was again a four-game series; and as was the case in New York, if they could win all four, they would jump over the Pirates into first place.

Hope for a sweep ended in the first game. Pitching before a large and enthusiastic Forbes Field crowd, Babe Adams stymied the Giants for the second time in six days. Team captain Max Carey's three hits, Clyde Barnhart's two triples, and Rabbit Maranville's three runs batted in paced the 6–3 triumph. The loser was Douglas, who had beaten the Pirates twice earlier, including a one-hitter back on June 4.

The loss dropped the Giants to four games back; yet this day, July 25, was the day that turned the Giants from a very good team into one of the best teams of the era. They accomplished this when Phillies' owner William Baker, saying he "could no longer endure the sight of Meusel," agreed to trade him to New York.[16] In return Philadelphia received rookie outfielder Curt Walker; Butch Henline, a promising catcher playing at Indianapolis of the American Association; and $30,000. McGraw had used several center fielders this season. In addition to Walker, there had been Lee King, Eddie Brown, and the recently added Casey Stengel and Bill Cunningham. But adding Meusel to an outfield that already had George Burns and Ross Youngs made it the best one in the National League.

In another move, McGraw removed veteran left-hander Rube Benton from the active roster, despite a 5-2 record and a 2.88 earned run average. Benton was yet another of McGraw's crew of hard drinkers, and rumor had it that the Giants released him because of his failure to keep in condition, despite numerous warnings from his manager. Benton vehemently denied the allegation, as did owner Stoneham.

"It is an injustice to Benton that the erroneous report got about that he was not keeping in condition," Stoneham said. "This story was all wrong. No one has done better this year than Benton to keep in training. He violated no club rule whatsoever. In justice to him this story should be corrected. We were over the player limit and had to cut down, and Benton had not been delivering. That's all."[17]

Because Irish Meusel was a rising star and because the Phillies did not appear to get equal value in return, the trade elicited the predictable complaints from Pittsburgh and other cities around the league that McGraw was trying to buy a pennant. Some called for action from Commissioner Landis. But Landis, who in June had vetoed McGraw's

21. On July 25, 1921, the Giants made their most important addition of the year when they acquired Irish Meusel in a trade with the Philadelphia Phillies. Meusel was batting .353 for the Phillies, but owner William Baker claimed he "could no longer endure the sight of him" (Pietrusza, *Judge and Jury*, p. 185). *Private collection of Michael Mumby.*

attempts to get Heinie Groh, allowed the deal to stand. The commissioner's biographer could not justify this inconsistency. "Perhaps, like a bad umpire, Landis had decided to 'even up' on his calls."[18] Landis would admit later that "the Meusel deal never should have gone through."[19]

Two weeks earlier on July 13, Landis had witnessed the fruition of his order to McGraw and Stoneham to sell their Havana racetrack and gambling interests. And while Landis had ordered Stoneham to stop inviting Arnold Rothstein to his Polo Grounds box in this summer of '21, he did not require the Giants' owner to end his business dealings with the reputed underworld kingpin. Stoneham would even join the National League's Board of Directors in 1924 while under indictment for illegal stock dealings, revealing Landis's contrasting treatment of owners and players.[20]

Despite Landis's acquiescence to the Meusel trade, much of the rest of the baseball establishment reacted negatively. The *Sporting News*, always on the lookout for what it perceived to be a pro–New York bias among the owners, was quick to find fault with the trade. On the front page of its August 4, 1921, edition, under the headline "Reward for 'Indifference,'" it wrote,

> Mr. William Baker of the Phillies says Emil (Irish) Meusel acted so "indifferent" concerning the success of the team that he couldn't endure the sight of him any longer, so last week, a few days before the time limit for making such deals, Baker traded his great hitter and capable outfielder to the New York Giants for a rookie bench warmer and a catcher who isn't even in the big leagues.
>
> Of course nobody believes Mr. Baker when he says he had to rid the Phillies of Meusel for the team's good. If that really was the case he would be subject to severe censure for thus rewarding a bad actor. As it is, the only censure is that it aids John McGraw's Giants when they need aid so badly. As for Meusel, the innocent cause of the rumpus, it's all to his advantage any way you look at it. He goes from a club that any real ball player is ashamed to associate with to a possible contender. He is dead certain to land as high as third money. He's saying nothing in his own defense regarding Baker's charges against him—probably does not think any remarks are necessary.[21]

The issue of late-season, seemingly one-sided acquisitions would arise again a year later. Then, it would involve both New York teams and come, coincidentally, at the expense of both teams from St. Louis, the home of the *Sporting News*. In late July 1922 the Yankees and Giants were in close races with the Browns and Cardinals. On July 23 the Yanks acquired third baseman Joe Dugan from the Red Sox, and a week later, the Giants got pitcher Hugh McQuillan from the Braves.

Shortly after those deals were completed, Cardinals vice president and field manager Branch Rickey echoed the disapproval many owners and fans had about them. Speaking at a Rotary Club luncheon in St. Louis, Rickey alluded to the wealth of the two New York teams and asked, "How can those teams without unlimited resources in their deposit boxes have a chance to compete fairly?"[22] And while Landis again failed to react, allowing each of those trades to stand, the owners did take action. First, they moved the trading deadline from July 31 to June

22. Giants coach Hughie Jennings said of George Burns, "He is as good a player as ever drew on a spiked shoe. There's nothing he doesn't or cannot do well on a ball field" (Puff, "Silent George Burns," p. 123). *National Baseball Hall of Fame Library, Cooperstown, New York.*

15. Then, they changed the rules to allow each team in the league, in their reverse order in the standings, the option of claiming any player involved in a trade made after that June 15 deadline.

Irish Meusel was twenty-eight years old and in his fourth full season. An above-.300 hitter the past two seasons, he was batting .353 with twelve home runs and fifty-one runs batted in at the time of the trade. In addition to trailing only George Kelly in home runs, he was third in the league in both batting average and slugging percentage. He presented just one problem for McGraw: he was not a center fielder. Meusel lacked both the speed and the throwing arm of his younger brother Bob, who patrolled right field for the Yankees.

McGraw solved the dilemma by moving George Burns from left field to center and installing Meusel in left. Burns, the Giants' full-time left fielder since 1913, was among the outstanding defensive players of his day. In a 1920 *Sporting News* article, John B. Sheridan ranked Burns as the fourth best outfielder of all time, placing him behind only Tris Speaker, Ty Cobb, and Jimmy Sheckard. "I am one of those who think that Burns has been greatly underrated in New York and elsewhere," Sheridan wrote. "He is one of the great outfielders of all time. I have never seen him play a bad game of baseball."[23]

Playing left field was difficult at the Polo Grounds because for much of the game a player would be staring into the sun.[24] Burns overcame the problem by wearing a long-billed cap and using tinted glasses. He claimed that he could tell from the sound of the bat where the ball was heading. Based solely on that sound, he would turn his back on the ball and head to the spot where he knew it would come down.[25] At one time, the Ajax Flypaper Company had a billboard beyond the center field bleachers at the Polo Grounds that said, "Last year Giant left fielder George Burns caught 198 flys, but Ajax Flypaper caught 19 billion, 865 million, etc. flies."[26]

McGraw was never among those who underrated Burns. "He is a marvel in every department of play, a superb fielder, a wonderful thrower, a grand batsman and with few peers in baseball history as a run scorer," he said. "That boy has more natural playing strength than any outfielder I've seen in a number of years. He may never be a Ty Cobb or a Tris Speaker, but by playing strength I mean he is more proficient in

23. Three of these four Giants outfielders joined the team in July. Casey Stengel (*left*) and Irish Meusel (*right*) came in trades with the Phillies, while Bill Cunningham (*second from left*) was purchased from the Seattle Rainiers of the Pacific Coast League. Only Ross Youngs (*second from right*) was a member of the Giants on opening day. *Private collection of Michael Mumby.*

all the things required of an outfielder."[27] Coach Hughie Jennings agreed with his manager: "He is as good a player as ever drew on a spiked shoe. There's nothing he doesn't or cannot do well on a ball field."[28]

Known as Silent George, Burns was a quiet, even-tempered man who managed to play his entire career without ever being ejected from a game. Despite the difference in their temperaments, Burns was one of the few players that McGraw liked personally, calling him "one of the most valuable ball players that ever wore the uniform of the Giants."[29] The fans loved him, too, especially those who sat behind him in the left-field bleachers, which they had christened "Burnsville."

Along with praising Burns's ability, McGraw also praised him as "the easiest player to handle that ever stepped upon a field."[30] So while some veterans might have balked at switching positions, it was no surprise that Burns, among the least temperamental of men, made the switch willingly.

After losing the first game at Pittsburgh, the Giants won the next three, leaving them just one game behind the Pirates. A tenth-inning triple by Bill Cunningham, who played center field in New York's 9–8 win in the second game of the series, drove in the winning run. Whitey Glazner was the loser—it was just the second loss for the rookie against nine wins. George Kelly hit his seventeenth home run, while the teams combined to hit seven triples in a park known for its proclivity for three-baggers.

Coach Hughie Jennings deserved part of the credit for turning around this game, and perhaps the season. Midway through the contest, with the Giants looking listless and beaten, Jennings was seen exhorting the troops in the dugout. Pep talks work only if you have the talent to back them up, and this may have been the boost the Giants needed.

Meusel arrived the next day to a warm welcome from his new teammates. McGraw stationed him in left, with Burns in center, and batted him sixth, behind Frisch, Kelly, and Youngs, giving the Giants a fearsome lineup. He had a single in three at bats and stole a base, as Nehf won his thirteenth game of the season, 4–1. The Giants' outfield alignment surprised those who had expected Meusel to play right field, as his brother did, with Youngs, the best athlete of the bunch, moving to center. While McGraw did not specifically say so, the feeling around the Giants was that putting Burns in center was an experiment. If he adjusted well, he would stay there. If not, he would go back to left field, Youngs would move to center, and Meusel would play right field. Burns did adjust well, and Youngs would continue to play all his games in right.

Wilbur Cooper, the league's top winner, pitched well in suffering his fifth defeat, which dropped his record to 17-5. Youngs, with 4 hits in 4 at bats, raised his batting average to .367 and his on-base percentage to .449, second in both categories to Rogers Hornsby. Pirates owner Barney Dreyfuss protested the game, saying that umpire Bill Klem had failed to enforce the infield fly rule in the fourth inning, allowing the Giants to get a double play that ended a Pirates' rally. Dreyfuss alleged the missed call changed the complexion of the game, but league president John Heydler disallowed the protest.

Meusel made his initial impact as a Giant in the final game of the series, getting three hits in a 6–4 win. Trailing, 4–2, Frankie Frisch doubled home the tying and winning runs, as the Giants pushed across four ninth-inning runs to win their third straight game at hostile Forbes Field. Phil Douglas replaced ineffective starter Jesse Barnes with one out in the third inning and pitched through the eighth, allowing one run on five hits. Rosy Ryan closed it out with a one-two-three ninth. Glazner went the distance for Pittsburgh, getting his third loss of the season and his second of the series.

The summer heat, present throughout the series, and the importance of the games fueled the intensity of the competition. Both sides were guilty of displays of temper toward the opposition—Grimm threatened Nehf after a pitch he felt was too close to him—and toward the umpires. President Heydler suspended McGraw and Rawlings on the morning after the Giants' 9–8 win on July 26. The charge was excessive profanity directed at umpire Klem following the game. While McGraw missed a few games, coaches Jennings and Cozy Dolan ran the club. Heydler allowed McGraw to return after he went to Chicago to apologize. He was back on the bench and in charge when the Giants moved on to Cincinnati.

July 27 was an especially difficult day for McGraw. In addition to the suspension, he had to go to court to post a $3,000 bond to avoid having an Alleghany County, Pennsylvania, sheriff's deputy arrest him. The case involved a man named George Duffy, who was suing McGraw for $20,000. Duffy claimed that on June 3, during the Giants' last visit to Pittsburgh, a drunken McGraw had severely beaten him in a room at the Hotel Schenley, where the Giants had been staying.[31]

Berating umpires and getting into drunken fistfights were McGraw staples; but a little-noted incident that same day revealed another side of the Giants' manager, his loyalty and respect for players from the past. He brought Amos Rusie, the great Giants' pitcher of the 1890s, back from Seattle, where he had been working as a steamfitter, and gave him a job under Arthur Bell, the superintendent of the Polo Grounds. Rusie joined former big leaguers Jennings, Dolan, Jesse Burkett, Bill Dahlen, Art Devlin, and Dan Brouthers on the Giants' 1921 payroll.

Rusie was recognized as the hardest-throwing pitcher of his day. Historians often cite his blazing speed as the reason why the pitching mound was moved back to sixty feet and six inches in 1893. He offered these opinions on the differences between the mostly slap-hitting game of John

McGraw's playing days and the Babe Ruth–led slugging game of 1921: "Yes, things have changed considerably since then," said Rusie, who won 245 games between 1889 and 1898 and was a frequent opponent of McGraw's Baltimore Orioles. "In the old days the Polo Grounds stands were wooden affairs, not nearly so large as the steel ones now. The 'L' trains were drawn by steam engines then, and there wasn't any subway. Instead of taxis the sports used hansom cabs. But it's the same old game."[32]

But after getting his first look at Ruth, whom he called the greatest figure in baseball, Rusie was not so sure it was the same old game. "It's been nineteen years since I saw a major league game," he said. "The game surely has taken long strides. Back in my day we had some heavy hitters, but none of them could hold a candle to Ruth. I refer to Wagner, Lajoie, and Ed Delahanty."[33]

Then and now, most players talk about the great players of their day as being better, or at least as good as, the current players. Rusie was an exception to the rule in his praise of Ruth. But then again, neither Rusie nor anyone else had ever seen a player quite like the Babe.

On the evening of July 28, after the smoke and fury of the four games in Pittsburgh had cleared, the Pirates' lead over New York had dwindled to a single game. Both teams had 34 losses, but the Pirates had 60 wins and the Giants had 58. Boston was now six back. After adding Rawlings and Meusel, the Giants felt they had no weaknesses and expected they would soon pass the Pirates and go on to win the pennant.

NL STANDINGS AT CLOSE OF PLAY OF JULY 28, 1921

TEAM	G	W	L	T	PCT	GB
Pittsburgh Pirates	94	60	34	0	.638	-
New York Giants	92	58	34	0	.630	1.0
Boston Braves	90	52	38	0	.578	6.0
Brooklyn Dodgers	95	49	46	0	.516	11.5
St. Louis Cardinals	91	44	47	0	.484	14.5
Chicago Cubs	91	40	51	0	.440	18.5
Cincinnati Reds	91	38	53	0	.418	20.5
Philadelphia Phillies	90	26	64	0	.289	32.0

17 "You can't play your outfielders in the middle of the next block"

After beating the Athletics on July 5, the Yankees headed to Chicago to begin their second western road swing of the season. They would not meet the league-leading Indians for another two weeks, at the end of their trip. The Yanks stopped off for exhibition games in Rochester and Pittsburgh on their way out west. They lost both games, but Miller Huggins played few of his regulars and started second-line pitchers. The Yanks still drew huge crowds because one star who did play was the one fans wanted to see, Babe Ruth.

In Chicago the Yankees continued to have difficulty with the lowly White Sox. As the *New York Times* put it, "The Yanks happened along, and the mackerel suddenly became a whale."[1] Chicago's little lefty, Dickie Kerr, beat them for a fourth time this season on July 8, 4–1, to end New York's eight-game winning streak. To add to the embarrassment, Kerr stole home, an exceedingly rare accomplishment for a pitcher.[2]

The next day, Carl Mays was sailing along with an 8–0 lead, when he suddenly weakened in the seventh.[3] Though the Sox had closed to 9–5, Mays was still pitching at the start of the ninth. He gave up two more runs and retired only one Chicago batter before Miller Huggins finally replaced him. Waite Hoyt was brilliant in relief, but Chicago finally pushed across the winning run in the sixteenth inning.

A manager staying with his ace after he seemingly had lost his stuff was not unusual in 1921. Brooklyn manager Wilbert Robinson noted how many pitchers were blowing leads late this year. "Managers hate to show lack of confidence in a good pitcher. For that reason too many of them are permitted to stay and take their beatings," he said.[4] Robinson, who had a reputation of being one of the best handlers of pitchers, readily admitted that he was guilty of this himself. The concept of bringing in a fresh reliever to protect a lead was simply not accepted in the early 1920s.

On Sunday, July 10, Red Faber bested the Yanks for his seventeenth win of the season, more than half the White Sox's total at the time of thirty-three. More than sixty years later, he would receive the American League's retroactive Cy Young Award for 1921.[5] The Yanks did salvage the final game of the series, thanks to one of Rip Collins's best games of the year, a five-hitter. With home run number thirty-two, Ruth now had connected in every American League park this season.

As they left Chicago, the Yankees trailed the Indians by three games. Cleveland was proving to be an elusive target. Even a New York paper acknowledged the scrappiness of the defending champions. "It is the gamest aggregation of ballplayers ever banded together, and it is led by a manager of more personal magnetism than any leader in the game, save John Joseph McGraw of the Giants."[6]

The Tribe desperately needed to shore up their pitching, with the struggles of Duster Mails and what one paper called "The Mystery of Jim Bagby," who was now under the care of a chiropractor.[7]

On July 5 Allan Sothoron won his first game as an Indian. St. Louis had released him early this season; and after an ineffective stint in Boston, so had the Red Sox. Tris Speaker and Cleveland coach Jimmy McAllister had spotted a flaw in Sothoron's delivery, wherein he was tipping his pitches.[8] They felt they could correct this and also rectify his defensive weakness of throwing away bunts that he fielded, so the Indians had claimed him in late June.

After the Chicago series, critics in the New York press were quick to pounce on Miller Huggins yet again. In trying to explain why the Yanks lost to weak teams, George Daley wrote in the *New York World* that the team was suffering from "the lack of inspiring leadership. . . . He is without the personal magnetism so necessary in holding his men on a level they are quite capable of reaching."[9] Huggins also was without the patience to curry favor with reporters and fans alike.

Because Huggins was not a well man, perhaps these personal attacks and the recent losses affected his health. An attack of blood poisoning (as evidenced by a boil on his cheek, which was successfully lanced) forced him to take a leave of absence.[10] The *New York Evening Journal* ominously reported that Huggins was a very run-down and sick man who had not responded well to treatment.[11] Just eight years later, Huggins would develop a boil under his eye, resulting in erysipelas (blood poisoning) that would cause his death.

Before the final Chicago game, Huggins turned over the team to his coach, Charley O'Leary, and to his veteran shortstop, Roger Peckinpaugh. When manager Frank Chance had quit the Yankees in disgust late in the 1914 season, Peckinpaugh, who had joined the team the year before, took over as manager for the final twenty games of the season. Twenty-three years old at the time, he remains today the youngest Major League manager ever.[12] He never again received serious consideration, however, as the team's regular manager. The new Yankee owners were in the market for a manager both in 1915, when they bought the team, and again three years later, when they were looking for a man to replace Donovan. In both cases, they turned to managers with more experience.

Peckinpaugh, known as a player's player, had remained a respected informal clubhouse leader for the Yankees.[13] Now, seven years later, he took over the club in Huggins's absence. (Accounts had him, not O'Leary, running the ballclub.) The team's turnaround just happened to coincide with Huggins's taking a leave. "The club began to play as though it took some interest in the game, played faster, stronger, more aggressive ball than at any other time all season."[14]

Under Peckinpaugh the Yankees immediately won eight games in a row, sweeping both the Browns and the Tigers. On July 12 and 13 in St. Louis, the Yankees hammered two of their jinxes: Dixie Davis and Urban Shocker. In late May, when Davis had walked Ruth twice, St. Louis fans booed their pitcher. This time he pitched to the Babe and paid the price. Ruth homered against him twice.

The next day, Mays beat Shocker in an 11–1 massacre, and John E. Wray wryly noted in the *St. Louis Post-Dispatch* that the Yankee pitcher was "living proof that the lively ball in the hands of a good pitcher can still make the enemy play dead."[15]

In Detroit, fans were still buzzing over the mammoth home run that Harry Heilmann had hit earlier in the month off Boston's Joe Bush. A number of papers had reported that the drive had traveled 610 feet.[16] The other major topic of conversation was framed in a *Sporting News* editorial: Will Ty Cobb swallow his pride and direct his pitchers to walk Ruth? Will Detroit fans agree with such a strategy of not letting the Babe hit?[17]

Cobb himself would be available only for pinch-hitting. He had somehow spiked himself while sliding during the June 30 game in Cleveland.

After New York won the first two contests, both close affairs, the third game, played on July 18, was a New York blowout. Howard Ehmke had already walked Ruth four times (the Babe now had eighty-five walks for the season) when the Babe came up in the eighth. With the Yankees ahead, 8–1, Cobb let reliever Bert Cole—who had "more courage than Ehmke or less sense"—pitch to Ruth. The result was a piece of baseball history, "the master mauler's masterpiece."[18] It was arguably the longest home run Babe Ruth ever hit.[19] It cleared the center-field fence and was variously reported as having traveled anywhere from 560 feet to 610 feet and even longer. Miller Huggins, usually a man of few words and mostly understated comments, called it "the gosh-darnedest wallop that ever was made, any time, anywhere."[20]

In the final game with the Tigers, Ruth exhibited his versatility, showing a very different side of his game—his base running—as "he dashed as much as a man of his tonnage can dash."[21] He scored the winning run for the Yankees' eighth straight victory this way: He singled and took second when outfielder Chick Shorten bobbled the ball. Taking a big lead off second, Ruth drew a throw from catcher Eddie Ainsmith. It was wild; and the Babe came around to score, crashing into Ainsmith, who could not hold onto the ball. Ruth was not the only one to use speed and daring on the base paths. In the second inning, Chick Fewster scored all the way from second on a bunt.

The Yankees had completed the sweep and were now 11-1 against the Tigers this season. The *New York Globe and Commercial Advertiser* noted that while Cobb resented losing, his Tigers resented their manager's fiery methods. "Their morale is shot to pieces and cannot be restored except through a change of leadership."[22]

On July 16 nineteenth-century player and former manager and executive Arthur Irwin died at the age of sixty-three, under perhaps the murkiest and strangest circumstances of any man in Major League Baseball history. He had a long and rich career—as an infielder in the 1880s (when he popularized the padded glove), manager of Major and Minor League teams (including the New York Giants in 1896 and the Rochester Hustlers in 1919, where he managed George Kelly), and Yankee scout

(1908–12) and business manager (1913–14).[23] Sam Crane claimed that Irwin had discovered more future stars than any other scout.[24]

Irwin is the only Major League ballplayer whose death did not occur in any country. He was diagnosed with a terminal illness just a few weeks earlier and resigned as the Hartford Senators manager. (Probably cancer, the illness had caused him to lose sixty pounds in the previous few weeks.) Shortly before Irwin received his diagnosis, a promising New York youngster named Lew Lewis had played twelve games for Irwin's Eastern League team. "Lew Lewis" was actually the alias of Lou Gehrig, used to protect his college eligibility at Columbia University. Earlier in the spring, Irwin had arranged for Gehrig to have a tryout with the New York Giants, but John McGraw was too preoccupied with other matters to focus much on the youngster. It was then that Irwin persuaded Gehrig to join his Hartford team.[25]

On the night of July 16, Irwin fell overboard the steamship *Calvin Austin*, which was heading from New York to Boston. An apparent suicide, his body was never recovered. But there was more to his tragic demise. "Death, which often places an eternal seal on life's mysteries, reversed its role last week," wrote the *New York Globe and Commercial Advertiser*.[26] The shocking tabloid story of Irwin's dual life soon emerged. He had two longtime families, one in Boston (a wife and three children, including a thirty-seven-year-old son) and one in New York (a wife and a twenty-four-year-old son). Neither family was aware of the other, and both apparently accepted the explanation that a baseball manager and scout is on the road a lot, even during the off-season.

Upon arriving in Cleveland on July 20, the Yankees were just one game out of first place. They had won sixteen of their past nineteen games, including the eight straight with Huggins on the sidelines. Huggins's detractors now thought they could force a change at the helm; they were vocal as never before. In the *New York Tribune* W. J. Macbeth wrote, "Writers with the club say that under Peckinpaugh it was one of the most formidable machines ever seen. . . . It is up to Huggins to make good in like fashion or gracefully retire."[27] Even Babe Ruth (or his ghostwriter) chimed in with praise in his syndicated column: "Unlimited credit belongs to Roger Peckinpaugh for the way he handled the club during the absence of Miller Huggins."[28]

24. Yankee co-owner Til Huston enjoyed nights on the town with New York sportswriters and Yankee players, especially Babe Ruth. In the summer of 1921, Huston—who never wanted to hire Miller Huggins as manager—was the source of newspaper stories of dissension within the Yankee clubhouse. *Private collection of Steve Steinberg.*

Hugh Fullerton contributed to the controversy. He wrote that there was a good chance the Yankees would replace Huggins. He explained that unnamed "experts" feel that Huggins is "a 'wet blanket' sort of manager whose manner and actions tend to discourage the players, while Peckinpaugh is an inspiring leader." Yet Fullerton tried to maintain a balanced approach, noting that Huggins deserved a fair chance to succeed.[29]

Some papers reported that players unhappy with Huggins would meet with Colonel Huston. As Frank Graham wrote in his Yankee history, "When Hug admonished the players for some of their pranks off the field, they simply laughed at him. . . . They had reason to believe that any shackles placed on them by Huggins would be struck off by Cap [Huston]."[30] The insurgents would request that Peckinpaugh be installed as the team's regular manager. Ironically, Peckinpaugh was loyal to Huggins, despite the fact that he served as a rallying point for the insurgents.

Walter Trumbull, sports editor of the *New York Herald*, was one writer who did not rush to judgment. He wrote that the Yankees had a number of temperamental players, and he recognized the difficult and delicate situation that both Huggins and the team were in. "It is easy enough to say that a real manager would handle the trouble makers, but the only way to handle some of them would be to get rid of them, and breaking up a club in the heat of the race doesn't win pennants."[31]

In the meantime, Huggins did return to manage the Yankees as they met the Indians for the first of two four-game series in the next thirteen days. In the opener, they again handily beat Cleveland's ace, Stan Coveleski, 7–1. New York (55-31) climbed into a virtual tie with Cleveland (56-32) for first place. Years later, Indians pitcher George Uhle revealed that Coveleski was tipping his pitches in 1921.[32] At least, the Yankees seemed to have figured him out.

Frank Baker knocked in five runs, and the usually taciturn Yankee third baseman was almost gloating after the game. "We have the Indians whipped. . . . We showed their other pitchers what is in store for them," he said.[33]

The thirty-five-year-old Baker was in the twilight of his career. He had led the American League in home runs for four straight seasons, starting with 1911. Baker was a reluctant hero, a consummate professional who did his job quietly. He was not a flashy player, nor did he relish the spotlight. One New York newspaper wrote that he "hasn't enough ginger to keep him warm even when the thermometer is soaring around the century mark."[34]

More than once with the Yankees, Baker had considered retiring to his farm and family on Maryland's Eastern Shore, before signing his contract. His Hamlet-like ambivalence became an annual rite of spring: would he give up baseball and return to private life?[35] While Baker had some solid seasons for the Yankees after joining them at age thirty, he never came close to his dominant offensive years with the Athletics.[36] Though Baker appeared to be somewhat slow and awkward, he was still a terrific third baseman, as reflected in his fielding numbers, including those he garnered with New York.[37]

On July 21 the Indians returned the favor and blasted the Yankees out of first place, 17–8, in a game that featured an amazing sixteen doubles.

Tris Speaker hit his league-leading thirty-sixth two-bagger in the game. Cleveland shortstop Joe Sewell hit three of them—in his first full season, the Alabaman would hit .318 with a .412 on-base percentage. Years later, he would win the American League's retroactive Rookie of the Year Award.[38] The win was even sweeter because it came against Mays, whom the Tribe knocked out in the third inning. The teams then had an odd, scheduled off day in the middle of the series; and the Yanks played an exhibition game in Akron.

In the third game of the series, on Saturday, Allan Sothoron pitched a three-hit gem, a 3–0 victory that was a testament to Speaker's judgment and to the veteran hurler's moxie. It was a bitterly fought contest, as the Yankees repeatedly tried to rattle Sothoron, including the use of personal taunts.[39]

Sothoron had a reputation for throwing an assortment of freak pitches, not simply the spitball. Cleveland sportswriter Ed Bang had noted in early 1920, "What this bird didn't know about doctoring the ball wasn't worthwhile."[40] Bang considered him the king of American League trick twirlers, even more of a master than Chicago's Eddie Cicotte had been. The Yankees challenged almost every one of Sothoron's pitches, claiming he was throwing, among other tricks, an emery ball.

Umpire Brick Owens found nothing wrong with the balls. And the more the Yankees razzed the Cleveland pitcher, the better he pitched. There were few Yankee highlights. In the first inning, Ruth hit the ball so hard off the right-field wall that it bounced back to first baseman Doc Johnston, who threw Ruth out trying for a double.[41]

The Yankees did manage a split in the series, as Bob Shawkey won for the second time in the four games. Again Frank Baker was the hitting star, coming through with a bases-loaded single after Ruth was intentionally passed. Carl Mays shut the door with two innings of scoreless relief—the third time he finished for Shawkey on this road trip.

As the Yankees headed home after a successful 10-5 road trip, they stopped in Cincinnati on July 25 for an exhibition game against the Reds. Once again it was a limited lineup, as Huggins sent pitchers Mays, Hoyt, Shawkey, and Quinn ahead to New York. The 20,000 fans got what they came for, and more: Babe Ruth hit, not one, but two long home runs, one of which cleared the center-field fence. Both came off former Cleveland left-hander Fritz Coumbe.

Two years earlier almost to the day (July 18, 1919), a Ruth home run off Coumbe had led directly to a managerial change. Lee Fohl was then the skipper of the Indians. They were leading late in the game, 7–3, when the Red Sox loaded the bases. Fohl brought Coumbe into the game. Apparently, center fielder Tris Speaker, whose suggestions Fohl took on a regular basis, had signaled for Fohl to bring in a different pitcher. When Coumbe gave up a bases-loaded home run to the Babe, which led to an 8–7 Red Sox win, Fohl had managed his last game as an Indian. He soon resigned, and Speaker took over as manager. One of his first moves was to send Coumbe to the Minors.

The Yankees returned to the Polo Grounds on July 27 and split two games with the Browns. Shocker won the first, holding "the so-called 'Murderers' Row' spellbound," wrote Damon Runyon, "with a sling so slow you could almost see the elastic in the ball as it gradually eased its way over the plate."[42] Carl Mays once again faltered late, giving up four runs in the last two innings.

Babe Ruth was hitless; but Shocker walked him intentionally two times, which brought razzes from the crowd. Earlier in July, the Babe (or his ghostwriter) had a feature in *Collier's* magazine entitled, "Why I Hate to Walk." He concluded by saying that he hoped the fans, who wanted action, would keep pitchers honest with "that humiliating weapon of torture—the razzberry."[43] Yet after this game, Browns manager Lee Fohl matter-of-factly explained that while the fans wanted to see Ruth hit, his Browns were trying to win games and move up in the standings. He went on to explain, "Anytime you give that big fellow a good ball he is going to knock it right out of the park. You have a chance with almost any other player in the world except Ruth. You can't play your outfielders in the middle of the next block, and therefore, one must protect himself."[44]

Before the next game, Browns starter Dixie Davis bet Eddie Bennett, the little Yankee mascot, a suit of clothes that he would go the distance.[45] But Davis did not survive New York's four-run third inning. The Yankees won, 6–0, behind Waite Hoyt's four-hitter, and Bennett won his suit. Just a few days earlier, perhaps in response to the disappointment expressed by some New York sportswriters about Hoyt's less-than-spectacular season, Miller Huggins was raving about his young pitcher, "one of the greatest prospects in the league. I wouldn't swap him for another pitcher in the league, and I bar none."[46]

Hoyt was just shy of his sixteenth birthday and still at Brooklyn's Erasmus Hall High School when the Giants signed him in August 1915. The pitching prodigy had earned the nickname "the Schoolboy Wonder."[47] In the next few years, he moved around to a number of Minor League teams and appeared in only one game for the Giants, pitching one inning in 1918.[48] Frustrated over not getting more opportunities with the Giants, Hoyt had some run-ins with McGraw. After refusing to report to his assigned Minor League teams in both 1918 and 1919, Hoyt quit Organized Baseball and joined a shipbuilding team, the Baltimore Dry Docks.

He ended up in Boston late in 1919 after Barrow, who was then the Red Sox manager, acquired his rights from New Orleans and promised to use him as a starter. Injuries had limited him to only twenty-two starts during his two seasons in Boston. While at the time of the trade Hoyt seemed "unpredictable at best, and unmanageable at worst," it was Hoyt's talent and potential that drove Barrow and Huggins to acquire him.[49]

Ruth had only a single in that 6–0 shutout of the Browns, but it was the start of what would be the longest consecutive-game hitting streak of his career, twenty-six games. Coincidentally, Ruth was in the midst of his longest home run drought of the season, eleven days, from July 19 to July 29.[50]

Less than a week after the Yankees and Indians met in Cleveland, the two teams squared off in the Polo Grounds. On Saturday July 30 before more than 35,000 fans, Stan Coveleski was sharp against the Yankees for the first time this year, twirling a seven-hitter for his seventeenth win of the season, as the Indians cruised, 16–1. Bob Shawkey, who had already beaten Coveleski twice this year, was knocked out in the third inning. He gave up eight runs and endured booing by the impatient New York fans. William B. Hanna wondered why Huggins did not pull Shawkey earlier. "He had nothing." Yet Hanna went on to criticize the fans' lack of sportsmanship, noting that the razzing of the home team was a practice "as contemptible as it is prevalent."[51]

Coveleski was an extremely quiet man of Polish heritage. He had averaged more than twenty-two wins for the Indians the past four seasons. He had a reputation as a control pitcher, explaining, "Why should I throw eight or nine balls to get a man out when I got away with three or four."[52] Ironically, he led the league in strikeouts in 1920 with 133.

He came from the Pennsylvania coal-mining town of Shamokin, not far from where fellow spitballers Ed Walsh and Jack Quinn, as well as Hughie Jennings, had grown up. For these men, whose families knew only the dangerous work of the mines, baseball was more than an enjoyable and somewhat lucrative career. It could be quite literally a lifesaver. As Coveleski explained to Larry Ritter more than forty years later, "There was nothing strange in those days about a twelve-year-old Polish kid in the mines for 72 hours a week at a nickel an hour. What was strange was that I ever got out of there."[53]

The Yankees closed out July the next day behind Carl Mays's 12–2 two-hitter, his sixteenth victory. Mays helped his own cause by knocking in four runs. His sixth-inning double knocked Allan Sothoron out of the game. The Babe greeted reliever Ray Caldwell with his thirty-eighth home run later that inning. Shaking off a recent leg injury, Speaker made a spectacular catch of a sinking liner on the wet grass, and his momentum carried him into a somersault. The play brought the New York crowd to its feet, cheering.

New York then beat Jim Bagby in the third and final game (scheduled as a four-game set, the final game of this series would be rained out). Hoyt again went the distance; and Frank Baker had the hot hand with the bat, smacking a double and a home run. George Uhle pitched a perfect final two innings for the Indians, and some in Cleveland's press (as well as in the New York papers) wondered why Speaker had not started Uhle in the first place.[54]

Uhle, who came to the Indians straight from starring on the Cleveland sandlots, was one of the best-hitting pitchers of all time, with a .289 career batting average. He did not start any of the seven games against New York in July through August 1, nor would he start against New York in their other three meetings in August. Yet he had beaten the Yankees in May and had pitched well against them in June. He started twenty-eight games in 1921 and won sixteen. Years later, Tris Speaker acknowledged that he should have started Uhle more often against the Yankees in 1921 and took full responsibility for those decisions.[55]

The Yankees drew more than 80,000 fans for the three-game July-August set, despite damp and drizzly weather on Sunday. The Yankees were drawing extremely well in 1921; on the road, they played to many crowds overflowing onto the field. They also had a number of sellouts at home. While their 1921 attendance was a few thousand fans behind their numbers from 1920, that previous year had been spectacular. Sam Murphy of the *New York Evening Mail* had noted in 1920 that big crowds did not concern the magnates as much as did the thousands turned away at the ballpark gates. Yet unlike other clubs, Murphy pointed out, the Yankees (and the Giants, for that matter) refused to let overflow crowds onto the field, at the cost of a considerable loss of revenue. The two Yankee colonels, wrote Murphy, had decided that "crowds on the playing field are better for the boxoffice than the game."[56]

The Yankees again would lead the Major Leagues in attendance by a large margin in 1921 with 1,230,696 attendees, compared to 1,289,422 in 1920. The Giants would finish second with 973,477, up from 929,609 in 1920. One wonders just how high the New York teams' attendance would have been had they allowed fans onto the field.[57]

By taking two of three from the Indians, the Yankees had drawn to within a game of first place on the evening of August 1. At 59-35, they had played four fewer games than the 62-36 Indians. Washington was in third place, ten games back.

Both New York teams had to feel good about their chances if their pitching could hold up. For the Yankees, Ruth continued to feast on opposing pitching; he had gone 6-9 in the Cleveland series (including two home runs and a triple), along with four walks. As Chet Thomas, who caught for the Indians during Steve O'Neill's injury in the spring, said, "I am not so certain now that Ruth is human. At least he does things that you couldn't expect a mere batter with two arms and legs to do. I can't explain him. Nobody can explain him. He just exists."[58]

AL STANDINGS AT CLOSE OF PLAY OF AUGUST 1, 1921

TEAM	G	W	L	T	PCT	GB
Cleveland Indians	98	62	36	0	.633	-
New York Yankees	94	59	35	0	.628	1.0
Washington Senators	103	54	48	1	.529	10.0
Detroit Tigers	101	48	52	1	.480	15.0
St. Louis Browns	95	44	51	0	.463	16.5
Boston Red Sox	95	43	52	0	.453	17.5
Chicago White Sox	97	43	54	0	.443	18.5
Philadelphia Athletics	99	36	61	2	.371	25.5

18 Lay off Huggins and Hope Nothing Happens to the Babe

As July wound down, the fortunes of both New York teams were on the upswing. John McGraw had addressed the weaknesses on his team with the additions of Johnny Rawlings and Irish Meusel. Now Miller Huggins had done the same, bolstering the Yankees' shaky outfield defense with the acquisition of Elmer Miller, the mystery center fielder he had been pursuing. The deal was a complex three-way transaction among the Yankees, Miller's St. Paul Saints of the American Association, and the Boston Red Sox.[1] The Yanks sent Ping Bodie, approaching age thirty-four, to the Red Sox, who in turn sent outfielder Tim Hendryx to the Saints.[2] St. Paul also got Yankee pitcher Tom Sheehan and Yankee outfielder Tom Connelly.[3]

The thirty-one-year-old Miller had a reputation as a fine outfielder, but he had not yet matched his Minor League batting success at the Major League level.[4] Playing with the Yankees for parts of four seasons (1915–18), he had averaged only .233. The Yankees had acquired him from Mobile in 1915, where he was known as the Ty Cobb of the Southern League, stealing thirty-eight bases and hitting .326. The Yanks sent him to Baltimore of the International League for the first half of the 1916 season, where he was an immediate sensation, batting .338. For the past three seasons, he had been with St. Paul and had hit well above .300 each year. Some wondered if Miller was one of those players who hit well at all levels except the Majors.[5] Questions centered on his lack of confidence at the plate as well as his inability to hit a big league curve ball, the bane of many an unsuccessful Major Leaguer.

There never was any question about Miller's fielding, which would soon earn him the nicknames "Ball Hawk" and "Antelope" in the New York press. "Speaker doesn't cover much more ground than Miller," wrote one New York paper.[6] Miller arrived not a moment too soon. Chick Fewster had lost track of fly balls in a couple of key games in

25. Elmer Miller returned to the Yankees after an absence of almost three years and filled a gaping hole in the team's outfield defense. His outstanding fielding was instrumental in the Yankees winning the pennant. *Private collection of Dennis Goldstein.*

late July, and he had been suffering from both dizzy spells and stomach problems.[7]

The Miller deal also marked the close of Ping Bodie's Major League career. His 1920 season had ended in early September when he broke his ankle in an exhibition game in Pittsburgh. He had batted only .172 with no home runs for the Yankees this season. One of the game's most colorful characters, Bodie refused to report to Boston.[8] But the deal was not contingent on Bodie's signing and still went through. Instead, he returned to the West Coast, where he would play for the Vernon Tigers of the Pacific Coast League the next two seasons.[9]

Meanwhile, a surprising postscript to the disappointing 1918 trade that brought Duffy Lewis and Ernie Shore to the Yankees from the Red Sox was emerging. In mid-May 1921 that same Vernon club returned Shore to the Yankees, who then released him. He had never come close to recapturing the magic he had with Boston from 1914 to 1917, even though he was still only thirty years old.

In mid-June the Washington Senators released Lewis, who was hitting an anemic .186. "The rise of Lewis was meteoric. His fall was swift and sudden," wrote the *New York Sun*.[10] Lewis also made his way to the Pacific Coast League, where he found the success that had eluded Shore. As a member of the Salt Lake City Bees, Lewis began to feast on the league's pitching. Lewis hit safely in thirty straight games and would have a .403 batting average in that rarified air in 1921. He took over as player-manager of the Bees for the following three years.[11]

The Yankees were also hoping to land veteran left-handed pitcher Jim "Hippo" Vaughn for the stretch run.[12] Vaughn had been a teammate of Jack Quinn on the 1910 Yankees, when Quinn won eighteen games and Vaughn thirteen. Both men faltered in 1911; and by late 1912 they found themselves in the Minors, Vaughn at Kansas City and Quinn at Rochester.

In mid-July 1921 Vaughn walked out on his Chicago Cubs and signed a deal with a semipro team in Beloit, Wisconsin. A few days later, Commissioner Landis put him on the ineligible list, ending any possibility of a deal with the Yankees. Vaughn landed on the list for playing with a Beloit team that had played against outlaws, players whom Landis had declared ineligible.[13]

Early August also saw the ebb and flow of the 1921 pennant races briefly and dramatically interrupted. On the second day of the month, a jury found the eight Chicago Black Sox not guilty of charges of conspiring to lose ball games in the 1919 World Series. Yet the next day, Landis banned them from Organized Baseball. In his famous statement, he declared, "Regardless of the verdict of juries, no player that throws a ballgame, no player that entertains proposals or promises to throw a game, no player that sits in a conference with a bunch of crooked players and gamblers where the ways and means of throwing games are discussed, and does not promptly tell his club about it, will ever play professional baseball. . . . Just keep in mind that regardless of the verdict of juries, baseball is entirely competent to protect itself against the crooks both inside and outside the game."[14]

Hugh Fullerton, one of the few reporters who spoke out about the scandal shortly after the 1919 World Series ended, now saluted the judge as the savior of baseball, who was determined to save the game regardless of the economic costs to the owners.[15] Yet surely even Fullerton realized that by narrowing his primary focus to this one incident (the

1919 Series) and these eight men, Landis was solidifying "the mythology of this episode as being aberrational, even inexplicable."[16] This public relations masterstroke enabled baseball to put aside this one event and continue to move forward. As Charles Alexander wrote in his history of the national pastime, "If somewhat self-contradictory, frequently despotic and nearly always arrogant and bombastic, Landis was also probably indispensable under the circumstances."[17]

A few sportswriters took a broader view. Sid Mercer put the Black Sox affair in perspective and said the game would survive: "A hundred years from now they will be doing the same thing. The times change, but not the men."[18] William McGeehan added his social commentary, that fans should not be surprised or outraged, since sports reflects society as a whole: "The trouble lies in the fact that we make demigods of our professional athletes."[19]

Whether Mercer and McGeehan could be called cynics or realists, they were in the overwhelming minority in the press. Virtually all newspapers hailed Landis's action as the end of a sorry chapter. Landis understood the power of the press and equated the importance of sportswriters with that of the ballplayers themselves.[20] He, in turn, had enormous influence to shape public opinion on baseball matters. In the National Agreement of January 1921, which laid out the commissioner's powers, the owners pledged loyalty to him and agreed not to criticize him in public.[21]

Baseball also had the benefit of Babe Ruth's prodigious hitting feats. His timing could not have been better for the national pastime. As the Black Sox affair unfolded, Ruth's surging popularity drowned out the negative news. He was not only changing the way the game was being played, he was becoming the face of the game and its savior in the minds of many.[22]

The Yankees hosted the Tigers, starting on August 4; and for the first time this season, Detroit won a series from New York, taking two of three games. Ty Cobb celebrated his return to the lineup (having recovered from his spike wound) with a triple and a home run in an 8–3 win over Bob Shawkey. Cobb accused Shawkey of throwing an illegal pitch in the game, delaying the proceedings and irritating the New York hurler, just before Cobb hit the triple.[23] An added feature for the fans was a pregame contest between Babe Ruth and Harold Lentz, the world champion surf caster. The Babe would try to hit a baseball farther than Lentz could cast a four-ounce slug. Both men had reached at least 450 feet in the past.[24]

The next day, Carl Mays and catcher Wally Schang led New York to a win. Schang's three-run inside-the-park home run over Cobb's head in the eighth inning broke the game open. One New York daily called the Yankee backstop the game's smartest catcher on the base paths.[25] The steady Schang had already anchored two World Series winners, the 1913 Athletics and the 1918 Red Sox; and he brought experience and strong defense behind the plate to the Yankees. He also added a powerful bat to the lineup. He would hit .316 in 1921, his third straight season above .300. Schang would have one of the league's highest on-base percentages this year, achieving a .428 mark.

Yet in spite of his well-rounded game, Schang garnered remarkably few headlines after he left the Athletics. Fred Lieb called him the best catcher on the two New York clubs: "We prefer Schang [to Snyder and Smith, the Giants' catchers] because he is faster than Snyder, and on the whole more aggressive and active. There are a lot of persons who consider Schang the most valuable player on the Yankees."[26]

The rubber match of the series was a thriller, won by the Tigers, 9–8, despite two dramatic Yankee rallies. Elmer Miller had arrived at the Polo Grounds for the game but could not play until Hendryx reported to St. Paul. Ruth's three-run homer in the sixth, his thirty-ninth, brought New York back to within a run; it would be his first of six home runs in eight games. Back-to-back triples by Frank Baker and Bob Meusel in the eighth pulled the teams even at eight. But in the ninth inning, Ruth muffed Chick Shorten's bases-loaded fly that let the go-ahead run score. The *New York Tribune* wrote that the Babe was so intent on throwing the ball home that he lost focus on catching it first.[27]

Ruth was not the only Yankee who had problems in the field this day. Chick Fewster misjudged yet another ball, Cobb's fly that went for a triple in the seventh.[28] Wally Pipp misplayed one ground ball and showed poor judgment on another by trying to make the out at first base himself, rather than throwing to his pitcher. Back in July one sportswriter had noted that the Yankees first baseman was having more and more trouble with grounders. Pipp was "pitifully weak on batted balls. . . . He seems to live in constant dread of making errors."[29]

Wally Pipp was the first major signing of the new Yankee owners in early 1915, and he immediately paid dividends. Pipp led the American League in home runs in both 1916 and 1917. Like his counterpart at the other end of the infield, Frank Baker, Pipp had been a very proficient fielder, though in 1921 he was starting to cover less ground.[30] He was also similar to Baker in another regard: Pipp went about his work without flair. "He possesses every quality that goes to make a star player excepting the 'old pep.'"[31] Pipp would occupy first base for more than a decade, until Lou Gehrig won the job from him in 1925.

The Indians dropped three straight in Washington on August 4 (in a doubleheader) and August 5, when Senators pitchers held them to only a run in each game. Walter Johnson, who was getting stronger as the season wore on, won the first contest; and the Senators' winning streak reached eleven games the next day. They solidified their hold on third place, only seven games out of first. The Yankees moved into first place by a half game on the fifth. The next day, when they lost the final game to Detroit and the Indians beat the Senators in their final game, the top two teams traded places. It was becoming increasingly clear that the American League race was going to be tight the rest of the way.

Chicago was the next visitor to the Polo Grounds, and Rip Collins and Bob Shawkey tossed back-to-back shutouts. Collins's one-hitter bested Red Faber, 2–0, in a rain-shortened game that went five innings. Elmer Miller made his debut and was impressive as the lead-off hitter, with a walk and a hit. He also made a fine catch of an Eddie Collins drive. Eddie Collins was having another superb year, showing few signs of slowing down at age thirty-four. The team's scrappy manager, Kid Gleason, made it clear that his depleted club was conceding nothing: "Whoever wins this here pennant will have to make a fight of it so far as the Sox are concerned."[32]

Red Faber would play his entire twenty-year career in a White Sox uniform, with this one exception. The team's uniforms were not loaded onto the train from Boston, and the White Sox wore the Yankees' gray road attire for the game. The smallest men on the club, Ray Schalk and Dickie Kerr, looked odd in the larger Yankee uniforms.

Miller's arrival allowed Fewster, whose mental and physical health had been poor, to take a break. One New York paper suggested that he take time off to rest his body and relieve the strain he seemed to be under.[33] Jacob Ruppert suggested that he go to Maine and forget baseball for the rest of the year.[34] Fewster did not take him up on the offer.

The Yankees gave up the momentum generated by the Collins and Shawkey shutouts when they dropped the next two games to the Sox. Chicago beat the Yankees' top two hurlers, Hoyt and Mays; in one of the games, Dickie Kerr won his fifth victory of the season over the Yanks.

In the fifth and final game of the series on August 10, two Frank Baker home runs and Ruth's forty-second drove the Yankees to victory. Baker had a huge day—he also singled and walked twice, scoring three times and knocking in five runs. Just a couple of days earlier, Damon Runyon had marveled at the condition of this aging slugger: "He is always in perfect physical condition. He does not smoke. He does not drink. He eats simple food and plenty of it. At thirty-five, the age when the average player is about through, Baker is in his prime."[35]

The Babe was also showing his versatility. As he had done two days earlier, he both bunted for a base hit and homered. He took pleasure in fouling up defenses that were stacked to the right side of the infield. "Imagine a bunt trickling down the third base foul line," he said with a relish, "with a team in that formation."[36]

The Chicago series showed yet again how unpredictable the Yankees' ballclub could be—after this series, New York's season record against the Sox was 7-10. "Good one day, bad the next. Like a million dollars for one hour, like a Mexican cent the next sixty minutes. The word steadiness isn't in their vocabulary," wrote the *New York World*.[37] On August 10 the *New York American* reported that one of the Yankee owners (presumably Huston) soon might remove Miller Huggins as manager. The paper noted that Huggins had developed only two players on the club (Meusel and Collins) and that this was a veteran team that needed a different kind of leader.

One paper repeated a quip by one of the Yankee players that suggested Huggins's aloofness and lack of warmth. Playing with the manager names Pat Moran of the Cincinnati Reds and Kid Gleason of the

26. Miller Huggins was not a well man, and the pressures of the 1920 and the 1921 pennant races were more than he could handle. He was seriously ill after the 1920 season and took leave of the Yankees during 1921 spring training and again in the middle of the 1921 season. Huggins and the Yankees also wore black armbands at the end of the 1920 season to pay tribute to Ray Chapman, who suffered his fatal beaning in a game against the Yankees. SDN-062204, *Chicago Daily News negatives collection, Chicago History Museum.*

White Sox, it stated, "You can pat Moran and kid Gleason, but you can't hug Miller."[38] Both Moran and Gleason were considered down-to-earth and approachable men.

The standard refrain of Huggins's critics had been "Of course the Yankees should win the pennant. They have Babe Ruth. How can they not win?" But, as Hugh Fullerton noted, the Yankees were not a great ballclub. "It is great in spots, weak in others, indifferent in others. He has had to keep switching, patching, and making changes. . . . Huggins has not had an entirely square shake out of the box."[39] Damon Runyon was even more to the point: Surely Huggins deserved some credit for leading a winning club that was in the fight for first place.[40]

Joe Vila, one of Huggins's few friends in the New York press, was scathing toward the complaining players. He found the report that some Yankees were convening a meeting to review the possible firing of their manager outrageous if it was in fact true.[41] He elaborated in his column in the *Sporting News* a few days later, accusing some members of the team of sabotaging their skipper. They wanted the lenient and laid-back Roger Peckinpaugh to take over the club, so they could then do as they wanted. Vila also chastised the "grandstand managers," whom he derisively called "pinheads," for wanting "to hurl him [Huggins] into outer darkness" whenever the Yankees lost a game.[42]

Jacob Ruppert, who remained Huggins's biggest booster, quickly informed the press that his manager was there to stay. The rebels among the players (who reportedly included Ruth) quickly backtracked and denied that they were undermining Huggins.[43] They even professed indignation that they were being accused unjustly. Once Ruppert had staked out his position, the press became more balanced and at times even came to Huggins's defense.

Harry Schumacher of the *New York Globe and Commercial Advertiser* noted that there were few "mental giants" on the Yankees. He then listed the team's "naturally 'smart' players." There were only five, he said: Ruth, Peckinpaugh, Baker, Mays, and Shawkey.[44] Perhaps Walter Trumbull of the *New York Herald* had the best and final (at least for now) word for Huggins's critics: "If anything should happen to Mr. Ruth there wouldn't be enough left of the Yanks to bring home. So please, everybody, lay off Miller Huggins and twist your left finger that nothing happens to the Babe."[45]

The Yankees were in Philadelphia on August 11 to begin a long road trip; they would not return to the Polo Grounds until September 1.[46] They took three of four games from the Athletics, including a Saturday doubleheader sweep that drew an enormous crowd of more than 30,000 to Shibe Park. The *Philadelphia Inquirer* reported that another 10,000 fans were turned away; a number of papers mentioned that this was the A's biggest crowd since 1914, when they last won a pennant. All this to see their last-place 40-66 team lose twice, including another game to Carl Mays. Of course, the primary reason the fans came was to see Babe Ruth, who thrilled them with home runs on Thursday and Friday. Tilly Walker hit his third home run in three games for the Athletics; he would finish the 1921 season with twenty-three, fourth best in the league.

New York's one loss in the series came on Friday, and it stung. Not only did the Yanks waste Ruth's monstrous clout that cleared the center-field bleachers, but they also blew a 5–0 lead. Waite Hoyt lost his second game in a week; Huggins may have been guilty of staying with him too long. Hoyt remained on the mound until he had given up six runs and the lead, yet Huggins may have been sending a message: that he believed in his young hurler.

The Yankees then headed west to Chicago, playing exhibition games in Columbus, Louisville, and Indianapolis along the way. New York papers were critical of the club for scheduling meaningless games that generated revenue but denied the players time to rest for the games that really counted.[47] There were also injury risks to these meaningless games. "The management cannot see any farther than the shekels that will be drawn in by the hippodroming."[48] Yankee owner Til Huston felt compelled to respond. He explained that the Yankees had the highest payroll in baseball. In addition, fans deserved a chance to see the Yankees, the biggest attraction in baseball history.[49]

The Yanks lost two of three to the White Sox, even though this time they avoided Dickie Kerr, who was sidelined by arm trouble. Carl Mays lost the second contest, 7–6, one the *Chicago Daily Tribune* called the most exciting game in Chicago since the war, which was saying a lot since the pennant races of 1919 and 1920 had provided Chicago fans with plenty of thrills. And once again, a Ruth home run (number forty-six) went for naught. That three-run blow gave the Yankees the lead, yet it was shrouded in controversy. The ball appeared to have curved foul, and White Sox catcher Ray Schalk was ejected for arguing the call with umpire Frank Wilson.[50] The Sox then rallied for three runs in the eighth, in what one newspaper called "the seemingly inevitable collapse . . . Mays retreating under fire."[51] Scoring six runs against Faber was a rarity; still, he gutted out the win. If Faber had a slump in 1921, this was it. In the past week, he had been inconsistent in splitting two decisions against the Indians. His earned run average was still a league-best 2.40.

In that second game against Chicago, Bill Piercy made his first appearance in weeks; and the Sox rocked him for four runs in one and one-third innings. Harry Hooper, a star outfielder on the championship Boston Red Sox teams of 1912, 1915, 1916, and 1918, celebrated his recent return to the Chicago lineup from a broken hand with three hits, including two doubles. The White Sox had acquired Hooper this spring to add a marquee name to their depleted roster, and he responded with a .327 batting average in 1921.

As the Yankees arrived in St. Louis, the local fans were still talking about Dixie Davis's victory in Washington eleven days earlier. Davis went the distance in a nineteen-inning game, pitching no-hit ball for the final nine innings. They were also talking about George Sisler's hot bat. He had recently strung together ten straight hits, just one short of the record Tris Speaker had set a year earlier.

In the opening game on August 20, Waite Hoyt beat Davis; but it was a costly win for New York since Frank Baker strained a leg muscle rounding third base in the first inning. Baker had aggravated an old charley horse; and he would play only sparingly the rest of the year, almost exclusively as a pinch hitter. Aaron Ward again moved back to third base and veteran utility man Mike McNally took over at second. While these moves did not hurt the team's defense (it may have even improved somewhat since the infield now had more speed and range), the offense would suffer. Baker had been swinging a hot bat after a slow start this season, and the Yankees would miss his firepower.[52]

On Sunday the twenty-first, the Browns swept a doubleheader, beating the recently ineffective Rip Collins in the second game, 10–0. Yet the real fireworks came in the first game, won by Urban Shocker. An unusual sequence of events triggered the tumult in the Yankees' sixth inning, with the Browns leading. After Ward doubled, Shocker walked McNally and apparently hit Schang, loading the bases. Shocker was upset with the call and hurled the ball to the ground, as the Browns were arguing the hit-batsman call with umpire Tom Connolly. Seeing an opening as the ball rolled away, Ward broke for the plate. Shocker retrieved the ball and threw to catcher Hank Severeid, who tagged Ward out.

After Connolly consulted with the other arbiter, Dick Nallin, the call was reversed. The play was ruled dead, and Ward was returned to third. At this point, Shocker became furious and got into a tussle with manager Huggins. One St. Louis account said that Shocker "jabbed and slapped little Hug with his glove."[53] As Huggins swung at the Browns' pitcher, a large policeman defused the conflict by forcibly grabbing the diminutive Yankee skipper by the collar and dragging him back to the dugout.[54] After New York tied the score that inning, the Browns rallied to win.

The pennant hopes of the Yankees were slipping away as New York fell two and a half games behind Cleveland. While the Yankees picked up a game on the Tribe the next day, they headed into Cleveland with their pitching staff in tatters. The *New York Evening Journal* lamented, "Huggins hasn't a flinger, not a single, solitary hurler of consistently steady skill. All have degenerated into in-and-outers of the most pronounced type."[55] Damon Runyon suggested that the Yankees could clinch the 1921 pennant if they had one great pitcher—a Faber, for example—even if they had to trade Ruth to get him.[56] But the Babe was too valuable a gate attraction, Runyon concluded, beyond his skill on the playing field. "A pennant is a lovely thing to have, to be sure, but so is the money that Ruth brings in. . . . The big town likes Ruth. He is cut to its measure. There may be pennants in other years. There is only one Ruth."[57]

In mid-August, as the Indians continued to hold first place, Tris Speaker seemed to be keeping his team going with sheer tenacity and dogged determination more than anything else. On August 8 Allan Sothoron tossed eleven and two-thirds innings of relief, including a scoreless last nine, in a thirteen-inning win. On August 12 the Tribe drove Red Faber from the mound after four innings in Stan Coveleski's victory. When Faber came back after one day's rest, they lost to him, 4–1.

When the Yankees arrived at Cleveland's Dunn Field for the first of three games on August 23, they were one and a half games behind. Huggins called on Jack Quinn to start, a surprise choice since the veteran had not started a game since July 10 in Chicago. Perhaps it was a hunch on the beleaguered skipper's part. The spitballer responded with an impressive five-hitter. Quinn had his spitter working this day; his pitches were breaking down. The Indians were beating his pitches into the ground all afternoon, as reflected in first baseman Pipp's eighteen put-outs as well as in Ward's nine assists and Peckinpaugh's six.

On the 1909 Yankees, Quinn was a teammate of fellow spitballer Jack

27. Jack Quinn won eighteen games for the Yankees in 1910 and again in 1920. The spitballer was not nearly as effective in 1921 and was dropped from the rotation. Yet Huggins gave him the start for two of the season's biggest games, both against the Indians, in late August and in late September. The Yankees were one of only a handful of teams that memorialized Ray Chapman by wearing armbands. *Private collection of Dennis Goldstein.*

Chesbro, then in his final year in the big leagues. A year later, Quinn won eighteen games for New York. After recording losing records in 1911 and 1912 (allowing almost six earned runs per game in 1912) and approaching the age of thirty, Jack Quinn seemed near the end of his Major League career.

Yet he persevered for the next six seasons, primarily in the Minors and the Federal League.[58] When the Pacific Coast League suspended operations in the summer of 1918 because of shortages of both players and fans due to the military draft of World War I, both the White Sox and the Yankees signed him.[59] The dispute came before the National Commission that summer. Ban Johnson cast the deciding vote, awarding Quinn to the Yankees.[60] He became one of their key pitchers in 1919, with fifteen wins.

This seemingly minor Quinn ruling had far-reaching effects beyond the remarkable comeback and contributions of the hurler, who also won eighteen games in 1920. First, it was the final blow and firmed up the permanent break between two of the most powerful men in the American League, Ban Johnson and White Sox owner Charles Comiskey.[61] When the Yankees took on Johnson a few months later in the Carl Mays dispute, the league president was isolated and ultimately doomed as baseball's supreme ruler. Second, had Quinn remained with the White Sox in 1919, he may very well have provided Chicago manager Kid Gleason with another pitching option in the 1919 World Series, which then might have unfolded quite differently.[62]

Another veteran spitball pitcher, Ray Caldwell, was not nearly as sharp as Quinn was in the showdown between the American League's top two teams. He gave up home runs number forty-seven and number forty-eight to the Babe. Both times, Roger Peckinpaugh was on base; and both shots came off "cripples," balls thrown on 3-1 and 3-0 counts, respectively.

The Yankees moved into first place the next day with a tense 3–2 win, as Waite Hoyt bested Coveleski for his fifteenth win of the season. "The Flatbush redhead never pitched a better game in his whole life," gushed the New York Sun.[63] The Yanks played a fine game of inside baseball, showing once again that they could win without the long ball. Ruth, Meusel, and Pipp all stole bases. (In 1921 each would record seventeen stolen bases.) Ruth walked with two outs in the first inning, stole second, and scored on Meusel's single. In the second inning, Pipp walked, was sacrificed to second, and scored on McNally's single. The 2–2 tie was broken in the ninth when the Indians' defense broke down. Joe Sewell's throwing error allowed Elmer Miller to reach first. He advanced on Peckinpaugh's bunt and came home on Pipp's sacrifice fly, after Coveleski had walked the Babe to load the bases.

In the bottom of the ninth with a runner on second, Miller brought down a Charlie Jamieson drive to deep center, killing the rally. Just that morning, Babe Ruth had written in his column, "We don't wonder any more when a ball is hit to centre. We know he is going to get it. . . . Miller has added just about forty per cent to our ball club."[64]

Speaker formally protested the game. He claimed that in the top of the ninth with Miller on second, Peckinpaugh had interfered with catcher Steve O'Neill. The Yankee shortstop had bunted, and O'Neill had a hard time getting around the batter to the ball. His throw to third just missed getting Miller. Speaker came running in from center field to argue with umpire George Moriarty, who soon pulled out his watch and warned the Cleveland skipper to get on with the game. American League president Ban Johnson would again disallow the protest because the play was a judgment call by the umpire.

The Indians moved back into first place by a half game on Thursday the twenty-fifth with a 15–1 beating of the Yankees. It was the third time in a little over a month that Cleveland had scored fifteen or more runs against New York. As was the case in the 16–1 game on July 30, Bob Shawkey was the victim. In the earlier game, he gave up seven runs in two and two-thirds innings; today he allowed eight in four and two-thirds innings. In both games, Rip Collins was totally ineffective in relief.

The game's drama had little to do with the outcome. Allan Sothoron was pitching for the Tribe, and the Yankees repeatedly accused him of tampering with the ball. There were more complaints in 1921 about Sothoron than about any other pitcher. The charge was that he was nicking the ball with his fingernails and "winging it." Hugh Fullerton, an outspoken critic of cheating in baseball, actually saluted the Cleveland pitcher if indeed he was doctoring the ball. "If Sotheron [sic] has been nicking the ball he is a smart pitcher, smarter than most of us have given him credit for being. . . . If now the pitchers are getting smart enough to cheat only when it counts [as opposed to all the time], it seems a move toward the good, no matter how immoral."[65]

Fullerton went on to say that most of Sothoron's success was probably due to the fact that he was part of a fighting and hustling team. On this day, that fighting and hustling almost cost Sothoron and the Indians the game, even with their big lead. Harry Harper came in to relieve Collins in the eighth; it was his first appearance since breaking his finger in May. Whether the result of his being rusty or angry about the score, he hit two Indians: Larry Gardner in the arm, and Steve O'Neill in the back, after Shawkey had hit Sewell. O'Neill then picked up the ball and threw it back at Harper, and a bench-clearing brawl was underway.

Ultimately, umpires Ollie Chill and Moriarty ejected O'Neill and Yankee pitcher Bill Piercy (but not Harper) from the game. When the fiery O'Neill refused to leave, Moriarty once again pulled out his watch, threatening to forfeit the game to New York if O'Neill did not leave the field. O'Neill did, and the Indians added an exclamation point with four more runs. Moriarty then became the target of pop bottles when Harper resumed pitching; and when approximately a thousand fans converged onto the field after the game, he and Chill needed a police escort, as did the Yankees.

It was an ugly game for the Yankees. The pitching was atrocious, and Bob Meusel made four errors. The *New York Times* reached back to a children's story to describe New York's performance: "The Yankees are like the little girl in the rhyme who, when she was good, was very, very good, but when she was bad she was horrid."[66]

During this series, Huggins announced that the Yankees had acquired pitcher Tom "Shotgun" Rogers from Buffalo of the International League, where he had posted a 15-9 record this season. He had pitched without much distinction for the Browns and the Athletics from 1917 to 1919, but his claim to fame had occurred in 1916. That year, he won twenty-four games for Nashville, leading the Southern Association in wins.[67] In June his fastball hit Mobile third baseman Johnny Dodge in the head. Dodge, a former member of the Phillies and the Reds, died from the "fatal fastball" on June 19, the only upper-tier Minor League player to be killed on the playing field.[68] Like Carl Mays after the 1920 Chapman beaning, Rogers was able to compose himself and continue pitching at a high level that season. Less than a month after he beaned Dodge, Rogers tossed a perfect game against Chattanooga.

Thus, for the final weeks of the 1921 season, the Yankees had a trio touched by beanball tragedy: Mays and Rogers, whose pitches had killed players, and Chick Fewster, who had narrowly escaped death from his spring 1920 beaning.

The Yankees ended their long western road trip with a weekend series in Detroit. The Tigers had gained a modicum of respectability by taking the series in New York earlier in the month; but as August wore on, fourth place and the first division were slipping away. On August 20 Ty Cobb had released Donie Bush, the team's regular shortstop for more than a decade and the last link to the pennant-winning team of 1909 other than Cobb. (Although Bush had been slowing down, the Senators picked him up on waivers.) His release marked the end of an era in Detroit baseball, and many Tiger fans were not happy with the move. "It was Bush who made the Detroit team. . . . There never has been a greater lead-off man than Donie," wrote Hugh Fullerton.[69]

On Friday, August 26, the Yankees showed no signs of carryover from the Thursday slaughter in Cleveland. They easily handled Howard Ehmke's pitching with fifteen hits and a 10–2 win. Ironically, only one Yankee went hitless; and that was Babe Ruth, thus ending his consecutive-game hit streak at twenty-six. Elmer Miller hit a home run, and the Yankees hit four doubles. As his first month with New York was coming to an end, Miller was proving to be everything that was expected of him in the field, and more than was expected of him at the plate. He would hit .298 in 1921.

The Tigers did win the final game of the series from Waite Hoyt. The Babe got three doubles in the loss. In doing so, he was into another streak; this time he would have nine straight games with an extra-base hit. The Yankees finished their road trip with a decent if not spectacular 10-7 record. As they caught their train back east on Sunday night, their record stood at 73-46. The Indians had just swept New York's next opponent, the Washington Senators. In the final game of that series, Joe Wood had three hits and knocked in all three runs, including a home run that broke a 2–2 tie. Cleveland's record was now 76-46, good for a one-and-a-half-game lead. Already, fans in both cities were anticipating the final meeting of the two clubs, a four-game set in New York the final week of the season.

On August 23 when the Yankees came to Cleveland and the Giants were about to host the Pirates, the *New York Evening Telegram* bemoaned the prospects of an all-Manhattan World Series, noting that the New York teams seemed to lack the pluck and guts that Cleveland and Pittsburgh were showing. "Both clubs have shown the lack of the sublime fire, the spirit that conquers." But, the paper noted, there were still games to be played. "And a pennant race is not over until it is over."[70]

AL STANDINGS AT CLOSE OF PLAY OF AUGUST 28, 1921

TEAM	G	W	L	T	PCT	GB
Cleveland Indians	122	76	46	0	.623	-
New York Yankees	119	73	46	0	.613	1.5
Washington Senators	126	65	60	1	.520	12.5
St. Louis Browns	123	63	60	0	.512	13.5
Boston Red Sox	120	58	62	0	.483	17.0
Detroit Tigers	127	59	67	1	.468	19.0
Chicago White Sox	122	52	70	0	.426	24.0
Philadelphia Athletics	123	43	78	2	.355	32.5

As the National League pennant race heated up, so too did the tempers of the players and spectators. In Pittsburgh, where the fans had a long-standing antipathy toward John McGraw and the New York Giants, the intensity of those late-July Giants-Pirates games at Forbes Field had them in a frenzy.

"Sportsmanship is an unknown quantity to the rabid rooters of the team. Any way to win a ball game seems to be their motto," wrote Walter St. Denis.[1] In addition to the vicious verbal assaults, bleacherites had used peashooters to pelt Giants outfielders. St. Denis contrasted the behavior of Pittsburgh fans with that of New York fans. "New York rooters have played fair with every opponent that has hit here, even the Pirates. They have applauded the fine plays of the visitors as readily as they have those of their own players. Their display of sportsmanship on all occasions has been something that is worthy of copy by the fans of other cities."[2]

While St. Denis was writing specifically about fans of the Giants when he used the term "New York rooters," his words applied equally to fans of the Yankees. So too did his prognostication for what lay ahead. "It's a tough road that the Giants have to travel, and just for that reason they deserve the support of everyone who glories in calling himself a New Yorker. They have proved their fighting qualities and the spirit to do even when all is against them."[3]

Will Wedge offered another reason why the Giants' road to a pennant would be a difficult one. His theory was that because every other player in the National League wanted to play for the Giants, they did their best in games against the New Yorkers to impress McGraw. "The Polo Grounds stands out as the 'La Scala'—the Metropolitan Opera House of the baseball profession," wrote Wedge. He further stated that a player feels he has not really made it until he plays at the Polo Grounds in a Giants' uniform.[4]

Fresh off their three wins in Pittsburgh, the Giants moved on to Cincinnati, where, as July turned to August, they would play the seventh-place Reds six times in four days. Manager McGraw viewed this series as an opportunity for his team to take over first place and perhaps even to put some daylight between themselves and the Pirates. In the eyes of some in the New York press, the Giants were already in a more favorable position than the Pirates. Sam Crane believed that Pirates manager George Gibson, along with many of his players, had lost some confidence following their three straight home losses to New York. Also, said Crane, the pressure of having been the front-runners all season appeared to be wearing the Pirates down.[5]

The Reds' fans who "greeted" the Giants at Redland Field seemed even more anti–New York in their partisanship than the Pirates' fans in Pittsburgh had been. "It may be that the Western fans are a unit against the pennant going to the East again."[6] The truth, however, was that this antipathy to the Giants went beyond a mere East-West split. There was no comparable antagonism among western-city fans toward the three other eastern clubs: Boston, Brooklyn, and Philadelphia.

The New York club held a special place in the hearts of National League fans. For years, it had been the league's most detested team; and John McGraw, the league's most reviled manager. It was no different in Cincinnati, where two years earlier the Reds had held off the Giants' challenge and had gone on to win their first pennant. They had declined precipitously since then, but the players and the fans still took particular pleasure in beating the New Yorkers whenever they met. The Giants' success and McGraw's truculent, combative personality shared much of the blame for the club's unpopularity. However, the primary reason for the opposition was the interlocking "NY" on their caps, an emblem that announced to all that this team represented New York City. As it is today, New York was then the wealthiest, most urbanized city in the nation. In an America increasingly shedding its agricultural roots, that distinction was enough to engender fear, suspicion, and antipathy.

That 1919 pennant race between the Reds and Giants was a touchstone of the East-West antagonism, wrote the New York Times:

The Giants, to the embittered Buckeye fan, came to personify the malignant destiny which thwarted all the efforts of Midwestern virtue. And so the struggle which is now at its height has quite a different meaning in Cincinnati from that which is given to it in New York. To the Giants this is a pennant race like any other; they may win, they may lose; it is all in a day's work, and they are calloused to victory no less than to defeat. But to Cincinnati, it is the wiping out of an ancient wrong, the correction of old injustice, the final vindication of the principles of eternal truth. The Giants can expect no mercy from those who are merely demonstrating the ultimate triumph of right over the forces of evil.[7]

McGraw had rejoined the team in Cincinnati after a quick trip to Chicago to speak to John Heydler about the suspensions imposed on Johnny Rawlings and him. Heydler had lifted them; but while Rawlings was in the lineup, McGraw chose to watch the game from the grandstand, allowing coaches Hughie Jennings and Cozy Dolan to run the team.

Always looking for ways to bolster his club, McGraw made a move to strengthen his pitching for the season's final two months. He brought back twenty-two-year-old right-hander Pat Shea from St. Paul, where Shea had a 9-10 record for the American Association Saints. In return, New York sent Rube Benton to St. Paul.[8]

Shea had first appeared in the Majors as a nineteen-year-old in 1918, pitching in three games for Connie Mack's Philadelphia Athletics. In 1920 Shea finished 27-7 and pitched 298 innings for the Toronto Maple Leafs, where he was a teammate of Rosy Ryan. Scouts were calling the redheaded youngster one of the very best pitchers in the Minor Leagues, leading the Giants to spend $12,000 to purchase his contract. Shea showed well in spring training; nevertheless, on April 21 McGraw sold him to the White Sox via the interleague waiver rule. The deal fell through, and Shea remained with the Giants but never appeared in a game. McGraw had sent him to St. Paul on May 15.

While he was in Chicago meeting with Heydler, McGraw encountered Buck Weaver, one of the White Sox players charged with throwing the 1919 World Series. The meeting between the two men set off rumors that if Weaver were to be cleared of wrongdoing, he would sign with the Giants. Quite naturally, McGraw, no stranger to accusations of tampering, denied that he made Weaver an offer. They had talked about inconsequential things, McGraw said. Weaver had shaken hands with him and told him he hoped the Giants would win the pennant.

Slim Sallee, a former Red, got the Giants off to a good start in Cincinnati with his sixth win of the season, all of which were in relief, and the 174th and final win of his big league career. The victory enabled New York to cut Pittsburgh's lead from a game to a half game, as the Pirates' contest with the Braves was postponed because of wet grounds.

By merely splitting the next day's doubleheader on July 30, New York missed an opportunity to take undisputed possession of first place. Boston's Joe Oeschger, on his way to the only twenty-win season of his career, opened the door with a 1–0 shutout of the Pirates and Wilbur Cooper. The Giants had to settle for being tied with Pittsburgh at 60-35, with the Braves now just five back. In the second game, George Kelly hit his eighteenth home run of the season, providing the most dramatic hit of the day. Experienced onlookers called Kelly's drive to left field the longest ever hit in a regular-season game at Redland Field. The honor of hitting the longest in any game here, as it was in almost every park he played in, belonged to Babe Ruth. The Babe had played an exhibition game here against the Reds earlier in the week and hit two, one to right and one to center, that were even longer.

Fred Toney's poor performance in the opening-game loss appeared to be the cause of his between-games tussle with Ross Youngs.[9] The fight began in the Giants' dugout after the six-feet-one, 195-pound Toney "made a caustic remark about Youngs's work in right field." Youngs, five inches shorter and thirty pounds lighter, came back with a comment about Toney's mediocre pitching and threw the first punch.[10]

The fight then spilled out onto the field in front of the dugout before several teammates separated them, with Youngs appearing the more anxious for the tussle to continue. Neither man would say specifically what caused the fight; nor fortunately for the Giants, did Toney or Youngs (the league's second-leading hitter) suffer any injuries from it.

Much to the delight of a large, boisterous Sunday crowd—the final day of July brought the Giants even more disappointment and frustration. They squandered late leads in both games and went down to two crushing, extra-innings, one-run defeats. The damaging double blow to the Giants' pennant hopes would engender "little weeping or wailing outside Manhattan," wrote W. A. Phelon, the Cincinnati correspondent for the *Sporting News*, recognizing the dislike of the Giants outside New York City.[11]

In the sixth inning of the first game that day, the locals precipitated a near riot when umpire Cy Rigler failed to rule interference on Giants base runner George Kelly.[12] The fans believed that Kelly, running from second to third, had deliberately let Edd Roush's throw hit him, causing the ball to roll into the Giants' dugout and permitting two runs to score. The good people of Cincinnati showed their "disagreement" with Rigler's call by throwing debris, including bottles, onto the field. Luckily, no one was hit during the outburst that to Will Wedge resembled "the good old days of Redland rowdyism."[13]

Art Nehf went all the way in the second game, allowing only five hits. Nehf was pitching in front of his wife Elizabeth, who made the trip from Washington, Indiana, and claimed she had never before seen her husband lose a game. Nehf's downfall was issuing two walks in the eleventh inning, both of which turned into runs. Heinie Groh's single to left brought in the tying run; and when the ball went through left fielder Irish Meusel's legs, in came the winning run.[14] An earlier Reds run was the result of Youngs's misplaying Roush's routine fly to right, which turned into a triple. Youngs seemed to have trouble with the sun again today, which may well have been the reason for Toney's between-games rant the previous day.

While the Giants were splitting the six games in Cincinnati, rain curtailed the Pirates' series with the Braves to just two games, which they split. As a result, when the Giants left Cincinnati, they were in the same place in the standings that they had been in when they arrived, a game behind the Pirates. Yet the reality was that they were actually in a worse position. Instead of having played two fewer games than Pittsburgh, with two fewer wins, they now had played two more games than the Pirates, with two more losses.

Four wins in their last five games had allowed the fifth-place Cardinals to move to within a win of .500. The situation had been much different in mid-June, when the Giants had last played in St. Louis and the Cardinals had been in third place. The St. Louis papers had been critical of Cardinals manager Branch Rickey and wondered how much

28. Branch Rickey was the Cardinals' business manager and field manager. He had the Giants and Yankees in mind when he asked, "How can those teams without unlimited resources in their deposit boxes have a chance to compete fairly?" (Lowenfish, *Branch Rickey*, 135). *St. Louis Cardinals Hall of Fame Museum.*

more their former manager, Miller Huggins, might have been able to do with the team. Huggins may have been under siege by the New York press, but he was still remembered fondly and respected by St. Louis sportswriters. However, Rickey's club would reach the break-even point and exceed it against the Giants. Only Toney's 2–1 win in the final game prevented a four-game Cardinals sweep.

After scoring three runs in the first inning of the first game, the Giants tallied only five more runs over the next thirty-five innings. Ross Youngs, batting .350 when the Giants began this trip, reached as high as .370 during the St. Louis series. However, Youngs had little help from his high-powered teammates against the Cardinals. The worst offender was Irish Meusel, who went hitless in fourteen at bats during the four games and left many runners on base. With a paltry .200 batting average, no extra-base hits, and no runs batted in since joining the team, Meusel had so far been a major disappointment.

A two-run homer by Austin McHenry was the big blow in the Cardinals' 3–2 win on August 3. McHenry's home run was his thirteenth of the season, breaking the three-way tie that had existed among him, Meusel, and Rogers Hornsby behind leader George Kelly's eighteen. At age twenty-five, McHenry had blossomed into one of the National League's brightest stars. He would finish the season second in slugging percentage and third in batting average, runs batted in, extra-base hits, and total bases. Rickey would later call him one of the best left fielders ever. McHenry's average would fall from .350 in 152 games in 1921 to .303 in just 64 games in 1922. The decline was the result of a brain tumor, which would lead to McHenry's far-too-premature death in November 1922.

Max Flack of the Cubs and Hod Ford of the Braves also hit home runs on August 3, raising the National League total to a record 316. (The National League's previous full-season record was 314, set in 1911.) With the American League having hit 319, the two leagues now had a combined total of 635, establishing a new Major League home run record—a remarkable accomplishment given that there were still two months to play.[15]

A pair of shutouts the next day combined to increase the Giants' deficit to three and a half games. While Earl Hamilton and the Pirates were blanking the Phillies, Bill Pertica was defeating Art Nehf, 1–0, another

29. Left-handed hitter Earl Smith shared the Giants' catching duties with Frank Snyder. A hard-drinking, hot-tempered Arkansan, Smith feared no one, including McGraw, whom he despised. *Private collection of Michael Mumby.*

tough loss for the little left-hander. A sixth-inning single by Hornsby, leading the league with a .414 average, brought Joe Schultz home with the game's only run. In Schultz's next at bat, in the eighth inning, a Nehf pitch hit him behind the ear, precipitating yet another of the ugly on-field chaotic situations that seemed endemic to the Giants.

As Schultz, their right fielder, lay unconscious on the ground, several Cardinals players began shouting at Nehf, accusing him of throwing a beanball, either on his own or on orders from McGraw.[16] Then, after Schultz was taken from the field, the action shifted to the respective catchers, Frank Snyder of the Giants and Pickles Dillhoefer of the Cardinals.[17] The two, who had been squabbling all game, started up again. The six-feet-two Snyder discarded his mask and glove, went over to the five-feet-seven Dillhoefer, and took three swings at him before umpire Ernie Quigley could step between them. Quigley threw both men out—Dillhoefer, who had initiated the incident with his words, and Snyder, who had done the punching.

The Sportsman's Park crowd did not view Quigley's dual ejections as equal justice. They started howling at Snyder and throwing pop bottles at the onetime Cardinal as he headed to the Giants' bench. Casey Stengel, who had barely seen any action on the field since joining the Giants, tried to come to Snyder's rescue. But he too was cursed by the fans; and when one spat at him, Stengel responded by punching him in the face. Quigley ejected Stengel after he threw the punch, as bottles continued to rain down on the Giants' dugout before the police finally restored order.

Because McGraw had suspended Earl Smith, the man who shared the catching duties with Snyder, rookie Alex Gaston replaced Snyder behind the plate. The suspension, McGraw said, was because Smith, who had little use for his manager, had been insubordinate and had repeatedly broken training rules. Before suspending Smith a few days earlier, McGraw had indicated his displeasure with him in a most obvious way. The left-handed-batting Smith had looked less than ready to play, striking out twice in two at bats against right-hander Bill Doak. When he was next due up, McGraw sent up right-handed-hitting Eddie Brown to bat for him. It was the first time that McGraw had removed Smith for a right-handed batter against a right-handed pitcher. When Smith cursed at McGraw after the game in front of the whole club, he left the manager no choice but to suspend him. McGraw (and his club) were accustomed to being the targets of vicious verbal abuse on the road, but he could not allow it from one of his own.

Three policemen took up posts near the Giants' bench for the final game in St. Louis. Nothing untoward happened on the field, but the fans unleashed profanity-laced tirades at pitcher Toney and catcher Snyder all afternoon. The Giants held a 2–1 lead, thanks to a two-run triple by Frisch; but in the home eighth, St. Louis had runners at first and third with nobody out. The next three batters were Hornsby, Jack Fournier, and McHenry, making the likelihood of a tie game almost a certainty, and a Cardinals' lead a distinct possibility. Toney, however, was equal to the task. He used a Carl Mays–like underhanded delivery to catch the great Hornsby looking at a third strike, and he then got Fournier on a Bancroft-to-Rawlings-to-Kelly double play. The *New York Times* writer used his usual florid prose in describing Toney's final pitch to Hornsby: "He switched his usual overhand delivery and took to that manner of workmanship espoused by Carl Mays. He whirred his arms high into the air, brought the right one earthward in one tremendous sweep and shot a dazzling underhand fast one toward the region of the plate."[18]

Pittsburgh's win over Philadelphia prevented the Giants from gaining any ground.[19] Beginning on August 6, the Pirates would host the Dodgers for four games, while the Giants, trailing by three and a half games, would play four in Chicago, where the Cubs had a new manager. Three days earlier, Cubs president William Veeck had announced that catcher Bill Killefer, who had been a replacement manager for an ill Johnny Evers earlier in the week, would take over permanently.

Evers had had problems with a number of his players—reports said they had laid down on him, just as some Yankees were reported to have done with Miller Huggins—and was fired on August 3. Evers's dismissal ended his long and sporadic association with the Cubs that dated back to 1902. His career as a player—mostly for the Cubs—would earn him a place in the Hall of Fame.[20] He also served as a player-manager for the Cubs in 1913, leading them to a third-place finish. Chicago had brought him back this year as a replacement for Fred Mitchell, who had taken the managerial job with the Braves. Evers left with a 41-55 record and the Cubs in sixth place.

New York lost the opening and closing games at Cubs Park, both to rookie Virgil Cheeves, but won the middle two for a split in the series. This second trip west for the Giants was shaping up much like the first. They had opened both trips by winning three of four from Pittsburgh and then faltered against the weaker Reds, Cubs, and Cardinals. "They put everything they have into beating the good clubs," said one observer, "and when they meet the weak boys, they've nothing left and prove easy picking."[21] Finishing this second western trip with a 9-9 record, their deficit, which had shrunk to a game after leaving Pittsburgh, was back up to three games.

Bright spots for the Giants in Chicago included Irish Meusel finally breaking out of his slump with five hits in the series, Art Nehf's fourteenth win, and George Kelly's nineteenth home run. Meanwhile, Brooklyn took three of four from Pittsburgh to move five wins above the .500 mark for the first time since May 18. The Dodgers-Pirates series featured four well-pitched games, in which neither team hit a home run. Babe Adams's ninth consecutive victory accounted for Pittsburgh's lone win, while Leon Cadore won twice for Brooklyn. Burleigh Grimes, whose record stood at 16-6 going into the series, also defeated Wilbur Cooper (18-7) in a showdown between the former teammates—now the league's two winningest pitchers.[22]

On August 11 the Giants returned home for a doubleheader against the Dodgers. They would play twenty-six of their next twenty-eight games at the Polo Grounds, while facing each of the National League's seven other teams. (The two road games in that stretch would be across the East River in Brooklyn.) Wilbert Robinson's club had come to life with thirteen wins in its last nineteen games. At 56-51, the Dodgers had climbed to fourth place. But they still trailed the Pirates by eleven games, and their chances of repeating as National League champions were fading.

With just seven weeks left in the season, both New York teams were in second place. Both were getting good work from their pitching staffs, although the Giants appeared "steadier afield than the Yankees."[23] The Giants trailed Pittsburgh by two and a half games and had fewer home games left than the Pirates. With the last long home stand of the season about to start, the Giants had to be "up and doing right away."

The Yankees, only a percentage point behind Cleveland, were in a much better position. They would be at home for most of September, while the Indians would be on the road. Playing the last three weeks of the season almost exclusively at the Polo Grounds "heightens the chances of the Huggins clan to win this year's American League flag."[24]

Evidently assuming the Yankees would win, Walter St. Denis issued a call for every New Yorker to pull for the Giants and give the city its first all–New York World Series: "New York wants the world series to itself this year, and that's why every mother's son in the city is rooting so hard for McGraw's boys to be up and doing their very best all the time, and get in there with the Yanks this fall."[25]

Whether every one of New York's "mother's sons" was rooting for McGraw and the Giants is debatable, especially those "mother's sons" who were Yankee fans. What is not debatable, however, is the sense of entitlement that New Yorkers had, as reflected by St. Denis: "The city is deserving of the best the national game provides, and the owners of the two clubs, who have shown gameness throughout, should cut in with the spoils of the world's championship games."[26]

A crowd of 32,000—many of whom had come over from Brooklyn, as they always did when the Dodgers played at the Polo Grounds—attended the August 11 doubleheader. With passionate fans on both sides, the noise level was extremely high throughout both games. "If more howling was ever concentrated in a single place on a single afternoon, history says nothing about it. When the Giants' supporters were not clamoring, thousands of robust Flatbush baritones and tenors were in action."[27]

Both sides had much to cheer about, as each team had ten hits in the first game and seventeen in the second. Burns had a combined six hits for New York, and Frisch had five. But Meusel again struggled, going hitless in nine at bats. In the opener, four Giants' errors led to three unearned runs and a 5–3 Brooklyn win. Pat Shea pitched the ninth inning, retiring all three batters in his Giants' debut.

The second game went back and forth before the Giants finally won it, 6–5, in thirteen innings. Frisch, who had a two-run homer in the first game, won it with a triple to left off Sherry Smith. The split cost the Giants a game in the standings, as Pittsburgh's doubleheader sweep of the Cubs raised their lead to three and a half games.

Seeing the Giants fall further back pleased the Brooklyn rooters, though Sam Crane could not understand why. "Brooklyn baseball fans are disloyal to their own big city when they root for the Pittsburgh Pirates to head the Giants off," wrote Crane. "I have seen how strong is the antagonism to the Giants in the West. It is rabid to a degree, but I am free to acknowledge that Brooklyn fans are more rabid against the Giants than are the fans of the West."[28]

Evidently, Crane was either unaware or unwilling to acknowledge the deep-seated hostility fans in Brooklyn felt toward the Giants. He pointed out how "loyal New Yorkers" had rooted for Wilbert Robinson and the Dodgers to defeat Cleveland in the previous year's World Series, but he speculated that Brooklynites would not have rooted for the Giants under similar circumstance. Missing from Crane's analysis was the high regard everyone had for Wilbert Robinson, as opposed to the hatred fans in all other National League cities, including those in the borough of Brooklyn, had for John McGraw.

Therefore, Dodger fans were ecstatic the next day when they helped drop the Giants another game behind Pittsburgh. With each team using its best pitcher, Burleigh Grimes bested Art Nehf, 3–1. Zack Wheat had a two-run single in the first inning, and that was all that Grimes would need. Making good use of his fastball and spitball, Grimes held the Giants to four hits (three of them by Frisch) in gaining his seventeenth win of the season. That still left him two behind Wilbur Cooper, who won his nineteenth while beating the Cubs. Pittsburgh made it four straight over Chicago the following day, but the Giants kept the Pirates' lead at four and a half with a 4–3 win behind Toney's five-hitter.

Philadelphia followed Brooklyn into the Polo Grounds for an abbreviated two-game series, and again McGraw would be facing a rookie manager. Kaiser Wilhelm, a former pitcher in the National and Federal leagues, had replaced Bill Donovan at about the same time that Bill Killefer had replaced Evers in Chicago. The Giants won the first game, 8–2, behind Phil Douglas, with Philadelphia's only two runs coming on first baseman Ed Konetchy's home run. The Phillies had picked up the thirty-five-year-old Konetchy on waivers from Brooklyn back on July 4. Playing in seventy-two games for the Phillies in this, his fifteenth and final big league season, Konetchy would bat .321 with eight home runs.

Frisch, who had gone 10 for 19 in the four games against Brooklyn, continued his red-hot pace. He had two more hits, including a first-inning three-run home run, and four runs batted in. Despite Kelly's home runs and Youngs's lofty batting average, it was Frisch, the local boy, who played with an engaging joie de vivre and generated the most excitement among Giants' fans.

The game was one of the odder ones of the season, featuring several instances of farce and one of near tragedy. The farcical moments were a result of a steady rain that threatened to wipe out the Giants' early lead. That inspired the New Yorkers to do what they could to speed things up, including failing to run out ground balls, while on the other side, the Phillies made five errors in an attempt to slow things down.

Philadelphia pitcher Jimmy Ring was responsible for the most egregious attempt to get umpire Charlie Moran to call the game. It came in the fourth inning, with the Giants ahead, 5–0, and the rain coming down hard. Johnny Rawlings and Frank Snyder were the first two batters, and each made out on the first pitch. Douglas wanted to do the same, but the first pitch was ten yards wide of the plate and the second sailed over his head. Moran went to the mound to warn Ring, but the pitcher just laughed at him. "This ball is too slippery to pitch," he said. "Why don't you call the game?"[29] Douglas eventually walked; and when Ring hurled the ball into center field, Douglas continued to second, then made his way toward third, where Goldie Rapp tagged him out. After the Phillies batted in the top of the fifth inning, it became an official game; and the pace of play returned to normal.

The near tragedy occurred in the eighth inning and again centered on Ring. Manager Wilhelm had kept his pitcher on the mound for the entire game; so when Ring batted in the top of the eighth with his team trailing, 6–0, he was probably not in the best frame of mind. When a Douglas pitch came in dangerously high and tight, Ring flung his bat at the Giants' pitcher. The bat missed its intended target and landed near second base. Ring then headed toward the mound, before cooler heads intervened. Such an incident usually results in an ejection, but umpire Moran let Ring stay in the game.

During the home eighth, while the Giants were adding two more runs, Ring, out of frustration and perhaps retaliation, threw several pitches at the head of George Burns. One finally connected with its target, and Burns collapsed with blood flowing from his nose. Memories of Ray Chapman's beaning just under a year ago on this same field surely were on everybody's mind. Even Ring seemed genuinely distraught as he gathered with players from both sides around an unconscious Burns. To everyone's relief, Burns got up and seemed okay, although Bill Cunningham went in to run for him. Moran again failed to eject Ring, who went back to the mound accompanied by a chorus of boos.

Burns missed the next two games, both one-run losses, with Cunningham going 1 for 10 as his replacement in the leadoff spot and in center field. Konetchy, who had gone 4-4 against Douglas, went 4-4 again to help Lee Meadows edge Jesse Barnes, 2–1. It was a listless effort by the Giants; and the one thing the fans had to cheer was the return of Earl Smith, who made his first appearance in twelve days. Warmly welcomed when he batted for Barnes in the seventh, Smith showed his appreciation with a solid single to center.

The western clubs were set to make their third and last visit to New York beginning on August 17; but before that, the Giants had one game to play with Brooklyn. Three days earlier, Burleigh Grimes had beaten them and Art Nehf, 3–1. Now the two aces were matched again; and while it was a much different kind of game, the result was the same, a victory for the Dodgers. Grimes went the distance in raising his record to 18-6.

The back-to-back one-run losses to the Phillies and the Dodgers left the Giants five and a half games behind Pittsburgh and fighting to hold off third-place Boston, who had closed to within two games of them. McGraw's club had played at a mediocre .500 pace over the last month, and some in the press were beginning to write them off.

"The race is more than two-thirds run and the Giants have made practically no gain on the leaders the past month. If it were not for the resourcefulness and indomitable fighting spirit of McGraw, I would say the task of overcoming the Pirates were well nigh impossible," wrote one sportswriter.[30] Collyer's Eye, a gambling weekly, told their readers that despite the addition of Bancroft, Rawlings, and Meusel, the Giants did not have the look of a pennant winner. Nor could they compare with previous National League champions, citing "Frank Chance's Cubs, the old Pittsburgh Pirates and other McGraw teams."[31]

While John McGraw remained outwardly confident, everyone connected to the Giants knew that the club would have to improve on the .500 pace of the last month if it hoped to catch the Pirates. Three games with Cincinnati and four with St. Louis would precede Pittsburgh's five-game visit, which would begin on August 24. If the Giants could not reduce the Pirates' five-and-a-half-game lead before then, their chances of overtaking the frontrunners would suffer a serious setback.

The Cincinnati series started well, with a 6–3 win over the always-troublesome Rube Marquard. George Kelly's home run with three men on in the first inning, his twentieth four-bagger of the season, was the big blow for the Giants. Long George now had three of the five bases-loaded home runs hit in the National League this season. George Burns, with three stitches over his left eye, returned to action and had three hits and two runs scored. Defensively, the Giants made two more double plays, giving them eighteen in their last eight games. Not even the old-timers in the press box could recall a similar streak.

However, the best news for McGraw to come out of this game, and the one with the greatest possible long-term significance, was the performance of Pat Shea. Working in relief of starter Fred Toney, Shea pitched five and one-third hitless, scoreless innings to gain his first Major League win. A year earlier, Duster Mails had joined the Indians late in the season and won seven games without a loss to help Cleveland win a pennant. Perhaps Shea could do the same for the Giants.

In addition, Shea's impressive outing may have influenced McGraw's decision not to seek other pitching assistance. Although McGraw denied them, there had been reports that the Giants had offered owner Jack Dunn of the Baltimore Orioles the lofty sum of $150,000 for pitcher–first baseman Jack Bentley, pitcher Jack Ogden, and outfielder Otis Lawry. "I know nothing about a deal with the Baltimore club for any players," McGraw said. "As for paying $150,000 for a trio of minor leaguers, I would not give that sum to Jack Dunn for his entire club."[32]

The win allowed the Giants to pick up a half game on the idle Pirates and to increase their lead to three and a half games over the third-place Braves, losers of a doubleheader to Chicago. But when Pittsburgh won two one-run games at Philadelphia the next day, while Dolf Luque was beating the Giants, the lead was up to six and a half games. "New York's world's series hopes now rest almost entirely on the Yankees," wrote Fred Lieb.[33]

On August 19 Jim Mutrie, often called "the Father of New York Baseball," watched from the press box as the Giants won the final game from the

Reds. Mutrie, now seventy, had managed the New York Metropolitans of the American Association in 1883–84, when the Association was a Major League. He took over the Giants in 1885—their third year of existence—and managed them through 1891. It was Mutrie who had given the team the name "Giants." While acknowledging that there were some great teams playing now, Mutrie expressed his dislike of pinch hitters. "There is one thing I object to strongly," he said. "I do not think that men should be taken out for pinch hitters. In our day it was a battle royal—a picked nine against a picked nine."[34]

The Giants' goal now was to try to pick up some ground in their four games with the Cardinals, before the Pirates came to town. At the end of July New York had lost three of four very contentious games at Sportsman's Park. Unfortunately for the Giants, they caught Branch Rickey's St. Louis club at a bad time. The 56-56 Cardinals had just begun a streak in which they would win thirty-one of their final forty-one games. In winning three of the four games at the Polo Grounds, they dealt what seemed to be a deathblow to the Giants' pennant hopes.

Bill Doak, the spitball-throwing right-hander, allowed only a first-inning run in winning the opener, 10–1. A twenty-game winner in 1920, Doak would lead the National League in winning percentage (.714) and earned run average (2.59) in 1921. The loss, combined with Pittsburgh's victory at Boston (Wilbur Cooper's twentieth win of the season), increased New York's deficit to seven games. For the Giants to win the pennant, they would have to win twenty-six of their remaining thirty-six games and hope the Pirates could do no better than split theirs. However, should the Pirates continue at their current .652 pace, then the Giants would have to win thirty-one of the remaining thirty-six. At this point, their chances of finishing third seemed more likely than their chances of finishing first. They had a two-and-a-half-game lead over Boston, but that was only because they had played five more games and won them all (69-48 vs. 64-48).

On Sunday the twenty-first, the citizens of New Rochelle, New York, honored their neighbor Frankie Frisch as part of the large gathering that watched Toney give the Giants their lone win of the series. Frisch stole his league-leading forty-second base, one of five steals the Giants had against catcher Eddie Ainsmith. The Russian-born veteran (born Edward Anshmedt) had been Walter Johnson's longtime catcher in Washington. Released by the Tigers on July 23, he was signed by the Cardinals on August 4. In addition to the stolen bases, Ainsmith also allowed two passed balls, which led to his receiving a lot of razzing from the Giants. At one point, he became so annoyed at what he was hearing that he threw off his mask and started toward the Giants' bench. He never got there because Burt Shotton, the Cardinals' Sunday manager, and some of his players ran from the dugout to intercept him, aided by umpires Hank O'Day and Ernie Quigley.[35]

Despite the win, August had so far been a disastrous month for the Giants. Since July 30, when they were tied with Pittsburgh for first place, the Pirates had picked up six and a half games by going 15-5 while the Giants, with the day's win, were 10-13.

McGraw gave Pat Shea his first start the next day, and any hope of Shea duplicating Mails's 7-0 record of 1920 went quickly by the wayside. He pitched five innings and allowed all six St. Louis runs, while Bill Pertica, who had shut out the Giants in St. Louis, did it again, allowing just three hits. Pittsburgh's win at Boston increased their lead to a season-high seven and a half games.

George Kelly hit his twenty-first home run in the fourth game of the series, but it mattered little in St. Louis's victory. Mademoiselle Suzanne Lenglen, the great French tennis star, who was attending her first Major League game, graced the Polo Grounds that afternoon. "Ever since I became interested in sports I have been eager to see your great American game," said Lenglen, who was in the United States to play some exhibition matches. "It might surprise Americans to know that we in France read much concerning the national sport of this country. The fame of your Babe Ruth is well known to us. We have heard a great deal of other noted players such as Speaker and Cobb and Hornsby."[36] She met McGraw in the Giants' dugout and then sat in a box behind first base, eating peanuts and drinking soda pop and seemed excited by what she saw. In return, the fans greeted her with great applause. Rogers Hornsby presented her with a baseball, and Hughie Jennings taught her some of the rudiments of the game.

Meanwhile, Giants fans were doing some anticipating of their own. Frontrunner Pittsburgh was invading the Polo Grounds for a five-game, do-or-die series that would begin with a doubleheader on August 24. Most newspapers, both in and out of New York, were conceding the pennant to the Pirates, whose lead was a comfortable seven and a half games. With less than six weeks left, it was crucial that the Giants win at least four of the five games, while there was little or no pressure on the Pirates. Sportswriter Ed Balinger, who covered the Pittsburgh club from 1903 through 1946, wrote, "If the worst comes to the worst, and the Pirates lose three out of the five, they'll still leave New York six and a half games to the good."[37]

NL STANDINGS AT CLOSE OF PLAY OF AUGUST 23, 1921

TEAM	G	W	L	T	PCT	GB
Pittsburgh Pirates	117	76	41	0	.650	–
New York Giants	120	70	50	0	.583	7.5
Boston Braves	114	65	49	0	.570	9.5
Brooklyn Dodgers	120	62	58	0	.517	15.5
St. Louis Cardinals	116	59	57	0	.509	16.5
Cincinnati Reds	118	53	65	0	.449	23.5
Chicago Cubs	117	47	70	0	.402	29.0
Philadelphia Phillies	118	38	80	0	.322	38.5

20 "Let's go get 'em while the getting's good"

Ed Balinger's assessment of the pennant race was much different from the prevailing wisdom of a few weeks earlier. When July ended with the Giants and Pirates tied for first place, the eight games remaining between the two teams—the upcoming five in New York and the three in Pittsburgh in mid-September—figured to be the major factor in deciding the National League's eventual winner.

However, because so much had happened in the intervening three and a half weeks, the series at the Polo Grounds now appeared likely to be simply a coronation for the Pirates. Since July 30, when both teams had records of 60-35, George Gibson's high-flying Buccaneers had won sixteen of twenty-two, while the stumbling Giants had lost fifteen of twenty-five. On August 24, when a Wednesday doubleheader kicked off the series, the 76-41 Pirates held a seven-and-a-half-game lead over the Giants, a lead many in the press thought close to insurmountable.

The general feeling was that the Giants had to win all five games to get back in the race.[1] While discussing the Pirates pitching staff, Walter Trumbull wrote that "If the Pittsburgh team gets into the world's series, and there appears to be small doubt that it will, it will be interesting to watch the work of the veteran and the youngster."[2]

The youngster was Whitey Glazner, a rookie who would go 14-5 this season. The veteran was Babe Adams, who, with a record of 12-3, would pitch the opening game of the doubleheader. Wilbur Cooper, still the league's top winner with a record of 20-8, would be Gibson's starter in the second game. John McGraw would counter with Art Nehf and Phil Douglas, whose records stood at 14-8 and 10-8, respectively. That the Giants had won ten of the fourteen games already played between the two teams this season now meant nothing. If they hoped to stay in the race, New York would have to win at least four of these next five games. Certainly, the Pirates were not expecting such a one-sided result. They seemed supremely confident that Pittsburgh, the city they represented, would be returning to the World Series for the first time in twelve years. Owner Barney Dreyfuss had even begun the process of adding more bleacher and grandstand seats to Forbes Field for the World Series games he expected to host.

For John McGraw, Dreyfuss's longtime antagonist, the situation was quite the opposite. McGraw's floundering team appeared on the verge of completing its fourth consecutive season without a pennant, a stretch of futility exceeded only by his 1906–10 teams. The New York press that had mostly fawned on him for so many years now seemed more interested in the exploits of Yankee slugger Babe Ruth. Miller Huggins, McGraw's managerial counterpart on the Yankees, was accustomed to hearing criticism in New York; but McGraw was not. Now, however, he had begun to hear grumbling from the fans and from certain segments of the press that it was he who was mainly responsible for the Giants' poor play. Even some of his players had been voicing complaints about his managerial style, though not openly and at nowhere near the level Huggins was getting from his players. Though still in uniform, McGraw had taken to running the club from the bench, with Hughie Jennings replacing him as the third base coach. Some players disagreed with the move. "McGraw ought to be on the coaching lines actively directing the club," said one unnamed player.[3]

McGraw, in turn, was unhappy both with the way his team had been playing and with the way various Pirates players, including Rabbit Maranville, Charlie Grimm, and Dave Robertson, had shown their contempt for him. McGraw's displeasure led him to prepare his team for the season's biggest series in his own inimitable way. Following the 10–7 loss to St. Louis the day before the opening of the Pittsburgh series, he called a team meeting and unleashed a brutal tirade directed against his players. He told them that despite having the potential to be one of the best clubs he had ever managed, they were now becoming one of the worst. Pointing to the success of the Ruth-led Yankees, he said that a Giants-Yankees World Series would rank among the greatest sporting events ever. In addition, he added, it would put a lot of money in all their pockets.

"Now it's gone," he screamed. "Gone because you're all a bunch of knuckle-headed fools! Pittsburgh is going to come in here tomorrow

30. Rabbit Maranville poses for teammate Wilbur Cooper, Pittsburgh's leading pitcher. Despite his taste for the "high life," Maranville was having an outstanding season. In late August he cautioned his league-leading Pirates teammates not to start their victory celebrations too early. *National Baseball Hall of Fame Library, Cooperstown, New York.*

laughing at us. Pittsburgh is going to take it all! Pittsburgh! A bunch of banjo-playing, wisecracking humpty-dumpties! You've thrown it all away! You haven't got a chance! And you've got only yourselves to blame!"[4]

The next day, McGraw stood quietly in a corner of the dugout before the first game of the doubleheader, while his players sat close-mouthed on the bench watching the Pirates laughing and joking their way through batting and fielding practice. First baseman Grimm, one of the "banjo-playing, wisecracking humpty-dumpties" McGraw had referred to, sat in the Pittsburgh dugout strumming his ukulele.[5] Then, as if to add insult to injury, manager Gibson ordered all his men to gather for team pictures to be used for the 1921 World Series program. The gesture by Gibson, who had coached under McGraw in 1918–19, surely irritated his former mentor; and it clearly upset one of his own star players, Rabbit Maranville. "Pictures for what?" said the Pirates' veteran shortstop. "Wait until we win the pennant before we have our pictures taken."[6]

Maranville had been a major contributor to the Pirates' success, both on defense, which they had expected, and on offense, which they had not. He was having the best offensive season of his ten-year career, batting .318, far above his previous high of .267 for the 1919 Braves.[7] As if on cue, the speedy Maranville opened the first game by lining a Nehf pitch for a double off the glove of leaping third baseman Frankie Frisch. He eventually scored the first run of the series on a sacrifice fly by Max Carey.

The Nehf-Adams matchup figured to be an excellent one. Nehf had beaten the Pirates four times this season without a loss. However, Adams had been tough on the Giants too; and he had been pitching very well of late. Runs figured to be hard to come by; so when Irish Meusel smacked a two-run home run in the second, the largest weekday crowd thus far this season rose to its feet to cheer. Not only had the Giants taken the lead, but a Meusel home run had provided it. It was the thirteenth for Meusel, but it was his first as a Giant. That was very different from the first half of the season, prior to his trade from Philadelphia, when he and George Kelly had been running first and second in the home run race. At one time, Meusel led Kelly, eleven to nine.

Once ahead, the Giants would not surrender the lead. Nehf allowed another run, in the fifth, reducing New York's lead to 3–2; but that would be all the Pirates would get. Adams left after the seventh, with Pittsburgh trailing, 6–2, before the Giants jumped on Whitey Glazner for four eighth-inning runs to make the final score 10–2. Kelly added his twenty-second home run, Meusel scored four runs, and every other Giant regular except Dave Bancroft hit safely. Nehf's five-hitter raised his record to 15-8 and to 5-0 against Pittsburgh. He had been the last pitcher to defeat Adams, back on May 24; and in doing it again, he ended Adams's nine-game winning streak.

As effective as Nehf had been in the opener, Phil Douglas was even more so in the nightcap. He tossed a five-hit, 7–0 shutout—his third shutout of the season.[8] Douglas's best pitch was the spitball. He had learned to throw it from one of the best, Ed Walsh of the White Sox, when Douglas was a rookie with that club in 1912. Along with the spitter, Douglas also threw a fastball, a good curve, and an excellent change of pace. Giants catcher Frank Snyder, who spent sixteen seasons in the National League, called Douglas "the best right-handed pitcher I ever caught."[9]

The second game bore a certain resemblance to the first. It too was a low-scoring affair until the Giants broke it open with a big inning, this time a five-run sixth. Wilbur Cooper matched Douglas's shutout pitching through four innings before the Giants pushed across a run in the fifth on singles by Johnny Rawlings, Frank Snyder, and George Burns. Burns also had the big blow an inning later. His three-run inside-the-park home run, on a drive to deep right-center, gave him four runs batted in for the game.

Meusel drove home the final run in the eighth with his fifth hit of the afternoon, a triple off Lyle Bigbee. Lyle, the older brother of Pirates left fielder Carson Bigbee, was making his Pirates debut. Meusel had begun the day batting a measly .231 since joining the Giants. But beginning with this afternoon's magnificent performance against the Pirates and carrying through until the season ended, he would be the offensive force the Giants had hoped for when they got him from Philadelphia. He would bat .405 through the rest of the season, raising his average as a Giant to .329 and his combined batting average to .343, the sixth highest in the National League.[10]

The New York fans headed for the exits, buoyed by the two wins. Their heroes had taken two full games off the Pirates' lead, cutting it to five and a half games. More than a month of the season remained. If they could win the next three, or even two of the three, they would be back in the pennant race. Meanwhile, third-place Boston failed to take advantage of the Pirates' two losses when they dropped a pair of one-run games to the visiting Cardinals. The Braves remained nine and a half games behind Pittsburgh, and they were now four behind the Giants. And, for those who dreamed of the first all–New York World Series, there was more good news. The Yankees' 3–2 win at Cleveland had moved them into first place in the American League, a half game ahead of the Indians.

The Giants' players were in the clubhouse after the sweep, celebrating their refutation of McGraw's words with their deeds, when the manager walked in. "I told you fellows last night that you didn't have a chance," he said. "Well I was wrong. You have a chance, a bare chance. . . . If my brains hold out."[11] Recalling the incident years later, George Kelly said, "It's a good thing he got out then or he might have been skulled by a shower of bats."[12]

There are days in each baseball season, both at the personal and the national levels, when "real life" intrudes and the importance of the pennant races gets put in its proper perspective. August 24, 1921, was such a day. While Giant fans were celebrating their two wins over the Pirates and Yankee fans were rejoicing in their win over the Indians that vaulted them into first place, disaster struck the United States on both sides of the Atlantic.

In Hull, England, the dirigible ZR-2, in the process of being transferred to the U.S. Navy, exploded in midair and broke apart, with the pieces of the huge airship landing in the Humber River. Forty-four of the forty-nine men on board died in the explosion, including seventeen men of the U.S. Navy and twenty-seven men of the Royal Navy. Meanwhile in Hoboken, New Jersey, across the Hudson River from Manhattan, a fire destroyed two army piers and scorched the steamship *Leviathan*. Firemen from New Jersey and New York, with an assist from a favoring wind, were able to keep the fire from spreading into the city of Hoboken. They were also able to save the caskets of 1,500 U.S. Army dead that the ship was returning from the battlefields of Europe to their families in America. A day later, the United States would sign a peace treaty with Germany, officially ending hostilities between the two nations.

Had the tongue-lashing McGraw inflicted on his players before the doubleheader played a part in the Giants' turnaround? Perhaps it had resonated with Meusel, who had been underperforming and may have needed this kind of spark. Yet it is difficult to imagine McGraw's harangue had much effect on any of the other regulars, all of whom were veterans and knew how important this series was.

Sixty-three years later, Kelly, whose memory at age eighty-eight may have dimmed, claimed he did not remember the speech. "We didn't have that pep talk and all that kind of baloney," he said. "That was a lot of baloney in my days. I never heard McGraw come out and get on a speech to fire people up. You had to come out there and be fired up to win the ball game."[13]

As for the two pitchers, Nehf was a serious professional who did not need a pep talk, and Douglas, detesting McGraw as he did, probably paid no attention.

Still, part of a manager's role is to address his players en masse, whether negatively and sarcastically, as McGraw had done, or positively, as Gibson did before the game the next day. "All right, we looked lousy yesterday and lost two games, but we're still five and a half games in front and finishing the season at home," said the usually easy-going Gibson in an attempt to cheer his players. "Now let's go out there and win today."[14]

Not content to trust in words alone, Gibson shook up his batting order. He put Carson Bigbee in the lead-off spot, dropped Maranville down to number three, moved Clyde Barnhart from the cleanup spot to sixth, and inserted hot-hitting Dave Robertson in Barnhart's place. The moves proved futile. Fred Toney held the revamped Pirates lineup to single runs in the fourth and ninth innings as the Giants won again, 5–2. Toney's sixth consecutive win, which followed his five-game losing streak, brought his season record to 15-8 and again tied him with Nehf for the team lead. He also had the game's biggest hit, a second-inning home run into the right-field upper deck (Babe Ruth territory) that accounted for three of the Giants' five runs against Johnny Morrison. Earl Smith, batting in front of Toney, had a bases-loaded single that accounted for the first two runs of the inning.

After the game, the people filing out of the Polo Grounds seemed to have a new awareness that this race was not yet over. Barney Dreyfuss, who attended all five games, must have had a similar feeling as he saw his team's lead slip a bit more, down to four and a half games. Giants fans were left wondering how their team could do so well against the strong Pirates yet play so spottily against some of the league's weaker teams. If only they had won more of those games, they would now be ahead in the race.

After defeating them three times in two days, the Giants players too suspected that the strain of leading the race for so long was beginning to tell on the Pirates. "Let's go get 'em while the getting's good," said reserve outfielder Casey Stengel.[15] Moreover, that specter of doubt settling over the Pirates was now being echoed in the Pittsburgh newspapers, like this item in the *Pittsburgh Press*: "It had been confidently hoped that when the team arrived here that a couple of battles would settle the little matter of which is the best team in the National League beyond a doubt. But the doubt still lingers, in fact is more evident than for some time."[16]

That doubt grew stronger the next day when, despite an outstanding performance by Earl Hamilton, the Pirates lost again. Hamilton allowed only five hits but ended up a 2–1 loser to Phil Douglas in a game that featured outstanding defensive plays for both sides. Douglas, pitching with one day's rest, got out of more tight scrapes than Harry Houdini. This was only fitting since Houdini, the world's best-known escape artist, was among the Friday crowd of 18,000, an above-normal size for a weekday.

Unlike the previous three games, this one was tense and nerve-racking right from the start. Bigbee and Carey began the first inning with singles. Maranville then sacrificed them into scoring position, but Douglas kept them there. In the third, Pittsburgh had two on with none out and then loaded the bases with two out, but George Cutshaw's grounder to Bancroft ended the inning. The Pirates made a final attempt to tie the game in the eighth. One-out singles by Cutshaw and Barnhart put the potential tying and winning runs on base. But Douglas had enough left to get Grimm on a fly to Meusel and Walter Schmidt on a grounder to Bancroft.

Shufflin' Phil allowed ten hits but only the one run, thanks to a sensational double play in the sixth started by Dave Bancroft. New York was up, 2–0, when the Pirates scored their one run on singles by Maranville, Cutshaw, and Barnhart. They still had runners at first and third with one out, when Grimm hit a low liner to the shortstop side of second base. The ball looked as if it would get into the left-center-field gap for at least a double, scoring both base runners. However, Bancroft dove, speared it with one hand, and then threw to Kelly to double Barnhart off first.

The Giants had far more trouble with Hamilton than they had experienced with Adams, Cooper, or Morrison. Their two fourth-inning runs came on a one-out walk to Bancroft, a triple by Frisch (the game's only extra-base hit) that sailed over Robertson's head in right-center, and Ross Youngs's infield single. Youngs's hit was a sharp grounder that took a bad hop and bounced off the shoulder of second baseman Cutshaw. (In an attempt to bolster his offense, Gibson had inserted Cutshaw at second base in place of the slumping Cotton Tierney.)[17]

McGraw had told his players following the doubleheader that they had a chance if his brains held out. In truth, his brains, or maybe more correctly his baseball instinct, were a big part of this win. The preseries plan was for Rosy Ryan to start this game, but Ryan had hurt his arm

31. Despite fines, suspensions, and unexcused absences—alcoholic pitcher Phil Douglas was one of the best-liked players on the Giants' team. In 1921 he accounted for some of the most significant wins in their history. *Private collection of Dennis Goldstein.*

in his last outing and was unable to pitch. That left Jesse Barnes and Pat Shea. McGraw was reluctant to start either one: Barnes had not pitched well recently, and Shea, he felt, was too inexperienced. But before he could make a decision, Phil Douglas spoke up: "Let me go in there this afternoon, and I'll beat those fellows."[18] Aware that Douglas had already beaten Pittsburgh four times this season, McGraw played a hunch that he could do it again.

Maybe that is what happened and maybe it's not. In another version of the story, McGraw approached Douglas in the clubhouse thirty minutes before game time and said, "Douglas, you work." "But Mac, I worked day before yesterday. Are you sure I can go in there and lick 'em again?" responded Douglas, clearly not as confident of victory in this version. "Phil, you work," replied McGraw, ending the discussion.[19]

In whatever way McGraw came to choose Douglas, obviously he had made the right choice. Rabbit Maranville summed up the feelings of the Pirates' players after their fifth loss to Douglas this season. "We have seen too much of the Shuffler," Maranville grumbled. "There ought to be a law against a fellow as big and as smart as that having all that stuff."[20]

With the lead now down to three and a half, McGraw came back with his ace, Nehf, in the fifth game of the series. Gibson might have come back with Cooper or Adams on short rest, but evidently he did not wish to show any sign of panic to his players. Instead, he chose Hal Carlson, a fourteen-game winner in 1920 who had only been a spot starter with a 2-4 record this season. Yet, it was unlikely that Carlson, a veteran of the Battle of the Argonne Forest, would feel any undue pressure in pitching a baseball game.

Changes in momentum are often subtle and cannot be measured, but the 38,000 fans at the Polo Grounds this Saturday had a sense that it had shifted sharply in favor of the Giants. That sense was correct and reinforced this afternoon. Nehf, who had pitched a five-hitter in the first game of the series, pitched a four-hitter in this one. Supported by a large, enthusiastic crowd—whose deafening roars lent a World Series–like atmosphere to the game—the Giants came away with a 3–1 victory and a stunning sweep of the five-game series. Nehf's win raised his record against Pittsburgh to 6-0, the only such record by any pitcher against any team in the National League at this point in the season.

For the second time at a Giants' home game this year, it was necessary to lift the screens in center field to allow for more patrons. The screens were there to provide batters with a better background, and their absence may have been partially responsible for the lack of hitting in this game. Nehf allowed only four hits, while the Giants managed only six, all singles, against Carlson, Jimmy Zinn, and Whitey Glazner.

With any luck, Nehf could have had a shutout. Two of the Pirates' hits came in the first, when Maranville hit a bloop single and Possum Whitted followed with a short fly to center. Burns tried to make a shoestring catch, but the ball landed in front of him. Whitted made a double out of it (the game's only extra-base hit) as Maranville scored. While Burns often made that play successfully, chances are if he had let Whitted's hit fall in for a single, the Pirates would not have scored. Then again, stellar defense by his teammates, particularly Bancroft and Frisch, aided Nehf on several occasions.

Frustrated by Carlson, who had made that one run stand through six innings, the fans standing for the seventh-inning stretch were screaming and imploring the Giants to indeed make it the "lucky seventh." When Frisch and Youngs hit one-out singles, they came alive, cheering for Kelly at least to tie the game. Long George disappointed by popping out to Cutshaw; but Meusel came through with a sharp single to right, his eighth hit in sixteen at bats in the five games.[21] Frisch scored easily; and when right fielder Carey juggled the ball, Youngs, running at full speed with two out, also scored. Frisch's sacrifice fly off Glazner in the eighth gave New York an insurance run.

Giants pitching, which had been suspect for much of the season, had been spectacular throughout this series. Nehf, Douglas, and Toney had thrown five complete games and had allowed the league-leading Pirates a total of only six runs. In beating the Pirates for the eighth consecutive time, the Giants raised their season's record against them to 15-4. Pittsburgh's lead, which had been seven and a half games on August 23, was now just two and a half games on August 27. "Not bad," said McGraw after the sweep. "But Pittsburgh is still in first place."[22]

Indeed they were; and with the Braves now ten games behind, the Cardinals eleven, and the Dodgers thirteen, it would be strictly a two-team race to the finish. And, as the newspapers in Pittsburgh were quick to point out, despite the five losses in New York, the numbers still favored the Pirates. With a record of 76-46, they still had four fewer losses than the 75-50 Giants. That meant the Giants would need Pittsburgh to lose five more games than they would over the remaining month to finish first.

Moreover, the Pirates also had the advantage of playing twenty-two of their remaining thirty-two games at home, while the Giants would be on the road for nineteen of their remaining twenty-eight. As the Pirates headed to Brooklyn and the Giants welcomed the Cubs, it remained to be seen how much psychological damage the Giants had inflicted on the Pirates in these five games. As New York sportswriter Arthur Robinson reminded his readers after the sweep, "Take nothing for granted in baseball."[23]

NL STANDINGS AT CLOSE OF PLAY OF AUGUST 27, 1921

TEAM	G	W	L	T	PCT	GB
Pittsburgh Pirates	122	76	46	0	.623	-
New York Giants	125	75	50	0	.600	2.5
Boston Braves	120	65	55	0	.542	10.0
St. Louis Cardinals	122	65	57	0	.533	11.0
Brooklyn Dodgers	124	64	60	0	.516	13.0
Cincinnati Reds	123	55	68	0	.447	21.5
Chicago Cubs	121	49	72	0	.405	26.5
Philadelphia Phillies	123	41	82	0	.333	35.5

"It is no time in which to count
McGraw and his men out of any race"

The debate between those who believe that good managers make for good teams and those who believe that good teams make for good managers has always been a part of baseball. The former usually cite leadership as their primary argument and John McGraw as their primary example. The latter most often mention talent on the diamond as their main point. In 1921 Miller Huggins was their most prominent example. Babe Ruth, not his taciturn little skipper, made the Yankees a good team, they said.

Being a good leader, of course, does not necessarily mean that those you lead hold you in affection. Again, John McGraw is a prime example. Throughout his thirty-one years as manager of the Giants (1902–32), many of his players disliked him and some actually hated him, including Earl Smith and Phil Douglas of the 1921 squad.

Similarly, many Yankee players disliked and resented Miller Huggins. Yet, like McGraw, Huggins had kept his team in the pennant race all season long. As Labor Day approached, an all–New York City World Series remained a real possibility.

It had been McGraw's pep talk to a seemingly beaten Giants team, along with his continued bold and adroit use of his pitching staff, which had helped his players engineer the August 24–27 five-game sweep of the Pirates. Picking up five games in four days had moved the Giants to within striking distance of Pittsburgh. They had come close earlier this season, only to falter against the league's weaker teams. With the seventh-place Cubs coming to the Polo Grounds for three games, beginning on August 28, the chance to falter was again present.

This time, however, the rejuvenated Giants took advantage of their opportunity. By winning all three games from Chicago, they were able to cut another game off the lead, as the Pirates lost one of their three games in Brooklyn.

The New Yorkers got well-pitched complete games from Jesse Barnes in the opener and from Art Nehf in the closing game. Fred Toney was ineffective in the middle game, but three and two-thirds innings of solid relief work by Slim Sallee and three more by Pat Shea saved the day.

Roommates Frankie Frisch and Ross Youngs, the two speediest men on the team, each hit a key triple in Barnes's 4–2 victory. Grover Alexander was the losing pitcher for Chicago, which enabled the Giants to even their lifetime record against the great right-hander at 25-25.[1] Nehf's win in the final game was his seventeenth of the season and the eighth straight for the team. Trailing, 3–0, the streak appeared in jeopardy until the Giants exploded for five runs in the eighth inning. Four of the runs came on two-run home runs by Earl Smith and Dave Bancroft. Until then, the closest the Giants had come to scoring against Speed Martin was in the third inning when they had runners at first and third and nobody out. That rally ended suddenly when second baseman Zeb Terry snared Nehf's liner and turned it into the first and only triple play of the 1921 season at the Polo Grounds.

Over in Brooklyn, Pittsburgh had won the first game of their three-game series with the Dodgers, ending the Pirates' losing streak at six. (A loss to the Braves had preceded the five losses to the Giants.) A large Sunday crowd saw Johnny Morrison defeat Burleigh Grimes, 2–0, preventing Grimes from getting his twentieth win of the season. In another great pitching duel the next day, Brooklyn's Dutch Ruether edged Wilbur Cooper, 1–0. A dropped throw at first base by Cooper in the last of the ninth allowed Hy Myers to score the game's lone run. The loss by Cooper was the sixth in his last nine decisions and dropped the record of the league's only twenty-game winner to date to 20-10. It also shaved a game off the Pirates' lead, which was now down to one and a half games. Dave Robertson, who hit for the cycle, helped Whitey Glazner and the Pirates win the final game.

In an age before radio broadcasts—much less BlackBerrys, cell phones, and other handheld forms of instant communication—fans in ballparks learned how their team's competitors were faring by watching the scoreboard. Scoreboard watching had been a part of baseball since the inception of scoreboards and was particularly prevalent during closely contested, late-season pennant races.[2] Now that the Giants were back in the race, scoreboard watching at their home games had returned. It had been very much a part of the Chicago series and would continue until they or the Pirates captured the pennant. And as September rolled around, when the Yankees were at home in the Polo Grounds, they started posting the Pirates' scores in addition to those of American League games. (They had already been posting the Giants' scores for a number of years, as the Giants had been doing with the Yankees' scores.)

While tracking the scores of other games is mostly associated with fans, players do it, too, though in a more surreptitious manner. The press reported several Giants players sneaking peeks at the Polo Grounds scoreboard to see how the Dodgers were doing against Pittsburgh. No doubt, the Pirates' players were doing the same at Ebbets Field, monitoring the progress of the Giants-Cubs games.

Still, scoreboard watching remained primarily a fan diversion, which had been on full display at the two New York parks over the past three days. The Dodgers' 1–0 victory over Cooper on Monday set off the loudest cheers of the afternoon at the Polo Grounds. It was strange hearing Giants fans cheering a Brooklyn win and even stranger hearing fans at Ebbets Field cheering for the Giants.

While the fans of each team hated the other, the hatred seemed to be stronger among Dodger fans. Under manager Ned Hanlon, the Dodgers (or Superbas) had been the far-superior team at the turn of the century, winning pennants in 1899 and 1900.[3] That began to change with the arrival of John McGraw in 1902, and since then the Giants had usually fielded better teams than the Dodgers. Also fueling the stronger feelings on the Brooklyn side was the borough's inferior place in the city's power structure, as compared to that of Manhattan.

Nevertheless, many Dodger fans apparently were rooting for the Giants to overtake Pittsburgh and win the pennant. Their animosity toward the Pirates and their owner Barney Dreyfuss dated back to 1900, when a bitter rivalry developed between Brooklyn and Pittsburgh as the two teams battled for the pennant. Dreyfuss often criticized Hanlon's leadership and his players' courage, and even tried to intimidate them before a key series in May 1900 by ordering police to surround the visitors' bench. Then, after Brooklyn finished first and Pittsburgh second, the Pirates, still believing they were the better team, challenged the Dodgers to what the press called a "world's championship series."

32. Spitballer Burleigh Grimes of Brooklyn led the National League in wins (22), complete games (30), and strikeouts (136) in 1921. He defeated the Giants four times and the Pirates three times. *Culver Pictures.*

The *Pittsburgh Chronicle-Telegraph* agreed to award a silver cup to the winner of the best-of-five series, in which Pittsburgh would host all five games. Hanlon thought so little of the idea that he went home to Baltimore and chose outfielder Joe Kelley to run the team. Brooklyn won the Chronicle Cup series in four games, led by two dominating performances by "Iron Man" Joe McGinnity.[4] Before the series, the Brooklyn players had decided that if they won, they would draw straws to see who got to keep the actual cup. But after McGinnity's two commanding complete-game outings, they reversed themselves and awarded it to the Iron Man unanimously.[5]

Both New York and Pittsburgh had off days on August 31, 1921, before resuming play the next day—the Pirates at home with St. Louis and the Giants at Brooklyn. The eight-game winning streak that ended the Giants' home stand raised their record at the Polo Grounds to a sparkling 50-23 (a .685 winning percentage). Their road record, however, where they would play nineteen of their remaining twenty-five games, was a mediocre 28-27. The Pirates, by comparison, would have the advantage of playing twenty-two of their final twenty-eight games at home.

New York's road record dropped to an even .500 after Burleigh Grimes defeated them, picking up his twentieth win of the season. Grimes would capture two legs of the pitcher's Triple Crown in 1921, leading the National League with twenty-two wins (tied with Wilbur Cooper) and 136 strikeouts.[6] More than six decades later, baseball historians would award Grimes the National League's retroactive Cy Young Award for 1921.[7]

Yet despite the Giants' loss, in which they were victimized by a triple play for the second consecutive game, the New Yorkers picked up a half game on floundering Pittsburgh. The Pirates' return to Forbes Field, after more than two weeks on the road, did not provide any change in their fortunes. St. Louis's Bill Pertica and Bill Sherdel defeated them in both ends of a doubleheader. The two wins allowed the Cardinals to pass the Braves, who had been playing poorly in recent weeks, and take over third place. The Pirates' situation got even worse the next day, when Jesse Haines beat Hal Carlson, 1–0, dealing the slumping leaders their second consecutive shutout. With the Giants idle, Pittsburgh's lead was now a mere half game. Both teams had seventy-eight wins; but the Giants had fifty-one losses, one more than the Pirates had.[8]

The momentum had clearly shifted in the Giants' favor, both on and off the field. "I think the Giants have the more nerve and the better morale," wrote Sam Crane.[9] "[George] Gibson's men are not playing pennant ball," wrote Joe Vila. "They have 'cracked' and their manager will experience much difficulty in pulling them together again."[10]

A small sidebar in the *New York Times* of September 3 gave further indication of the sense of impending doom surrounding the Pirates' chances. There had been plans to shift the football game between the University of Pittsburgh and West Virginia University, scheduled for Forbes Field on October 8, to October 15 in order to avoid a possible conflict with the Pirates hosting a World Series game. Those plans had been temporarily put aside now that Pittsburgh's winning the pennant was no longer anywhere near a sure thing. They became even less of a sure thing that afternoon, when Barnes beat the Dodgers in a game called after seven innings because of rain. With the Pirates being rained out against St. Louis, they had fallen into a virtual tie with the Giants.[11]

A day later, Pittsburgh's lead was back up to a full game after they won, 2–1, in twelve innings at Cincinnati. Both pitchers, Glazner for the Pirates and Dolf Luque of the Reds, went the distance. Meanwhile, in the Giants' opener of a four-game home series with the Braves, Boston's Joe Oeschger, aided by a tie-breaking three-run home run by Billy Southworth, beat Art Nehf, 6–3. Oeschger's twentieth win of the season tied him with Burleigh Grimes and Wilbur Cooper for the league lead. Although Boston had dropped to fourth place behind St. Louis, the incentive was there for them to move back ahead of the Cardinals. Third-place finishers received a share of the World Series revenue; fourth-place finishers did not.

On September 5 one of the largest crowds in Polo Grounds history attended the Labor Day doubleheader with the Braves. The Giants' management had to lock the gates to prevent the additional 25,000–60,000 fans (depending on which newspaper estimate one read) that jammed the streets around the park from pouring in. Extra police and the New York City Fire Department had to be called in, and several women fainted in the crush of activity.

Had they allowed at least some of those turned away to take up positions on the field, the Giants could have added many thousands of dollars to their coffers. However, unlike the practice used at many other parks, where ropes were spread across the outfield and fans were allowed to stand behind them, owner Charles Stoneham refused to do so. Not allowing fans on the field was a protocol the Giants had followed ever since the late John Brush owned the team. "I want a clear field for my players," Brush had said. "As long as I live there will be no spectators allowed on the playing field of the Polo Grounds."[12] The Giants' tenants, the Yankees, also followed the Brush philosophy regarding outfield standees.

The first game was a back-and-forth thriller won by Boston, 6–5. Fred Toney took a 1–0 lead into the top of the seventh (a lead he had provided with his third home run of the season), when the Braves rallied for two runs. The Giants retook the lead with three in the home seventh, only to have the Braves load the bases with one out in the eighth. When Toney's first two pitches to Southworth were off the mark,

McGraw gave the signal to shortstop and captain Dave Bancroft to inform Toney that he was finished for the day. Toney appeared upset at the decision and was probably more so when Southworth, the hero of the previous day's game, struck again. He lined reliever Slim Sallee's first pitch off George Kelly's glove for a two-run double. Boston added two more runs in the inning off Sallee, enough to withstand a ninth-inning run by the Giants and come away with the victory.

With Rosy Ryan still having arm problems and Phil Douglas "unavailable," McGraw turned to Pat Shea in the second game. Arthur Robinson had this to say about Douglas's unavailability: "Shufflin' Phil Douglas, who pitched and won two games in three days for the Giants while they reached out desperately at the coattails of the Pirates, has been of little use. The two games he won seem to have spoiled him, and [coach] Cozy Dolan now spends some of his time as the errant pitcher's chaperone."[13]

Shea rewarded McGraw's faith in him and revived the dispirited crowd with a route-going 5–3 win. It would be the only complete game of his career. Pittsburgh maintained its one-game lead by also splitting a doubleheader in a pair of 2–1 games at Cincinnati. Eppa Rixey of the Reds went thirteen innings to capture the morning game, with the winning run scoring on a walk, a steal of second, and successive errors by catcher Art Wilson and rookie third baseman Pie Traynor.[14] Wilbur Cooper earned his twenty-first win in the afternoon game, keeping him tied with Brooklyn's Burleigh Grimes, who defeated Philadelphia.

Meanwhile, in St. Louis on Labor Day, the Cardinals took a doubleheader from Chicago, giving them eighteen wins in their last twenty-one games. Although they were still seven and a half games behind Pittsburgh, the Branch Rickey–led Cardinals could not be counted out. They would play their last seventeen games at home, with the final eight against the two teams ahead of them: three against New York and five against Pittsburgh. Two more wins against Chicago on September 6 moved the Cardinals to just six and a half games behind idle Pittsburgh.

A disappointing 6–2 loss to spitballer Dana Fillingim in the final game of the Boston series dropped the Giants one and a half games behind the Pirates. Losing three of four to the Braves had seemingly halted whatever momentum they had gained from their eight-game winning streak. However, the Boston series would be the final one the Giants would lose this season.

On September 7 the reliable Art Nehf and the unpredictable Phil Douglas downed the dreadful last-place Phillies, 7–2 and 13–4, in a doubleheader at Philadelphia. Solo home runs by Cy Williams and Ed Konetchy accounted for the only runs off Nehf, who won his eighteenth game of the season. Williams and Konetchy each homered again in the second game, but their blows had little impact.[15] Nineteen Giants hits, including four each by Frisch and Meusel, plus four Philadelphia errors turned the game into a rout for the New Yorkers. With Pittsburgh not scheduled, the Giants, at 82-54, picked up a full game on the 80-51 Pirates and again trailed them by just a half game.

Neither club was scheduled to play the next day, although the Pirates used this third consecutive "off day" to play an exhibition game in nearby Connellsville, Pennsylvania. Pittsburgh's three idle days allowed manager Gibson to come back with his ace, Wilbur Cooper, against the Cubs. Cooper had started the Pirates' most recent game, winning the second game of the Labor Day doubleheader. Going for his twenty-second win, he allowed the Cubs four runs in the first inning, on the way to an 8–5 loss.

That same Friday, September 9, the Giants began a critical three-game weekend series with Brooklyn. The first two games would be at the Polo Grounds; and the final one, on Sunday at Ebbets Field.[16] Wilbert Robinson's club had been the most difficult to defeat for McGraw. The fifth-place Dodgers had taken eleven of the eighteen games played between the interborough rivals this season.

Robinson surprised the Giants by using Leon Cadore on Friday, instead of his ace, Grimes, despite it being Grimes's turn in the rotation. The ploy was both unsuccessful and short-lived. After George Burns and Dave Bancroft opened the home first with singles, Robby quickly replaced Cadore with Dutch Ruether. Burns had three hits, as did Meusel, in Fred Toney's complete-game victory. Meusel also contributed the key defensive play of the game, throwing Ernie Krueger out at the plate in the seventh inning when the Giants' lead was only 3–2. At 83-54, the Giants were now a half game ahead of the 80-52 Pirates, though Pittsburgh still led in winning percentage, .60606 to .60583.

Cooper's loss the day before gave Grimes the opportunity to take over the league lead in wins when he faced the Giants on Saturday. His chances for number twenty-two looked strong against a team he had already beaten four times this season. However, the New Yorkers scored three runs in the first inning, which, along with a strong performance by Jesse Barnes, was enough to defeat Grimes, 3–1. Pittsburgh's Johnny Morrison's shutout of the Cubs kept the standings of the top two teams unchanged, despite the Giants' attempt to affect them off the field. They had appealed to John Heydler to reverse his decision on the May 28 game that Pittsburgh had lost to the Reds, which the Pirates then won when the last one and a half innings were replayed on June 30. A nice try, but it failed when Heydler stood by his original decision.

On September 11 at Ebbets Field, the Giants pummeled four Brooklyn pitchers for twenty hits in an 11–3 win. Staked to a 5–0 lead, starter Phil Douglas gave up a run in the third inning and was facing a bases-loaded, no-out situation, when McGraw replaced him with Toney. Pitching with one day's rest, Toney allowed two of the inherited runners to score but then held the Dodgers scoreless over the final six innings.

That evening, Sunday, September 11, the Giants boarded a train to Cincinnati to begin their final western swing. It had been a long, difficult road; but they were in first place at last. What had seemed inevitable ever since they swept the Pirates in late August had finally transpired. The thumping of the Dodgers, combined with Pittsburgh's loss to Rube Marquard and the Reds, gave New York undisputed possession of the top spot. They not only had a one-and-a-half-game lead, but they also now led in winning percentage, 612 to .604.

The Giants' chances of retaining that lead appeared grim after eight innings of the first game against the Reds. The scoreboard showed the Pirates beating the Braves, while New York was trailing Dolf Luque, 3–0. But this Giants team had an offense that could explode at any time. They rallied to tie in the ninth, before Kelly's single and Meusel's triple won it in the twelfth. Pat Shea, with four scoreless innings in relief, earned his fourth victory of the season.

Two more wins at Cincinnati followed, complete-game efforts by Douglas and Barnes. McGraw was especially pleased at getting such a strong effort from Douglas. The unreliable alcoholic had won only one game since winning two in the big August series with Pittsburgh. When sober, however, he was as good a pitcher as there was in the game.

"Douglas, when he is in the mood, can beat any team in the National League, for which reason thousands of New York fans hope that, for the rest of the season, he will attend strictly to business."[17]

McGraw and the Giants also found it particularly satisfying to defeat Eppa Rixey and Rube Marquard on successive days. Both veteran left-handers had always been extremely tough against them. Meanwhile, Jack Scott of Boston defeated Pittsburgh and Wilbur Cooper on the fifteenth, increasing the Pirates' deficit to two and a half games.

Having won eight straight and eighteen of the last twenty-two, the Giants were a confident bunch when they moved on to Pittsburgh on September 16. The players were now looking forward to the World Series, hoping it would be against the Yankees, currently leading the Indians by a half game in the fiercely contested American League race. McGraw, of course, did not want his team looking that far ahead. His job continued to be keeping them focused on winning the National League pennant. Still, his players believed that if they could win two of three in Pittsburgh, which would stretch their lead to three and a half games, the Pirates would be unable to catch them.

Fred Toney's two-hitter won the opener, 5–0, his best-pitched game and only shutout of 1921. The win was Toney's third in the past week and his eighteenth of the season, tying him with Nehf for the team lead. The subject of continuous taunts from the frustrated partisan crowd, Toney held the Pirates hitless until George Cutshaw doubled with two out in the seventh inning. Toney's opponent, Earl Hamilton, gave up all five runs in the third inning, as the Giants batted around. When Whitey Glazner retired Meusel on a fly ball to Max Carey, finally ending the inning, the capacity crowd, growing ever more frustrated, greeted their heroes with derisive jeers.

Five innings later, that frustration turned to violence. Charlie Grimm led off the eighth with a single, Pittsburgh's second hit. The next batter, Walter Schmidt, hit a ground ball to second baseman Johnny Rawlings; but umpire Barry McCormick called Grimm out for interfering with Rawlings as he tried to field the ball. The fans exploded in anger and began showering McCormick with pop bottles, including one that struck his head. The police finally restored order; nevertheless, a squad of twenty-five of them escorted McCormick off the field when the game ended. Afterward, many of the yellow "I'm a Pirates Rooter" buttons worn by the fans during the game littered the streets surrounding Forbes Field. Two weeks remained in the season; and though the Giants' lead was far from insurmountable, there seemed to be a pervading sense in Pittsburgh that the race was over.

Still, that sense of gloom did not prevent a crowd estimated at more than 30,000 from coming out on Saturday. They came despite an intermittent rain that had been falling all morning. A half hour before the scheduled three o'clock start, the skies finally cleared. Because of the overflow of fans, several thousand watched while standing behind ropes in the outfield. If a sense of impending doom had gripped the crowd the day before, Art Nehf's performance intensified it today. He reclaimed his place as the Giants' win leader with his nineteenth, easily handling the Pirates, 6–1. He had now beaten Pittsburgh, the Giants' closest rivals for the pennant, seven times this season without a loss. Moreover, Nehf was in the midst of an eleven-game winning streak against the Pirates that began in 1920 and would extend into 1922.

Possum Whitted's home run in the fourth inning gave the home team the early lead, but it would be the only run they would score. Hal Carlson had the Giants shut out through six innings, before they tied it in the seventh. Ross Youngs blasted a ground-rule triple into the overflow crowd in center, and Meusel scored him with a sacrifice fly. Frisch drove in two runs with a triple in the eighth, before the Giants put the game out of reach with three more in the ninth.

The Giants' win was their tenth straight overall as well as their tenth straight against Pittsburgh. They raised their season record against the Pirates to 16-5, a remarkable spread between two contending teams. With a four-and-a-half-game lead, New York was now clearly in command. They had ten scheduled games remaining, while Pittsburgh had thirteen.[18] If the Giants just split those ten games, they would finish at 95-59. The Pirates would have to win eleven of thirteen games to tie and twelve of thirteen to win the pennant outright.

Back at the Giants' headquarters in the Schenley Hotel, McGraw called Christy Mathewson at Saranac Lake to inform him of the team's big win. Keeping Mathewson, his friend and all-time favorite player, up to date on the Giants' progress was a regular part of McGraw's routine. Several other Giant officials and some of the writers covering the team also got on the phone to exchange pleasantries with the ailing former hero. Matty was still at the Saranac Lake sanatorium, trying to recover from the tuberculosis he had contracted reportedly because of a gassing incident during the war. Plans were under way for a benefit game to honor Mathewson before the Giants' final home game with Boston on September 30.

Knowing they could just about clinch the pennant with another win over the Pirates, the Giants had to put that potential knockout blow on hold the next day. Because of the Pennsylvania blue laws prohibiting baseball on Sundays, the players were forced to spend the day sitting around at the hotel, a most unwelcome interruption for a team brimming with confidence and anxious to play. McGraw would not come out and say the race was over, but he too was obviously confident that it was. "I have a strong team and they ought to win," he said. "If they can not win with the lead they now possess, they do not deserve the pennant."[19]

On Monday, September 19, Phil Douglas faced Babe Adams in the final meeting of the season between the two clubs. Pittsburgh's disappointing losses the last two days, along with this being a workday, held the crowd at Forbes Field to a still-respectable 18,000. Douglas had beaten the Pirates four times this season, including twice in the August sweep in New York. He pitched well again today; but he came up short, losing a tough 2–1 decision to Adams. Douglas allowed single runs in the sixth and seventh, both of which were unearned due to errors by Burns and himself. He allowed only four hits in seven innings, before McGraw removed him for a pinch hitter. McGraw then sent Toney, his best pitcher of late, out to pitch the eighth, an indication of how much McGraw wanted to win this game.

Adams raised his record to 14-4, while ending both the Giants' overall winning streak and their streak against Pittsburgh at ten games. At thirty-nine, Adams was now the oldest player in the National League, a distinction he would retain until he played his final game on August 11, 1926.[20] One of the game's all-time great control pitchers, he would lead the National League with the fewest walks per nine innings for the third year in a row in 1921 with a stingy 1.01.

Although losing the final game in Pittsburgh slowed the Giants temporarily, their lead was still three and a half games. The press and the fans in New York were again hailing John McGraw for his managerial

33. After the Pirates surrendered what had once been a substantial lead, Pirates manager George Gibson denied he had lost control of his players. He also refused to blame the "free spirits" on the team for the collapse. *National Baseball Hall of Fame Library, Cooperstown, New York.*

genius, while those in Pittsburgh were placing much of the blame for the Pirates' monumental collapse on Gibson, an easy target. Both his managerial strategy and his "handling" of the freewheeling Pirates, so praised prior to the late-August disaster at the Polo Grounds, were now being roundly denounced.

Following Adams's 2–1 win, a beleaguered Gibson spoke to the press in defense of his team and himself: "The Pirates have not quit. We are not out of the pennant race by any means and do not intend giving up until the last game is played." He reminded them that all teams suffer slumps during the season and that Pittsburgh's "unfortunately came at a period in the race when it hurt the most."[21]

Gibson went on to defend his players against charges of excessive carousing and drinking. "While I do not lay claim to having a Sunday school team, I know that these Pirates take better care of themselves than 90 percent of all the ball clubs in the business," he said.

"As for Walter Maranville, let me say right here that he has done more individually for the team than anybody imagines. It would be impossible to give him too much credit for his work. Speaking of the management, I have had absolute control over every player on the team, and I take all responsibility for every game that has been lost."[22]

Following the Giants' August sweep of the Pirates, the questions about McGraw's leadership that had surfaced in the press a few days earlier disappeared. Those who covered sports in New York City were now lavish in their praise of his leadership. "Where there is a mathematical chance it is no time in which to count McGraw and his men out of any race."[23]

McGraw and his Giants did not let up. Their three-week spurt remains among the most remarkable in pennant-race history. On the morning of August 24, they trailed Pittsburgh by seven and a half games. But by winning twenty of their next twenty-four, they had gained eleven games on the Pirates, transforming a seven-and-a-half-game deficit into a three-and-a-half-game advantage.

Damon Runyon saluted McGraw for instilling in his men "the determination to keep going in the face of all obstacles."[24] Miller Huggins credited that resolve to McGraw's "faculty of influencing a player into a feeling of intense loyalty to the team as a unit the moment he joins it." That, said Huggins, "is real leadership."[25]

NL STANDINGS AT CLOSE OF PLAY OF SEPTEMBER 19, 1921

TEAM	G	W	L	T	PCT	GB
New York Giants	145	90	55	0	.621	-
Pittsburgh Pirates	142	85	57	0	.599	3.5
St. Louis Cardinals	144	82	62	0	.569	7.5
Boston Braves	144	77	67	0	.535	12.5
Brooklyn Dodgers	142	70	72	0	.493	18.5
Cincinnati Reds	144	66	78	0	.458	23.5
Chicago Cubs	143	57	86	0	.399	32.0
Philadelphia Phillies	146	48	98	0	.329	42.5

22 Ascent to First and Then a Demoralizing Loss

On the morning of August 30, the Yankees trailed the Indians by one and a half games, but they did have the schedule in their favor. They would play twenty-four of their remaining thirty-two games at the Polo Grounds, including eighteen of their last twenty. The Tribe would play only five of their last thirty-two games at home; their final twenty-one games would be played in front of mostly hostile fans.[1] The next three weeks would seem like one long yet dramatic prelude leading up to the final act, the showdown in New York between the league's top two teams, from September 23 to 26.

The Yankees stopped off for two games in the nation's capital to close out August before returning home for four more with the Senators. New York had not faced Washington for more than two months, and the third-place Senators had a couple of new looks. They had picked up Donie Bush, who was now their shortstop and lead-off hitter. They also had an evolving situation with their manager, George McBride. In a freak accident during a practice on July 27, McBride was hit in the face by a ball tossed by outfielder Earl Smith.[2] He was knocked unconscious and spent three weeks in the hospital, suffering from paralysis of the lower jaw, vertigo, and fainting spells. While he would remain as manager for the balance of the season, health problems would limit McBride's role; and the Senators' veteran outfielder and team captain, Clyde Milan, would serve as acting manager.[3]

By sweeping the six games from the Senators while the Indians were splitting their series with the Tigers, the Yankees stormed into first place. They ended the Washington series on September 3 with a record of 79-46 (.632), while the Tribe was two games back at 78-49 (.614). New York pitchers had given up a total of only twenty-two runs against the Senators, and nine of them came in Rip Collins's shaky 17–9 victory. Miller Huggins displayed a rare outburst of optimism bordering on cockiness after the series: "We have the Indian sign on the Clevelands, and they know it. I think right now the pennant is as good as won, but we are going to keep on fighting right up to the end."[4]

The highlight of the series for the Yankees was a September 1 double-header sweep of the Senators' best pitchers, George Mogridge and Walter Johnson. Bob Shawkey and Harry Harper beat them, 6–3 and 8–1, respectively. Shawkey's effort was encouraging after his 15–1 thrashing by the Indians a week earlier. Harper's performance, in his first start since May 13, was both surprising and satisfying for Yankee fans. Perhaps the Yanks would have a lefty for the stretch run after all.

Among those in attendance for Waite Hoyt's four-hit win the next day were several members of the New York Giants, who had an off day in their Ebbets Field series with the Dodgers. They saw Babe Ruth, Bob Meusel, and Roger Peckinpaugh hit home runs. It was the second straight day that Meusel homered. On Saturday it was Ruth's turn to homer on back-to-back days. "Sometimes Babe looks foolish on a slow ball, and [pitcher Harry] Courtney fed him one. Babe fed it to a fan in the upper deck," wrote the *New York Times*.[5] It was his fiftieth of the season, a milestone that only he had ever reached.

The final game of the series, scheduled for Sunday, September 4, was rained out and would not be made up. The Yankees would play only 153 games in 1921. The Babe was in the midst of one of his long-ball hot streaks, hitting home runs on September 2, 3, 5, 7, 8, and 9. The rainout may have cost him a good chance to hit another home run, preventing him from hitting sixty in 1921.

Next up for the Yankees were five games with the Red Sox, starting with a Labor Day doubleheader at Fenway Park and ending with a mid-week doubleheader at the Polo Grounds. In the first game, a Shawkey shutout, New York pounded Sam Jones. Jones, who had come to Boston as a throw-in to the April 1916 deal that sent Tris Speaker to Cleveland, was now emerging as one of the league's best pitchers. He would win twenty-three games this year for a Red Sox team that would win only seventy-five.

The Yankees lost the second game, another poor Collins start, ending their winning streak at seven. Meusel achieved an American League record (for an outfielder) of four assists in the losing effort.[6] He would lead the league in outfield assists this year (tied at twenty-eight with the

34. Mike McNally was a valuable reserve infielder for the 1921 Yankees, especially with his glove. A quiet and unassuming player, he backed up Frank Baker at third base. *Private collection of Michael Mumby.*

Browns' Jack Tobin) and in 1922. The Yankees' final game of the year in Boston was a classic pitching duel between Waite Hoyt, who formerly played for the Red Sox, and Joe Bush, a future Yankee. Bush was coming back from a serious arm problem suffered in 1919; and on the strength of his new pitch, the forkball, he would win sixteen games in 1921. On this day, he came out on top, 2–1.

Back in New York, where the Yankees swept the Wednesday, September 7, twin bill, Mike McNally had twelve assists at third base. As a part of the trade that brought Waite Hoyt and Wally Schang to New York, McNally provided the Yankees with just what they had hoped for when they acquired him: infield reserve depth. Minooka Mike had been the captain of a famous Pennsylvania sandlot team, the Minooka Blues, whose catcher was the Cleveland Indians' star backstop, Steve O'Neill. McNally was known for his speed, most notably for scoring Boston's winning run in the fourteenth inning of a 1916 World Series game.[7]

He was also one of the many players who were wonderful with the glove but could not hit well enough to play every day. Only now, his glove had been so good that he was playing regularly. Burt Whitman wrote in the *Boston Herald*, "Mike is fielding brilliantly at the hot corner, and he is infinitely faster on his feet than was the venerable Baker."[8] Frank Baker had rejoined the Yankees when they came to Washington, after recuperating for a week at his Maryland farm. Yet McNally's terrific play had reduced Baker's role to that of a pinch hitter.[9]

The Babe also starred on September 7. In the second game, he hit his fifty-second home run and made a spectacular over-the-shoulder catch of an Eddie Foster drive. Just two days earlier, Ruth had chased a foul ball all the way to the dugout railing and caught it. With the sweep, the 82-48 Yankees were now only a game up on the 82-50 Indians, who had won four of their last five contests.

The Yankees then traveled to Philadelphia, where they split the first two games of a Thursday-to-Saturday series. The Babe homered in both games, numbers fifty-three and fifty-four for the season, the latter tying his 1920 record. On Saturday Philadelphia jumped out to a 3–0 lead in first inning on Tilly Walker's home run, his third in their last two games. Walker, a teammate of Carl Mays and Babe Ruth on the 1916 and 1917 Red Sox, had replaced Tris Speaker as Boston's center fielder in 1916.

In 1918, after the Red Sox traded him to the Athletics, Walker tied the Babe for the league lead with eleven home runs.

The Athletics' three first-inning runs were all they would score. The Yanks fought back and buried them, 19–3. Eleven of their twenty-four hits came in the ninth inning, when they were already up, 10–3. The first five Yankees who batted that inning—Schang, Mays, Miller, Peckinpaugh, and Ruth—all got hits, including Ruth's bases-clearing triple. Later in the inning, the same five Yankees again hit safely.[10] Schang, the Yanks' only starter who was a switch hitter, had five hits in the game. Mays got the win, his sixteenth in a row against the Athletics.

In early September two Columbia University psychologists had run a series of tests on Babe Ruth, establishing his superior physical and mental skills. Hugh Fullerton's article on the tests had just appeared in *Popular Science Monthly*.[11] Fullerton wrote that the results revealed the Babe's almost perfect coordination between eye, brain, and muscle. This, and not mere slugging strength, was the source of his terrific performance.[12] As the Babe wrote in his column (one in which his ghostwriter really seemed to capture the Babe's voice), "They harnessed me with wires and tubes until I felt like a cross between a fire horse and a deep-sea diver. . . . It's too deep for me. . . . I don't know any more why or how I knock home runs now than I did before."[13]

After the Philadelphia series, the Yankees returned home for a Sunday doubleheader with the Red Sox. The games drew 42,000, the largest ever at the Polo Grounds. (One paper also noted that 40,000 more fans were turned away.)[14] They came hoping to be part of history, to see the Babe set a new record with home run number fifty-five. But they would go home disappointed. Ruth had two singles and four walks on the day, but no home runs. Instead, the long ball that sent the crowd into pandemonium came off the bat of Bob Meusel. It came late in the second game and gave New York its first lead of the afternoon. Fans spilled onto the center-field grass in celebration, and manager Huggins had to go out and plead with them to return to their seats—or risk the Yankees' forfeiting the game. "Straw hats, shredded programmes, seat cushions, and wadded newspapers literally filled the air."[15] That night, groundskeeper Henry Fabian disposed of the hats with a giant bonfire.[16]

(It was customary at the time for men to toss their summer straw hats onto the field late in the season, in celebration of a feat by a member of the home team.)

Another highlight of the second game, which gave New York a split on the day, was Bill Piercy's strong start following his lengthy absence due to arm trouble. After months of inaction, Harper and Piercy had won three games since September 1. Mike McNally sparkled again in the field, with eleven assists in the two games. "The Giants have their Frisch; the Yankees have their McNally," wrote the *New York Tribune* after the game. "Mike was a wonder."[17]

Chicago followed Boston into New York for the final two meetings between the clubs. The seventh-place Sox were twenty-eight and a half games behind the first-place Yankees, yet they had beaten the New Yorkers twelve times in their twenty games this year. And now they would prove tough again, splitting the series.

Dickie Kerr would finish the season barely over .500, at 19-17. His earned run average would rise to 4.72, almost one and a half runs higher per game than he had allowed in 1920. Yet on September 13, the little lefty beat the Yankees for the sixth time this season. The Yankees seemed to be nervous, "very Pittsburgh, to state it plainly."[18]

Kerr had help from Chicago outfielder Harry Hooper. Hooper walked and scored in the first inning. After the Yankees tied the game, Hooper homered in the third. After they tied it again, he homered in the fifth. He singled and scored in the seventh and then walked in the eighth, forcing in a run. Now thirty-four years old, Hooper, the former Red Sox star whom John McGraw once called "one of the most dangerous hitters in a pinch that the game has ever known," could still hit.[19]

The next day, the White Sox hit Bob Shawkey early and often, jumping out to leads of 7–1 and 8–2. It was one of the strangest games ever played at "the Brush Stadium."[20] Chicago pitchers literally hit the Yankees all afternoon. The game featured five hit batsmen, four of them Yanks. The one White Sox victim, Amos Strunk, was knocked unconscious by a Rip Collins pitch. The White Sox pitching staff would finish the season with an earned run average of 4.94, the worst in the Majors in 1921.

The in-and-out Shawkey pitched awkwardly; his movement seemed forced and constricted.[21] This season had to be frustrating for Shawkey, who had been such a key member of the Yankees' pitching staff since he joined the team in 1915. A twenty-game winner in three of his previous four seasons, Shawkey's earned run average had ranged between 2.21 and 2.72; this year it was above 4.00.[22]

Shawkey was one of the many talented young pitchers developed by Connie Mack. He won fifteen games for the pennant-winning 1914 Athletics at the age of twenty-three. In June 1916 Mack sold him to the Yankees for only $3,000.[23] Shawkey would go on to win 168 games for the Yanks, including twenty-four in 1916 and twenty in both 1919 and 1920. A good-natured and even-tempered man and a keen student of the game, Shawkey willingly spent time helping younger pitchers. After he won ten games in a row in the 1919 season, one paper noted that Shawkey was the hardest-working Yankee, coaching the younger pitchers when he wasn't on the mound himself.[24]

Fueled by Bob Meusel's two home runs, the Yankees rallied and won the game. Meusel was having a fine season and would have been "the reigning sensation was it not for the Babe," wrote Damon Runyon.[25] Meusel was on his way to a season of twenty-four home runs, 136 runs batted in, and a .318 batting average. Meusel's nonchalant personality brought him criticism in his rookie season and would detract from recognition of his play on the field throughout his excellent career. "Largely because of his seeming lack of dash and personal magnetism, Meusel is seldom given the credit that he probably deserves."[26]

Bob Meusel, a Coast League star from California, hit .328 with forty doubles and eleven home runs in his 1920 rookie season.[27] "I know of no slugger who can hit the ball harder than Meusel, excepting, of course, Babe Ruth and possibly Joe Jackson," said Miller Huggins that year.[28]

Meusel had started the 1920 season at third base, where he played forty-five games.[29] He moved to the outfield when Duffy Lewis hurt his knee on June 13, and Aaron Ward then came off the bench to replace Meusel at third. Meusel had plenty of time to adapt to the new position since Lewis would be out for almost two months. Meusel had a hard time tracking fly balls in the outfield; yet once he caught the ball, he had a rifle arm getting it back to the infield. His arm was quickly recognized as one of the best in baseball, as reflected by his ten outfield assists in only sixty-four games.

From the start, there was talk of Meusel's laid-back personality. The *New York Evening Telegram* called it "lackadaisical spirit."[30] Sam Crane wrote in the *New York Evening Journal*, "He lacks the good old pep. . . . He must show more interest in his work."[31] In part, the impression Meusel gave was a function of his size and style. His future teammate Waite Hoyt wrote in a letter sixty years later that Meusel "appeared lazy in running because, being six three in height, he took long loping strides. He never appeared in a hurry—and wasn't. I suppose that was mistaken for indifference—and possibly he was to a degree—but he wanted to win."[32]

Yet there was some basis for believing that Meusel had an "attitude problem" in his rookie season. He kept late hours and was so indifferent about playing for the Yankees that he said he did not care if he was in the Coast League or the American League.

When Meusel reported for spring training 1921, his attitude was more serious; even Miller Huggins acknowledged that. "I think Meusel is an entirely changed man," Huggins declared. "He was little more than a boy last year."[33] Meusel was a Yankee holdout in early March 1921, not because he wanted more money, but because he objected to the "good behavior" clause Ed Barrow and Miller Huggins had put in his contract. Management wanted to ensure that Meusel would remain focused; he eventually accepted the contract and signed.[34]

Huggins still had to find the best spot for Meusel. He had to get the young slugger's bat in the lineup, while minimizing his defensive shortcomings. "There is just one way that Meusel would fit perfectly into my ball club now," Huggins told Sid Mercer, with uncanny foresight. "If we could get them to change the rules so as to let a pinch-hitter bat for a pitcher each time, what a job that would be for this big fellow."[35]

Much of the early-September drama in the American League centered on Cleveland, not New York. On September 1, while the Tribe was suffering a crushing twelve-inning defeat, Stan Coveleski pulled ligaments in his side. Initial reports said that he might be done for the year. But the pain subsided after a few days, and he returned to action nine days later. Coveleski pitched well on September 10 against St. Louis, but he and his team ran into Urban Shocker, who shut out the Tribe on three hits, 2–0. Shocker may have taken special pleasure in beating his old

35. Cleveland right-hander Ray Caldwell was one of Tris Speaker's most impressive reclamation projects, an exceptionally talented pitcher whose drinking had seemingly ended his career in 1919. After winning twenty games for the 1920 Indians, Caldwell had an up-and-down season in 1921, when he "fell off the wagon." *Private collection of Mark Stang.*

team, the Yankees. But he proved to be an "equal opportunity" pitcher, beating the Yanks' rivals too.

Ray Caldwell had recently been suspended for "breaking training rules" and might never have pitched for the Indians again. The hard-drinking pitcher had gone off the wagon a number of times during his career, sometimes for extended periods.[36] Under Tris Speaker's tutelage, he seemed to have moderated his behavior since coming to Cleveland two years earlier.

But Caldwell had won only four games so far this year; and his earned run average rose to 4.90 in 1921, more than a run higher than his 1920 mark. Joe Vila, who had criticized Caldwell's antics over the years, wrote, "The erratic hurler evidently has forgotten Speaker's friendly act and soon will leave fast company forever."[37]

Yet predictions of Caldwell's demise were premature. The *Cleveland Plain Dealer* soon carried an open letter the pitcher had sent to his manager, offering to pitch without pay for the rest of the season. "Spoke [Speaker's nickname], it is impossible for me to stay away any longer without trying to make some reparation to you and the boys . . . to do my share to help the club win the pennant."[38]

On September 7 Caldwell went to the bullpen and warmed up on his own initiative. When Speaker needed a reliever in the ninth inning, fans were stunned to see Caldwell running to the mound, since his letter would not appear in the paper until the following day. He came in with the bases loaded and struck out the last two Detroit batters to preserve a 5–4 win. In the next two weeks, Caldwell's pitching would help keep the Indians in the pennant race.

Cleveland rallied for an 8–4 win in its final game of the season in St. Louis on September 11. It was a costly victory because Speaker slipped rounding first base, injuring his knee and putting himself out of action and on crutches.[39]

After ripping off seven straight wins, the Yankees had won only six of their next eleven games. In the meantime, the Indians had won seven of ten after they split the six games with the Tigers. On September 14 New York's lead was down to a mere half game. Cleveland's record stood at 86-52 (.623), while the Yankees were at 86-51 (.628). Both teams had doubleheaders on Thursday the fifteenth. This had been an off day for both on their original schedules, but rainouts had to be made up as the season was winding down.

The Indians crushed Philadelphia, 17–3, just five days after the Yankees had thrashed the Athletics, 19–3. A's starter Arlas Taylor was a true cup-of-coffee player. This was his only appearance in a Major League game. He started and gave up five runs in two innings. Interestingly, he had one strikeout, that of Joe Sewell, the hardest man to strike out in baseball history.[40] In the second game of the doubleheader, Ray Caldwell tossed his only shutout of the year. The Tribe now had a six-game winning streak.

The Yankees kept pace by sweeping their doubleheader with the third-place Browns. Bob Meusel's third-inning bases-loaded home run in the opening game with the Browns brought New York back from a 4–0

36. The 1921 edition of Murderers' Row was anchored by Babe Ruth (*left*). The aging Frank Baker (*middle*), who was thirty-five years old that year, was relegated to the bench most of the season. Baker's nine home runs were overshadowed by the twenty-four of Bob Meusel (*right*). The Yankees scored 948 runs, over 100 more than the Giants. *Transcendental Graphics/theruckerarchive.com.*

deficit, and two innings later Ruth's homer gave the Yankees the lead. The Babe hit his record-breaking fifty-fifth home run off Billy Bayne. Little Eddie Bennett, the Yankee mascot, jumped onto Ruth's back as he crossed the plate. The *Sporting News* reported that 30,000 straw hats were tossed onto the field.[41]

Ruth had been pressing since getting his fifty-fourth homer six days earlier. He had been seeing some decent pitches, especially the way Meusel was swinging the bat behind him in the lineup. For the past five weeks (August 9–September 15), they each had fourteen home runs. In his poem, "The Narrow Squeak," Grantland Rice described the nightmare that pitchers facing the Yankees' one-two power punch had:

Last night I dreamed that I was pitching
Against the Yankee team.
And two were on and two were out
In this soul-gripping dream.
And when I looked around again
I almost hit the mat.
For a fellow named George Herman Ruth
Was strolling up to bat.

And then I thought—"I'll walk this boob
And so clamp on the lid."
And then I looked around and saw
What I had went and did.
For all I had to handle now
Was Meusel in his prime.
But just before I choked to death,
I woke up just in time.[42]

New York would not see their former nemesis, Dixie Davis, any more this year. He had just lost a classic 1–0 game to Walter Johnson the day before, in which Johnson faced only twenty-seven men. Johnson gave up only three infield hits. However, the three base runners were erased by a pick-off and a triple play. Johnson was serving notice that he had a lot more baseball left in his arm, even though this was his second straight subpar year.

Johnson would finish with seventeen wins and lead the league in strikeouts for the tenth time. He continued to win with a deceptive delivery. As Detroit outfielder Sam Crawford told historian Larry Ritter about Johnson more than forty years later, "He had such an easy motion it looked like he was playing catch. That's what threw you off. He threw so nice and easy—and then swoosh, and it was by you."[43]

On Friday the sixteenth, Bob Shawkey faced off against Urban Shocker for the fourth time this year. Shocker had given up two home runs to Elmer Smith on September 5, and today the Babe went long on him for number fifty-six.[44] Other than this at bat, Shocker had no trouble with Ruth and struck the slugger out three times. He had little problem with the Yankees either, on the way to his twenty-fifth win of the year.

The Indians moved back into first place that same day for the first time in September, albeit by only a half game. George Uhle shut out the Senators, 2–0, and Joe Wood led the way. Wood made a great catch of a Sam Rice drive in the seventh and then broke up a scoreless game with a two-run triple in the eighth. He had been flirting with a .400 batting average during much of the 1921 season, before finishing with a .366 batting average in 194 at bats.

Unlike the Pittsburgh Pirates, who faded so badly once the Giants closed in on them, the Indians refused to crumble. While the Yankees and Indians were certainly thinking of their showdown now only a week away, they still had other business to attend to. Cleveland had two more games in Washington, a day off, and then three at Fenway Park, while the Yankees had a day off before hosting Detroit for four games.

On September 17 the Indians increased their lead to a full game over the idle Yankees. It was their eighth win in a row, and it was Allan Sothoron's twelfth victory with Cleveland in an improbable comeback season. He pitched 178⅓ innings for three teams in 1921 (144⅔ of them with the Indians) and did not give up a single home run. In the post-Deadball Era (since 1920), this is still the most innings a pitcher has thrown in a season without giving up a home run.[45]

The Detroit Tigers arrived in New York mired in the second division, in sixth place, with their manager Ty Cobb's frustration boiling over. The most excitement they were generating was the tight batting-title race between Cobb and teammate Harry Heilmann. The latter had led for most of the year; but by September 1 Cobb (.394) had closed to within three percentage points of Heilmann (.397). He would get no closer. The student had learned his lessons well from his teacher. As Cobb would later say in his autobiography, "In all modesty, I could teach hitting."[46]

Heilmann would beat out Cobb for the batting title, .394 to .389. And the Tigers would finish 1921 with the highest batting average in either league, .316. Cobb's cast of characters was very similar to the Tigers' club that Hughie Jennings had managed in 1920. Yet that team had hit only .270.[47]

As the 1921 season drew to a close and the Tigers' slide continued, Detroit sportswriter E. A. Batchelor explained Cobb's lack of success as a manager this way: "Like so many other great performers, he was impatient with stupidity, lack of ambition, and lack of what he considered normal baseball ability. The result was that he proved to be a poor teacher and that he never could get his team imbued with real team spirit."[48]

In the seventh inning of the opening game, Cobb ordered his pitcher, Dutch Leonard, to bunt. When Leonard twice failed to execute by fouling off pitches, Cobb pulled him for a pinch hitter. The Yankees won the game, 4–2, thanks to great catches by Elmer Miller of drives off the bats of Heilmann and Bobby Veach, both times with Cobb on base.

On the same day, Sunday, September 18, Stan Coveleski had a good outing for Cleveland, but he ran into Walter Johnson's brilliant two-hitter. The Yankees moved back into first place by percentage points. Their record stood at 89-52 (.631), while the Tribe's was 90-53 (.629).

The Yankees' game the next day was potentially devastating for the team and its manager. They jumped out to a 4–0 lead against the Tigers, with Carl Mays in control and seemingly on the way to his twenty-sixth win. Suddenly Mays tired as he had in late innings a number of times this season. In the seventh, he escaped with two deep fly balls hit to Ruth and a fine stop by Aaron Ward. In the eighth, the Yanks "collapsed as though they had been hit by several lightning bolts and a few twelve-shot shells."[49] Mays gave up two hits and two walks, yielding one run. Although Mays had retired one batter, Huggins, who this season often seemed to stick too long with his ace, moved quickly and replaced him with Shawkey. Mays did not leave quietly, arguing that he should not be pulled. Only after Yankee coach Charley O'Leary came to the mound did Mays finally depart.

With the bases loaded, Shawkey induced a comebacker; but in trying to force the runner at the plate, he hurled it so hard at catcher Wally Schang that the ball bounced away and two more Tigers scored.[50] Cobb then singled and Veach tripled. Shawkey, who had been ineffective against both the White Sox and the Browns on this home stand, had reached the nadir of his Yankee career. Huggins again had a short leash and called for Hoyt; Shawkey, who had not gotten anyone out, threw the ball away in disgust and marched off the mound. Hoyt gave up a single, a double, and another single, before finally retiring the side.

A 4–0 lead had become an 8–4 deficit in one inning. Boos and hoots filled the Polo Grounds. Reporters started writing their columns, panning Huggins for pulling Mays and inserting Shawkey, though he was choosing from limited and imperfect choices. Hugh Fullerton wrote, "A manager has about as much chance of pleasing the fans as he has of developing two Ty Cobbs and three Walter Johnsons a season."[51] The Tigers went on to win, 10–6, with Howard Ehmke getting the win in relief. The *Detroit News* declared, New York "is almost ready to follow the Pittsburgh Pirates on a long plunge down the chutes."[52]

Miller Huggins had experienced many difficult losses in his baseball career, but this may have been the toughest. The crushing defeat, which pushed the Yankees out of first place (by a half game since the Indians were idle), was the final blow. The curses of the fans, the hostility of the press, the rebellion from his own players, and now this collapse on the field. Looking back on this period, Huggins later said, "I would not go through those years again for a million dollars. . . . Money and honors are nothing compared with peace of mind and health. I was a sick man during a good part of the time, perhaps sicker than my friends knew."[53]

Huggins wrote out his letter of resignation after the game and submitted it to his biggest supporter, Yankees co-owner Jacob Ruppert.[54]

AL STANDINGS AT CLOSE OF PLAY OF SEPTEMBER 19, 1921

TEAM	G	W	L	T	PCT	GB
Cleveland Indians	143	90	53	0	.629	-
New York Yankees	142	89	53	0	.627	0.5
St. Louis Browns	144	74	70	0	.514	16.5
Boston Red Sox	139	69	70	0	.496	19.0
Washington Senators	143	70	72	1	.493	19.5
Detroit Tigers	147	71	75	1	.486	20.5
Chicago White Sox	142	58	84	0	.408	31.5
Philadelphia Athletics	140	47	91	2	.341	40.5

Jacob Ruppert refused to accept Miller Huggins's resignation. As a businessman, Ruppert understood the dangers of replacing a manager based on pressure from his subordinates (the players) and outside parties (the press). He recognized how unreasonable New York sportswriters could be and the impossibly high expectations that came with managing the Babe Ruth–led Yankees.

Finally, and perhaps most importantly, Ruppert believed in Huggins's skills as a baseball leader. Ruppert saw in Huggins "a man worthy of confidence, a man hung on the cross of propaganda, which was as cruel as it was false, and as unfounded as it was detrimental to the cause of the Yankees."[1] Miller Huggins was Ruppert's man. Despite Til Huston's strong reservations, Huggins would continue to manage the Yankees. As Joe Vila wrote shortly after the 1921 season, "It was Ruppert's words of encouragement in the darkest hours that kept Huggins from losing his nerve."[2]

Huggins's September 19, 1921, letter of resignation was not reported at the time and has never been widely disseminated. Two New York evening papers related the story, with very different interpretations. Fred Lieb gave his account more than a year after the event. He mentioned it while covering the story of Huston's decision to sell his 50 percent share in the Yankees to Ruppert.[3]

Lieb's article discussed Huston's poor relationship with Huggins and noted that Huston, who never wanted to hire Huggins in the first place, did not want to retain him after the 1921 World Series (or the 1922 Series, for that matter). Lieb noted that Huggins came close to leaving the Yankees in the last month of the 1921 season, after Carl Mays blew a big lead late to Detroit. Lieb continued, "He wrote out his resignation, which Ruppert would not accept."[4]

The other account came from sportswriter Ed Van Every, just two

37. Jacob Ruppert hired Miller Huggins and stood by him despite opposition to the Yankee manager from many quarters. He refused to accept Huggins's resignation after the team's late-game collapse on September 19. The loss dropped New York out of first place, but the next day they were back in first . . . for good. *Courtesy of the Boston Public Library, Print Department.*

weeks after the end of the 1921 World Series. Quoting a reliable source, he wrote that the September 19 loss to the Tigers had triggered an upheaval on the Yankees. The owners and the players blamed Huggins for the defeat, and "Miller tendered his resignation."[5]

Yet it is here that Van Every's story takes a very different turn than Lieb's: Van Every wrote that Huggins no longer ran the team after that September 19 game, though he was consulted out of courtesy. Roger Peckinpaugh and Babe Ruth were now directing the Yankees, he said. The change was confirmed by the fact that Huggins did not appear in the third base coach's box after that game, including the World Series.

Two reports state that Huggins resigned, yet they then diverge dramatically. Other newspapers were silent on the matter. Lieb's account seems more plausible for a number of reasons.

First, there is no evidence that anyone other than Huggins was making all the key decisions for the Yankees after the September 19 game. During the 1921 World Series, extensive press coverage by countless reporters from across the country covered Huggins's moves and quoted him extensively. All the accounts point to Huggins as the man very much at the helm of the Yankees.

Second, Huggins was signed to manage the Yankees for the 1922 season (after Van Every's column had appeared), even though they had lost the 1921 World Series. Had Huggins been retained as a mere figurehead in September simply to minimize any disruption to the team, he certainly would not have been brought back as manager for the following year.

Third, Van Every's conclusions may have been wishful and inaccurate thinking. He had been very critical of the Yankees' skipper and had been predicting Huggins's firing for some time. In the article, he wrote, "You will never convince some observers other than that the Yanks won in spite of Huggins." He predicted that Huggins would be gone and declared that it would be no surprise if Babe Ruth would manage the Yankees.

Huggins's future was a key element in the murky, behind-the-scenes power struggle between the Yankee co-owners. They probably fought over whether to sign Huggins for each season from 1918 through 1923. Ruppert seemed to have had the upper hand every step of the way—Huggins repeatedly returned as Yankees manager—with the battle not ending until Ruppert finally bought out Huston in 1923. Upon taking full control that May, Ruppert sent a brief telegram to his team, which was on the road at the time. It read, simply, "I am now the sole owner of the Yankees. Miller Huggins is my manager."[6]

On Tuesday, September 20, Harry Harper started for the Yankees and had his third strong outing since returning to action, a complete-game 4–2 victory. One New York paper called Harper's performance against the Tigers nothing less than "a dazzling return to form."[7] Perhaps it was more than a return, since he was now pitching better than he had at the start of the season. The Yankees needed his strong effort because the Indians were leading the Red Sox, 4–1, that afternoon.

Late in the Yankee game, with New York also up, 4–1, an enormous roar rolled through the Polo Grounds. Huggins wondered what had triggered the outburst, until he turned to the outfield wall. The fans were scoreboard watching, and now so were the Yankees. The scoreboard operator had just posted a "6" for the Red Sox in the eighth.[8] Boston had rallied and held on for an improbable 7–4 win. Tris Speaker's Indians had suffered an eighth-inning collapse, similar to that of the Yankees against Detroit just twenty-four hours earlier.

Back in New York in the ninth inning, the Tigers put two men on base with no outs. However, Huggins was taking no chances that his team would let another game slip away. He had starters Carl Mays, Jack Quinn, Rip Collins, and Bill Piercy warming up, ready to win this contest at all costs. After the previous day's loss, Huggins probably felt he had no choice. But his concerns were put to rest when Harper steadied after giving up a run. Just as quickly as the Yanks had dropped out of first place the day before, they were back on top, by a half game.

Cleveland rebounded on Wednesday, beating Boston and Sam Jones. Since the Yankees were rained out (the Indians played their game in Boston in a steady rain), the Tribe moved into a virtual tie for first place. Their record stood at 91-54 (.628), while the Yankees were at 90-53 (.629).

There was more drama on Thursday, the day before the Cleveland–New York showdown. Late that afternoon, it looked likely that the Yankees would fall a game behind the Tribe. The Indians were cruising with an 8–2 lead, while the Yankees were trailing the Tigers, 5–1. Suddenly the Red Sox again rallied to send the game into extra innings. This time they mounted their attack against Allan Sothoron, bunting ten times and rattling him into making two throwing errors.[9]

In New York, Bob Shawkey, once again ineffective, was knocked out in the third inning. But the Yankees fought back. Jack Quinn gave them a chance to do so, by giving up only three hits in six and one-third innings of relief. He even hit a home run in the third (one of eight he would hit in his twenty-three-year career) after Wally Schang had tripled, closing the gap to 5–3. An inning later, New York took the lead on the way to a 12–5 win. The heart of the Yanks' lineup—Peckinpaugh, Ruth, and Meusel—were a combined 0-13. The fireworks instead came from the bottom of the order: Aaron Ward and Schang went a combined 5-5, with a double, three triples, and a home run.

The Indians survived the Red Sox's comeback to eke out a twelve-inning win. Tris Speaker appeared in a game for the first time since his injury back on September 11, pinch-hitting in the twelfth. He grounded out to the right side, moving the eventual game-winning runner to third; yet he almost collapsed from pain while running to first.

Ty Cobb's Tigers finished their season series against the Yankees with only 5 wins, against 17 losses. Their overall record of 71-82 would relegate them to sixth place, and Cobb's rookie season as a manager had not been an easy one. "Cobb's congenital rage widened. A snarl became his habitual mode of expression."[10] At some point in his six-year managerial career, perhaps as early as 1921, Cobb realized, as he later would write in his autobiography, "I wish now I'd never stuck my head in the noose that the Tiger management represented."[11]

In the heat of a baseball game, even when the pennant is not on the line, tempers often run short and fists sometimes fly. The clashes are usually between members of the opposing teams or sometimes between teammates, although in the early 1920s, players still occasionally fought with umpires. Such scrapes had been much more common in the late nineteenth century, when umpires were not as respected or as supported by league management.

On September 24, 1921, Ty Cobb was at the center of one of the game's more notorious fights. During the course of Washington's win over the Tigers, he was called out on attempted steals of second base and home plate. Cobb was so angered by the calls that he challenged umpire Billy Evans to a fight. After the game the two men met under the grandstand, took off their shirts, and fought. Reportedly, Cobb got in more punches, and the men parted on good terms. Fellow umpire George Hildebrand, who had been the one to call Cobb out at home, reported the incident to the American League office; and Cobb was suspended indefinitely.[12]

While hotheaded ballplayers were usually involved in such fights, even more-polite men took swings at arbiters too. Just two months earlier in St. Louis, mild-mannered Browns star George Sisler lost control during a loss to the Red Sox. He was so upset over a call made by Hildebrand, who had called him out on a close play at first base, that he began swinging at the umpire and swiping his glove at him. Hildebrand kept dodging and later said that he ejected the usually soft-spoken Sisler more for his bad language than for his swings.[13]

In the summer of 1920 at Fenway Park, the Yankees' easy-going pitcher, Bob Shawkey, had also tussled with Hildebrand. Shawkey lost his temper after the umpire called some borderline pitches balls, resulting in a walk that forced in a run. After Hildebrand made a strike three call on a Shawkey pitch, the hurler sarcastically took off his cap and bowed to the umpire. When Hildebrand tossed him out of the game, Shawkey swung at him; and the umpire swung back, hitting Shawkey with his mask. In both cases, aberrations in the careers of Sisler and Shawkey, the offenders were suspended. While they were two of the game's real gentlemen of their era, they were also fiercely competitive men. Whether the matter was retiring a batter or winning a game, emotions were hard to keep in check. When there was a pennant at stake, the battles became even more spirited and feelings ran even higher.

The four-game showdown series at the Polo Grounds between Cleveland and New York would start with the Yankees leading by a mere .002. Uncertainty hung in the air. "There is no telling from one inning to the next just what a Yankee pitcher will do these days," wrote Harry Schumacher on the eve of the series.[14] He went on to predict that the team with the stronger—or the "less inferior"—pitching would win the series. The *Cleveland Plain Dealer* admitted it did not know who would win the American League pennant. But the paper did know that the Indians would fight until the last out of the series. "The Indians are a team which never quits. They do not know how."[15]

They would have to know how to win without their leader on the playing field. The Tribe announced that Speaker probably would not play in New York. The Yankees would be without Frank Baker; his mother had died on Thursday. This came on top of the deaths of his wife a year ago and his mother-in-law earlier this year.

A World Series–like atmosphere permeated this series. The Yankee office was besieged for tickets, but the reserved seats were sold out early in the week. About 20,000 grandstand and bleacher tickets would go on sale before each game on a first-come, first-served basis.

A crowd estimated at between 32,000 and 36,000 fans turned out for the first game on Friday, September 23. The featherweight boxing champion Clevelander Johnny Kilbane wore a regulation Indians jersey as he warmed up with catcher Steve O'Neill before the game.

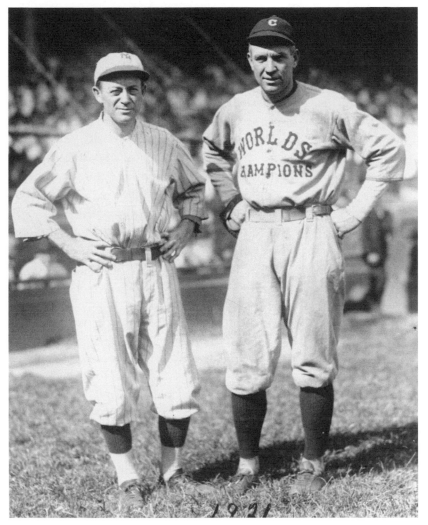

38. On Friday, September 23, the Yankees and Indians opened a four-game series at the Polo Grounds; the two teams were in a virtual tie for first place. Here the two managers, Huggins and Speaker (wearing his 1921 "Worlds Champions" uniform), pose for cameras during the series. *Private collection of Steve Steinberg.*

The two managers, Speaker and Huggins, posed somewhat awkwardly for photographers. The Indians received an ovation from the New York fans when they came out onto the field. The biggest cheers were directed toward player-manager Speaker. Joe Vila said he could not recall such a warm welcome for a visiting team in his long newspaper career.[16]

"It was the greatest game ever played"   291

Stan Coveleski started for Cleveland, and Waite Hoyt got the nod from Huggins. Both men were on their game and went the distance, each giving up only six hits. Coveleski held the Yankees hitless through three innings; Hoyt struck out the side in the first. The Indians were very suspicious throughout the game, constantly accusing Hoyt of tampering with the ball. The *New York Herald* said they were even suspicious that Wally Pipp's bat may have been loaded with nails.[17]

Cleveland struck first, scoring two runs in the fourth. After Larry Gardner singled, Joe Sewell drove a ball that bounded past Ruth in left field for a triple. The *Herald* also noted that Ruth did not play the ball very well. Sewell then scored on a Hoyt wild pitch.

Then the Babe took over. Before the game, Speaker said that the only way to pitch to Ruth with men on base was *not* to pitch to him, but rather to walk him.[18] He did walk in the first, though no one was on base. He would come up three more times, each with the bases empty. Each time he would double and score.

These were not ordinary doubles. In the fourth and sixth innings, the Babe hit the ball with such force that it crashed off the gloves of infielders Sewell and Wambsganss, respectively. Speaker had his outfielders playing so deep for Ruth that they could not get to the deflected balls in time to hold Ruth to singles. Daring base running on the slugger's part turned what should have been singles into doubles. Heywood Broun vividly described Ruth barreling into second: "He looked like [335-pound former president] William Taft pursued by bloodhounds."[19]

Pipp was a force at the plate, driving in three runs in three different at bats. In the fourth inning, his double scored Ruth and closed the gap to 2–1. In the sixth, after Bob Meusel's single had scored Ruth and tied the game, Pipp's single brought Meusel home and gave New York a 3–2 lead. All six Yankee hits came from these three men in the middle of the lineup. In the eighth, Pipp's sacrifice fly scored Ruth for the Yankees' fourth and final run.

After scoring twice in the fourth, the Indians got only two more hits, none of which were in the last three innings. Speaker hobbled to the plate to pinch-hit in the ninth. He popped out to shortstop Roger Peckinpaugh to end the game, a 4–2 Yankee win. Broun captured the tension in the air in the Polo Grounds: "It was a crowd which seemed to pray under its breath and sometimes curse. . . . Nobody can shout very well when he is holding his breath."[20]

"Having led with his ace and failed, Speaker is now forced to do some gambling."[21] Reporters speculated that he would pitch Duster Mails or Ray Caldwell the next day. Down a game in the series and the standings, Speaker finally let George Uhle start against the Yankees for the first time since June 8. Miller Huggins would have started Carl Mays; but since Harry Harper would not pitch on Sundays, Harper got the start for the second game, on September 24.

The game almost did not take place. The Indians complained that the Yankees had only one of the center-field screens in place. Because Uhle threw right-handed and Harper was a southpaw, the screen to the left of dead center would let the Yankees pick up right-hander Uhle's release of the ball, but the Indians would lose left-hander Harper's in the shirtsleeves of the fans. When Speaker threatened to take his team off the field, the umpires ordered the Yankees to raise the entire screen.[22] In front of a crowd estimated at 35,000–40,000 fans, the game was on.

Harper may have not pitched on Sundays, but some observers said he did not pitch on Saturdays either, at least not on this Saturday. Uhle and the Indians defeated the Yankees, 9–0. The *New York Herald* ominously noted, "Once Harry loses his control, it's a total loss."[23] Harper walked three men in the third and three more in the fourth. He did not survive that inning, giving up five runs in three and one-third innings. Bob Shawkey was ineffective in relief, giving up four more runs the rest of the way.

Speaker started for the first time since his injury in St. Louis; he went 0-4. Joe Evans, who platooned in left field with veteran Charlie Jamieson and faced left-handed pitchers, batted leadoff. His third-inning single resulted in the game's first run, and his bases-loaded double an inning later brought home three more.[24] The New York outfield made three errors, two by Elmer Miller (on the same play) and one by Ruth, when he dropped "Tioga" George Burns's fly.[25] Uhle tossed a four-hitter, though he too walked six. The pitcher had a most unusual batting line, showing that he had a good eye, as well as a good swing. Despite coming away with no official at bats, Uhle did manage to score three runs off three walks and a sacrifice. His efforts again pushed the Tribe back into a virtual tie for first place. Once more, two very different Yankee teams had shown up in just two days. As Dan Daniel put it, "King for one day; jesters for another."[26]

On Sunday, there was such a rush of fans for the third game that the grandstand was full by one o'clock. Though 40,000 fans turned out for the game, the Yankees claimed they could have sold 75,000 tickets, despite the threatening weather.[27] It rained intermittently throughout the game, and fans in the bleachers made umbrellas out of their newspapers.

Mays, who had been pushed back a day, started for the Yankees. His opponent was Ray Caldwell, who had given up just one run in his last two starts combined. This afternoon, Caldwell did not survive the second inning, as the Yanks built up a 5–0 lead. Mails came in and ended the rally, but New York added two more runs in the third inning.

Mays was not particularly sharp, and these were the never-say-die Indians. They pushed across four runs in the fourth to make it a ball game, 7–4. Now it was the Tribe's turn to change their colors overnight. The Yankees scored eight runs in their half of the fourth, as Mails faced a nightmarish fourteen men. After six singles, two walks, three errors, and a triple, Mails was able to strike out Ruth—and that was only the inning's first out.

Perhaps Speaker wanted to conserve his pitchers for the next game; perhaps he was making a point and wanted Mails to get through the inning. By its end, Mails was done, and so were the Tribe, down 15–4. The *Cleveland Plain Dealer* lamented the turnaround, writing that it was hard to believe the world champions had played so poorly.[28]

When the game was over, the Yankees had won, 21–7. Mays had his twenty-sixth win, a thirteen-hitter. Bob Meusel and Chick Fewster hit home runs, Meusel and Elmer Miller had triples, and Meusel alone had five runs batted in. New York sportswriter George Daley, who went by the pseudonym Monitor, simply said, "The Yanks executed another of their famous form reversals."[29] The Babe was not much of a factor, with a single and a couple of walks. He was busy, however, in the third base coach's box, waving home Yankee after Yankee coming around to score. Ruth enjoyed occupying that role and did so often during the 1921 season.

The series, and perhaps the season, came down to the fourth and final game, on Monday. A Cleveland victory would pull the Indians back into a virtual tie and leave the pennant race up for grabs. A New York win would give the Yankees a commanding two-game lead, with just a handful of games left in the season. The only question was which pitchers Huggins and Speaker would select to start. Many observers expected to see Waite Hoyt (on two days' rest, after winning the opening game) and Allan Sothoron.

Huggins did have one problem. "The Shocker menace complicates things," wrote Sid Mercer.[30] The Yankees would have a game against the Browns the following day to make up the September 17 rainout. Shocker, who had defeated the Yanks on September 16, would start against them again. Damon Runyon noted a most unusual, almost bizarre occurrence: Shocker of the Browns was working out and warming up along the Indians' sideline before this Monday game, almost taunting the Yankees and reminding them and their fans that he was getting ready for them.[31] Inexplicably, Huggins held Hoyt back for tomorrow, even though today's game was the head-to-head match between the two leading teams.

In his history of the Yankees, Frank Graham describes the scene that unfolded in the Yankees' clubhouse before this game. Huggins called a team meeting and asked his pitchers who they thought should start against the Tribe. This was a stark contrast to McGraw's telling Phil Douglas in Pittsburgh in late August, "Phil, you work." Graham explains, "The pitchers didn't know what to say. None of them ever had heard a manager talk like that. It was the manager's place, not theirs, to make decisions. Bewildered, they looked at each other. No one wanted to be the first to speak. . . . The discussion lengthened, grew heated. It ended in a decision to pitch Quinn."[32]

Old Jack Quinn, who had started only twelve games all year, got the nod to start the Yankees' biggest game of the season. Most New York reporters had concluded that the aging spitballer's career was coming to an end. A few weeks earlier, newspapers reported that he would pursue a career as a big league umpire in 1922.[33] Perhaps Huggins was drawing on Quinn's stunning August 23 win over Cleveland, though he had not started a game since then. Speaker decided to go with his ace, Stan Coveleski, on two days' rest.

While Saturday's and Sunday's games had started at two o'clock, the Monday game would have the usual weekday start time of three thirty. With the end of daylight saving time the past weekend, a long game would brush up against the shadows of dusk. The day's crowd was variously estimated between 28,000 and 35,000. There was so much interest in this series that Western Union was sending the play-by-play to numerous cities across the country, as it would normally do only for World Series games.

The Indians jumped on Quinn immediately. They scored three times in the first inning on three hits, a walk, and a hit batter. Huggins was quick with his hook, scrapping tomorrow's plans by bringing in Hoyt for long relief today. Hoyt walked the dangerous Steve O'Neill and then struck Coveleski out with the bases loaded to end the inning. Hoyt then struck out the side in the second and gave up only two hits in the next three innings. He was doing his job well, giving the Yankees a chance to get back into the game.

Ruth put New York on the scoreboard in the bottom of the first with his fifty-seventh home run. In the third inning, his double was the key blow in a three-run rally: a one-out walk to Peckinpaugh, Ruth's double, and then singles by Meusel and Pipp. After New York had tied the score at three, Coveleski joined Quinn on the sidelines. After Ruth's double, Huggins sent Fewster in to pinch-run for the Babe, who had been troubled by a bad leg. Ruth waved him off.[34] In came George Uhle, the star of the second game, to pitch on one day's rest. He gave up a sacrifice pop-up to Aaron Ward (Meusel scored on the fly) and then retired the side. He then turned back the Yankees—three up, three down—in the fourth.

As Hoyt and Uhle settled in, it appeared that they might each continue to cool the opposition's bats. Then in the bottom of the fifth, Ruth struck again; and again it was Peckinpaugh on board. Ruth's third hit in the game was his second home run of the day, number fifty-eight; and New York's lead was now 6–3.

The Indians struck back immediately with two runs in the sixth. George Burns, who would finish the season with a .361 batting average, hit a triple (his second of four hits on the day). He brought Joe Sewell home and soon scored himself. It was now a 6–5 game. Hoyt and Uhle had been roughed up but remained in the game. Speaker and Huggins had only so many pitching cards to play, and these two seemed as good as any sitting on the benches.

Both teams continued to score. Wally Schang's two-run home run gave New York an 8–5 lead after six innings, but the Indians matched that with two runs in the seventh. Speaker started the rally with an infield hit, a vicious drive that deflected off Hoyt's pitching hand. Whether the play injured Hoyt or simply unsettled him, he wavered and walked Steve O'Neill and Elmer Smith. Trying to rattle the young pitcher and question his courage, the Indians started chanting, "Yellow Hoyt! Yellow Hoyt!" from their dugout.[35]

Once again, George Burns struck the key blow, a bases-loaded single that scored two. It was now an 8–7 game. Elmer Miller's pinpoint throw from deep center field nipped Sewell, trying to go from first to third, to end the inning. Miller had already made a fine catch of a Burns fly in the third (the only time Burns was retired all day), ending that inning with Sewell on second base.

The Indians' eighth was a strange, muddled series of events. Having already walked three men, Hoyt had become discouraged by umpire Bill Dinneen's calling of balls and strikes and asked to be taken out of the game.[36] Huggins ignored his young pitcher and sent him back out. After Hoyt gave up a one-out walk to Joe Evans, shortstop Peckinpaugh came to the mound and suggested that Hoyt leave the game.

Coach Charley O'Leary came rushing to the mound and told Hoyt to continue pitching. Peckinpaugh then "scowled and said a lot of caustic things to nobody in particular."[37] Charlie Jamieson then sent a drive to deep center field that Miller somehow hauled in, and his throw kept Evans at first. Bill Wambsganss then doubled, sending Evans to third. Now, with Speaker coming up, Huggins had seen enough. He pulled Hoyt. There was no newspaper report of Peckinpaugh's reaction to the move.

Carl Mays took over on the mound. Speaker hit a sinking liner that seemed destined to drop in and give the Indians a 9–8 lead. But Elmer Miller, "a recruit outfielder with the dust of minor league diamonds still clinging to his spikes," somehow reached the ball. He made a shoestring catch just before the ball would have touched the ground.[38] The Yankees' lead was safe, at least for another inning.

Elmer Miller had saved the day for New York, as he had many others since joining the team. He had made fifty catches since joining the Yankees, wrote Frank O'Neill, catches that no other American Leaguer, with the possible exception of Tris Speaker or Sam Rice, could have made.[39] Hindered by his knee injury and unable to swing with his full weight on his bad leg, Speaker had managed just one infield hit in the entire series. The best he could do was 1-13. Even the Yankees had to wonder how different the series might have been had Speaker been at full strength.

After Guy Morton faced only three Yankees in the eighth, Mays had to protect the lead of one run in the game and a potential two games in the pennant race. The late-afternoon shadows were enveloping the Polo Grounds. Larry Gardner, who already had scored twice in the game, worked Mays for a one-out walk.[40] After Sewell forced him at second, the Indians were down to their last out. Burns then came through with his fourth hit of the day, pushing Sewell to second. Steve O'Neill now came to the plate, and Joe Wood stepped into the on-deck circle to pinch-hit for Morton.

Perhaps Tris Speaker and Miller Huggins flashed back to a game in Cleveland a little more than a year earlier—August 13, 1920, to be exact. Speaker faced Mays with two outs in the ninth and the Yankees clinging to a 4–3 lead. It was getting so dark that a haze had settled on the field. "An umpire of sufficient nerve would have called the game on account of darkness," wrote the *New York World*.[41] On a 2-2 count, Mays struck Speaker out to end the game.

All eyes in the stadium were now on O'Neill. All eyes except two—those of one of the Yankees' owners, Jacob Ruppert. He simply could not bear the tension of watching the game's final moments. He walked to the Yankees' bullpen, where backup catcher Fred Hofmann updated him, pitch by pitch, on O'Neill's at bat.[42]

With the count 3-2 and Sewell and Burns running on the pitch, sportswriter Frank O'Neill (who was of no relation to the batter) described what happened: "O'Neill could barely see it [the pitch] and fearing that perhaps Bill Dinneen would call the third strike, took a game man's chance and swung."[43] He missed as the ball tailed into the dirt, and the Yankees had prevailed. They had beaten the Indians for the fourteenth time in twenty-two games this year. Heywood Broun summed up the remarkable game this way: "It was the greatest baseball game ever played. . . . A masterpiece can always be identified by the hush which follows. . . . His [Mays's] performance approached its climax in the midst of a silence acute as any ever paid to a great tragic actor."[44]

For the second time in four days, Waite Hoyt had gotten the win, his nineteenth, while Stan Coveleski had taken the loss. Tris Speaker had not followed his own advice of walking the Babe with a man on base. One Cleveland paper noted that had the Tribe walked Ruth four times in this game, they would probably have won by a score of 7–4.[45]

Ruth batted .727 in the series. He made sixteen plate appearances and got on base thirteen times; in eleven at bats, he totaled eighteen bases.[46] His teammate Frank Baker, with an eerily prescient eye to the early-twenty-first century, had this to say about the Babe: "There has never been anybody like him and I don't believe there ever will be anybody like him. . . . Some time the ball parks may be smaller than they are now and then perhaps some husky slugger will come to the fore who may break Babe's present record. But that doesn't mean anything. Put Babe in some ball parks right now and he would average a home run a day."[47]

AL STANDINGS AT CLOSE OF PLAY OF SEPTEMBER 26, 1921

TEAM	G	W	L	T	PCT	GB
New York Yankees	148	94	54	0	.635	-
Cleveland Indians	150	93	57	0	.620	2.0
St. Louis Browns	151	78	73	0	.517	17.5
Washington Senators	149	76	72	1	.514	18.0
Boston Red Sox	146	72	74	0	.493	21.0
Detroit Tigers	152	71	80	1	.470	24.5
Chicago White Sox	150	59	91	0	.393	36.0
Philadelphia Athletics	148	52	94	2	.356	41.0

24   The Giants Clinch and the Repercussions Get Ugly

After the Giants and Yankees each won their September series against their main rival, both New York teams had taken control of their respective pennant races. In the September 22 issue of the *Sporting News*, three days after the Giants finished in Pittsburgh and just a day before the Indians came to New York, Joe Vila noted the surprising turn of events. If there was to be an all–New York World Series, he pointed out, few had expected the Giants to get there first.

With the pennant now within their grasp, the Giants continued their western road trip. Moving from Pittsburgh to Chicago on September 20, they split a pair of games with the seventh-place Cubs. Trailing Grover Alexander after seven innings of the first game, they tied the score on George Kelly's twenty-third (and final) home run of the season.[1] Chicago had tallied all their runs off Jesse Barnes, who left in the fifth. From then on, Pat Shea, Slim Sallee, and Art Nehf held the Cubs scoreless until Nehf allowed the game winner in the tenth. The Pirates, rained out at home, now trailed by three games, but had only one more loss than the Giants.

Nehf had been effective in relief—despite the loss—but was less so a day later when McGraw started him against the Cubs. Phil Douglas, who relieved Nehf, was worse. Shea retired the only batter he faced and picked up a cheap win when the Giants scored four times in the eighth inning to overcome a 7–5 deficit. Fred Toney—McGraw's most reliable pitcher of late, both as a starter and a reliever—nailed down the win with two hitless innings.

The weather was still bad in Pittsburgh, where the previous day's rained-out game with the Dodgers was to be made up as part of a doubleheader. Brooklyn's Clarence Mitchell shut out the Pirates in the first game, called after seven innings because of the rain. With the second game being called off, the Giants' win combined with the Pirates' loss to increase New York's lead to four games.

A travel date on September 22 and a rainout in St. Louis on the twenty-third kept the Giants off the field for two days; nevertheless, they did gain a slight victory. American League president Ban Johnson and National League president John Heydler met in Commissioner Landis's office in Chicago for a coin toss to determine which league would host the World Series opener. Johnson called heads, but the coin came up tails.

During the two days the Giants did not play, the Pirates, barely breathing, split a doubleheader with Brooklyn and defeated Philadelphia, cutting the lead to three and a half games. The Cardinals, seven and a half games behind, were now out of the race. Nevertheless, the three games they would play against the Giants were of great importance to them, as they still had a chance to overtake Pittsburgh and finish second.

The Cardinals' Bill Doak was leading the National League with a 2.61 earned run average, slightly ahead of Babe Adams and Burleigh Grimes, when he faced the Giants on September 24. A crowd of 15,000 turned out on a very hot and muggy Saturday afternoon in St. Louis. With Fred Toney as Doak's opponent, it figured to be a low-scoring game. However, each team scored four runs in the first three innings, before the Cardinals eventually won, 8–4. While Doak, now 15-6, was touched for four runs, three were unearned; and so his league-leading earned run average actually dropped to 2.54.

Meanwhile, Pittsburgh's win over Philadelphia kept them four ahead of the Cardinals, while reducing the Giants lead to two and a half games. With a week left in the season, the Pirates still had an outside chance to finish first.

Given that the Cardinals had only a faint hope of finishing second, Sunday's crowd, with many forced to stand behind ropes, was surprisingly large. Irish Meusel's ground-rule double into the standees drove in two of the Giants' three first-inning runs, on the way to a 5–2 victory. Meusel, who had four hits off Doak the day before, had four more today; and he also drove in four of the Giants' five runs. His performance raised his batting average to .343, fourth best in the National League behind three Cardinals: Rogers Hornsby, Austin McHenry, and Jack Fournier. Douglas went the distance in the Giants win, making his record 15-9 on the season.

With each day's results, the mathematics of the pennant race changed, and time had almost run out on the Pirates' hopes. If New York could win just three of their five remaining games, they would finish with a record of 95-59 and clinch at least a tie. Pittsburgh would then have to win all seven of their games to reach that mark.

The Giants were to play an exhibition game in Indianapolis on Monday the twenty-sixth but had to cancel so that they could make up Friday's rained-out game with the Cardinals. Art Nehf returned to form with a 4–1 win over Bill Pertica, as he reached the twenty-win mark for the second consecutive season. Among the five hits Nehf allowed was Hornsby's forty-second double of the season, tying Kelly for the most in the National League. St. Louis, which had made two errors on Saturday and four on Sunday, made five more today, although three of the Giants' four runs were earned.

Nehf's victory, combined with Pittsburgh's loss to the Phillies, moved the Giants four games ahead. They now needed just one win to assure a tie; however, for the Pirates to tie, they would have to win all six of their games, provided the Giants won only one more.

After defeating the Cardinals on the twenty-sixth, the Giants quickly shed their uniforms for street clothes. They then piled into a fleet of automobiles that took them to St. Louis's Union Station, where they boarded the *Empire State Express* for the grueling thirty-hour ride that would bring them to New York the next day. "Every Giant on the team is rooting for the Yankees to win the pennant, not because of any feeling that the Hugmen will be easier to defeat than the Indians, but for the reason that they will not be obliged to go West again if the Yankees win. They detest railroad journeys."[2]

As the Giants headed home, John McGraw canceled the exhibition games scheduled for September 29 and 30 against the International League's Orioles in Baltimore, preferring to rest his players over any gate receipts the team might have earned from those games. Instead, he held a couple of morning practice sessions at the Polo Grounds.

While McGraw was satisfied with the overall physical condition of the team, several of his players were hurting, most seriously Dave Bancroft and Earl Smith, both with fingers badly bruised in the St. Louis series. Additionally, two of his best players, Frankie Frisch and Ross Youngs, had suffered leg injuries early in the season. He wanted to make sure all were rested and ready for the World Series.

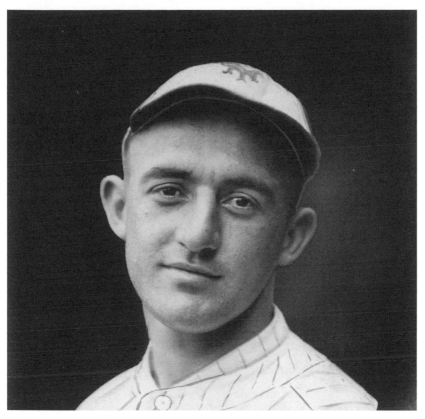

39. Signed out of Fordham University in the Bronx, twenty-two-year-old Frankie Frisch's spectacular play made the native New Yorker especially popular among Giants fans. One reporter called Frisch a "tower of strength on defense" and perhaps their "most important cog" on offense (Walter St. Denis, *New York Globe and Commercial Advertiser*, September 28, 1921). *Private Collection of Dennis Goldstein.*

Frisch in particular would have to be at full strength for the Giants to be successful. Only recently having turned twenty-three, he had become the Giants' most valuable player. "Frisch has already established himself as one of the greatest infielders the game has ever produced. With Frisch on third, the Giants are the class of their league; without him they are just a baseball club; a better baseball club than the average, of course, but not the sort of club that captures pennants. He is not only a tower of strength on defense, but one of the vital cogs, perhaps the most important cog, in their offensive machinery."[3]

Frankie Frisch had taken a much different path to stardom than most players, one that took him directly from college to the Major Leagues with no Minor League stops in between. A native New Yorker, he signed with the Giants after starring in baseball, football, basketball, and track at Fordham University in the Bronx. A natural leader, he captained the baseball, basketball, and football teams at Fordham. Frisch's best sport may have been football. A speedy 155-pound halfback, he earned a spot on Walter Camp's second team in Camp's 1918 All-America selections.[4]

In today's world Frisch, who left school in 1919, would be a high draft choice by both the National Football League and Major League Baseball. However, there was no organized professional football in 1919, nor was there a draft in baseball. Several teams, including the hometown Yankees, the Detroit Tigers, and the Boston Red Sox, tried to sign Frisch, a shortstop who had batted close to .500 during Fordham's 1919 season. However, the Giants had the inside track. Frisch's baseball coach at Fordham was Art Devlin, McGraw's third baseman for the Giants from 1904 through 1911.

Frisch's play and his leadership qualities as team captain convinced Devlin that he would be a successful Major Leaguer—and then some. On Devlin's recommendation, McGraw signed the youngster for a $200 bonus and a salary of $400 to play for the Giants for the remainder of the 1919 season. "He is another Eddie Collins," raved Devlin after the signing. "He is a natural ball player and next year will be one of the greatest in the game."[5] "McGraw wanted to sign me up with the club two years before I finally came," Frisch later revealed. "Of course, I was flattered by the offer, but I didn't want to join just then."[6]

Frisch's father, Franz, a German immigrant who had grown wealthy manufacturing lace and linen, opposed the signing. Not surprisingly, he was unhappy with the idea of his son leaving college for a career in baseball. He finally agreed to young Frisch joining the Giants but hoped it would be only for the summer.

"There was an unusual clause in the contract, though," Frisch reminisced many years later. "It said that if I failed to make good with the Giants after two years, I would be given my unconditional release. That was pretty good thinking for a dopey college kid," he added.[7] The clause would prove unnecessary, as Frisch's speed on the bases and in the field made the local youngster an immediate favorite with the Polo Grounds crowds.

He did not hit much that first year (.226 in 190 at bats), but he filled in admirably at second base when Larry Doyle was injured in August. Blessed with quickness and dexterity, Frisch was a natural athlete. Nevertheless, while the playing fields of Fordham were only a short distance from the Polo Grounds, it was a long way from college baseball to the Major Leagues. To bridge that gap and to refine Frisch's raw talent, McGraw spent many hours tutoring his young recruit in the fine arts of batting and sliding. He called Frisch "the most promising young player who has broken into the game in years."[8]

McGraw was pleased by his players' confidence regarding the upcoming World Series, a series they now fully believed they would play against the Yankees. "One of the finest features of this remarkable spurt of the Giants in the last month is that it has left them in such excellent condition of mind and body."[9]

He was especially proud of the way the team had come back against the Pirates, principally because they had done so in head-to-head competition. Moreover, they had overcome the disadvantage of having to play so many late-season games on the road.[10]

The actual clinching, which came on Thursday, September 29, was anticlimactic and lacked any sense of drama. Pittsburgh had won on the twenty-seventh while the Giants were idle, cutting the lead to three and a half games. Neither team played on the twenty-eighth. The Giants were also idle on the twenty-ninth; but when Pittsburgh lost both games of a doubleheader at St. Louis, the Pirates were eliminated.[11]

By winning his seventh league pennant, McGraw broke the tie that had existed since 1917 with the Athletics' Connie Mack for most pennants won. Much of the credit for this one belonged to McGraw, mainly for his deft handling of a pitching staff that was not as dominant as those of many of his previous winners. Offensively, he had quickly realized that the squad he had opened the season with was not strong enough to win the pennant. The acquisitions of second baseman Johnny Rawlings and outfielder Irish Meusel, in separate deals with the Phillies, had turned a good team into a very good team. McGraw, always the master psychologist, had seen his team go 23-9 since his locker-room speech before the Pirates' series in late August.

After three days of not playing, the newly crowned National League champions concluded their home season with a game against the Boston Braves on Friday, September 30. A crowd in excess of 25,000 was on hand, not so much to see the game, but to see the event that preceded it. The Giants had arranged to play a benefit game between the current team and some of their great stars of the past. The purpose was to raise money for their former star pitcher Christy Mathewson.

The squads played five innings, with the old-timers winning, 2–0. The fans got what they came to see, so their disappointment was not too great when rain ended the regularly scheduled game after one inning.[12] In addition to the gate receipts, money was raised by advance donations and the sale of Mathewson-related souvenirs. In all, Mathewson reportedly received almost $50,000 from the event, which at the time was by far the most anyone had ever received from a benefit game.[13]

The Giants concluded their season by splitting a doubleheader at Philadelphia and losing at Brooklyn. McGraw used these games to give his regulars just enough playing time to keep them sharp and line up his pitching rotation for the Yankees.

New York's spectacular comeback and Pittsburgh's woeful collapse were not without repercussions. Manager Gibson's defense of his team and of himself had not satisfied Pirates owner Barney Dreyfuss, who blamed the downfall on having too many fun-loving spirits on the club. Dreyfuss was furious that his team had allowed itself to be humiliated by McGraw and the Giants. The enmity between the two men had an extensive history. In one memorable incident during a game at the Polo Grounds back in May 1904, McGraw had shouted such gross obscenities at Dreyfuss that the Pirates' owner felt compelled to report it to National League president Harry Pulliam. Pulliam fined McGraw a hefty $150 and suspended him for fifteen days, though he eventually rescinded both penalties. In June of that year, Pittsburgh fans attacked the Giants players as they were returning to their hotel from Exposition Park, the Pirates' home field.[14]

Now, seventeen years later, the mutual distrust between the two National League titans was as great as ever. Charges had surfaced that the Pirates had somehow been drugged during their August series in New York. A *Sporting News* editorial discussed the rumor that friends of McGraw had enticed Pirate players to speakeasies during their late-August visit to the big city and plied them with alcohol. Yet that very column noted there was little substance to the report, as was also the case with the drugging story.[15]

Still, McGraw was taking no chances. When the Giants made their mid-September visit to Pittsburgh, he ordered his players to drink only bottled water. His combative personality and us-against-the-world view fed both the Pittsburgh rumors and his own fears of their possible retaliation. Nevertheless, Dreyfuss would later say, "After the Pirates lost those five games in a row, there were rumors that something was wrong. It is generally understood that some of the Pittsburgh players broke training rules at that time and their actions in a large part were blamed for the collapse of the team and the loss of the pennant."[16]

Losing the 1921 pennant to the Giants was so devastating to Dreyfuss that he later alleged that the Giants had collected money to give to certain Brooklyn players if they would beat the Pirates. The series he had in mind was the three games between the Pirates and the Dodgers from August 28 through 30, following the Pirates' loss of five games at the Polo Grounds. If it was true—and both McGraw and Dodgers manager Wilbert Robinson vigorously denied it—it was not very successful. The Pirates defeated the Dodgers in two of those three games.

Several years later, Pittsburgh sportswriter Ralph S. Davis blamed what he called "the joy riding Bucs of that year" for the loss of the pennant. "It wasn't the 'bearing down' of rival clubs against them that thwarted the Buccaneers that year so much as it was a failure of Dreyfuss' athletes to tread the straight and narrow pathway and keep themselves in playing condition," Davis wrote. "Joy rides were numerous, and the Pirates were a dandy bunch of .500 hitters in the Midnight League," he added. "On the other hand, the eyes that shone brightest at night were sometimes dim in the afternoon, and rival pitchers had little difficulty in putting over the fooler on Pittsburgh batters."[17]

A much more serious allegation appeared late in 1921. An article appeared in the September 3, 1921, issue of Henry Ford's anti-Semitic newspaper, the *Dearborn Independent*, entitled "Jewish Gamblers Corrupt American Baseball." The *Dearborn Independent* had been blaming all of America's and the world's problems on the Jews, and this time it was baseball's turn. Painting with a broad brush and including everyone with a Jewish-sounding name connected to baseball in any way, the article claimed that Jewish gamblers and Jewish owners had corrupted the game. In doing so, it made no distinction between a known gambler, such as Arnold Rothstein, and a respected owner, such as Barney Dreyfuss.

From there, the story evolved into the Jewish owner, Dreyfuss, having his team deliberately lose the pennant to the Giants in exchange for money from Jewish gambling interests. But even the *Sporting News*, whose own editorial page was not immune from anti-Semitic remarks, balked at this allegation.[18] Under a headline that read "Pirates Were Just Not of High Class," it editorialized, "The stuff is ridiculous on the face of it, and none but the most evil mind could imagine, none but the most perverted sporting editor give space to such guff."[19]

FINAL NL STANDINGS, OCTOBER 2, 1921

TEAM	G	W	L	T	PCT	GB
New York Giants	153	94	59	0	.614	-
Pittsburgh Pirates	154	90	63	1	.588	4.0
St. Louis Cardinals	154	87	66	1	.569	7.0
Boston Braves	153	79	74	0	.516	15.0
Brooklyn Dodgers	152	77	75	0	.507	16.5
Cincinnati Reds	153	70	83	0	.458	24.0
Chicago Cubs	153	64	89	0	.418	30.0
Philadelphia Phillies	154	51	103	0	.331	43.5

On the morning of Tuesday, September 27, the day after the Cleveland series, the 94-54 Yankees (.635) had a hard-earned two-game lead over the 93-57 Indians (.620). The Yanks had five games to play (they would not make up the game rained out at Washington), while the Tribe had but four. New York sent Harry Harper to the mound that afternoon against St. Louis's Urban Shocker. The visiting Browns struck early with George Sisler's two-run home run in the first. After giving up three hits in that inning, Harper settled down and allowed only four more the rest of the way.

It did not matter. Shocker had all the runs he needed in crafting his twenty-seventh win of the season. "Shocker never was greater in all his career, and his performance was worthy of the masters," wrote Frank O'Neill.[1] The Babe did drive a ball to the wall in the first, but Jack Tobin hauled it in for nothing more than a long out. Through eight innings, Shocker gave up only three singles, and no Yankee reached second base.

In the ninth inning, New York mounted a rally. Wally Schang led off with an infield hit; and with two outs, Roger Peckinpaugh singled. After seeing firsthand what the Babe had done to the Indians the day before, Shocker and the Browns decided to put the potential winning run on base. Shocker walked Ruth intentionally, tossing four wide ones to load the bases. He then retired Bob Meusel on a fly ball to nail down the 2–0 victory.[2] After the game, John McGraw asked the sports editor of the *St. Louis Times* what Shocker had been throwing on this day. "Slow balls," replied Sid Keener.

The Indians, who were now one and a half games behind New York, were idle until Thursday the twenty-ninth, when they would start their final series of the season, four games in Chicago. The Yankees would face the Athletics three times (Thursday and Friday in Philadelphia and

40. Bob Shawkey won twenty games three times in his first four full seasons with the Yankees. Now that they were approaching their first World Series, Shawkey was having his poorest season and was no longer the reliable pitcher they could count on. *Photo by Charles M. Conlon. Private collection of Steve Steinberg.*

Saturday in New York) and then close out the season against the Red Sox in the Polo Grounds.

Triples by Mike McNally and Elmer Miller and a home run by Peckinpaugh fueled Bob Shawkey's 5–0 shutout of the A's on Thursday. The New York press played up the win as Shawkey's comeback. Dan Daniel wrote that Miller Huggins was "sending up fervent prayers that Shawkey retain the form he showed yesterday."[3] Yet the newspapers overlooked the fact that it came against the Athletics, who had the lowest batting average in either league this season. They also ignored Shawkey's four walks. He was still struggling with his control.

While the Yankees were closing in on their first-ever pennant, Huggins was getting no respite from criticism. Fans taunted him during the game, yelling, "Hey, Miller, where are you going next year—Rochester?"[4] Huggins was simply fated to be an unsympathetic figure in the eyes of many New York reporters and fans alike. Under a front-page photo of the Yankee skipper that week, the *Sporting News* wrote, "The Mite

Manager fights his way through, sans diplomacy, sans personality, and makes it harder for himself; that's not his fault: he was born that way."[5]

The Yankees finally got some help from their nemesis, White Sox pitcher Dickie Kerr. He shut out the Indians by the same 5–0 score that Shawkey had beaten Philadelphia with, pushing the Tribe two and a half games back. (At 93-58, the Indians could reach ninety-six victories only if they won their three remaining games, while the Yankees' win-loss record was already at 95-55.) Cleveland won a critical game on Friday, as Stan Coveleski bested Red Faber. When New York's Friday game was rained out, some Yankee fans and players thought they had clinched the pennant.[6] But they soon learned that the Philadelphia rainout would have to be made up Saturday in New York.[7] The Yankees needed another win or a Cleveland loss to clinch the pennant.

Returning to the Polo Grounds, the Yankees started Carl Mays in the first game of Saturday's doubleheader. It was fitting that New York's best pitcher would go for the pennant clincher, which would also tie him with Shocker for the league lead in wins with twenty-seven. New Yorkers were surprised that rookie Jim Sullivan, who had made his Major League debut just three days earlier, got the start for the A's. (He would pitch for them for three seasons and never win a Major League game.) Connie Mack held back his leading pitcher, Eddie Rommel, for the second game. If the Athletics were going to derail the Yanks' pennant train, they would have to win both games.

Giants pitcher Fred Toney and catcher Earl Smith were among the 26,000 fans who saw Philadelphia stun Mays with five hits in the fourth inning to take a 3–1 lead. The Yankees then used their speed to remind people that they could win without home runs, or even extra-base hits. On a double steal in the fifth, Wally Schang scored to close the gap. An inning later, Wally Pipp tied the game by stealing second and coming around to score on two throwing errors. The Yanks took the lead in the seventh, when Mike McNally scored all the way from first on a hit-and-run single by Schang. Elmer Miller then got his third hit of the game, scoring Schang and completing the scoring for the 5–3 win.

When Miller caught Chick Galloway's fly ball for the final out, the New York Yankees had won their first American League pennant. Damon Runyon called the season-long struggle between the Yanks and Indians one of the fiercest pennant battles in baseball history.[8] After the clincher, the Polo Grounds reverberated with waves of cheers. Some of the kudos were directed to a somewhat forlorn and unsmiling figure. Runyon captured the surreal scene: "Miller Huggins, the little manager of the New York club, tramped across the yard in the wake of his men, his head bowed in a characteristic attitude. In happiness or sorrow Huggins is ever something of a picture of dejection. The crowd cheered him as his familiar Charley Chaplin feet lugged his small body along, and Huggins had to keep doffing his cap."[9] With all the criticism that had been hurled Huggins's way, he surely could not be blamed if he felt some bitterness.[10]

McNally's daring dash highlighted the value of this classic utility man. With Frank Baker's absences during the season, McNally played in forty-nine games at third base (Aaron Ward also played thirty-three games at third) and sixteen at second. His role should not be overlooked. "If ever a single man saved a team, Mike McNally had saved the Yanks," wrote Frank O'Neill.[11]

The White Sox rallied from a 4–0 deficit and beat the Tribe on Saturday, 8–5. The Yankees' anticlimactic second game was an odd one. After they staked Waite Hoyt to a 5–0 lead against Rommel, Jack Quinn relieved Hoyt in the fifth inning. Babe Ruth then took over on the mound in the eighth inning with a 6–0 lead. The Athletics scored six runs off him to knot the score. While Ruth finished the game and got the win in the eleventh, the blown lead cost Waite Hoyt what would have been his twentieth win of the season.[12]

The Yankees closed the season on Sunday, October 2, with a win over the Red Sox, while Cleveland lost again in Chicago. The Indians finished four and a half games back, a number hardly indicative of how close and hard fought the race had been. The Browns held onto third place, just a half game ahead of the Senators.[13]

Cleveland sportswriter Ed Bang felt that Tris Speaker's managerial performance in 1921 was more impressive than that of 1920, when the Tribe had won it all.[14] Stuart M. Bell looked back on the season in the *Cleveland Plain Dealer*: "The Indians most of the time had a wreck of a championship ball club. . . . He piloted an almost pitcherless, and for two months, an almost catcherless ball club. . . . Nobody but Tris Speaker could have done it."[15]

While Speaker was garnering accolades for finishing second, Huggins was getting grudging approval at best. Yet it was now time, said Runyon, to give Miller Huggins his due. "He is entitled to all the credit and the glory that goes with the leadership of a pennant winning ball club. He is entitled to an apology from those who have belittled his efforts."[16]

FINAL AL STANDINGS, 1921

TEAM	G	W	L	T	PCT	GB
New York Yankees	153	98	55	0	.641	-
Cleveland Indians	154	94	60	0	.610	4.5
St. Louis Browns	154	81	73	0	.526	17.5
Washington Senators	154	80	73	1	.523	18.0
Boston Red Sox	154	75	79	0	.487	23.5
Detroit Tigers	154	71	82	1	.464	27.0
Chicago White Sox	154	62	92	0	.403	36.5
Philadelphia Athletics	155	53	100	2	.346	45.0

PART 3   The Postseason

26 Prelude to the World Series, Part 2

The story line of the 1921 World Series was succinct and direct. Two New York teams were vying for the hearts of New Yorkers, attempting to lay claim to baseball supremacy in the nation's largest city. Two of the biggest personalities in the history of the game were leading these teams into the Series. "Big Series Resolves Itself to Question of Ruth versus McGraw," read the headline in the Boston Herald.[1]

In addition to having taken New York by storm the past two seasons, Babe Ruth had captured the attention of people throughout the country, and not only of baseball fans. He did so in part with his record-setting home run feats. But he had much more—an exuberant joie de vivre and behavior that pushed conventional boundaries. Both were made to order for the early 1920s, a time of breaking free from constraints and having a good time.

Ruth was so genuine and so unbridled in his enthusiasm for baseball and for life that his drinking and carousing only added to his allure. Grantland Rice captured the Babe's persona well when he wrote, "Ruth, the man-boy, was the complete embodiment of everything uninhibited."[2] After the devastating Great War, Americans wanted to enjoy themselves. Sports became "an American obsession," and celebrities (in sports and in entertainment) became the focus of great attention and adulation.[3]

In a time of increasing urbanization and mass production, the Babe was one of the biggest and most inimitable heroes of the times, one who appealed to people of all ages. He was "a screaming symbol, saying 'I won't go'—to some, the last gasp of the rugged individual."[4]

Ford Frick was a young New York sportswriter who covered the Yankees in the 1920s and would serve as the commissioner of baseball from 1951 to 1965. Frick knew Ruth well and even was one of the Babe's ghostwriters. "Most of us lack the nerve to defy the conventions which we secretly detest. When we find a man who has such nerve, then we put him on a pedestal of notoriety. While we question his judgment at times, we admire his daring and his originality. That's Babe Ruth."[5] This was the man who would spearhead the Yankees' attack in the upcoming Series.

New York drama and literary critic Heywood Broun conveyed Ruth's impact, in an article in *The Nation* during Ruth's first season in New York. Broun related a story about the famous New York Baptist preacher John Roach Straton (1875–1929). Straton dies and goes to heaven, where he meets the "ruler of the realm," as thousands of fans are attending a Sunday ball game at the Polo Grounds. "Let New York be destroyed," cries the preacher. "Delay not thy wrath." But the ruler sees that it is the ninth inning of a tie game, with two men on base and Ruth coming to the plate. "The time has not come," declares the King.[6] While some may have found Broun's article humorous and others may have seen it as irreverent, it resonated because of Ruth's enormous appeal. It seemed that everyone wanted to see the Babe hit.

Everyone except John McGraw. As demeaning as the Giants' skipper had been in the past about Ruth's long-ball style (having stated, "We pitch to better hitters than Ruth in the National League"), McGraw was a realist. A week before the postseason, he said, "It's a tough proposition to go against Ruth. I'm not silly enough to say that my pitchers will prevent Ruth from hitting out of the park."[7] A week later, he elaborated, "We shall take no liberties with a slugger like Ruth." McGraw made it clear that in threatening situations, he would not hesitate to walk the Babe, even though the fans would not like it. "Ruth is the man we must beat," he declared. "I will not be swerved by any sentiment from the grandstand. It will not disturb me at all."[8]

One reporter noted that Giants pitchers were not afraid of pitching to the Babe. "But, then, there are people who are not afraid of rattlesnakes, and it is a well known scientific fact that rattlesnakes bite those who are not afraid of them just as readily as those who are afraid."[9]

While Giants pitchers may have been eager for the challenge of pitching to Ruth, doing so would not be their decision to make. McGraw controlled his team to such an extent that he often called every pitch from the bench. Back in the spring of 1914, after winning three straight National League pennants, McGraw spoke openly about his heavy-handed style: "It has been said of me that 'The Giants are McGraw.' I admit that to a great extent that is true. It is my policy to build a team that is a machine, and my relation to it is always to have my hand on the lever that controls things."[10] McGraw had given little indication in the intervening seven years that he had changed his philosophy.

Analysts and prognosticators considered the Series a toss-up; and the odds, which hovered around even money, reflected the closely matched abilities of the two teams. Dan Daniel declared that this World Series between two of the gamest clubs ever was "the hardest ever to dope. To tell the truth, there is no edge either way."[11] As humorist Bugs Baer put it, "Teams look as evenly matched as [sic] set of false teeth."[12]

Refusing to pick a winner, a *Sporting News* editorial added what has often been true in the postseason, that this Series between two such evenly matched teams might be decided by a break.[13] Sam Crane observed that an obscure player often emerges as the star of the World Series. He even offered up a possible candidate, the Giants' Johnny Rawlings, "one of the gamest men who ever played the bag [second base]."[14] Fred Lieb suggested that Waite Hoyt might emerge as the star, since the Brooklyn youngster was eager to gain revenge on the Giants, who originally had signed him and then let him go.[15]

Hugh Fullerton presented some of the most detailed analyses of the upcoming event. He predicted that the early games would be low scoring, with hitting taking over as the Series got deeper into the pitching rotations. He went so far as to pick the winner of each game, based on projected pitching matchups. He said the Yanks would win the first two games but would eventually lose the Series, as the Giants would win the final three contests.[16]

The press, which had set up headquarters at the new Commodore Hotel, made the battle between Miller Huggins's sluggers and McGraw's pitchers the focus of most of their stories.[17] Mainly they talked about Ruth. The Babe had hit fifty-nine home runs to break his own record set a year earlier, while also establishing new single-season Major League highs in runs (177), runs batted in (171), and total bases (457).[18]

Seemingly forgotten by much of the press was that the Giants also had their league's home run leader, perhaps because George Kelly's twenty-three paled next to Ruth's fifty-nine. One exception was Harry A. Williams of the *Los Angeles Times*, who seemed cognizant that the Giants had some long-ball hitters of their own and predicted the Series would set a record for the number of home runs. Then, echoing McGraw's frustration with the long-ball style of play, Williams added, "Baseball has switched from a science to a wild scramble."[19]

While the Yankees had the better hitting, the Giants had plenty of offensive weapons too. The Giants had hit seventy-five home runs in 1921, more than any previous two World Series opponents combined; yet it seemed hardly worth mentioning compared to the Yankees' record-setting total of 134.[20] The numbers were illuminating. The Giants hit .298 with 1,575 hits in 1921, and the Yankees hit .300 with 1,576 hits. Yet, because of their power, the Yankees scored 108 more runs—948 compared to the Giants' 840—to set a new twentieth-century high.

The consensus was that with Art Nehf, Phil Douglas, Fred Toney, and Jesse Barnes, the Giants had better and deeper starting pitching, though their earned run average of 3.55 was only third best in the National League, lagging behind those of Pittsburgh and Cincinnati. The Yankees were led by veterans Carl Mays and Bob Shawkey, who respectively won twenty-seven and eighteen games, and by twenty-one-year-old newcomer Waite Hoyt, who won nineteen. The Yanks' pitching staff had the lowest earned run average in the American League, at 3.82.

In the dawning of the Lively Ball Era, many felt the Series would be dominated by hitting. "Playing for a run is a forgotten art," wrote umpire-columnist Billy Evans.[21] Yet John McGraw felt that some things never change, regardless of the era. "Pitching will, as it has so many times in the past, decide the championship," he declared.[22]

John McGraw believed that his Giants had a stronger all-round set of starters than the Yankees had. "We are going into the series with plenty of confidence, but we are not boasting," he said.[23] Not surprisingly, Miller Huggins thought his team had the edge. In Carl Mays, whose twenty-seven wins this season had come on the heels of twenty-six victories in 1920, the Yanks clearly had the best pitcher on either club. "My pitchers are all in good shape for the series with the Giants," said the Yankee skipper. "Ruth, Meusel, and the rest of my hitters will bat their way to victory."[24]

Many of those analyzing the teams' respective strengths felt that the Giants had a big—and perhaps decisive—edge in the dugout, where

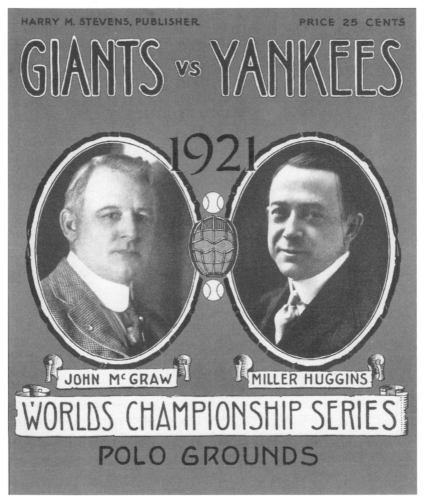

41. An all–New York World Series was finally at hand. While the program cover featured the two managers, most people saw the games as a showdown between Babe Ruth and John McGraw. Because the Giants' manager called all the pitches his hurlers threw, he would determine if Ruth would get anything decent to swing at. *Private collection of Steve Steinberg.*

they believed McGraw was clearly superior to Huggins. Sam Crane, for example, said that the Giants' manager was more creative and more of a risk taker, while Huggins was more deliberate and predictable.[25] The Giants also had the advantage of discipline that came from their manager's iron hand. The Yankees, on the other hand, openly challenged and disregarded their manager, often deciding on their own what to do.[26] Such a style might prove fatal in a short series. Yet it seems somewhat paradoxical, if not contradictory, for sportswriters to consider the Giants the smarter and more resourceful club, when their players did little thinking on their own with McGraw pulling the levers from the dugout.

William Hanna was in the distinct minority of New York reporters in recognizing Huggins's quiet and hidden strengths. "Tactically Huggins plays second fiddle to nobody, nor is he behind anybody in quick grasp of openings," he declared.[27]

New Yorkers had been talking about a Giants-Yankees World Series since spring training; and now that it was here, it gripped this normally blasé city with a sense of enthusiasm and anticipation. Finding a New York City baseball fan who had no opinion on the outcome was difficult, and finding one who professed neutrality was near impossible. "As a result of this family feud, Manhattan seethes tonight with arguments, debates, and scraps."[28] Even the governor, Nathan L. Miller, voiced his preference. Though he risked antagonizing millions of voters by doing so, Miller announced that he was rooting for the Giants, citing the fact that both he and McGraw were born in Cortland County, New York.[29]

Though not directly involved, those whose allegiance was to Brooklyn, the city's third team, also had a rooting interest, one that centered on being for or against the Giants and had little to do with the Yankees. Some Dodger fans were for McGraw's club simply out of loyalty to the National League. Others loathed McGraw enough to want him humbled regardless of the opposition. With Ruth now the most popular man in baseball and McGraw perhaps the most hated, there was no doubt the vast majority of fans in other cities across America were hoping for a Yankees victory.

While there was some muttering that an all–New York Series would not generate much interest across the country, the unprecedented crush for press credentials and game tickets belied such comments. Tickets were in such demand that Yankees co-owner Til Huston grumbled, "I know I'm going to be an unpopular cuss after this series, and the worst of it is I can't do a thing about it."[30]

Revelations about the fixed Reds–White Sox World Series of 1919 were only a year old, as news of the plot had first surfaced in September 1920.

Nevertheless, there was extremely heavy betting on the Series, and the press reported it in detail.[31] Professional gamblers gave the Yankees a slight edge based on their superior offense; but because bettors considered the teams evenly matched, both clubs had vast amounts of money wagered on them.

With Nehf and Mays expected as the probable Game 1 starters, there was a last-minute switch in the odds to favor the Giants. The thinking behind this shift was that bettors felt that if Nehf lost the opener, the Giants could come back, but if Mays lost it, the Yankees could not.

No less an authority on baseball gambling than Hugh Fullerton, the Chicago reporter who broke the story of the 1919 World Series fix, reported in his syndicated column that this 1921 World Series was seeing the heaviest postseason betting ever.[32] The professionals who ran the gambling establishments went even further than Fullerton. They felt certain that the amount of money wagered on the 1921 World Series would exceed that of any previous sporting event.

Almost hourly the odds shifted back and forth, as money poured into the various gambling venues around the city. Newspapers reported the odds given and the individual bets placed on Wall Street, along Broadway; at the Jamaica, New York, racetrack; and at various well-known betting parlors.[33] A number of bets centered on Ruth himself—such as, Who would get more walks in the Series, Babe Ruth or the entire New York Giants' team?

Among those professional gamblers monitoring the betting was Arnold Rothstein, acknowledged by observers as the only gambler who had the brains, bankroll, and chutzpah to devise such a scheme as fixing a World Series. Yet, in a ludicrous miscarriage of justice, Rothstein had recently avoided indictment for any involvement in the 1919 fix.

Rumors along Broadway indicated that Rothstein was betting on the Giants to defeat the Yankees. Given his involvement in some shady dealings with Giants owner Charles Stoneham and his onetime partnership with McGraw in a billiards parlor, Rothstein might have been expected to be backing the Giants. If he was, it would not be for any reasons of friendship or sentiment. Arnold Rothstein's only sentiment was for money, so his "rooting" interest would lie only where there was money to be made.

Interest in the Series extended even to Paris, France, home to a growing American expatriate colony disproportionately made up of people with ties to New York. The Longchamp racetrack reported that among Parisian bettors the Yankees were slightly favored, just as they were among New Yorkers.

Meanwhile, back home, as the two teams prepared to do battle at the Polo Grounds, the New York City Police Department was making preparations of its own. The police had experience handling Sunday and holiday games at the Polo Grounds, but they suspected an exceptional crush of fans would be attempting to purchase game-day tickets. Their job would be to get the spectators in and out of the park as efficiently as possible while dispersing the overflow crowd unable to get in. Aware of the excitement this first–New York World Series was generating and knowing how exhilarated the fans were about it, the police department assigned three hundred men to the job of maintaining order, the largest police contingent ever assigned to any ballpark.

Inspector Cornelius F. Cahalane was in charge of this huge force, whose primary duty would be to maintain order among the crowds in line for the 20,000 unsold seats. The remaining seats consisted of 9,000 in the unreserved upper deck, priced at \$3.30, and 11,000 bleacher seats, which sold for \$1.10.[34] Strips of reserved-seat tickets to four games had a face value of \$22.00 (\$5.50 each), and the scalpers were getting between \$44.00 and \$60.00 for the set of four.[35]

Additionally, the police would be responsible for controlling and directing the ever-growing number of people coming to the park by automobile. However, once the fans were in the park, the police department's responsibilities would end. The custom in New York was to not have uniformed policemen inside the park but rather to have employees of the home team responsible for crowd control. Plainclothes detectives would also be present, mainly to look for ticket speculators. Capacity crowds of about 37,000 were expected for each game; but because of the large police presence and "the usual good nature of New York crowds," no trouble was expected at the games.[36]

For the limited few with access to the new wireless technology of radio, stations wjz in Newark, New Jersey, and wbz in Springfield, Massachusetts, would be broadcasting the games. Station kdka in Pittsburgh had done the first broadcast of a baseball game—a Pirates-Phillies game on August 5, 1921; but this would be the first time World Series games would be "on the air." More fans would follow the games via a medium that had become popular in many of the nation's biggest cities. Several New York City newspapers had set up boards outside their offices that would allow thousands of people in the streets to follow the play-by-play action.

Baseball's first World Series, back in 1903, had been a best-of-nine affair. There was no Series in 1904, thanks to the intransigence of McGraw and Brush; but all those between 1905 and 1918 had been best of seven. With the 1919 regular-season schedule reduced from 154 games to 140, the leagues revived the nine-game format for the Series between the Cincinnati Reds and the Chicago White Sox; and they continued that format in 1920 for the Cleveland-Brooklyn Series, even though both leagues had returned to the 154-game schedule. The 1921 season would again follow the nine-game format for what would be the final time.

In 1919 the scheduled sequence of games had been two at Cincinnati, three at Chicago, two at Cincinnati, and two at Chicago. In 1920 it was three at Brooklyn, four at Cleveland, and two back at Brooklyn. But because all the games of the 1921 World Series would be played at the same park, the Polo Grounds, there would be no off days; and the Giants and the Yankees would simply alternate as the home team.[37] The Giants would assume that role in Games 1, 3, 5, and 7; and the Yankees, in Games 2, 4, 6, and 8. As such, the home team would wear their home whites, occupy the first base dugout, and bat last. The home team for a ninth game, if one would be needed, had not yet been addressed.[38]

New Yorkers could revel in an all New York City World Series, with the world champion sure to come from the city. Just a year earlier, Brooklyn had represented the National League, but that was different. As the Sporting News editorialized, "The distinctive Gotham obsession is that anything bearing the New York label is or should be the only thing worth while—and both ball clubs of late years have been incorporated as part of New York's best in everything. Brooklyn is the more populous borough, but it is not and never will be 'New York.'"[39]

Back in 1915 Miller Huggins was a third-year manager who had led the Cardinals to a surprising third-place finish in 1914. No less an authority than John McGraw was impressed with the young skipper: "Miller Huggins is my ideal of a real leader. . . . He can take a player who has shown only a mediocre supply of ability on some team and transform him into a star with his club. . . . He will make a high mark as a manager in baseball one of these days."[40]

When Huggins took over as the manager of the Yankees after the 1917 season, someone told McGraw, "Now you have a man who will go 50/50 with you in New York." To which he replied, "No man will ever go 50/50 with me there."[41] Perhaps it was arrogance; perhaps it was his belief, confirmed over the years, that he and his Giants had a virtual birthright over New York. Yet now with the rise of the Yankees, led by the Babe, New York was in play. And the Yankees were going for much more than "50/50."

This was more than a civil war, even more than what Judge Landis called a "historic occasion" in "the greatest city in the country."[42] Joe Vila wrote of the significance of this Series for the two franchises: "The New York teams must battle not only for gold, but for the magnetism that goes with victory. . . . New Yorkers have little use for losers. That is why the clans of McGraw and Huggins now are prepared for a desperate grapple."[43]

27   GAME 1, Wednesday, October 5

"Who said the Yanks were slow and
clumsy and dull?"

The night before the first game of the Series was cool, damp, and windy; nevertheless, hundreds of people camped out at the Polo Grounds waiting for the thousands of unreserved upper-grandstand and bleacher tickets that would go on sale the next morning. Many had brought along wooden crates on which to sit and doze; though as the night wore on and the temperature dropped, many used the boxes for bonfires. Two soldiers brought canned heater stoves and a percolator in a baby carriage. Hot dog and coffee vendors did a brisk business.[1]

These were the "real fans," those who attended games during the year, wrote the *New York Evening Post*.[2] Yet the truth was that many of those in line were unemployed, hoping to sell their places for $5 the following morning.[3] While the police announced that they would not allow such "spot sales," such a practice would be as hard to prevent as the scalping of the tickets themselves.

This first all–New York City World Series had captured the attention of fans far beyond the confines of Manhattan Island. For only the second time since 1903, all World Series games would be played in the same city. (In 1906 the Chicago White Sox had defeated the favored crosstown Cubs.) Approximately five hundred reporters, more than half of them from outside New York City, had come to the Polo Grounds to cover the Series. Before the game, photographers on the field outnumbered the players by about three to one.

Yet despite the intense fan interest and demand for tickets, the game was not sold out. There were a few thousand empty seats, what one paper called a "fan shortage."[4] In part, the crowd was reduced because of the weather, which continued to be damp and chilly, compounded by a threat of rain. But reports in the morning papers, predicting an enormous onslaught of fans that would overwhelm the ballpark, were a bigger factor in keeping the crowd down. The New York City Police Department also believed those reports. To maintain order and avoid a mob scene, they kept non–ticket holders away from the immediate area around the Polo Grounds after one o'clock, one hour before game time. Thousands of people thus missed the opportunity to see the opening game, a pitching gem in an age of slugging.

Many celebrities were present, including former New York governor Al Smith, playwright George M. Cohan, and songwriter Irving Berlin. Also at the game were former Giants star John Montgomery Ward and former Yankees owner Frank Farrell. Gambler Arnold Rothstein and attorney William J. Fallon, his frequent defender, also attended. Tickets were expensive—box seats were $6.60 and reserved seats were $5.50, compared to regular-season prices of $1.50 and $1.10, respectively.

One very special guest was not a celebrity, at least not in 1921. Jim Mutrie, a pioneer of New York baseball, had managed the Giants to pennants in 1888 and 1889. He had fallen on hard times and was now reduced to selling newspapers on Staten Island. Giants coach Hughie Jennings had tracked down the forgotten baseball man this past summer and brought him to the Polo Grounds. "We're going to take care of him," declared John McGraw, again displaying his less-publicized generous side. The Giants put Mutrie on their payroll, where they would keep him for the rest of his life, providing him with $25 a week.[5]

The throng was what Heywood Broun called a "50/50 crowd," seeming to root for both teams equally, because the gathering was "bereft of any threat of alien invaders."[6] Ed Brewster, the stadium's Western Union man, noted that the $1.10 fans of the regular season were absent today. "The prices have attracted largely the type of spectator who likes to go places just because the tariff is high and the event consequently 'fashionable.'"[7] Broun agreed, noting that because of both the high ticket prices and the general public's limited access to them, "thousands of fans had been replaced by spectators." The fans cheered when Babe Ruth, whom even the "spectators" knew, made a hit; and they also cheered when he made an out.

Humorist and critic Irvin S. Cobb wrote, "With both the contending outfits locally owned, there is no sharp division of sentiment in the populace, no pronounced spirit of rivalry to bring out popular exuber-

42. The "Star Ball Player" board set up at Times Square for the 1921 World Series was even larger than this one, where fans watched the 1919 Series at the same location. *Private collection of Michael Mumby.*

ance."[8] Sid Mercer explained the lack of partisanship a little differently: "In this conflict the visiting team is always a home team, and New Yorkers do not like to pan a home team. What seems like a lack of rooting is merely the effect of thousands of persons trying to be neutral."[9]

Both teams were listed as "New York" on the scoreboard. For the "visiting" Yankees, it was written in yellow; and for the "home" Giants, in white. For the second straight year, brothers were facing off in the Series.[10] Irish and Bob Meusel were the focus of the media before the game, and photos of the two of them side by side would run in many papers.

The crowd of just over 30,000 fans did generate the largest gate in baseball history up to that point, more than $100,000. Even more people followed the play-by-play action in front of the big game boards (sometimes called Play-O-Graph boards) that many of the major New York City newspapers provided than were in the Polo Grounds itself.

The *New York Times'* "Star Ball Player" board at Times Square measured fifteen feet in height and twenty feet in width, covering an entire floor on the north side of the Times Building on 43rd Street. It was the largest such device ever set up for this purpose and drew a crowd of about 15,000. The east and west sides of Broadway, as far north as 45th Street, were a mass of humanity; and the overflow crowd spilled up to 50th on 7th Avenue as well as on Broadway. The *Times* board so disrupted traffic in the area that the paper would discontinue it after the second game.

A similar board, called the "Wonder Score Board," was set up at Madison Square Garden at 26th Street and Madison Avenue. It was billed as the greatest invention since wireless telegraphy; and for fifty cents these boards would allow fans to see depictions of players hitting the ball, running the bases, and getting put out.

More than 10,000 fans watched the combined *Herald-Sun* board, a joint effort of the two competing newspapers, on the south side of the landmark Stewart Building, at the corner of Broadway and Chambers in lower Manhattan. The *New York Herald* explained why watching a ball game on an electric scoreboard was so exciting:

> Watching an actual game is tame by comparison. There your eyes do the work. Nothing is left for the back of your head to do. But watching the *New York Herald*'s score board poured kerosene upon your imagination and the electric sparks that traced the ball and the hitter touched it off in explosions. . . . And then watch that ball leave the pitcher and bobble down toward the plate. . . . And right there you get the thrill supreme. Yesterday that mob squealed—not roared, but squealed—when the lamps told them that the ball had reached Ruth.[11]

Broun conveyed the thrill of the boards by telling of a conversation he overheard at the Polo Grounds during the regular season. Two newsboys were watching the Yanks rally and take the lead over the Indians. One said to the other, "Gee what would you give to be in Times Square right now?" As Broun explained, "with nothing but chalk and blackboard to follow, the shifts came with a dramatic suddenness denied to those who see every move."[12]

The newspaper scoreboard was patented back in 1889 by an editorial writer of the *New York World*, Edward Van Zile. Five thousand fans had

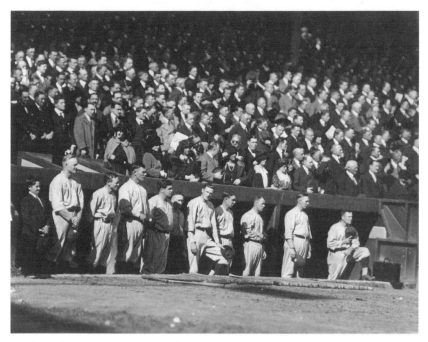

43. The Yankees stand at attention in the visitors' (third base) dugout for the singing of "The Star-Spangled Banner" before the start of Game 1. Miller Huggins is third from the left, Babe Ruth is fifth from the left, and Jack Quinn is standing between them. Note that Huggins and Quinn are standing on a higher step than Ruth is. *Private collection of Michael Mumby.*

watched the progress of that year's postseason series between St. Louis of the American Association and New York of the National League. The crowds had prevented horse carts from operating in the area, just as they now disrupted automobile traffic. At that time, players on the diamond board were denoted with colored pegs rather than light bulbs. Until the 1921 Series, Van Zile had not watched a World Series game on a newspaper board since 1888.[13] These Play-O-Graph boards would soon become obsolete due to the explosive rise of radio in the 1920s.

However, few people owned a radio in the fall of 1921. Those who did heard the first broadcasts of World Series games on the Westinghouse Network. A reporter phoned the plays into Newark station WJZ, where Tommy Cowan re-created the games for his listeners.[14] Not until the 1922 World Series would the games be broadcast live, directly from the ballpark. Grantland Rice, teaming with sportswriter William McGeehan, would call those games.[15]

Miller Huggins expected the Giants would start left-hander Art Nehf, their lone twenty-game winner, and therefore had his lone southpaw, Harry Harper, toss batting practice. Instead, John McGraw selected Phil Douglas, 15-10 during the regular season, to face the Yankees' ace, Carl Mays. Some observers were surprised with the choice. No doubt thinking of Douglas's drinking problems, Burt Whitman said, "See if you can recall any great [World Series] pitching by athletes who were not sound as a new walnut in matters of habits."[16] Yet Douglas was sound on this day, yielding just five hits in eight innings. Remarkably, not a single Giants outfielder had a putout. Mays himself called Douglas's performance "the best spitball pitching I've seen all year. Twice as good as anything I saw Coveleskie do."[17]

Yet Mays was even better. His submarine delivery befuddled the Giants all afternoon. His ball, wrote Damon Runyon, "seems to cling to the ground as it travels, so low is it moving . . . only to suddenly rise."[18] Mays was hitting the corners and effectively mixing in his slow ball. He threw but eighty-six pitches, with no walks. Former Athletics pitcher Eddie Plank, the winningest left-hander in history to that point, told Mays afterward that his control in this game was the best he had ever seen a pitcher exhibit.[19]

Third baseman Frankie Frisch was the lone bright spot in the Giants' lineup. Frisch, who had 211 hits during the regular season, went 4-4, including a triple.[20] (Johnny Rawlings's seventh-inning single was the Giants' only other hit.) In the fourth inning, Frisch, the National League's stolen base leader, displayed his speed and daring by stealing second after two straight pitchouts. While the Giants made no official errors, they were not sharp in the field, making the kind of mistakes that writer and analyst Bill James has called "Defensive Misplays"[21] Led by the infield, the Yankees' defense, on the other hand, was flawless. Shortstop Roger Peckinpaugh had nine assists and was a "ball-playing centipede," in the words of Grantland Rice.[22] Aaron Ward was almost as good at second base. In the seventh inning, he made three difficult plays in retiring the side.

Elmer Miller led off the game for the "visiting" Yankees with a hit, a bouncing ball up the middle, one that second baseman Rawlings could have reached, in the eyes of some observers. After Peckinpaugh sacrificed Miller to second, the Polo Grounds grew very quiet as Ruth, who had batted in a record 171 runs during the season, stepped into the batter's box. When the Babe lashed the first pitch to center field, a line drive over second base, the crowd exploded. The Yankees had scored the first World Series run in their history. This would be Ruth's only hit on the day, though Douglas challenged him all afternoon, striking him out twice and walking him on a 3-2 pitch. "Just remember, don't give that big baboon anything but low curves," McGraw had warned his pitchers.[23]

The game's decisive play, and its most dramatic, came in the top of the fifth. Mike McNally, whose outstanding play had relegated Frank Baker to the Yankees' bench, doubled to start the inning and was sacrificed to third by Wally Schang. Then, after Mays struck out, McNally stunned the crowd when he took off for home. He had but five steals all season, in eleven attempts. After sliding home safely, head first, he now had his sixth. Irvin S. Cobb blamed Douglas for the steal, noting that he had "insisted on winding himself up as a grandfather's clock before delivering the ball."[24]

In modern times, critical plays are routinely replayed and dissected on television with the help of instant replay. In 1921 plays were seen but once, and analysis was based on fleeting impressions and recollections. Not surprisingly, others saw the theft differently than Cobb. Sam Crane thought the problem was Douglas's throw, not his windup.[25] H. G. Salsinger felt that McNally had stolen because of catcher Frank Snyder, as did Fred Lieb—both felt that Snyder was out of position, a little too far from the plate.[26] The *New York American* account said that home plate umpire Cy Rigler raised his hand upward, as if to call McNally out, before suddenly moving both hands horizontally for the "safe" call.[27]

There was also some confusion as to who called the steal. The Babe, who was coaching at third, suggested in his syndicated column that he sent McNally.[28] Miller Huggins told reporter Frank O'Neill that he (Huggins) had not sent McNally.[29] The most likely explanation is that the often overlooked and always underrated McNally simply took off on his own. "Did you get a signal from the bench?" he was asked afterward. "No," he replied. After noticing Douglas's big windup, "I just stole home."[30] Most papers reported that this was only the second steal of home in World Series play, the other being Ty Cobb's in 1909. Yet McNally's was actually the fifth such postseason theft.[31] For the Yankees, it was their third steal of home all year, dating back to when Chick Fewster and McNally had done so in May.

The Yankees added a third and final run in the sixth inning on a strange play in which Yankees outfielder Bob Meusel was both hero and goat. After Peckinpaugh led off with an infield hit and moved to second on a passed ball, Meusel blasted a one-out triple to left. Peckinpaugh scored, but Giants coach Cozy Dolan, watching the play unfold from his perch in the first base dugout, shouted to first baseman George Kelly to get the ball and step on first. Kelly did so, and umpire George Moriarty called Meusel out for failing to touch first base.

Meanwhile, the Giants never had two men on base at the same time. In the fourth inning, Kelly came up with one out and Frisch on third, but he struck out. The Giants pulled Douglas for a pinch hitter in the eighth; and Jesse Barnes pitched the ninth, when he was touched for a couple of hits and McNally stole another base. The Yankees had the win, 3–0. "Who said the Yanks were slow and clumsy and dull?" asked one sportswriter.[32] McGraw's men had been beaten at their own game.

The Yankees Again Win
with an Inside Game

The teams switched uniforms and dugouts for the second game. The Yankees were now wearing their home whites and were in the first base dugout, while the Giants were in their road grays and occupied the third base dugout. With warmer weather and no threat of rain, the bleachers were full, though there were some empty seats in the upper grandstand. The makeup of the crowd had not changed much from the first game. Police inspector William G. McGrath was emphatic: "The real fans aren't coming to this series. I know them."[1] One fan, however, seemed vaguely familiar; reporters finally recognized Jack Chesbro, winner of forty-one games for the 1904 New York Americans, who had fallen just short of the pennant. Chesbro had also been a teammate of current Yankee Jack Quinn on the 1909 Yanks. He retired after that season and had not seen the Yankees play since.

Art Nehf (20-10), bypassed for Phil Douglas in Game 1, got the nod for the Giants. Joe Vila had noted that the only American League lefty who compared favorably to Nehf was Dickie Kerr, who had great success against the Yankees this season.[2] Nehf's opponent was Waite Hoyt (19-13), "the Schoolboy Wonder," who had just turned twenty-two in September. Hoyt had originally been signed by the Giants, leading Joe Vila to declare that "McGraw knows him like a book."[3] Columnist Westbrook Pegler suggested that McGraw was not worried about facing his ex-pitcher: "Knowing Hoyt as well as your collar button knows your Adam's apple, the Giants anticipate with relish the opportunity."[4]

Hoyt had been inconsistent during the season, certainly not in the same class as Carl Mays. He had twenty-one complete games in his thirty-two starts; Mays, by comparison, had thirty complete games in thirty-eight starts. Perhaps that was why one sportswriter called Hoyt

44. The Giants thought they could rattle Waite Hoyt, the young Yankee pitcher who was once a Giant. Yet he showed remarkable composure and pitched three great World Series games in 1921. Here he relaxes with his parents and sister before one of the games. *Private collection of Michael Mumby.*

"a sort of five-inning slabster."[5] The Giants felt they could fluster the young pitcher, as the Cleveland Indians seemed to have done a couple of weeks earlier. During warm-ups the day before the start of the Series, Ross Youngs made a point of walking past Hoyt and saying to Frankie Frisch in a loud voice, "So that's the young punk who expects to beat us."[6] McGraw had told friends that the Giants would "murder" Hoyt's fastball.[7]

For the second straight day, baseball seemed to be in a time warp, playing the low-scoring "inside game" of the Deadball Era. Two of the best-hitting teams in this year of record-setting hitting managed a combined five hits, though both pitchers had control problems. Nehf walked seven men and Hoyt passed five, yet both men pitched terrific games. The Giants were unable to rattle the Yankee youngster, who exhibited a "nonchalance and coolness that was amazing," in the words of Philadelphia reporter Gordon Mackay.[8]

Frankie Frisch continued to shine for the Giants at third base. He made several dazzling plays in the field to bail Nehf out of trouble in the early innings. In the first, after Elmer Miller and Ruth had walked, Frisch leapt high in the air to rob Bob Meusel of an extra-base hit and double Miller off second to end the inning. In the second inning, with Wally Pipp on second, McNally hit a hard shot to third that knocked Frisch down. Somehow he was able to tag Pipp from a sitting position. Hugh Fullerton called these "two of the most astounding plays ever in a world's series."[9] Yet taken as a whole, the Yankees' defense was once again virtually airtight, while the Giants' cracked again at key points in the game.

In the third inning, the Giants got their first safety when Ruth and shortstop Roger Peckinpaugh did not communicate and nearly collided, as Johnny Rawlings's pop fly to short left dropped in. In the bottom half of the inning, Hoyt got the Yanks' first hit. In the fourth, Aaron Ward got a fluke base hit on a checked swing when the ball hit his bat and fell just beyond Rawlings's outstretched glove. McNally then hit a double play ball back to the mound, but Nehf threw wide to shortstop Dave Bancroft, who then made a poor throw to first. Everyone was safe. Nehf then walked Schang to load the bases.

Hoyt followed with a grounder to Rawlings at second, who chose to get the sure out at first, though by some accounts he had a good chance to nab Ward at the plate. The Yankees had taken a 1–0 lead on an accidental hit and a questionable decision not to make a throw home. McNally, continuing to run with abandon, tried to score all the way from second on the play and was thrown out. He had also been thrown out trying to steal in the first inning.

Nehf was pitching much more carefully to Ruth than Douglas had done. In the fifth inning, he walked the Babe for the third time, two of them at least semi-intentionally. The crowd was razzing Nehf for issuing the passes to the slugger, but McGraw was not perturbed. Nehf explained afterward, "We are fighting for a world title, and we are not out there to give any home run hitting opportunities to anybody."[10] If anyone was getting frustrated, it was the Babe: "I can't knock home runs if the Giant pitchers walk me, but I can run the bases."[11] He did just that, stealing second and third in quick succession. He then was attempting a steal of home when Bob Meusel swung at the pitch and grounded to short to end the inning. Ruth's slides would prove to be costly.[12] He reaggravated an injury to his left elbow, which would soon get infected.[13]

The teams exchanged taunts throughout the afternoon, hurling vulgarities and obscenities at each other regarding ethnicity, physical characteristics, family members, and anything else they felt might upset their opponents. At one point, home plate umpire George Moriarty threatened to clear the Yankees' bench if the players did not stop. He directed his most pointed warning toward Braggo Roth, who was known for his big mouth. Considered one of the biggest off-season acquisitions, Roth's knee injury had made him mostly a nonfactor. While he would not appear in the Series, Roth was a vocal contributor to the proceedings.[14] The leader of the Giants' bench jockeys was Casey Stengel, a midseason acquisition who also would not appear in this World Series.

Behind the plate for the Giants was combative Earl Smith, who in the words of a veteran observer, Detroit's H. G. Salsinger, was "notorious for his 'riding' habits. He is abusive to an unbearable degree . . . obnoxious even on a ball field, where they deal in rough verbal passages."[15] Throughout the game, Smith and Bob Meusel were having an ongoing verbal feud. At one point, Meusel accused Smith of tipping his bat (an old catchers' trick, going back to the early days of the game). The catcher's response was to call Meusel "yellow."[16] Their war of words continued each time Meusel came to bat.

Through eight innings, the Giants had only the Rawlings hit, a misplayed short fly ball. The Yankees padded their lead by adding two runs in the eighth, once again taking advantage of Giants defensive lapses. Inexplicably, Frisch, who had been brilliant in the field, muffed an easy Peckinpaugh pop-up when he crowded Bancroft on the play. After the Babe hit into a force play, Meusel singled to center—the game's first clean hit. Ruth slid into third, just beating the throw but further aggravating his injury. Meusel took second base on the throw. Irvin S. Cobb made a pointed reference to the Babe's girth, noting that "Mr. Ruth can run faster than any fat man in this country has run since Mr. Taft made his first race for President."[17]

Wally Pipp then hit a grounder to Rawlings. The Giants' second baseman again chose to throw to first, even though he again may have had a play at the plate. Meusel, who reached third on the play, then shouted to Smith that "he was coming," an indication that he was about to steal home. As he took off for the plate on the first pitch to Aaron Ward, it was obvious he was gunning for Smith because he did not go into a slide. In the words of Grantland Rice, Meusel was "yearning for personal contact with Earl Smith."[18] Nehf got the ball to his catcher in plenty of time; but Smith—perhaps fearing a collision with the big Yankee outfielder—let the ball get away before Meusel arrived. Under the scoring rules of the day, the catcher was charged with a passed ball; and Meusel was credited with a steal of home. The two men continued to trade insults after Meusel had scored, and Moriarty had to separate them. After the game, Commissioner Landis would fine Smith (but not Meusel) $200 for "profane and obscene language."

Frisch got a one-out single in the ninth, the only clean hit Hoyt gave up all afternoon in his two-hit effort. Ross Youngs followed with a walk, finally giving the Giants two base runners in an inning. George Kelly, the National League home run champion, came to the plate with a chance to tie the game. He hit the ball hard, but third baseman McNally made a terrific stop (he had also robbed Kelly of a hit in the seventh) and started the game-ending double play. Kelly, who again was hitless, had also ended the first game by grounding into a double play. The Yankees' infield continued to shine: Peckingpaugh and Ward had flawlessly handled thirty-three chances in the two games.

For the fourth straight World Series game, the National League had failed to score.[19] For the second straight day, the Giants had been shut out by the score of 3–0. Hoyt confessed that he was indeed pitching for a purpose beyond winning for the Yankees: "I wanted to go out and show McGraw that I was a real pitcher and remind him of a day in 1916 [when the Giants had sent him down to the Minors]."[20] Years later, after his illustrious career, Hoyt chose this game as "my greatest day in baseball."[21]

The Yankees had surprised the Giants with a style of play that the Giants had not expected.[22] John McGraw told Fred Lieb after the game, "Losing two shutouts is bad enough, but having them steal home on me in two successive days, that's what really hurts."[23] He also commented on the amazing amount of "stuff" Hoyt had—speed, an effective slow ball, and a deceptive curve. Sid Mercer aptly noted that Hoyt was not good enough for McGraw in 1916, but was "too good" for the Giants today.[24] McGraw tried to maintain a positive front. "I am anything but discouraged. . . . Of course, when a team isn't hitting, it looks bad."[25]

Reporters swarmed around Miller Huggins after the game, asking for his explanation of how the Yankees had seized a 2-0 Series lead. He matter-of-factly and somewhat wryly replied, "I don't see why people should so be awfully surprised by our showing in the first two games of this series."[26] The Yankees were able to win low-scoring pitching duels during the regular season, even when their big bats were quiet. He compared the games to the taut first game against the Indians a couple of weeks earlier, when Hoyt had edged Stan Coveleski, 4–2. Huggins had subtly changed tactics in these first two games. In the face of sharp pitching, he had the Yankees sacrifice and hit and run a number of times, rather than swing away all the time. McGraw, on the other hand, had the lead-off hitter on base three times; yet he never called for the sacrifice, a tactic he disdained.

Hugh Fullerton had predicted that Mays and Hoyt would win the first two games, and the results had "followed the dope." Yet the outlook was not bleak for the Giants, in his opinion. First, the rest of their pitching staff was stronger and deeper than that of the Yankees. Fred Toney and Jesse Barnes, for example, stacked up well against Bob Shawkey and Harry Harper. He also felt that Mays and Hoyt probably would not duplicate their exceptional performances the next time around, since the Giants would be more familiar with them. "New York's Giants' darkest hour is just before dawn," he declared.[27]

But Fullerton's Series outlook was in the minority. The focus of the New York press was on the Giants and their leader, and it was mostly negative. The *Sporting News* criticized the Giants in the second game (and McGraw by implication) for "one of the sorriest spectacles we ever saw . . . a world's record for brainless batting in a pinch." They repeatedly swung at the first pitch despite Hoyt's control problems.[28] The talk on Broadway that night was that the Giants' day had passed and that John McGraw should consider resigning.[29] Such chatter confirmed the impatience of New York City baseball fans, who wanted a winner. McGraw's Giants had lost their last four World Series and were heading in the wrong direction in the fifth.

29 GAME 3, Friday, October 7

The Giants' Offense Comes Alive

The Giants were facing long odds when they took the field for the start of Game 3.[1] No team had ever won a World Series after losing the first two games, although the nine-game format used this year made their situation less dire than it would have been under the seven-game format. Well aware of the Giants' perilous position of having to win five of the next seven games, oddsmakers installed the Yankees, who needed to win just three, as prohibitive 7–2 favorites to take the Series.

Those who had predicted a Giants victory cited most often their superior pitching as the reason, yet it was the Yankees' pitching that had dominated the first two games. Back-to-back shutouts by Carl Mays and Waite Hoyt, in which they allowed a combined seven hits, had completely stifled the National League's highest-scoring team.

"They're not hitting, and they are not playing the kind of ball that wins games," said John McGraw, stating the obvious. "There also have been several close decisions given against the Giants," he added. "I thought [George] Burns was safe on his steal in the eighth inning [of the second game]."[2] Yet neither McGraw nor his players appeared disheartened. Their ability to make up a huge deficit was what had gotten them to the World Series. McGraw said his team was not discouraged over the two losses. He claimed that it would make them fight even harder, while announcing, "I am going to pitch Toney tomorrow."[3]

That was McGraw speaking calmly to the press. His words to his players had a much different tone. Furious at being humiliated in successive games by a team he detested and being shut out by Hoyt, a pitcher he had discarded, McGraw vented his frustration in the clubhouse after the second game. In a tirade reminiscent of the one before the late-August series against Pittsburgh, McGraw berated his players for getting so close to a championship and then failing him and disgracing them-

45. Fred Toney had been one of the Giants' most reliable pitchers down the stretch. But as American League observers predicted, reliance on his fastball made him ineffective against the Yankees. *Private collection of Michael Mumby.*

selves. Despite his five hits in two games, Frankie Frisch bore the brunt of McGraw's attack.[4] George Kelly, hitless so far in the Series, heard his manager repeat something to him he had been hearing all season, "Do something brilliant."[5] Perhaps it was coincidence, but McGraw's diatribe worked just as his previous one had.

Toney (18-11) had been McGraw's most reliable pitcher during the season's final weeks; but he had not pitched since September 24, a stretch of thirteen days, and had never appeared in a World Series. Because he relied so much on his fastball, Toney was also the one Giants pitcher American League observers felt would be the easiest for the Yankees to handle. "Anybody but Toney," they said. "The Yanks will murder him; they'll make a monkey out of him."[6] After the game, H. G. Salsinger would write, "A pitcher that pitched as Toney pitched yesterday will be wrecked by a club like the Yanks, the Cleveland Indians, the Tygers or the Browns. Those clubs would never lose a game batting against Toney."[7] Nevertheless, in spite the American Leaguers' assessment of Toney, or perhaps unaware of it, McGraw had chosen to start the thirty-two-year-old veteran.

In contrast to Toney's long layoff, Bob Shawkey, Miller Huggins's choice, had pitched the Yanks' final regular-season game just five days earlier. Shawkey, purchased from the Athletics in June 1915, was the Yankee pitcher with the longest continuous term of service.[8] Yet despite winning 18 games with only 12 losses, he had struggled much of the season. "He is not, in his present form, even a fair major league pitcher," wrote Hugh Fullerton.[9]

The efforts of both veteran hurlers were similarly disappointing; each failed to survive the third inning. Both Toney and Shawkey were charged with four runs, before McGraw and Huggins turned the pitching duties over to relievers Jesse Barnes and Jack Quinn. Toney had retired the Yanks in order in the top of the first, but he yielded a lead-off double to Bob Meusel in the second. Nothing came of it. After being sacrificed to third, Meusel tried to score on Aaron Ward's grounder to second, but Johnny Rawlings's throw nailed him at the plate. McNally's force of Ward would be the last out Toney recorded in the game. In the third inning, Shawkey's single followed Wally Schang's lead-off walk and preceded another single by Elmer Miller, which drove home the game's first run.

A walk to Roger Peckinpaugh loaded the bases for Babe Ruth. For the Yankee fans in the crowd, it was the ideal situation—bases loaded, no-body out, and the Babe coming to bat. On the other side, those rooting for the Giants feared that just one of his mighty swings could all but end their hopes of winning the Series. Toney had fanned Ruth in the first inning; and now, with no place to put him, McGraw signaled Toney to pitch to him again. The count went full before the Babe ripped a single to center, scoring Shawkey and Miller. He had driven home two runs instead of the four Yankees fans had hoped for, but McGraw had seen enough of Toney and replaced him with Barnes. Later in the inning, Peckinpaugh scored to give the Yanks a commanding 4–0 lead.

Trailing two games to none and down by four runs, the Giants' situation was indeed bleak. "About as bad as Abie Cohen's chances of being elected chief of the Ku Klux Klan," wrote Fullerton in a "humorous" aside reflective of the times.[10] However, there was hope. Shawkey had not been sharp in the first two innings, allowing three singles and a walk. A double play, a caught stealing, and a spectacular catch by Aaron Ward of a Rawlings line drive had prevented the Giants from scoring; but whether Shawkey could make that lead stand up the rest of the way was questionable.

As it turned out, the lead did not survive the third inning. Barnes opened with a single and went to third on a one-out single by Dave Bancroft, the first safety of the Series for the Giants' captain. Shawkey then became the first pitcher in World Series history to walk three consecutive batters: Frankie Frisch to load the bases; Ross Youngs, scoring Barnes to end the Giants' streak of twenty consecutive scoreless innings; and George Kelly, scoring Bancroft. Like McGraw in the top of the inning, Miller Huggins had finally seen enough of his starting pitcher and summoned Quinn. Frisch and Youngs, recipients of the first two walks, later scored, tying the game.

Seemingly dead after the top of the inning, the Giants now had new life. Their rebirth, according to many Yankee rooters in the crowd, was more attributable to Huggins than to the National Leaguers' bats. Quinn had begun warming up after Bancroft's hit, and the Yankee fans had begun screaming for Huggins to bring him in while Shawkey was pitching to Frisch. "'Take him out,' they shouted, but the midget manager decided to keep his robust pitcher in."[11] On the other side, the Giants' fans were ecstatic, finally getting their chance to whoop and holler.

The clamoring for Shawkey's exit grew even louder with each of the three walks he issued, before Huggins at last made his move. The consensus among sportswriters and fans was that Huggins had stayed far too long with a pitcher who did not appear sharp and lacked control. It was, most felt, the type of tactical error McGraw would never make.

The New York writers, ever critical of Huggins, took advantage of this perceived blunder to again question his managerial ability. "No one could understand why Huggins was permitting Shawkey to remain in the box," wrote Damon Runyon in a typical comment.[12]

Fullerton went even further. "Shawkey had no business trying to pitch a world series game," he said.[13] Perhaps Huggins felt he owed Shawkey the opportunity to work his way out of trouble; he had been the Yankees' ace for a number of years. Sid Mercer wrote of the poignancy of the pitcher's failure, which he called "deplorable. . . . Here is a veteran of stout heart and cunning brain whose arm is failing him. . . . Shawkey cannot say that Huggins did not go the limit for him."[14] Runyon suggested an explanation for Huggins's hesitancy to remove Shawkey. Knowing how shaky his pitching staff's depth was, Runyon speculated, Huggins was hoping Shawkey could get into the sixth or seventh inning with the game close and then bring in his ace, Carl Mays. That way, Mays could still start in the fourth or fifth game, which would not be the case had he relieved in the third.[15]

For the next three innings, Barnes and Quinn held the hitters in check, as the score remained tied at 4–4. Then, leading off the seventh, Quinn hit a long, wind-aided drive that seemed good for at least three bases if it did not clear the outfield fence altogether. But center fielder George Burns raced back and, "with the combined grace of Speaker and effectiveness of Sam Rice," caught the ball, causing the crowd to erupt in cheers.[16]

In the home seventh, the Giants finally displayed the type of offense that had gotten them here. Against Quinn and Rip Collins, the Giants exploded for eight runs on eight hits, both of which were World Series records.[17] In leading the attack, Frisch and Youngs set several individual Series marks. Frisch was the first player to score twice in an inning.[18] Youngs, with a double and a bases-loaded triple, became the first player to have two hits in an inning as well as the first to have two extra-base hits in an inning.[19] His five total bases in an inning was also a record.[20]

After silently witnessing the feebleness of the Giants' offense in the first two games, their fans finally had a chance to explode. "They tore up newspapers and tossed them, hats and even overcoats into the air in a frenzy of joy."[21]

The Giants' big inning ended what had been a memorable performance by Quinn. "By every theatrical and fictional law, Jack Quinn should have been assigned to a heroic role. He was the oldest man on the field. He came first to the Yankees eleven years ago and since then has been down to the minors and back again. . . . But he was only a three innings' hero."[22]

Each team scored single runs in the eighth to make the final score 13–5. The combined eighteen runs set a Series record—as did the Giants' twenty hits, which included four each by George Burns and Frank Snyder.[23] After Toney's departure, Barnes, touched for two hits in an inning of work in the opener, turned in a magnificent performance. Over the final seven innings, he held the Yankees to one run on four hits while striking out seven, one of the best long-relief efforts in World Series history.

Still, the Yankees were not dismayed by their crushing defeat, at least not outwardly. Huggins said, "We will get going again tomorrow." And when asked if he was discouraged, he responded, "Why should I be, with the odd game tucked away and two pitchers [Mays and Hoyt] who have conclusively proved they could stop the Giants to call upon?"[24]

GAME 4, Sunday, October 9

The Giants Finally Get to
Carl Mays, or So It Seems

Colonels Ruppert and Huston may have been disappointed when they mingled with owner Charles Stoneham and other Giants officials at the Commodore Hotel in mid-Manhattan after the third game. Nevertheless, the magnates from both clubs had to be rejoicing at what was turning into a record-setting financial haul for World Series play. The fans had paid more than $350,000 to view the first three games; and if the Series went the full nine games, a $1 million payoff seemed possible.

But gate receipts were not the only financial sphere where records were being set. "The betting on this series has been the heaviest in the history of baseball," wrote Hugh Fullerton. "The great bulk of it, of course, is non-professional."[1] As he had for the past two years, Fullerton continued to use his column to rail against the ongoing evils of gambling, a subject about which most sportswriters had been silent most of the year.

"New York is a gambling city. Almost every one gambles," he wrote, estimating that millions had been bet on the Series. Much of the betting was taking place at the Commodore Hotel, which was the headquarters of both teams. Men crowded the lobbies, "betting, talking betting, and offering to bet." Fullerton concluded that as long as such large amounts of money were being bet, sooner or later there would be "a recurrence of the 1919 episode."[2]

The Yankees' loss in Game 3 had their fans sniping at Miller Huggins again, just as Giants' fans had been sniping at John McGraw for his team's losses in the first two games. The most recent attacks on Huggins were the result of his reluctance to remove an obviously ineffective Shawkey. Now he was faced with choosing a pitcher for Game 4, a choice between Harry Harper and Carl Mays. Harper was the Yanks' lone left-hander; but he had failed miserably in the last big game he pitched, which had been against Cleveland.

"I can't tell yet," Huggins replied when asked who would get the start. "I want to think it over and study the situation. I have both Harper and Mays available and may not decide until game time which to use. I can't tell you yet, because I honestly do not know myself."[3] That may have been true; but knowing that another loss would tie the Series and shift the momentum sharply in the Giants favor, Huggins decided to go with his ace, Mays.

The Yankee skipper also had to deal with the possibility that Ruth's injury, an abscess that had developed near his left elbow, would prevent him from playing. "We have won without Ruth before," he said, "and if we are called on to do it we can win without him again."[4] If he were without his great slugger, said Huggins, he would use Chick Fewster in Ruth's spot in left field and move Wally Schang into Ruth's third-place slot in the batting order.

Huggins's decision to start Mays was reinforced when rain washed out the game scheduled for Saturday, giving Mays an extra day's rest.[5] The World Series rules of the day specified that a postponed game be made up before the teams switched parks. That, of course, was unnecessary here; but it did mean the Yankees would remain the home team for Game 4. It also meant that people with tickets for Saturday's rained-out game could use them only on Sunday. Similarly, people with tickets for Sunday's game would have to wait until Monday to use them—if they could, since for some (if not many) Sunday was their only day off from work.

With a big Saturday crowd expected, Commissioner Landis was reluctant to have the game called. However, as conditions worsened, he agreed with umpire Ollie Chill's decision not to risk the chance of a player being injured on the muddy field. "I hope the disappointed ones will note those boys slipping and realize that no game could possibly be played," said the judge. Nevertheless, Landis remained solicitous of the dilemma the postponement posed for many fans. "When I look over at those bleachers [which were packed], and think that there are many men and boys who can get away to a game only on Saturday afternoon, I want to make certain that it is a physical impossibility to go ahead before a final decision is reached."[6]

The Yankees had just begun taking batting practice, and somewhere between 20,000 and 30,000 fans were already in their seats when the game was called. McGraw, still relishing his Game 3 triumph, expressed disappointment at the delay. "The Giants hit their stride in yesterday's game and we were all set to ride roughshod over the Yankees this afternoon."[7] He said he planned to come back with Douglas, setting up a rematch of the Game 1 starters; but it depended on how Douglas looked. "I always like to look over my pitchers when they are warming up. It is then that I get the best line on how much stuff they have on the ball."[8]

Sunny and pleasant weather returned for Sunday's game, when the largest crowd to date, 36,372, saw the Giants finally catch up with Carl Mays. Trailing, 1–0, and looking helpless against him through seven innings, they erupted for three eighth-inning runs on the way to a 4–2 win. Irish Meusel began Mays's downfall with a long triple to left-center and scored on Johnny Rawlings's single, tying the score and ending the Giants' skein of sixteen consecutive scoreless innings against the Yankees' ace. Perhaps in retaliation, Mays would send Rawlings sprawling in his next at bat with a pitch near his head, eliciting boos and hisses from the crowd. After Snyder reached first, when Mays slipped on a wet spot on the grass going for his bunt, Douglas sacrificed the two runners over.

With George Burns at the plate, Mays shook off Schang's call for a curve ball and instead delivered a fastball. Burns hit it past the drawn-in infield, just out of Peckinpaugh's reach. Two runs came in, and the Giants had a 3–1 lead. With Burns's hit, "the crowd was roaring wildly and the air was so filled with flying paper that it looked like a snowstorm."[9] "One of the quietest, most gentlemanly and least colorful players in the game," as one account described Burns, had come through in the clutch yet again.[10] The Giants added a run in the ninth when Kelly doubled (his first hit of the series) and scored on Meusel's single.

Meanwhile, Douglas, with excellent control of his spitball, pitched a brilliant seven-hitter, allowing no walks while striking out eight. Schang's RBI triple in the fifth accounted for the Yankees' only run, until Ruth, playing in defiance of his doctors' orders, hit a one-out home run in the ninth to make the final score 4–2. (The Babe also had a single and struck out once.) Douglas then retired Bob Meusel and Pipp to end the game and even the Series at two games apiece. Afterward, the voluble Casey

Stengel could not restrain his enthusiasm. "We've got 'em tottering now and we'll have them hanging on the ropes after tomorrow's game."[11]

Despite the Babe's home run, winning the past two games may have made McGraw more confident in his pitchers' ability to handle him. "Nobody can say that my pitchers are not allowing Ruth to hit the ball. We're pitching to him, and we are going to pitch to him in the remaining games," he said.[12]

When Ruth first took his place in left field at the start of the game with bandages on his left elbow, his throwing arm, an enormous roar rolled through the Polo Grounds. The press, however, had a mixed reaction to his appearance. Most raved about his gameness for playing while hobbled. Grantland Rice applauded the Babe's playing "in defiance of all orders . . . his mangled elbow, that looked like a veal cutlet, breaded."[13]

But there were some dissenting voices among those covering the game. One wrote that the Babe "loafed" and played "slovenly" on Irish Meusel's eighth-inning triple, which should have been only a double. "Any warrior with two hands is better than a general with one."[14] Another suggested that a fielder with a good arm would have held Burns to a single on his game-winning blow, while noting that sometimes gameness can degenerate into foolishness.[15]

Mays's performance also came in for criticism. In his column "The Listening Post," Walter Trumbull wrote that "If Mays could have lasted just two more innings the Yankees would be in a very enviable position this morning."[16] True enough. Mays's eighth-inning collapse had indeed prevented the Yankees from taking a commanding 3-1 lead in the Series.

However, what caused that collapse remains a matter of controversy to this day. The source for the controversy is sportswriter Fred Lieb, who was elected president of the Baseball Writers Association of America that very day. In both J. G. Taylor Spink's 1947 book on Commissioner Landis (said to have been ghostwritten by Lieb) and Lieb's 1977 retrospective of twentieth-century baseball history, Lieb told a story of intrigue and corruption centering on Carl Mays's performance in that fourth game.

Lieb claimed that, on the night following the game, former reporter George Perry, who was then the personal secretary of Jacob Ruppert, along with a well-known (but unnamed) Broadway actor called on Lieb at the press hospitality suite in the Commodore Hotel. Perry told of the bizarre circumstances surrounding the Giants' eighth-inning rally. Mays had had a no-hitter through five innings and a two-hitter though seven. The actor's story was that Mays had been offered a bribe by gamblers before the game.

At the start of the eighth inning, Marjorie Mays signaled her husband that she had received the bribe money and that he now should throw the game. Mays supposedly disregarded Huggins's signal to serve up a fastball to lead-off hitter Irish Meusel and instead threw a slow curve that Meusel hit for a triple to start the Giants' rally. He then gave up the three runs on four hits in that inning, and the Giants took a 3–1 lead. Mays gave up another run on three hits in the ninth.

The three men (Lieb, Perry, and the actor) awakened Colonel Huston and then Judge Landis and related the story to them. The commissioner directed Lieb to refrain from making the story public while he put a detective on Mays for the remainder of the Series. The detective was unable to uncover anything incriminating.[17] To his dying day, Mays maintained that it was the Ray Chapman incident that kept him out of the Baseball Hall of Fame. However, Lieb, who was a member of the Hall's Veterans' Committee from 1966 to 1980, said that the question mark that kept Mays out of the Hall revolved around his performance in that eighth inning on October 9, 1921, not Ray Chapman.

When a biography of Mays, very sympathetic to the pitcher, came out in 1972, it was Fred Lieb who reviewed the book in the *Sporting News*.[18] Lieb admitted in that review, "I confess that my view of Mays was slanted by Miller's [Miller Huggins's] strong dislike, even hatred, for his powerful underhanded pitcher."[19] (Lieb's use of the word "underhanded" in this quote refers to Mays's throwing style, not his character.)

So what do we make of this remarkable tale? Was Mays guilty of doing what the Chicago Black Sox had done just two years earlier? He was already one of the most disliked players in the game. His easygoing teammate, Bob Shawkey, called him a "stinker" decades after their playing days, when the conflicts and competitive juices should have receded.[20] If anyone in baseball had enemies who might try to disgrace him, it was Carl Mays.

Nevertheless, questions remain. If Mays did decide to take a payoff in exchange for letting down and serving up easy pitches to hit, why would the fix involve a midgame payment and a signal from the stands? Why not exchange the money, or at least the down payment, before the game, rather than the ludicrous plan of a midgame transfer of money and a handkerchief-waving signal from Mrs. Mays?

On the other hand, this was not the only story that alleged Mays's connection to gamblers. In late 1917 he was sued for breach of contract for reneging on a gambling debt of hundreds of dollars that he owed to Joseph "Sport" Sullivan, a well-known Boston gambler who was later indicted in the Chicago Black Sox scandal. The case was dismissed on a technicality.[21] Then in early 1927, during the commissioner's investigation of the Ty Cobb–Tris Speaker affair, Mays would be back in the news regarding a story that he had bet against his Yankees during a series in Boston in June 1922.[22] The lowly Red Sox beat the eventual pennant winners four straight games at that time, June 22–24, including a game in which Mays blew a 4–0 lead.[23]

Yet there is no direct evidence of a 1921 World Series Game 4 fix. More importantly, Mays's late-game fade was not all that unusual. Despite Mays's outstanding 1921 season, he had weakened in the late innings in numerous games. His devastating collapse against Detroit on September 19 was merely the most recent of many collapses the Yankee ace suffered during the 1921 season.[24]

So it seems likely that on October 9 Carl Mays simply ran out of gas in the eighth inning as he had done a number of times that year.[25] By the sixth inning, he was throwing more slow balls and varying the speed of his pitches more than he had earlier. In the seventh, Mike McNally bailed him out with a spectacular stop of a Frank Snyder drive, and a double play got him out of the inning. Through it all, as through the tough days after Ray Chapman was killed, Mays remained unflappable. "Mays is not the nervous type. He is almost phlegmatic in his temperament. . . . He is the type that would sleep soundly, dreamlessly on the eve of going to the guillotine."[26]

Then came the eighth. Some writers did not see it coming. But others did. Henry Edwards noted, "Instead of keeping the ball low and working the corners, he [Mays] was getting it up above the knees and when he did they killed it."[27]

By the eighth inning, he was abandoning his underhand delivery for a sidearm one. Hugh Fullerton, who uncannily predicted Mays would

46. Carl Mays was not a popular player either with fans or players, including his own teammates. But how he could pitch. In the 1921 World Series, his sweeping underhand delivery befuddled the Giants for sixteen innings of shutout ball until the fateful eighth inning of Game 4. *National Baseball Hall of Fame Library, Cooperstown, New York.*

win in his first World Series start in 1921 and lose his second, said, "Mays pitched exactly the sort of game he figured to pitch, weakened toward the end just as he figured to weaken."[28] Yet no one could paint a more vivid picture than Heywood Broun: "Yes, Mays was weakening and he knew it. He needed another day of rest. His equipment was just two innings short of victory. Like a tired prize fighter he tried to save every possible ounce of effort. He wasted nothing, because he realized that he did not have enough. Bit by bit he crumbled. Anybody who has ever seen camels being loaded in the straw department of a wholesale granary will have no trouble in picturing the sudden downfall of Mays."[29]

That downfall was no surprise to McGraw. "As for Mays," he said, "it was only a question of when the Giants would get to him. They were hitting him all along, but not hitting him just right. That eighth inning rally was bound to come."[30]

With the series tied at two games each, it was now a best-of-five series; but the momentum, as reflected by the oddsmakers, had shifted unmistakably to the Giants. The National Leaguers had two major factors in their favor. First, Ruth's participation in the rest of the Series remained doubtful; and despite Huggins's assurances, the Yankees were not the same team without the Babe. Secondly, based on Barnes's sensational outing and Shawkey's miserable performance in Game 3, plus the availability of Nehf, Toney, Douglas, and Pat Shea, the Giants now clearly held the edge in pitching.

31 GAME 5, Monday, October 10

Ruth's Gameness and Hoyt's Guts

Game 5 featured a rematch between Game 2's starters, Waite Hoyt and Art Nehf. For Hoyt, it was clear from the first inning that he was not going to have as easy a time as he had in that first matchup. While his control had improved—he had walked five in that first encounter—he did not seem to have as much "stuff" on his pitches. Before the game, an unnamed Giant said his team was confident in facing Hoyt this second time. "Now that we know what he's got we'll be able to time our swing. I expect to see the Giants roll up quite a score this afternoon."[1]

Babe Ruth overruled his doctors and again started in left field, though it was obvious that he was nowhere near 100 percent. In addition to his infected elbow, he had a bad knee and a charley horse in his leg. Joe Vila, a frequent critic of Ruth, was upset with the Babe's toying with the fans and the press. The Yankees had said he probably would not play in the fourth game; yet not only did he play, he even hit a home run. Vila felt he was being played for a fool by Ruth, telling his readers one thing and then having the opposite occur.

The veteran reporter, one of the most opinionated and senior of New York's sportswriters, suggested that the Babe's injuries were being exaggerated and overdramatized: "Ruth possibly enjoyed the trick he played on the fans by going into the game after the report had been spread that he had been forced out of the series by an operation on his 'infected elbow.' . . . Further reports of the Bambino's indisposition will be taken with plenty of salt."[2] Vila insinuated that Ruth was pleased to avoid the pressure of playing in the World Series.

In his biography of the Babe, Marshall Smelser said of Vila suggesting that Ruth had faked the injury, "this may be the most doltish remark ever made about Ruth."[3] Ruth really had no business being in the lineup for this game. An incision near his elbow had allowed doctors to drain the pus out of his infected wound, but he was in a severely weakened state.

Vila's perspective was in the distinct minority of the coverage, though even the *Sporting News* could not resist sarcasm, simply unable to accept the possibility that Ruth could play with such pain and injuries. "Nothing but death it would seem can relieve the wretched cripple from his sufferings," the paper wrote in an editorial.[4]

After Nehf retired the Yankees in order in the top of the first inning, George Burns led off for the Giants and reached first when Mike McNally bobbled his grounder (the third baseman's second error in as many days). After Dave Bancroft forced Burns, Frankie Frisch got a hit up the middle that Hoyt deflected off his bare hand, causing a split middle finger that probably bothered him throughout the game. Ross Youngs then walked to load the bases. George Kelly followed with a pop-fly single that center fielder Elmer Miller played conservatively, unlike the daring defense he had displayed in the last few weeks of the season. Bancroft scored, but Frisch had to hold up to see if the ball would be caught. Hoyt had not been hit hard; but with one run already in, the bases loaded, and only one out, he was in deep trouble. As the dangerous Irish Meusel stepped to the plate, Jack Quinn started warming up in the Yankees' bullpen.

John McGraw had been roundly criticized for letting Hoyt off the hook in Game 2, with the Giants repeatedly swinging at his first pitches. Now, with a 1-1 count, Meusel kept glancing back to the dugout to get McGraw's signal. Hoyt's control had betrayed him a number of times in Game 2; so McGraw directed Meusel not to swing, hoping Hoyt might walk in a run. But the next pitch was a change-up for strike two. Rather than wasting a pitch, Hoyt followed with a big, slow curve. Umpire Cy Rigler called strike three to retire the dangerous Giants outfielder with the bat on his shoulder. Hoyt's slow curve was effective throughout this game. When he induced Rawlings to hit a ground ball to shortstop that forced Kelly at second, the inning was over. Instead of having a big inning, the Giants had come away with only one unearned run.

In the second inning, the Yankees abandoned their usual big-inning strategy from the regular season. They instead played for one run at a time—inside baseball—just as they had in the first two games. After Bob

47. At twenty-eight, Irish Meusel (*left*) was three years older than his brother Bob (*right*). Playing for the Giants and Phillies this season, Irish batted a combined .343, with fourteen home runs and 87 runs batted in. Bob, in his second season with the Yankees, was the more powerful hitter. He had twenty-four home runs and 136 runs batted in to go along with his .318 average. *Library of Congress, Prints and Photographs Division, George Grantham Bain Collection,* LC-B2-5562-7.

Meusel led off with a single to right, Huggins instructed Wally Pipp to move the runner over, which he did. As Nehf was fanning Aaron Ward for out number two, Meusel took off for third. Catcher Earl Smith's throw was there in time for what should have been an inning-ending double play, but Frisch dropped the ball. When Meusel saw it rolling away, he took off for home. However, Frisch recovered the ball and threw it to Smith in time to retire the Yankee daredevil. Once again, Meusel and Smith collided. But this time, unlike in Game 2, the Giants' catcher held on to the ball. It was clear that Huggins was going to continue to test the Giants' defense and not wait for a big inning.

With two outs in the bottom of the second, Burns bunted safely; and Bancroft followed with a single to right. Burns, running on the play, easily reached third. Bob Meusel then displayed that he had an active brain as well as an accurate arm. He bluffed a throw to second, where the ball would usually be thrown after a single. As Bancroft turned the corner at first, Meusel whipped the ball to first baseman Wally Pipp. Bancroft was now trapped; and during the rundown, Burns broke for home. Pipp's throw to catcher Wally Schang was in time, and once again Hoyt had squirmed out of trouble.

In the top of the third, the Yankees came from behind for the first time in the Series and tied the score at one. After McNally walked, Schang doubled (that was a generous call, though, since he took second on the throw to third) and moved McNally to third. After Hoyt grounded out (the runners holding), Miller hit a fly to short left. While Irish Meusel's arm was not in the same class as his brother's, his throw home appeared to have a chance to get McNally. Yet Giants shortstop Dave Bancroft, who was having a terrible series at the plate (he had just 1 hit in 18 at bats so far in the Series), now made a blunder in the field, inexplicably cutting off the throw. McNally scored, and the Yankees had pulled even. Bancroft later defended his action, saying the throw was off-line. Most observers saw the play differently. So far in the Series, Bancroft had been anything but a "Beauty."[5]

The Giants came right back in the bottom of the third. Frisch led off with his second single of the day. After Youngs forced him at second and Kelly struck out, Irish Meusel doubled Youngs to third base. Again the Giants had a runner ninety feet away; and again they failed to score, as Hoyt retired Johnny Rawlings on a pop-up. Just the first three innings had generated more excitement than many entire games.

Leading off the top of the fourth, with McGraw's infielders and outfielders playing deep, Ruth stunned the Giants and the crowd with a hit that traveled less than ninety feet. The game's mightiest slugger laid down a bunt toward third base and reached first just ahead of Frisch's throw. A few Giants let first base umpire George Moriarty know what they thought of his call. After the Series, McGraw was equally emphatic.

"I shall always claim that Ruth was out at first by two feet on his 'safe' bunt which caused so much damage."[6]

The bunt was so unexpected, it stunned just about everyone in the Polo Grounds. As Damon Runyon explained, "It was as if you had been anticipating the collapse of the Woolworth Building and saw but the drift of a feather."[7] Heywood Broun called it "a gorgeous piece of character acting," since the Babe had taken some mighty practice swings when he had stepped into the batter's box.[8]

When Bob Meusel followed with a double (a ball that his brother misplayed, as it bounced over his head and almost hit a policeman stationed at the wall), Ruth never hesitated at third and scored on the play. He staggered into the dugout, collapsed, and passed out. Dr. George Stewart revived him with spirits of ammonia.[9] The fans had no idea that the Babe had passed out. Announcer George Levy ran to the press box and shouted to the reporters, "Ruth has fainted on the bench."[10] Typewriters suddenly went silent; and the area, usually buzzing with activity, became very quiet. Sid Mercer spoke for many (though not for Joe Vila) when he wrote, "Surely no greater exhibition of gameness has ever been featured in baseball."[11]

Meusel later scored on a Ward sacrifice fly, giving the Yankees a 3–1 lead. The inning ended when Burns made his second spectacular catch of the Series, robbing Mike McNally at the wall of what seemed like a sure triple.

When the Yankees took the field in the bottom of the inning, there was no Ruth. After a delay of a minute or two, the Babe staggered out of the dugout and took his place in left field. He would finish the game; and while he struck out three times, it was his bunt single that had made the difference. Baseball record keeper Al Munro Elias, "that demon with the statistics," noted that the Babe now had eight strikeouts in the Series, a total that no one had ever amassed in only five games.[12]

The Giants put the lead runner on base in both the fourth and the sixth, but again McGraw refused to call for the sacrifice.[13] Neither runner, Smith in the fourth or Kelly in the sixth, got as far as second base. McGraw held his ground against "any irresponsible second guesser who may happen to take a fling at me." He declared, "I know the value of a sacrifice as well as the next man. I also know when, in my opinion, another style of offense is preferable."[14]

In the eighth inning, Hoyt was in trouble yet again. After Youngs hit a one-out single, Kelly got a base hit to right field. Then, as he had done in the second inning, Bob Meusel snuffed out the Giants' rally. He threw a rifle shot to Ward at second, nabbing Kelly as he tried for two bases. Hoyt then retired Irish Meusel on a pop foul that Wally Pipp caught at the box seat railing.

The Giants tried to rattle Hoyt all afternoon. "Tutored by the genial McGraw," they used such coarse and vulgar language that "it may be imagined and is better not depicted."[15] When words did not have an effect, the Giants resorted to props. In a scenario difficult to imagine today, someone on the Giants' bench (Rumor said it was Casey Stengel) threw a bar of soap at the Yankees' pitcher, after Hoyt had grounded out in the fifth. Just days earlier, Hoyt had signed an endorsement contract with a brand of soap. The irrepressible Stengel then yelled at Hoyt to wash his neck with it.[16] The Yankees' pitcher picked up the bar of soap and hurled it back from where it came, where, in Hoyt's words, "it just shaved McGraw's ear."[17] On this day, as in his previous start, he would not be unnerved. "Hoyt was invincible," wrote Dan Daniel, "imperturbable, a pitcher always courageous, if not always baffling, but most effective when the outlook turned darkest."[18]

Hoyt had to face down a final threat in the ninth when Johnny Rawlings led off with a double. Miller Huggins quickly had a few pitchers start to warm up. Yet a pop-up and two strikeouts later, Hoyt had the win, 3–1; and the Yankees had the World Series lead, 3-2. He had given up ten hits and faced base runners in seven different innings, including five in which the lead-off hitter got on base. Hoyt was repeatedly great "in the pinches," leading veteran umpire Billy Evans to declare that he had just watched the best right handed pitcher in the American League.[19] He also proved the uncanny Hugh Fullerton to be less than perfect; the scribe had predicted Hoyt would lose this game.

Art Nehf was again terrific in defeat. After Ruth's lead-off bunt in the fourth, he gave up only two hits the rest of the game. Once again, his batters had failed him, as had his base runners. Manager McGraw gave his players a tongue-lashing after the game, and with good reason. As Walter Trumbull put it, the Giants "ran bases with all the skill of a fat lady with the asthma racing for a street car."[20] If they had respected Meusel's arm—they were well aware of his throwing ability—they might have had the big innings that McGraw was playing for. Yet Meusel was by no means the only Yankees star in the field. At second base, Aaron Ward had now handled forty-two chances without an error in the five games.

Polo Grounds concessionaire Harry M. Stevens was selling 21,000 hot dogs and 3,000 bags of peanuts a game; yet he was complaining that the drama of the games was hurting his sales, because the fans were so focused on the action on the field that they were not buying food.[21] Born in England, Stevens had started at the Polo Grounds in 1894, with the help of Giants manager John Montgomery Ward.[22] He took over the catering at New York's Saratoga Race Track in 1902 at the request of William C. Whitney and now had the food concession at a number of ballparks, race tracks (horse, auto, and bicycle), and arenas, primarily in the Northeast.[23] Known at ballparks for ice cream and scorecards, as well as hot dogs and peanuts, Stevens was a familiar figure at Polo Grounds games. "Baseball without Harry," wrote Damon Runyon, "would be as dull and dreary as ham hocks and cabbage without the ham."[24]

After the game, Huggins spoke to reporters about Ruth's bunt and dash around the bases: "It was an exhibition of gameness that will go down through history."[25] Yet it now appeared certain that the Yankees would be without the inspirational slugger for the rest of the Series. The Babe's personal physician, Dr. George King, told reporters that Ruth should not have played in the last two games and that he would risk losing his arm if he continued to play.[26]

Ruth's attending physicians ran a more detailed and frightening statement, especially since this was long before the advent of antibiotics: "The glands have taken up the poison, as is usual, but the swelling has reached such proportions that if the arm is used it will force the poison into the system, when the poisoning would become general. When blood poisoning becomes general throughout the system, the seat of the trouble must be removed, and that means amputation. Ruth will not play again in the series."[27]

His doctors would not even allow Ruth to suit up to coach third base, afraid he would talk Huggins into playing him. The Babe's arm was in such bad shape that he could not steer his own car. Someone would have to drive him to the ballpark.

Even though the Yankees now had the Series lead, Sid Mercer was quite pessimistic about their chances, especially in Game 6. "Huggins is just one jump ahead of a desperate situation," he noted. "As Ethel Barrymore would say, Huggins, when he surveys his pitchers, points to Mays and Hoyt and exclaims, 'That's all there is. There isn't any more.'"[28]

This Series had been unpredictable and full of surprises. The Yankees had won three low-scoring contests, while the Giants struck in Game 3 with two big rallies. Each team was resourceful enough to bounce back just when it appeared to be beaten—the Giants in Game 3 and the Yankees in Game 5. Game 5 had so many dramatic plays that the fans went home "in a state of nervous collapse," in the words of Sid Mercer. "If the boys continue to play those close games the undertakers will win the series."[29]

The Series Is Evened, but
without Ruth—Is It Really Even?

Before the start of the sixth game, silent-film star Mae Murray (fresh off two hit movies with Rudolph Valentino) appeared on the field and revealed her sentiments by spending most of her time with the Yankees. For this sixth game, both the Giants and the Yanks had to reach beyond their top two pitchers. John McGraw decided to come back with Fred Toney despite his poor showing four days earlier. Miller Huggins turned to left-hander Harry Harper, his talented yet inconsistent nine-year veteran. As Sid Mercer wrote about Harper's shortcomings before his Series start, "The Hackensack lefthander is temperamental. He is a most self-conscious boxman [pitcher] and is inclined to loss of aplomb and control when things are breaking badly for him."[1]

Just before the start of the game, home plate umpire George Moriarty chased Babe Ruth from the Yankee dugout, saying that someone in civilian clothes had no place on the bench.[2] Ruth would spend the rest of the game in the press box, a rather forlorn figure, helpless to contribute to his team. "The pluckiest player who ever took part in the baseball classic" would not be contributing, probably not for the rest of the Series.[3] The Babe told reporters, "It isn't often that I have been able to view a game from this angle, and I can't say that I relish it very much."[4]

Huggins decided to put Chick Fewster (rather than Braggo Roth) in left field in place of Ruth and had him leading off, moving Elmer Miller down to the Babe's third spot in the batting order. It paid off right away when Fewster made a long run to catch a Ross Youngs foul fly in the left-field corner, tumbling near the wall as he caught the ball to end the first inning. The Yankees fell on Toney quickly with three runs on a lead-off walk to Fewster and singles to Miller, Bob Meusel, and Aaron Ward. Perhaps half-jokingly, Ring Lardner declared, "If you want to see

Toney pitch, you half [*sic*] to get there by 2 o'clock."[5] Down, 3–0, with two outs in the first, McGraw did not wait. He brought in Jesse Barnes, the pitching star of the third game.

One newspaper noted, "Harper is one of those pitchers who is very, very good when good and very, very bad when bad."[6] On this afternoon, he was bad. He got through the first inning without any damage but was hammered in the second. Irish Meusel hit a two-run home run that just cleared the right-field wall, the Giants' first home run of the Series. Moments later Frank Snyder homered to the left-field bleachers. Just like that, the Giants had evened the score, coming from behind as they had in the third game. *Spalding's Guide* editor John B. Foster wrote in the *Daily News*, New York City's newest daily, that Harper's nerves "were so palpable that they stuck out like the arms of a cactus."[7] Harper was done for the day after he gave up a hit to Barnes, the opposing pitcher. Huggins brought in Bob Shawkey, hoping that he would be sharper than he had been in Game 3. The first man to face him, George Burns, singled; but Shawkey got out of the inning with the score still knotted at three.

The Yankees struck back immediately and with the most unlikely of heroes. In the bottom of the second, after a one-out single by Shawkey, Fewster, "frail and nervous, filled up the tremendous gap made by the withdrawal of Ruth."[8] He had hit but one home run during the 1921 season; yet he sent a high fastball into the left-field seats to give the Yanks a 5–3 lead, triggering an enormous outburst of cheers. Damon Runyon noted, "He has a hole in his head [referring to Fewster's spring 1920 near-fatal beaning], but his heart is quite intact."[9]

Only one home run in the first five games, and now three in one inning. That, declared Al Munro Elias, was a World Series record. Heywood Broun described the display of power in his inimitable way. Psychiatrists such as Sigmund Freud and Carl Jung, he noted, "have pointed out that suppressed things are apt eventually to pop out with great violence. The suppressed desire for home runs was lifted from the subconscious yesterday."[10]

After Fewster's blow, Slim Sallee began to warm up. For the sixth straight game, he would not be touched for a hit . . . in the bullpen.[11] As Ring Lardner joked, "It was rumored round last night that Slim Sallee, who has been warming up for two years, is pretty near ready."[12] But

Barnes settled down, retiring Roger Peckinpaugh and Elmer Miller on ground balls to end the inning; and Slim Sallee sat down in the bullpen yet again. Sallee, the thirty-six-year-old left-hander, had led the Giants this season with thirty-seven relief appearances and finished nineteen games; but he would not appear in the Series (though he would warm up in the remaining games too) or ever again in a Major League game.

In the top of the third, with one out and Kelly on first, Irish Meusel sent a ball to deep left. Fewster turned his back to the plate and caught up with the ball at the wall, making another catch the Babe never would have made. Both Shawkey and Barnes got through the third inning without much damage, each giving up but one hit. The Yankees maintained their 5–3 lead.

Hugh Fullerton wrote that the true test of a game team is whether it can rally from behind more than once in a game.[13] In the fourth inning, the Giants again struck back. After Snyder and Barnes started the inning with singles, Mike McNally threw low to first on Burns's attempted sacrifice to load the bases. This was a rare Giants' sacrifice and McNally's third error in three games. A two-run single by Dave Bancroft tied the game, and the Giants added two more runs for a 7–5 lead before the inning was over.

Shawkey again was not up to the task, and this had to be terribly disappointing to him. The ace of the Yanks' pitching staff for many years finally had reached baseball's highest level. Yet now "he finds that his good right arm is not equal to the demand. His back hurts him, his face is pinched, and his nerves cry aloud."[14] Inexplicably, Miller Huggins failed to make a move to the bullpen, the same approach he had taken in Game 3 for which he had been so severely criticized. Perhaps he wanted to give Shawkey every possible chance to recover. Perhaps he felt he had to hold Mays back for the seventh game; and unlike McGraw, he did not have a Slim Sallee or Pat Shea in the bullpen. Perhaps he felt the Yanks would reach Barnes again. Perhaps all of the above.

In the bottom of the fourth, Barnes continued to pitch effectively, having settled down after the Fewster home run. He struck out the side, though he did walk two batters, giving him five outs in a row via the strikeout. Known as a fastball pitcher and one the Yankees were expected to feast on, Barnes repeatedly fooled them with a terrific curve ball, one that kept breaking downward and catching a corner of the plate. He also mixed in a tantalizing slow ball.

48. After relieving starter Fred Toney in the first inning of Game 6, Jesse Barnes allowed the Yankees just two runs and four hits in eight and one-third innings. He struck out ten batters, setting a relief record that would stand for forty-five years. *Private collection of Steve Steinberg.*

In the fifth, Barnes struck out the first two Yankees, giving him seven consecutive outs that were strikeouts. H. G. Salsinger was moved to write, "No single delivery in a World Series has ever been as deceptive as this curve ball that Barnes used."[15]

Frank Baker pinch-hit for Shawkey in the eighth. Ten years earlier, when he was with the Athletics, Baker had earned his nickname, "Home Run," by helping win two World Series games with dramatic home runs off Rube Marquard and Christy Mathewson. Surely the memory of those blows flashed through the mind of John McGraw, the manager Baker had victimized in October 1911. Now at age thirty-five, Baker had been consigned to the role of bench warmer and was easily retired on a grounder to Johnny Rawlings at second.

Bill Piercy pitched the top of the ninth for the Yankees, giving up two hits but no runs. Barnes then put an exclamation point on his performance in the bottom of the inning. Three Yankees came up; all were retired on pop-ups to Rawlings.

When the game was over, the Giants had an 8–5 victory; and they had knotted the Series at three games apiece. The Circleville Cyclone, as Barnes was known for the tiny Kansas town that he came from, gave up only four hits in Game 6 and only two in the last seven and two-thirds innings. (All four Yankee hits reportedly came off fastballs.) He also struck out ten Yankees, a relief record that would stand for forty-five years.[16] In sixteen and one-third innings of relief in this Series, he had fanned eighteen men and given up only three earned runs on ten hits. Frank Graham called Barnes, the first man to win two Series games he did not start, the greatest relief pitcher in World Series history.[17]

As they had done with Jack Quinn in the third game, the Giants' comeback eclipsed a stirring story that had emerged earlier in the game. Hugh Fullerton noted that "we had a story all made up then with Chick Fewster as the hero."[18] Then, as the Giants came back and Barnes throttled the Yankee bats, Fewster's exploits (at bat and in the field) were washed away.

During the game, umpire Moriarty continued to deal with players hurling verbal abuse from the dugouts. He tossed Earl Smith and Casey Stengel during the game, and he also ejected former Giants third baseman Hans Lobert from the Giants bench.[19] Lobert, who would join the Giants as a full-time coach in 1928, was now the baseball coach at the U.S. Military Academy at West Point and was providing coaching advice to McGraw's already top-heavy brain trust of coaches—Hughie Jennings, Jesse Burkett, and Cozy Dolan. Moriarty seemed to be "a vigilance committee of one," since none of the other umpires was having such problems, resulting in ejecting players.[20]

Not all of the dugout remarks were directed at players of the opposing team. Throughout the Series, there had been complaints from both teams about the officiating, especially the calling of balls and strikes. Many observers found Moriarty's calls on balls and strikes wanting. "The work of the poetic Moriarty behind the plate was glaringly inefficient, although impartially so."[21] (Moriarty also wrote poetry, some of which appeared in *Baseball Magazine*.) Veteran reporters felt that Oliver Chill and Moriarty, both of whom were American League umpires, were the weakest of the group, though McGraw singled out Cy Rigler for his poor work behind the plate.[22] After the Series, sportswriter Frank Graham would note that Ernest Quigley was clearly the best of the group.[23]

After this game, even Hugh Fullerton weighed in on the issue: "The umping in this series has not been first class, and it has caused considerable disgruntlement."[24] Without rating the four umpires, Fullerton complained that the league presidents were selecting World Series arbiters either to spread the wealth or based on years of service. (Rigler was the most senior of the four, having served in the National League since 1906.) Fullerton noted that the best umpire in each league at calling balls and strikes—Bill Klem of the National and Billy Evans of the American, who were also two of the most respected arbiters in the game—was not selected for this year's World Series.

There was more drama after the game, when an agitated Babe Ruth confronted Joe Vila in the press room over his questioning the Babe's "alleged injury." As the Babe explained, "To be called a quitter and a fake by a writer is more than I intend to stand for."[25] Fred Lieb described it as a "violent argument" between the Yankee star and the veteran fifty-four-year-old sports editor of the *New York Sun*.[26] Vila was so fearful of physical injury when Ruth confronted him that he held his typewriter as a shield against blows that never came. (Vila is credited with introducing the typewriter to ringside, at the 1898 Gentleman Jim Corbett–Tom Sharkey heavyweight title fight.) Ripping off his bandages to reveal his ugly elbow abscess, the Babe shouted to him, "You're accusing me of not having any guts. Now, if *you* have any, print a picture of my arm with this hole in it and let your readers see my side of it."[27]

The *New York Sun* did not do so, nor did it apologize to Ruth. Instead, Vila continued his line of attack the next day: "Ruth, it seems, is no different from other baseball stars who consider praise and flattery belongs to them as a matter of course but are unable to stand criticism without showing themselves in their true colors."[28] Most reporters rallied to Ruth's defense. Sid Mercer, for example, commented that the Babe "administered a well deserved call to a smug 'expert'" who had been saying the injury was a myth. The consensus among the sportswriters was that the Babe was done a big injustice and deserved an apology.[29] Ruth may have made his point in the press box, but it remained doubtful he would be scoring any more points on the playing field this October.

One fan in attendance who was disappointed that Ruth did not play was Willie Keeler, a member of the original 1903 Yankees. After the game, he made his way almost unnoticed to the Giant clubhouse to congratulate John McGraw. "I want to see Mac win, of course," said Keeler, McGraw's teammate on the great Baltimore Oriole teams of the 1890s. Keeler was experiencing shortness of breath and chest pains, and this was the last game he ever saw.[30]

Huggins himself had little to say after the game: "I have no alibi to offer for today's defeat. . . . When a pitcher is able to strike out ten men in a game and get every member of your batting order, why try to explain away defeat?"[31] John McGraw had brought his Giants back again, and he again did it with his controlling style. Every one of his players, including Frankie Frisch and George Burns, could not use his own judgment when at the plate. "Close observers will notice that after almost every pitch and especially when there are runners on the bases, the Giant batters never fail to turn to the bench for instructions."[32]

Sid Mercer summed up the Yankees' predicament, as the Series was now reduced to a best two of three. "If the Giants win the world's series, it will be because Miller Huggins could not find a third pitcher to collaborate with Mays and Hoyt." Huggins did have Mays and Hoyt lined up for Games 7 and 8. If the Series were to go the full nine games, the Yankees would have few promising pitching options. For that reason, Mercer noted, Huggins "remains just one step ahead of dire necessity."[33]

33 GAME 7, Wednesday, October 12

"Give me another game against those
Yankees, and they'll get even less"

Miller Huggins may have disliked Carl Mays for his occasional insubordination; but Mays, with twenty-seven wins and seven saves, had been his best pitcher all season. The twenty-nine-year-old right-hander had appeared in more games (totaling forty-nine this season) and thrown more innings (336⅔) than any other Major League pitcher in 1921. And with the exception of that one poor inning in Game 4, he had been extremely effective against the Giants. Furthermore, Huggins had no viable alternative, and so he chose Mays to start Game 7. John McGraw would come back with Phil Douglas, who had split the two previous games in which he had opposed Mays.

Douglas would later report that he had a bad cold and had not gotten a good night's sleep: "I was ill all morning and at that time I thought I would be unable to pitch." He said his condition improved about noon; and when he got to the clubhouse, he told McGraw he was ready to take on the Yankees.[1] McGraw was probably happy just to hear that his often unreliable pitcher had spent the night in bed.

Despite the chilly weather, another turnaway crowd was on hand, helped by the twin holidays of Columbus Day and Yom Kippur, which gave New Yorkers the excuses they needed to skip work and school. Police inspector Cornelius Cahalane estimated that 50,000 disappointed fans were turned away after the gates of the Polo Grounds closed at noon.[2] Still, the owners of both teams, continuing their long-held policy, did not allow overflow fans onto the playing field. The huge gathering pushed the total gate receipts for the Series past $800,000—more than $80,000 in excess of the previous high mark, which was set in 1919 by the Reds and White Sox in eight games.

Before the game, statistician Al Munro Elias compared the two pitchers: "Douglas and Mays are even up, but Douglas has pitched the better ball. I think he is due to win a close one today. The Giants are now fairly familiar with the peculiar Mays delivery, and think they can hit it. On the other hand, the Yanks may know that Douglas is going to pitch a spitter and yet they can't hit it."[3] After his Game 4 win, Douglas had declared, "Give me another game against those Yankees, and they will get even less."[4]

Both pitchers lived up to pregame expectations. Each had a strong outing in a game that was close, hard fought, and went down to the last batter. "So strenuous was the combined rooting that many patrons were in a state of collapse at the finish of the contest," wrote Sam Crane.[5] Yet the New York Times saw it differently, saying the game lacked "the succession of thrills, the highly tense situations and the outstanding hero that might be expected in a low-score battle of its kind."[6] Mays and Douglas had been so dominant that the Times labeled the game "for the most part drab, due to the mastery which two pitchers held from start to finish over the opposing batsmen."[7] While the Times may have been correct in saying the game lacked a hero, it certainly did provide a "goat," perhaps more than one.

The Yankees scored first, as they had in five of the previous six games, when Mike McNally's second-inning single drove in Wally Pipp, who had doubled. McNally then tore ligaments in his shoulder sliding into second on the next play, and another Yankee starter was finished for the Series.

Mays had prevented a run in the first inning, with a sensational barehanded catch of Ross Youngs's line drive with Dave Bancroft on third. However, sloppy play later on by the Yankee defense allowed the Giants to tie the score in the fourth. Youngs had an infield single on a ball hit to second that Aaron Ward failed to handle cleanly. It was scored a hit, a decision that surprised the fans and the press, who almost unanimously thought Ward should have been charged with an error. Then, as the next batter, George Kelly, was striking out swinging, Youngs took off for second. His steal attempt was successful, perhaps due to "Schang's sloppy work in making the throw."[8]

Irish Meusel's soft fly ball, which Elmer Miller misjudged and played "in an atrocious manner," brought Youngs home with the tying run.[9] In the next inning, George Burns's fly rolled off Miller's glove and was generously ruled a double. Miller redeemed himself somewhat with a strong throw to Ward, who relayed the ball to Frank Baker, who tagged Burns, trying for three bases. Baker had taken over at third base for the injured McNally.

The score remained tied at one until the seventh, the most dramatic inning of the game. In the top of the inning, the Yankees threatened Douglas, who had been getting stronger as the game progressed. With two down and nobody on, Baker and Schang hit singles to center. A wild pitch put both runners in scoring position. The Yankee fans were on their feet, screaming in anticipation; but Douglas escaped by getting Mays on an easy ground ball to Rawlings. Mays batted .343 for the Yankees in 1921, yet he could manage only 1 hit in 9 at bats in the World Series.

Mays was not so fortunate under similar circumstances in the bottom of the seventh inning. He too retired the first two batters and seemingly had retired the third. But second baseman Ward let him down again. He booted Johnny Rawlings's routine grounder, allowing Rawlings to reach base. This time the official scorer did charge Ward with an error. Ward had fielded sensationally in the first five games before making an error in Game 6. That one had not hurt; but like his earlier bobble in the fourth inning today, this one did. Frank Snyder then smacked a liner into left-center for a double, which if handled cleanly, would have forced Rawlings to stop at third. But when Miller had trouble picking up the ball, third base coach Hughie Jennings waved Rawlings home with what would be the game-winning run.

"It was a sure enough single. . . . He [Miller] groped here and there as if the pill were a huge ball of quicksilver. And when he did get it he threw it as if it were a 16-pound shot."[10] Some reporters questioned Huggins's decision to pitch to the dangerous Giants catcher—who would hit .364 in this Series—rather than walk him and pitch to Douglas. Then again, it may not have been Huggins's decision. Perhaps in cases such as this, he let the veteran Mays decide whom to pitch to. Or given the manager's seeming lack of control over his free-spirited team, it is possible that he ordered an intentional walk, but Mays ignored the order.

Elmer Miller was normally a sure-handed fielder who had made a number of outstanding defensive plays during the season, and Bob Meusel's throwing arm had no equal. Neverthess, H. G. Salsinger, who covered the Tigers and was more familiar with the American League, was not impressed. Salsinger, praised the superiority of the Giants' outfield, especially George Burns and Ross Youngs. "Their work has sparkled all through the series," he wrote, "while that of the Yanks is just what it has been all season long. The Yank outfielders look mussy on any tough chance."[11] As for Miller, "Elmer won the pennant but he helped 'blow' the world series," wrote sportswriter Burt Whitman.[12]

The Yanks got the potential tying run aboard with two outs in both the eighth and the ninth, but neither Meusel nor Schang could deliver. "Douglas waved them out of the way as if he were brushing cobwebs from a garden bush," wrote Grantland Rice.[13] Douglas would not confirm or deny the rumor that McGraw had called him into his office after the game and presented him with a check for a substantial sum of money. He did say, though, "I'd like to get after them again today."[14] The *Washington Post* was among those who considered Douglas to be McGraw's greatest reclamation success. "Shufflin' Phil is McGraw's masterpiece in a long career of baseball miracles," it declared.[15]

Sam Crane believed that baseball was better off for Douglas having reestablished his reputation. "The pastime needs just such instances of real 'come backs' as Phil has accomplished."[16] Crane was a bit premature in his praise. Events would later show Douglas to be less than the "worthy fellow, respected and honored," Crane had claimed him to be.

Hugh Fullerton may have hit the mark more accurately when he noted that, had Douglas "kept in condition" during his career, "he would have been one of the great pitchers of all time."[17] Just ten months later, yet another of Douglas's drinking binges would lead to a series of events that would result in his lifetime banishment from the game.

Grantland Rice—who often wrote about fate, fame, and destiny in his long journalistic career—lamented Aaron Ward's sudden reversal of form. It was vintage Rice:

Gibraltar has fallen. Verdun has collapsed. The Chinese wall has crumbled to yellow dust. . . . Fate at times has a mocking way of leading some hapless human to within a stride of the far summit and then suddenly rolling his broken body down the rocky slope to the deep ravine below. . . . The difference between being a hero and a goat in this fickle, pallid existence is frequently a matter of ten or twenty

49. Aaron Ward sparkled in the field in the first five games of the Series. Then he stumbled in Game 6, and his fielding mistakes cost the Yankees Game 7. *Private collection of Steve Steinberg.*

minutes. . . . We are all wards of Fate, but the fate of Ward has been an even harder blow than the tragedy of the crippled Ruth.[18]

In the sixth inning, perhaps ten or twenty minutes before Ward's crucial error, he had made three difficult and terrific stops on ground balls to give Mays a three-up, three-down inning. "From a pitching standpoint the game will rank among the greatest in the long history of world's series play," wrote the *New York Times*.[19] Mays, in particular, had given his team another excellent outing—one earned run, six hits (two or three of which could easily have been scored as errors), and seven strikeouts—only to lose the game in the late innings. When it was over, Miller Huggins lauded Mays's effort: "In all my years in baseball I don't think I ever felt so sorry for a pitcher who lost a ball game as I felt for Carl Mays this afternoon. It was a wonderful performance by Mays, one of the greatest games he ever pitched."[20] This time no one could fault him for the defeat. Physical and mental errors by his Yankee teammates had turned what should have been a 1–0 victory into a 2–1 loss. In twenty-six innings in this World Series, Mays had not walked a single man.

Mays's reaction to Ward's and Miller's seventh-inning miscues was obvious to all. His face was "a perfect mirror of the disgust he felt over the failure that seemed destined to mark one of his greatest efforts on the mound."[21] Nevertheless, Mays was philosphical in defeat. "I pitched good ball and the Giants seldom gave me any trouble," he said. "Good luck was with the other fellow, and I lost a tough ball game."[22] True enough; the National Leaguers had gotten the breaks and took full advantage of them.

Capitalizing on breaks, even forcing them, was the way McGraw liked his clubs to play. "The players are all on their toes," he said after the game. "They proved that this afternoon. They were awake to all opportunities and that is the way to win ball games."[23] Evidently, McGraw had also added his voice to those with complaints about the officiating. A young reporter named Nat Fleischer had a scoop.[24] Fleischer reported that, should there be a Game 9, McGraw would formally protest the use of the existing umpires and demand different arbiters for the decisive game.[25]

For the first time in the Series, the Giants had the lead, four games to three; and as McGraw proudly pointed out, they had trailed in each win. "One of the things that pleases me most about the work of the Giants in the series thus far is that in each of the four games we have won we have had to come from behind to clinch the victory," he said. "It proves as nothing else could the fine fighting spirit of the Giants."[26]

The National Leaguers received more good news after the game when a coin tossed by Commissioner Landis determined that they would be the home team if there should be a ninth game. McGraw had made the correct call on the toss; nevertheless, he had no plans to play a ninth game. "If the Giants are not the world champions by sundown tomorrow, I shall be greatly disappointed," he said.[27]

Still, a ninth game was a distinct possibility; and should there be one, McGraw had several good options but would likely turn to Jesse Barnes. Miller Huggins also had several options, but they were not as strong as McGraw's. In the words of Sid Mercer, Huggins was now "just one hop ahead of the undertaker."[28] If Hoyt should beat the Giants in Game 8, whom would the Yankee skipper call on to face Barnes?

34 GAME 8, Thursday, October 13

"New York and baseball are proud
of the Yanks and the Giants"

For Game 8, cold and windy weather, along with the possibility that there might be a ninth and deciding game the next day, made for the smallest crowd of the Series, less than 26,000. The Polo Grounds' lower deck was mostly full, but there were many empty seats in the upper grandstand and in the bleachers.

As was his custom, John McGraw was evasive in revealing his starting pitcher. Three years later, prior to the Giants' World Series opener against Washington, McGraw would explain his practice of not naming pitchers until the day of the game.[1] Rather than notifying his starter the day before, he said, "how much better, in my opinion, it is to relieve such a strain as this by witholding my choice until a few minutes before the big test. Let 'em all have a good night's sleep."[2] McGraw said it would likely be Jesse Barnes, who had given him two outstanding relief performances, or Art Nehf, who had pitched two strong games but lost them both. The vast majority of reporters covering the Series expected it would be Nehf, and they would prove to be correct.

At five feet nine and a half, Nehf was not overpowering; but he did have a respectable fastball complemented by an excellent curve ball and the ability to keep hitters off balance by changing speeds. Nehf was all business on the mound, employing a simple workmanlike windup in delivering the ball to the batter. He was also an above-average fielder who participated in eleven double plays in 1920, breaking the Major League record of ten for pitchers set in 1905 by Addie Joss of the Indians and Nick Altrock of the White Sox.[3]

Intelligent and well spoken, Nehf had attended Rose-Hulman Institute of Technology in Terre Haute, Indiana, and was therefore not the typical, poorly educated player of this era. Harry A. Williams of the *Los Angeles Times* described Nehf as "a college man. He reads a lot and is more likely to discuss subjects other than baseball with reporters on train trips. He seems high strung on days he pitches. His usual pregame meal is apple pie and a glass of milk."[4]

For Miller Huggins the choice was easy. It would be Waite Hoyt, who had won his two previous starts convincingly. So just as Carl Mays and Phil Douglas had faced each other for the third time in Game 7, Hoyt and Nehf would do the same in Game 8. Douglas had lost his first encounter with Mays before winning the next two. Now for the Yankees to stay alive, Hoyt, who had beaten Nehf and the Giants twice, would have to win a third time.

Hoyt was hindered somewhat by a blister that had formed on a finger of his pitching hand, probably from the Frankie Frisch smash that he had stopped with his bare hand in Game 5. The blister had been lanced and treated with iodine, and was extremely painful. Also, the nail of that split finger was lifting with every pitch. Still, pitching with the injured finger and with the specter of his team's elimination hanging over him, the twenty-two-year-old Hoyt continued to dominate the Giants' batters. He was beaten mainly because the Yankee defense failed him, just as it had Mays the day before. They allowed the Giants to score an unearned run in the first inning, a run that Nehf made stand up for a 1–0 victory.[5] After four consecutive losses to American League teams, John McGraw and the Giants had their first World Series triumph since 1905.

While the one run the Giants scored was unearned, Hoyt was not completely blameless. He issued first-inning walks to Dave Bancroft and Ross Youngs, and he was particularly upset with the ball four call to Youngs by Oliver Chill, an American League umpire. Hoyt may have had good reason to be upset. Analyzing the Series in *Baseball Magazine*, W. A. Phelon described that ball four to Youngs as "one miscalled pitch—a perfect strike."[6] Thus, when George Kelly came to bat with two men out, the Giants had runners at first and second. Hoyt seemed to have escaped when Kelly hit a routine ground ball to shortstop, but the ball went through the legs of Roger Peckinpaugh. Bancroft scored what would be the final run of the 1921 World Series and the only run of this eighth game.

50. The two veteran shortstops and team captains, Dave Bancroft (*left*) and Roger Peckinpaugh (*right*), each hit less than .200 in the 1921 World Series. In the first inning of Game 8, Peckinpaugh misplayed a ground ball and allowed Bancroft to score the game's only run. *Private collection of Dennis Goldstein.*

Peckinpaugh had handled forty-two consecutive chances cleanly in the Series, but he could not handle the forty-third. "As long as I live I shall never forget the error I made in the first inning of yesterday's game," Peckinpaugh said after the game. "Like the man who lost his head on the guillotine, I must resign myself to my fate. I envy the man who lost his head—the big lucky stiff," added the despondent Yankee captain.[7]

Most game accounts simply said that Peckinpaugh had booted the ball; some said that it had gone right through his legs. Sid Mercer and Damon Runyon noted that the shortstop deflected the ball just enough to allow Bancroft to score from second base.[8] But a handful of sportswriters were far more critical of Peckinpaugh. John Foster asked his readers to "Imagine this infielder missing the ball completely and, turning around, dazed and stupefied, pursuing it disconcertingly into left field."[9] A staff writer for the *New York Tribune* was even more damning: "Picking on Peckinpaugh is a form of malicious cruelty, but did you notice how Roger stood still and looked at the ball after it had ambled between his legs? Reminded us of a man trying to make a misbehaved pup retrieve."[10]

Peckinpaugh's error, while costly, certainly seemed something the Yanks could overcome, even without Babe Ruth in the lineup. But as it turned out, they could not. A Series that had begun with the Giants going scoreless in the first twenty innings would end with the Yankees going scoreless in the final sixteen. (In addition to Nehf's shutout in Game 8, Douglas had held them without a run after the second inning of Game 7.) Hugh Fullerton had correctly predicted that the Giants would win the Series in eight games, but he expected this game to be a high-scoring affair between two tired pitchers.[11] Perhaps so did John McGraw and Miller Huggins. Both managers had their starters on a short leash. McGraw had Slim Sallee and Jesse Barnes "throwing leisurely," starting in the first inning, and Fred Toney and Phil Douglas started to warm up in the fifth. Likewise, Huggins had Jack Quinn warm up early and Mays warm up later in the game.[12]

The American Leaguers came closest to scoring in the fourth, when two-out singles by Aaron Ward and Wally Pipp and a walk to Frank Baker loaded the bases. Nehf's first two pitches to Wally Schang were balls. The next one may have been ball three; but Schang, perhaps over-

51. Art Nehf was the Giants' only twenty-game winner in 1921. The college-educated left-hander was "all business" on the mound. He possessed both an outstanding curve ball and the ability to keep hitters off balance by changing speeds. *Private collection of Michael Mumby.*

eager to put the Yankees ahead, swung at it. The result was a fly ball to center fielder George Burns that stranded the three runners. H. G. Salsinger blamed Schang's swing on Miller Huggins's lack of leadership: "The Giants listen to a smart manager, and the Yanks listen to nobody."[13]

Nehf and Hoyt continued to hold their opponents scoreless, but the Yankees did not go quietly. Pipp was due to lead off the home ninth; but while the crowd watched and waited, he remained in the dugout. As Nehf continued to warm up, a roar went through the crowd. Babe Ruth had emerged from the dugout and was heading to the plate to bat for Pipp. In uniform for the first time since Game 5, Ruth had been coaching at third base during the game. Almost every man, woman, and child in the Polo Grounds was now standing. The Giants' fans were up in anticipation of a Series victory; the Yankee fans were up hoping the Babe could hit just one more home run, one that would keep their team alive. McGraw yelled something to his captain, shortstop Bancroft, who relayed the message to Nehf: "Steady, and don't groove one for him. He's anxious and he'll bite."[14]

Nehf's first pitch was a curve ball that the Babe fouled back, agony showing on his face from his wound and the pain caused by the ferocity of the swing. Nehf's next offering was another curve ball that Ruth took for strike two. After taking a third hook for a ball, Ruth connected on yet another curve ball but hit a grounder to first baseman George Kelly, who outraced him to the bag.

That Nehf had thrown the Babe four consecutive curve balls was no accident. In an interview from his home in Phoenix more than a quarter century later, Nehf reminisced about pitching to Ruth. "I'll never forget Babe Ruth," he said. "I can still see him up there at the plate, and when I'd see him I would remember McGraw's order that he was never to get a fastball anywhere close to the plate."[15]

As the injured hero headed for the dugout, the fans rewarded him both for the unbelievable offensive year he had had and for the gameness he had shown, with the most prolonged cheering of the Series. The fans of both teams were letting Ruth know just how much they appreciated what he had contributed to baseball's revival. The dejection felt by Yankee rooters quickly turned to hope again when Ward drew Nehf's fifth walk of the game (he allowed only four hits). That set up one of

52. Journeyman second baseman Johnny Rawlings had an outstanding World Series, with ten hits and a .333 batting average. He "exemplifies what can be done, especially in tight places, by a player of ordinary ability possessed of a spirit that won't be downed," said Babe Ruth (*New York American*, October 16, 1921). *Library of Congress, George Grantham Bain Collection, Prints and Photographs Division, LC-B2-5543-4.*

the more spectacular game-ending (and in this case, Series-ending) defensive plays ever.

Baker followed the walk to Ward by ripping a 2-1 pitch that appeared headed between Kelly and Johnny Rawlings into right field. However, Rawlings, who had sparkled the entire Series for the Giants, made a spectacular play to retire Baker. Rawlings later recalled what went through his mind as Nehf faced Baker: "Baker was a tough left-handed pull hitter, and I would have been playing him over toward first anyway. But with a man on first, I figured he'd be trying to hit behind him and edged over even more. It was a good thing I did, because Frank hit right through the hole. I was lucky to get my glove on the ball, but I did, fielded it cleanly, but fell down and threw to Kelly at first base on my knees to get Baker."[16]

Meanwhile, Ward never stopped running, continuing around second base and headed for third. When Kelly saw what was happening, he whipped the ball across the diamond to third baseman Frankie Frisch, who put the tag on Ward. Umpire Ernie Quigley gave the out sign, completing the double play and ending the Series. No World Series had ever ended with a double play before; and only one, in 1947, has since.[17]

"It was the hit-and-run, of course, and Wardie [Aaron Ward] was off at the crack of the bat," remembered Rawlings. "He saw where the ball was hit and never even hesitated at second, but kept right on for third, figuring it for a single. Kelly was on his toes, too, and Long George, with that great arm of his, whipped the ball across the diamond to Frisch at third. Frankie put the ball on Ward as he slid in, and we were the champions of the world."[18]

Kelly did indeed possess a "great arm," powerful and accurate. In fact, McGraw thought so highly of Kelly's throwing ability, he would use him as a cutoff man, having him rush into the outfield on long hits to handle relays. The National League's home run king may have had a poor Series at the plate (where he tied a World Series record with ten strikeouts), but he excelled in the field. For his part, Ward had violated one of the cardinal rules of baseball. He had made the third out at third base. That the out had ended both the game and the Series only compounded his blunder.

The sudden and dramatic end of the game stunned the fans, and an eerie silence hovered over the Polo Grounds. "It required the crowd more than one minute to realize that the game and series were over and even when the players started leaving the field the vast mob did not realize that the end had come."[19] Nehf later called the ninth inning the most thrilling he had ever pitched. "I knew I had victory and the title within my reach when I walked out to the mound for the ninth. I was not disturbed when Ruth came to the plate instead of Pipp. The biggest moment came when Ward walked and Baker stepped to the plate. I remembered that Baker beat Mathewson in a world's series by making a home run in the ninth inning. I pitched carefully to Baker and when Rawlings stopped the ball it took a great load off my mind."[20]

Fans rushed onto the field, surrounding McGraw and his players as they tried to make their way to the clubhouse. Once there, with the pressure of the long season finally over, the Giants let loose, congratulating one another as winners always do. "I have the greatest baseball club in the world. And undoubtedly the gamest," shouted McGraw over all the whooping and hollering.[21]

But the festivies in the Giants' clubhouse were just a prelude to what was to come.

That night, in the Giants' suite at the Waldorf, McGraw and Charles Stoneham were hosts at a celebration that will never be forgotten by those who attended it—including one Giant player who had never been known to take a drink before, but was carried out stiff as a board, along about five o'clock of the morning after. There were hams and chickens and turkeys for the guests that night—or steaks for those who wanted them. And rye and Scotch and gin and champagne. . . . The sun was high over Fifth Avenue and Thirty-fourth Street as the last of the guests emerged and tottered homeward.[22]

Rawlings, whose lead-off doubles in the second and fourth had failed to result in a run, was one of a number of heroes of this World Series. Babe Ruth's column described a postseason phenomenon that exists to this day. Rawlings's performance "exemplifies what can be done, especially in tight places, by a player of ordinary ability possessed of a spirit that won't be downed. . . . At the same time I predict that next season he [Rawlings] will fall right back into his ordinary swing."[23]

Still, the best overall performance of the 1921 World Series was provided by Waite Hoyt, the hard-luck loser of Game 8. Grantland Rice lamented that Hoyt's "masterpiece of grim courage" would soon be forgotten in "the shadows of another Lost Cause."[24] Although often overlooked, Hoyt's pitching in this Series remains among the best in World Series history. Over the course of twenty-seven innings, the National League's most prolific offense had failed to score a single earned run against him. His 0.00 earned run average for twenty-seven innings duplicated that of Christy Mathewson in 1905 and has not been equaled since. An unearned run in each of his last two starts was all that prevented Hoyt from matching Mathewson's three shutouts against the Philadelphia Athletics in that 1905 Series.

Changes in various aspects of the game often can make comparing accomplishments from one era to those of another meaningless. However, a comparison of the offenses of the 1905 Athletics and the 1921 Giants makes Hoyt's pitching effort perhaps the more impressive one. The Deadball Era A's team that Mathewson faced had a team batting average of .255, with twenty-four home runs and 623 runs scored. The 1921 Giants, playing in a much more high-scoring era, had a .298 team batting average, hit seventy-five home runs, and scored 840 runs. Holding such a team without an earned run for three complete games was a truly remarkable feat. Despite his valiant effort, Hoyt was very disappointed at the outcome. "I gave the best I had," he said after the game.[25]

The press mostly praised the players on both teams. They had accomplished "great deeds in this series—deeds that have done much to bring back our great American pastime to the confidence of the fans," wrote Ed Van Every.[26] The games had been intense and, for the most part, well played. Van Every echoed the feelings of all New Yorkers when he wrote, "New York and baseball are proud of the Yanks and the Giants."[27]

The relative depth of the teams' pitching had been the difference. The Giants had gotten strong efforts from three men: Nehf, Douglas, and Barnes; the Yankees, on the other hand, received them from only two: Hoyt and Mays. Sid Mercer equated the Giants' advantage to that of a checkers player with three kings facing a player with two kings and a plain checker.[28]

The season-long talk of a new slugging-dominated game was getting a second look as baseball entered the Hot Stove League months. Some observers wondered about the extent to which the game really was entering a new era of slugging. Fred Lieb asked rhetorically, "What became of the lively ball during the series? Was it used only when Toney, Harper and Shawkey pitched, or on the day in which the Giants batted out lively hits?"[29] In the six games in which Toney, Harper, and Shawkey did not pitch, the teams combined to average a mere 3.3 runs per game. Joe Vila, who often sneered at the excesses of slugging, surely felt satisfaction when he wrote, "Pitching, not the quality of the ball, was responsible for batting records that insulted the intelligence of sensible baseball students."[30]

This first all–New York World Series drew 269,976 fans, breaking the Series record set by the Giants and Red Sox in 1912. The total gate receipts of $900,233 also set a Series record, topping the 1919 mark established by the Reds and White Sox. Both previous records had been set in an eight-game series.[31] Those who tracked such things said that money bet on the Series, both legally and illegally, exceeded $1 million.

The Giants' victory was also an individual triumph for John McGraw in his "war" with Babe Ruth. "I signaled every pitch to Ruth," he said after Game 8, reveling in having prevented the Babe from continuing his season-long heroics. "It was no secret. You could see [Frank] Snyder or [Earl] Smith turn and look at the bench before signaling the pitcher. We pitched only nine curveballs and three fastballs to Ruth during the entire Series. All the rest were slowballs, and of the twelve of those, eleven set him on his ear."[32]

McGraw's boasting aside, many fans wondered if the outcome would have been different had Ruth not been hurt. Yet even early in the Series, the Babe had not been very effective. McGraw ordered his pitchers to toss Ruth curve balls away from the heart of the plate, and the overanxious slugger often flailed at them. The Babe struck out eight times; five other times, McGraw's pitchers walked him. However, he did bat .313, drive in a team-high four runs, and hit one of the Series's four home runs (two were hit by each team).

As is so often the case, if some plays had gone differently, it could have changed the outcome of the Series. Yet "there never was a decisive battle fought in the history of the world that might not have been fought differently. It is useless to dwell on what might have happened. We know what did happen."[33]

Epilogue

When the 1921 season ended, New York ruled the baseball world; and John McGraw was its king. For the first time since 1905, the Giants were champions of the world. McGraw's handling of his team, particularly his pitching staff, had been remarkable. He had rallied his team after losing the first two games, and his Giants then won five of the next six. As Hugh Fullerton noted, "I have warned them often enough that this Giant team is dangerous when it gets started, and it fights like an inspired team once an opening is discovered."[1] Remarkably, Fullerton had predicted that the Yankees would win the first two games and that the Giants would storm back and win the last three to capture the Series.

While McGraw (at least outwardly) disparaged what Fullerton called the Yankees' "brute force system" led by Babe Ruth's home runs, he believed in scoring runs in clusters, as reflected in his general disdain of the sacrifice and decreasing emphasis on the stolen base. Fullerton described McGraw's system as "'hitting for a bunch.' That is, he believes in getting 'one big inning,' and scoring a flock of runs at a time."[2] The Giants' dramatic comebacks in Games 3 and 6 of the Series reflected what the *1922 Reach Official American League Base Ball Guide* called "McGraw's season-long system of winning the games in one or two innings."[3]

John McGraw may not have embraced the long ball, but he did embrace the Lively Ball Era far more than is commonly recognized. Just two years later he would express his strategy in clear terms: "Most ball games are won in a single inning. Sooner or later, by one method or another, you are able to mass your attack where it counts and by one vigorous assault win the game."[4] Recognizing that the game was changing, McGraw had displayed the ability to adapt to the new style of play.

Although injuries and McGraw's pitchers had limited Ruth's impact on the 1921 World Series, the Babe remained enormously popular. Additionally, he had the good fortune of playing in the nation's largest city. In the 1920s, a time of rising consumerism, New York was becoming "the most commercially and culturally creative place on earth—committed as never before or since to the intoxicating dreams of capitalism and commerce."[5] The entertainment industry was also experiencing enormous growth led by celebrities, including sports stars, who became household names.

Ruth was on the cutting edge of both these trends. "The Babe endorsed everything from baseballs and baseball caps to cigars and cars, pronouncing Packards, Reos, and Cadillacs the best car on the road, sometimes in the same issue of the same magazine."[6] And Jerome Charyn explained Ruth's appeal: "The nation cottoned to him because he was outsized, the greatest, most flamboyant gargoyle in a city of gargoyles—fast and furious, like Broadway itself. The twenties crystallized around the Babe."[7]

This was the man little Miller Huggins had been trying to control for the past two seasons. Pulitzer Prize–winning historian Bruce Catton has explained that this Yankees team was different from those of the late 1920s. The 1921 Yanks "were still a gang rather than a team; a gang of all-stars, most of whom had been bought ready-made who never felt they had any special need for a manager."[8] One wonders, had McGraw foreseen the new style of play that was emerging in 1919, would he have attempted to acquire the Babe?

The *Boston Herald*'s Burt Whitman, who had followed Ruth closely when he played for the Red Sox, recognized the obvious as well as the not so obvious. "Of course, 'Hug' cannot handle the big fellow. Nobody has been able to handle the Colossus. . . . Yet, in fairness to Huggins, let it be said that even John McGraw could not handle Babe Ruth."[9] However, McGraw had a long track record of acquiring unmanageable stars, from Bugs Raymond to Hal Chase to Phil Douglas, almost relishing the challenges as he did the rewards should he succeed in keeping them on the straight and narrow.

It was against this backdrop of Ruth's awesome popularity and outsized personality that he decided to go on a postseason barnstorming tour with teammates Bob Meusel and Bill Piercy. (The Babe's arm had healed quickly; his recuperative powers were remarkable.) Such a series of games could be extremely lucrative for a team led by a big star, as McGraw's Cuban exhibitions had been for the Giants a year earlier after he added Ruth to the tour. Yet there was just one problem: Ruth's 1921 tour was forbidden. World Series participants were barred from barnstorming.

The ban had been instituted after the late-1910 exhibition series some members of the world champion Philadelphia Athletics had played in Cuba. The A's were embarrassed by their Cuban competition, losing most of their games on the tour, which one reporter called "a joy ride from start to finish."[10] To avoid future embarrassment, in January 1911 the National Commission banned such tours by world champions. A few years later they extended the rule to the World Series losers. Calling into question the fairness of the regulation was the fact that star players could paradoxically make more money by not being on a World Series team and barnstorming than they could by participating in the Series.

Judge Landis expressly warned Ruth and the others who were to join him not to go on the tour. Carl Mays and Wally Schang backed down; but the Babe, Meusel, and Piercy (as well as former Yankee Tom Sheehan) did not. The Yankee owners were unable to either convince or pay off Ruth to cancel the tour. After his Red Sox had won the World Series back in 1916, Ruth did barnstorm. He was fined a mere $100, and his World Series ornament was withheld.[11] Sportswriter Gene Fowler noted, "Mr. Ruth always made his own rules. Rather, he had but one rule: never to go halfway in anything, on or off the baseball diamond."[12]

But 1921 was not 1916. Landis may have understood that the rule was unfair, but it was the law. And so was he. One has to wonder what advice Ruth's agent, Christy Walsh, gave him on this matter. Perhaps the Babe knew what he was doing in taking on the commissioner. He expected to earn at least $1,000 per game, more than enough to cover a fine. The lines were drawn. Leigh Montville wrote in his Ruth biography that the Babe "had not been told no in a long time," while Landis "was an expert in saying no."[13]

Public opinion quickly moved toward Landis's position. Damon Runyon's comments were typical. "The issue is Ruth or Landis and the authority of baseball, and it is not conceivable that Ruth can prevail in such an encounter. . . . Even prima donnas must realize that there are limits beyond which they cannot go."[14] Joe Vila probably relished seeing the Babe on the wrong side of the issue: "Mr. Ruth, once glorified, has come to a realization of what it means to have public sentiment lined up almost solidly against him."[15]

Well before the end of the tour and the end of October, Ruth called it off; and Yankee co-owner Til Huston paid off the promoters. Ruth cancelled the rest of the tour in part because the weather was miserable, in part because Minor League teams would not furnish their ballparks for the tour's games after Landis had threatened them, and perhaps in part because the Babe now realized which way the wind was blowing. But it was too late. In early December, Landis announced his decision, fining the players their withheld World Series shares and suspending them until May 20, 1922.[16] (Apparently, they eventually got their World Series money, $3,362 each.)[17] Landis framed the matter as "a mutinous defiance intended by the players to present the question: who is the bigger—baseball, or any individual in baseball?"[18]

Yet the real issue may have been who was bigger, Ruth or Landis. Syndicated columnist Robert Edgren went further and called Landis's pronouncement "bunk." In 1921, as had been the case for many years, he wrote, "business has been bigger than the game. . . . 'The game' has been purely a commercial proposition, not a sporting proposition at all."[19]

Landis's consolidation of power was now complete. He would modify the barnstorming ban the following year.[20] As for the Babe, he now had limits placed on his behavior. He would still do very well financially during the offseason. Walsh had booked Ruth for a four-month vaudeville tour at $3,000 a week.[21] However, the Yankees would not fare as well. Dan Daniel wrote, "There were many who believed that Judge Landis had done nothing less than assess the Yankees one perfectly good pennant [in 1922]."[22] Without Ruth drawing fans into the ballparks, American League teams, especially the Yankees, would suffer a substantial loss of gate receipts totaling hundreds of thousands of dollars.

Circumstances (and his personality) continued to prevent Miller Huggins from dealing with the Babe as decisively as Landis had done. In late October, newspapers wrote that Huggins was seriously ill with tonsillitis. Hugh Fullerton noted at the time, "Huggins was a very sick man during much of the season this year, and his management was handicapped by this fact."[23] One report went so far as to say that during his illness, "in his delirium, Huggins is said to have fought over again the losing battles of the world's series, 'managing' the club from his bed."[24] Rumors swirled that either White Sox manager Kid Gleason or his star second baseman Eddie Collins would take over as the Yankees'

53. After the season, the Giants traded longtime fan favorite George Burns to Cincinnati for Heinie Groh (seen here with his wife, Ruby, at the 1922 World Series). Judge Landis had vetoed the trade of Groh to the Giants during the season but allowed this one to go through. *Culver Pictures.*

manager for 1922.[25] In mid-December many were surprised and some were disappointed when the Yankees announced that Miller Huggins had been signed to manage the team for the 1922 season.

As Christmas approached, the two best teams in baseball took big steps toward becoming even stronger than they were in 1921. John McGraw struck first with a dramatic double stroke. "McGraw . . . is on the rampage and no one may assume to predict his limits," wrote Dan Daniel.[26] Despite Johnny Rawlings's terrific play in the Series, McGraw finally acquired Cincinnati star third baseman Heinie Groh. In return, McGraw had to part with veteran outfielder George Burns, seldom-used catcher Mike Gonzalez, and a substantial amount of cash.[27]

Sam Crane described Burns, a longtime Polo Grounds favorite, as "beloved as no other player has been since Christy Mathewson." Sid Mercer, Crane's colleague at the *New York Evening Journal*, noted the poignancy of a situation that required such a wonderful player as Burns to be "sold down the river as a crowning reward for ten years of faithful service to his New York club."[28]

A month earlier the Cardinals' Branch Rickey had declared that the sale of Groh to the Giants "would be one of the worst crimes ever committed against baseball."[29] Yet the teams that were screaming the loudest, the Cardinals and the Cubs, had themselves been trying hard to land the Reds' third baseman. Judge Landis had canceled the trade of Groh to the Giants earlier in the year. This time he had no objections.

The arrival of Groh meant that Frankie Frisch would move back to second base in 1922. Rawlings would be relegated to the bench. Yet despite the demotion, Rawlings reflected the fierce loyalty McGraw's players felt toward their leader (as well as, perhaps, toward the likelihood of more World Series checks). "Yes, I expect to sit on the bench next season, and I don't care where I play or where I sit so long as I'm playing or sitting for McGraw."[30]

The next day, McGraw announced that the Giants had acquired Coast League star Jimmy O'Connell from the San Francisco Seals for $75,000. In acquiring the twenty-year-old (who would stay with the Seals for one more season), McGraw was getting a man who hit for average (.337 in 1921) and had both power and speed (seventeen home runs and twenty-three stolen bases in 1921). Sam Crane wrote that McGraw may have acquired an "embryo Sultan of Swat."[31]

Just two weeks later the Yankees engineered a major deal of their own. Again, it was with the Red Sox. They sent their captain and World Series goat, Roger Peckinpaugh, along with pitchers Jack Quinn, Bill Piercy, and Rip Collins to Boston for another fine shortstop, Everett Scott, and two of the league's best pitchers in 1921, Joe Bush and Sam Jones. Huggins seemed to have addressed his team's pitching weakness, doubling his number of dependable starters from two to four in one move.[32]

At thirty-eight, Quinn appeared to be at the end of the line. No one remotely foresaw that he would win 122 more Major League games in a career that would run until he would turn fifty. The most that could be said about Piercy and Collins was that they had "potential." Although they were "endowed with exceptional natural talents," they were "temperamentally lacking."[33] Meanwhile, Jones and Bush, both of whom were twenty-eight years old, had respectively won twenty-three and sixteen games for the fifth-place Red Sox in 1921.

Scott for Peckinpaugh brought the Yankees a younger, better-fielding shortstop in exchange for a better-hitting one. Despite the fact that

Huggins said that Red Sox owner Harry Frazee had insisted on getting Peckinpaugh, his departure was "not to be mourned by Huggins."[34] More than a half century later, Peckinpaugh explained, "The Babe was openly knocking Huggins down as manager and boosting me to be manager of the club. He made no bones about it. During the winter they got rid of me."[35]

Then there was *the error.* As Monitor explained in his column in the *New York World*, after the Yankees' shortstop had booted Ross Youngs's ground ball in the first inning of Game 8, it rolled no more than fifty feet away.[36] Dave Bancroft was still thirty feet from third base. Peckinpaugh could have easily held him at third or thrown him out at home, had Bancroft tried to score. Instead, he just stood there in disgust.

While in no way questioning the integrity of the Yankee captain, Monitor continued, "From inside sources, it is learned that 'Peck' practically fired himself. He has been on the baseball market since the evening of Oct. 13, 1921. One play, one disastrous lapse in one crowded half second ended the career of Peckinpaugh with the Yankees. . . . I have talked to dozens of players, managers, sporting writers and oldtime baseball men since the game and they all agree on the same thing—that Peckinpaugh had a chance to retrieve himself, to make a wonderful play, which should be expected of a Captain of a World's Series team."[37]

Howls of outrage that the New York teams were cornering the market on talent and "buying" the pennants rolled across the country. John McGraw added fuel to the controversy. After spending a fortune on two deals in two days, he announced, "We are ready to purchase any player who looks as if he could help us win another pennant next season. . . . The fans of New York want the best there is—they are entitled to it."[38]

Damon Runyon noted a reality of baseball, that it takes two willing partners to consummate a trade. Club owners "have made a practice of selling off their best ball players for fat prices, then assembling clubs of low-priced, low-salaried players."[39] Runyon's observation gave New York writers ammunition to defend the actions of their teams. George Daley explained, "So long as they put a price on players, so long will these players go to the highest bidder. . . . If not the Giants then some other club would have paid a price only slightly less."[40]

Sid Keener, sports editor of the *St. Louis Times*, gave a very different perspective, speaking on behalf of the fans of long-suffering, uncompetitive teams. "It may be said that both New York teams 'bought their pennants,' but for the fans isn't it better to buy and win than not to buy and lose?"[41]

During the 1921 holiday season, John McGraw must have felt that he was sitting on top of the world. He had won the World Series, vanquishing the Yankees while handcuffing their slugger, the mighty Ruth. Moreover, he had pushed the Yankees out of the Polo Grounds by refusing to renew their lease beyond 1922. This would give him total control of the great ballpark, including many more lucrative Sunday playing dates. McGraw, who would prove to be a better manager than prognosticator, said, "They'll have to build a park in Long Island City or the far edges of the Bronx. They'll starve to death wherever they go."[42]

Yet with the growth of New York City and the corresponding expansion of the subway system, the Bronx was evolving and growing. "As a demographer, McGraw was stuck at the turn of the century."[43] Years later Jacob Ruppert would say, "Yankee Stadium was a mistake. Not my mistake, but the New York Giants."[44] Arthur Daley put it both simply and bluntly by suggesting that McGraw "never made a more egregious blunder in his life."[45] Even *Baseball Magazine* saw what McGraw did not see. In a pair of 1921 editorials, the monthly wrote, "In New York, at least, baseball has not only outgrown the 40,000 stage, but has already entered upon an era of expansion where crowds of fifty or even sixty thousand would not be a rarity," calling the construction of the Polo Grounds in 1911, "a forward-looking move that seemed radical to the point of rashness only yesterday . . . conservative and inadequate today."[46]

A small, one-paragraph article appeared in many papers on December 17, 1921, noting that the last obstacle to the construction of the Yankees' stadium had been removed. The New York City Board of Aldermen had approved the Yanks' plans to close a road that ran through the site. Charles Stoneham and John McGraw had more than met their match with the Tammany connections of Jacob Ruppert and Til Huston. Yankee Stadium would become a much bigger and more impressive ballpark than the Polo Grounds. "Ruppert knew he had to build a playpen large enough and dramatic enough to exhibit his performers," wrote Ray Robinson and Christopher Jennison in their book on the stadium. "He was aware, too, that a bountiful postwar economy and an increasing acceptance of Sunday baseball underlined the need for a large park."[47]

The Giants would repeat as world champions in 1922 in even more impressive fashion. They would beat the Yankees in the World Series in just five games, four wins and a tie (a game called because of darkness), as the Series returned to a best-of-seven format.[48] After a healthy Ruth hit only .118 in that Series, Joe Vila declared the Babe was "the biggest kind of bust. . . . The Exploded Phenomenon didn't surprise the smart fans, who long ago realized that he couldn't hit brainy pitching."[49]

Yet the Yankees were steadily laying the groundwork for the stronger franchise, both on and off the field. They were developing an organization that was ahead of its time. They had Ed Barrow for a skilled business manager—a position separate from that of field manager—and an ownership that removed itself from the day-to-day running of the club. As Henry Fetter has noted in *Taking on the Yankees*, "Stoneham made money from his team, but Ruppert built a dynasty."[50]

During the decade of the 1920s, the Giants would earn $2 million, distribute $1.5 million in dividends, and pay off a $280,000 loan. The Yankees would earn $3 million and pay out not a penny in dividends.[51] Instead, the Yankees plowed the money back into the franchise by building the new stadium and acquiring top Minor League prospects. All this occurred while Prohibition was severely curtailing Ruppert's primary source of income outside of baseball, his brewery. The dry law was still the law of the land, as it would be for another dozen years. In less than two years, it had dramatically undercut respect for the law and generated growth in the black market for liquor.

When Yankee Stadium opened in April 1923, Will Wedge of the *New York Globe and Commercial Advertiser* wrote, "The Broadway of the theatres sets the standard of the town in only having eyes and attention and attendance for a 'hit.' An out and out 'winner' is the town's only love."[52] The Yankees would finally win their first world championship that year, beating the Giants in six games. Ruth would hit .368 with three home runs, and Heywood Broun would write his memorable line, "The Ruth is mighty and shall prevail."[53] While McGraw's Giants would win a fourth straight pennant in 1924, it would be his last and the Giants' last until 1933, a few months before McGraw's death. The

Yankees, led by Ruth and managed by Huggins, would win three more pennants and two World Series in the late 1920s.

The Dodgers—geographically the third New York team, though never regarded as such by most of the denizens of Manhattan or Brooklyn—would fade to the second division. With the exception of a late rush in 1924 that would fall just short of the pennant (won by the Giants), that is where they would remain for most of the next two decades. A year after they finally reconciled, both John McGraw and Dodgers manager Wilbert Robinson would complete their last full season at the helms of their respective clubs in 1931. The Dodgers would not capture another National League pennant until 1941.

In January 1924, after the New York teams had captured three straight World Series, an editorial in *Baseball Magazine* took note of the anti–New York feeling across the country. While stating that the New York clubs had done "nothing dishonorable," the monthly wrote, "The Big City is unpopular elsewhere on the circuits because it is the Big City. Furthermore, the fans in other towns, whether rightly or wrongly, see in the continued domination of New York, the clear cut shadow of the dollar sign. The New York Clubs are the wealthiest. Therefore they can pay the most money. Therefore they get the best players. Therefore they win. . . . But the general welfare of the Major Leagues as a whole seems to require a keener competition than the New York Clubs have recently encountered."[54]

By 1927 Miller Huggins was making statements remarkably similar to McGraw's comments of 1921: "It is our desire to have a pennant winner each year indefinitely. New York fans want championship ball, and the Yankees can be counted on to provide it. We are prepared to outbid other clubs for young players of quality."[55] The Yankees would meet and defeat the Giants again in 1936 and 1937, long after Huggins had passed from the scene, and again in 1951, continuing their dominance of the national pastime. Moreover, the Giants had already lost the attendance war and would never again seriously challenge the Yankees at the gate. Marshall Smelser wrote of the irony: "John McGraw had brought Huston and Ruppert together and advised them to buy the Yankees. Together they built a team that humbled McGraw."[56]

The ascendancy of the Yankees over the Giants also signaled their rise, and that of New York City, to the top of the baseball world. In

1921 New York had its first world championship in sixteen years. In the next sixteen, the city would have eight more championships; and the Yankees would win six of them. Once regarded as New York's "other team," the Yankees would remain preeminent for much of the twentieth century.

Appendix 1   1921 Yankees and Giants Regular Season Batting and Pitching

1921 NEW YORK YANKEES REGULAR SEASON BATTING

	G	AB	R	H	2B	3B	HR	RBI	BB	SO	HBP	SH	SB	CS	AVG	OBP	SLG
Frank Baker	94	330	46	97	16	2	9	71	26	12	4	9	8	5	.294	.353	.436
Ping Bodie	31	87	5	15	2	2	0	12	8	8	0	2	0	1	.172	.242	.241
Rip Collins	28	56	4	11	0	1	0	6	3	18	0	2	0	0	.196	.237	.232
Tom Connelly	4	5	0	1	0	0	0	0	1	0	0	0	0	0	.200	.333	.200
Al DeVormer	22	49	6	17	4	0	0	7	2	4	0	2	2	0	.347	.373	.429
Alex Ferguson	19	19	1	4	0	0	0	2	0	5	0	0	0	0	.211	.211	.211
Chick Fewster	66	207	44	58	19	0	1	19	28	43	6	7	4	4	.280	.382	.386
Harry Harper	8	16	1	2	0	0	0	1	1	4	0	0	0	0	.125	.176	.125
Chicken Hawks	41	73	16	21	2	3	2	15	5	12	0	1	0	1	.288	.333	.479
Fred Hofmann	23	62	7	11	1	1	1	5	5	13	1	0	0	0	.177	.250	.274
Waite Hoyt	43	99	8	22	1	1	0	7	2	17	0	9	0	0	.222	.238	.253
Carl Mays	51	143	18	49	5	1	2	22	4	7	1	8	0	0	.343	.365	.434
Mike McNally	71	215	36	56	4	2	1	24	14	15	0	11	5	6	.260	.306	.312
Bob Meusel	149	598	104	190	40	16	24	136	34	**88**	2	12	17	6	.318	.356	.559
Elmer Miller	56	242	41	72	9	8	4	36	19	16	3	6	2	2	.298	.356	.450
Johnny Mitchell	13	42	4	11	1	0	0	2	4	4	0	1	1	0	.262	.326	.286
Roger Peckinpaugh	149	577	128	166	25	7	8	71	84	44	2	33	2	2	.288	.380	.397
Bill Piercy	14	28	2	6	2	0	0	2	1	7	2	0	0	0	.214	.290	.286
Wally Pipp	153	588	96	174	35	9	8	98	45	28	1	33	17	10	.296	.347	.427
Jack Quinn	33	41	4	9	2	0	1	4	3	9	0	2	0	0	.220	.273	.341
Tom Rogers	6	3	1	1	1	0	0	0	0	0	0	0	0	0	.333	.333	.667
Braggo Roth	43	152	29	43	9	2	2	10	19	20	2	3	1	2	.283	.370	.408
Babe Ruth	152	540	**177**	204	44	16	**59**	171	145	81	4	4	17	13	.378	**.512**	**.846**
Wally Schang	134	424	77	134	30	5	6	55	78	35	5	6	7	4	.316	.428	.453
Bob Shawkey	38	90	13	27	2	1	1	11	2	13	0	8	0	0	.300	.315	.378
Tom Sheehan	13	8	3	5	0	0	0	1	0	0	0	2	0	0	.625	.625	.625
Aaron Ward	153	556	77	170	30	10	5	75	42	68	8	29	6	8	.306	.363	.423
Total	153	5250	**948**	1576	284	87	**134**	863	575	571	41	190	89	64	.300	.374	**.464**

Bold numbers indicate league leader. Source: Retrosheet

1921 NEW YORK YANKEES REGULAR SEASON PITCHING

	G	GS	CG	SHO	GF	SV	IP	H	BFP	HR	R	ER	BB	SO	SH	WP	HBP	BK	W	L	ERA
Rip Collins	28	16	7	2	4	0	137.1	158	641	6	103	83	78	64	14	6	10	0	11	5	5.44
Alex Ferguson	17	4	1	0	7	1	56.1	64	258	4	40	37	27	9	11	1	4	0	3	1	5.91
Harry Harper	8	7	4	0	1	0	52.2	52	235	3	23	22	25	22	10	4	2	0	4	3	3.76
Waite Hoyt	43	32	21	1	7	3	282.1	301	1201	3	121	97	81	102	25	3	5	1	19	13	3.09
Carl Mays	**49**	38	30	1	10	**7**	**336.2**	332	1400	11	145	114	76	70	22	2	9	0	**27**	9	3.05
Bill Piercy	14	10	5	1	3	0	81.2	82	354	4	40	27	28	35	7	3	7	1	5	4	2.98
Jack Quinn	33	13	6	0	7	0	119	158	542	2	61	50	32	44	22	2	5	0	8	7	3.78
Tom Rogers	5	0	0	0	5	1	11	12	53	1	9	9	9	0	3	0	1	0	0	1	7.36
Babe Ruth	2	1	0	0	1	0	9	14	49	1	10	9	9	2	0	0	0	0	2	0	9.00
Bob Shawkey	38	31	18	3	6	2	245	245	1053	15	131	111	86	126	27	2	7	1	18	12	4.08
Tom Sheehan	12	1	0	0	9	1	33	43	154	1	23	20	19	7	2	0	1	0	1	0	5.45
Total	153	153	**92**	8	60	15	1364	**1461**	5940	51	706	579	470	**481**	143	23	51	3	98	55	**3.82**

Bold numbers indicate league leader. Source: Retrosheet

Appendix 1 *1921 Yankees and Giants Regular Season Batting and Pitching*

1921 NEW YORK GIANTS REGULAR SEASON BATTING

	G	AB	R	H	2B	3B	HR	RBI	BB	SO	HBP	SH	SB	CS	AVG	OBP	SLG
Dave Bancroft	153	606	121	193	26	15	6	67	66	23	4	22	17	10	.318	.389	.441
Jesse Barnes	42	92	8	19	0	1	0	6	3	3	0	4	1	2	.207	.232	.228
Rube Benton	18	21	1	3	1	0	0	1	1	4	0	2	0	0	.143	.182	.190
Joe Berry	9	6	0	2	0	1	0	2	1	1	0	0	0	0	.333	.429	.667
Eddie Brown	70	128	16	36	6	2	0	12	4	11	4	3	1	0	.281	.324	.359
George Burns	149	605	111	181	28	9	4	61	**80**	24	6	7	19	20	.299	.386	.395
Red Causey	9	3	1	1	0	0	0	0	0	0	0	0	0	0	.333	.333	.333
Joe Connolly	2	4	0	0	0	0	0	0	1	1	0	0	0	0	.000	.200	.000
Bill Cunningham	40	76	10	21	2	1	1	12	3	3	1	3	0	1	.276	.313	.368
Phil Douglas	40	81	7	16	2	0	1	10	3	12	0	5	1	0	.198	.226	.259
Frankie Frisch	153	618	121	211	31	17	8	100	42	28	1	26	**49**	13	.341	.384	.485
Alex Gaston	20	22	1	5	1	1	0	3	1	9	0	0	0	0	.227	.261	.364
Mike Gonzalez	13	24	3	9	1	0	0	0	1	0	0	2	0	0	.375	.400	.417
Bud Heine	1	2	0	0	0	0	0	0	0	0	0	0	0	0	.000	.000	.000
Butch Henline	1	1	0	0	0	0	0	0	0	1	0	0	0	0	.000	.000	.000
Claude Jonnard	1	1	0	0	0	0	0	0	0	1	0	0	0	0	.000	.000	.000
George Kelly	149	587	95	181	42	9	**23**	122	40	73	3	17	4	12	.308	.356	.528
Lee King	39	94	17	21	4	2	0	7	13	6	1	2	0	2	.223	.324	.309
Wally Kopf	2	3	0	1	0	0	0	0	1	1	0	0	0	0	.333	.500	.333
Jim Mahady	1	0	0	0	0	0	0	0	0	0	0	0	0	0	-	-	-
Irish Meusel	62	243	37	80	12	6	2	36	15	12	2	4	5	9	.329	.373	.453
John Monroe	19	21	4	3	0	0	1	3	3	6	1	0	0	0	.143	.280	.286
Art Nehf	42	89	9	18	2	0	0	5	7	10	0	8	0	0	.202	.260	.225
Pat Patterson	23	35	5	14	0	0	1	5	2	5	0	0	0	1	.400	.432	.486
Pol Perritt	5	3	0	0	0	0	0	0	0	2	0	0	0	0	.000	.000	.000
Goldie Rapp	58	181	21	39	9	1	0	15	15	13	0	7	3	11	.215	.276	.276
Johnny Rawlings	86	307	40	82	8	1	1	30	18	19	4	13	4	4	.267	.316	.309
Rosy Ryan	36	45	2	9	1	0	0	1	5	11	0	3	0	1	.200	.280	.222
Slim Sallee	37	22	2	8	1	0	0	0	0	2	0	4	0	0	.364	.364	.409
Hank Schreiber	4	6	2	2	0	0	0	2	1	1	0	0	0	0	.333	.429	.333
Pat Shea	9	9	0	1	0	0	0	1	0	2	0	0	0	0	.111	.111	.111
Earl Smith	89	229	35	77	8	4	10	51	27	8	1	4	4	3	.336	.409	.537
Frank Snyder	108	309	38	99	13	2	8	45	27	24	4	4	3	4	.320	.382	.453
Casey Stengel	18	22	4	5	1	0	0	2	1	5	0	0	0	1	.227	.261	.273
Fred Toney	42	86	11	18	1	0	3	12	2	13	0	1	1	0	.209	.227	.326
Curt Walker	64	192	30	55	13	5	3	35	15	8	0	7	4	3	.286	.338	.453
Ross Youngs	141	504	90	165	24	16	3	102	71	47	1	18	21	17	.327	.411	.456
Walter Zink	2	1	0	0	0	0	0	0	0	1	0	0	0	0	.000	.000	.000
Total	153	5278	**840**	1575	237	93	75	748	**469**	390	33	166	137	114	.298	.359	.421

Bold numbers indicate league leader. Source: Retrosheet

1921 NEW YORK GIANTS REGULAR SEASON PITCHING

	G	GS	CG	SHO	GF	SV	IP	H	BFP	HR	R	ER	BB	SO	SH	WP	HBP	BK	W	L	ERA
Jesse Barnes	42	31	15	1	6	6	258.2	298	1076	13	108	89	44	56	34	2	3	0	15	9	3.10
Rube Benton	18	9	3	1	4	0	72	72	297	2	28	23	17	11	9	2	0	0	5	2	2.88
Red Causey	7	1	0	0	6	0	14.2	13	65	0	8	4	6	1	2	0	0	0	1	1	2.45
Phil Douglas	40	27	13	**3**	7	2	221.2	266	956	17	119	104	55	55	35	4	2	1	15	10	4.22
Claude Jonnard	1	0	0	0	1	1	4	4	15	0	0	0	0	7	0	0	0	0	0	0	0.00
Art Nehf	41	34	18	2	5	1	260.2	266	1067	**18**	116	105	55	67	30	5	2	0	20	10	3.63
Pol Perritt	5	1	0	0	3	0	11.2	17	56	0	9	5	2	5	1	0	0	0	2	0	3.86
Rosy Ryan	36	16	5	0	14	3	147.1	140	597	6	72	61	32	58	15	3	1	0	7	10	3.73
Slim Sallee	37	0	0	0	19	2	96.1	115	405	7	48	39	14	23	17	0	0	0	6	4	3.64
Pat Shea	9	2	1	0	4	0	32	28	125	2	13	11	2	10	3	0	3	0	5	2	3.09
Fred Toney	42	32	16	1	9	3	249.1	274	1054	14	112	100	65	63	38	4	4	1	18	11	3.61
Walter Zink	2	0	0	0	1	0	4	4	21	0	3	1	3	1	1	1	0	0	0	0	2.25
Total	153	153	71	9	79	**18**	1372.1	1497	5734	79	636	542	**295**	357	185	21	15	2	94	59	3.55

Bold numbers indicate league leader. Source: Retrosheet

AMERICAN LEAGUE BATTING LEADERS—1921

GAMES	PLATE APPEARANCES	AT BATS
155 Jimmy Dykes PHI	731 Jack Tobin STL	671 Jack Tobin STL
154 Six players	726 Whitey Witt PHI	629 Whitey Witt PHI
	715 Joe Judge WAS	622 Joe Judge WAS
	709 Lu Blue DET	613 Jimmy Dykes PHI
		613 Ernie Johnson CHI

RUNS	HITS	DOUBLES
177 Babe Ruth NY	237 Harry Heilmann DET	52 Tris Speaker CLE
132 Jack Tobin STL	236 Jack Tobin STL	**44 Babe Ruth NY**
128 Roger Peckinpaugh NY	216 George Sisler STL	43 Harry Heilmann DET
125 George Sisler STL	211 Baby Doll Jacobson STL	43 Bobby Veach DET
124 Ty Cobb	207 Bobby Veach DET	**40 Bob Meusel NY**

TRIPLES	HOME RUNS	RUNS BATTED IN
18 Howard Shanks WAS	**59 Babe Ruth NY**	**171 Babe Ruth NY**
18 George Sisler STL	**24 Bob Meusel NY**	139 Harry Heilmann DET
18 Jack Tobin STL	24 Ken Williams STL	**136 Bob Meusel NY**
16 Three players	23 Tilly Walker PHI	128 Bobby Veach DET
	19 Harry Heilmann DET	120 Larry Gardner CLE

WALKS	STRIKEOUTS	HIT BY PITCH
145 Babe Ruth NY	**88 Bob Meusel NY**	18 Bucky Harris WAS
103 Lu Blue DET	**81 Babe Ruth NY**	15 Jimmy Dykes PHI
84 Roger Peckinpaugh NY	75 Jimmy Dykes PHI	13 Johnny Mostil CHI
80 Joe Sewell CLE	69 Bibb Falk CHI	11 Joe Sewell CLE

SACRIFICE HITS	STOLEN BASES	BATTING AVERAGE
43 Bill Wambsganss CLE	35 George Sisler STL	.394 Harry Heilmann DET
41 Donie Bush DET-WAS	29 Bucky Harris WAS	.389 Ty Cobb DET
35 Stuffy McInnis BOS	25 Sam Rice WAS	**.378 Babe Ruth NY**
34 Eddie Mulligan CHI	22 Ty Cobb DET	.371 George Sisler STL
	22 Ernie Johnson CHI	.362 Tris Speaker

ON BASE PERCENTAGE	SLUGGING AVERAGE	ON BASE PLUS SLUGGING
.512 Babe Ruth NY	**.846 Babe Ruth NY**	**1.359 Babe Ruth NY**
.452 Ty Cobb DET	.606 Harry Heilmann DET	1.051 Harry Heilmann DET
.444 Harry Heilmann DET	.596 Ty Cobb DET	1.048 Ty Cobb DET
.439 Tris Speaker CLE	.561 Ken Williams STL	.990 Ken Williams STL
.429 Ken Williams STL	.560 George Sisler STL	.977 Tris Speaker

TOTAL BASES
457 Babe Ruth NY
365 Harry Heilmann DET
334 Bob Meusel NY
327 Jack Tobin STL
326 George Sisler STL

Bold entries indicate Yankee players. Source: Gillette and Palmer, *The ESPN Baseball Encyclopedia*, 5th ed.; and Retrosheet

AMERICAN LEAGUE PITCHING LEADERS—1921

GAMES	GAMES STARTED	COMPLETE GAMES
49 Carl Mays NY	40 Stan Coveleski CLE	32 Red Faber CHI
47 Bill Bayne STL	39 Red Faber CHI	**30 Carl Mays NY**
47 Urban Shocker STL	38 Sam Jones BOS	30 Urban Shocker STL
46 Eddie Rommel PHI	**38 Carl Mays NY**	28 Stan Coveleski STL
	38 Urban Shocker STL	

SHUTOUTS	GAMES FINISHED	SAVES
5 Sam Jones BOS	21 Bill Burwell STL	**7 Carl Mays NY**
4 Red Faber CHI	20 Jim Middleton DET	7 Jim Middleton DET
4 George Mogridge WAS	20 Allan Russell BOS	4 Four players
4 Urban Shocker STL	18 Three players	

WINS	WINNING PERCENTAGE	INNINGS PITCHED
27 Carl Mays NY	**.750 Carl Mays NY**	**336.2 Carl Mays NY**
27 Urban Shocker STL	.692 Urban Shocker STL	330.2 Red Faber CHI
25 Red Faber CHI	.640 Joe Bush BOS	326.2 Urban Shocker STL
23 Stan Coveleski CLE	.639 Stan Coveleski CLE	315.0 Stan Coveleski CLE
23 Sam Jones BOS	.625 Red Faber CHI	308.2 Dickie Kerr CHI

FEWEST HITS PER GAME	FEWEST WALKS PER GAME	STRIKEOUTS
7.97 Red Faber CHI	2.01 Bob Hasty PHI	143 Walter Johnson WAS
8.63 Joe Bush BOS	**2.03 Carl Mays NY**	132 Urban Shocker STL
8.88 Carl Mays NY	2.06 George Mogridge WAS	**126 Bob Shawkey NY**
9.00 Bob Shawkey NY	2.07 Jim Bagby CLE	124 Red Faber CHI
9.03 Walter Johnson WAS	2.12 Tom Zachary WAS	120 Dutch Leonard DET

OPPONENTS BATTING AVERAGE	OPPONENTS ON BASE PERCENTAGE	EARNED RUN AVERAGE
.242 Red Faber CHI	.297 Red Faber CHI	2.48 Red Faber CHI
.257 Carl Mays NY	**.303 Carl Mays NY**	3.00 George Mogridge WAS
.260 Joe Bush BOS	.313 George Mogridge WAS	**3.05 Carl Mays NY**
.263 Bob Shawkey NY	.319 Urban Shocker STL	**3.09 Waite Hoyt NY**
.263 Walter Johnson WAS	.326 Walter Johnson WAS	3.22 Sam Jones BOS

Bold entries indicate Yankee players. Source: Gillette and Palmer, *The* ESPN *Baseball Encyclopedia,* 5th ed.; and Retrosheet

NATIONAL LEAGUE BATTING LEADERS—1921

GAMES	PLATE APPEARANCES	AT BATS
154 Rogers Hornsby STL	699 Ray Powell BOS	652 Ivy Olson BRO
153 Five players	**698 Dave Bancroft NY**	632 Carson Bigbee PIT
	698 George Burns NY	624 Jimmy Johnston BRO
	695 Ivy Olson BRO	624 Ray Powell BOS

RUNS	HITS	DOUBLES
131 Rogers Hornsby STL	235 Rogers Hornsby STL	44 Rogers Hornsby STL
121 Dave Bancroft NY	**211 Frankie Frisch NY**	**42 George Kelly NY**
121 Frankie Frisch NY	204 Carson Bigbee PIT	41 Jimmy Johnston BRO
114 Ray Powell BOS	203 Jimmy Johnston BRO	38 Ray Grimes CHI
111 George Burns NY	201 Austin McHenry STL	37 Austin McHenry STL

TRIPLES	HOME RUNS	RUNS BATTED IN
18 Rogers Hornsby STL	**23 George Kelly NY**	126 Rogers Hornsby STL
18 Ray Powell BOS	21 Rogers Hornsby STL	**122 George Kelly NY**
17 Carson Bigbee PIT	18 Cy Williams PHI	102 Austin McHenry STL
17 Frankie Frisch NY	17 Austin McHenry STL	**102 Ross Youngs NY**
17 Charlie Grimm PIT	16 Jack Fournier STL	**100 Frankie Frisch NY**

WALKS	STRIKEOUTS	HIT BY PITCH
80 George Burns NY	85 Ray Powell BOS	8 Jack Fournier STL
71 Ross Youngs NY	81 Frank Parkinson PHI	7 Rogers Hornsby STL
70 Max Carey PIT	**73 George Kelly NY**	6 Five players
70 Ray Grimes CHI	55 Ray Grimes CHI	
66 Dave Bancroft NY		

SACRIFICE HITS	STOLEN BASES	BATTING AVERAGE
36 Milt Stock STL	**49 Frankie Frisch NY**	.458 Rogers Hornsby STL
35 Billy Southworth BOS	37 Max Carey PIT	.352 Edd Roush STL
34 Bill Terry CHI	28 Jimmy Johnston BRO	.350 Austin McHenry STL
33 Jake Daubert CIN	26 Sammy Bohne CIN	.346 Walton Cruise BOS
		.343 Jack Fournier STL
		.343 Irish Meusel PHI-NY

ON BASE PERCENTAGE	SLUGGING AVERAGE	ON BASE PLUS SLUGGING
.458 Rogers Hornsby STL	.639 Rogers Hornsby STL	1.097 Rogers Hornsby STL
.411 Ross Youngs NY	.531 Austin McHenry STL	.924 Austin McHenry STL
.409 Jack Fournier STL	**.528 George Kelly NY**	.914 Jack Fournier STL
.406 Ray Grimes CHI	**.515 Irish Meusel PHI-NY**	**.895 Irish Meusel PHI-NY**
.395 Max Carey PIT	.512 Les Mann STL	**.884 George Kelly NY**

TOTAL BASES

378 Rogers Hornsby STL
310 George Kelly NY
305 Austin McHenry STL
302 Irish Meusel PHI-NY
300 Frankie Frisch NY

Bold entries indicate Giants players. Source: Gillette and Palmer, *The ESPN Baseball Encyclopedia*, 5th ed.; and Retrosheet

NATIONAL LEAGUE PITCHING LEADERS—1921

GAMES	GAMES STARTED	COMPLETE GAMES
47 Jack Scott BOS	38 Wilbur Cooper PIT	30 Burleigh Grimes BRO
46 Joe Oeschger BOS	37 Eppa Rixey CIN	29 Wilbur Cooper PIT
45 Hugh McQuillan BOS	36 Dolf Luque CIN	25 Dolf Luque CIN
44 Dana Fillingim BOS	36 Rube Marquard CIN	21 Three players
44 Mule Watson BOS	36 Joe Oeschger BOS	

SHUTOUTS	GAMES FINISHED	SAVES
3 Eight players	26 Lou North STL	7 Lou North STL
	22 Huck Betts PHI	6 **Jesse Barnes NY**
	19 Hal Carlson PIT	5 Hugh McQuillan BOS
	19 Slim Sallee NY	4 Four players

WINS	WINNING PERCENTAGE	INNINGS PITCHED
22 Wilbur Cooper PIT	.714 Bill Doak STL	327.0 Wilbur Cooper PIT
22 Burleigh Grimes BRO	**.667 Art Nehf NY**	304.0 Dolf Luque CIN
20 Art Nehf NY	.629 Burleigh Grimes BRO	302.1 Burleigh Grimes BRO
20 Joe Oeschger BOS	**.625 Jesse Barnes NY**	301.0 Eppa Rixey CIN
19 Eppa Rixey CIN	**.621 Fred Toney NY**	299.0 Joe Oeschger BOS

FEWEST HITS PER GAME	FEWEST WALKS PER GAME	STRIKEOUTS
8.23 Whitey Glazner PIT	1.01 Babe Adams PIT	136 Burleigh Grimes BRO
8.72 Babe Adams PIT	1.18 Grover Alexander CHI	134 Wilbur Cooper PIT
9.12 Joe Oeschger BOS	**1.53 Jesse Barnes NY**	102 Dolf Luque CIN
9.16 Bill Pertica STL	1.55 Bill Hubbell PHI	94 Hugh McQuillan BOS
9.18 Art Nehf NY	1.60 Bill Doak STL	

OPPONENTS BATTING AVERAGE	OPPONENTS ON BASE PERCENTAGE	EARNED RUN AVERAGE
.250 Whitey Glazner PIT	.272 Babe Adams PIT	2.59 Bill Doak STL
.251 Babe Adams PIT	.306 Whitey Glazner PIT	2.64 Babe Adams PIT
.267 Bill Pertica STL	**.311 Art Nehf NY**	2.77 Whitey Glazner PIT
.270 Mule Watson BOS	.312 Dolf Luque CIN	2.78 Eppa Rixey CIN
.271 Art Nehf NY	.313 Bill Doak STL	2.83 Burleigh Grimes BRO

Bold entries indicate Giants players. Source: Gillette and Palmer, *The* ESPN *Baseball Encyclopedia,* 5th ed.; and Retrosheet

Appendix 3   *1921 World Series Box Scores*

WORLD SERIES GAME 1, WEDNESDAY, OCTOBER 5, 1921

NEW YORK YANKEES

	AB	R	H	PO	A	E
Miller cf	4	1	1	0	0	0
Peckinpaugh ss	3	1	1	1	9	0
Ruth lf	3	0	1	4	0	0
B. Meusel rf	4	0	0	1	0	0
Pipp 1b	2	0	0	17	0	0
Ward 2b	3	0	1	3	5	0
McNally 3b	4	1	2	0	0	0
Schang c	2	0	0	1	1	0
Mays p	3	0	1	0	3	0
Total	28	3	7	27	18	0

NEW YORK GIANTS

	AB	R	H	PO	A	E
Burns cf	4	0	0	0	0	0
Bancroft ss	4	0	0	1	3	0
Frisch 3b	4	0	4	1	4	0
Youngs rf	3	0	0	0	0	0
Kelly 1b	4	0	0	14	1	0
I. Meusel lf	3	0	0	0	1	0
Rawlings 2b	2	0	1	3	5	0
Snyder c	3	0	0	7	1	0
Douglas p	2	0	0	0	3	0
Smith[a]	1	0	0	0	0	0
Barnes p	0	0	0	0	0	0
Total	30	0	5	26[b]	18	0

a. Flied out for Douglas in eighth inning.

b. Schang out; hit by batted ball in seventh inning after walking.

Yankees	100	011	000-3	
Giants	000	000	000-0	

Runs batted in—Ruth, B. Meusel. *Two-base hits*—McNally. *Three-base hits*—Frisch. *Sacrifice hits*—Peckinpaugh, Pipp, Schang, Youngs. *Stolen bases*—McNally (2), Frisch. *Double plays*—Frisch, Rawlings, and Kelly; Peckinpaugh, Ward, and Pipp. *Left on base*—Yankees, 5; Giants, 5. *Earned runs*—Yankees, 3. *Struck out*—by Mays, 1; by Douglas, 6; by Barnes, 1. *Bases on balls*—off Douglas, 4. *Hit by pitcher*—by Mays (Rawlings). *Hits*—off Douglas, 5 in 8 innings; off Barnes, 2 in 1 inning. *Passed ball*—Snyder. *Losing pitcher*—Douglas. *Umpires*—Rigler (NL), Moriarty (AL), Quigley (NL), and Chill (AL). *Time of game*—1:38. *Attendance*—30,202. *Gate receipts*—$103,965.

Source: Retrosheet. Checked against and coordinated with
Sporting News, Official World Series Records; and the *New York Times*.

Appendix 3   *1921 World Series Box Scores*

NEW YORK GIANTS   **NEW YORK YANKEES**

	AB	R	H	PO	A	E			AB	R	H	PO	A	E
Burns cf	3	0	0	1	0	0		Miller cf	3	0	0	1	0	0
Bancroft ss	4	0	0	3	3	0		Peckinpaugh ss	3	0	0	3	1	0
Frisch 3b	4	0	1	3	2	1		Ruth lf	1	1	0	0	0	0
Youngs rf	2	0	0	2	0	0		B. Meusel	4	1	1	1	0	0
Kelly 1b	4	0	0	12	2	0		Pipp 1b	3	0	0	14	0	0
I. Meusel lf	2	0	0	0	0	0		Ward 2b	4	1	1	4	7	0
Rawlings 2b	3	0	1	2	2	0		McNally 3b	3	0	0	0	3	0
Smith c	3	0	0	1	1	0		Schang c	2	0	0	4	2	0
Nehf p	2	0	0	0	3	1		Hoyt p	3	0	1	0	2	0
Total	27	0	2	24	13	2		Total	26	3	3	27	15	0

Giants	000	000	000-0
Yankees	000	100	02X-3

Runs batted in—Pipp, Hoyt. *Stolen bases*—Ruth (2), B. Meusel. *Double plays*—Frisch and Rawlings; Rawlings, Kelly, and Smith; McNally, Ward, and Pipp. *Left on base*—Yankees, 6; Giants, 5. *Earned runs*—Yankees, 1. *Struck out*—by Hoyt, 5. *Bases on balls*—off Nehf, 7; off Hoyt, 5. *Passed ball*—Smith. *Umpires*—Moriarty (AL), Quigley (NL), Chill (AL), and Rigler (NL). *Time of game*—1:55. Attendance—34,939. *Gate receipts*—$115,320.

Source: Retrosheet. Checked against and coordinated with
Sporting News, Official World Series Records; and the *New York Times*.

Appendix 3 *1921 World Series Box Scores*

NEW YORK YANKEES

NEW YORK GIANTS

	AB	R	H	PO	A	E			AB	R	H	PO	A	E
Miller cf	5	1	1	2	0	0		Burns cf	6	1	4	1	0	0
Peckinpaugh ss	3	1	0	4	2	0		Bancroft ss	5	1	1	3	2	0
Ruth lf	3	0	1	1	0	0		Frisch 3b	2	3	2	2	1	0
Fewster[a]	0	1	0	0	0	0		Youngs rf	3	2	2	0	1	0
B. Meusel rf	3	0	2	1	0	0		Kelly 1b	3	1	0	7	1	0
Pipp 1b	3	0	0	12	0	0		I. Meusel lf	5	2	3	2	0	0
Ward 2b	4	0	2	1	5	0		Rawlings 2b	5	0	2	3	5	0
McNally 3b	3	0	0	0	2	0		Snyder c	5	1	4	8	2	0
Schang c	2	1	1	2	2	0		Toney p	0	0	0	0	1	0
DeVormer c	1	0	0	1	0	0		Barnes p	5	2	2	1	1	0
Shawkey p	1	1	1	0	0	0		Total	39	13	20	27	14	0
Quinn p	2	0	0	0	1	0								
Collins p	0	1	0	0	0	0								
Rogers p	0	0	0	0	1	0								
Baker[b]	1	0	0	0	0	0								
Total	31	5	8	24	13	0								

a. Ran for Ruth in eighth inning.

b. Flied out for Rogers in ninth inning.

Yankees	004	000	010-5
Giants	004	000	81X-13

Runs batted in—Miller, Ruth (2), Pipp, Ward, Kelly, Bancroft, Youngs (4), I. Meusel (3), Rawlings (3), Snyder. *Two-base hits*—B. Meusel, Youngs, I. Meusel, Burns. *Three-base hits*—Burns, Youngs. Sacrifice hits—Pipp, Bancroft. *Stolen bases*—Burns, Frisch, I. Meusel. *Double plays*—Ward and Pipp; Quinn, Peckinpaugh, and Pipp. *Left on base*—Giants, 10; Yankees, 5. *Earned runs*—Giants, 13, Yankees, 5. *Struck out*—by Toney, 1; by Barnes, 7; by Quinn, 2; by Rogers, 1. *Bases on balls*—off Shawkey, 4; off Toney, 2; off Barnes, 2; off Quinn, 2; off Collins, 1. *Hit by pitcher*—by Barnes (McNally). *Wild pitch*—Barnes. *Hits*—off Toney, 4 in 2 innings (pitched to five batters in third inning); off Barnes, 4 in 7 innings; off Shawkey, 5 in 2 1/3 innings; off Quinn, 8 in 3 2/3 innings (pitched to five batters in seventh inning); off Collins, 4 in 2/3 inning; off Rogers 3 in 1 1/3 innings. *Winning pitcher*—Barnes. *Losing pitcher*—Quinn. Umpires—Quigley (NL), Chill (AL), Rigler (NL), and Moriarty (AL). *Time of game*—2:40. Attendance—36,509. *Gate receipts*—$119,007.

Source: Retrosheet. Checked against and coordinated with *Sporting News, Official World Series Records*; and the *New York Times*.

Appendix 3 *1921 World Series Box Scores*

WORLD SERIES GAME 4, SUNDAY, OCTOBER 9, 1921

NEW YORK GIANTS

	AB	R	H	PO	A	E
Burns cf	4	0	2	0	0	0
Bancroft ss	4	0	0	4	1	1
Frisch 3b	4	0	0	1	3	0
Youngs rf	4	0	1	1	0	0
Kelly 1b	4	1	1	9	0	0
I. Meusel lf	4	1	2	0	0	0
Rawlings 2b	4	1	2	1	4	0
Smith c	4	1	1	10	2	0
Douglas p	2	0	0	1	2	0
Total	34	4	9	27	12	1

NEW YORK YANKEES

	AB	R	H	PO	A	E
Miller cf	4	0	0	1	0	0
Peckinpaugh ss	4	0	1	2	6	0
Ruth lf	4	1	2	2	0	0
B. Meusel rf	4	0	0	1	0	0
Pipp 1b	4	0	1	17	0	0
Ward 2b	2	0	0	1	7	0
McNally 3b	3	1	1	1	2	1
Schang c	3	0	2	2	1	0
Mays p	3	0	0	0	3	0
Total	31	2	7	27	19	1

Giants	000	000	031-4
Yankees	000	010	001-2

Runs batted in—Burns (2), I. Meusel, Rawlings, Ruth, Schang. *Two-base hits*—Burns, Kelly. *Three-base hits*—Schang, I. Meusel. *Home run*—Ruth. *Sacrifice hits*—Douglas, Ward. *Double play*—Ward, Peckinpaugh, and Pipp. *Left on base*—Giants, 4; Yankees, 3. *Earned runs*—Giants, 4; Yankees, 2. *Struck out*—by Douglas, 8; by Mays, 1. *Umpires*—Chill (AL), Rigler (NL), Moriarty (AL), and Quigley (NL). *Time of game*—1:38. *Attendance*—36,372. *Gate receipts*—$118,527.

Source: Retrosheet. Checked against and coordinated with
Sporting News, *Official World Series Records*; and the *New York Times*.

Appendix 3   *1921 World Series Box Scores*

WORLD SERIES GAME 5, MONDAY, OCTOBER 10, 1921

NEW YORK YANKEES

	AB	R	H	PO	A	E
Miller cf	3	0	1	2	0	0
Peckinpaugh ss	4	0	1	3	3	0
Ruth lf	4	1	1	2	0	0
B. Meusel rf	4	1	2	1	2	0
Pipp 1b	3	0	0	6	1	0
Ward 2b	3	0	0	5	3	1
McNally 3b	2	1	0	1	1	0
Schrang c	3	0	1	7	1	0
Hoyt p	3	0	0	0	1	0
Total	29	3	6	27	12	1

NEW YORK GIANTS

	AB	R	H	PO	A	E
Burns cf	5	0	1	2	0	0
Bancroft ss	4	1	1	3	1	0
Frisch 3b	4	0	2	1	6	1
Youngs rf	3	0	1	0	0	0
Kelly 1b	4	0	3	11	1	0
I. Meusel lf	4	0	1	3	0	0
Rawlings 2b	4	0	1	0	2	0
Smith c	3	0	0	6	1	0
Nehf p	3	0	0	1	1	0
Snyder[a]	1	0	0	0	0	0
Total	35	1	10	27	12	1

a. Struck out for Nehf in ninth inning.

Yankees	001	200	000-3
Giants	100	000	000-1

Runs batted in—Miller, B. Meusel, Ward, Kelly. *Two-base hits*—Schang, I. Meusel, B. Meusel, Miller, Rawlings. *Sacrifice hits*—Miller, Pipp, Ward. *Double play*—Schang and Ward. Left on base—Giants, 9; Yankees, 3. *Earned runs*—Yankees, 3; Giants, 0. Struck out—by Hoyt, 6; by Nehf, 5. *Bases on balls*—off Hoyt, 2; off Nehf, 1. *Umpires*—Rigler (NL), Moriarty (AL), Quigley (NL), and Chill (AL). *Time of game*—1:50. *Attendance*—35,758. *Gate receipts*—$116,754.

Source: Retrosheet. Checked against and coordinated with *Sporting News*, *Official World Series Records*; and the *New York Times*.

Appendix 3 *1921 World Series Box Scores*

NEW YORK GIANTS   **NEW YORK YANKEES**

	AB	R	H	PO	A	E		AB	R	H	PO	A	E
Burns cf	3	1	1	0	0	0	Fewster lf	3	2	1	5	0	0
Bancroft ss	5	0	2	0	2	0	Peckinpaugh ss	5	0	0	3	1	0
Frisch 3b	4	2	0	1	2	0	Miller cf	5	1	1	1	0	0
Youngs rf	5	0	1	2	0	0	B. Meusel rf	3	1	1	2	0	0
Kelly 1b	4	1	3	7	1	0	Pipp 1b	4	0	1	2	0	0
I. Meusel lf	4	1	2	2	0	0	Ward 2b	4	0	1	3	1	1
Rawlings 2b	5	0	0	5	2	0	McNally 3b	4	0	0	3	0	1
Snyder c	4	2	2	10	0	0	Schang c	2	0	1	8	3	0
Toney p	0	0	0	0	0	0	Harper p	0	0	0	0	0	0
Barnes p	4	1	2	0	0	0	Shawkey p	3	1	1	0	0	0
Total	38	8	13	27	7	0	Baker[a]	1	0	0	0	0	0
							Piercy p	0	0	0	0	0	0
							Total	34	5	7	27	5	2

a. Grounded out for Shawkey in eighth inning.

Giants	030	401	000-8
Yankees	320	000	000-5

Runs batted in—Bancroft (2), Frisch, Kelly (2), I. Meusel (2), Snyder, Fewster (2), B. Meusel, Ward (2). *Home runs*—I. Meusel, Snyder, Fewster. *Sacrifice hit*—Burns. *Stolen bases*—Frisch, Pipp. *Double play*—Schang and McNally; Schang and Ward. *Left on base*—Giants, 8; Yankees, 7. *Earned runs*—Giants, 6; Yankees, 5. *Struck out*—by Barnes 10; by Harper, 1; by Shawkey, 5; by Piercy, 2. *Bases on balls*—off Toney, 1; off Barnes, 4; off Harper, 2; off Shawkey, 2. *Hits*—off Toney, 3 in 2/3 inning; off Barnes 4 in 8 1/3 innings; off Harper, 3 in 1 1/3 innings; off Shawkey, 8 in 6 2/3 innings; off Piercy, 2 in 1 inning. *Winning pitcher*—Barnes. *Losing pitcher*—Shawkey. *Umpires*—Moriarty (AL), Quigley (NL), Chill (AL), and Rigler (NL). *Time of game*—2:31. *Attendance*—34,283. *Gate receipts*—$112,234.

Source: Retrosheet. Checked against and coordinated with
Sporting News, Official World Series Records; and the *New York Times*.

Appendix 3 *1921 World Series Box Scores*

WORLD SERIES GAME 7, WEDNESDAY, OCTOBER 12, 1921

NEW YORK YANKEES

	AB	R	H	PO	A	E
Fewster lf	4	0	1	0	0	0
Peckinpaugh ss	4	0	2	0	4	0
Miller cf	3	0	0	2	1	0
B. Meusel rf	4	0	0	1	0	0
Pipp 1b	4	1	1	13	0	0
Ward 2b	3	0	0	0	4	1
McNally 3b	1	0	1	0	2	0
Baker 3b	3	0	2	1	0	0
DeVormer[a]	0	0	0	0	0	0
Schang c	4	0	1	7	0	0
Mays p	3	0	0	0	2	0
Total	33	1	8	24	13	1

NEW YORK GIANTS

	AB	R	H	PO	A	E
Burns cf	4	0	2	2	0	0
Bancroft ss	4	0	1	2	2	0
Frisch 3b	4	0	0	2	3	0
Youngs rf	3	1	1	2	0	0
Kelly 1b	3	0	0	13	0	0
I. Meusel lf	3	0	1	0	1	0
Rawlings 2b	3	1	0	2	3	0
Snyder c	3	0	1	3	0	0
Douglas p	3	0	0	1	5	0
Total	30	2	6	27	14	0

a.Ran for Baker in ninth inning.

Yankees	010	000	000-1
Giants	000	100	10X-2

Runs batted in—McNally, I. Meusel, Snyder. *Two-base hits*—Peckinpaugh, Bancroft, Pipp, Burns (2), Snyder. *Sacrifice hit*—Ward. *Stolen base*—Youngs. *Left on base*—Yankees, 7; Giants, 4. *Earned runs*—Yankees, 1; Giants, 1. *Struck out*—by Mays, 7; by Douglas, 3. *Bases on balls*—off Douglas, 1. *Wild pitch*—Douglas. *Umpires*—Quigley (NL), Chill (AL), Rigler (NL), and Moriarty (AL). *Time of game*—1:40. *Attendance*—36,503. *Gate receipts*—$118,974.

Source: Retrosheet. Checked against and coordinated with
Sporting News, Official World Series Records; and the *New York Times*.

Appendix 3   *1921 World Series Box Scores*

NEW YORK GIANTS   **NEW YORK YANKEES**

	AB	R	H	PO	A	E		AB	R	H	PO	A	E
Burns cf	4	0	1	3	0	0	Fewster lf	3	0	0	2	0	0
Bancroft ss	3	1	0	0	4	0	Peckinpaugh ss	2	0	0	2	2	1
Frisch 3b	4	0	0	2	3	0	Miller cf	4	0	1	1	0	0
Youngs rf	2	0	1	0	0	0	B. Meusel rf	4	0	0	2	0	0
Kelly 1b	4	0	0	13	1	0	Pipp 1b	3	0	1	11	0	0
I. Meusel lf	4	0	1	1	0	0	Ruth[a]	1	0	0	0	0	0
Rawlings 2b	4	0	3	4	4	0	Ward 2b	3	0	1	0	2	0
Snyder c	2	0	0	4	0	0	Baker 3b	3	0	0	1	3	0
Nehf p	4	0	0	0	0	0	Schang c	3	0	0	8	1	0
Total	31	1	6	27	12	0	Hoyt p	3	0	1	0	3	0
							Total	29	0	4	27	11	1

a. Grounded out for Pipp in ninth inning.

Giants	100	000	000-1
Yankees	000	000	000-0

Runs batted in—none (run scored on Peckinpaugh's error). Two-base hits—Rawlings (2). Sacrifice hits—Snyder (2). Stolen base—Youngs. Double plays—Bancroft, Rawlings, and Kelly; Rawlings, Kelly, and Frisch. Left on base—Giants, 9; Yankees, 7. Earned runs—none. Struck out—by Nehf 3; by Hoyt, 7. Bases on balls—off Nehf 5; off Hoyt, 4. Wild pitch—Nehf. Umpires—Chill (AL), Rigler (NL), Moriarty (AL), and Quigley (NL). Time of game—1:58. Attendance—25,410. Gate receipts—$95,452.

Source: Retrosheet. Checked against and coordinated with
Sporting News, Official World Series Records; and the *New York Times*.

Appendix 4   *1921 Yankees and Giants World Series Batting and Pitching*

	G	AB	R	H	2B	3B	HR	RBI	BB	SO	HP	SH	SF	SB	CS	BA	OBA	SA
Frank Baker	4	8	0	2	0	0	0	0	1	0	0	0	0	0	0	.250	.333	.250
Rip Collins	1	0	0	0	0	0	0	0	0	0	0	0	0	0	0	.000	.000	.000
Al DeVormer	2	1	0	0	0	0	0	0	0	0	0	0	0	0	0	.000	.000	.000
Chick Fewster	4	10	3	2	0	0	1	2	3	3	0	0	0	0	0	.200	.385	.500
Harry Harper	1	0	0	0	0	0	0	0	0	0	0	0	0	0	0	.000	.000	.000
Waite Hoyt	3	9	0	2	0	0	0	1	0	1	0	0	0	0	0	.222	.222	.222
Carl Mays	3	9	0	1	0	0	0	0	0	1	0	0	0	0	0	.111	.111	.111
Mike McNally	7	20	3	4	1	0	0	1	1	3	1	0	0	2	2	.200	.273	.250
Bob Meusel	8	30	3	6	2	0	0	3	2	5	0	0	0	1	2	.200	.250	.267
Elmer Miller	8	31	3	5	1	0	0	2	2	5	0	0	1	0	0	.161	.206	.194
Roger Peckinpaugh	8	28	2	5	1	0	0	0	4	3	0	1	0	0	1	.179	.281	.214
Bill Piercy	1	0	0	0	0	0	0	0	0	0	0	0	0	0	0	.000	.000	.000
Wally Pipp	8	26	1	4	1	0	0	2	2	3	0	3	0	1	1	.154	.214	.192
Jack Quinn	1	2	0	0	0	0	0	0	0	1	0	0	0	0	0	.000	.000	.000
Tom Rogers	1	0	0	0	0	0	0	0	0	0	0	0	0	0	0	.000	.000	.000
Babe Ruth	6	16	3	5	0	0	1	4	5	8	0	0	0	2	1	.313	.476	.500
Wally Schang	8	21	1	6	1	1	0	1	5	4	0	1	0	0	0	.286	.423	.429
Bob Shawkey	2	4	2	2	0	0	0	0	0	1	0	0	0	0	0	.500	.500	.500
Aaron Ward	8	26	1	6	0	0	0	4	2	6	0	2	1	0	0	.231	.276	.231
Total	8	241	22	50	7	1	2	20	27	44	1	7	2	6	7	.207	.288	.270

Source: baseball reference.com. Checked against and coordinated with the *New York Times*.

	G	GS	CG	GF	IP	H	SO	BB	HB	R	ER	HR	WP	W	L	SV	SHO	ERA
Rip Collins	1	0	0	0	0.2	4	0	1	0	4	4	0	0	0	0	0	0	54.00
Harry Harper	2	1	0	0	1.1	3	1	2	0	3	3	2	0	0	0	0	0	20.25
Waite Hoyt	3	3	3	0	27.0	18	18	11	0	2	0	0	0	2	1	0	1	0.00
Carl Mays	3	3	3	0	26.0	20	9	0	1	6	5	0	0	1	2	0	1	1.73
Bill Piercy	1	0	0	1	1.0	2	2	0	0	0	0	0	0	0	0	0	0	0.00
Jack Quinn	1	0	0	0	3.2	8	2	2	0	4	4	0	0	0	1	0	0	9.82
Tom Rogers	1	0	0	1	1.1	3	1	0	0	1	1	0	0	0	0	0	0	6.75
Bob Shawkey	2	1	0	0	9.0	13	5	6	0	9	7	0	0	0	1	0	0	7.00
Total	8	8	6	2	70.0	71	38	22	1	29	24	2	0	3	5	0	2	3.09

Source: baseball-reference.com. Checked against and coordinated with the *New York Times*.

1921 NEW YORK GIANTS WORLD SERIES BATTING

	G	AB	R	H	2B	3B	HR	RBI	GW	BB	SO	HP	SH	SF	SB	CS	BA	OBA	SA
Dave Bancroft	8	33	3	5	1	0	0	3	0	1	5	0	0	1	0	1	.152	.171	.182
Jesse Barnes	3	9	3	4	0	0	0	0	0	0	0	0	0	0	0	0	.444	.444	.444
George Burns	8	33	2	11	4	1	0	2	0	3	5	0	1	0	1	1	.333	.389	.515
Phil Douglas	3	7	0	0	0	0	0	0	0	0	2	0	1	0	0	0	.000	.000	.000
Frankie Frisch	8	30	5	9	0	1	0	1	0	4	3	0	0	0	3	0	.300	.382	.367
George Kelly	8	30	3	7	1	0	0	4	0	3	10	0	0	0	0	1	.233	.303	.267
Irish Meusel	8	29	4	10	2	1	1	7	0	2	3	0	0	0	1	2	.345	.387	.586
Art Nehf	3	9	0	0	0	0	0	0	0	1	3	0	0	0	0	0	.000	.100	.000
Johnny Rawlings	8	30	2	10	3	0	0	4	0	0	3	1	0	0	0	1	.333	.355	.433
Earl Smith	3	7	0	0	0	0	0	0	0	1	0	0	0	0	0	1	.000	.125	.000
Frank Snyder	7	22	4	8	1	0	1	3	0	0	2	0	2	0	0	1	.364	.364	.545
Fred Toney	2	0	0	0	0	0	0	0	0	0	0	0	0	0	0	0	.000	.000	.000
Ross Youngs	8	25	3	7	1	1	0	4	0	7	2	0	1	0	2	1	.280	.438	.400
Total	8	264	29	71	13	4	2	28	0	22	38	1	5	1	7	9	.269	.326	.371

Source: baseball-reference.com. Checked against and coordinated with the *New York Times*.

1921 NEW YORK GIANTS WORLD SERIES PITCHING

	G	GS	CG	GF	IP	H	SO	BB	HB	R	ER	HR	WP	W	L	SV	SHO	ERA
Jesse Barnes	3	0	0	3	16.1	18	2	6	1	3	3	1	1	2	0	0	0	1.65
Phil Douglas	3	3	2	0	26.0	17	2	5	0	6	6	1	1	2	1	0	0	2.08
Art Nehf	3	3	3	0	26.0	8	1	13	0	6	4	0	1	1	2	0	1	1.38
Fred Toney	2	3	0	0	2.2	1	5	2	0	7	7	0	0	0	0	0	0	23.63
Total	8	8	5	3	71.0	44	38	27	1	22	20	2	3	5	3	0	1	2.54

Source: baseball-reference.com. Checked against and coordinated with the *New York Times*.

1. Prelude to the World Series

1. On July 2, 1921, Dempsey defended his title by knocking out Carpentier in the fourth round at Jersey City. The fight drew more than 90,000 people; and the gate, estimated at more than $1.6 million, was the first million-dollar gate in boxing history.

2. Shortly after McGraw's announcement, Chicago Cubs president Jim Hart announced that, should his team win the pennant, they too would refuse to play against the American League in a World Series.

3. When the new American League began to challenge the established National League in 1901, John McGraw became the manager of the American League's Baltimore team. But McGraw, a product of the rough-and-tumble National League of the 1890s, had problems with the strict discipline imposed by AL president Ban Johnson. In mid-1902 McGraw abandoned the Orioles and the American League and signed to manage the New York Giants of the National League. McGraw's desertion was a big part of the collapse of the Baltimore franchise. The next year, the club moved to New York and began playing at Hilltop Park.

4. *Sporting News*, October 13, 1906.

5. Originally, this postseason matchup was called the World's Championship Series. While the 's had dropped off the first word by 1921 and the middle word had been dropped, leaving the event as simply the World Series, some reporters still used the older name. The *Reach Guide* used World's Series through 1930, and the *Sporting News* used it from 1942–63.

6. That Ruth was the game's greatest attraction is indisputable. Yet a profile in the *New Yorker* of March 28, 1925, began with these two sentences: "John McGraw is baseball. He is the incarnation of the American national sport."

7. Goldblatt, *Giants and the Dodgers*, 27.

8. *New York Times*, October 2, 1921.

9. Sid Mercer, *New York Evening Journal*, October 3, 1921.

10. Although the team was known as the Dodgers for most of their years in Brooklyn, some newspapers called them the Robins during Wilbert Robinson's tenure as manager (1914–31) as a mark of respect for Robinson.

11. *New York World*, October 4, 1920.

12. *New York Times*, October 4, 1920.

13. Joe Vila, quoted in Lee Allen, *Giants and the Dodgers*, 113–14.

14. In his effort to incorporate a different culture in the American League, President Johnson included these strictures in a May 8, 1901, directive to all club owners in his league: "Clean Ball is the Main Plank in the American League platform, and the clubs must stand by it religiously. There must be no profanity on the ball field. The umpires are agents of the League and must be treated with respect. I will suspend any Manager or player who uses profane or vulgar language to an Umpire, and that suspension shall remain in force until such time as the offender can learn to bridle his tongue. Rowdyism and profanity have worked untold injury to baseball. To permit it would blight the future of the American League" (Light, *Cultural Encyclopedia of Baseball*, 22).

15. Hynd, *Giants of the Polo Grounds*, 220.

16. Creamer, *Babe*, 82. Creamer claims that when Dunn tried to sell Lefty Grove to the Giants, McGraw would have nothing to do with the Orioles, and so Dunn sold Grove to Connie Mack's Philadelphia A's. Dunn may have sold Ruth to Boston as a gesture of appreciation toward Joseph Lannin, the owner of the Red Sox. Lannin had helped save the International League during the Federal League war with his financial backing of the Buffalo and Providence clubs and by helping Dunn meet his payroll in Baltimore (Ruth, *Babe Ruth Story*, 31).

17. Creamer, *Babe*, 190.

18. Creamer, *Babe*, 190.

19. Ruth pitched one game for the Yankees in 1920 and two in 1921.

20. McGraw did not use the sacrifice bunt as much as other teams. The Giants' 166 sacrifice hits in 1921 were the third lowest in the National League and were 23 fewer than the Yankees. Tris Speaker's Cleveland Indians led both leagues in sacrifice hits in 1921 with 232. To advance runners, McGraw preferred to use the hit-and-run, an offensive tactic introduced by the Baltimore Orioles teams he played on in the 1890s.

21. McGraw, *My Thirty Years in Baseball*, 207.

22. Editorial, *Sporting News*, October 13, 1921; and *Detroit News*, October 5, 1921.

23. The New York Giants of the National League did play the Brooklyn Bridegrooms of the American Association in the 1889 postseason. However, Brooklyn was not part of New York City at that time. The Giants, led by home run slugger Roger Connor, won the Series, 6-3.

24. *Philadelphia Inquirer*, October 10, 1921.

2. Baseball Confronts the Black Sox Scandal

1. *Sporting News*, October 16, 1919, quoted in Fleitz, *Shoeless*, 198.

2. Murdock, *Ban Johnson*, 188.

3. William McGeehan, *New York Tribune*, October 22, 1920, quoted in Cottrell, *Blackball, the Black Sox, and the Babe*, 240.

4. Crepeau, *Baseball*, 16.

5. Veeck Jr., *Hustlers' Handbook*, 298. The colorful Veeck owned the Cleveland Indians, St. Louis Browns, and Chicago White Sox between 1946 and 1981.

6. The upstart league had thought it had a sympathetic judge to hear its case. Landis had a reputation for standing up for the underdog; he had gained fame for fining Standard Oil Company $29 million in 1907, at the height of President Theodore Roosevelt's trust-busting campaign. The award was overturned upon appeal, as were a number of Landis's other decisions.

7. While the clause gave players no freedom to choose the teams they played for, its abolition might create havoc in baseball, the owners argued. The result, they claimed, would be a concentration of the best players on the wealthiest teams. Landis recognized Organized Baseball's vulnerability if the clause were abolished. He also realized that if he ruled quickly in Organized Baseball's favor, a higher court would possibly overturn his decision on appeal.

8. As part of the settlement, the Federal League dropped its lawsuit. But one of its teams, the Baltimore Terrapins, miffed that it was not allowed to join the Major Leagues, filed their own lawsuit. The case eventually made its way to the United States Supreme Court. Its landmark 1922 ruling, which still protects Organized Baseball today, declared that baseball is not interstate commerce and thus is exempt from antitrust claims.

9. Koppett, *Leonard Koppett's Concise History*, 161.

10. *New York Times*, November 29, 1920. Landis's remarks did not garner a lot of national media attention at the time. The judge was in New York for the Army-Navy football game at the Polo Grounds, where he spoke to reporters before returning to Chicago.

11. Voigt, "Chicago Black Sox," 65–76.

12. Spink, *Judge Landis*, 99.

13. Pietrusza, *Judge and Jury*, 177.

14. Pietrusza, *Judge and Jury*, 175. Moreover, the powerful Landis did have some constraints. If he were to go too far, the owners could fire him.

15. Koppett, *Leonard Koppett's Concise History*, 148.

16. An Internet search for "Buck Weaver" or "Clear Buck Weaver" brings up numerous articles and Web sites that advocate Weaver. The same is true for a "Joe Jackson" search on the Internet.

17. Pietrusza, *Judge and Jury*, 194. Many more players had "guilty knowledge" of the fix and were not punished.

18. Herzog, "From Scapegoat to Icon," 133.

19. Rice, *Tumult and the Shouting*, 106.

20. "Penalties and Psychology," *Sporting News*, December 23, 1920.

21. W. J. Macbeth, *New York Tribune*, quoted in *Sporting News*, January 6, 1921.

22. *New York Herald*, January 13, 1921.

23. *New York Herald*, January 14, 1921.

24. *New York Evening Journal*, February 17, 1921.

25. Grantland Rice, *New York Tribune*, October 14, 1920, quoted in Fountain, *Sportswriter*, 179.

26. *New York Tribune*, January 11, 1921.

27. *New York Herald*, April 10, 1921.

28. *Washington Post*, March 15, 1921.

29. Carney, *Burying the Black Sox*, 237, 152.

30. White, *Creating the National Pastime*, 97, 104.

31. Veeck Jr., *Hustlers' Handbook*, 296–97.

3. The Shady Side of Baseball's Flagship Franchise

1. The Giants easily withstood the challenge of New York's American Association team (1883–87) but were outdrawn by the city's Players League entry in 1890, almost all of whose stars had been members of the 1889 world champion Giants. The Players League folded after one season, and most of the Giants' players who had left returned to the team in 1891.

2. Throughout his career, the press almost always called Ross Youngs by the name Young, minus the *s*. However, his correct name is Youngs, which is the name we use in this book.

3. This fifth and final incarnation of the Polo Grounds was located in the north Harlem section of Manhattan, on the west side of 8th Avenue between 157th Street and 159th Street. Beyond center field was the Harlem River, which separated Manhattan from the Bronx.

4. Golden, "From *For 2 Cents Plain*," 132.

5. Charyn, *Gangsters and Gold Diggers*, 38–39.

6. Pietrusza, *Rothstein*.

7. Sinclair was already involved in sports as the owner of a very successful stable of racehorses and had been one of the leaders of the Federal League. In 1915 he had been the principal backer of that league's Newark Peppers, who had relocated from Indianapolis to take advantage of the New York market. In 1929 Sinclair would spend six months in prison in the aftermath of the Teapot Dome Scandal.

8. At the time, it was the largest baseball transaction ever, more than double the price Jacob Ruppert and Til Huston had paid for the Yankees just four years earlier.

9. *New York Times*, January 15, 1919.

10. Alexander, *John McGraw*, 209.

11. Hynd, *Giants of the Polo Grounds*, 211.

12. Quoted in Jacob A. Stein, "Great Mouthpiece." In addition to being Arnold

Rothstein's lawyer, Fallon was also the lawyer of choice for many of the country's top crime figures. Included in his roster of clients was the notorious gambler and thief Nicky Arnstein, the husband of Broadway star Fannie Brice.

13. On August 7, 1920, a drunken McGraw had gotten into a fistfight with another patron at the club.

14. Pietrusza, *Rothstein*, 184. Rothstein would be fatally shot in a Manhattan hotel on November 3, 1928, dying the next day without revealing any information about his assailant.

15. The flamboyant Sloane had been America's leading jockey in the 1890s. In 1901 England had banned him for betting on races in which he was involved. Racing authorities in the United States upheld the ban, ending Sloane's career. McGraw's pal George M. Cohan based the title character in his 1904 musical, *Little Johnny Jones*, on Sloane.

4. Ruppert and Huston Arrive, Ready to "Go to the Limit"

1. The team was known as the Highlanders or simply the New York Americans at first. They played their games at Hilltop Park in upper Manhattan, at 168th and Broadway. By 1906 many New York City newspapers and fans were already calling them the Yankees.

2. Perhaps Farrell's biggest mistake was supporting New York's talented yet corrupt first baseman, Hal Chase, in his showdown with manager George Stallings late in the 1910 season. Stallings had turned the team around, from a last-place finish in 1908 to second place in 1910. To make matters worse, Farrell then appointed Chase as manager. One of the most crooked players in baseball history, Chase was responsible for fixing many games and managed the Yankees to a sixth-place finish in 1911. Stallings would lead the "Miracle" Boston Braves to a dramatic turnaround and world championship just four years later, in 1914.

3. Smelser, *Life That Ruth Built*, 123.

4. Frank Graham, *New York Yankees*, 23.

5. Smelser, *Life That Ruth Built*, 124. Smelser notes that Ruppert had gone to see Walter Johnson's Senators and Ty Cobb's Tigers play the Yankees.

6. Frank Graham, *New York Yankees*, 23. Graham notes (21) that National League owners had approached Ruppert about buying the struggling Giants in 1900, but he was not interested. Smelser provides a different account in which Ruppert actually bid on the Giants at that time but lost out to John Brush (*Life That Ruth Built*, 123).

7. Ruppert was elected four times on the Tammany slate (1899–1907) and was a regular contributor to Tammany fundraising campaigns. In 1911 he was elected president of the United States Brewers' Association (*New York Times*, October 21, 1911).

8. The number has variously been reported as $450,000 and $460,000. In his January 19, 1939, column in the *Sporting News*, written shortly after the death of Colonel Ruppert, J. G. Taylor Spink stated that the American League contributed $50,000 of the purchase price. There was also mention of the league's making up a difference in price in the *Atlanta Constitution*, December 25, 1914, and in the *New York Times*, January 1, 1915. Michael Haupert and Kenneth Winter have shed more light on the matter ("Yankees Profits and Promise," 199–200). They note that the Yankees had $300,000 of debt at the time, which the new owners assumed. Therefore, Ruppert and Huston probably paid no more than $160,000 in cash and then settled the debt at considerably less than one hundred cents on the dollar, conclude Haupert and Winter.

In April 1911 the New York Giants' Polo Grounds burned down; and while it was being rebuilt as a concrete structure, the Highlanders graciously let the Giants play in their ballpark. In 1913 the Giants returned the favor by leasing their Polo Grounds to the American Leaguers.

9. *New York Evening Telegram*, March 26, 1918.

10. *St. Louis Times*, June 11, 1914.

11. *New York Times*, January 13, 1939. Damon Runyon wrote sarcastically at the time that the Yankees "looked like a dandy investment, except that Mr. Farrell has no team and no park to offer" (*Chicago Daily Tribune*, December 18, 1914).

12. Donovan had success as a manager in the high minor leagues. He won the International League pennant in 1914 with Providence (where Carl Mays won twenty-four games for him) and the Eastern League pennant in 1922 with New Haven.

13. Ironically, the Yankees' owners took over when McGraw and the Giants were in a long stretch of only limited success. The Giants won only one pennant from 1914 to 1920, in 1917. They lost that World Series to the Chicago White Sox, a cast that was very similar to the Black Sox that lost the fixed Series two years later.

14. While Huggins is listed in baseball databases as five feet six and 140 pounds, he was much smaller—a number of sources have him around five feet two and a half and 125 pounds. Huggins's sister Myrtle said in the article "Mighty Midget" that he weighed 125 pounds. "He is only an inch or so above five feet . . . he looks not unlike a jockey grown old," wrote Henry F. Pringle ("Small Package," 25). Sid Keener wrote that Huggins was five feet four and 135 pounds (*St. Louis Times*, May 5, 1919). Huggins himself wrote, "I weigh just 120 pounds, and I never weighed much more or much less." Miller Huggins, "Serial Story of His Baseball Career," chap. 14, *San Francisco Chronicle*, January 29, 1924; this article also appeared in many other papers.

15. Sid Keener, *St. Louis Times*, June 27, 1914.

16. Damon Runyon, *Sporting News*, April 18, 1918.
17. Hugh Fullerton, *New York Evening Mail*, August 15, 1921.
18. Sam Crane, *New York Evening Journal*, December 20, 1918.
19. *New York Globe and Commercial Advertiser*, November 8, 1917.
20. The deal never panned out for the Yankees, even though it seemed to favor them when it was made. Lewis and Shore had starred on the 1915 and 1916 championship Red Sox. After the trade, Lewis played just two more full seasons in the majors; and Shore won only seven more games, even though he was just twenty-seven years old when he joined the Yankees. Caldwell had won thirty-seven games for the 1914–15 Yankees. The Red Sox would trade Caldwell to Cleveland during the 1919 season, and he would make a spectacular comeback with the 1920 Indians.
21. They acquired him on July 29 for pitchers Allan Russell and Bob McGraw plus $40,000. For details on this trade, the Lewis-Shore deal, and the other Yankees–Red Sox trades of 1918 to 1923, see Steinberg, "Curse of the . . . Hurlers?"
22. Levitt, *Ed Barrow*, 154.
23. *New York Evening Journal*, December 19, 1918.
24. His son, Robert Wagner, also had a long career in New York City politics, including serving as mayor of the city from 1954 to 1965. Though the younger Wagner was a devoted Giants fan, it was during his administration that the city lost its two National League teams, when the Dodgers and Giants moved to California in 1958.
25. Hank Thormahlen and George Mogridge, who were the Yanks' third and fourth starters in 1919, would drop down a slot in 1920 with the acquisition of Mays.
26. Robert Ripley, *New York Globe and Commercial Advertiser*, June 12, 1918. In the first week of the 1918 season, *Globe* sportswriter Sid Mercer had used the phrase. "Murderers' Row brutally maltreated the great Walter Johnson," he wrote on April 16.
27. Fred Lieb, *New York Sun*, June 23, 1918.
28. In *Before They Were the Bombers*, Jim Reisler notes that the new Yankee owners also secured the rights to three other players: Joe Berger from the White Sox, Elmer Miller from the Cardinals, and Walter Rehg from the Red Sox (238). Of these three men, only Miller played for the Yankees, from 1915 to 1918. And he would make a dramatic return to New York during the 1921 season.

    The Tigers sold Pipp and High to the Yankees for $5,500. Detroit wasn't making too great a sacrifice. Neither man had played much for the Tigers. Pipp hit only .161 in a brief 1913 stint with them. As Sid Mercer wrote sarcastically in the *New York Globe and Commercial Advertiser*, "The generous magnates were willing to palm off their shoddy goods on the new 'suckers.'" (May 31, 1918). High played slightly more than three seasons for New York.

29. It was one of Huggins's few trading errors, and he would reacquire Urban Shocker seven years later.
30. Bozeman Bulger, *New York Evening World*, n.d., Bill Loughman private collection.

5. "You can't compare him with anybody else. He's Babe Ruth."

1. Douglas, *Terrible Honesty*, 24.
2. In their Ruth biographies, both Marshall Smelser and Kal Wagenheim discuss the many nicknames writers came up with for Ruth. Among the more colorful sobriquets "to describe the indescribable" Ruth, as Wagenheim puts it, were "the Mauling Mastodon"; "the dauntless devastating demon"; and one of Damon Runyon's monikers, "the diamond-studded ball-buster" (Wagenheim, *Babe Ruth*, 66, 71). Perhaps most apropos is the chapter entitled "Into the Arms of the Mythmakers" in Ken Sobol's book, *Babe Ruth and the American Dream*.
3. His fourteen-inning, 2–1 win over Brooklyn in 1916 remains the longest complete game in Series history. Ruth also set a record for pitching twenty-nine consecutive, scoreless innings in the World Series, a mark that was later broken by Whitey Ford.
4. Walter Trumbull, *New York World*, July 23, 1915.
5. Tilly Walker of the Athletics tied Ruth's league-leading total of eleven. In 1919 Ruth far outpaced the field. His twenty-nine blasts were followed by Walker, the Yankees' Frank Baker, and George Sisler of the St. Louis Browns, each of whom hit ten. The leader in the National League, the Phillies' Gavy Cravath, had only twelve.
6. *Boston Daily Globe* and *New York Times*, September 25, 1919.
7. After Ruth was hailed for breaking Freeman's mark of twenty-five on September 8, statistician Al Munro Elias pointed out the "real" record of twenty-seven set by Williamson (*Hartford Courant*, September 25, 1919). But National League president John Heydler had announced even before Ruth hit number twenty-six that the league did not recognize Williamson's mark, despite its appearance in a record book (*Boston Daily Globe*, September 9, 1919). It was only 180 feet down the left-field line in Chicago's White Stocking Park (also known as Lake Front Park) in 1884. The year before, balls hit out of the park were doubles (Lowry, *Green Cathedrals*, 48). Home run historian David Vincent has noted that the NL passed a rule in 1888 stating that a ball hit over a fence less than 210 feet from home plate would be ruled a double, and the league increased that distance to 235 feet in 1892 and to 250 feet in 1926 (*Home Run*, 12–13, 46). One thing was clear: after Ruth hit number twenty-eight, he was the clear single-season home run record holder.
8. *Atlanta Constitution*, September 27, 1919. By comparison, Mark McGwire's 1998 seventieth home run ball went for about $3 million, while Barry

Bonds's 2001 seventy-third home run ball brought $450,000. A 1928 Babe Ruth home run ball was sold for around $26,000 in 2006.

9. In 1918 Ruth had walked out on his team, jumping to a shipbuilding team. In 1919 he had almost come to blows with his manager, Ed Barrow.

10. Daniel, *Real Babe Ruth*, 40–41. Daniel recounts the detailed conversation he had with Ruppert, shortly before the latter's death in 1939.

11. *New York Times*, February 5, 1918.

12. Ruth, "Secret of My Heavy Hitting," 420.

13. Ruppert, "Ten Million Dollar Toy," 18.

14. The 1919 Red Sox finished in fifth place, twenty and a half games out of first place, after winning the World Series in 1918. Frazee explained that Ruth "had become impossible and the Boston club could no longer put up with his eccentricities. . . . Twice before he has jumped the club and revolted. He refused to obey orders of the manager and became so arrogant that discipline in his case was ruined" (Stout and Johnson, *Red Sox Century*, 146). The Boston press was fairly evenly split on the deal at the time, in no small part because Frazee said he would use the money to acquire players. There was by no means an overwhelming outcry over the sale.

15. There were conflicting reports of the sale price. For example, the January 6, 1920, *New York Times* said it was $125,000. The loan was not made public until late in 1920. It was a personal loan from Ruppert to Frazee.

16. *New York Evening Telegram*, May 13, 1920. These were the three biggest stars of the silent films at the time.

17. Broun, "Sweetness and Light in Baseball," 64.

18. "Along Came Ruth" was the name of a 1914 Irving Berlin tune. Ten years later, Edward Cline directed a silent film, a comedy, of the same name. Both were about a girl named Ruth, and neither the song nor the movie had anything to do with Babe Ruth.

19. Neil Sullivan, *Diamond in the Bronx*, 6.

20. Creamer, *Babe*, 217.

21. Montville, *Big Bam*, 125.

22. State senator and future New York City mayor Jimmy Walker sponsored the bill. With so many men working six days a week, the attendance at Sunday games would easily exceed that of any other day of the week. Sharing the Polo Grounds meant that the Giants would have approximately twelve Sunday games. Having the ballpark to themselves, the Giants would have about nineteen Sunday dates. Each Sunday date was worth around $37,000 at the time, according to the *New York Herald*, February 6–7, 1921.

23. *New York Tribune*, May 5, 1919, quoted in Fetter, *Taking On the Yankees*, 71. The Giants hosted this first Sunday game and lost to the Phils, 4–3. Richard Crepeau suggests in *Baseball: America's Diamond Mind* that the battle over Sunday baseball, while framed at the time as a religious issue, also had class overtones (153).

24. The Giants increased the Yankees' rent from $65,000 a year to $100,000 a year (Riess, *Touching Base*, 124, 129).

25. The ten-acre lot, just across the Harlem River from the Polo Grounds, was sold to the Yankees for $625,000. Construction by the White Construction Company began in May 1922. Eleven months and $2.5 million later, it opened, on the Yankees' opening day of 1923.

26. Baker sat out the entire 1915 season because of a salary dispute with his manager, Connie Mack. He sat out the 1920 season because of the death of his wife.

27. April 29, 1920, article in Aaron Ward file, National Baseball Library and Archives, Cooperstown, New York.

28. Batting helmets would not become mandatory until 1971. Researcher Bill Deane notes that "rules addressing helmets evolved between the late 1950s and early 1980s." "SABR-L," online research forum post, October 13, 2006.

29. For example, an editorial in the May 3, 1917, *Sporting News* had accused the Red Sox in general and Dutch Leonard and Carl Mays in particular. "Charges are made that the Red Sox pitchers are again using the 'bean ball.' They are indulging in their specialty of hitting opposing batters in the head, without regard to consequences. . . . They are pitchers of high ability, schooled in control, as their records show," wrote the paper.

30. Had Barry Bonds hit 14.6 percent of the National League's home runs in 2003, the season he hit seventy-three, he would have hit 494 circuit blasts that year.

31. Ruth's 1920 slugging percentage would be the highest of his career; he would exceed his 1920 on-base percentage only in 1923 with .545. Ruth would never hold the single-season record for on-base percentage. That mark was held by Giants manager John McGraw, who had a .547 in 1899, until Ted Williams broke it in 1941 with a .553 mark. (Throughout virtually his entire playing career, McGraw benefited from the rule that all foul balls not caught on the fly did not count as strikes.) Barry Bonds would break both these marks with a slugging percentage of .863 in 2001 and on-base percentages of .582 in 2002 and .609 in 2004.

32. During his career, Coveleski's name had the letter *e* on the end of it. The letter was dropped years later. As with many European names (Coveleski was of Polish heritage), there are numerous possible spellings. He was born Stanislaus Kowalewski.

33. Gallico, *Farewell to Sport*, 40.

34. Intentional walks were not tracked until 1955.

35. Thorn et al., *Total Baseball*, 2420. The 1919 season did have fourteen fewer games than 1920, 140 rather than the usual 154. The owners thought, incorrectly it turned out, that the public would return only slowly to the game after the war.

36. Haupert and Winter, "Yankees Profits and Promise," 201. The Giants earned a profit of $296,803 in 1920 (Riess, *Touching Base*, 77).
37. Dan Levitt has worked extensively with the Yankees' financial records at the National Baseball Hall of Fame Library in Cooperstown, New York, including general ledger records ("Players Bought and Sold") and Player Card files. He notes that since Ruth's 1920 bonus was paid in February 1921, some sources have reported his 1921 salary as $30,000. The Babe was also paid a bonus of $50 for each home run he hit in 1921. Dan Levitt, e-mail message to Steve Steinberg, June 18, 2006.
38. Damon Runyon, *Sporting News*, December 9, 1920.
39. Sanborn, "Consider the Pitchers," 475.
40. Spitball pitchers were originally given a one-year exemption from the ban, for 1920. After the 1920 season, they were granted the right (by a grandfather clause) to use the pitch for the rest of their careers.
41. As the 1920 season progressed, the owners were concerned about the extra expense of using a lot of balls; and Ban Johnson told umpires to back off and be more frugal in their use of baseballs (*New York Times*, August 19, 1920). That was the case until August 1920, when Ray Chapman was killed. Chapman might have had a difficult time spotting the darkened ball in the afternoon shadows of the Polo Grounds in New York. Henceforth, the umpires were instructed to replace scuffed and soiled balls.
42. Tests conducted during the 1920s did not reveal significant changes in the composition of the ball. For example, widely publicized tests done by Columbia University chemistry professor Harold A. Fales concluded that 1914, 1923, and 1925 balls had similar elasticity (*New York Times*, July 16, 1925). He did note the "tighter, thinner, and all but seamless cover" of the 1925 ball, whose countersunk seams prevented pitchers from getting a good grip on the ball.
43. Lane, "Much Discussed Menace," 505.
44. In an unpublished paper, researcher Bob Schaefer has uncovered a May 9, 1949, interview of George Reach in the *Philadelphia Evening Bulletin*. He suggested that his family's A. J. Reach & Company, which manufactured baseballs for the American League, from time to time adjusted the resiliency of the ball. Reach, who was eighty-one years old at the time of the interview, had a reputation of impeccable integrity; and during the 1920s he had repeatedly denied any such alterations were made. The higher grade of yarn, which had more spring and could be wound tighter, coupled with mechanical improvements in the winding and sewing machines, can reconcile officialdom's claim that there was no plot to change the ball with its increased resiliency. Attempts to improve the quality of the ball had generated its greater spring.
45. See Steinberg, "Spitball and the End of the Deadball Era."

46. Sanborn, "Consider the Pitchers," 475.
47. *New York Evening Telegram*, August 22, 1920.
48. Hoefer, "Reign of the Wallop," 375.
49. Huston was a captain when he bought the Yankees, a commission he earned in the Spanish-American War. By 1919 he was a colonel, after serving in France in World War I. Ruppert was called "colonel" ever since he was given that title when appointed to the position on the staff of New York governor David B. Hill.
50. Gallico, *Golden People*, 39.

6. The Giants Fail to Get Rogers Hornsby

1. Lane, "Kelly's Place in the 'Greatest Infield,'" 452.
2. Cubs Park opened in 1914 as Weeghman Park, home of the Chicago Whales of the Federal League. After the Federal League folded, the Cubs began playing there in 1916. It was renamed Wrigley Field in 1927.
3. The Cubs suspected Hendrix was involved and released him in February 1921. He never played another Major League game.
4. Kauff's last Major League season was in 1920. Although a jury would acquit him of involvement in an auto theft scheme, Commissioner Landis banned Kauff from baseball for life. The Giants would release Benton in July 1921, calling him an "undesirable" player.
5. Alexander, *John McGraw*, 216.
6. Chase and Zimmerman were eventually blacklisted for life. Reporting on Zimmerman's departure, the *Sporting News* said he "was doubtless uncouth, vulgar and altogether unreliable, but even so he has some of the qualities that excite a certain sort of admiration."
7. *Sporting News*, March 11, 1920, quoted in Alexander, *John McGraw*, 218.
8. Zimmerman had made $6,500 in 1919; the Giants offered him $2,100 for 1920.
9. *New York Sun*, March 9, 1921.
10. *New York Sun*, March 9, 1921.
11. Curran, *Mitts*, 33.
12. *Washington Post*, February 22, 1921.
13. *New York Globe and Commercial Advertiser*, June 10, 1920.
14. Bancroft played 42 games at shortstop for the Phillies and 108 for the Giants in 1920. His 598 assists broke Rabbit Maranville's Major League record of 574 assists with the 1914 Boston Braves. Since 1920 only Glenn Wright, with 601 for the 1924 Pirates, and Ozzie Smith, with 621 for the 1980 Padres, have exceeded Bancroft's mark.
15. Grantland Rice, *New York Tribune*, January 21, 1921.
16. The Chalmers Motor Company awarded a new automobile to one player from the National League and to one from the American League. In 1910

the Chalmers Award went to the league batting champion, but from 1911 to 1914 it was an early version of the current Most Valuable Player Award. The voting was done by one sportswriter from each Major League city.

17. Lesch, "Larry Doyle," 58.
18. Heywood Broun, *Literary Digest*, February 25, 1928, 58, quoted in Lowenfish, *Branch Rickey*, 172.
19. *New York World*, December 30, 1920.
20. Alexander, *Rogers Hornsby*, 62.
21. *New York World*, December 30, 1920. Six years later, in December 1926, McGraw would trade Frisch to St. Louis for Hornsby.
22. *New York Evening Mail*, December 30, 1920.
23. *St. Louis Post-Dispatch*, November 1, 1920.
24. Dan Daniel, *New York Herald*, January 5, 1921.
25. *New York World*, December 10, 1920.
26. Roush, who like Groh had played briefly for McGraw, was also unhappy in Cincinnati. But just before the season started, a rumored four-for-one trade with the Giants fell through; and Roush remained with the Reds.
27. In the 1914 World Series, Maranville batted .308 in the Braves' four-game sweep of the Philadelphia Athletics.
28. *Washington Post*, February 11, 1921.
29. Two of the Giants' best pitchers, Jesse Barnes in 1918 and Art Nehf in 1919, had come to New York in trades with Boston.
30. Oscar C. Reichow, *Sporting News*, February 5, 1920, quoted in Crepeau, "Urban and Rural Images," 31.

7. Ed Barrow Comes to New York

1. Lieb, "Business Directors," 491.
2. Ruth explained, "I had sense enough to realize that I couldn't win, even if I beat him" (*Babe Ruth Story*, 76). Robert Smith summed up the situation well: "That was the Babe all over, as the current phrase had it. He would talk as tough as any man alive, and tougher than most. But he was not a fighter. He wanted people to like him" (*Babe Ruth's America*, 67).
3. Sid Mercer, *New York Evening Journal*, October 29, 1920.
4. Levitt, *Ed Barrow*, 177-78.
5. Barrow, *My Fifty Years in Baseball*, 110.
6. Frank Graham, *New York Yankees*, 57.
7. Barrow, *My Fifty Years in Baseball*, 126.
8. Bob Quinn of the Browns, Branch Rickey of the Cardinals, and William Veeck Sr. of the Cubs had similarly broad authority.
9. Sportswriter Fred Lieb used the phrase "The Rape of the Red Sox" as the title for chapter 15 of his 1947 team history, *The Boston Red Sox* (178–92). He considered the Ruth sale and this December 1920 deal as part of that

plundering. Yet in the *New York Evening Journal* of September 29, 1931, Lieb declared that December 1920 trade as one of the most even deals that the Yankees made with Red Sox owner Frazee.

10. The Ernie Shore–Duffy Lewis trade of two years earlier, the Carl Mays deal of 1919, and the Babe Ruth acquisition were the other three.

11. One of the other two Yankees, pitcher Hank Thormahlen, had been a top prospect. After he won twenty-five games for the International League's Baltimore Orioles in 1917, owner Jack Dunn sold him to the Yankees, comparing him to another former Orioles pitcher. "He is as good a pitcher as Babe Ruth," he told the *New York Globe and Commercial Advertiser* (May 17, 1918). Yet after two promising seasons with New York, Thormahlen proved undependable for Huggins in 1920. He would not turn things around in Boston and won only one more big league game. The fourth Yankee player in the deal, outfielder Sam Vick, tore up his knee that winter and appeared in only forty-four more games. He is the answer to the following trivia question: who was the Yankees' starting outfielder in 1919 whose spot Babe Ruth took in 1920?

12. Burt Whitman, *Boston Herald*, December 16, 1920.

13. Joe Vila, *Sporting News*, December 23, 1920.

14. Lane, "Biggest Trade of Recent Years," 432–33.

15. Sam Crane, *New York Evening Journal*, December 16, 1920.

16. *Boston Post*, December 16, 1920.

17. John Kieran, *New York Times*, June 17, 1929.

18. W. J. Macbeth, *New York Tribune*, December 16, 1920. Miller Huggins later said that trading away Ruel was his biggest trading blunder, thinking that he was just too small at five feet nine and 150 pounds. "If I ever had a son, I'd like him to be like Muddy," said Huggins. "But I simply couldn't see him as a catcher" (quoted in *New York Journal-American*, November 7, 1945). Ruel went on to a long baseball career and was the starting catcher of the 1924 and 1925 Washington Senators. He later became a baseball executive as the general manager of the Detroit Tigers and later as the assistant to Commissioner Happy Chandler.

19. *New York Evening Mail*, April 9, 1921.

20. Burt Whitman, *Boston Herald*, December 16, 1920.

21. *New York World*, December 20, 1920.

22. Mogridge would find success in Washington, where he went on to win sixty-eight games.

23. Lewis would play in only twenty-seven more Major League games.

24. Roth went to Cleveland as a minor figure in the big trade that brought Shoeless Joe Jackson to the White Sox. Roth led the AL with seven home runs that year (1915), the lowest American League total ever for a league leader. Detroit's Sam Crawford also led with seven (1908), as did Red Murray of the

Giants (1909). The leader with the lowest post-1900 total is Tommy Leach, with six for the 1902 Pirates.

25. Joe Vila, *New York Sun*, January 3, 1921.

26. *New York Tribune*, March 10, 1921.

27. Pitcher Bob McGraw, catcher Truck Hannah, and infielder Ham Hyatt also accompanied Shore in the trade with Vernon. Hyatt had played for the Yankees only in 1918, though they still controlled his contract. McGraw had gone to the Red Sox in the Carl Mays deal but rejoined the Yankees for the 1920 season. Shore's last big league appearance was with the 1920 Yankees.

28. *New York Evening Telegram*, January 28, 1921.

29. The Yankees gave Vernon two more players they controlled, pitcher Slim Love and shortstop Roy Corhan. Vernon let O'Doul go to the San Francisco Coast League team, and the Yankees did recall him for the 1922 season. O'Doul would never win a game for the Yanks. That summer of 1922, he would be one of the players they sent to Boston in the Joe Dugan deal. In the late 1920s and early 1930s, O'Doul would become a feared hitter for the Phillies and the Dodgers, including a .398 batting average with a National League record of 254 hits with Philadelphia in 1929. He did win one game as a Major League pitcher, for the 1923 Red Sox.

30. Harry A. Williams, *Los Angeles Times*, January 29, 1921.

31. *Sporting News*, November 17, 1932.

32. *New York Evening Journal*, May 9, 1924.

33. Kelley, *They Too Wore Pinstripes*, 108. Ray Kelly died in 2001.

34. Many ballplayers would spend a week or two in Hot Springs in late February on their way to spring training. They worked off their excess weight by sitting in the resort town's spring-fed hot baths and by walking in the rolling hills nearby. Two of their favorite hotels, the Arlington and the Majestic, still serve the public today.

35. *Sporting News*, January 6, 1938.

36. Sportswriters Ford Frick (who would later serve as president of the National League and commissioner of baseball) and Bill Slocum of the *New York American* were two of Ruth's main writers, or ghosts. Ruth said about Slocum, "He writes more like me than anyone I know" (*Sporting News*, January 13, 1938).

37. John McGraw and Miller Huggins would join the syndicate in the next two years, and Notre Dame football coach Knute Rockne soon became another member.

8. "We fear only Cleveland"

1. *New York Evening Telegram*, January 3, 1921.

2. *New York Herald*, March 21, 1921.

3. *New York Globe and Commercial Advertiser*, April 13, 1921.

4. *New York Evening Telegram*, April 11, 1921.

5. Green, *Forgotten Fields*, 70–71.

6. Editorial, *Sporting News*, December 9, 1920.

7. Billy Evans, *Atlanta Constitution*, November 14, 1920. Evans had been an Ohio sportswriter before his umpiring career and became a widely distributed columnist during his umpiring career. He would later become a Major League general manager (Indians and Tigers), farm director (Red Sox), league president (Southern Association), and even the general manager of a National Football League club.

8. *Sporting News*, November 25, 1920. Many spitball pitchers chewed on the bark of the slippery elm tree to increase saliva, the key element of the spitter.

9. *Sporting News*, November 18, 1920.

10. *Atlanta Constitution*, Nov. 14, 1920.

11. Another factor that may have aided these pitchers was the fact that the new standard player contract, approved as part of the 1921 National Agreement, gave players the right to appeal directly to Commissioner Landis. The owners had to realize that the spitball pitchers might take their case to Landis, arguing for their right to earn an honest livelihood. As a federal judge, Landis had a reputation for standing up for the little guy. The magnates did not want to open a Pandora's box of labor relations.

12. *New York Sun*, September 17, 1924.

13. Krichell had played eighty-seven games as a catcher for the St. Louis Browns in 1911–12. He joined Yankee scouts Bobby Gilks and Bob Connery. Connery was one of Miller Huggins's closest confidantes and had been scouting for Huggins in St. Louis when he discovered and signed Rogers Hornsby. Krichell later ran the Yankees' scouting organization. During his long career, Krichell signed many Yankee stars, including Lou Gehrig and Whitey Ford.

14. Lerner, *Dry Manhattan*, 162.

15. Lerner, *Dry Manhattan*, 99.

16. Sanborn, "What Prohibition Hasn't Done," 525.

17. Johnston, "Beer and Baseball," 23.

18. *New York World*, February 6, 1921

19. *New York World*, May 9, 1921.

20. James P. Sinnott, *New York Evening Mail*, May 15, 1920.

21. Ed Van Every, *New York Evening Mail*, February 7, 1921.

22. *New York Evening Journal*, April 20, 1921. Baker's transgression was that Upland might have played against ineligible players, a serious offense in the eyes of the commissioner. Landis extended his reach and power by threatening to eject from Organized Baseball players who competed against men who had already been banished from the game, such as the Black Sox. Baker was reinstated at least in part because of a lucky break. Upland had been scheduled to play Heinie Zimmerman's All Stars the previous September,

but the game was rained out. Would Landis have banned Frank Baker, had he participated in a game against the blacklisted Zimmerman?

23. Sparks, *Frank "Home Run" Baker*, 220.
24. *Shreveport Journal*, January 31, 1921.
25. Sid Mercer, *New York Evening Journal*, March 1, 1921.
26. Damon Runyon, *New York American*, April 14 and 25, 1921.
27. Creamer, *Babe*, 236. Creamer also tracks Ruth's weight during his career (324).
28. Broun, "Sweetness and Light in Baseball," 64.
29. Lane, "Can Babe Ruth Repeat?" 556–57.
30. *New York World*, April 7, 1921.
31. Hugh Fullerton, *New York Evening Mail*, April 14, 1921.
32. Fred Lieb, *New York Evening Telegram*, March 3, 1921.
33. Grantland Rice, *New York Tribune*, April 6, 1921.
34. Ralph Davis, *Pittsburgh Press*, quoted in *Cleveland Press*, August 31, 1921.
35. *New York Evening Journal*, October 22, 1920.
36. Grantland Rice, *New York Tribune*, April 6, 1921.
37. "Dusting them off" means throwing so close to batters that they literally had to hit the dirt to avoid being hit.
38. *San Francisco Chronicle*, July 11, 1974. In 1915 and 1916 Mails pitched a few games for Brooklyn, where he had an 0-2 record and walked fourteen batters in twenty-two and a third innings, though—surprisingly—he did not hit a single man. Mails then spent four years in the Minors, before Cleveland acquired him from Sacramento of the Coast League late in the 1920 season.
39. Mails did not qualify for the 1920 American League earned run average title (a minimum of ten complete games were required), which was won by the Yankees' Bob Shawkey with a 2.45 mark, followed by Cleveland's Stan Coveleski with a 2.49. Mails also did not hit a batter in Cleveland in 1920.
40. Billy Evans, *Sporting News*, January 27, 1921. It is not known if Evans was referring to the former Philadelphia Athletics pitcher's skill on the mound or to his eccentricities—perhaps both.
41. Backup infielder Harry Lunte initially took over for Chapman but was soon injured. When Bill Wambsganss broke his arm, once again Lunte was his substitute. And once again, he went down with an injury.
42. Phelon, "Who Will Win the Pennants?" 560. He compared the Indians to recent pennant winners who didn't repeat, the 1914 Braves and the 1919 Reds.
43. University of Alabama professor James S. Thomas told the story of the university's baseball program in an August 1921 article in *Baseball Magazine* entitled "Where Ball Players Graduate from College to the Majors."
44. Hugh Fullerton, *Washington Post*, April 11, 1921.
45. Lane, "The Shadow of New York," 397.
46. Ultimately the Yankees would get Dugan, but not until July 1922. Mack trad-

ed Dugan to the Boston Red Sox in January of that year, and Harry Frazee then traded him to New York in the heat of the pennant race that summer.

47. *New York Evening Telegram*, January 19, 1921.
48. Hugh Fullerton, *New York Evening Mail*, August 4, 1921. Connie Mack was able to get American League owners to adopt a rule before the 1920 season prohibiting "managers, club owners and agents" from "negotiating for the services of a player of another club, without permission, under a penalty of $1,000 for the first offense and expulsion from the league for the second offense" (Foster, *Spalding's Official Base Ball Guide, 1920*, 33). But as Mack and other owners realized, tampering was very difficult to prove.
49. William B. Hanna, *New York Herald*, April 3, 1921.

9. "I do not fear any club in the National League"

1. *New York Times*, October 2, 1920.
2. As part of Commissioner Landis's war on gambling, one of his first orders of business was to tell McGraw and Stoneham to sell their interest in the track and casino within six months. They sold in July 1921.
3. The Tigers won the American League pennant in each of Jennings's first three seasons as manager and had not won since. They lost the World Series to Chicago in 1907 and 1908 and to Pittsburgh in 1909.
4. Jennings's managerial experience would lead to press speculation that McGraw was getting ready to retire and that Jennings would become the Giants manager in 1921.
5. Former Major League infielder Jack Barry replaced Burkett at Holy Cross in 1921. Barry would hold that position for forty years and be among the initial class of inductees to the American Baseball Coaches Association Hall of Fame.
6. Burkett had eleven, including two seasons with Cleveland better than .400: .405 in 1895 and .410 in 1896. McGraw had nine, and Jennings had five.
7. Pietrusza, Silverman, and Gershman, *Baseball*, 558. McGraw would pay Burkett's 1921 World Series share out of his own pocket (Dewey and Acocella, *New Biographical History of Baseball*, 48).
8. *Washington Post*, March 10, 1921.
9. *Chicago Daily Tribune*, February 18, 1921.
10. The National League had twelve teams from 1892 to 1899. When they contracted down to eight teams before the 1900 season, they provided an opening for the rise of the American League. Three of the contracted teams—Baltimore, Cleveland, and Washington DC—joined the AL in 1901. (The other contracted team was in Louisville.)
11. Frank Jackson, "Crossing Red River," 87.
12. *New York American*, March 5, 1921.
13. Alexander, *Ty Cobb*, 132.

14. *Detroit Free Press*, March 28, 1917, quoted in Alexander, *Ty Cobb*, 132.
15. McGraw would add Dolan to his coaching staff in 1922. Dolan had played third base for the Yankees in 1911 and 1912.
16. *New York American*, March 5, 1921.
17. In return for Kauff, the Giants got outfielder Vern Spencer. Spencer appeared in forty-five games for them in the second half of 1920, but that would be his only Major League experience.
18. *Sporting News*, quoted in Jones, "Benny Kauff."
19. Jones, "Benny Kauff."
20. Jones, "Benny Kauff."
21. Hugh Fullerton, *Atlanta Constitution*, April 17, 1921.
22. Hugh Fullerton, *Atlanta Constitution*, April 17, 1921.
23. *New York Globe and Commercial Advertiser*, April 1, 1921.
24. Hugh Fullerton, *New York Evening Mail*, January 27, 1921.
25. *New York Herald*, March 22, 1921.
26. Grantland Rice, *New York Tribune*, April 10, 1921.
27. *New York Times*, April 13, 1921.
28. In 1920 Adams gave up only .62 walks per nine innings. No other pitcher was even close; the league's second best was his teammate Wilbur Cooper, with 1.43 per nine innings. The Yankees' Jack Quinn led the American League with a 1.71 mark.
29. Richard Guy, *Sporting News*, April 7, 1921.
30. *New York Tribune*, April 10, 1921.
31. *New York Times*, April 10, 1921.

10. "My job is to knock 'em a mile"

1. "Huggins Fails to Have Popularity," *New York Sun*, June 15, 1919.
2. *New York Evening Telegram*, April 2, 1921.
3. *New York Evening Telegram*, November 29, 1921.
4. Bill Slocum, sixth of six undated columns on Miller Huggins from late September or early October 1929, originally appearing in *New York American*, Miller Huggins file, *New York Journal-American* morgue files, Harry Ransom Humanities Research Center, University of Texas at Austin.
5. Sid Mercer, *New York Evening Journal*, October 29, 1920.
6. Spatz, *New York Yankee Openers*, 82.
7. All the uniform descriptions in this book are based on Okkonen, *Baseball Uniforms*.
8. Damon Runyon, *New York American*, April 14, 1921.
9. Ruth, *Babe Ruth Story*, 35.
10. He hit fourteen, eleven, and ten batters, respectively.
11. The Tigers won that September 15 game, to draw within a game of Boston. But the Red Sox held on to win the 1915 pennant, edging Detroit by two and a half games.

12. *New York Herald*, July 2, 1916. Ironically, in his long career as a pitcher, Griffith had hit 102 batters. Although he hit his last batter more than a century ago, Griffith still ranks in the top sixty all time.

13. *New York Sun*, June 23, 1917.

14. *Sporting News*, May 30, 1918. Speaker and Mays were teammates on the 1915 Red Sox. The *Boston Daily Globe's* May 21, 1918, account of the May 20 beaning of Speaker said that the force of the impact of the ball hitting Speaker's skull sent it careening into the grandstand.

15. Meany, *Yankee Story*, 29–30.

16. Barrow, *My Fifty Years in Baseball*, 106.

17. Mays, "My Attitude," 575.

18. This was Ruth's second 5-5 day. Back on May 9, 1918, he did so against Washington. Ruth pitched a complete game that day (a ten-inning 4–3 loss) and batted fourth.

19. Bodie hit .295 with a career-high .446 slugging percentage in 1920. Despite missing the last three weeks of the season due to an ankle injury, he had seven home runs and seventy-nine runs batted in.

20. The Pacific Coast League was called simply the "Coast League" in 1921. Bodie's thirty home runs had set a new Coast League record.

21. It was Ping, when asked by reporters what it was like to room with Babe Ruth, who made the immortal remark, "I don't know. I never see him. I room with his suitcase" (Seymour, *Baseball*, 431).

22. The Baer remark has been told and retold countless times. In 1919 Bodie stole fifteen bases for the Yankees. In 1920 he stole six bases and was caught stealing fourteen times.

23. Mercer, "Supreme Value of 'Color,'" 424.

24. *New York Globe and Commercial Advertiser*, March 8, 1918.

25. Lieb, *Connie Mack*, 196.

26. Ruth and Meusel would hit home runs in the same game forty-seven times in their careers. Ruth typically batted third in the order and Meusel hit fifth, with first baseman Wally Pipp at cleanup until 1925, when Lou Gehrig replaced him.

27. *New York American*, April 22, 1921.

28. *Sporting News*, March 24, 1938, Eddie Rommel file, National Baseball Library and Archives, Cooperstown, New York.

29. Ed Summers, star of the 1908 and 1909 pennant-winning Tigers, threw it and credited an old-timer of the 1880s who taught him the pitch (Quigley, *Crooked Pitch*, 110). Peter Morris suggests that Eddie Cicotte and Nap Rucker may have invented the pitch in 1905 (*Game of Inches*, vol. 2, 156).

30. Rommel gave up twenty-one home runs in 1921 and tied Urban Shocker's total as the most given up by a pitcher since 1901.

31. *Baseball Magazine*, quoted in *Literary Digest*, September 18, 1920, 83.

32. *New York American*, April 21, 1921.

33. Murdock, *Baseball Players and Their Times*, 154. His reputation aside, Ruth was always much more than a slugger, as his .376 batting average in 1920 confirmed.

34. *New York Times*, April 14, 1921.

35. Farmer, "Carl Mays Dominates the A's," 67–68.

36. *New York Evening Telegram*, March 17, 1921.

37. *New York World*, April 17, 1921.

38. Only twice previously had Johnson's earned run average exceeded two runs a game, and those were 2.21 (1917) and 2.22 (1909).

39. *Sporting News*, April 14, 1921. Both Wood's and Walsh's pitching careers were cut short by arm injuries.

40. *Washington Times*, April 26, 1921.

41. *New York Herald*, April 26, 1921.

42. *New York Globe and Commercial Advertiser*, April 26, 1921.

43. Undated newspaper article in the Fewster file at the *Sporting News*.

44. While a number of players were seriously beaned over the years, liners were not required until 1958; and helmets did not become mandatory until 1971 (Morris, *Game of Inches*, vol. 1, 445).

45. James P. Sinnott, *New York Evening Mail*, April 11, 1921.

46. Sid Mercer, *New York Evening Journal*, April 27, 1921.

47. *New York Herald*, April 18, 1921.

48. *New York Herald*, April 28, 1921.

49. *New York Globe and Commercial Advertiser*, April 22, 1921.

50. *New York Herald*, April 22, 1921.

51. Obituary of Aaron Ward, *Sporting News*, February 8, 1961.

52. He had the best range of AL third basemen that year (Gillette and Palmer, ESPN *Baseball Encyclopedia*).

53. Fred Lieb, *New York Evening Telegram*, April 28, 1921.

54. Baker led the league in home runs in 1911, 1912 (tied with Tris Speaker), 1913, and 1914. Roth was the leader in 1915, and Pipp captured the honors in 1916 and 1917. Ruth then rounded out the decade, leading the AL in 1918 (tied with Tilly Walker of the A's), 1919, and 1920.

55. The stadium was named after team president and owner Clark Griffith, a star pitcher of the 1890s and the first manager of the New York Americans, from 1903 to 1908. Griffith had managed the Senators from 1912 to 1920.

56. *New York Evening Telegram*, May 6, 1921.

57. *New York Evening Telegram*, March 29, 1921.

58. Dan Daniel, *New York Herald*, May 9, 1921.

59. *Boston Daily Globe*, May 3, 1921, quoted in *New York Herald*, May 4, 1921.

60. Hugh Fullerton, *New York Evening Mail*, April 27, 1921. While Fullerton does not give a specific date for this particular Ruth-Huggins confrontation,

it appears to be the Yankees' 8–4 win over the Red Sox on April 20. In the seventh inning, the game was tied at 1–1. After a walk to Peckinpaugh, Ruth hit the home run that sent New York ahead. The way the pitchers were going at the time Ruth came up, it may have been reasonable for Huggins to play for one run by ordering Ruth to bunt.

The *New York Tribune* of April 21, 1921, provided a different perspective on the incident. The paper said that Ruth had dared pitcher Allan Russell to "groove one," which he apparently did; and "the Hercules of Swatdom" effectively won the game for the Yankees with his blast.

61. Damon Runyon, *New York American*, May 6, 1921.
62. James K. McGuinness, *New York Evening Telegram*, May 9, 1921.
63. John Barleycorn is the personification of beer and whiskey and refers to the cereal-crop rye.
64. Hugh Fullerton, *New York Evening Mail*, May 6, 1921.

11. "This home run business is being carried too far"

1. Smith managed the team for six and a half weeks after succeeding first-year manager Horace Fogel in early June. The Giants had employed thirteen different managers following Jim Mutrie's seven-year run (1885–91) and before McGraw stepped in.
2. *New York Times*, April 13, 1921.
3. Williams based his estimate of 15 percent on how much harder it was for the Giants to win on similar estimates made for the Cardinals and Browns. It was accepted as "scientific fact," he said, that in St. Louis the enervating heat was the cause. Williams served as president of the Pacific Coast League from 1924 to 1931 and also served as the league's publicity director and secretary for many years.
4. Harry A. Williams, *Los Angeles Times*, December 20, 1920.
5. Williams noted that the great success of the Yankees in 1920 had put them in a position similar to that of the Giants among American League fans.
6. The opening day crowd represented approximately a tenth of the Phillies' 1921 total attendance of 274,000.
7. The Phillies would finish last again, with a record of 51-103. They were 25-62 under Donovan, who would be replaced by Kaiser Wilhelm in July.
8. Clark, *One Last Round*, 24.
9. Clark, *One Last Round*, 37.
10. Clark, *One Last Round*, 37.
11. John Lardner, "That Was Baseball," 140.
12. *Sporting News*, November 25, 1920.
13. *New York Evening Journal*, April 16, 1921.
14. *New York Evening Journal*, February 4, 1921.
15. Patriots' Day, April 19, is an official holiday in Massachusetts that celebrates the Revolutionary War battles of Lexington and Concord.

16. Saves did not become an official statistic until 1969. However, baseball statisticians have gone back and awarded them retroactively to pitchers who finished winning games without earning the win themselves.

17. For some old-timers in the crowd, MacArthur's presence reminded them that when the Giants played their first home opener, back in 1883, another famous general had attended, Ulysses S. Grant.

18. *New York Times*, April 22, 1921.

19. Lange was at the height of his career when he left baseball after the 1899 season. He did so to satisfy his future father-in-law, who did not want his daughter to marry a ballplayer. However, the couple later divorced.

20. Spatz, *Bad Bill Dahlen*, 25–26.

21. Pietrusza, Silverman, and Gershman, *Baseball*, 594.

22. *Sporting News*, January 8, 1958.

23. *Daguerreotypes, Sporting News*, October 17, 1935.

24. Despite missing the last month of the season, Kelly's fifteen home runs led the International League.

25. Hynd, *Giants of the Polo Grounds*, 215.

26. Nineteen twenty was the first year that runs batted in became an official Major League statistic.

27. Lee Allen, *Giants and the Dodgers*, 113.

28. Hynd, *Giants of the Polo Grounds*, 122.

29. When eighteen-year-old McGraw joined the Baltimore Orioles as a rookie in 1891, his most welcoming teammate was twenty-eight-year-old Robinson, the team's established catcher. Now, Robinson at fifty-eight was the oldest manager in the National League, and McGraw at forty-eight was the second oldest.

30. Semchuk, "Wilbert Robinson," 302.

31. Pietrusza, Silverman, and Gershman, *Baseball*, 979.

32. *New York Evening Journal*, May 4, 1921.

33. John J. Ward, "Kelly Seven, Ruth Six," 341.

34. Westbrook Pegler, *Atlanta Constitution*, May 4, 1921.

35. John B. Foster, *New York Daily News*, May 4, 1921.

36. Cliff Wheatley, *Atlanta Constitution*, May 4, 1921.

37. *New York Tribune*, May 23, 1921.

38. Fuzzy Woodruff, *Atlanta Constitution*, May 7, 1921.

39. Hugh Fullerton, *New York Evening Mail*, May 16, 1921.

12. The Trials and Tribulations of John McGraw

1. Parrish, *Anxious Decades*, 158–59.

2. Mercer, "Supreme Value of 'Color,'" 423–24.

3. McGraw, *My Thirty Years in Baseball*, 23.

4. Bishop, "Rube Benton," 254.

5. James J. Long, *Sporting News*, May 12, 1921.

6. McGraw mistook Boyd for another actor, Walter Knight. Actually, McGraw was not even supposed to be in the Lambs Club, as he was still under a three-month suspension for having gotten into a fight with Knight.

7. The William Boyd in the brawl was William H. Boyd, not to be confused with William L. Boyd, another actor, who later went on to play Hopalong Cassidy in films.

8. McGraw missed several games with his injury and assigned the running of the team to coach Hughie Jennings.

9. The *New York American* pointed out that enforcement was much tougher and quicker at an East Side café, for example, than at a West Side club with more "respectable" members (quoted in Lerner, *Dry Manhattan*, 111).

10. Perrett, *America in the Twenties*, 177.

11. Franklin P. Adams, "Prohibition Is an Awful Flop," quoted in Perrett, *America in the Twenties*, 405.

12. Sam Crane, *New York Evening Journal*, May 9, 1921.

13. A player's OPS, determined by the sum of on-base percentage and slugging average, is a modern-day method of measuring offensive output.

14. Youngs reached safely 281 times from his 204 hits, 75 walks, and 2 times hit by a pitch.

15. Sam Crane, *New York Evening Journal*, April 19, 1918.

16. *New York Times*, March 18, 1921.

17. *New York Herald*, March 18, 1921.

18. *Sporting News*, quoted in Crepeau, *Baseball*, 197.

19. Case number 46447, New York Supreme Court for the First District, New York County (Manhattan).

20. The *New York Evening Journal* said that Douglas's early-season absence was due to abscesses in both ears.

21. Bill Watkins, Arthur Irwin, and Fred Lake had preceded Gibson.

22. Rabbit Maranville, *New York Herald*, May 24, 1921.

23. Rabbit Maranville, *New York Herald*, May 24, 1921.

24. *New York Evening Mail*, March 31, 1921.

25. Bescher's decline was as precipitous as Perritt's. After hitting .263 in his first year in St. Louis, he hit .235 in 1916 at the age of thirty-two, although he did also steal thirty-nine bases. (His eighty-one stolen bases with Cincinnati in 1911 stood as the modern NL record until Maury Wills broke it in 1962.) As a part-time player the following year, he hit only .155.

26. Perritt appeared in a total of nineteen games for the 1919–20 Giants and in a combined nine games for the Giants and Tigers in 1921. Detroit released him in July 1921, ending his Major League career.

27. Sam Crane, *New York Evening Journal*, June 1, 1921.

28. Sam Crane, *New York Evening Journal*, June 1, 1921.

13. Cobb and Speaker Await as the Yankees Head West

1. U.S. Bureau of the Census. *Population of the 100 Largest Cities*.
2. The 1915 Tigers are one of only four teams that played a 154-game schedule and won one hundred or more of them but did not win a pennant. The others are the 1909 Cubs, the 1942 Dodgers, and the 1954 Yankees.
3. Stump, *Cobb*, 321.
4. Ruth also received a $5,000 bonus in both 1920 and 1921.
5. Alexander, *Ty Cobb*, 158–59.
6. Sher, "Georgia Peach," 107.
7. Hoefer, "Will Ty Make Good," 447.
8. Damon Runyon, *Sporting News*, February 3, 1921.
9. The intentional base on balls (IBB) was not tracked as a separate statistic in Ruth's era. Moreover, even a review of newspaper play-by-play accounts does not always provide an answer. A pitcher could have pitched carefully to Ruth and not given him a decent pitch to swing at, resulting in a semi-IBB.
10. John B. Sheridan, *Sporting* News, June 2, 1921.
11. Damon Runyon, *New York American*, April 25, 1921.
12. This article was printed in the *New York Evening Telegram*, July 30, 1920. Ruth had set a new record with 150 walks in 1920. By comparison, the National League leader, George Burns of the Giants, had only 76.
13. This was Sutherland's fourth win of the young season. He would win only two more games in 1921, and he would finish his big league career with just those six victories.
14. H. G. Salsinger, *Detroit News*, May 14, 1921.
15. *New York Sun*, May 12, 1921; and *New York Globe and Commercial Advertiser*, May 12, 1921.
16. He did it playing for Minneapolis on July 5, 1915, in a game against St. Paul. Harper had tossed a no-hitter against the Saints a few weeks earlier and struck out ten or more men in each of eight games in May and June.
17. Damon Runyon, *New York American*, May 25, 1915.
18. Billy Evans, *Detroit News*, September 21, 1921. Evans was an Ohio sportswriter before his umpiring career and became a widely distributed columnist during his umpiring career.
19. Ed Bang, *Collyer's Eye*, February 19, 1921. Bang freelanced for this gambling weekly.
20. A right-handed batter tends to have a higher batting average over time against a left-handed pitcher than a left-handed batter has against that pitcher, and vice versa.
21. John B. Sheridan, *Sporting News*, May 5, 1921.
22. Linkugel and Pappas, *They Tasted Glory*, 20.
23. *Sporting News*, April 21, 1921.
24. In one of the games, Uhle set an American League record for a pitcher of six

runs batted in, which has since been broken. Baseball Library, "Charlton's Baseball Chronology, April 28," http://www.baseballlibrary.com/chronology/thisday.php?month=4&day=28.

25. *New York Evening Telegram*, May 13, 1921.

26. *New York Globe and Commercial Advertiser*, May 14, 1921.

27. The ballpark was also known as League Park. It took on the name of its owner, "Sunny" Jim Dunn (no relation to Baltimore Orioles owner Jack Dunn), who purchased the team early in 1916. He died in 1922; and his wife sold the Indians in 1927, when the ballpark again became known as League Park (Ritter, *Lost Ballparks*, 105).

28. *Cleveland Plain Dealer*, May 15, 1921.

29. *New York Tribune*, May 15, 1921.

30. *New York Sun*, June 10, 1921.

31. Jensen, "Tris Speaker," 436.

32. *Cleveland Plain Dealer*, June 21, 1921.

33. The Yanks had played four fewer games because of the rain in the East, and they were actually ahead by a few percentage points.

34. *New York Globe and Commercial Advertiser*, May 20, 1921.

35. "Yankees with Wrecked Mound Staff Sweep into First Place," *New York Evening Journal*, May 16, 1921.

36. *New York Times*, May 17, 1921.

37. Wagenheim, *Babe Ruth*, 75.

38. Damon Runyon, *New York American*, May 25, 1921.

39. Cliff Wheatley, *Atlanta Constitution*, June 3, 1921.

40. Editorial, *Sporting News*, May 26, 1921.

41. Meany, *Baseball's Greatest Pitchers*, 47.

42. Joe Williams, May 23, 1958, in Dickie Kerr file, National Baseball Library and Archives, Cooperstown, New York.

43. This single-season hit mark would stand until the Seattle Mariners' Ichiro Suzuki had 262 hits in 2004.

44. *Sporting News*, July 22, 1920.

45. Lane, "Urban Shocker," 381.

46. *New York Sun*, May 23, 1921.

47. Joe Vila, *Sporting News*, May 26, 1921.

48. *New York Evening Telegram*, May 28, 1921.

49. *New York Globe and Commercial Advertiser*, June 3, 1921. Reese once explained, "If the soreness is in the elbow it's a speedball pitcher nine times out of ten; if it's in the shoulder, a curve ball pitcher" (Anderson, "Bonesetter Reese," 19).

50. *New York Evening Telegram*, December 15, 1920. This was Davis's fourth season in the Majors, when he finally broke through and won eighteen games for the Browns. He had failed to win a game in brief stints with the 1912 Reds, the 1915 White Sox, and the 1918 Phillies.

51. *New York Evening Telegram*, March 7, 1921.

52. *New York Times*, May 25, 1921.

53. Players who appear in the Major Leagues for only a few games are said to have been there only long enough to have a cup of coffee, hence the term. Fohl fit this description well; he appeared in only five games, in 1904–5.

54. *New York Globe and Commercial Advertiser*, March 2, 1921.

55. *St. Louis Globe-Democrat*, May 26, 1921. The incident was not reported in the New York press.

56. *New York Evening Journal*, May 24, 1921.

57. *New York Evening Journal*, May 27, 1921.

58. *New York Evening Telegram*, May 24, 1921.

59. *Sporting News*, June 15, 1968.

60. *New York Times*, May 31, 1921.

61. *New York Herald*, June 2, 1921.

62. *New York Globe and Commercial Advertiser*, June 4, 1921.

63. Not every team used their ace in this way. While Mays made eleven relief appearances and Shocker made nine, Faber made only four and Coveleski, three. John McGraw—who used closers, including Doc Crandall earlier in the Deadball Era—used all of his starters in relief in 1921: Douglas came in thirteen times; Barnes, eleven; Toney, ten; and Nehf, seven.

64. Smelser, *Life That Ruth Built*, 371.

65. *New York Sun*, June 3, 1921.

66. Sam Crane, *New York Evening Journal*, June 3, 1921.

67. There was virtually no mention that year of the true career leader, Roger Connor, who had hit 138 home runs in an eighteen-year career, from 1880 to 1897. Twelve of those seasons, and the bulk of those homers, came as a member of the New York Giants.

68. Lane, "Wizard of the Dope," 509.

69. Sam Crane, *New York Evening Journal*, June 6, 1921.

70. *New York Evening Journal*, May 27, 1921.

14. "The Yanks are the best worst team in either league"

1. Lane, "Extraordinary Career of Howard Ehmke," 546.

2. Lane, "All America Baseball Club of 1920," 354. See also Lane, "All-America Baseball Club of 1921," 620.

3. Hugh Fullerton, *New York Evening Mail*, June 8, 1921.

4. The average price of a new Ford (the company that had more than half of U.S. new-car sales at the time) was dropping after 1910 and into the early 1920s. By 1924 the Ford Model T sold for only $290. Microsoft Encarta, "Automobile Industry," *Online Encyclopedia 2009*, Microsoft Corporation, 1997–2009, http://encarta.msn.com/encyclopedia_761563934_3_24/ Automobile_Industry.html (accessed July 4, 2009; site now discontinued).

5. Hugh Fullerton, *New York Evening Mail*, June 15, 1921.

6. The account of Ruth's day in court and jail is drawn primarily from the *New York Herald*, June 9, 1921.

7. *New York American*, June 9, 1921. While Speaker formally protested the ruling and thus the game's outcome, he did not prevail since it was a judgment call by the umpire, not the misinterpretation of a rule.

8. *New York Evening Journal*, June 9, 1921.

9. Actually, the Giants did not perform that poorly; they won ninety-six games. But they were up against the Chicago Cubs and their record-setting 116-win season.

10. *New York World*, June 8, 1921.

11. At the time, both pitchers were flirting with the Federal League. The story of the proposed trade is told by Joe Vila, *New York Sun*, March 16, 1919; and by Fred Lieb, *New York Evening Telegram*, January 15, 1922.

12. Steinberg, "Ray Caldwell," 719.

13. Lewis, *Cleveland Indians*, 104–5.

14. *New York Evening Telegram*, June 26, 1921.

15. Dan Daniel, *New York Herald*, June 11, 1921. Ruth would not break Roger Connor's record of 138 career home runs until July 18, although there would be no mention of this record at the time.

16. Simon, "Larry Gardner," 438.

17. Bagby would drop from a 31-12 record and a 2.89 ERA in 1920 to 14-12 with a 4.70 ERA in 1921. Quinn would go from an 18-10 record with a 3.20 ERA in 1920 to 8-7 with a 3.78 ERA in 1921.

18. *Atlanta Constitution*, June 3, 1921.

19. Sid Mercer, *New York Evening Journal*, May 12, 1921.

20. Cobb, "What I Think of My New Job," 387. With the magazine's lengthy lead time, it is possible Cobb was interviewed before this June series. The article almost certainly was written before the Yankees and Tigers met in mid-July.

21. *New York Herald*, June 12, 1921. Cleveland was hitting above .320, and the Yankees were only in the .270s at the time.

22. Lane, "Terrific Slugging," 414.

23. Damon Runyon, *New York American*, May 26, 1921.

24. Honig, *Baseball When the Grass Was Real*, 119.

25. This would be the sixth of eight seasons Speaker would lead the league in two-base hits. He still holds the career record of 792 doubles.

26. He also would score 128 runs; both totals were career highs. And both would be third best in the league, though far behind baseball's leader—the Babe, who had 145 and 177, respectively.

27. For example, the March 16, 1920, *Evening Telegraph* rated him number one, with Buck Weaver the next best. For many years, there had been no discussion of who was the game's best shortstop. Now that Honus Wagner was no

longer playing (he had retired after the 1917 season), the mantle of baseball's best shortstop was open for discussion. By the end of the 1920 season, Grantland Rice of the *New York Tribune* was calling Dave Bancroft of the Giants the game's best shortstop.

28. *New York Sun*, June 22, 1919.
29. Heywood Broun, *New York World*, October 6, 1921.
30. Sam Crane, *New York Evening Journal*, June 13, 1921.
31. Cobb, *My Life in Baseball*, 215.
32. Ironically, Leonard was traded to the Yankees in the 1918 Caldwell deal; but after a contract dispute with them, he was sold to the Tigers. Late in 1926 Leonard would touch off a firestorm when he accused both Cobb and Speaker of fixing a 1919 ball game.
33. Ruth would pitch and win two more games, in 1930 and 1933, after Cobb had retired.
34. Frank O'Neill, *New York Sun*, June 14, 1921.
35. *New York American*, May 18, 1921.
36. Boston's Bill Bradley also hit four in four days in 1902 and eleven that season.
37. *New York Evening Journal*, June 14, 1921.
38. H. G. Salsinger, *Detroit News*, June 14, 1921.
39. Hugh Fullerton, *New York Evening Mail*, May 31, 1921.
40. *New York Evening Telegram*, May 9, 1921.
41. *New York American*, June 14, 1921.
42. Stump, *Cobb*, 328.
43. Walter Trumbull, Listening Post, *New York Herald*, June 20, 1921.
44. Walter Trumbull, Listening Post, *New York Herald*, June 25, 1921.
45. Sammons, *Beyond the Ring*, 67.
46. *New York Evening Journal*, June 29, 1921.
47. Lieb, *New York Evening Post*, June 28, 1927.
48. Gould, "Game of Golf Hurt Batting?" 499–500.
49. Hugh Fullerton, *New York Evening Mail*, June 25, 1921.
50. *New York World*, June 16, 1921.
51. *New York Herald*, June 16, 1921.
52. Hugh Fullerton, *New York Evening Mail*, June 20, 1921.
53. *New York Evening Mail*, June 17, 1921. There had been suggestions that the Black Sox also threw some 1920 games before they were suspended in late September, even though the team stayed in the pennant race until the end of that season (Asinof, *Eight Men Out*, 145–48).
54. Burt Whitman, *Boston Herald*, June 21, 1921.
55. *New York Globe and Commercial Advertiser*, June 23, 1921.
56. Henry Thomas, *Walter Johnson*, 176.
57. Eaton, "Babe Ruth's Latest," 491.

58. Harry Schumacher, *New York Globe and Commercial Advertiser*, June 22, 1920.

59. *New York Evening Mail*, June 10, 1921.

60. *Washington Times*, June 25, 1921.

61. In the 1911 World Series, Baker's home runs in Games 2 and 3, off Rube Marquard and Christy Mathewson, respectively, were the key blows in the A's defeat of McGraw's Giants.

62. *New York Globe and Commercial Advertiser*, June 28, 1921.

63. *New York World*, July 6, 1921.

64. *New York Times*, July 6, 1921. See also Kermisch, "From a Researcher's Notebook," 126–27.

15. Setbacks on the Road and in the Commissioner's Office

1. On May 28 Pittsburgh lost a ten-inning home game to the Cincinnati Reds, 4–3. However, Pirates manager George Gibson protested the result. National League president John Heydler eventually upheld the protest and ordered the game to be continued on June 30 with the Reds leading, 3–2, after seven and a half innings. In the interim, newspapers treated this game as a loss for the Pirates, and the standings for this time period reflected that decision. On June 30 the Pirates rallied to win the game, 4–3.

2. In 1934 Pennsylvania became the last state to allow professional baseball to be played on Sunday.

3. Pirates manager George Gibson was the catcher on that 1909 team.

4. In December 1920 the Giants had offered veteran catcher Frank Snyder and another unnamed player to Philadelphia for Rixey, a pitcher who had always been tough on the New Yorkers. But the Phillies traded him to Cincinnati for pitcher Jimmy Ring, who had won seventeen games in 1920, and outfielder Greasy Neale. Rixey would win one hundred games for the Reds over the next five seasons and was elected to the Baseball Hall of Fame by the Veterans Committee in 1963. Conversely, no Giants pitcher during that five-year period achieved comparable success or was elected to the Hall of Fame. Neale went on to a successful career coaching the National Football League's Philadelphia Eagles and was elected to the Pro Football Hall of Fame in 1969.

5. Spink, *Judge Landis*, 89.

6. Spink, *Judge Landis*, 90.

7. *New York Times*, June 12, 1921.

8. Sam Crane, *New York Evening Journal*, June 18, 1921.

9. Hugh Fullerton, *New York Evening Mail*, June 16, 1921.

10. Lane, "Famous Landis-Groh Decision," 414, 431, 432.

11. Sam Crane, *New York Evening Journal*, June 18, 1921.

12. Sam Crane, *New York Evening Journal*, June 18, 1921.

13. Murdock, *Ban Johnson*, 207.
14. Schupp had won sixteen games for St. Louis in 1920 and twenty-one for McGraw's last pennant winner in 1917, but those were the only seasons he was used primarily as a starter. The Giants traded him to the Cardinals in June 1919 for catcher Frank Snyder.
15. The first time was in 1884, when conditions were markedly different. On September 20 of that year, both Jimmy Macullar and Oyster Burns of Baltimore as well as Podge Weihe of Indianapolis each hit two home runs in a game. All three men played in the American Association.
16. *New York Herald*, June 14, 1921.
17. *New York Evening Journal*, July 12, 1921.
18. Sam Crane, *New York Evening Journal*, June 8, 1921.
19. In 1920 there were 4,893 runs scored in the National League and 5,869 runs scored in the American League. In 1921 those totals climbed to 5,632 in the NL and 6,303 in the AL.
20. *New York Evening Mail*, June 10, 1920.
21. *New York Globe and Commercial Advertiser*, June 17, 1921.
22. *Sporting News*, May 19, 1921.
23. *Sporting News*, June 2, 1921.
24. *New York Evening Journal*, June 25, 1921; and *New York Herald*, June 25 and June 29, 1921.
25. In the late 1930s the American League would settle on using earth from the Delaware Valley farm of former player Lena Blackburne, from near Pennsauken Creek in Palmyra, New Jersey. (The National League began using the "rubbing mud" in the 1950s.) Umpires still use that same mud today to remove the gloss from baseballs.
26. McGraw's combined record (as a player and as a manager) of 131 ejections was broken in 2007 by Bobby Cox.
27. Society for American Baseball Research, SABR *Baseball List and Record Book*, 367. The total of career ejections by umpires and of managers and players remains a work in progress.
28. Hugh Fullerton, *New York Evening Mail*, June 18, 1921. This may or may not have been true. It is more likely that Fullerton had a "sense" that Klem moved games along more quickly than other umpires, rather than his having compared the actual times of games.
29. By comparison, as of June 20, five teams in the higher-scoring American League had scored more runs than the Giants: Cleveland (387), Detroit (387), New York (332), Washington (326), and St. Louis (320).
30. While the "Fordham Flame" did not catch on, the "Fordham Flash" would; and Frisch would forever be known by that nickname.
31. A fifth game, scheduled for Tuesday, June 28, was rained out.
32. Clark, *One Last Round*, 45.

33. Clark, *One Last Round*, 42.
34. Clark, *One Last Round*, 44–45.
35. *New York Sun*, July 1, 1921.

16. The Giants Solidify Their Lineup

1. Benito Santiago is the current rookie record holder. Santiago hit safely in thirty-four consecutive games for the 1987 San Diego Padres.
2. Creamer, *Stengel*, 134.
3. Robertson was in government service in Norfolk during 1918 and played just one game with the Giants in 1919. He refused to remain with the team after a preseason deal in which McGraw traded him to Washington did not work out. In July McGraw sent him to the Cubs in the deal that brought Phil Douglas to New York. Robertson's twelve home runs in 1916 and 1917 tied him for the lead with Cy Williams of Chicago in 1916 and Gavy Cravath of Philadelphia in 1917.
4. On August 1, 1919, the Giants had obtained Nehf from the Braves in exchange for pitchers Joe Oeschger, Red Causey, and Johnny Jones, catcher Mickey O'Neil, and $55,000.
5. A fuller discussion of Vaughn's exit from the Cubs can be found in Finkel's "Hippo Vaughn."
6. Joe Vila, *New York Sun*, June 16, 1921.
7. *New York Times*, July 2, 1921.
8. Lane, "Home-Run Epidemic," 372–73.
9. Hugh Fullerton, *New York Evening Mail*, July 27, 1921.
10. *New York American*, July 13, 1921.
11. Damon Runyon, *New York American*, July 11, 1921.
12. Damon Runyon, *New York American*, July 10, 1921.
13. *New York Times*, July 14, 1921.
14. In addition to Frisch winning the stolen bases title in 1921, George Burns of the Giants led in both 1914 and 1919.
15. Rothe, "Shortened No-Hitters," 54.
16. Pietrusza, *Judge and Jury*, 185.
17. *New York Globe and Commercial Advertiser*, July 26, 1921. That Benton "had not been delivering" was not true. He had had very few poor outings all season.
18. Pietrusza, *Judge and Jury*, 185.
19. Spink, *Judge Landis*, 91.
20. Koppett, *Leonard Koppett's Concise History*, 154.
21. "Reward for 'Indifference,'" *Sporting News*, August 4, 1921.
22. Lowenfish, *Branch Rickey*, 135.
23. Puff, "Silent George Burns," 123–24.
24. In his three years as a Yankee when they played at the Polo Grounds

(1920–22), Babe Ruth played the majority of his games in left field. Ruth was the everyday left fielder for the Yankees in 1921, playing there in 134 games.

25. Curran, *Mitts*, 161.
26. Fetter, *Taking On the Yankees*, 59.
27. Puff, "Silent George Burns," 123.
28. Puff, "Silent George Burns," 123.
29. Lesch, "George Burns," 77.
30. Puff, "Silent George Burns," 123.
31. McGraw and Duffy settled the suit out of court after the season.
32. *Hartford Courant*, August 7, 1921.
33. *Los Angeles Times*, August 23, 1921.

17. "You can't play your outfielders in the middle of the next block"

1. *New York Times*, July 9, 1921.
2. Gettelson, "Pitchers Stealing Home," 12. Only twenty-two pitchers had done so through 1975.
3. Short on pitchers, White Sox manager Kid Gleason started former Lehigh College star Cy Twombly. He played only in 1921, with a career mark of 1-2. Twombly was hit hard, and another rookie, Jack Wieneke, relieved him. He too pitched in the Majors only in 1921 and had a career record of 0-1.
4. *New York Evening Journal*, July 16, 1921.
5. Faber is the consensus winner of the retroactive American League Cy Young Award for 1921 (Gillette and Palmer, ESPN *Baseball Encyclopedia*, 1806). See also, Thorn et al., *Total Baseball*, 726; and Spatz, "Retroactive Cy Young Awards," 3.
6. *New York Evening Mail*, July 28, 1921.
7. *New York Sun*, July 14 and 21, 1921.
8. Ed Bang, *Collyer's Eye*, July 30, 1921.
9. *New York World*, July 11, 1921.
10. *St. Louis Times*, July 16, 1921.
11. *New York Evening Journal*, July 16, 1921.
12. The Yankees split those twenty games he managed. He would later manage the Cleveland Indians, from 1928 to 1933 and in 1941.
13. F. C. Lane explained in *Baseball Magazine* that "player's players" were "men whose work, while not often recognized at its true value by press or spectator, has earned the respect of other players" (Lane, "Roger Peckinpaugh," 533).
14. *New York Globe and Commercial Advertiser*, July 18, 1921.
15. John E. Wray, *St. Louis Post-Dispatch*, July 14, 1921. Such remarks could be seen as offensive since Mays did bean Ray Chapman just a year earlier, resulting in the only death on the playing field in Major League history.
16. The *New York Herald* and the *New York Tribune* were just two of these papers.

17. *Sporting News*, June 23, 1921.

18. *New York Globe and Commercial Advertiser*, July 19, 1921.

19. Bill Jenkinson forcefully promotes this position in his book *The Year Babe Ruth Hit 104 Home Runs* (211–13). The *New York World* and the *New York Sun* reported the ball went a distance of 560 feet; the *Chicago Daily Tribune*, 610 feet. Henry Bullion of the *Detroit Free Press* measured Heilmann's drive at 515 feet and Ruth's at 590 feet, according to Foster, *Spalding's Official Base Ball Guide, 1922*, 29.

20. *New York Globe and Commercial Advertiser*, July 19, 1921. If Huggins saw the home run, as this quote suggests, he would have traveled to Detroit during his recovery, even though he had not yet resumed his duties as manager of the Yankees. Coincidentally, this was also the home run that set a new career record of 139, breaking Roger Connor's 138. Yet there was no mention in the press of this milestone since Gavy Cravath, whom the Babe had passed back in June, was considered the career leader at the time.

21. *New York Herald*, July 20, 1921.

22. *New York Globe and Commercial Advertiser*, July 16, 1921.

23. Morris, *Game of Inches*, vol. 1, 427.

24. Sam Crane, *New York Evening Journal*, July 22, 1921. Frank Chance, the Yankees' manager in 1913–14, had a very different opinion. When he resigned in September 1914, Chance blamed his failure to build the Yankees into a winner on Irwin's incompetence as a scout (*Sporting News*, September 17, 1914).

25. Frank Graham, *Lou Gehrig*, 36–40; and Eig, *Luckiest Man*, 29–32. Graham specifically mentions Irwin as the go-between in getting Gehrig both the Giants' tryout and the Hartford offer. Eig details Gehrig's brief stay in Hartford. Both books cover the difficulties Gehrig then had regaining his college eligibility at Columbia. Fred Lieb relates that McGraw himself told Gehrig that it would be all right for him to use an assumed name while playing for Hartford (*Baseball as I Have Known It*, 169–70).

26. *New York Globe and Commercial Advertiser*, July 21, 1921.

27. W. J. Macbeth, *New York Tribune*, July 25, 1921.

28. Babe Ruth, *New York American*, July 28, 1921.

29. Hugh Fullerton, *New York Evening Mail*, July 16, 23, and 25, 1921.

30. Frank Graham, *New York Yankees*, 63.

31. Walter Trumbull, "Listening Post," *New York Herald*, July 27, 1921.

32. Murdock, *Baseball Players and Their Times*, 136.

33. *New York Sun*, July 21, 1921.

34. *New York Evening Journal*, March 11, 1918.

35. He did play semipro ball with Upland, Pennsylvania, of the Delaware County League in 1915, when he sat out the season in a contract dispute with his manager, Connie Mack, and in 1920, when he cared for his daughters after the death of his wife.

36. In four seasons with the A's, from 1911 to 1914, he had a batting average of .334. With the Yankees, he reached the .300 mark only once, batting .306 in 1918. He would hit nine home runs in 1921 with only 330 at bats. His career high was twelve home runs in 1913.

37. In 1917 Baker led all AL third basemen in put-outs and assists. In 1918 he led in put-outs and fielding percentage. In 1919 he led in both put-outs and double plays. Baseball experts now consider put-outs and assists, which reflect the ground a fielder covers, better measures of a fielder's worth than fielding percentage. A player can have a high fielding percentage by covering only his immediate area and not venturing beyond it. Other factors can affect the numbers, including a team's type of pitchers—such as fly ball pitchers—and field conditions.

38. While there was no voting for Rookie of the Year until 1947, Sewell is a consensus winner of the hypothetical or retroactive American League Rookie of the Year Award for 1921 (Gillette and Palmer, ESPN *Baseball Encyclopedia*, 1807). See also, Thorn et al., *Total Baseball*, 727; and Spatz, "SABR Picks 1900–1948 Rookies of the Year," 3.

39. *New York Tribune*, July 24, 1921.

40. Ed Bang, *Collyer's Eye*, February 28, 1920.

41. While some accounts say that outfielder Elmer Smith threw out Ruth, the *New York Times* (July 24, 1921) was very detailed in its account, stating that the ball was hit so hard off the wall that it eluded Smith and bounded all the way back to first baseman Johnston.

42. Damon Runyon, *New York American*, July 28, 1921.

43. Ruth, "Why I Hate to Walk," 33.

44. *St. Louis Times*, July 28, 1921.

45. *New York Evening Journal*, July 29, 1921. Also, the *St. Louis Times* (July 29, 1921) reported that Davis promised he would go more than six innings and win the game. Either way, Davis lost the bet.

46. *St. Louis Times*, July 25, 1921.

47. Hoyt went to Brooklyn's Ebbets Field one day, hoping to pitch batting practice for the Dodgers. He did not get that chance, but he caught the eye of the New York Giants' catcher and scout Red Dooin, according to Meany, *Baseball's Greatest Pitchers*, 108. In his Hoyt biography, William Cook accounts for the youngster's early career. Hoyt pitched in amateur and semipro games the summer of 1915 and pitched for Erasmus Hall again in the spring of 1916, before leaving school that May to join his first pro team. That June, he signed a regular playing contract with the Giants (Cook, *Waite Hoyt*, 7–11).

48. Between 1916 and 1919, Hoyt was assigned to Mt. Carmel, Hartford, Lynn, Memphis, Montreal, Nashville, Newark, Rochester, and New Orleans.

49. Steinberg, "Curse of the . . . Hurlers," 66.

50. Ruth and the Yankees played in seven games during this stretch. His longest

home run drought in terms of games was nine, during nine days from August 24 through September 1. Bob Meusel was now also in the midst of his longest home run drought, which ran from July 12 through August 8.

51. William B. Hanna, *New York Herald*, July 31, 1921.

52. Levitt, "Stan Covelelski," 690.

53. Ritter, *Glory of Their Times*, 110.

54. *Cleveland Plain Dealer*, August 2, 1921. See also the *New York Globe and Commercial Advertiser*, August 2, 1921.

55. Lewis, *Cleveland Indians*, 140.

56. *New York Evening Mail*, August 11, 1920.

57. Total Major League attendance in 1921 was 8,607,312, down 5.6 percent from 9,120,875 attendees in 1920. The next-highest 1921 attendance figures belonged to the Indians and the Pirates, whose numbers lagged far behind those of New York, less than 750,000 each. Attendance figures are from Thorn et al., *Total Baseball*, 2421.

58. Leverett T. Smith Jr., "Changing Style of Play," 132.

18. Lay off Huggins and Hope Nothing Happens to the Babe

1. Huggins had played Minor League ball in St. Paul from 1901 to 1903; and his manager from that time, Mike Kelley, was still the skipper of the Saints. Huggins and Kelley had become close friends. In early 1925 Huggins would buy a minority interest in the Saints.

2. Hendryx had led the American Association in hitting in 1919, with a .368 batting average for Louisville. He was a former Yankee (1915–17) who hit .328 for the 1920 Red Sox but had fallen to .241 this season. He would hit .341 for St. Paul in 1922 and would not return to the Majors.

3. Sheehan, who appeared in twelve games with a 1-0 record for New York, would lead the American Association in both wins and earned run average in 1922 and 1923 before returning to the Majors with Cincinnati and Pittsburgh (Davids, *Minor League Baseball Stars*, 120). Sheehan had control problems in New York, walking nineteen men in thirty-three innings. Connelly had only five at bats with the 1921 Yanks, plus one more in 1920; and thus his big league career would end with a .167 batting average. The *New York Globe and Commercial Advertiser* reported on August 1, "He developed the temperament of an established prima donna."

4. Baseball records show his date of birth as July 28, 1890. But his death certificate lists it as July 28, 1888.

5. *New York Evening Mail*, August 4, 1921.

6. *New York Evening Telegram*, August 3, 1921.

7. Fewster's recent fielding mistakes were noted in the August 1 and August 3, 1921, editions of the *New York Globe and Commercial Advertiser*. The *New York Evening Mail* reported on his ongoing health issues on August 15, 1921.

8. The February 18, 1922, *New York American* reported that Bodie refused to report because the Yankees would not guarantee him a 1921 World Series share. In early 1922 Bodie would apply to the commissioner for reinstatement with good standing, the first step in his return to the Major Leagues. Landis refused to do so, citing Bodie's refusal to report to the Red Sox.

9. Bodie's power would return in Des Moines in 1924 and Wichita Falls in 1925, when he would hit thirty-two and thirty-seven home runs, respectively, in his late thirties. He had more than two hundred hits and hit over .340 each of those years (Hoie and Bauer, *Historical Register*, 27).

10. *New York Sun*, June 18, 1921.

11. *New York Evening Telegram*, July 25, 1921. Lewis certainly found his batting stroke and eye out west. He would hit .362, .358, and .392 in the years 1922–24, respectively (Armour, "Duffy Lewis," 452).

12. *New York World*, July 24 and 27, 1921.

13. Finkel, "Hippo Vaughn."

14. Spink, *Judge Landis*, 84.

15. Hugh Fullerton, *New York Evening Mail*, August 9, 1921.

16. White, *Creating the National Pastime*, 104.

17. Alexander, *Our Game*, 132.

18. Sid Mercer, *New York Evening Journal*, July 14, 1921.

19. William McGeehan, *New York Herald Tribune*, December 28, 1926. McGeehan's comments came more than five years later, when gambling intruded back into the spotlight. Ty Cobb and Tris Speaker were accused (and later exonerated) of fixing a 1919 game.

20. Lieb, "Baseball," 393.

21. Pietrusza, *Judge and Jury*, 174. The final language of that agreement was worked out by a committee of four lawyers: George Wharton Pepper of Philadelphia, John Conway Toole of New York, James C. Jones of St. Louis, and Landis himself. See Spink, *Judge Landis*, 75.

22. Spatz, *New York Yankee Openers*, 81.

23. Stump, *Cobb*, 331–32.

24. *Detroit News*, August 4, 1921. Lentz's best cast of 440 feet fell 60 feet short of Ruth's blast to the center-field bleachers.

25. *New York World*, August 6, 1921.

26. Fred Lieb, *New York Evening Telegram*, September 26, 1922, written prior to the 1922 Giants-Yankees World Series.

27. *New York Tribune*, August 7, 1921.

28. Fewster also had misplayed Urban Shocker's drive, which went for a double on July 27. He did the same with Doc Johnston's drive on July 30, which went for a three-run inside-the-park home run. Fewster then had problems with another Cobb fly that went for a triple on August 4.

29. Harry Schumacher, *New York Globe and Commercial Advertiser*, July 15, 1921.

Gillette and Palmer's ESPN *Baseball Encyclopedia* confirms that Pipp had a significant drop in both fielding runs and range in 1921 from 1920 (830).

30. Pipp led American League first basemen in put-outs and double plays four times and in assists twice. The ESPN *Baseball Encyclopedia* rates him as having the best numbers for range and throwing among American League first sackers in both 1918 and 1919 (830). His fielding runs and range, which fell off markedly in 1921, would remain low in both 1922 and 1923.

31. *New York Evening Journal*, March 11, 1918.

32. *New York Sun*, August 9, 1921.

33. *New York Globe and Commercial Advertiser*, August 15, 1921.

34. *New York Herald*, August 11, 1921.

35. Damon Runyon, *New York American*, August 8, 1921.

36. Babe Ruth, *New York American*, August 28, 1921.

37. *New York World*, August 9, 1921.

38. *New York Evening Mail*, August 9, 1921.

39. Hugh Fullerton, *New York Evening Mail*, August 15, 1921.

40. Damon Runyon, *New York American*, August 9, 1921.

41. Joe Vila, *New York Sun*, August 11, 1921.

42. Joe Vila, *Sporting News*, August 18, 1921.

43. *New York Globe and Commercial Advertiser*, August 11, 1921.

44. Harry Schumacher, *New York Globe and Commercial Advertiser*, August 11, 1921.

45. Walter Trumbull, Listening Post, *New York Herald*, August 26, 1921.

46. The Yankees had been scheduled to play single games in Philadelphia on Saturday, August 13, and Monday, August 15, with an off day on Sunday (due to the state's blue laws). They got the A's to change the Monday game to half of a doubleheader on Saturday. This enabled them to play exhibitions on Sunday, Monday, and Tuesday, before their next league game in Chicago on Wednesday.

47. *New York Herald*, August 18, 1921.

48. *New York Evening Telegram*, August 14, 1921.

49. *New York Evening Mail*, August 15, 1921.

50. After 1930 a home run was determined fair or foul by where it left the playing field. Previously, the ruling was based on where the ball was when it left the umpire's sight.

51. *New York Globe and Commercial Advertiser*, August 19, 1921.

52. Baker hit .294 in 1921. For the two months preceding this injury, from June 22 until August 20, he hit a torrid .339 according to the league's day-by-day logs.

53. *St. Louis Times*, August 22, 1921.

54. All of the papers covering the game had accounts of the melee, though there were variations of just what happened. Most reports suggested that the scene

had an almost comical ending, with the sight of the little Yankee manager being hauled away from the conflict by a big law officer.

55. *New York Evening Journal*, August 23, 1921.
56. While Mays would win twenty-seven games and Faber only twenty-five in 1921, there is little doubt that the latter was the better pitcher this season. Not only had Faber won on a team with only sixty-two wins, he also had the edge in most statistical categories, including earned run average (2.48 compared to Mays's 3.05).
57. Damon Runyon, *New York American*, August 22, 1921.
58. Quinn pitched for Rochester of the International League (1912–13); the Boston Braves (1913); Baltimore of the Federal League (1914), where he had twenty-six wins; and Vernon, California, of the Pacific Coast League (1917), where he had twenty-four wins.
59. The Coast League's players became free agents. After getting the approval of the National Commission, Chicago negotiated directly with Quinn and signed him. He sparkled for them late that season, going 5-1. In the meantime, the Yankees purchased the rights to Quinn from the Vernon, California, club.
60. With somewhat convoluted logic, the commission ruled that the players were free agents since the league had shortened its season (so the owners wouldn't have to pay them for the part of the season not played out). However, when the league would resume play, the players would then revert back to their teams, under the reserve rule that bound a player to the same team year after year. So Vernon ultimately retained Quinn's rights, which the Yankees then acquired.
61. Murdock, *Ban Johnson*, 156–57.
62. Two of the Black Sox were pitchers, Eddie Cicotte and Lefty Williams. With Red Faber out of action with the flu and a lame arm late in the 1919 season, Gleason had only Dickie Kerr to fall back on as a capable and honest starting pitcher; and Kerr did win two World Series games. Assuming that Quinn would not have joined in the conspiracy (he had a reputation as a straight shooter), Black Sox historian Gene Carney suggests that Quinn would have provided Gleason with another pitching option and possibly prevented the Series from being thrown, had Quinn remained with the White Sox (*Burying the Black Sox*, 208).
63. *New York Sun*, August 25, 1921.
64. Babe Ruth, *New York American*, August 24, 1921.
65. Hugh Fullerton, *New York Evening Mail*, September 12, 1921.
66. *New York Times*, August 26, 1921.
67. He was tied in wins with Dickie Kerr of Memphis and Scott Perry of Atlanta.
68. Lemke, "Rogers' Fatal Fastball," 56–59.
69. Hugh Fullerton, *New York Evening Mail*, August 29, 1921.
70. *New York Evening Telegram*, August 23, 1921.

19. A Terrible August for the Giants . . . So Far

1. Walter St. Denis, *New York Globe and Commercial Advertiser*, August 1, 1921.
2. Walter St. Denis, *New York Globe and Commercial Advertiser*, August 1, 1921.
3. Walter St. Denis, *New York Globe and Commercial Advertiser*, August 1, 1921.
4. Will Wedge, *New York Globe and Commercial Advertiser*, August 4, 1921.
5. Sam Crane, *New York Evening Journal*, August 1, 1921.
6. Sam Crane, *New York Evening Journal*, July 30, 1921.
7. *New York Times*, August 17, 1921, quoted in Crepeau, "Urban and Rural Images," 321.
8. Though McGraw had already released Benton, who then signed with the Kansas City Blues of the American Association, the Giants had a ten-day window on Benton's services and were able to recall him in order to send him to St. Paul for Shea.
9. Toney allowed six runs (five of which were earned), ten hits, and three walks in four innings.
10. *New York Herald*, July 31, 1921.
11. W. A. Phelon, "Reds Help in Burial of McGraw's Hopes," *Sporting News*, August 25, 1921, quoted in Crepeau, "Urban and Rural Images," 321.
12. Cy Rigler umpired in the National League for thirty years, from 1906 to 1935. He was more than six feet tall, weighed more than 250 pounds, and had played right tackle for the original Massillon (Ohio) Tigers professional football team.
13. Will Wedge, *New York Globe and Commercial Advertiser*, August 1, 1921.
14. Batting .302 at the time, Groh would finish the season with a .331 batting average in ninety-seven games.
15. *Boston Daily Globe*, August 4, 1921.
16. Schultz left the game and sat out for a few days, but he was not seriously injured.
17. This would be Dillhoefer's final season. He would die at age twenty-eight on February 23, 1922, of typhoid fever.
18. *New York Times*, August 6, 1921.
19. The August 5, 1921, Pirates-Phillies game featured the first play-by-play broadcast of a baseball game. Harold W. Arlin, a Westinghouse foreman, was the announcer, using a telephone to report the play-by-play over a special three-station hookup on KDKA in Pittsburgh, Pennsylvania; WJZ in Newark, New Jersey; and WBZ in East Springfield, Massachusetts.
20. With only 1,659 hits and an unimpressive .270 lifetime batting average, the selection of Evers is one of the more controversial Hall of Fame choices.
21. *Atlanta Constitution*, August 5, 1921.
22. After Grimes went 3-16 in 1917, his first full season, the Pirates traded him to Brooklyn, along with pitcher Al Mamaux and shortstop Chuck Ward, for second baseman George Cutshaw and outfielder Casey Stengel. Wilbert Robinson's skill with pitchers had turned Grimes into one of the game's best.

23. Walter St. Denis, *New York Globe and Commercial Advertiser*, August 11, 1921.

24. Walter St. Denis, *New York Globe and Commercial Advertiser*, August 11, 1921.

25. Walter St. Denis, *New York Globe and Commercial Advertiser*, August 11, 1921.

26. Walter St. Denis, *New York Globe and Commercial Advertiser*, August 11, 1921.

27. *New York Times*, August 12, 1921.

28. Sam Crane, *New York Evening Journal*, August 13, 1921.

29. *New York Herald*, August 15, 1921.

30. Ed Van Every, *New York Evening Mail*, August 11, 1921.

31. E. G. Brands, *Collyer's Eye*, August 13, 1921.

32. *New York Herald*, August 20, 1921.

33. Fred Lieb, *New York Evening Telegram*, August 19, 1921.

34. *New York Herald*, August 20, 1921.

35. Because of a promise he made to his mother, Branch Rickey had never played or managed on Sundays.

36. *New York Times*, August 23, 1921.

37. Lieb, *Pittsburgh Pirates*, 190.

20. "Let's go get 'em while the getting's good"

1. Will Wedge, *New York Globe and Commercial Advertiser,* August 24, 1921.

2. Walter Trumbull, "Listening Post," *New York Herald*, August 24, 1921.

3. *New York Evening Mail*, August 27, 1921.

4. Hynd, *Giants of the Polo Grounds*, 222.

5. Hynd, *Giants of the Polo Grounds*, 222.

6. Maranville, *Run, Rabbit, Run*, 48.

7. Maranville would finish the season at .294, the second-highest full-season batting average of his twenty-three-year career.

8. Douglas's three shutouts tied him for the league lead with Cincinnati's Dolf Luque and Boston's Joe Oeschger.

9. John Lardner, "That Was Baseball," 142.

10. From August 24 through October 2, Meusel would have 51 hits in 126 at bats.

11. Hynd, *Giants of the Polo Grounds*, 222.

12. Hynd, *Giants of the Polo Grounds*, 222.

13. George Kelly, interview by Norman Macht (chairman of the Society for American Baseball Research's Oral History Committee), April lo, 1984.

14. Lieb, *Pittsburgh Pirates*, 190.

15. *New York American*, August 26, 1921.

16. *Pittsburgh Press*, August 26, 1921.

17. The thirty-four-year-old Cutshaw, who shared the second base position with

Tierney, was having by far the finest offensive year of his career. A lifetime
.265 hitter, he would bat .340 in ninety-eight games in 1921.

18. Dan Daniel, *New York Herald*, August 27, 1921.
19. Arthur Robinson, *New York American*, August 27, 1921.
20. Clark, *One Last Round*, 51.
21. Meusel's brother, Bob, also had a big day. He hit two long home runs in
    Detroit to lead the Yankees to a 7–5 win.
22. Hynd, *Giants of the Polo Grounds*, 223.
23. Arthur Robinson, *New York American*, August 28, 1921.

21. "It is no time in which to count McGraw and his men out of any race"

1. *New York Times*, August 29, 1921.
2. The first modern scoreboard was erected at White Stocking Park in Chicago
   in 1880 (Morris, *Game of Inches*, vol. 2, 95).
3. During the time Ned Hanlon managed the Brooklyn team (1899–1905),
   sportswriters began calling them "the Superbas," a reference to a popular
   vaudeville act of the time known as Hanlon's Superbas.
4. McGinnity won the first game, 5–2, and the fourth game, 6–1.
5. Spatz, *Bad Bill Dahlen*, 86.
6. Bill Doak of the Cardinals would lead in the third category with an earned
   run average of 2.59. The concept of a Triple Crown for pitchers did not exist
   until after World War II.
7. Gillette and Palmer, ESPN *Baseball Encyclopedia*, 1806. See also, Thorn et al.,
   Total Baseball, 726; and Spatz, "Retroactive Cy Young Awards," 3.
8. In a statistical oddity, the Yankees and Indians also each had seventy-eight
   wins. New York's one-game lead in the American League race was due to
   their having forty-six losses while Cleveland had forty-eight.
9. Sam Crane, *New York Evening Journal*, September 3, 1921.
10. Joe Vila, *New York Sun*, September 3, 1921.
11. Pittsburgh's winning percentage was .609 (78-50), while the Giants' percent-
    age was .608 (79-51).
12. *New York Evening Journal*, September 6, 1921.
13. Arthur Robinson, *New York American*, September 7, 1921.
14. On September 1 the Pirates had recalled Traynor from Birmingham of the
    Southern Association, where the future Hall of Famer was batting .336.
15. Cy Williams had been in a three-way tie with St. Louis' Austin McHenry and
    Jack Fournier for third place in the National League home run race. His two
    home runs this day gave him eighteen, just two behind another Cardinal,
    Rogers Hornsby, and four behind the leader, George Kelly. Konetchy hit five
    of his eleven home runs this season—his last in the Majors—against the Gi-
    ants. He had one off Toney, one off Nehf, and three off Douglas.
16. Because their September 30 game with Boston was rained out, these would
    be New York's final two home games of the season.

17. Joe Vila, *New York Sun*, September 12, 1921.
18. The Giants would play only nine of those ten games. Their scheduled game against Boston at the Polo Grounds on September 30 was rained out and not made up.
19. *New York Evening Journal*, September 19, 1921.
20. Adams had been the third-oldest player in the National League when the season began. However, since then, the two men older than him—Phillies pitcher Kaiser Wilhelm, who was now the team's manager, and Reds outfielder Dode Paskert—both had played their final games. Kaiser Wilhelm made his final Major League appearance on August 26, and Dode Paskert made his on May 27.
21. *Pittsburgh Post*, September 20, 1921.
22. Gibson's specific defense of Maranville stemmed from his reputation as the leader of the Pirate partiers. A story in the September 10, 1921, *New York Evening Journal* said that Maranville, assisted by Charlie Grimm, started a premature pennant celebration in late August when the Pirates were in Boston prior to their being swept by the Giants. Whether that late-August party was a premature pennant celebration is unknown. However, it was Maranville who protested the Pirates premature photo session for the World Series program when the Pittsburgh team was at the Polo Grounds.
23. Walter St. Denis, *New York Globe and Commercial Advertiser*, August 30, 1921.
24. Damon Runyon, *New York American*, September 19, 1921.
25. Miller Huggins, "Serial Story of His Baseball Career," *San Francisco Chronicle*, January 28, 1924.

22. Ascent to First and Then a Demoralizing Loss

1. The Yankees had played only fifty-three games at home at this point, winning thirty-four of them. They had won thirty-nine of their sixty-six on the road. The Indians had played nineteen more games at home than New York and had won two of every three, for a 48-24 record. They had played only fifty games on the road, winning twenty-eight.
2. Ohioan Earl Smith, an outfielder, was no relation to Arkansan Earl Smith, the Giants' catcher. The former played seven seasons, more than four with the St. Louis Browns, while the catcher played twelve years.
3. After 1921 McBride would be out of baseball until 1925, when he would return as coach of Ty Cobb's Tigers. Milan would take over as Washington's manager in 1922 (Able, "George McBride," 748).
4. *Sporting News*, September 8, 1921.
5. *New York Times*, September 4, 1921.
6. There was virtually no mention of Meusel's feat in the press. He threw out two base runners at home plate, one at first base, and one at second.

7. McNally had been inserted as a pinch runner in what is still the longest game in World Series history. The winner of that 2–1 contest was Babe Ruth, who went the distance as Boston defeated Brooklyn in Game 2.

8. Burt Whitman, *Boston Herald*, September 5, 1921.

9. *New York Evening Journal*, September 12, 1921. The ESPN *Baseball Encyclopedia* by Gillette and Palmer lists McNally with a fielding range of 132 (where 100 is the base) in 1921 and with fourteen fielding runs, both very impressive numbers.

10. That tied an American League record, set by the A's in 1902, of five men getting two hits in the same inning. Today's Major League record of seven men getting two hits in an inning was set by the Cincinnati Reds in 1989.

11. *New York Times*, September 11, 1921. The *Popular Science Monthly* article appeared in the magazine's October issue. The results are discussed at length in Leigh Montville's biography of the Babe, *Big Bam: The Life and Times of Babe Ruth* (136–38).

12. Hugh Fullerton, *New York Evening Mail*, September 10, 1921.

13. Babe Ruth, *New York American*, September 15, 1921.

14. *New York World*, September 12, 1921.

15. *New York Globe and Commercial Advertiser*, September 12, 1921.

16. *New York Evening Journal*, September 12, 1921.

17. *New York Tribune*, September 12, 1921.

18. *New York Herald*, September 14, 1921. "Very Pittsburgh" is a jab at the collapsing Pirates in their NL pennant race.

19. Zingg, *Harry Hooper*, 449. This 1921 season was the first of five solid years that Hooper would have in Chicago.

20. *New York World*, September 15, 1921. John T. Brush (1845–1912), the owner of the Giants, rebuilt the Polo Grounds after a fire in 1911 and gave it this name. But the name did not take hold, and it was usually referred to as the Polo Grounds.

21. *New York Herald*, September 15, 1921.

22. These numbers do not include the 1918 season, when Shawkey served in the U.S. Navy and pitched in only three games. His 1921 earned run average was 4.08.

23. Dan Levitt, Yankees financial records, National Baseball Library and Archives, Cooperstown, New York.

24. *New York World*, July 6, 1919. Four days later, Stan Coveleski and the Cleveland Indians stopped Shawkey's ten-win streak with a 2–0 win over New York.

25. Damon Runyon, *New York American*, September 16, 1921.

26. *New York Globe and Commercial Advertiser*, September 6, 1921.

27. While the Rookie of the Year Award was not instituted until the 1940s, Bob Meusel was awarded the Hypothetical Rookie of the Year Award for 1920.

Using several measures and factors, Bill Deane, an expert in baseball award voting, selected these recipients (Thorn et al., *Total Baseball*, 727). Meusel also won the ESPN *Baseball Encyclopedia* 1920 Ex Post Facto Rookie of the Year Award (Gillette and Palmer, 1807), as well as the Retroactive Rookie of the Year Award that Lyle Spatz conducted for SABR (Society for American Baseball Research) in 1985 ("SABR Picks 1900–1948 Rookies of the Year," 2–4).

28. John J. Ward, "Bob Meusel," 486.

29. Meusel had played ninety-six games at third base with Vernon in 1919.

30. *New York Evening Telegram*, August 9, 1920.

31. Sam Crane, *New York Evening Journal*, August 5, 1920.

32. Waite Hoyt to Bill Ayrovainen, October 1980, private collection. Society for American Baseball Research member Bill Ayrovainen has closely studied Bob Meusel.

33. *New York Evening Mail*, March 14, 1921.

34. Meusel's contract called for a $4,000 salary plus a $1,000 bonus if the Yankees finished in third place or better, "provided he pays strict attention to training rules and keeps himself in good physical condition during the season; it being further understood and agreed that Manager Huggins shall be the sole judge in these matters." Mastro Auctions, "Bob Meusel's 1921 Player Contract," Auction Catalogue, April 2007.

35. *New York Evening Journal*, March 29, 1921.

36. *Cleveland Plain Dealer*, September 6, 1921. Newspapers were cryptic in discussing a player's drinking problems. Another term they used, one that showed up in the *Cleveland Press* the same day, noted that Caldwell had "fallen by the wayside."

37. Joe Vila, *New York Sun*, September 7, 1921.

38. Ray Caldwell, open letter to Tris Speaker, *Cleveland Plain Dealer*, September 8, 1921.

39. The injury was described as a painful contusion of the knee joint (*Cleveland Plain Dealer*, September 12, 1921) and as torn knee ligaments (*New York Sun*, September 24, 1921).

40. Joe Sewell struck out only once every 62.56 at bats—far better than the second-place player, Lloyd Waner, who struck out once every 44.92 at bats. Tris Speaker is number eight on the all-time list, with one strikeout per 35.90 at bats. Sports Reference, "Career Leaders and Records for AB per SO," *Baseball-Reference*, http://www.baseball-reference.com/leaders/at_bats_per_strikeout_career.shtml.

41. *Sporting News*, September 22, 1921.

42. *Boston Daily Globe*, September 16, 1921.

43. Ritter, *Glory of Their Times*, 57.

44. Smith's blows were part of a record-setting streak. In three games on Sep-

tember 4 and 5, he had seven extra-base hits in a row—three doubles and four home runs. He still holds the record for the most consecutive at bats with extra-base hits.

45. Also in 1921 Eppa Rixey of the Philadelphia Phillies gave up only one home run, a hit by Clyde Barnhart that got lost in the tarp next to the stands down the right-field line as he rounded the bases. Since Rixey pitched 301 innings that year, only that freak home run kept his record from being even better than Sothoron's.

46. Cobb, *My Life in Baseball*, 208.

47. The American League's batting average in 1921 (.292) had risen slightly from 1920 (.284).

48. Lieb, *Detroit Tigers*, 165.

49. *New York Tribune*, September 20, 1921.

50. The error was charged to Schang, though the throw seemed to have been the culprit. The *New York Evening Telegram* of September 20, 1921, noted that Shawkey was so close to Schang that he could have handed the ball to him.

51. Hugh Fullerton, *Atlanta Constitution*, August 29, 1921.

52. *Detroit News*, September 20, 1921.

53. As told by Fred Lieb, *New York Evening Telegram*, December 26, 1924.

54. As told by Fred Lieb, *New York Evening Telegram*, December 12, 1922.

23. "It was the greatest game ever played"

1. Frank O'Neill, *New York Sun*, January 26, 1924.

2. Joe Vila, *Sporting News*, November 3, 1921.

3. Fred Lieb, *New York Evening Telegram*, December 12, 1922. Huston's sale to Ruppert would not be consummated until May 1923.

4. Lieb did have a couple of facts wrong. He wrote that the game was in Detroit. He also said that Huggins was blamed for not lifting Mays earlier in that game, when the reality was that this was one time that Huggins did have a quick hook with Mays.

5. Ed Van Every, *New York Evening Mail*, October 24, 1921.

6. Smelser, *Life That Ruth Built*, 279.

7. *New York Globe and Commercial Advertiser*, September 21, 1921.

8. *New York American*, September 21, 1921.

9. *Boston Daily Globe*, September 23, 1921.

10. Curran, *Big Sticks*, 188.

11. Cobb, *My Life in Baseball*, 196.

12. Alexander, *Ty Cobb*, 160.

13. *St. Louis Times*, July 25, 1921. See also Huhn, *Sizzler*, 121.

14. Harry Schumacher, *New York Globe and Commercial Advertiser*, September 22, 1921.

15. *Cleveland Plain Dealer*, September 23, 1921.

16. Joe Vila, *Sporting News*, September 29, 1921.

17. *New York Herald*, September 24, 1921. Hoyt did not have a reputation of defacing the ball; the Indians were probably trying to unsettle him. The paper gave no reason why the Tribe thought Pipp might have been using a loaded bat.

18. *Cleveland Plain Dealer*, September 24, 1921.

19. Heywood Broun, *New York World*, September 24, 1921.

20. Heywood Broun, *New York World*, September 24, 1921.

21. *New York Evening Journal*, September 24, 1921.

22. *Cleveland Plain Dealer*, September 25, 1921.

23. *New York Herald*, September 25, 1921.

24. The right-handed-hitting Evans would hit .333 in 1921; the left-handed-hitting Jamieson would hit .310.

25. The Indians' "Tioga" George H. Burns had a career batting average of .307 with 2,018 hits in sixteen seasons. The Giants' George J. Burns had a career mark of .287 with 2,077 hits in fifteen seasons.

26. Dan Daniel, *New York Herald*, September 25, 1921.

27. *New York Tribune*, September 26, 1921.

28. *Cleveland Plain Dealer*, September 26, 1921.

29. George Daley, *New York World*, September 26, 1921.

30. Sid Mercer, *New York Evening Journal*, September 25, 1921.

31. Damon Runyon, *New York American*, September 28, 1921. Perhaps the Indians were looking for any edge, and Shocker offered them a way to rattle the Yanks. The midwestern bias against the Yankees that Cleveland and Shocker's St. Louis team shared along with Shocker's brashness and his antipathy for the New York team that had traded him away help explain this incident.

32. Frank Graham, *New York Yankees*, 68.

33. *Boston Daily Globe*, July 19, 1921; and *New York Evening Telegram*, July 22, 1921.

34. *New York Evening Journal*, September 27, 1921.

35. *New York World*, September 27, 1921.

36. *New York Herald*, September 27, 1921.

37 *New York Tribune,* September 27, 1921.

38. Wilbur Wood, *Cleveland News*, September 27, 1921.

39. Frank O'Neill, *New York Sun*, October 3, 1921.

40. Gardner would finish the season scoring 101 runs and driving in 120.

41. *New York World*, August 14, 1920.

42. Frank Graham, *New York Yankees*, 69. Damon Runyon gave a different account in the September 28 *New York American*. He wrote that Ruppert retired to his office near the end of the game and that Ed Barrow informed him of the game's outcome.

43. Frank O'Neill, *New York Sun*, September 27, 1921.

44. Heywood Broun, *New York World*, September 27, 1921. In the *1945 Baseball Register*, Fred Lieb included this game in his list of the ten greatest games ever played (27–29). "Ten Outstanding Games."

45. *Cleveland News*, September 27, 1921.

46. Ruth now had 167 runs batted in. He would get one more run batted in on October 1 and three more in the season's final game the following day, to finish with 171. No one had ever driven in that many runs in a season. Lou Gehrig would break that mark just six years later (175 in 1927). Hack Wilson would then set a new record three years after that (191 in 1930), which still stands as the all-time mark.

47. John J. Ward, "Will 'Home Run' Baker Repeat?" 538. Waite Hoyt would make similar remarks years later.

24. The Giants Clinch and the Repercussions Get Ugly

1. Kelly's home run total of twenty-three was enough to lead the National League; but despite the early-season predictions, it was still short of Ed Williamson's league mark of twenty-seven in 1884.

2. Sam Crane, *New York Evening Journal*, September 28, 1921.

3. Walter St. Denis, *New York Globe and Commercial Advertiser*, September 28, 1921.

4. In 1889, known as the Father of American Football, Camp began naming the best collegiate players at each of the eleven positions.

5. Lane, "Frank Frisch," 681.

6. John J. Ward, "Frank Frisch," 522.

7. Pietrusza, Silverman, and Gershman, *Baseball*, 385.

8. John J. Ward, "Frank Frisch," 522.

9. *New York Times*, September 28, 1921.

10. *New York Times*, September 28, 1921.

11. With three games remaining against each other, St. Louis was in a position to tie Pittsburgh for second place if they won all three. But each team won one game, and the other ended in a tie. So the Pirates finished second, three games ahead of the Cardinals.

12. Playing for the Giants' old-timers were pitchers Hooks Wiltse and Jeff Tesreau; catchers Roger Bresnahan and Jack Warner; first basemen Fred Tenney and Fred Merkle; second basemen Larry Doyle and Billy Gilbert; shortstop Bill Dahlen; third basemen Art Devlin and Hans Lobert; and outfielders Jesse Burkett, Moose McCormick, and Red Murray.

13. Almost four years later to the day (October 7, 1925), Mathewson would die at Saranac Lake at age forty-five.

14. Spatz, *Bad Bill Dahlen*, 143.

15. Editorial, *Sporting News*, September 29, 1921.

16. *New York Times*, January 4, 1927.

17. Ralph S. Davis, *Sporting News*, January 13, 1927.

18. A relatively recent example of the *Sporting News'* anti-Semitic content was the weekly's coverage of the Black Sox scandal, as noted in Nathan, *Saying It's So*, 32–36.

19. "Pirates Were Just Not of High Class," *Sporting News*, December 8, 1921.

25. A Pennant for the Yankees, At Last

1. Frank O'Neill, *New York Sun*, September 28, 1921.

2. Sid Keener, *St. Louis Times*, September 28, 1921. The game also meant a lot to the Browns. They were just a half game ahead of Washington in the battle for third place (and thus third-place money). They would finish third, ahead of the Senators by that same margin.

3. Dan Daniel, *New York Herald*, October 1, 1921.

4. *New York World*, September 30, 1921.

5. *Sporting News*, September 29, 1921.

6. With a record of 95-55, they would have finished no worse than 95-57 if they lost their last two games. The Indians were at 93-58, and winning their last three games would leave them at 96-58. In that case, New York would still win by .002, recording a .625 winning percentage compared to Cleveland's .623. The Yankees would play only 153 games in 1921.

7. *New York World*, October 1, 1921. Ironically, it was the Yankees who had triggered a change in league rules after the 1919 season. They had wanted to make up a game against the Red Sox as they battled the Tigers for third place, but the Yanks were unable to do so. New York did still edge Detroit by a half game. The new rule said that if two teams met after a rainout, even in the other team's city, the game would have to be made up (Foster, *Spalding's Official Base Ball Guide, 1920*, 33).

8. Damon Runyon, *New York American*, October 2, 1921.

9. Damon Runyon, *New York American*, October 2, 1921. This was not the only comparison of Huggins to the silent-film star. Harry Schumacher wrote in the *New York Globe* that the little manager "Chaplined to the dugout through the applause" (October 3, 1921).

10. Harry Schumacher, *New York Globe and Commercial Advertiser*, October 3, 1921.

11. Frank O'Neill, *New York Sun*, October 3, 1921.

12. In 1921 a pitcher did not have to pitch at least five innings to get a win. This game also cost Hoyt in his pocketbook. Almost sixty years later, he recalled that he lost "a nice raise" in salary for 1922, by not winning twenty games in his first year as a Yankee when Ruth blew the 6–0 lead (Williams, "Waite Hoyt's Deprived Win," 86–87).

13. Since 1918 second- and third-place teams had shared in the World Series

money. In 1921 members of the second-place teams each earned about $750, and members of the third-place teams each earned about $500 (*New York Times*, October 11, 1921).

14. Ed Bang, *Collyer's Eye*, November 26, 1921.
15. Stuart M. Bell, *Cleveland Plain Dealer*, October 4, 1921.
16. Damon Runyon, *New York American*, October 3, 1921.

26. Prelude to the World Series, Part 2

1. *Boston Herald*, October 4, 1921.
2. Rice, *Tumult and the Shouting*, 114.
3. Frederick Lewis Allen, *Only Yesterday*, 69. See also Frederick Lewis Allen, *Big Change*, 133.
4. Crepeau, *Baseball*, 91.
5. Ford Frick, *New York Evening Journal*, June 19, 1924.
6. Broun, "A Bolt from the Blue," 128. In the early-twentieth century, religious conservatives known as Sabbatarians believed Sunday should be a day of religious observance, not to be desecrated by professional baseball games. The Sabbatarians led the battle against Sunday baseball, but the ban was slowly overturned state by state, with Pennsylvania the last state to relent, late in 1933. See Bevis, *Sunday Baseball*.
7. *St. Louis Times*, September 28, 1921.
8. *St. Louis Post-Dispatch*, October 5, 1921; and *St. Louis Times*, October 5, 1921.
9. Harry Cross, *New York Evening Post*, October 5, 1921.
10. *Baltimore Sun*, May 31, 1914.
11. Dan Daniel, *New York Herald*, October 3, 1921.
12. Bugs Baer, *New York American*, October 4, 1921.
13. Editorial, *Sporting News*, October 6, 1921.
14. Sam Crane, *New York Evening Journal*, October 4, 1921.
15. Fred Lieb, *New York Evening Telegram*, October 2, 1921.
16. Hugh Fullerton, *Atlanta Constitution*, September 29, 1921.
17. Built in 1920 at the corner of East 42nd Street and Lexington Avenue, the Commodore Hotel was named for Commodore Cornelius Vanderbilt.
18. Ruth's 457 total bases is still the Major League record. His 177 runs scored is still the American League record and the post-1900 Major League record.
19. Harry A. Williams, *Los Angeles Times*, October 5, 1921.
20. The 63 home runs by World Series foes Cleveland (35) and Brooklyn (28) in 1920 had set the record that the Yankees and Giants, with 209, obliterated in 1921.
21. Billy Evans, *Philadelphia Inquirer*, October 1, 1921.
22. *New York Times*, October 2, 1921.
23. *New York Times*, October 2, 1921.
24. *Washington Post*, October 3, 1921.

25. Sam Crane, *New York Evening Journal*, October 3, 1921.

26. H. G. Salsinger, *Detroit News*, October 5, 1921.

27. William Hanna, *New York Herald*, October 2, 1921.

28. *Philadelphia Inquirer*, October 4, 1921.

29. Cortland is a small rural county situated between Syracuse, Ithaca, and Binghamton.

30. *New York Evening Journal*, October 1, 1921.

31. The October 3 *New York Times* reported that stockbroker James O'Brien was hosting a dinner at the Ambassador Hotel that night to celebrate his winning $100,000 for successfully picking the Yankees and Giants at odds of 4–1 to win their leagues' pennants back in July when neither club was in the lead.

32. Hugh Fullerton, *New York Evening Mail*, October 8, 1921.

33. Although gambling was illegal in New York, the law, like Prohibition, was openly flaunted. And, again like Prohibition, it was protected by Tammany Hall–controlled judges and police.

34. The higher-priced $6.60 box seats and $5.50 reserved lower-grandstand seats had sold out quickly.

35. *Cleveland Plain Dealer*, October 2, 1921.

36. *New York Times*, October 2, 1921.

37. This was the first time that all games of the World Series would be played at the same park. The second time would be the following year, 1922, when the Yankees and Giants would repeat as pennant winners. The third and last time would be in 1944, when the St. Louis Browns and the St. Louis Cardinals played all the games at Sportsman's Park, the home field they shared.

38. After Game 7 the commissioner would hold a coin toss at the Giants' office in the Polo Grounds that would determine the home team if a ninth game was needed. Commissioner Landis flipped the coin, and the Giants won.

39. Editorial, *Sporting News*, September 22, 1921.

40. *St. Louis Post-Dispatch*, June 23, 1915.

41. *Sporting News*, September 22, 1921.

42. *New York Times*, October 4, 1921.

43. Joe Vila, *New York Sun*, October 5, 1921.

27. Game 1, Wednesday, October 5

1. *New York Sun*, October 5, 1921.

2. *New York Evening Post*, October 5, 1921.

3. *Sporting News*, October 13, 1921.

4. *New York Tribune*, October 6, 1921.

5. *New York World*, October 7, 1921; and *New York Globe and Commercial Advertiser*, October 7, 1921. Mutrie would stay on the Giants' payroll longer than his benefactor. He outlived McGraw by almost four years.

6. Heywood Broun, *New York World*, October 6, 1921.

7. Ed Brewster, *New York Globe and Commercial Advertiser*, October 6, 1921.

8. Irvin S. Cobb, *New York Times*, October 7, 1921.

9. Sid Mercer, *New York Evening Journal*, October 7, 1921.

10. In the 1920 World Series, third baseman Jimmy Johnston of the Dodgers played against his brother, first baseman Doc Johnston of the Indians.

11. *New York Herald*, October 6, 1921.

12. Broun, "Sweetness and Light in Baseball," 64.

13. *New York Herald*, October 12, 1921. E. A. Grozier, Joseph Pulitzer's personal secretary (the *New York World* was a Pulitzer paper), paid Van Zile $250 for his patented invention. Grozier earned enough money from the invention to buy a controlling interest in the *Boston Post*.

14. White, *Creating the National Pastime*, 207; and Halberstam, *Sports on New York Radio*, 137–40.

15. Curt Smith, *Voices of the Game*, 8–11. In 1923 Graham McNamee would take over the World Series broadcasts.

16. Burt Whitman, *Boston Herald*, October 3, 1921.

17. *New York Herald*, October 6, 1921.

18. Damon Runyon, *New York American*, October 6, 1921.

19. Grayson, *They Played the Game*, 127. Plank's 326 career wins now ranks third among left-handers, behind Warren Spahn (363) and Steve Carlton (329).

20. Frisch finished second to Rogers Hornsby of St. Louis, who led the National League with 235 hits.

21. James defines a Defensive Misplay as "a specific event, objectively observable, which has a negative cost to the defense." He notes that there are about fifty-five different Defensive Misplays. Examples include a fielder going back on a ball that lands in front of him and an outfielder chasing a ball to the wall and having the ball then bounce over his head. Bill James, e-mail message to Steve Steinberg, December 12, 2007.

22. Grantland Rice, *New York Tribune*, October 6, 1921.

23. Hynd, *Giants of the Polo Grounds*, 224.

24. Irvin S. Cobb, *New York Times*, October 6, 1921.

25. Sam Crane, *New York Evening Journal*, October 6, 1921.

26. H. G. Salsinger, *Detroit News*, October 6, 1921; and Lieb, *Story of the World Series*, 146.

27. *New York American*, October 6, 1921.

28. Babe Ruth, quoted in Ring Lardner, *Boston Daily Globe*, October 7, 1921.

29. Frank O'Neill, *New York Sun*, October 6, 1921.

30. *New York World*, October 6, 1921.

31. Besides Cobb's swipe on October 9, 1909, George Davis of the White Sox did it on October 13, 1906; the Giants' Buck Herzog did so on October 14, 1912; and the Boston Braves' Butch Schmidt stole home on October 9, 1914. All three of those steals of home were on the front end of double steals.

32. Cullen Cain, *Washington Post*, October 6, 1921.

28. Game 2, Thursday, October 6

1. *New York Herald*, October 7, 1921.
2. Joe Vila, *New York Sun*, October 3, 1921. Kerr had a 19-17 record in 1921. He started seven games against the Yankees and won six of them.
3. Joe Vila, *Sporting News*, October 6, 1921.
4. Westbrook Pegler, *Atlanta Constitution*, October 6, 1921.
5. Marshall Hunt, *New York Daily News*, October 5, 1921.
6. Carmichael, *My Greatest Day in Baseball*, 89.
7. Heywood Broun, *New York World*, October 7, 1921.
8. Gordon Mackay, *Philadelphia Inquirer*, October 7, 1921.
9. Hugh Fullerton, *Atlanta Constitution*, October 7, 1921.
10. *New York Herald*, October 7, 1921.
11. *New York American*, October 7, 1921.
12. Grantland Rice, *Boston Daily Globe*, October 7, 1921. In this account, Grantland Rice wrote that Ruth "was in the act of pilfering the plate."
13. There were varying accounts as to when the Babe first injured the elbow. One report mentioned that he had hurt it against the Indians a couple of weeks earlier; another referred to a slide in the first game of the World Series when he was sacrificed to second in the fourth inning.
14. *New York World*, October 7, 1921.
15. H. G. Salsinger, *Detroit News*, October 7, 1921.
16. *Boston Daily Globe*, October 7, 1921.
17. Irvin S. Cobb, *New York Times*, October 7, 1921. While reporters enjoyed comparing Ruth's weight to that of the former president (1909–13), in reality the slugger weighed far less, even when he was overweight. Ruth probably carried about 230 pounds during the 1921 season. Taft weighed about 330 pounds while president, though he dropped 60 to 70 pounds soon after he left office. Taft was now back in the public eye, having taken his seat as the chief justice of the U.S. Supreme Court that summer.
18. Grantland Rice, *New York Tribune*, October 7, 1921.
19. Cleveland's Duster Mails (1–0) and Stan Coveleski (3–0) had also shut out the Brooklyn Dodgers in the final two games of the 1920 World Series.
20. *New York Herald*, October 7, 1921.
21. Carmichael, *My Greatest Day in Baseball*, 88–92.
22. Harry Cross, *New York Evening Post*, October 7, 1921.
23. Lieb, *Story of the World Series*, 146.
24. Sid Mercer, *New York Evening Journal*, October 7, 1921.
25. *New York Times*, October 7, 1921.
26. *New York Tribune*, October 7, 1921.
27. Hugh Fullerton, *Atlanta Constitution*, October 7, 1921,

28. *Sporting News*, October 13, 1921.

29. Joe Vila, *Sporting News*, October 13, 1921.

29. Game 3, Friday, October 7

1. The game drew the largest crowd of the Series, 36,509; and the gate receipts of $119,007 constituted the richest purse ever for a baseball game.

2. *Boston Daily Globe*, October 7, 1921.

3. *Boston Daily Globe*, October 7, 1921.

4. Hynd, *Giants of the Polo Grounds*, 225.

5. Hynd, *Giants of the Polo Grounds*, 225.

6. H. G. Salsinger, *Detroit News*, October 8, 1921.

7. H. G. Salsinger, *Detroit News*, October 8, 1921.

8. Jack Quinn had pitched for the Yankees from 1909 to 1912 before returning in 1919.

9. Hugh Fullerton, *Atlanta Constitution*, October 8, 1921.

10. Hugh Fullerton, *Atlanta Constitution*, October 8, 1921.

11. *Philadelphia Inquirer*, October 8, 1921.

12. Damon Runyon, *New York American*, October 8, 1921.

13. Hugh Fullerton, *Atlanta Constitution*, October 8, 1921.

14. Sid Mercer, *New York Evening Journal*, October 8, 1921.

15. Damon Runyon, *New York American*, October 9, 1921.

16. Burt Whitman, *Boston Herald*, October 8, 1921.

17. Both records were broken on October 12, 1929, when the Philadelphia Athletics scored ten runs on ten hits in the seventh inning against the Chicago Cubs in a comeback from an 8–0 deficit for a 10–8 victory.

18. Frisch's double was the first of the record-setting ten he would accumulate in World Series play.

19. The only player since Youngs to have two extra-base hits in one inning of a World Series game is Matt Williams of the Arizona Diamondbacks. On November 3, 2001, Williams had two doubles in the third inning against the New York Yankees.

20. The only player since Youngs to have five total bases in one inning of a World Series game is Al Simmons of the Philadelphia Athletics. On October 12, 1929, Simmons had a single and a home run in the seventh inning against the Chicago Cubs.

21. Henry Edwards, *Cleveland Plain Dealer*, October 8, 1921.

22. Heywood Broun, *New York World*, October 8, 1921.

23. Both records have since been broken.

24. *New York Times*, October 8, 1921.

30. Game 4, Sunday, October 9

1. Hugh Fullerton, *New York Evening Mail*, October 8, 1921.

2. Hugh Fullerton, *New York Evening Mail*, October 8, 1921.

3. *Cleveland Plain Dealer*, October 8, 1921.
4. *New York Times*, October 9, 1921.
5. Actually, Huggins now had no choice but to start Mays, as Harper would not pitch on Sundays, per his contract.
6. *New York American*, October 9, 1921.
7. *New York American*, October 9, 1921.
8. *New York American*, October 9, 1921.
9. *New York American*, October 10, 1921.
10. *Atlanta Constitution*, October 10, 1921.
11. *New York World*, October 11, 1921.
12. *New York World*, October 11, 1921.
13. Grantland Rice, *New York Tribune*, October 10, 1921.
14. Gordon Mackay, *Philadelphia Inquirer*, October 10, 1921.
15. Walter Trumbull, "Listening Post," *New York Herald*, October 10, 1921.
16. Walter Trumbull, "Listening Post," *New York Herald*, October 10, 1921.
17. Spink, *Judge Landis*, 96–97; and Lieb, *Story of the World Series*, 147–48.
18. See McGarigle, *Baseball's Great Tragedy*.
19. Fred Lieb, *Sporting News*, December 9, 1972.
20. Honig, *Man in the Dugout*, 169.
21. *Louis Bennett v. Carl Mays*, Superior Court, Commonwealth of Massachusetts, November 15, 1917, quoted in Cottrell, *Blackball*, 96–97.
22. In late December 1926 Commissioner Landis investigated charges by former Detroit pitcher Dutch Leonard that Cobb and Speaker had agreed to fix and bet on a late-September 1919 game between the Tigers and the Indians. In January 1927 Landis exonerated them.
23. *New York Evening Journal*, January 15, 1927. Commissioner Landis thought this situation serious enough to reprimand the Yankees for betting on games and meeting with gamblers (*Sporting News*, July 6, 1922).
24. On April 25 against Washington, Mays had a no-hitter for seven innings but gave up five runs in the eighth and ninth innings and lost, 5–3. On May 2 against Boston, he had a one-hitter through seven innings in a scoreless game with Boston but gave up four hits in the last two innings and lost, 2–1. On June 1 against Washington, Mays gave up five runs in the ninth and lost, 8–7. On June 10 against Cleveland, he allowed two runs in the seventh and three in the ninth, and the Yankees lost in eleven, 8–6. On June 20 against Boston, Mays led, 5–3, after seven innings and allowed three runs in the eighth inning, although the Yankees did win in the tenth. On July 9 against Chicago, he allowed a total of eight runs in the seventh, eighth, and ninth innings; and the White Sox eventually won in the sixteenth inning, 10–9. On July 27 against St. Louis, Mays gave up four total runs in the eighth and ninth in a 7–5 loss. On August 18 against Chicago, he had a 6–4 lead but again gave up three runs in the eighth and lost, 7–6.

25. Mays had thirty complete games in 1921, tied for second in the AL with Urban Shocker. Red Faber led the league with thirty-two. Faber completed 82 percent of his starts, and Shocker and Mays each completed 79 percent of theirs.

26. Burt Whitman, *Boston Herald*, October 10, 1921.

27. Henry Edwards, *Cleveland Plain Dealer*, October 10, 1921.

28. Hugh Fullerton, *Atlanta Constitution*, October 10, 1921.

29. Heywood Broun, *New York World*, October 10, 1921. Broun's syndicated column was also carried in the *Boston Daily Globe*, with a slight variation of words. In that account, this quote ended with perhaps a better choice of words: "no trouble in picturing the gradual disintegration of Mays."

30. *New York Herald*, October 10, 1921.

31. Game 5, Monday, October 10

1. *New York Globe and Commercial Advertiser*, October 10, 1921.

2. Joe Vila, *New York Sun*, October 10, 1921.

3. Smelser, *Life That Ruth Built*, 224.

4. Editorial, *Sporting News*, October 13, 1921.

5. Bancroft had earned the nickname "Beauty" as a Minor League player for his habit of shouting the term on each good pitch his pitcher delivered to the opposition.

6. Lane, "How John McGraw Won Out," 590.

7. Damon Runyon, *New York American*, October 11, 1921.

8. Heywood Broun, *Boston Daily Globe*, October 11, 1921.

9. *New York Evening Telegram*, October 10, 1921.

10. *New York Evening Journal*, October 11, 1921.

11. Sid Mercer, *New York Evening Journal*, October 11, 1921.

12. *Philadelphia Inquirer*, October 11, 1921.

13. Jerome O'Leary, *Boston Daily Globe*, October 11, 1921.

14. Lane, "How John McGraw Won Out," 589.

15. Gordon Mackay, *Philadelphia Inquirer*, October 11, 1921.

16. *New York Times*, October 11, 1921

17. Carmichael, *My Greatest Day in Baseball*, 90. In Hoyt's account of Game 2, which he related to Carmichael years later, he placed this "soap incident" in that October 7 game. However, at least three day-of-game newspaper accounts (in the *New York Times*, the *New York Herald*, and the *Brooklyn Daily Eagle* of October 11, 1921) place the incident in Game 5.

18. Dan Daniel, *New York Herald*, October 11, 1921.

19. Billy Evans, *New York Sun*, October 11, 1921. Evans was merely an observer and columnist for this Series.

20. Walter Trumbull, "Listening Post," *New York Herald*, October 11, 1921.

21. *New York Herald*, October 13, 1921.

22. Fred Lieb, *Sporting News*, November 18, 1926.

23. *New York Evening Telegram*, August 11, 1918.

24. Damon Runyon, *New York American*, January 17, 1915.

25. *New York Times*, October 11, 1921.

26. *New York Morning Telegraph*, October 11, 1921. The *St. Louis Globe-Democrat*, October 11, 1921, notes that there were two physicians by the name of King who tended to Ruth: Dr. George W. King, who was his personal doctor, and Edward King, who was one of the club's doctors. The other Yankees team doctor whose name surfaces during the 1921 season is George D. Stewart.

27. *New York Evening Telegram*, October 11, 1921.

28. *New York Evening Journal*, October 12, 1921. Barrymore's line was from *Sunday*, a popular 1904 play she starred in. The line became famous the world over, closely associated with Barrymore, one of the leading actresses of the time. She explained in her autobiography, "It was just thrown in to get me off the stage politely. It meant nothing; it had nothing to do with anything. But it has become a universal saying, given many different meanings, some of them deep, some of them sinister—gangsters use it just before they pull the trigger" (Barrymore, *Memories*, 146).

29. Sid Mercer, *New York Evening Journal*, October 11, 1921.

32. Game 6, Tuesday, October 11

1. Sid Mercer, *New York Evening Journal*, October 11, 1921.

2. "There is a rule that no player not in uniform, except the captain and manager of the team, may sit on the players' bench during the progress of the game" (*St. Louis Globe-Democrat*, October 12, 1921).

3. Sam Crane, *New York Evening Journal*, October 11, 1921.

4. *New York Times*, October 12, 1921.

5. Ring Lardner, *Boston Daily Globe*, October 12, 1921.

6. *New York World*, October 11, 1921.

7. John B. Foster, *New York Daily News*, October 12, 1921.

8. Harry Cross, *New York Evening Post*, October 12, 1921.

9. Damon Runyon, *New York American*, October 12, 1921.

10. Heywood Broun, *New York World*, October 12, 1921.

11. *Cleveland Plain Dealer*, October 14, 1921. The bullpens were in fair territory, in left-center and right-center field.

12. Ring Lardner, *Boston Daily Globe*, October 12, 1921.

13. Hugh Fullerton, *Atlanta Constitution*, October 12, 1921.

14. *St. Louis Globe-Democrat*, October 12, 1921.

15. H. G. Salsinger, *Detroit News*, October 12, 1921.

16. On October 5, 1966, Moe Drabowsky of the Baltimore Orioles struck out eleven Los Angeles Dodgers in six and two-thirds innings of relief.

17. Frank Graham, *New York Sun*, October 12, 1921.
18. Hugh Fullerton, *Atlanta Constitution*, October 12, 1921.
19. *New York World*, October 12, 1921.
20. *New York Sun*, October 12, 1921.
21. Gordon Mackay, *Philadelphia Inquirer*, October 12, 1921.
22. Lane, "How John McGraw Won Out," 590.
23. Frank Graham, *New York Sun*, October 15, 1921. Ernie Quigley served as a National League umpire from 1913 to 1937, officiating in six World Series, and then became NL supervisor of umpires and public relations director. He would also serve for many years as a college basketball and football referee and was elected to the Basketball Hall of Fame in 1961.
24. Hugh Fullerton, *New York Evening Mail*, October 11, 1921.
25. *New York American*, October 12, 1921.
26. Lieb, *Story of the World Series*, 148–49.
27. Ruth, *Babe Ruth Story*, 102.
28. Joe Vila, *New York Sun*, October 12, 1921.
29. Sid Mercer, *New York Evening Journal*, October 12, 1921.
30. Solomon, *Where They Ain't*, 256. Just over ten years after his father died of heart disease, Willie Keeler would succumb to the same ailment on New Year's Day 1923.
31. *New York Times*, October 12, 1921.
32. *Chicago Daily Tribune*, October 12, 1921.
33. Sid Mercer, *New York Evening Journal*, October 12, 1921.

33. Game 7, Wednesday, October 12

1. *St. Louis Post-Dispatch*, October 13, 1921.
2. *New York Evening Telegram*, October 12, 1921.
3. *New York Evening Journal*, October 12, 1921.
4. *New York Herald*, October 10, 1921.
5. Sam Crane, *New York Evening Journal*, October 13, 1921.
6. *New York Times*, October 13, 1921.
7. *New York Times*, October 13, 1921.
8. Hugh Fullerton, *New York Evening Mail*, October 13, 1921.
9. Gordon Mackay, *Philadelphia Inquirer*, October 13, 1921.
10. Burt Whitman, *Boston Herald*, October 13, 1921.
11. H. G. Salsinger, *Detroit News*, October 13, 1921.
12. Burt Whitman, *Boston Herald*, October 13, 1921.
13. Grantland Rice, *New York Tribune*, October 13, 1921.
14. *New York Evening Journal*, October 13, 1921.
15. *Washington Post*, October 13, 1921.
16. Sam Crane, *New York Evening Journal*, October 13, 1921.
17. Hugh Fullerton, *Atlanta Constitution*, October 13, 1921.

18. Grantland Rice, *New York Tribune*, October 13, 1921.

19. *New York Times*, October 13, 1921.

20. *New York Times*, October 13, 1921.

21. *New York Times*, October 13, 1921.

22. *St. Louis Post-Dispatch*, October 13, 1921.

23. *Washington Post*, October 13, 1921.

24. A few months later, Nat Fleischer would start a boxing publication he would call *Ring Magazine* and go on to write more than fifty books on that sport. Sportswriter Dan Daniel helped Fleischer start the magazine and was a regular contributor to it.

25. Nat Fleischer, *New York Evening Telegram*, October 13, 1921.

26. *Washington Post*, October 13, 1921.

27. *Washington Post*, October 13, 1921.

28. Sid Mercer, *New York Evening Journal*, October 13, 1921.

34. Game 8, Thursday, October 13

1. McGraw, however, had believed that Christy Mathewson had no problem knowing the night before he was to pitch, and started this policy only after Mathewson left the Giants. According to the *Atlanta Constitution* of October 16, 1921, Miller Huggins followed the same policy. Huggins did not name his starting pitcher until just before the game so that "none of the hurlers would have a chance to become unnerved."

2. *New York American*, October 2, 1924.

3. The previous National League high was nine, set by George Suggs of the 1911 Reds. (Jesse Barnes, Nehf's teammate, also had nine for the 1920 Giants.) Bob Lemon of the 1953 Cleveland Indians is the current record-holder, with fifteen. Curt Davis of the 1934 Philadelphia Phillies and Randy Jones of the 1976 San Diego Padres hold the National League record, with twelve.

4. Harry A. Williams, *Los Angeles Times*, October 5, 1921.

5. Nehf would also shut out the Yankees, 1–0, in Game 3 of the 1923 World Series, making him the only pitcher with two 1–0 World Series wins. There would not be another 1–0 win in the World Series until the opening game in 1948, when Johnny Sain of the Boston Braves beat the Cleveland Indians by that score.

6. Phelon, "How the Championship," 613.

7. *New York American*, October 14, 1921.

8. Sid Mercer, *New York Evening Journal*, October 14, 1921; and Damon Runyon, *New York American*, October 14, 1921.

9. John Foster, *New York Daily News*, October 14, 1921.

10. *New York Tribune*, October 14, 1921.

11. Hugh Fullerton, *Atlanta Constitution*, October 14, 1921.

12. H. G. Salsinger, *Cleveland Plain Dealer*, October 14, 1921.

13. *Detroit News*, October 14, 1921.
14. *New York Herald*, October 14, 1921.
15. Interview by the Associated Press, *Florence (sc) Morning News*, October 3, 1948.
16. Hynd, *Giants of the Polo Grounds*, 226.
17. In the ninth inning of 1947's Game 7, Brooklyn's Bruce Edwards bounced into a 6-4-3 double play that retired Eddie Miksis at second. The Yankees won the game, 5–2.
18. Hynd, *Giants of the Polo Grounds*, 227.
19. H. G. Salsinger, *Detroit News*, October 15, 1921.
20. *St. Louis Post-Dispatch*, October 14, 1921. Baker's home run off Mathewson in Game 3 of the 1911 World Series actually just tied the game at 1–1. The Athletics then went on to defeat the Giants, 3–2, in eleven innings.
21. *Sporting News*, October 20, 1921.
22. Frank Graham Jr., *Farewell to Heroes*, 21–22.
23. Babe Ruth, *New York American*, October 16, 1921.
24. Grantland Rice, *Boston Daily Globe*, October 14, 1921.
25. *St. Louis Post-Dispatch*, October 14, 1921.
26. Ed Van Every, *New York Evening Mail*, October 14, 1921.
27. Ed Van Every, *New York Evening Mail*, October 14, 1921.
28. Sid Mercer, *New York Evening Journal*, October 14, 1921.
29. Fred Lieb, *New York Evening Telegram*, October 15, 1921.
30. Joe Vila, *New York Sun*, October 15, 1921.
31. The 1912 Series was a best of seven, but a tie game made an eighth game necessary.
32. Hynd, *Giants of the Polo Grounds*, 227.
33. Walter Trumbull, Listening Post, *New York Herald*, October 14, 1921.

35. Epilogue

1. Hugh Fullerton, *Atlanta Constitution*, October 10, 1921.
2. Hugh Fullerton, *New York Evening Mail*, October 10, 1921.
3. Richter, *Base Ball Guide, 1922*, 157.
4. McGraw, "Why a Baseball Game," 532.
5. Kenneth T. Jackson, "Modern World Took Shape," 317.
6. Douglas, *Terrible Honesty*, 65.
7. Charyn, *Gangsters and Gold Diggers*, 41.
8. Catton, "Yankees," 792.
9. Burt Whitman, *Boston Herald*, October 4, 1921.
10. Harry Schumacher, *New York Globe and Commercial Advertiser*, October 18, 1921.
11. Creamer, *Babe*, 132. Marshall Smelser describes the ornament as a diamond-studded miniature gold baseball. There is no mention of whether Ruth ever did receive it (Smelser, *Life That Ruth Built*, 145).

12. Fowler, *Skyline*, 107.
13. Montville, *Big Bam*, 143.
14. Damon Runyon, *New York American*, October 18 and 19, 1921.
15. Joe Vila, *Sporting News*, October 27, 1921.
16. The winners' share was just over $5,000. Initial newspaper computations were based on dividing the winners' and losers' pools by twenty-five. However, partial shares were often awarded to the support staff—such as scouts, trainers, and even players who were traded away during the season. The Giants did not reveal the exact amount of each share. Had the Yankees divided their pool by twenty-five, it would have totaled $3,510 each. Such clubhouse decisions were often contentious. The *Boston Daily Globe* reported on October 15, 1921, that coach Frank Roth, catcher Al DeVormer, and pitchers Bill Piercy and Tom Rogers had stormed out of a Yankees meeting, upset with their World Series shares.
17. Spink, *Judge Landis*, 103–4.
18. *New York World*, December 6, 1921.
19. Robert Edgren, *St. Louis Post-Dispatch*, December 17, 1921.
20. Under the revised rules, barnstorming would be allowed only until the end of October and subject to written permission by the commissioner. Ruth would legally barnstorm after playing in the 1922 World Series.
21. Part of the show was self-deprecatory. At one point, Ruth is delivered a telegram. "'Bad news from Judge Landis,' he moans. '75 cents collect.'" Later, he explains the key to hitting is keeping your eye on the ball. He is then asked, "Where was your eye that day when Nehf was pitching?" Giants fans in the audience loved that line(*St. Louis Star*, November 8, 1921).
22. Dan Daniel, *New York Herald*, December 6, 1921. The Yankees then embarked on an almost desperate search for an outfielder to help plug the holes created by the six-week absence of Ruth and Meusel. Norm McMillan, Elmer Miller, and Chick Fewster would constitute the Yankee outfielders for opening day 1922. (The club would soon trade all three to the Red Sox. Miller and Fewster, along with Johnny Mitchell, were traded in the Joe Dugan deal in July 1922; and McMillan went in the Herb Pennock trade of January 1923.) The quest for an outfielder included pursuit of Detroit's Bobby Veach, before the Yankees finally settled on Whitey Witt. An unusual option Huggins pursued was to "rent" Salt Lake City's player-manager, and former Yankee, Duffy Lewis until June 1 for $25,000. But the Bees turned the Yankees down (*St. Louis Star*, January 18, 1922). Lewis would bat .362 that year for Salt Lake.
23. Hugh Fullerton, *New York Evening Mail*, October 31, 1921.
24. *St. Louis Star*, October 24, 1921.
25. *New York World*, October 23 and November 15, 1921. A multiplayer trade in which the Yankees would acquire Collins to play second base was an ongoing story in late 1921 as well as in 1922.

26. Dan Daniel, *New York Herald*, December 8, 1921.

27. The amount has been reported as low as $50,000 and as high as $150,000, with $100,000 often mentioned.

28. Sam Crane, *New York Evening Journal*, December 8, 1921; and Sid Mercer, *New York Evening Journal*, December 9, 1921.

29. *St. Louis Globe-Democrat*, December 9, 1921.

30. *New York Globe and Commercial Advertiser*, January 17, 1922.

31. Sam Crane, *New York Evening Journal*, December 9, 1921.

32. This assumed that Bob Shawkey would not return to form, although he would win fifty-two games in the next three seasons.

33. Harry Schumacher, *New York Globe and Commercial Advertiser*, December 21, 1921.

34. *New York Herald*, December 21, 1921.

35. Murdock, *Baseball between the Wars*, 8.

36. Monitor was the pseudonym of sportswriter George Daley. Peckinpaugh's erratic defensive play in the 1925 World Series would overshadow his blunder in the 1921 Series. Playing for Washington, he made eight errors in the Series, including two crucial ones in the Series-deciding Game 7 loss to Pittsburgh.

37. George Daley, *New York World*, December 27, 1921.

38. *New York Herald*, December 9, 1921.

39. Damon Runyon, *New York American*, November 9, 1921.

40. George Daley, *New York World*, December 12, 1921.

41. Sid Keener, *St. Louis Times*, October 18, 1921.

42. Daley, *Inside Baseball*, 63.

43. Neil Sullivan, *Diamond in the Bronx*, 43. Sullivan notes that between 1900 and 1920, Manhattan's population remained at around 2 million, while the Bronx, Queens, and Staten Island grew from a combined .5 million to 1.9 million. The Bronx alone now had about .7 million inhabitants.

44. Ritter, *East Side, West Side*, 173.

45. Daley, *Inside Baseball*, 63.

46. Editorial, *Baseball Magazine*, April 1921, 506; and Editorial, *Baseball Magazine*, July 1921, 338.

47. Robinson and Jennison, *Yankee Stadium*, 12.

48. While the National League owners wanted to continue with the best-of-nine format, the American League magnates were willing to return to the best of seven. Landis felt that the longer series dragged on too long and dissipated fan interest, pointing to the low attendance of the final game of 1921 to support his case. He also felt the longer Series smacked of commercialism. At the December 1921 winter meetings, Landis broke the tie between the two leagues; and the World Series has been a best-of-seven contest ever since.

49. Joe Vila, *Sporting News*, October 19, 1922.

50. Fetter, *Taking On the Yankees*, 89.
51. Fetter, *Taking On the Yankees*, 89.
52. Will Wedge, *New York Globe and Commercial Advertiser*, April 23, 1923.
53. Broun, "1923," 42.
54. Editorial, *Baseball Magazine*, January 1924, 344.
55. *Sporting News*, August 4, 1927.
56. Smelser, *Life That Ruth Built*, 288–89.

Bibliography

Able, Stephen. "George McBride." In Jones, *Deadball Stars of the American League*, 747–48.

Alexander, Charles C. *John McGraw*. New York: Viking, 1988.

———. *Our Game: An American Baseball History*. New York: Henry Holt, 1991.

———. *Rogers Hornsby: A Biography*. New York: Henry Holt, 1995.

———. *Spoke: A Biography of Tris Speaker*. Dallas: Southern Methodist University Press, 2007.

———. *Ty Cobb*. New York: Oxford University Press, 1984.

Allen, Frederick Lewis. *The Big Change: America Transforms Itself, 1900–1950*. New York: Harper and Brothers, 1952.

———. *Only Yesterday: An Informal History of the 1920s*. New York: Perennial Classics, 2000. Originally published in New York by Harper and Row, 1931.

Allen, Lee. *The American League Story*. New York: Hill and Wang, 1965.

———. *The Giants and the Dodgers: The Fabulous Story of Baseball's Fiercest Feud*. New York: Putnam, 1964.

———. *Hot Stove League*. Mattituck NY: A. S. Barnes, 1955.

———. *The National League Story*. New York: Hill and Wang, 1961.

———. *100 Years of Baseball*. New York: Bartholomew House, 1950.

Anderson, Dave, Murray Chass, Robert Creamer, and Harold Rosenthal. *The Yankees: Four Fabulous Eras of Baseball's Most Famous Team*. New York: Random House, 1979.

Anderson, David W. "Bonesetter Reese." *Baseball Research Journal*, no. 30 (2001): 18–19.

Appel, Marty. "New York Yankees: Pride, Tradition, and a Bit of Controversy." In *Encyclopedia of Major League Baseball: American League*, edited by Peter O. Bjarkman, 250–92. New York: Carroll and Graf, 1993.

Armour, Mark. "Duffy Lewis." In Jones, *Deadball Stars of the American League*, 451–52.

Asinof, Eliot. *Eight Men Out*. New York: Holt, Rinehart, and Winston, 1963.

———. *1919: America's Loss of Innocence*. New York: Donald I. Fine, 1990.

"The Babe Ruth Epidemic in Baseball." *Literary Digest*, June 25, 1921.

Bak, Richard. *Cobb Would Have Caught It: The Golden Age of Baseball in Detroit*. Detroit: Wayne State University Press, 1991.

———. *Peach: Ty Cobb in His Time and Ours*. Ann Arbor: Sports Media Group, 2005.

Baldassaro, Lawrence. "Before Joe D: Early Italian Americans in the Major Leagues." In Baldassaro and Johnson, *American Game*, 92–115.

Baldassaro, Lawrence, and Richard A. Johnson, eds. *The American Game: Baseball and Ethnicity*. Carbondale: Southern Illinois University Press, 2002.

Banks, Ed. "Jack Dunn, the Man with the Eagle Eye." *Baseball Magazine*, May 1922.

Barrow, Edward G. *My Fifty Years in Baseball*. With James M. Kahn. New York: Coward-McCann, 1951.

Barrymore, Ethel. *Memories: An Autobiography*. New York: Harper and Brothers, 1955.

Bevis, Charlie. *Sunday Baseball: The Major Leagues' Struggle to Play Baseball on the Lord's Day, 1876–1934*. Jefferson NC: McFarland, 2003.

Bielawa, Michael J. "The Manager Who Disappeared." *Fate*, March 2008.

Bishop, Bill. "Rube Benton." In Simon, *Deadball Stars of the National League*, 253–54.

Boren, Steve. "The Bizarre Career of Rube Benton." *Baseball Research Journal*, no. 12 (1983): 180–83.

Bready, James H. *The Home Team: Our Orioles 25th Anniversary Edition*. N.p.: self-published, 1979.

Broun, Heywood. "A Bolt from the Blue." *Nation*, July 31, 1920.

———. "1923: New York Yankees 4, New York Giants 2." In Einstein, *Baseball Reader*, 42–46.

———. "Sweetness and Light in Baseball." *Vanity Fair*, October 1921.

Brown, Warren. *The Chicago White Sox*. New York: Putnam, 1952.

Burns, Rick, and James Sanders. *New York: An Illustrated History*. New York: Alfred A. Knopf, 1999.

Camp, Walter. "They Shall Not Pass!" *Collier's Weekly*, October 13, 1921, pages 9 (2).

———. "The Truth about Baseball." *North American Review* 213 (April 1921): 483–88.

Carmichael, John P., ed. *My Greatest Day in Baseball*. Lincoln: University of Nebraska Press, 1996. Originally copublished in New York by Grosset and Dunlap and by A. S. Barnes, 1945.

Carney, Gene. *Burying the Black Sox: How Baseball's Cover-Up of the 1919 World Series Fix Almost Succeeded*. Washington DC: Potomac, 2006.

Carter, Paul. *The Twenties in America*. New York: Thomas Crowell, 1968.

Catton, Bruce. "The Yankees." In Jackson and Dunbar, *Empire City*, 788–97.

Chadwick, Bruce, and David Spindel. *The Bronx Bombers*. New York: Abbeville, 1991.

Charyn, Jerome. *Gangsters and Gold Diggers: Old New York, the Jazz Age, and the Birth of Broadway*. New York: Four Walls Eight Windows, 2003.

Clark, Tom. *One Last Round for the Shuffler*. New York: Truck, 1979.

———. *The World of Damon Runyon*. New York: Harper and Row, 1978.

Cobb, Ty. *My Life in Baseball*. With Al Stump. New York: Doubleday, 1961.

———. "What I Think of My New Job." *Baseball Magazine*, August 1921.

Cobbledick, Gordon. "Tris Speaker: The Grey Eagle." In Gallen, *Baseball Chronicles*, 71–87.

Cohen, Eliot. "Rose Out, McGraw In. Why?" *Baseball Research Journal*, no. 20 (1991): 6–7.

Cook, William A. *Waite Hoyt: A Biography of the Yankees' Schoolboy Wonder*. Jefferson NC: McFarland, 2004.

Cooper, Brian E. *Red Faber: A Biography of the Hall of Fame Spitball Pitcher*. Jefferson NC: McFarland, 2007.

Costello, James, and Michael Santa Maria. *In the Shadow of the Diamond: Hard Times in the National Pastime*. Dubuque IA: Elysian Fields, 1992.

Cottrell, Robert C. *Blackball, the Black Sox, and the Babe: Baseball's Crucial 1920 Season*. Jefferson NC: McFarland, 2002.

Creamer, Robert W. *Babe: The Legend Comes to Life*. New York: Penguin, 1974.

Crepeau, Richard C. *Baseball: America's Diamond Mind, 1919–1941*. Orlando: University Presses of Florida, 1980.

———. "Urban and Rural Images in Baseball," *Journal of Popular Culture* 9 (Fall 1975): 315–24.

Curran, William. *Big Sticks: The Batting Revolution of the Twenties*. New York: William Morrow, 1990.

———. *Mitts: A Celebration of the Art of Fielding*. New York: William Morrow, 1985.

———. *Strikeout: A Celebration of the Art of Pitching*. New York: Crown, 1995.

Daley, Arthur. *Inside Baseball: A Half Century of the National Pastime*. New York: Grosset and Dunlap, 1950.

Daniel, Dan. *Babe Ruth: The Idol of the American Boy*. Racine WI: Whitman, 1930.

———. *The Real Babe Ruth*. With anecdotes by H. G. Salsinger. St. Louis: Sporting News, 1948.

Davids, L. Robert, ed. *Minor League Baseball Stars*. Vol. 1. Cleveland: Society for American Baseball Research, 1984.

———, ed. *Minor League Baseball Stars*. Vol. 2. Cleveland: Society for American Baseball Research, 1985.

———, ed. *Minor League Baseball Stars*. Vol. 3. Cleveland: Society for American Baseball Research, 1992.

Deford, Frank. *The Old Ball Game*. New York: Atlantic Monthly, 2005.

Dewey, Donald, and Nicholas Acocella. *The Ball Clubs*. New York: Harper Collins, 1996.

———. *The Black Prince of Baseball: Hal Chase and the Mythology of the Game*. Toronto: Sport Classic, 2004.

Dewey, Donald, and Nicholas Acocella. *The New Biographical History of Baseball.* Chicago: Triumph, 2002.

Dickson, Paul. *Baseball's Greatest Quotations.* New York: Edward Burlingame Books, 1991.

———. *The New Dickson Baseball Dictionary.* New York: Harcourt Brace, 1999.

Douglas, Ann. *Terrible Honesty: Mongrel Manhattan in the 1920s.* New York: Farrar, Straus, and Giroux, 1995.

Dreifort, John E., ed. *Baseball History from Outside the Lines.* Lincoln: University of Nebraska Press, Bison Books, 2001.

Durso, Joseph. *Baseball and the American Dream.* St. Louis: Sporting News, 1986.

———. *Casey and Mr. McGraw.* St. Louis: Sporting News, 1989.

Eaton, Paul W. "Babe Ruth's Latest, the Super Home Run." *Baseball Magazine,* October 1921.

Eig, Jonathan. *Luckiest Man: The Life and Death of Lou Gehrig.* New York: Simon and Schuster, 2005.

Einstein, Charles, ed. *The Baseball Reader.* New York: Lippincott and Crowell, 1980.

Farmer, Ted. "Carl Mays Dominates the A's." *Baseball Research Journal,* no. 28 (1999): 67–68.

Ferber, Nat. *I Found Out.* New York: Dial, 1939.

Fetter, Henry D. *Taking On the Yankees: Winning and Losing in the Business of Baseball, 1903–2003.* New York: W. W. Norton, 2003.

Finkel, Jan. "Hippo Vaughn." *The Baseball Biography Project.* Society for American Baseball Research. http://bioproj.sabr.org/bioproj.cfm?a=v&v=l&bid=921&pid=14570.

Fitzgerald, Ed, ed. *The Book of Major League Baseball Clubs: The American League.* New York: A. S. Barnes, 1955.

———, ed. *The Book of Major League Baseball Clubs: The National League.* New York: Grosset and Dunlap, 1952.

Fleitz, David. *Shoeless: The Life and Times of Joe Jackson.* Jefferson NC: McFarland, 2001.

Foster, John B., ed. *Spalding's Official Base Ball Guide, 1920.* New York: American Sports, 1920.

———, ed. *Spalding's Official Base Ball Guide, 1921.* New York: American Sports, 1921.

———, ed. *Spalding's Official Base Ball Guide, 1922.* New York: American Sports, 1922.

Fountain, Charles. *Sportswriter: The Life and Times of Grantland Rice.* Bridgewater NJ: Replica Books, 2000.

Fowler, Gene. *The Great Mouthpiece: A Life Story of William J. Fallon.* New York: Covici Friede, 1931.

———. *Skyline: A Reporter's Reminiscence of the '20s.* New York: Viking, 1961.

Frick, Ford. *Games, Asterisks and People: Memoirs of a Lucky Fan*. New York: Crown, 1973.

Frommer, Harvey. *Big Apple Baseball: An Illustrated History from the Boroughs to the Ballparks*. Dallas: Taylor, 1995.

———. *A Yankee Century: A Celebration of the First Hundred Years of Baseball's Greatest Team*. New York: Berkley Books, 2002.

Gallagher, Mark. *The Yankee Encyclopedia*. Champaign IL: Sagamore, 1996.

Gallen, David, ed. *The Baseball Chronicles*. Edison NJ: Galahad Books, 1991.

Gallico, Paul. *Farewell to Sport*. Evanston IL: Holtzman, 1980.

———. *The Golden People*. New York: Doubleday, 1965.

Gay, Timothy M. *Tris Speaker: The Rough- and-Tumble Life of a Baseball Legend*. Lincoln: University of Nebraska Press, 2005.

Gershman, Michael. *Diamonds: The Evolution of the Ballpark*. Boston: Houghton Mifflin, 1993.

Gettelson, Leonard. "Pitchers Stealing Home." *Baseball Research Journal*, no. 5 (1976): 12–14.

Gilbert, Thomas. *The Soaring Twenties*. New York: Franklin Watts, 1996.

Gillette, Gary, and Pete Palmer, eds. *The ESPN Baseball Encyclopedia*. 5th ed. New York: Sterling, 2008.

Ginsburg, Daniel E. *The Fix Is In*. Jefferson NC: McFarland, 1995.

Goewey, Edwin. "What Babe Has Done to Baseball." *Leslie's Illustrated Weekly*, July 23, 1921.

Goldblatt, Andrew. *The Giants and the Dodgers: Four Cities, Two Teams, One Rivalry*. Jefferson NC: McFarland, 2003.

Golden, Harry. "From *For 2 Cents Plain: Only in America*." In Einstein, *Baseball Reader*, 132–34.

"Golf vs. Baseball as a Paying Profession." *Literary Digest*, April 9, 1921.

Gonzales, Raymond. "Pitchers Giving Up Home Runs." *Baseball Research Journal*, no. 10 (1981): 18–28.

Gould, James M. "Does the Game of Golf Hurt Batting?" *Baseball Magazine*, October 1925.

Graham, Frank. *Lou Gehrig: A Quiet Hero*. New York: Putnam, 1942.

———. *McGraw of the Giants: An Informal Biography*. New York: Putnam, 1944.

———. *The New York Giants: An Informal History*. New York: Putnam, 1952.

———. *The New York Yankees: An Informal History*. New York: Putnam, 1943.

Graham, Frank, Jr. *A Farewell to Heroes*. New York: Viking, 1981.

Grayson, Harry. *They Played the Game*. New York: A. S. Barnes, 1944.

Green, Paul. *Forgotten Fields*. Waupaca WI: Parker, 1984.

Greenberg, Eric Rolfe. *The Celebrant*. Lincoln: University of Nebraska Press, 1993.

Griffith, Clark. "Why the Spit Ball Should Be Abolished." *Baseball Magazine*, July 1917.

Gropman, Donald. *Say It Ain't So, Joe: The True Story of Shoeless Joe Jackson*. New York: Lynx Books, 1988.

Hailey, Gary. "Anatomy of a Murder." *National Pastime* 4, no. 1 (Spring 1985): 62–73.

Halberstam, David. *Sports on New York Radio: A Play-by-Play History*. Chicago: Masters, 1999.

Harper, William A. *How You Played the Game: The Life of Grantland Rice*. Columbia: University of Missouri Press, 1999.

Haupert, Michael J., and Kenneth Winter. "Pay Ball: Estimating the Profitability of the New York Yankees, 1915–1937." *Essays in Economic and Business History* 21 (Spring 2003): 89–102.

———. "Yankees Profits and Promise: The Purchase of Babe Ruth and the Building of Yankee Stadium." In *The Cooperstown Symposium on Baseball and American Culture*, edited by William M. Simons, 197–214. Jefferson NC: McFarland, 2003.

Herzog, William R., II. "From Scapegoat to Icon: The Strange Journey of Shoeless Joe Jackson." In *The Faith of 50 Million: Baseball, Religion and American Culture*, edited by Christopher H. Evans and William R. Herzog, 97–141. Louisville KY: Westminster John Knox, 2002.

Heydler, John. "Are the New Rules a Success?" *Baseball Magazine*, October 1920.

Heyn, Ernest V., ed. *Twelve More Sport Immortals*. New York: Bartholomew House, 1951.

———, editor. *Twelve Sport Immortals*. New York: Bartholomew House, 1951.

Hoefer, W. R. "The Reign of the Wallop." *Baseball Magazine*, July 1923.

———. "Will Ty Make Good as a Manager?" *Baseball Magazine*, February 1921.

Hoie, Bob, and Carlos Bauer, comps. *The Historical Register*. San Diego: Baseball Press Books, 1999.

Holway, John. *The Complete Book of Baseball's Negro Leagues: The Other Half of Baseball History*. Fern Park FL: Hastings House, 2001.

Honig, Donald. *Baseball When the Grass Was Real*. Lincoln: University of Nebraska Press, Bison Books, 1993. Originally published in New York by Coward, McCann and Geoghegan, 1975.

———. *The Man In the Dugout: Fifteen Big-League Managers Speak Their Minds*. Lincoln: University of Nebraska Press, Bison Books, 1995. Originally published in River Grove IL by Follett Publishing, 1977.

"How the World's Batting King Is Regarded by the King of Pitchers." *Literary Digest*, September 18, 1920.

Hoyt, Waite. "Babe Ruth: As I Knew Him." In Gallen, *Baseball Chronicles*, 25–44.

Huggins, Myrtle. "Mighty Midget." As told to John B. Kennedy. *Collier's Weekly*, May 24, 1930.

Huhn, Rick. *Eddie Collins: A Baseball Biography*. Jefferson NC: McFarland, 2008.

———. *The Sizzler: George Sisler, Baseball's Forgotten Great*. Columbia: University of Missouri Press, 2004.

Hynd, Noel. *The Giants of the Polo Grounds*. New York: Doubleday, 1988.

Istorico, Ray. *Greatness in Waiting: An Illustrated History of the Early New York Yankees, 1903–1919*. Jefferson NC: McFarland, 2008.

Jackson, Frank. "Crossing Red River: Spring Training in Texas." *National Pastime* 26 (2006): 85–91.

Jackson, Kenneth T. "Where the Modern World Took Shape, 1898–1929." In Burns and Sanders, *New York*, 300–307.

Jackson, Kenneth T., and David S. Dunbar, eds. *Empire City: New York through the Centuries*. New York: Columbia University Press, 2002.

James, Bill. *The Bill James Historical Baseball Abstract*. New York: Villard Books, 1986.

———. *The New Bill James Historical Baseball Abstract*. New York: Free Press, 2001.

James, Bill, and Rob Neyer. *The Neyer/James Guide to Pitchers*. New York: Fireside Books, 2004.

"A Japanese Baseball Invasion on the Way," *Literary Digest*, May 7, 1921.

Jenkinson, Bill. *The Year Babe Ruth Hit 104 Home Runs*. New York: Carroll and Graf, 2007.

Jensen, Don. "Tris Speaker." In Jones, *Deadball Stars of the American League*, 434–37.

Johnson, Lloyd, and Miles Wolff, eds. *The Encyclopedia of Minor League Baseball*. 3rd ed. Durham NC: Baseball America, 2007.

Johnston, Alva. "Beer and Baseball." *New Yorker*, September 24, 1932.

———. "The Ghosting Business." *New Yorker*, November 23, 1935.

Jones, David. "Benny Kauff." *The Baseball Biography Project*. Society for American Baseball Research. http://bioproj.sabr.org/bioproj.cfm?a=v&v=l&bid=986&pid=7293.

———, ed. *Deadball Stars of the American League*. Washington DC: Potomac, 2006.

Kahn, Roger. *A Flame of Pure Fire. Jack Dempsey and the Roaring '20s*. New York: Harcourt Brace, 1999.

Karst, Gene, and Martin T. Jones. *Who's Who in Professional Baseball*. New Rochelle NY: Arlington House, 1973.

Kelley, Brent E. *They Too Wore Pinstripes: Interviews with 20 Glory-Days New York Yankees*. Jefferson NC: McFarland, 1998.

Kermisch, Al. "From a Researcher's Notebook," *Baseball Research Journal*, no. 29 (2000): 126–28.

———. "A Vote for Dunn's Orioles," *Baseball Research Journal*, no. 6 (1977): 6–9.

Kerr, Dickie. File. National Baseball Library and Archives, Cooperstown, New York.

Kofoed, J. C. "The Hero of the 1921 World's Series." *Baseball Magazine*, December 1921.

Kohout, Martin Donell. *Hal Chase: The Defiant Life and Turbulent Times of Baseball's Biggest Crook.* Jefferson NC: McFarland, 2001.

Koppett, Leonard. *Koppett's Concise History of Major League Baseball.* Philadelphia: Temple University Press, 1998.

———. *The New Thinking Man's Guide to Baseball.* New York: Simon and Schuster, 1991.

Krueger, Joseph. *"Baseball's Greatest Drama."* Milwaukee: Classic, 1942.

Lane, F. C. "The All America Baseball Club of 1920." *Baseball Magazine,* December 1920.

———. "The All-America Baseball Club of 1921." *Baseball Magazine,* December 1921.

———. "Baseball's Dictator." *Baseball Magazine,* February 1921.

———. "Biggest Trade of Recent Years." *Baseball Magazine,* February 1921.

———. "Can Babe Ruth Repeat?" *Baseball Magazine,* May 1921.

———. "Carl Mays' Cynical Definition of Pitching Efficiency." *Baseball Magazine,* August 1928.

———. "The Extraordinary Career of Howard Ehmke." *Baseball Magazine,* May 1924.

———. "Extraordinary Career of 'Smoky' Joe Wood." *Baseball Magazine,* October 1921.

———. "The Famous Landis-Groh Decision." *Baseball Magazine,* August 1921.

———. "The Far Reaching Draft Problem." *Baseball Magazine,* February 1922.

———. "Flashing the World Series to Waiting Millions." *Baseball Magazine,* November 1922.

———. "Frank Frisch the Star of the World's Champions." *Baseball Magazine,* February 1922.

———. "Has the Lively Ball Revolutionized the Game?" *Baseball Magazine,* September 1921.

———. "The Home-Run Epidemic." *Baseball Magazine,* July 1921.

———. "How Babe Ruth Wins for the New York Yankees." *Baseball Magazine,* June 1921.

———. "How John McGraw Won Out." *Baseball Magazine,* December 1921.

———. "Huggins vs. McGraw." *Baseball Magazine,* December 1923.

———. "Kelly's Place in the 'Greatest Infield.'" *Baseball Magazine,* March 1924.

———. "The Man Who Led the Yankees to Their First Pennant." *Baseball Magazine,* December 1921.

———. "The Much Discussed Menace of the Lively Ball." *Baseball Magazine,* October 1929.

———. "'Red' Faber Who Wins with a Losing Club." *Baseball Magazine,* September 1921.

———. "Roger Peckinpaugh the Baseball Plodder Who Became a Star." *Baseball Magazine,* February 1920.

———. "The Sensational Rube Benton Affair." *Baseball Magazine*, May 1923.

———. "The Shadow of New York on the Baseball Diamond." *Baseball Magazine*, August 1923.

———. "Should the Spit Ball Be Abolished?" *Baseball Magazine*, June 1919.

———. "A Startling Baseball Tragedy: Ray Chapman's Tragic Death." *Baseball Magazine*, October 1920.

———. "The Terrific Slugging of Long Harry Heilmann." *Baseball Magazine*, September 1921.

———. "Urban Shocker: One of the Great Pitchers of 1920." *Baseball Magazine*, January 1921.

———. "Why Babe Ruth Has Become a National Idol." *Baseball Magazine*, October 1921.

———. "The Wizard of the Dope." *Baseball Magazine*, April 1923.

Lardner, John. "That Was Baseball: The Crime of Shufflin' Phil Douglas." *New Yorker*, May 12, 1956.

Lardner, Ring W. "Tyrus: The Greatest of 'Em All," In Gallen, *Baseball Chronicles*, 47–59.

Lemke, Bob. "Rogers' Fatal Fastball—Mishap or Manslaughter?" *Sports Collectors Digest*, February 11, 1994.

Lerner, Michael A. *Dry Manhattan: Prohibition in New York City.* Cambridge MA: Harvard University Press, 2007.

Lesch, R. J. "George Burns." In Simon, *Deadball Stars of the National League*, 77–78.

———. "Larry Doyle." In Simon, *Deadball Stars of the National League*, 58–60.

Levitt, Dan. *Ed Barrow: The Bulldog Who Built the Yankees' First Dynasty.* Lincoln: University of Nebraska Press, 2008.

———. "Stan Covelelski." In Jones, *Deadball Stars of the American League*, 690–92.

———. Yankees financial records. National Baseball Library and Archives, Cooperstown, New York.

Lewis, Franklin A. *The Cleveland Indians.* New York: Putnam, 1949.

Lieb, Frederick G. *Baseball as I Have Known It.* Lincoln: University of Nebraska Press, 1996. Originally published in New York by Coward, McCann, and Geoghegan, 1977.

———. "Baseball—the Nation's Melting Pot." *Baseball Magazine*, August 1923.

———. *The Baseball Story.* New York: Putnam, 1950.

———. *The Boston Red Sox.* New York: Putnam, 1947.

———. "The Business Directors of Baseball's Big Clubs." *Baseball Magazine*, October 1923.

———. *Connie Mack: Grand Old Man of Baseball.* New York: Putnam, 1945.

———. *The Detroit Tigers.* New York: Putnam, 1946.

———. "The Manager's Right-Hand Man." *Baseball Magazine*, September 1921.

———. *The Pittsburgh Pirates*. New York: Putnam, 1946.

———. *The Story of the World Series*. New York: Putnam, 1949.

———. "Ten Outstanding Games of Major League History." *Baseball Register*. St. Louis: Sporting News, 1945.

Liebman, Ronald. "Winning Streaks by Pitchers." *Baseball Research Journal*, no. 7 (1978): 35–42.

Light, Jonathan Fraser. *The Cultural Encyclopedia of Baseball*. Jefferson NC: McFarland, 1997.

Lindberg, Richard. *Who's on 3rd? The Chicago White Sox Story*. South Bend IN: Icarus, 1983.

Linkugel, Wil A., and Edward J. Pappas. *They Tasted Glory: Among the Missing at the Baseball Hall of Fame*. Jefferson NC: McFarland, 1998.

Lowenfish, Lee. *Branch Rickey: Baseball's Ferocious Gentleman*. Lincoln: University of Nebraska Press, 2007.

———. *The Imperfect Diamond: A History of Baseball's Labor Wars*. Rev. ed. New York: Da Capo, 1991. Originally coauthored by Lee Lowenfish and Tony Lupien and published in New York by Stein and Day, 1980.

Lowry, Philip J. *Green Cathedrals: The Ultimate Celebration of Major League and Negro League Ballparks*. New York: Walker, 2006.

Lynch, Michael T., Jr. *Harry Frazee, Ban Johnson, and the Feud that Nearly Destroyed the American League*. Jefferson NC: McFarland, 2008.

Mails, Duster. "The Pitcher Who Cinched Cleveland's First Pennant: An Interview with Duster Mails." *Baseball Magazine*, December 1920.

Maranville, Walter "Rabbit." *Run, Rabbit, Run*. Cleveland: Society for American Baseball Research, 1991.

Markey, Morris. "The Current Press." *New Yorker*, October 24, 1925.

———. "A Reporter at Large: Scandal." *New Yorker*, January 8, 1927.

———. "A Reporter at Large: A Yankee Holiday." *New Yorker*, May 22, 1926.

Mays, Carl. "My Attitude toward the Unfortunate Chapman Affair." *Baseball Magazine*, November 1920.

———. "What I Have Learned from Four World Series." *Baseball Magazine*, November 1922.

McCallum, John D. *Ty Cobb*. New York: Praeger, 1975.

McGarigle, Bob. *Baseball's Great Tragedy: The Story of Carl Mays, Submarine Pitcher*. Jericho NY: Exposition, 1972.

McGraw, John J. *My Thirty Years in Baseball*. Lincoln: University of Nebraska Press, Bison Books, 1995. Originally published in New York by Boni and Liveright, 1923.

———. "Why a Baseball Game Is Like a Battle." *Baseball Magazine*, November 1923.

McGraw, Mrs. John. *The Real McGraw*. Edited by Arthur Mann. New York: David McKay, 1953.

Meany, Tom. *Babe Ruth: The Big Moments of the Big Fellow*. New York: A. S. Barnes, 1947.

———. *Baseball's Greatest Hitters*. New York: A. S. Barnes, 1950.

———. *Baseball's Greatest Pitchers*. New York: A. S. Barnes, 1951.

———. *The Yankee Story*. New York: E. P. Dutton, 1960.

Mercer, Sid. "The Supreme Value of 'Color' in Baseball." *Baseball Magazine*, August 1920.

"Mister Muggsy," *New Yorker*, March 28, 1925.

Moffi, Larry. *The Conscience of the Game: Baseball's Commissioners from Landis to Selig*. Lincoln: University of Nebraska Press, 2006.

Montville, Leigh. *The Big Bam: The Life and Times of Babe Ruth*. New York: Doubleday, 2006.

Morris, Peter. *A Game of Inches: The Stories behind the Innovations That Shaped Baseball*. Vol. 1, *The Game on the Field*. Chicago: Ivan R. Dee, 2006.

———. *A Game of Inches: The Stories behind the Innovations That Shaped Baseball*. Vol. 2, *The Game behind the Scenes*. Chicago: Ivan R. Dee, 2006.

Mott, Frank Luther. *American Journalism*. New York: Macmillan, 1962.

Murdock, Eugene C. *Ban Johnson: Czar of Baseball*. Westport CT: Greenwood, 1982.

———. *Baseball between the Wars: Memories of the Game by the Men Who Played It*. Westport CT: Meckler, 1992.

———. *Baseball Players and Their Times: Oral Histories of the Game, 1920–1940*. Westport CT: Meckler, 1991.

Nathan, Daniel A. *Saying It's So: A Cultural History of the Black Sox Scandal*. Urbana: University of Illinois Press, 2005.

Okkonen, Marc. *Baseball Uniforms of the 20th Century*. New York: Sterling, 1991.

———. *The Ty Cobb Scrapbook*. New York: Sterling, 2001.

Palmer, Pete. "Home Park Effects on Performance in the American League." *Baseball Research Journal*, no. 6 (1978): 50–60.

Parrish, Michael E. *Anxious Decades: America in Prosperity and Depression 1920–1941*. New York: W. W. Norton, 1992.

Pease, Neal. "Diamonds Out of the Coal Mines: Slavic Americans in Baseball." In Baldassaro and Johnson, *American Game*, 142–61.

Perrett, Geoffrey. *America in the Twenties: A History*. New York: Simon and Schuster, 1982.

Pfeffer, Jeff. "How a Single Pitched Ball May Upset a Pennant Race." *Baseball Magazine*, June 1920.

Phelon, W. A. "How the Championship Was Lost and Won." *Baseball Magazine*, December 1921.

———. "Who Will Win the Pennants?" *Baseball Magazine*, May 1921.

Pietrusza, David. *Judge and Jury: The Life and Times of Judge Kenesaw Mountain Landis*. South Bend IN: Diamond Communications, 1998.

———. *Rothstein: The Life, Times, and Murder of the Criminal Genius Who Fixed the 1919 World Series*. New York: Carroll and Graf, 2003.

Pietrusza, David, Matthew Silverman, and Michael Gershman, eds. *Baseball: The Biographical Encyclopedia*. Kingston NY: Total Sports Illustrated, 2000.

Plunkitt, William L. "Brooklynites Natural-Born Hayseeds." In *Plunkitt of Tammany Hall: A Series of Very Plain Talks on Very Practical Politics*, edited by William L. Riordon, 27–29. Boston: Bedford/St. Martin's Press, 1993.

Porter, David L., ed. *Biographical Dictionary of American Sports: Baseball*. Rev. and exp. ed. 3 vols. Westport CT: Greenwood, 2000.

Povich, Shirley. *All Those Mornings at the Post*. Edited by Lynn Povich, Maury Povich, David Povich, and George Solomon. New York: Public Affairs, 2005.

———. "Walter Johnson: The Big Train." In Gallen, *Baseball Chronicles*, 89–108.

Prince, Carl E. *Brooklyn's Dodgers: The Bums, the Borough, and the Best of Baseball, 1947–1957*. New York: Oxford University Press, 1996.

Pringle, Henry F. "A Small Package." *New Yorker*, October 8, 1927.

Puff, Richard A. "Silent George Burns: A Star in the Sunfield." *Baseball Research Journal*, no. 12 (1983): 119–25.

"Pulling Grass Is Tris Speaker's Baseball Barometer." *Literary Digest*, December 11, 1920.

Quigley, Martin. *The Crooked Pitch: The Curveball in American Baseball History*. Chapel Hill NC: Algonquin Books, 1984.

Rader, Benjamin. *Baseball: A History of America's Game*. Urbana: University of Illinois Press, 1992.

Reisler, Jim. *Babe Ruth: Launching the Legend*. New York: McGraw-Hill, 2004.

———. *Before They Were the Bombers: The New York Yankees' Early Years, 1903–1915*. Jefferson NC: McFarland, 2002.

Reynolds, Quentin, comp. "Peanut Vendor." In *More than a Game*, compiled by A. Lawrence Holmes, 182–89. New York: Macmillan, 1967. Originally published in *Collier's Weekly*, October 19, 1935.

Ribowsky, Mark. *The Complete History of the Home Run*. New York: Citadel, 2003.

Rice, Grantland. "Ruth Is Stranger than Fiction." *Vanity Fair*, April 1921.

———. *The Tumult and the Shouting: My Life in Sport*. New York: A. S. Barnes, 1954.

Richard, Kenneth D. "Remembering Carl Mays." *Baseball Research Journal*, no. 30 (2001): 122–26.

Richter, Francis C., ed. *The Reach Official American League Base Ball Guide, 1921*. Philadelphia: A. J. Reach, 1921.

———, ed. *The Reach Official American League Base Ball Guide, 1922*. Philadelphia: A. J. Reach, 1922.

Riess, Steven A. "The Baseball Magnates and Urban Politics in the Progressive Era: 1895–1920." *Journal of Sport's History* 1, no. 1 (Spring 1974): 41–62.

———. *City Games: The Evolution of American Urban Society and the Rise of Sports*. Urbana: University of Illinois Press, 1991.

———. *Touching Base: Professional Baseball and American Culture in the Progressive Era*. Rev. ed. Urbana: University of Illinois Press, 1999.

Ritter, Lawrence S. *East Side, West Side: Tales of New York Sporting Life, 1910–1960*. New York: Total Sports, 1998.

———. "George McBride." *National Pastime* 4, no. 2 (Winter 1985): 42–45.

———. *The Glory of Their Times: The Story of the Early Days of Baseball Told by the Men Who Played It*. New York: William Morrow, 1984. Originally published in New York by Macmillan, 1966.

———. *Lost Ballparks: A Celebration of Baseball's Legendary Fields*. New York: Viking Penguin, 1992.

Robbins, Michael W., ed. *Brooklyn: A State of Mind*. New York: Workman, 2001.

Robinson, Ray, and Christopher Jennison. *Yankee Stadium: 75 Years of Drama, Glamour, and Glory*. New York: Penguin Studio, 1998.

Rommel, Eddie. File. National Baseball Library and Archives, Cooperstown, New York.

Rosenberg, Norman L. "Here Comes the Judge: The Origins of Baseball's Commissioner System and American Legal Culture." In Dreifort, *Baseball History from Outside the Lines.*, 104–21.

Rothe, Emil. "The Shortened No-Hitters." *Baseball Research Journal*, no. 6 (1977): 52–58.

Ruppert, Jacob. "The Ten-Million Dollar Toy." *Saturday Evening Post*, March 28, 1931.

Ruth, Babe. *Babe Ruth's Own Book of Baseball*. Lincoln: University of Nebraska Press, 1992. Originally published in New York by G. P. Putnam's Sons, 1928.

———. *The Babe Ruth Story*. As told to Bob Considine. New York: E. P. Dutton, 1948.

———. "Secret of My Heavy Hitting: An Interview with the King of Sluggers." By F. C. Lane. *Baseball Magazine*, August 1920.

———. "Why I Hate to Walk." *Collier's Weekly*, July 10, 1920.

Rygelski, Jim. "59 in '21," *Baseball Research Journal*, no. 27 (1998): 17–18.

Sammons, Jeffrey T. *Beyond the Ring: The Role of Boxing in American Society*. Urbana: University of Illinois Press, 1988.

Sanborn, Irving E. "Consider the Pitchers: They Shine Not Neither Shall They Spit." *Baseball Magazine*, September 1920.

———. "What Prohibition Hasn't Done for Baseball." *Baseball Magazine*, October 1920.

Sawyer, Ford. "The Champion Pinch Hitters of the Majors." *Baseball Magazine*, January 1921.

———. "Leading Pinch Hitters of the Past Five Years." *Baseball Magazine*, August 1921.

Schneider, Russell. *Tribe Memories: The First Century*. Hinkley OH: Moonlight, 2000.

Selko, Jamie. "Harry Who?" *National Pastime* 15 (1995): 45–50.

Semchuk, Alex. "Wilbert Robinson." In Simon, *Deadball Stars of the National League*, 301–2.

Seymour, Harold. *Baseball: The Golden Age*. New York: Oxford University Press, 1971.

Shalin, Mike, and Neil Shalin. *Out by a Step: The 100 Best Players Not in the Baseball Hall of Fame*. Lanham MD: Diamond Communications, 2002.

Shatzkin, Mike, ed. *The Ballplayers*. New York: Arbor House William Morrow, 1990.

Sher, Jack. "The Georgia Peach." In Heyn, *Twelve Sport Immortals*, 105–28.

———. "John McGraw: The Little Napoleon." In Gallen, *Baseball Chronicles*, 273–81.

Simon, Tom, ed. *Deadball Stars of the National League*. Washington DC: Brassey's, 2004.

———. "Larry Gardner." In Jones, *Deadball Stars of the American League*, 438–40.

Skipper, James K., Jr. *Baseball Nicknames: A Dictionary of Origins and Meanings*. Jefferson NC: McFarland, 1992.

Smelser, Marshall. *The Life That Ruth Built: A Biography*. New York: Quadrangle, 1975.

Smith, Curt. *Voices of the Game: The First Full-Scale Overview of Baseball Broadcasting, 1921 to the Present*. South Bend IN: Diamond Communications, 1987.

Smith, James D., III. "Harvest Seasons: Most Runs-Batted-In with Fewest Home Runs since 1920." *Baseball Research Journal*, no. 12 (1983): 130–32.

Smith, Leverett T., Jr. "The Changing Style of Play: Cobb vs. Ruth." In Dreifort, *Baseball History from Outside the Lines*, 122–41.

Smith, Robert. *Babe Ruth's America*. New York: Thomas Y. Crowell, 1974.

———. *Baseball*. New York: Simon and Schuster, 1947.

———. *Baseball in the Afternoon: Tales from a Bygone Era*. New York: Simon and Schuster, 1993.

Sobol, Ken. *Babe Ruth and the American Dream*. New York: Ballantine Books, 1974.

Solomon, Burt. *The Baseball Timeline*. New York: Dorling Kindersley, 2001.

———. *Where They Ain't: The Fabled Life and Untimely Death of the Original Baltimore Orioles, the Team That Gave Rise to Modern Baseball*. New York: Free Press, 1999.

Sowell, Mike. *The Pitch That Killed: Carl Mays, Ray Chapman and the Pennant Race of 1920*. New York: Macmillan, 1989.

Spatz, Lyle. *Bad Bill Dahlen: The Rollicking Life and Times of an Early Baseball Star*. Jefferson NC: McFarland, 2004.

———. *New York Yankee Openers: An Opening Day History of Baseball's Most Famous Team, 1903–1996*. Jefferson NC: McFarland, 1997.

——. "Retroactive Cy Young Awards." *Baseball Research Journal*, no. 17 (1988): 65–70.

——, ed. *The SABR Baseball List and Record Book*. New York: Scribner, 2007.

——. "SABR Picks 1900–1948 Rookies of the Year." *Baseball Research Journal*, no. 15 (1986): 2–4.

——. *Yankees Coming, Yankees Going: New York Yankee Player Transactions, 1903 through 1999*. Jefferson NC: McFarland, 2000.

Sparks, Barry. *Frank "Home Run" Baker: Hall of Famer and World Series Hero*. Jefferson NC: McFarland, 2006.

Speaker, Tris. "Tris Speaker, the Star of the 1920 Baseball Season." *Baseball Magazine*, December 1920.

Spink, J. G. Taylor. *Judge Landis and 25 Years of Baseball*. New York: Thomas Crowell, 1947.

Sporting News. *Official World Series Records, from 1903 through 1984*. St. Louis: Sporting News, 1988.

Stanton, Tom. *Ty and the Babe: Baseball's Fiercest Rivalry; A Surprising Friendship and the 1941 Has-Beens Golf Championship*. New York: St. Martin's Press, Thomas Dunne Books, 2007.

Stein, Fred. "New York Giants–San Francisco Giants: A Tale of Two Cities." In *Encyclopedia of Major League Baseball: National League*, edited by Peter O. Bjarkman, 303–41. New York: Carroll and Graf, 1993.

——. *Under Coogan's Bluff: A Fan's Recollections of the New York Giants under Terry and Ott*. Alexandria VA: Automated Graphics, 1979.

Stein, Irving M. *The Ginger Kid: The Buck Weaver Story*. Dubuque IA: Elysian Fields, 1992.

Stein, Jacob A. "The Great Mouthpiece." *Washington Lawyer*, April 2003. http://www.dcbar.org/for_lawyers/resources/publications/washington_lawyer/april_2003/spectator.cfm.

Steinberg, Steve. "The Curse of the . . . Hurlers?" *Baseball Research Journal*, no. 35 (2007): 63–73.

——. "Heralding Hug." In *New York Yankees Official 2005 Yearbook*, edited by Mark Mandrake, 246–268. Elmont NY: University Sports, 2005.

——. "Ray Caldwell." In Jones, *Deadball Stars of the American League*, 719–21.

——. "The Spitball and the End of the Deadball Era." *National Pastime* 23 (2003): 7–17.

Stout, Glenn, and Richard A. Johnson. *The Dodgers: 120 Years of Dodgers Baseball*. Boston: Houghton Mifflin, 2004.

——. *Red Sox Century: One Hundred Years of Red Sox Baseball*. Boston: Houghton Mifflin, 2000.

——. *Yankees Century: One Hundred Years of New York Yankees Baseball*. Boston: Houghton Mifflin, 2002.

Stump, Al. *Cobb: A Biography*. Chapel Hill NC: Algonquin Books, 1994.

Suehsdorf, A. D. "Irresistible Braggo Roth." *Baseball Research Journal*, no. 20 (1991): 43, 65.

Sullivan, George, and John Powers. *Yankees: An Illustrated History*. Englewood Cliffs NJ: Prentice-Hall, 1982.

Sullivan, Mark. *Our Times: The Twenties*. New York: Scribner's, 1935.

Sullivan, Neil. *The Diamond in the Bronx*. New York: Oxford University Press, 2001.

Tan, Cecilia. *The 50 Greatest Yankee Games*. Hoboken NJ: John Wiley, 2005.

Thomas, Henry W. *Walter Johnson: Baseball's Big Train*. Washington DC: Phenom, 1995.

Thomas, James S. "Where Ball Players Graduate from College to the Majors." *Baseball Magazine*, August 1921.

Thorn, John, Phil Birnbaum, Bill Deane, Rob Neyer, Alan Schwarz, Donald Dewey, Nicholas Acocella, and Peter Wayner, eds. *Total Baseball: The Ultimate Baseball Encyclopedia*. 8th ed. Wilmington DE: Sports Media, 2004.

Thornley, Stew. *Land of the Giants: New York's Polo Grounds*. Philadelphia: Temple University Press, 2000.

Tierney, John. "Brooklyn Could Have Been a Contender." In Jackson and Dunbar, *Empire City*, 407–21.

Tullius, John. *I'd Rather Be a Yankee: An Oral History of America's Most Beloved and Most Hated Baseball Team*. New York: Macmillan, 1986.

U.S. Bureau of the Census. *Population of the 100 Largest Cities and Other Urban Places in the United States: 1790 to 1990*. Prepared by the Population Division, U.S. Bureau of the Census. Washington DC, 1998. http://www.census.gov/population/www/documentation/twps0027.html (accessed July 4, 2009).

Veeck, Bill, Jr. *The Hustler's Handbook*. With Ed Linn. New York: Fireside Books, 1965.

Vincent, David. *Home Run: The Definitive History of Baseball's Ultimate Weapon*. Washington DC: Potomac Books, 2007.

Voigt, David Q. *American Baseball*. Vol. 2. Norman: University of Oklahoma Press, 1970.

——— "The Chicago Black Sox and the Myth of Baseball's Single Sin." In *America through Baseball*, 65–76. Chicago: Nelson-Hall, 1976. Originally published in *Journal of the Illinois State Historical Society* 62, no. 3 (Autumn 1969).

Wagenheim, Kal. *Babe Ruth: His Life and Legend*. New York: Henry Holt, 1974.

Walsh, Christy. *Adios to Ghosts*. Self-published, 1937.

———. *Baseball's Greatest Lineup*. New York: A. S. Barnes, 1952.

Warburton, Paul. "The 1921 AL Race." *National Pastime* 18 (1998): 103–6.

Ward, Aaron. File. National Baseball Library and Archives, Cooperstown, New York.

Ward, John J. "Bob Meusel, the Rookie Who Slugs Like Babe Ruth." *Baseball Magazine*, September 1920.

———. "Frank Frisch a Star Newcomer in Baseball." *Baseball Magazine*, October 1920.

———. "From the Sand Lots to the Majors." *Baseball Magazine*, September 1923.

———. "How Big Phil Douglas Came Through." *Baseball Magazine*, December 1921.

———. "Kelly Seven, Ruth Six!" *Baseball Magazine*, July 1921.

———. "The Man Who Rivalled Mathewson's Great Record." *Baseball Magazine*, December 1921.

———. "Will 'Home Run' Baker Repeat?" *Baseball Magazine*, November 1921.

White, G. Edward. *Creating the National Pastime: Baseball Transforms Itself, 1903–1953*. Princeton NJ: Princeton University Press, 1996.

Williams, Frank. "Waite Hoyt's Deprived Win." In *Grandstand Baseball Annual*, no. 13, edited by Joe Wayman, 86–87. Downey CA: Wayman, 1997.

Zingg, Paul J. *Harry Hooper: An American Baseball Life*. Urbana: University of Illinois Press, 1993.

275, 311; versus Yankees, 137, 157, 193–94, 211–12, 215–16, 275–76

Chill, Oliver, 221, 348, 368, 378

Cicotte, Eddie, 10, 41, 137

Cincinnati Reds, 41, 165–66, 176, 200, 225–26, 260–61, 263–64; versus Giants, 121–22, 164, 182–83, 227–28, 239, 263

Clarke, Fred, 164

Cleveland Indians, 59, 132, 134, 160–61, 194, 211, 217, 222–23, 277–79, 282–83, 288–90, 311–12; and 1920 season, 34–36; and Chapman fatality, 34–35, 134–35; and injuries, 145–46, 277, 279; prediction to win 1921 pennant, 67–68; uniforms, 148; versus Yankees, 134–36, 146–49, 151, 199–200, 202–3, 217, 219–21, 290, 292–99

Cobb, Ty, 78, 88, 106, *129*, 139, 155, 209; and batting race, 151–52, 282; and dislike for Mays, 88, 153; and dislike for Ruth, 128, 132, 152–54; and feud with McGraw, 75; and fight with Evans, 289; and fight with Herzog, 75; intensity of, 128–29, 132, 196; as manager of Tigers, 75, 128–29, 151, 153, 195–96, 282–83, 289; salary of, 128; tutoring hitters, 151, 282

Cohan, George M., 18, 328

Cole, Bert, 196

Collins, Eddie, 211, 392–93

Collins, Rip, 142, 149, 194, 211, 216, 220, 270–71, 275, 345, 394

Comiskey, Charles, 13, 41, 219

Connelly, Tommy, 95, 206, 454n3

Connery, Bob, 24, 434n13

Connolly, Tom, 171, 216

contract negotiations, 76, 277, 304

Coogan, Jackie, 86, *87*

Cooper, Wilbur, 123–24, 163, 181, 190,

227, 234, 236, 240, *245*, 247, 256, 259, 261–62, 264

Coumbe, Fritz, 200–201

Coveleski, Stan, 134, 136, 203, 217, 277, 283, 311, 428n32; and 1920 World Series, 36, 60; pitching against Yankees, 146, 199, 202, 219–20, 292, 295–96, 299; spitball of, 59–60

Cowan, Tommy, 331

Crane, Sam, 15, 126, 165–66, 169, 236

Cravath, Gavy, 44, 99, 143, 149

Crawford, Sam, 281

Crepeau, Richard, 225–26

Cruise, Walton, 168

Cunningham, Bill, 181–82, *189*, 190, 238

Cutshaw, George, 163, 250, 264, 459n17

Dahlen, Bill, 108, 191

Dauss, Hooks, 154–55

Davis, Dixie, 140, 143–44, 195, 201, 216, 281

Deadball Era, xii, xvii, 8, 32, 37, 38, 118, 128, 165, 169, 179, 181, 282, 336, 386, 429n45, 445n63

Dempsey, Jack, 3, 156, 159–60, 419n1

designated hitter, 277

Detroit Tigers, 128, 155, 164, 171–72, 195, 222, 279, 282, 289; versus Yankees, 130–32, 151–55, 196, 209–10, 222, 283–84, 287–88

Devery, Bill, 22

Devlin, Art, 191, 304

DeVormer, Al, 63, 479n16

Dillhoefer, Pickles, 232, 458n17

Dinneen, Bill, 153, 297

dirigible explosion, 248

dirty ball, 37, 170

Doak, Bill, 61, 240, 301

doctoring the ball, 37, 200, 220

Dodge, Johnny, 221

304; fielding of, 303; and football, 304; at Fordham University, 304; home runs of, 80, 235; nickname of, 449n30; and playing second base, 76, 119–20, 173, 305, 394; and playing third base, 42, 168, 173, 177; salary of, 304; signed by Giants, 76, 304; and stolen bases, 181, 240; as switch hitter, 77; as trade for Hornsby, 46–47; triples of, 121, 233, 250, 256, 265

Fullerton, Hugh, 68–69, 137, 157, 166; and Black Sox scandal, 10, 15–16, 208–9; on cheating, 220–21; and criticism of Ruth, 96, 155; on gambling, 347; on Huggins, 25, 198, 213–14, 284; and McGraw's handling of pitchers, 78–80; predictions on 1921 World Series, 319, 340, 352, 354, 360, 380, 389; and testing of Ruth, 274; on umpiring, 171, 365

Gallico, Paul, 35–36, 39
gambling, 10, 13, 16, 38, 40–41, 57, 114–15, 185, 307–8, 352
Gardner, Larry, 149
Gaston, Alex, 232
Gehrig, Lou, 197, 452n25
general manager, concept of, 25, 40, 43, 51, 53–54, 397
ghostwriters, 57–58, 317, 433n36
Gibson, George, 123, 225, 245, 249, 259, 267, 268
Glazner, Whitey, 190–91, 243, 246, 253, 256, 260
Gleason, Kid, 41, 211–13, 392–93
Golden, Harry, 5, 17
golf, 156–57
Gonzalez, Mike, 165, 393
Graney, Jack, 145

Grant, Eddie, 103, 126
Grant, George W., 49
Griffith, Clark, 88, 159
Grimes, Burleigh, 60, 81, 110, 178–79, 234, 236, 238, 256, 258, 259, 262–63, 458n22
Grimm, Charlie, 244–45, 250, 264
Groh, Heinie, 47–49, 165–66, 228, 393, 393–94
Grove, Lefty, 159, 420n16

Haines, Jess, 259
Hamilton, Earl, 162–63, 182, 250, 264
Hanlon, Ned, 74, 257
Hannah, Truck, 37
Harding, Warren G., 96, 121, 123–24
Harper, Harry, 65, 131, 275; and 1921 World Series, 363–64; pitching against Browns, 309; pitching against Indians, 221, 293; pitching against Senators, 271; pitching against Tigers, 131, 287–88; and thumb injury, 131, 139; traded to Yankees, 54–55
Harris, Sam, 18
Harriss, Slim, 90
Hart, Jim, 419n2
Hawks, Nelson "Chicken," 95, 141
Heilmann, Harry, 150, 151–53, 195, 282
Hempstead, Harry, 18–19
Hendrix, Claude, 41
Hendryx, Tim, 96, 206, 210, 454n2
Henline, Butch, 184
Herrmann, Garry, 165
Herzog, Buck, 75, 115
Heydler, John, 15–16, 71, 124, 137, 176, 190–91, 226, 263
High, Hugh, 27
Hildebrand, George, 289–90
home run "conspiracy," 111–12, 127
Hooper, Harry, 216, 275

Hornsby, Rogers, 43, *45*, 46–47, 111, 119, 151–52, 156–57, *167*, 167–68, 233, 241, 302

horseracing, 72, 185, 436n2

Houdini, Harry, 250

Hoyt, Waite, 58, 65, 91, 141, 201–2, 319, *336*; and 1921 World Series, 335–37, 339–40, 355–56, 358, 360, 378, 382, 386; accused of tampering with ball, 292; and finger injury, 378; pitching against Athletics, 90, 160, 215, 312; pitching against Browns, 143, 201, 216; pitching against Indians, 135, 147, 203, 219, 292, 296–98; pitching against Red Sox, 273; pitching against Senators, 96, 159; pitching against Tigers, 130, 222, 283; pitching against White Sox, 193, 212, 271; pitching against Yankees, 30; and Red Sox career, 55; relationship with McGraw, 202, 335, 339, 341, 453n47; signed by Giants, 202, 453n47; temperamental, 55; traded to Yankees, 54–55, 202

Huggins, Miller, *31*, *213*, *286*, *291*, *321*; and 1921 World Series, 340, 344, 347–48, 369, 375; and coaches, 61; criticism from his pitchers, 288, 295; disdained by Huston, xiii, 9, 53, 85, 212, 285; ejected from game, 148; evaluating talent, 93–95; fan appreciation of, 312; and fight with Shocker, 216–17, 456n54; and golf, 156; health of, xiii, 85–86, 194–95, 284, 392; leadership praised, 285, 313; leadership questioned, 65, 67, 382; managerial style of, 321–22; as manager of St. Louis Cardinals, 24, 230; molding a winning team, 25, 27–28, 30, 32, 39, 54–55, 69; personality of, 24–25, 212–13; physical ap-

pearance of, 424n14; press criticism of, xiii, 9, 28, 85, 194, 197, 212–13, 283–84, 287, 310–11, 344–45, 372; problems with Ruth, 96, 214, 392, 439n60; and relationship with his players, 9, 54, 67, 86, 96, 141, 153, 155, 198, 214, 255, 286; resignation letter of, 284–87; and rumors of his firing, 67; and support from Barrow, 53; and support from Ruppert, 9, 85, 214, 285–87

Huston, Tillinghast L'Hommedieu, xiii, 9, 22–24, *23*, 26, 51, 53, 59, 71, 85, *198*, 212, 215, 285, 287, 322, 392, 430n49, 464n3

Hylan, John F., 87, *87*, 121

immigrants, 5, 61, 117

inside baseball, 4, 7, 32–33, 38, 179, 219–20, 336, 356–57

Irwin, Arthur, 196–97

Jackson, Joe, 10, 41, 106

Jacobson, Baby Doll, 139, 141

Jennings, Hughie, 72, 128, 172, 189–91, 226, 241, 243, 328, 436n4, 442n8

Johnson, Ban, xiii, xvi, 3, 11, 13–14, 20, 26, 35, 135, 166–67, 170, 219–20, 419n3, 420n14

Johnson, Walter, 30, 90, 91–92, 95, 142, 158, 211, 271, 281, 283

Jones, Sam, 95, 158, 271, 394

Kauff, Benny, 42, 77–78, 430n4

Keeler, Willie, 369

Kelleher, John, 170

Kelly, George, 42, 76, 82, 102–3, *104*, 105–6, 118, 172–74, 178, 183, 228, 247–48, 263; and 1920 season, 75–76, 111; and 1921 World Series, 334, 339, 342, 349, 356, 360, 378,

Mays, Carl (*cont.*)
345, *353*; and 1921 World Series, 332, 348–52, 354, 370–72, 375; and bribe offer, 350–52; and Chapman fatality, 34–35, 134–36, 351; and gambling problems, 352; as a headhunter, 88, 349; hitting ability of, 87; and late-game collapses, 193, 352, 473n24; and personality difficulties, xiii, 88, 283; pitching against Athletics, 87, 91, 215, 274, 311; pitching against Browns, 144, 195, 201; pitching against Indians, 136, 149, 200, 203, 294, 297–98; pitching against Red Sox, 95–96, 158; pitching against Senators, 91–94, 96, 142; pitching against Tigers, 88, 130–31, 154–55, 210, 283, 285; pitching against White Sox, 193, 212, 215; and relationship with Huggins, 155, 351; and relationships with other players, 88, 153, 351; and submarine delivery, 88; traded to Yankees, xiii, 25–26, 167, 425n21

Mays, Marjorie, 351
McBride, George, 88, 95, 270
McCormick, Barry, 174, 264
McGeehan, William, 11, 209
McGinnity, Joe "Iron Man," 258
McGraw, Blanche, 42, 73, 115–16
McGraw, John, 9, 17, 23, *321*; and 1921 World Series, 336, 339, 350, 354, 369, 375; acts as business manager, 40, 43, 46–49; and antipathy toward Yankees, 4–5; berating his players, 73–74, 341–42, 360; and coaches, 72–73, 76, 109, 123, 191, 243, 367; dictatorial personality of, 98, 101, 174–75, 225, 326; as disciplinarian, 74–75; and disdain for Cobb, 75, 171; and disdain for Ruth,

xii, 7, 33, 387; disliked by his players, 174–75, 202, 232–33, 255; and enmity with Dreyfuss, 49, 306–7; and enmity with Robinson, 108–9; and facilitating sale of Giants, 18; and facilitating sale of Yankees, 22–23, *23*; and fistfight, 191; and golf, 156–57; and handling unmanageable players, 41–42, 78, 100–101, 114, 373, 390; and Lambs Club (New York City) drunken brawl, 115–17; leadership of, 268, 305; and loyalty to past players, 191, 328; managerial style of, 318–19, 321–22, 340, 359, 389; named manager of Giants, 17, 419n3; and opinion of Burns, 188–89; and opinion of Huggins, 325–26; as part owner of Giants, 18, 20; and pep talk, 244–45, 248, 255; and refusal to play 1904 World Series, 4; respect for Ruth, 318; and spring training, 73–76; and suspensions, 191, 226, 442n6; and tampering accusations, 47, 125, 166; and trades, 43, 176–77, 179, 181, 184–85; tutoring of Kelly, 106; views on gambling 41–42

McHenry, Austin, *167*, 167, 230, 233
McNally, Mike, 64, *272*, 311; and 1921 World Series, 333–34, 337, 339, 352, 356, 358, 365, 371; fielding of, 273, 275; as reserve infielder, 55–56, 216, 312; and stealing home, 142, 333, traded to Yankees, 54
McQuade, Francis X., 18–21, 47
McQuillan, Hugh, 110, 186
Meadows, Lee, 101–2, 105, 126–27, 183, 238
Mercer, Sid, 6, 35, 209, 329, 369
Meusel, Bob, 34, 67, 90, 219–20, *280*, 292, *357*; and 1921 World Series,